WYOMING ROAD TRIP
BY THE
MILE MARKER

Travel guide to Yellowstone/Grand Teton National Park, Devils Tower, Oregon/Mormon Trail, badlands, petroglyphs, waterfalls, camping, hiking, tourism and more...

Brook Besser

NightBlaze Books
Golden, Colorado

ISBN 978-0-9844093-0-3

Library of Congress Control Number: 2010923145

Manufactured in the United States of America

Special thanks to the following people: My wife Mianne who accompanied me for 5 weeks in Wyoming and supported my endless hours working on this book; my brother Brant and my daughter Brianna who each spent a week out on the road with me; my brother Brett who helped with my book summaries; my sister-in-law Sue who proofed many pages of the book; and the rest of my family for their support.

Cover design by Third Degree Designs

For additional information, photos and updates please visit:
www.wyomingroadtripbythemilemarker.com

HELP ME KEEP THIS GUIDE UP TO DATE

Every effort has been made by the author to make this guide as accurate and useful as possible. However, many things can change after a guide is published as well as researched information being inaccurate. I would much appreciate hearing from you concerning your experiences with this guide as well as any updates for improved accuracy. Please email any correspondences to:

brook@nightblazebooks.com

Thank you for your input and happy road tripping!

v1.2.1 - 07/2012

Contents

NOTE: Highways in italics are the "End of Highway" sections at the end of the chapters when traveling in the reverse direction

About the Book...4
How to Use the Book..5
Northwest Wyoming Map..8
Southwest Wyoming Map...9
Northeast Wyoming Map...10
Southeast Wyoming Map..11
Snowy Range Map...12
Yellowstone Map..13
Alcova/Pathfinder Reservoir Loop...............................14
Atlantic City Rd/CR-237 & South Pass City Rd/CR-479.........17
Brooklyn Lake Rd/FR-317...19
Brooks Lake Rd/FR-515..20
Buffalo Valley Rd/FR-30050...21
Casper Mountain Rd/Wy-251.......................................22
Chilton Rd...25
Cook Lake Recreation Area and Scenic Drive..............26
CR-406/Lakeshore Drive...27
CR-422/Phalow Ln & CR-44/Harmony Ln....................28
CR-44/Harmony Ln & CR-422/Phalow Ln....................28
Fossil Butte National Monument..................................29
FR-27/Ten Sleep Rd..30
FR-700/Vedauwoo Glen Rd..31
Fremont Lake Rd/Skyline Drive....................................32
Glendo Park Rd (Glendo State Park)............................34
Grand Teton National Park...36
Grayrocks Rd/Power Plant Rd/Wy-160.........................165
Greys River Rd/FR-10138...37
Gros Ventre Rd/FR-30400...38
Guernsey State Park - Lakeshore Drive/Wy-317..........40
Guernsey State Park - Skyline Drive.............................42
I-25...44
I-80...51
I-90...59
Jenny Lake Loop Rd: Grand Teton National Park.........63
Keyhole State Park via CR-205/CR-180........................64
Louis Lake Rd/FR-300/Wy-131....................................161
Moose-Wilson Rd/Wy-390...191
Oregon Trail Rd...66
Pilot Butte Wild Horse Tour...68
Seminoe-Alcova Back Country Byway..........................70
South Pass City Rd/CR-479 & Atlantic City Rd/CR-237....18
Sugarloaf Recreation Area/FR-346...............................73
Teton Park Rd: Grand Teton National Park..................74
Trail Lake Rd/CR-411..78
Union Pass Rd...80
US-14..81
US-14 (east)...86
US-14/16/20...87
US-14A..91
US-16..96
US-189...102
US-189/191..104
US-191...106
US-20/26..110
US-20/Wy-789 & US-16/20/Wy-789 & US-14/16/20/Wy-789 & US-310/Wy-789........................113
US-212 (Beartooth Scenic Byway)...............................118
US-26 & US-26/287...127
US-26 (I-25 to Nebraska)..121
US-26/287 & US-26...124
US-26/89..128
US-26/89/191...129
US-26/Wy-789 & Wy-789...196
US-287 (Lander to US-26)...132
US-287 (Laramie to Colorado)......................................133
US-287/Wy-789...134
US-30..137

US-30/287..138
US-310/Wy-789 & US-14/16/20/Wy-789 & US-16/20/Wy-789 & US-20/Wy-789.................................117
US-85..140
US-87/Wy-193..167
US-89..143
US-89/191/287...145
Wy-110/Devils Tower Rd (Devils Tower National Monument)..148
Wy-120...149
Wy-130 (Laramie to Wy-230)..151
Wy-130/Wy-230 (Walcott to Riverside)........................156
Wy-131/FR-300/Louis Lake Rd......................................158
Wy-133 & Wy-134..162
Wy-134 & Wy-133...162
Wy-135/136...163
Wy-160/Grayrocks Rd/Power Plant Rd.........................164
Wy-193/US-87...166
Wy-210/Happy Jack Rd...168
Wy-22...170
Wy-220...173
Wy-230 (Laramie to Colorado).....................................176
Wy-230 (Riverside to Colorado)...................................177
Wy-230/Wy-130 (Riverside to Walcott).......................157
Wy-24...178
Wy-28 (Farson to US-287)...179
Wy-28 (Wy-372 to Farson)..181
Wy-296 (Chief Joseph Scenic Highway).......................182
Wy-352/FR-10091..184
Wy-37 (Bighorn Canyon National Recreation Area)....187
Wy-372...189
Wy-390/Moose-Wilson Rd...190
Wy-70...192
Wy-789 & US-26/Wy-789...195
Yellowstone National Park...197
   Canyon Village to Fishing Bridge...........................199
   Canyon Village to Norris......................................213
   Canyon Village to Tower-Roosevelt.....................231
   East Entrance to Fishing Bridge.............................202
   Fishing Bridge to Canyon Village.........................201
   Fishing Bridge to East Entrance...........................204
   Fishing Bridge to West Thumb...............................205
   Madison to Norris..208
   Madison to West Entrance....................................234
   Madison to West Thumb.......................................240
   Mammoth Hot Springs to Norris...........................218
   Mammoth Hot Springs to North Entrance.............220
   Mammoth Hot Springs to Tower-Roosevelt...........210
   Norris to Canyon Village.......................................212
   Norris to Madison...209
   Norris to Mammoth Hot Springs............................214
   North Entrance to Mammoth Hot Springs..............219
   North Rim Drive...221
   Northeast Entrance to Tower-Roosevelt................223
   South Entrance to West Thumb..............................225
   South Rim Drive...227
   Tower-Roosevelt to Canyon Village......................229
   Tower-Roosevelt to Mammoth Hot Springs..........211
   Tower-Roosevelt to Northeast Entrance...............224
   Upper Terrace Drive...232
   West Entrance to Madison.....................................233
   West Thumb to Fishing Bridge..............................207
   West Thumb to Madison...235
   West Thumb to South Entrance.............................226
Glossary...242
Attractions at a Glance...243
Index..250

About the Book

This book is the culmination of my many years of traveling the wide open spaces of the western United States. For me there is nothing more liberating than escaping the crowds to a beautiful out-of-the-way destination. In the early days when I was dependent on the basic road atlas, a lot more time was spent driving than stopping. Other than National Parks, National Monuments, and a few other highlights, I didn't really know what was out there. With the advent of the internet, my vacation planning became more involved and eventually I would spend weeks planning my travels. The vacation planning began taking more time than the vacation itself!

When I was younger, camping on the side of the road or sleeping in a rest area was a viable option. However, as I grew older and had a family to travel with, finding reasonable places to camp before dark took on a greater significance. Unfortunately, the trusty road atlas only showed a few public campgrounds. All of this eventually led me to the idea of writing a detailed and easy-to-use travel guide.

During my vacation planning, I found a number of travel books that did an excellent job of explaining attractions in detail once you were there. Other books were very specific for an area or activity. Some books were broad, yet incomplete, with too much emphasis on lodging, restaurants and private campgrounds. For my family, the need was to easily identify and locate interesting attractions and know where to camp. I wanted to write a book that would provide the following:

- Make vacation planning fast and easy
- Be easy to use when out on the road
- Include primarily natural, scenic, and historic attractions
- Include all attractions that are within a reasonable distance from the main highway
- Provide necessary information to make decisions, but leave room for self-discovery
- Make attractions easy to locate
- Provide a complete list of camping areas
- Provide a comprehensive index to easily locate individual attractions by name

Referencing tourist attractions by the highway mile markers was a concept that I had been thinking about for a number of years, so in 2007 I decided to give the idea a test run. Since our summer vacation plans were taking us from Colorado through Wyoming to Glacier National Park in Montana, I mapped out a Wyoming tour that would take us to places that we had never visited. Being an Oracle programmer and seeing this project as data-intensive, storing the information in a database and generating the output seemed a natural approach.

The trip through Wyoming was quite interesting and served to further stimulate my interest in writing a book on Wyoming. Additional research uncovered an abundance of interesting natural, scenic, and historic attractions all around Wyoming. I created the database, designed the report format, and started plugging in my information. It was exciting to see the book start to take form. Little did I realize the scope of the project I had undertaken. However, I stuck with it, spending many weeks of my vacation time traveling around Wyoming and my spare time writing the book. Eventually, I took a year off work to allow the time needed to finish – 3 years after it all began.

This book will hopefully put to rest the perception that there is nothing but prairie and antelope (pronghorns) outside of Yellowstone and Grand Teton National Parks. This is most likely the result of driving across the state on I-25 and I-80. While there is an abundance of prairie and pronghorns, there are also 11 mountain ranges, 2 major National Parks, 2 National Monuments, canyons, badlands, and petroglyphs. Even the plains are sprinkled with dozens of interesting historic sites, primarily from the pioneer emigration of the 19th century. I have personally driven across Wyoming on I-80 at least a dozen times before writing this book, and it always did seem disinteresting. But, surprisingly there are over 20 attractions along or near this route, including hiking, biking, state parks, major historical sites, petroglyphs, geological areas, and wild horses. You could spend a week exploring just this part of the state!

Below are some of the many benefits of using this book:

- Attractions are laid out by the highway mile markers allowing you to keep ahead of your current location
- Detailed directions, GPS coordinates, and elevations are provided for:
    - Nearly 600 natural, scenic and historic attractions
    - Nearly 100 easily accessible hiking trails
    - Over 300 public campgrounds and dispersed camping areas
    - Over 30 rest areas
    - Over 60 RV dump stations
- A concise report style format with brief descriptions, condensed information, and a star rating system that allows for easily informed decisions about what to visit
- A comprehensive index that makes any attraction easy to locate in the book
- Complete coverage of Yellowstone and Grand Teton National Parks
- Makes an excellent companion book to longer, more in-depth books
- Pays for itself many times over in time and fuel savings

It was a long journey getting here, but my work is your gain. Happy Wyoming road tripping!

How to Use the Book

NOTE: It is highly advisable to read this chapter to understand the conventions used in this book.

1. Overview

This book is organized by **Chapters** that correspond to the **highways** in Wyoming. The highways are listed in alphabetical order, not by the highway number. For example, US-287 comes before US-30 even though the number 287 is greater than 30. The **Chapters** are subdivided into **Sections** that define each **Attraction** (separated by horizontal lines). Each **Attraction** is described by the **Mile Marker**, **Attraction Name**, **Description**, and **Attributes**, which are other pieces of information used to describe and locate the **Attraction**.

The book is most easily followed in the direction of increasing mile markers, i.e. reading the book front to back. However, it is just as likely that a highway will be traveled in the reverse direction. In this case the book would be followed from back to front, so keep in mind issues such as referring to "previous" or "next" sections whose context is from front to back. *See the sections below for more about following the book in forward and reverse direction.*

The directions in the book are very detailed and basic maps for highway orientation are provided. A free Wyoming map can be obtained from Wyoming Travel and Tourism or at the visitor centers. It may also be helpful to pick up a detailed Wyoming road atlas such as the DeLorme Atlas & Gazetteer.

2. Some Notes about Mile Markers

Since the book is based on highway mile markers, there are a few things to explain:

- The mile markers are green with white numbers and are located on the side of the highway where the mileages are increasing (following the book from front to back). They are double-sided to be seen in both directions, so if you are traveling in the opposite direction (following the book from back to front) they will be on the other side of the highway.
- Some highways and routes have no mile markers. For these cases the book displays the distances from both the start and the end of the highway separated by a slash. For example, using this convention on a 15.0 mile highway, the start is displayed as **MM: 0/15** and the end as **MM: 15/0**. Mile 8.0 would be displayed as **MM: 8.0/7.0**, meaning 8.0 mi from the start and 7.0 mi from the end. To keep track of the mileage the odometer can be zeroed out at either end of the highway.
- In a few cases the mile markers end along a route, but the route continues, e.g. a highway that enters a National Park. In this case, the mile markers will be shown both as if they did not run out, followed by starting at zero at the point where they did run out. For example, if the mile markers on a 15 mi route end at MM 7.0, with an entrance station at MM 7.8, the mile marker at the entrance station would display as **MM: 7.8 (0.0/7.2)**. The entry at MM 10 would display as **MM: 10.0 (2.2/5.0)**. In this example the odometer could be zeroed out at the beginning of the route, with the first part of the mile marker used for the entire route. Alternatively, the mile markers could be followed up to MM 7.8, where the odometer would be zeroed out and the second part of the mile marker (in parenthesis) would be used.
- When looking for a particular attraction on highways that are missing mile markers, it is a good idea to remain aware of where you are in relation to other nearby attractions and/or approximately how far that you have traveled along each highway. The maps in the front of the book also help.

3. Header, Footer, and Chapter Title

- The header and footer area on each page displays the **Highway**, **Mile Marker**, and **Page Number**.
- If the page is the beginning of a **Chapter**, the **Highway Name** is displayed below the header along with the direction of the highway. This is determined by the direction in which the **Mile Markers** increase. The directions use combinations of the following abbreviations:
     N=North, S=South, E=East, W=West, NE=Northeast, NW=Northwest, SE=Southeast, SW=Southwest
  For example: SW/NE means that the highway travels southwest to northeast.

4. Highway Descriptions and Highway Junctions

- At the start of every chapter is the **Highway Description** section that describes the highway in general and lists the most interesting attractions for quick reference. This is relevant when following the book from front to back with ascending mile markers.
- At the end of every chapter is the **Highway End** section. This not only shows the end mileage but, where applicable, serves as the **Highway Description** when following the book from back to front with descending mile markers. This describes the highway in general and lists the most interesting attractions for quick reference. For further clarity, if the highway names change along a route, the names will be reversed to display in the correct order. For example: the chapter for "Wy-160/Grayrocks Rd/Power Plant Rd" displays as "Grayrocks Rd/Power Plant Rd/Wy-160." *These reversed entries are listed in the Table of Contents and displayed in italics.*
- Following the **Highway Description** section, preceding the **Highway End** section, and at various points between are additional descriptions and directions for connecting highways. This provides an overview of each connecting highway without turning to the individual chapters. These highway connections are signified by "(see chapter)" after the highway name along with an Attraction Type of **Hwy Junction w/Chapter** or **Hwy Transition w/Chapter**. A "transition" is where the highway continues straight but the highway name changes.

5. Highway Naming

There are 5 different types of highway and road naming used in the state of Wyoming:

- **US-00** U.S. highways that run between states and are always paved.
- **Wy-00** Wyoming state highways that end at the state line and are always paved.
- **CR-00** County roads that change names between county lines and are generally gravel. These roads often are also named and have a street sign.
- **FR-00** National Forest roads that are generally gravel or dirt. These roads often transition from a county road at the National Forest boundary.
- **BLM-00** Bureau of Land Management roads that are generally gravel or dirt.

In many cases, two or more U.S. and Wyoming highways share common sections. In these cases the names are combined and separated by slashes, e.g. US-287/Wy-789. When multiple U.S. highways are combined, the "US-" prefix appears once, with the numerically sorted highway numbers separated by slashes, e.g. US-14/16/20. An extreme example is **Wy-789**, which runs south to north from Colorado to Montana and is shared with 6 U.S. highways.

These combinations of highways are named **Wy-789**, US-287/**Wy-789**, US-26/**Wy-789**, US-20/**Wy-789**, US-16/20/**Wy-789**, US-14/16/20/**Wy-789**, and US-310/**Wy-789**.

6. Attributes

Each **Section** is comprised of **Attributes**, which are the individual pieces of information that define the **Attraction** at the specified **Mile Marker**. The majority of these **Attributes** are defined textually; however, some are defined using a 1 to 6 star **Rating System** from *low* to *extra high* and defined as follows:

*	Low
**	Low/Medium
***	Medium
****	Medium/High
*****	High
******	Extra High *(only used for Cool Rating and only given in a few cases)*

6.1 Attraction Attributes

MM:	Highway Mile Marker to the tenth of a mile *(see section 2 above for more about Mile Markers)*
Dist:	Distance to the Attraction from the main highway
GPS:	GPS coordinates of the parking area or entrance for the Attraction
GPS2:	Optional GPS coordinates of the physical Attraction, if it is not at the parking area
Elev:	Elevation of the Attraction
Grid:	Used for estimating the location of an Attraction on the maps in the book or any physical map by a percentage to the right and down from the upper left corner. 0/0 is the upper left, 100/100 is the lower right, and 50/50 is the center. For example, Casper has a **Grid** of 67/55, which means it is 67% to the right and 55% down.
Land:	The entity that owns or manages the land where the Attraction is located. Some are abbreviated: BLM - Bureau of Land Management LDS - Church of Latter Day Saints (Mormon Church) NF - National Forest NM - National Monument NPS - National Park Service Wyoming G & F - Wyoming Game and Fish
Attraction:	The name of the place of interest at the specified Mile Marker. Under each Attraction is its description.
Type:	The type/category of the Attraction, e.g. Hiking Trail, Historic Site, Campground, etc.
Hours:	Hours and days that the Attraction is open, if limited. Unless otherwise stated, all hours are applicable 7 days a week
Crowds:	How crowded is the attraction? Rated from 1 - 5 stars (uncrowded=1, crowded=5)
Cool Rating:	How cool is the attraction (based on the author's opinion)? Rated from 1 - 6 stars (1=not cool, 6=Extra Cool). Combine this with the distance to travel to an attraction to help determine if it is worth your time.
[FEE AREA]	This is displayed when a fee is charged
Time:	The approximate time required to visit the Attraction, not counting driving time
Road Desc:	The description of the road surface, conditions, and restrictions. Unless otherwise noted: • All roads are paved and smooth • All gravel roads are reasonably smooth
Directions:	Detailed directions to the Attraction from the main highway • The directions use the following abbreviations: N=north, S=south, E=east, W=west, L=left, R=right. These are sometime combined, e.g. SW/L means southwest and left. • Since Interstate Highway exit ramps can be several tenths of a mile apart, the mileages are measured from the exit ramp closest to the direction being driven

Nearest Town:	Number of miles to drive and the direction to the nearest town. For example: Casper 14 NW (says Casper is 14 mi NW of the Attraction) Most Attractions do not include a nearest town, because the town is already listed as an Attraction at another Mile Marker. If there is not a "nearest town" at a highway junction, it means that the junction is already at a town.

6.2 Campground Attributes

For brevity, the Campground information is condensed to a single line, formatted as follows:

Campsites:	The number of campsites. If this is dispersed camping then "Dispersed" is displayed.
Shade:	Amount of shade rated from 1 to 5 stars (no shade=1, much shade=5)
Privacy:	General level of privacy per campsite rated from 1 to 5 stars (no privacy=1, much privacy=5)
RV Size:	Maximum RV length, in feet, that will fit in the largest parking areas. Values are: Tent, 20, 25, 30, 40, 40+

Other:	A compacted list of other campground information and amenities. For example:
	    1-877-444-6777:www.recreation.gov,Water,Electric,RVDump GRIZZLIES
	Would be interpreted as follows:
	• **1-877-444-6777:www.recreation.gov** - The phone number and web site for making reservations
	• **Water** - Drinking water is available
	• **Electric** - Electricity is available at some or all campsites
	• **RVDump** - An RV dump is located at the campground
	• ***GRIZZLIES** - The campground is in an area frequented by grizzly bears. Practice safe food storage
	• ***BEARS** - The campground is in an area frequented by black bears. Practice safe food storage
	* Practicing safe food storage means keeping food odors that will attract bears away from your camp.
	    Become familiar with these techniques before leaving home or ask a ranger.

Unless otherwise noted:
- All internal campground roads are gravel or dirt.
- All non-primitive campgrounds have a vault toilet, picnic tables, and fire rings or grills.

7. Conventions
- When you see a tilde in front of a number, this is shorthand for "approximately", e.g. "~10 mi" is the same as "approximately 10 miles".
- If an **Attraction** is followed by a direction indicator in parenthesis, e.g. (northbound), (heading southwest), etc., this means that the **Attraction** is only applicable if heading in that direction.

8. Book Indexes
- The book index is very detailed and is based on the **Attractions** and bolded words in the **Descriptions**.
- In addition, a section named "**Attractions at a Glance**" breaks down the **Attractions** per **Highway** by the following categories:
    - Attractions of Note
    - Campgrounds
    - Picnic areas and Rest Areas
    - Visitor Centers

This allows the reader to quickly and conveniently reference these most popular categories per highway without scanning through several pages of the book body.

9. Restrictions
- There are no photos included in this book. Grayscale photos do not accurately portray the beauty of Wyoming, plus they raise the price of the book. A fine collection of Wyoming photos are available at:
    www.wyomingroadtripbythemilemarker.com
- This book is not meant to be a comprehensive hiking guide. The book provides some of the better day hikes that are near the main highway while making the reader aware of longer trails that have trailheads near the main highways.
- This is the third minor update of this travel guide. Updates to previous versions plus any new information is available at:
    www.wyomingroadtripbythemilemarker.com

10. Abbreviations
- desc   description
- elev   elevation
- ft   feet
- hwy   highway
- mi   mile(s)
- sq   square, e.g. sq ft (square feet), sq mi (square miles)
- yds   yards

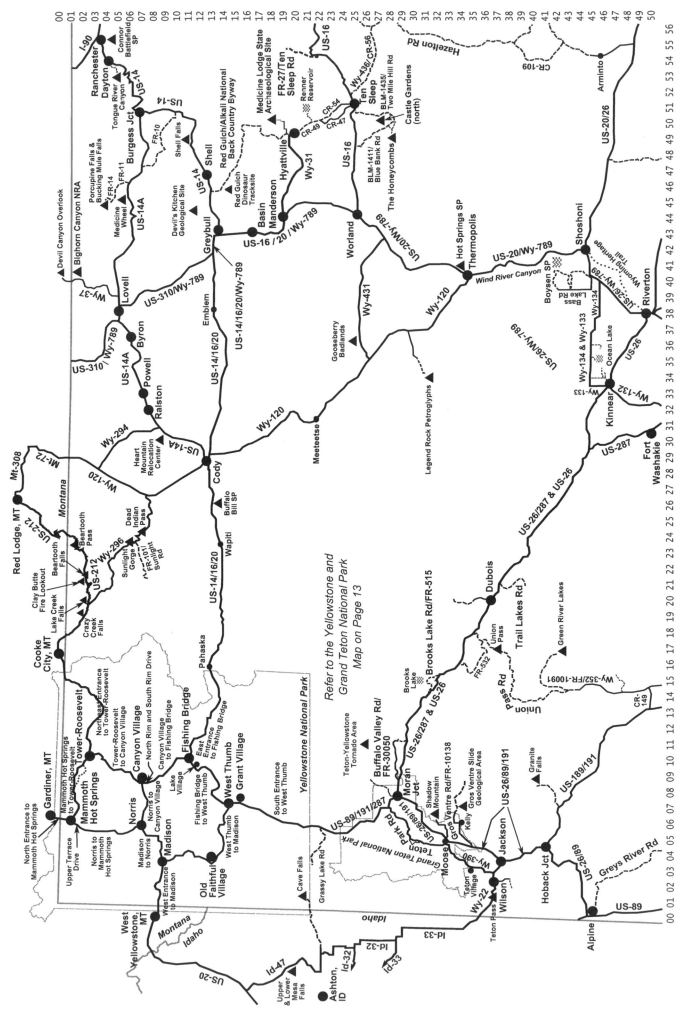

8   **Northwest Wyoming Map**

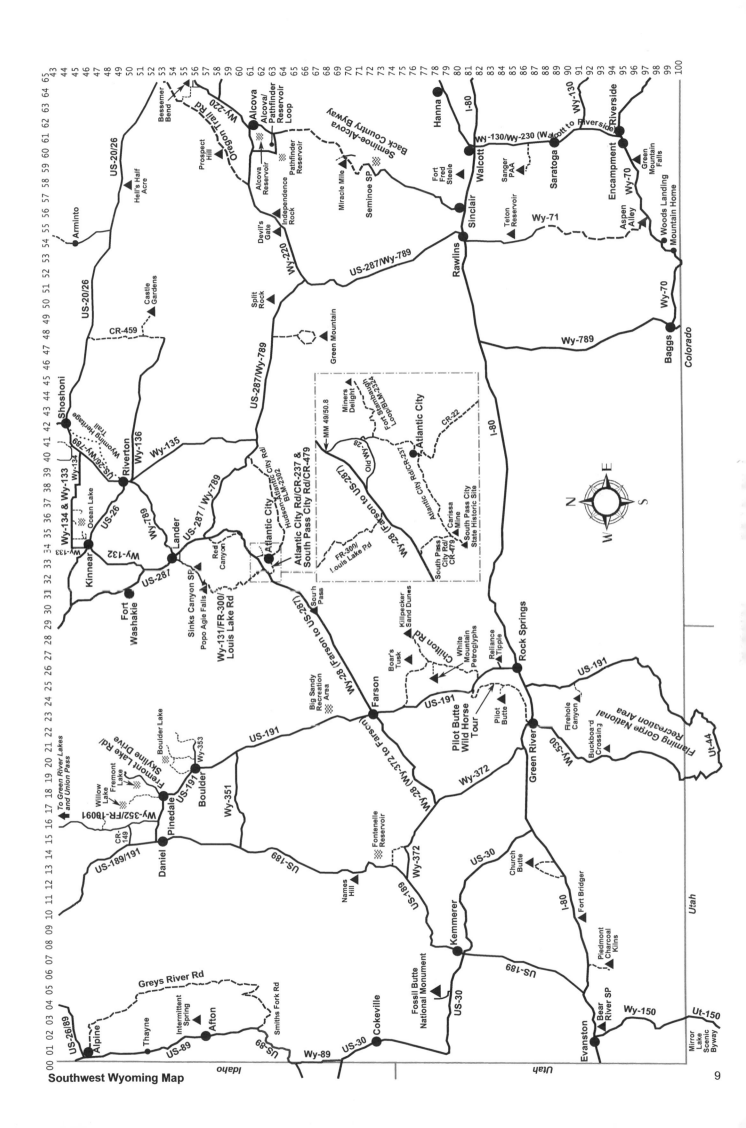

Southwest Wyoming Map

9

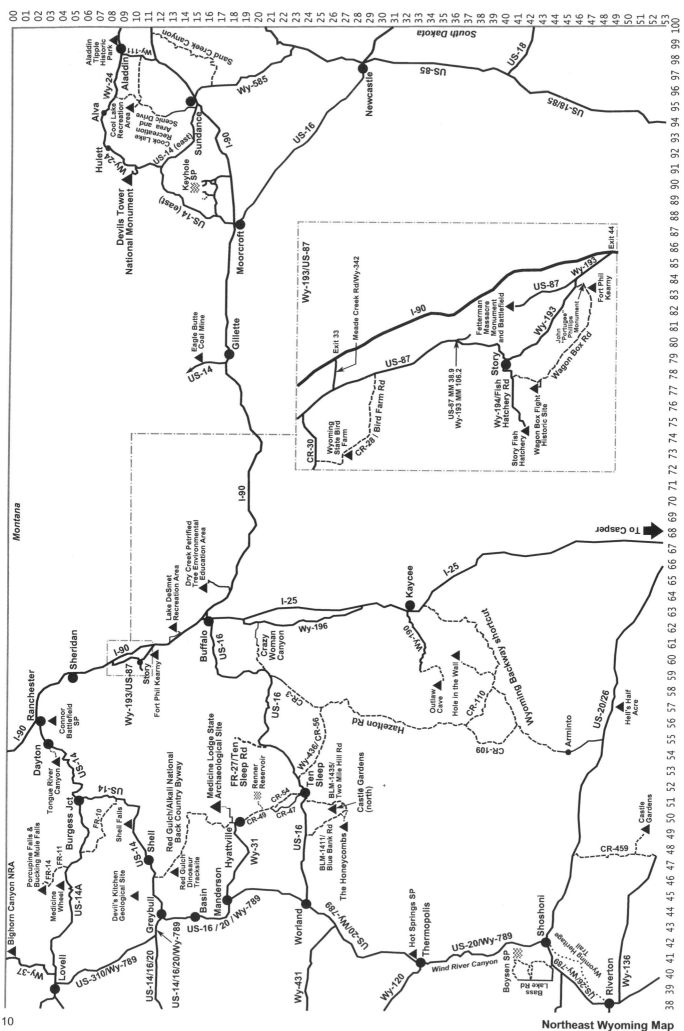

10

Northeast Wyoming Map

Nebraska

44 45 46 47 48 49 50 51 52 53 54 55 56 57 58 59 60 61 62 63 64 65 66 67 68 69 70 71 72 73 74 75 76 77 78 79 80 81 82 83 84 85 86 87 88 89 90 91 92 93 94 95 96 97 98 99 100

38 39 40 41 42 43 44 45 46 47 48 49 50 51 52 53 54 55 56 57 58 59 60 61 62 63 64 65 66 67 68 69 70 71 72 73 74 75 76 77 78 79 80 81 82 83 84 85 86 87 88 89 90 91 92 93 94 95 96 97 98 99 100

US-20

US-18/85

Lusk

US-85

Lingle

Torrington

Fort Laramie

US-26

Featherlegs Monument & Rawhide Buttes

Register Cliff

Fort Laramie National Historic Site

Wy-160/Grayrocks Rd

Power Plant Rd

Hawk Springs

Hawk Springs State Recreation Area

Pine Bluffs

I-80

US-18/20

Wy-270

Guernsey SP

Guernsey

Oregon Trail Ruts

US-26

US-85

Cheyenne

Glendo SP

Glendo Park Rd

Glendo

Wheatland

Wheatland Reservoir #1

Wy-34

I-25

I-80

Curt Gowdy SP

Wy-210/Happy Jack Rd

FR-700/ Vedauwoo Glen Rd

Douglas

Fort Fetterman

Wy-93

CR-27

I-25

Ayres Natural Bridge

Pole Mountain Trails

Wy-210

Yellow Pine CG

Happy Jack Trailhead

Aspen Trail

Summit Trail

Headquarters Trail

Tie City Trailhead

Pole Creek Trail

Summit Trailhead

FR-705

Summit Rest Area

Wy-210

Pole Mountain

Vedauwoo Recreation Area

Laramie

US-287

FR-105

National Historic Trails Interpretive Center

I-25

E 1st St

N Center St

Wy-258

US-20/26/87

S Wolcott St

Casper Mountain Rd/ Wy-251

Wy-258/SE/Wyoming Blvd

Edness Wilkins SP

US-20/26/87

Casper Mountain Rd/Wy-251

Casper Mountain

Muddy Mountain

Casper

I-25

US-20/26

Wy-220

MM 3.0

Wy-258

Fort Caspar

MM 6.1

US-20/26 Bypass

CR-202W Zero Rd to Oregon Trail Rd

US-20/26

Wy-220

CR-230

Wy-34

Wy-130 (Laramie to Wy-230)

CR-422/Phalow Ln

Lake Hattie

CR-44/Harmony Ln

Wy-230 (Laramie to Colorado)

Colorado

Medicine Bow

US-30/287

Rock River

Wy-13

I-80

FR-101/ Sand Lake Rd

Medicine Bow Peak

See Snowy Range map on next page

Wy-130 (Laramie to Wy-230)

Riverside

Wy-230 (Riverside to Colorado)

Wy-487

I-25

CR-505

Bessemer Bend

Alcova/ Pathfinder Reservoir Loop

Alcova

Wy-220

Oregon Trail Rd

Prospect Hill

Alcova Reservoir

Pathfinder Reservoir

Independence Rock

Devil's Gate

Seminoe-Alcova Back Country Byway

Miracle Mile

Seminoe SP

Hanna

Fort Fred Steele

Walcott

Sanger PAA

Saratoga

Encampment

Wy-70

Aspen Alley

Woods Landing Mountain Home

US-20/26

Arminto

Hell's Half Acre

Prospect Hill

Wy-220

Split Rock

US-287/Wy-789

Green Mountain

Sinclair

Rawlins

US-287/Wy-789

Wy-71

Wy-130/Wy-230 (Walcott to Riverside)

Wy-70

Castle Gardens

CR-459

Wy-789

Baggs

Shoshoni

Wyoming Heritage Trail

Riverton

Wy-136

Wy-135

US-26/Wy-789

US-20/26

I-80

N E S W

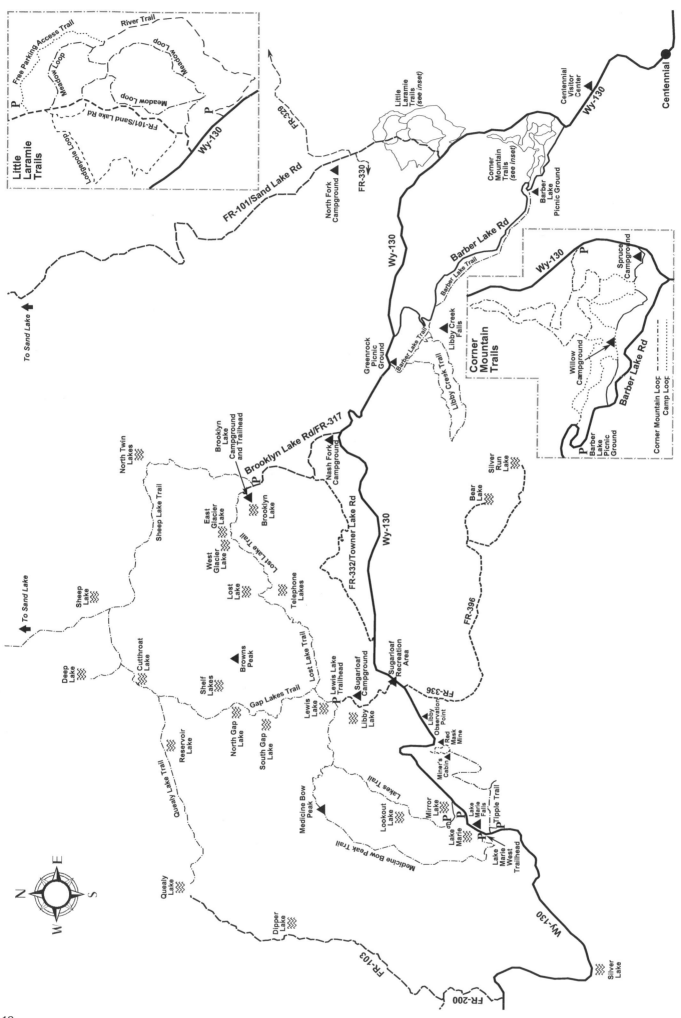

Little Laramie Trails

Free Parking Access Trail
River Trail
Meadow Loop
Meadow Loop
Meadow Loop
FR-101/Sand Lake Rd
Lodgepole Loop
P
P
Wy-130
FR-329

To Sand Lake

FR-101/Sand Lake Rd

North Fork Campground
FR-330

Little Laramie Trails *(see inset)*

Centennial Visitor Center
Wy-130
Centennial

Corner Mountain Trails *(see inset)*

Barber Lake Picnic Ground

Wy-130

Barber Lake Rd

Barber Lake Trail

Greenrock Picnic Ground

(Barber Lake Trail)

Libby Creek Falls

Libby Creek Trail

Corner Mountain Trails

Wy-130
P

Spruce Campground

Willow Campground

Barber Lake Rd

Barber Lake Picnic Ground
P

Corner Mountain Loop
Camp Loop

Brooklyn Lake Campground and Trailhead
P
Brooklyn Lake Rd/FR-317

Nash Fork Campground

North Twin Lakes

Sheep Lake Trail

East Glacier Lake
West Glacier Lake
Brooklyn Lake

Lost Lake Trail

FR-332/Towner Lake Rd

Wy-130

Bear Lake

Silver Run Lake

To Sand Lake

Sheep Lake

Deep Lake

Cutthroat Lake

Lost Lake

Telephone Lakes

Shelf Lakes

Browns Peak

Lost Lake Trail

Lewis Lake Trailhead
P

Sugarloaf Campground

Sugarloaf Recreation Area

FR-396

Gap Lakes Trail

Lewis Lake

Libby Lake

Libby Observation Point

Red Mask Mine

FR-336

Reservoir Lake

North Gap Lake

South Gap Lake

Qualy Lake Trail

Medicine Bow Peak

Lookout Lake

Lakes Trail

Miner's Cabin

Mirror Lake
P

Lake Marie Falls
P

Lake Marie

Tipple Trail
P

Lake Marie West Trailhead

Medicine Bow Peak Trail

N
E
S
W

Qualy Lake

Dipper Lake

FR-103

FR-200

Wy-130

Silver Lake

12

Snowy Range Map

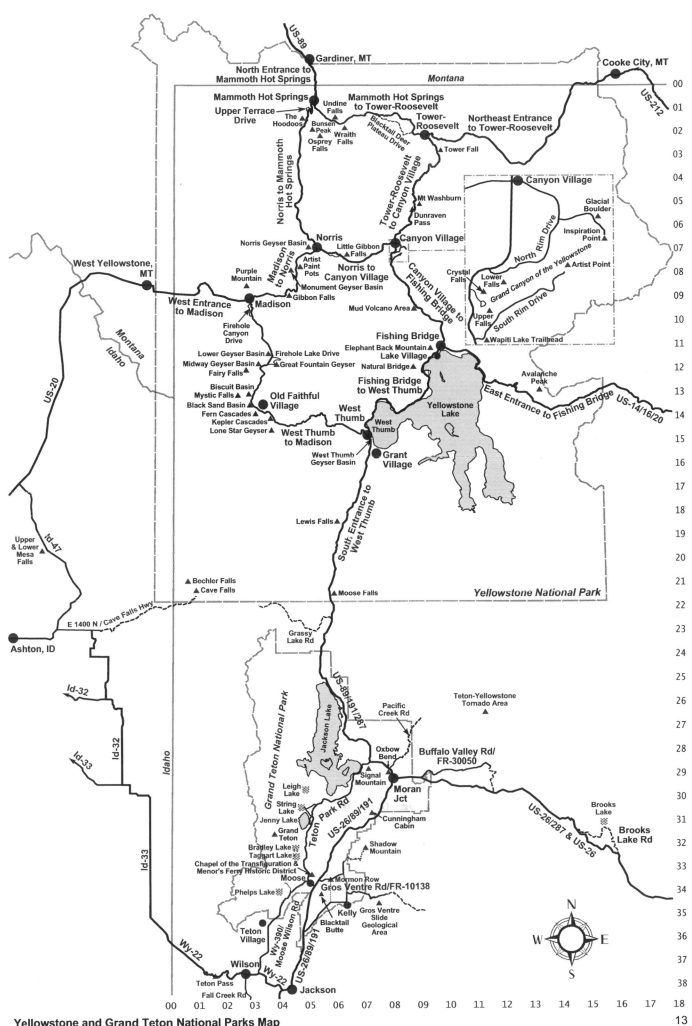

Yellowstone and Grand Teton National Parks Map

13

Alcova/Pathfinder Reservoir Loop   E/W

MM: 0.0/20.0 **GPS:** 42.56102/-106.72524 **Elev:** 5377 **Grid:** 62/61
Alcova/Pathfinder Reservoir Loop   **Type:** Highway Description
20 mi loop from **Wy-220** past **Alcova Reservoir**, **Fremont Canyon**, and **Pathfinder Reservoir**. This route starts at **Wy-220** MM 86.5 at the town of **Alcova** and ends at **Wy-220** MM 80.7, 5.8 mi west of the starting point. The campgrounds in the area are primarily for boaters and provide little shade. Highlights include: **Alcova Reservoir**, **Fremont Canyon Bridge and Overlook**, **Pathfinder Dam Overlook**, **Pathfinder Interpretive Center and Trail**.
Road Desc: CR-408 into and out of Fremont Canyon is steep and winding.
Directions: S on CR-407/Kortes Rd 7.0 mi; W on CR-408/Fremont Canyon Rd 6.8 mi; N on CR-409/Pathfinder Rd 6.2 mi.

MM: 0.0/20.0 **GPS:** 42.56102/-106.72524 **Elev:** 5377 **Grid:** 62/61
Wy-220 (see chapter)   **Type:** Hwy Junction w/Chapter
Directions: NE to Casper or SW to Rawlins from MM 86.5

MM: 0.0/20.0 **GPS:** 42.56102/-106.72524 **Elev:** 5377 **Grid:** 62/61
Alcova   **Type:** Town

MM: 0.9/19.1 **GPS:** 42.55033/-106.71652 **GPS2:** 42.54824/-106.71975 **Elev:** 5340 **Grid:** 62/61
Alcova Dam   **Type:** Dam
The fourth of 7 dams on the **North Platte River**, which was completed in 1938. The dam is earth-fill, 185 ft high and 763 ft long.
Cool Rating: * **Time:** Drive by **Directions:** Just west when driving over the North Platte River bridge.

MM: 3.0/17.0 **Dist:** 0.7 **GPS:** 42.53183/-106.71240 **Elev:** 5510 **Grid:** 62/62 **Land:** Bureau of Reclamation
Black Beach Campground: Alcova Reservoir   **Type:** Campground
Located on a point at the east end of **Alcova Reservoir** with nice views of the red hills along the shoreline. *Sheltered picnic tables. No trees.*
Crowds: **** **[FEE AREA]** **Road Desc:** Gravel
Directions: The turnoff is on CR-407/Kortes Rd (3.0 mi S of Wy-220 and 4.0 mi N of CR-408); NW on Black Beach Rd 0.7 mi.
Campsites: 14 **Shade:** * **Privacy:** * **RV Size:** 40'+ **Other:** None

MM: 5.0/15.0 **Dist:** 1.2 **GPS:** 42.52152/-106.74319 **Elev:** 5560 **Grid:** 62/62 **Land:** Bureau of Reclamation
Cottonwood Creek Campground: Alcova Reservoir   **Type:** Campground
A fairly large campground on the south shore of **Alcova Reservoir**. Dispersed sites are located near the lake, and better defined sites are up a hill above the pay station. Dozens of sites are scattered about the area in several loops. Some of the upper sites have a nice view of the lake. The camping areas near the lake fill fast, but the upper sites are less used. *Most of the sites are not level. Few sites have tables, but most have fire rings.*
Crowds: *** **[FEE AREA]** **Road Desc:** Gravel
Directions: The turnoff is on CR-407/Kortes Rd (5.0 mi S of Wy-220 and 2.0 mi N of CR-408); NW 1.2 mi to pay station; Continue straight to sites around the reservoir or turn right for sites above.
Campsites: Dispersed **Shade:** * **Privacy:** ** **RV Size:** 40' **Other:** None

MM: 5.0/15.0 **Dist:** 1.3 **GPS:** 42.52114/-106.74165 **Elev:** 5613 **Grid:** 62/62 **Land:** Bureau of Reclamation
Cottonwood Creek Dinosaur Trail   **Type:** Historic Site
In 1991 numerous dinosaur bones and the skeleton of a medium-sized dinosaur were discovered by 5th grade field science students in the sandstone ledges of the **Morrison Formation** south of **Alcova Reservoir**. A 0.3 mi round-trip hiking trail provides access to the site for further research and educational purposes and includes interpretive signs about the geology and fossils. The trail climbs steeply to a fine view of **Alcova Reservoir** and the surrounding area. The trail loops at the top and returns by the same route.
Cool Rating: * **Crowds:** * **Time:** 30 min **Road Desc:** Gravel
Notes: The trail is very steep and the footing is not good. Unless you are a geologist, the climb is more worth it for the scenic view than the geological information on the signs.
Directions: The turnoff is on CR-407/Kortes Rd (5.0 mi S of Wy-220 and 2.0 mi N of CR-408); NW 1.2 mi to pay station; Just before the pay station at Cottonwood Creek Campground NE/R 0.05 mi; S/R 0.1 mi.

MM: 7.0/13.0 **GPS:** 42.48322/-106.74944 **Elev:** 6043 **Grid:** 61/63
CR-407/Kortes Rd & CR-408/Fremont Canyon Rd   **Type:** Highway Junction
Directions: If heading S from Alcova, turn SW/R. If heading E from Fremont Canyon, turn N/L.

MM: 9.9/10.1 **GPS:** 42.47157/-106.79644 **Elev:** 5670 **Grid:** 61/63 **Land:** BLM
Fremont Canyon Bridge and Overlook   **Type:** Scenic Viewpoint
The **North Platte River** runs through a 120 ft deep gorge, which is spanned by the **Fremont Canyon Bridge**. Just north of the bridge along the canyon rim is a large parking area with a railed overlook, which provides views into the red-walled canyon as well as a good view the old steel truss bridge. This is a popular spot for rock climbers. Camping is allowed in the parking area. *No trees. 3 unshaded picnic tables. Picnic shelter. Vault toilet. Road noise.*
Cool Rating: **** **Crowds:** ** **Time:** 15 min
Directions: The turnoff is on CR-408/Fremont Canyon Rd (2.9 mi W of CR-407 and 3.9 mi E of CR-409); NE side of road.
Campsites: Dispersed **Shade:** * **Privacy:** * **RV Size:** 40'+ **Other:** None

MM: 12.7/7.3 **Dist:** 0.8 **GPS:** 42.46570/-106.84998 **Elev:** 5688 **Grid:** 60/63 **Land:** BLM
North Platte River access below Pathfinder Dam   **Type:** River Access Point
Access to the **North Platte River** below **Pathfinder Dam**. This area provides handicapped accessible fishing as well as a short walk to the **Swinging Bridge**, which is a highlight on the **Pathfinder Interpretive Trail** (see MM 13.8). *Vault toilet.*
Crowds: * **Road Desc:** Gravel
Directions: The turnoff is on CR-408/Fremont Canyon Rd (5.7 mi W of CR-407 and 1.1 mi E of CR-409); W 0.5 mi to river access turnoff; NW 0.3 mi to parking area.

MM: 12.7/7.3 *Dist:* 2.6 *GPS:* 42.45509/-106.87019 *Elev:* 5858 *Grid:* 60/64 *Land:* BLM
Dispersed Camping: Pathfinder Reservoir   *Type:* Campground
Primitive camping along the shore of **Pathfinder Reservoir** ending at a peninsula named **Woolf Point**. The shoreline is situated at the base of a mountain that extends along the peninsula, creating a lakeshore on both the north and the south sides. Continuing past the river access point *(previous section)* (MI 0.5) the road climbs 375 ft (MI 1.6) before descending 200 ft to a parking area with a vault toilet (MI 2.6). A primitive road continues another 1/2 mi to the tip of **Woolf Point**. Along the route are several primitive roads that lead to both the north and south lakeshore. Easy access roads are at MI 1.0, MI 1.1 and at the parking area at MI 2.6. Two other steep roads to the north shore are at MI 1.5 and MI 1.8. At MI 2.1 is a pullout with a nice view and a very steep road to the south lakeshore. At MI 2.2 is a steep road to **Woolf Point** on the south side of the mountain. *Some vault toilets.*
Crowds: ** *Road Desc:* Gravel, washboard sections. Primitive dirt access roads that are impassable when wet.
Directions: The turnoff is on CR-408/Fremont Canyon Rd (5.7 mi W of CR-407 and 1.1 mi E of CR-409); SW 2.6 mi to parking area.
Campsites: Dispersed *Shade:* * *Privacy:* * *RV Size:* 30' *Other:* None

MM: 13.6/6.4 *GPS:* 42.46953/-106.84913 *Elev:* 5920 *Grid:* 60/63 *Land:* Bureau of Reclamation
Pathfinder Dam Overlook   *Type:* Scenic Viewpoint
A 0.2 mi (one-way) hiking trail downhill to an overlook of the 214 ft tall **Pathfinder Dam**. Finished in 1909, this masonry dam is built between the narrow granite walls of **Fremont Canyon**. Interpretive signs are located at both the start and end of the trail. This is a highlight on the **Pathfinder Interpretive Trail** (see MM 13.8). **Pathfinder Reservoir** is the third of 7 reservoirs on the **North Platte River**.
Cool Rating: *** *Crowds:* * *Time:* 30 min
Directions: The turnoff is on CR-408/Fremont Canyon Rd (6.6 mi W of CR-407 and 0.2 mi E of CR-409); S side of road.

MM: 13.8/6.2 *GPS:* 42.47114/-106.85134 *Elev:* 5916 *Grid:* 60/63
CR-408/Fremont Canyon Rd & CR-409/Pathfinder Rd   *Type:* Highway Junction
Directions: If heading W from Fremont Canyon, turn N/R. If heading S from Wy-220, turn E/L.

MM: 13.8/6.2 *Dist:* 0.1 *GPS:* 42.47190/-106.85255 *Elev:* 5942 *Grid:* 60/63 *Land:* County
Pathfinder Interpretive Center   *Type:* Historic Site
This interpretive center is the former **dam tender's house** and contains exhibits relating to the construction of the **Pathfinder Dam**. *4 picnic tables, 2 on a covered porch.*
Hours: Access to the Interpretive Center is by appointment with the Natrona County Roads, Bridges and Parks Department.
Phone: 307-235-9325 *Cool Rating:* ** *Crowds:* * *Time:* 30 min
Directions: From the junction of CR-408 and CR-409; NW 0.1 mi.

MM: 13.8/6.2 *Dist:* 0.1 *GPS:* 42.47039/-106.85295 *Elev:* 5878 *Grid:* 60/63 *Land:* Bureau of Reclamation
Pathfinder Interpretive Trail   *Type:* Point of Interest
An interpretive loop trail that crosses **Pathfinder Dam**, descends into **Fremont Canyon**, then climbs out of the canyon to the dam overlook. Start the loop from a parking area at the beginning of the dam road. A self-guided tour pamphlet can be obtained at the **Pathfinder Interpretive Center** or by calling the reservation number *(see previous section)*.

Walking counterclockwise the trail passes the **spillway area** and crosses the **dam** to the south side of the canyon. Just to the south is an **earthen dike** originally built to stave off a catastrophe when unexpected high waters threatened to cut a new channel, bypassing the just-completed dam. A permanent dike was built in 1910-1911. At 1/4 mi is an overlook into the canyon where the **outlet tunnels** release water in the summer to meet the heavy irrigation demand downstream. The trail soon begins to descend to the bottom of the canyon where at 0.5 mi the river can be crossed on a **swinging bridge**. After scrambling across some boulders, the trail opens up and continues 0.3 mi to the **engineer's camp**, which contains building foundations and a single standing building that is believed to have been a jail. The trail then climbs rather steeply 0.4 mi up a rocky trail back to the top of the canyon, then to the parking area for the **Pathfinder Dam Overlook**. From the parking area a 1/2 mi round-trip trail leads to the best view of the dam *(see MM 13.6)*. Walk west along the road 0.3 mi back to the parking area. *Moderately easy; 1.4 mi loop with a 0.5 mi round-trip spur trail to the dam overlook; 240 ft elev loss to river, 100 ft elev loss to dam overlook.*

If short on time or unable to hike into the canyon, the following combination of driving and short hikes allow all of the points of interest to be seen, except the **engineer's camp**:
   1) Walk across the **Pathfinder Dam** to the **outlet tunnels** and back (0.5 mi)
   2) Drive to the **Pathfinder Dam Overlook** and hike down and back (0.4 mi) *(see MM 13.6)*
   3) Drive to the **North Platte River Access Area** and walk to the **swinging bridge** (0.2 mi) *(see MM 12.7)*
Easy; 1.1 mi round-trip; 100 ft elev loss to dam overlook.
Phone: 307-235-9325 *Cool Rating:* **** *Crowds:* * *Time:* 1.5 hrs
Notes: The dam walkway may be closed if there are heightened security concerns.
Directions: From the junction of CR-408 and CR-409; SW 0.1 mi to parking area on S side of road.

MM: 13.8/6.2 *Dist:* 0.3 *GPS:* 42.47048/-106.85795 *Elev:* 5900 *Grid:* 60/63 *Land:* Bureau of Reclamation
RV Dump: Pathfinder Reservoir   *Type:* RV Dump
No potable water.
Road Desc: Gravel *Directions:* From the junction of CR-408 and CR-409; SW 0.3 mi; N side of road.

MM: 13.8/6.2 *Dist:* 0.4 *GPS:* 42.46978/-106.85959 *Elev:* 5857 *Grid:* 60/63 *Land:* Bureau of Reclamation
Weiss Campground: Pathfinder Reservoir   *Type:* Campground
Near the northeast shore of **Pathfinder Reservoir**. *Few trees. Sheltered picnic tables. Boat ramp.*
Crowds: *** *[FEE AREA]* *Road Desc:* Gravel *Directions:* From the junction of CR-408 and CR-409; SW 0.4 mi.
Campsites: 12 *Shade:* * *Privacy:* * *RV Size:* 40'+ *Other:* None

MM: 13.8/6.2 *Dist:* 0.7 *GPS:* 42.47160/-106.86428 *Elev:* 5873 *Grid:* 60/63 *Land:* Bureau of Reclamation
Sage Campground: Pathfinder Reservoir   *Type:* Campground
Near the northeast shore of **Pathfinder Reservoir**. *Picnic shelters and a few trees in 5 sites nearest the lake. No shelters or trees in other 5 sites.*
Crowds: *** *[FEE AREA]* *Road Desc:* Gravel *Directions:* From the junction of CR-408 and CR-409; SW 0.7 mi.
Campsites: 10 *Shade:* * *Privacy:* * *RV Size:* 40'+ *Other:* None

MM: 13.8/6.2 *Dist:* 1.2 *GPS:* 42.46860/-106.87100 *Elev:* 5872 *Grid:* 60/63 *Land:* Bureau of Reclamation
Diabase Campground: Pathfinder Reservoir   *Type:* Campground
Near the northeast shore of **Pathfinder Reservoir**. *No trees. Picnic shelters. Marina. Boat ramp.*
Crowds: *** [FEE AREA] *Road Desc:* Gravel *Directions:* From the junction of CR-408 and CR-409; SW 1.2 mi.
Campsites: 10 *Shade:* * *Privacy:* * *RV Size:* 40' *Other:* None

MM: 16.4/3.6 *Dist:* 3.8 *GPS:* 42.49830/-106.90488 *Elev:* 5864 *Grid:* 59/63 *Land:* Bureau of Reclamation
Bishops Point Campground: Pathfinder Reservoir   *Type:* Campground
Near the north tip of **Pathfinder Reservoir**. *No trees. Sheltered picnic tables. Boat ramp.*
Crowds: * [FEE AREA] *Road Desc:* Gravel
Directions: The turnoff is on CR-409/Pathfinder Rd (2.6 mi N of CR-408 and 3.6 mi S of Wy-220); W on Bishop Point Rd 3.8 mi.
Campsites: 15 *Shade:* * *Privacy:* * *RV Size:* 40'+ *Other:* None

MM: 20.0/0.0 *GPS:* 42.55471/-106.83480 *Elev:* 6296 *Grid:* 60/61
Wy-220 *(see chapter)*   *Type:* Hwy Junction w/Chapter
Directions: NE to Casper or SW to Rawlins from MM 80.7

MM: 20.0/0.0 *GPS:* 42.55471/-106.83480 *Elev:* 6296 *Grid:* 60/61
End of Highway   *Type:* Highway End
20 mi loop from **Wy-220** past **Pathfinder Reservoir**, **Fremont Canyon**, and **Alcova Reservoir**. This route starts at **Wy-220** MM 80.7 and ends at **Wy-220** MM 86.5 at the town of **Alcova**, 5.8 mi east of the starting point. The campgrounds in the area are primarily for boaters and provide little shade. Highlights include: **Pathfinder Interpretive Center and Trail**, **Pathfinder Dam Overlook**, **Fremont Canyon Bridge and Overlook**, **Alcova Reservoir**.
Nearest Town: Alcova 5.8 E
Directions: S on CR-409/Pathfinder Rd 6.2 mi; E on CR-408/Fremont Canyon Rd 6.8 mi; N on CR-407/Kortes Rd 7.0 mi.

Atlantic City Rd/CR-237 & South Pass City Rd/CR-479   NE/SW

MM: 0.0/8.2   **GPS:** 42.52736/-108.72232   **Elev:** 8277   **Grid:** 33/62
Atlantic City Rd/CR-237 & South Pass City Rd/CR-479   **Type:** Highway Description
8.2 mi route that loops from **Wy-28** MM 49.0 southwest through **Atlantic City**, past **South Pass City**, and north back to **Wy-28**
MM 43.5. Highlights include: **Miner's Delight Ghost Town, Atlantic City, Willie Handcart Company Tragedy Memorial,**
Carissa Mine, South Pass City.
Road Desc: First 0.8 mi is paved. The rest is smooth gravel.
Directions: S on Atlantic City Rd/CR-237 2.7 mi; S/L on S Dexter Ave 0.2 mi; SW/R 3.7 mi on CR-237; N on South Pass City
Rd/CR-479 1.6 mi.

MM: 0.0/8.2   **GPS:** 42.52736/-108.72232   **Elev:** 8277   **Grid:** 33/62
Wy-28 (Farson to US-287) *(see chapter)*   **Type:** Hwy Junction w/Chapter
Directions: If heading northeast: N/R 1.5 mi to Wy-28; NE to Lander from MM 49. **If heading southwest:** SW/L 2.2 mi to
Wy-28; SW to Farson from MM 46.9.

MM: 0.6/7.6   **Dist:** 0.3   **GPS:** 42.51917/-108.71437   **Elev:** 8035   **Grid:** 33/62   **Land:** BLM
Big Atlantic Gulch Campground   **Type:** Campground
In the middle of a young aspen grove in a gulch between sagebrush hills. *Single loop. Short aspen trees don't offer much shade.*
Large sites. Level.
Crowds: ***   **[FEE AREA]**   **Road Desc:** Gravel   **Directions:** E on Fort Stambaugh Loop/BLM-2324 0.3 mi; N side of road.
Campsites: 8   **Shade:** **   **Privacy:** ***   **RV Size:** 30'   **Other:** Water BEARS

MM: 0.6/7.6   **Dist:** 2.8   **GPS:** 42.53171/-108.67738   **GPS2:** 42.53300/-108.67985   **Elev:** 8247   **Grid:** 34/62   **Land:** BLM
Miner's Delight Ghost Town   **Type:** Historic Site
Established as a gold mining camp in 1867 along with its sister camps **Atlantic City** and **South Pass City**. The camp was
originally named **Hamilton City** but was known as **Miner's Delight**, which was the name of the largest mine in the area. The name
was later officially changed. At its peak the town had 75 residents, but that number fell dramatically as gold mining became non-
cost effective in future years. In 1874 the mine shut down but reopened a short time later. The mine was shut down again in 1882
and the town was abandoned. The town was revived when there was an attempt to resume mining in 1907. During the Depression
some of the abandoned cabins were occupied by the jobless, and the town was inhabited as late as 1960. Adjacent to the parking
area is an old cemetery, which contains a single headstone for a person that lived from 1837-1875. The remainder of the cemetery
has some iron fences filled with sagebrush and young trees. A 1/4 mi trail passes 10 unrestored structures that are still standing
from the 1907 period.
Cool Rating: ***   **Crowds:** *   **Time:** 1 hr   **Road Desc:** Gravel
Directions: E/L on Fort Stambaugh Loop/BLM-2324 2.8 mi; N/L 80 yds to parking area.

MM: 0.8/7.4   **GPS:** 42.51820/-108.72090   **Elev:** 8107   **Grid:** 33/62
Pavement Ends (southbound)   **Type:** Pavement Change

MM: 0.9/7.3   **GPS:** 42.51591/-108.72217   **Elev:** 8110   **Grid:** 33/62   **Land:** BLM
Atlantic City Campground   **Type:** Campground
A nice campground on a forested hillside amid the sagebrush hills. *Single loop. Mixed forest. 3 pull-thrus.*
Crowds: ****   **[FEE AREA]**   **Directions:** W side of road
Campsites: 18   **Shade:** ****   **Privacy:** ****   **RV Size:** 40'   **Other:** Water BEARS

MM: 2.6/5.6   **GPS:** 42.49636/-108.73058   **Elev:** 7670   **Grid:** 33/63   **Land:** City
Atlantic City   **Type:** Historic Site
Established as a gold mining camp in 1867 along with its sister camps **Miner's Delight** and **South Pass City**. This camp was
established as a town in 1868 and since has experienced a continuing series of mining booms and busts, all but one tied to the
fortunes of gold. A brochure provides a detailed history of the town plus a 27 stop self-guided walking tour (including possibly the
oldest house in Wyoming). The brochure can be obtained from an information board at the northeast corner of **Main St** and
Geissler Ave and at the general store.
Cool Rating: ***   **Crowds:** *   **Time:** 1 hr   **Road Desc:** Partially paved

MM: 2.9/5.3   **Dist:** 7.9   **GPS:** 42.43970/-108.62318   **Elev:** 7346   **Grid:** 35/64   **Land:** BLM
Willie Handcart Company Tragedy Memorial   **Type:** Historic Site
In 1856 a group of 1,620 converts to the **Mormon** religion sailed to America intent on reaching **Salt Lake City** before winter.
Unable to afford wagons many of these destitute emigrants instead pushed small handcarts. Due to unforeseen delays, the fourth
group of 404 led by **James G. Willie** left Iowa City dangerously late on July 15. An early October blizzard and bitter cold trapped
the company on the east side of **Rocky Ridge**. A rescue party arrived on October 21, leaving men and supplies before moving on
in search of the **Martin Handcart Company** who had left even later on July 28 and were trapped by the same storm *(see Mormon
Handcart Historic Site on Wy-220 MM 56.5)*. After waiting until October 23 for more help, the **Willie Handcart Company** decided
to undertake the 5 mi climb over **Rocky Ridge** in a howling snowstorm and knee-deep snow. The 23 mi trek to a camp near **Rock
Creek** cost 15 lives, including 2 men who dug a circular grave to bury the original 13 who had died. On October 25 the company
moved on and was finally met by more rescue wagons near **South Pass**. They finally reached **Salt Lake City** on November 9, with
a loss of 77 members.

Follow a dirt path south 120 yds to a plaque and memorial at the unmarked burial site. Continuing another 220 yds leads to 2
additional fenced-in graves. The memorial and surrounding area is privately owned by the **Mormon** church. Across from the
memorial is the **Rock Creek Hollow** visitor center, which includes restrooms and a large private campground. This area is set up
to accommodate large groups that pull handcarts over **Rocky Ridge**, re-enacting the journey of their pioneer ancestors. These
treks commonly take place through July and early August. The site is hosted by members of the **Mormon** church who gladly help
visitors and explain the history of the handcart companies.
Cool Rating: **   **Crowds:** *   **Time:** 40 min   **Road Desc:** Gravel
Notes: The site is crowded during the handcart treks in July and early August.
Directions: At the end of S Dexter Ave keep left on Three Forks-Atlantic City Rd/CR-22 3.9 mi; Fork E/L on Lewiston Rd/CR-475
4.0 mi.

MM: 6.6/1.6 *GPS:* 42.47605/-108.79617 *Elev:* 8019 *Grid:* 32/63
South Pass City Rd/CR-479 *Type:* Highway Junction
This junction is 0.6 mi north of South Pass City.

MM: 6.6/1.6 *Dist:* 0.1 *GPS:* 42.47477/-108.79715 *Elev:* 7975 *Grid:* 32/63 *Land:* State
Carissa Mine *Type:* Historic Site
This was the largest and most productive mine in the area and the lifeblood of booming **South Pass City** *(see next section)*. The state has purchased this site and is in the process of restoration. 3 signs explain in detail the history of the mine and the restoration project. The mine area can be viewed more closely from a walking path.
Cool Rating: *** *Crowds:* * *Time:* 10-30 min *Road Desc:* Gravel *Directions:* SW on South Pass City Rd/CR-479 0.1 mi

---

MM: 6.6/1.6 *Dist:* 0.6 *GPS:* 42.46875/-108.80274 *Elev:* 7816 *Grid:* 32/63 *Land:* State
South Pass City State Historic Site *Type:* Historic Site
The discovery of the **Cariso Lode** near **South Pass** in June 1867 started **Wyoming**'s largest 19th century gold mining boom. **South Pass City** was the first of 3 area mining camps followed by **Atlantic City** and **Miner's Delight**. The nearby **Carissa Mine** was the largest and most productive of the area mines. As a result, **South Pass City** became a booming town growing to over 1000 residents. The town was incorporated in the summer of 1868, only to have the mining industry begin to slump in early 1869. An influx of capital temporarily revived the industry; however, by 1872 the population had dwindled to a few hundred as gold mining became non-cost effective. The town would boom and bust over the next several decades, during which time residents survived by diversifying into ranching, timber, and cottage industries. By 1949 the town was abandoned, fell into disrepair, and was subsequently run privately as a tourist attraction. The state purchased the town for restoration in 1966, and it later became a state historic site with accurately restored buildings furnished with original artifacts. Literature at the visitor center explains the history of the town and describes the buildings on the interpretive self-guided tour.
Hours: 9am - 6pm (May 15 - Sept 30) *Phone:* 307-332-3684 *Cool Rating:* *** *Crowds:* *** *Time:* 1 hr *[FEE AREA]*
Road Desc: Gravel *Directions:* SW on South Pass City Rd/CR-479 0.6 mi

---

MM: 8.2/0.0 *GPS:* 42.49295/-108.80993 *Elev:* 8264 *Grid:* 32/63
Wy-28 (Farson to US-287) *(see chapter)* *Type:* Hwy Junction w/Chapter
Directions: NE to Lander or SW to Farson from MM 43.5

MM: 8.2/0.0 *GPS:* 42.49295/-108.80993 *Elev:* 8264 *Grid:* 32/63
South Pass City Rd/CR-479 & Atlantic City Rd/CR-237 *Type:* Highway End
8.2 mi route that loops from **Wy-28** MM 43.5 south past **South Pass City**, northeast through **Atlantic City**, and north to **Wy-28** MM 49.0. Highlights include: **Carissa Mine**, **South Pass City**, **Willie Handcart Company Tragedy Memorial**, **Atlantic City**, **Miner's Delight Ghost Town**.
Directions: S on South Pass City Rd/CR-479 1.6 mi; NE/L 3.7 mi on CR-237; N/L on S Dexter Ave 0.2 mi; E/R then N on Atlantic City Rd/CR-237 2.7 mi.

Brooklyn Lake Rd/FR-317   S/N

MM: 0.0 **GPS:** 41.35706/-106.23280 **Elev:** 10150 **Grid:** 69/91 **Land:** NF
Brooklyn Lake Rd/FR-317   **Type:** Highway Description
1.9 mi road north from **Wy-130** to **Brooklyn Lake** with access to scenic hiking trails around **Browns Peak** and 2 campgrounds.
Notes: The road is gravel with washboard sections and somewhat narrow. It is usually open around July 1.

MM: 0.1 **GPS:** 41.35869/-106.23322 **Elev:** 10178 **Grid:** 69/91 **Land:** NF
Nash Fork Campground   **Type:** Campground
A nice campground near **Nash Fork Creek**, which consists of 2 loops with the majority of the campsites in the 2nd loop. *Conifer stands alternate with subalpine meadows. Spacious sites. 3 pull-thrus.*
Crowds: ***** **[FEE AREA] Notes:** Gets very cold and may not open until July. **Directions:** W/L side of road.
Campsites: 27 **Shade:** *** **Privacy:** **** **RV Size:** 30' **Other:** Water

MM: 0.8 **GPS:** 41.36192/-106.24279 **Elev:** 10355 **Grid:** 69/91 **Land:** NF
FR-332/Towner Lake Rd   **Type:** Highway Junction
A 2.9 mi forest road that connects **Brooklyn Lake Rd/FR-317** to **Wy-130** MM 38. A few dispersed camping areas are located along this route, although signs state that camping must be 500 ft from the road. Only **FR-332.A** to **Towner Lake** appears to allow you to get 500 ft from the road.
Road Desc: Dirt, rough & potholed, narrow **Directions:** W side of road.
Notes: Although I saw no other opportunities to get 500 ft from the road, there were plenty of people camping.

MM: 0.9 **GPS:** 41.36349/-106.24290 **Elev:** 10391 **Grid:** 69/91 **Land:** NF
St. Alban's Chapel   **Type:** Chapel
An outdoor chapel used by the **Episcopal Church**.
Hours: Sunday 10am service **Directions:** E side of road.

MM: 1.7 **GPS:** 41.37247/-106.24546 **Elev:** 10562 **Grid:** 69/91 **Land:** NF
Sheep Lake Trail   **Type:** Hiking Trail
A trail that rounds the northeast end of **Browns Peak** with options of a one-way trail to **Sand Lake** (which requires a shuttle from another trailhead on **FR-101/Sand Lake Rd**) or combining with other trails to create an 11.25 mi loop.

<u>Sheep Lake</u> - The trail heads north 1.6 mi climbing 130 ft to **North Twin Lakes** on the east end of **Browns Peak** (MI 1.6). The next 2.2 mi curves northwest across alpine tundra climbing another 300 ft along the exposed north slope of **Browns Peak** before turning north and descending 190 ft to a trail junction at the southwest end of **Sheep Lake** (MI 3.8).
<u>Sand Lake</u> – From the junction at **Sheep Lake**, continue north 4.4 mi passing 3 more lakes and descending 660 ft to **Sand Lake** (MI 8.2). *Moderate; 8.2 mi one-way; 440 ft elev gain, 660 ft elev loss.*
<u>Loop Trail</u> – From the junction at **Sheep Lake**, take the **Gap Lakes Trail** west 0.7 mi to the junction with the **Deep Lake Trail** (MI 4.5). Continue southwest 3.25 mi past **Cutthroat Lake**, **North Gap Lake**, and **South Gap Lake** (*see Gap Lakes Trail in chapter: Sugarloaf Recreation Area MM 1.0*) to the junction with the **Lost Lake Trail** (MI 7.75). Follow this trail northeast 1.75 mi climbing 130 ft to **Lost Lake** (MI 9.5). Continue 1.75 mi descending 340 ft past **West Glacier Lake** and **East Glacier Lake** to the **Brooklyn Lake Trailhead** (MI 11.25). *(See section below for a detailed description of the Lost Lake hike).* Follow the road south past the campground completing the loop. *Moderate; 11.25 mi loop; 900 ft total elev gain.*
Cool Rating: ***** **Crowds:** ** **Time:** 4-8 hrs **Directions:** Parking areas across from trailhead and just south on E side of road
Notes: Sand Lake is accessed from Wy-130 MM 31.2 heading north 17.2 mi on FR-101/Sand Lake Rd. It can also be accessed from I-80 exit 272 by taking Elk Mountain Arlington Rd W 1.1 mi and heading S on FR-111 and FR-101 14.1 mi.

MM: 1.9 **GPS:** 41.37424/-106.24693 **Elev:** 10600 **Grid:** 69/91 **Land:** NF
Lost Lake Trail   **Type:** Hiking Trail
A rocky trail that passes through forest, across subalpine meadows, and past 2 high mountain lakes to the clear and shallow **Lost Lake**. This is most commonly done as a 3.5 mi out and back; however, the trail continues 2.0 to the **Lewis Lake Trailhead** parking at the **Sugarloaf Recreation Area**. Using a shuttle vehicle allows a nice 3.75 mi one-way alternative.

The trail climbs gradually 100 ft in 1/4 mi above **Brooklyn Lake** and then climbs another 100 ft to **East Glacier Lake** (MI 0.6). A short spur trail accesses this beautiful lake, which is backed by a steep rocky slope of **Browns Peak**. Continue another 0.1 mi to a short and somewhat steep descent on a spur trail (0.1 mi round-trip) to **West Glacier Lake** (MI 0.7). *A shorter version of the hike can be made by turning around at either of these lakes.* Continue 0.3 mi to a footbridge over a lush creek (MI 1.0). The trail then continues 1/4 mi southwest along a smoother surface (MI 1.25) before beginning the final 100 ft ascent. In 1/4 mi (MI 1.5) a short spur trail forks left and climbs to an overlook of **Telephone Lakes**. Keeping right, the last 1/4 mi climbs to a trail junction near the west shore of **Lost Lake** (MI 1.75). Take the short trail to the right to reach the lake. *Moderate; 1.75 mi one-way (1.9 mi with side trails); 340 ft elev gain.*

The main trail continues west 1.75 mi with excellent views, passing the west **Telephone Lake** and several other small lakes to a junction with the **Gap Lakes Trail**. Turn left 1/4 mi to reach the **Lewis Lake Trailhead**. *Easy; 2.0 mi one-way; 170 ft elev loss.*
Cool Rating: ***** **Crowds:** ** **Time:** 2 hrs **Directions:** N side of road just before Brooklyn Lake Campground

MM: 1.9 **GPS:** 41.37414/-106.24703 **Elev:** 10590 **Grid:** 69/91 **Land:** NF
Brooklyn Lake Campground   **Type:** Campground
Located above the northeast shore of **Brooklyn Lake** at the southeast base of **Browns Peak**. The lake is popular for canoes. 2 trailheads are located adjacent to the campground (*see 2 previous sections*). *Small stands of conifers in an alpine meadow. All sites have a view of the lake. Fairly level.*
Crowds: ***** **[FEE AREA] Notes:** Gets very cold and may not open until July. **Directions:** End of road
Campsites: 19 **Shade:** *** **Privacy:** ** **RV Size:** 30' **Other:** 1-877-444-6777:www.recreation.gov,Water

Brooks Lake Rd/FR-515   SE/NW

MM: 0.0/9.5 **GPS:** 43.70587/-109.96506 **Elev:** 8359 **Grid:** 16/32 **Land:** NF
Brooks Lake Rd/FR-515   **Type:** Highway Description
9.5 mi road that begins at **US-26/287** MM 32.8, loops north and west past **Brooks Lake**, and returns to **US-26/287** MM 25.9. If continuing west on **US-26/287**, completing the loop west past **Brooks Lake** saves 7.3 mi, but the road narrows and is not recommended for RVs and trailers. **Brooks Lake** is situated in a beautiful valley surrounded by steep volcanic cliffs with 2 National Forest campgrounds, a trailhead, and a private lodge.
Road Desc: Gravel, washboarded.
Directions: N on FR-515 4.0 mi; Keep left at fork 0.9 mi to Brooks Lake; Continue S then W 4.5 mi to US-26/287 MM 25.9.

MM: 4.0/5.5 **GPS:** 43.74971/-109.99089 **Elev:** 9080 **Grid:** 15/31 **Land:** NF
FR-516   **Type:** Highway Junction
Side road that provides access to the northeast side of **Brooks Lake**.
Road Desc: Gravel **Directions:** Keep right at fork; N 1.0 mi.

MM: 4.3/5.2 **Dist:** 0.1 **GPS:** 43.75216/-109.99556 **Elev:** 9073 **Grid:** 15/31 **Land:** NF
Pinnacles Campground   **Type:** Campground
A scenic campground overlooking the southeast shore of **Brooks Lake** (see section below). Sites are spread along a road above **Brooks Lake** with an end loop away from the lake. Compared to **Brooks Lake Campground**, the sites are nicer, it is more expensive, and the views of the cliffs are not as good. Dense conifer forest. Good spacing between sites. Fairly level. 3 pull-thrus.
Crowds: ***** **[FEE AREA]** **Directions:** NE/R on FR-515.1G 0.1 mi
Campsites: 21 **Shade:** ***** **Privacy:** ***** **RV Size:** 30' **Other:** Water GRIZZLIES

MM: 4.9/4.6 **Dist:** 0.2 **GPS:** 43.75034/-110.00530 **Elev:** 9095 **Grid:** 15/31 **Land:** NF
Brooks Lake Campground   **Type:** Campground
A scenic campground near the south shore of **Brooks Lake** (see next section). The configuration is unusual with 4 sections: **1)** To the right, just past the entrance, are 3 sites along a road that parallels the entrance road, separated by trees. **2)** Another road to the right leads to 3 sites in a T-formation with good shade and privacy. Neither spur road has a turnaround for RVs. **3)** 2 sites are in the open along the north side of the main road with a hill blocking a view of the lake. **4)** The end loop has 2 pull-thrus on the south side and 4 parking areas close together on the north side that provide tenting options down the hill near the lake. Compared to **Pinnacles Campground**, the sites are not as nice, it is less expensive, and the views of the cliffs are better. Conifer forest. 2 pull-thrus.
Crowds: ***** **[FEE AREA]** **Directions:** W toward Brooks Lake Lodge and immediately N/R 0.2 mi; E/R into campground.
Campsites: 14 **Shade:** *** **Privacy:** ** **RV Size:** 40' **Other:** GRIZZLIES

MM: 4.9/4.6 **Dist:** 0.3 **GPS:** 43.75156/-110.00535 **Elev:** 9055 **Grid:** 15/31 **Land:** NF
Brooks Lake   **Type:** Lake
A medium-sized lake situated in a beautiful valley between 2 volcanic stratified cliff massifs anchored by **Mount Sublette** to the southwest and **Pinnacle Butte** to the southeast. The cliffs to the west are sometimes referred to as the **Brooks Lake Cliffs**, which form a smoother ridge than the spires of the **Pinnacle Buttes** to the east. The lake has excellent fishing with a large boat launch and 2 National Forest campgrounds on the south shore (see previous entries).
Cool Rating: **** **Crowds:** *** **Directions:** W toward Brooks Lake Lodge and immediately N/R 0.3 mi

MM: 4.9/4.6 **Dist:** 0.3 **GPS:** 43.75153/-110.00600 **Elev:** 9073 **Grid:** 15/31 **Land:** NF
Brooks Lake Trailhead   **Type:** Trailhead
Located on the southwest shore of **Brooks Lake** with 2 day hikes to the **Jade Lakes** (the most scenic) and **Upper Brooks Lake** (the easiest).

Jade Lakes - **Upper Jade Lake** is a beautiful green and deep lake below the towering **Brooks Lake Cliffs** (see previous section on Brooks Lake). Hike northwest around the southwest shore of **Brooks Lake** 0.8 mi to the junction with the **Jade Lakes Trail** (MI 0.8). Fork left and climb steeply uphill for 0.4 mi (MI 1.2). The trail then ascends more gradually 0.3 mi before crossing an open ridge 370 ft above **Brooks Lake** with a great view of the **Pinnacle Buttes** (MI 1.5). The trail re-enters the forest and climbs over a hill 0.5 mi to a small pond (MI 2.0). Continue 0.3 mi climbing gently through a meadow to the high point of the hike at 9,635 ft (MI 2.3). Drop steeply 100 ft to the east shore of **Upper Jade Lake** (MI 2.4). The trail continues 0.5 mi descending 100 ft to **Lower Jade Lake** (MI 2.9). Moderate; 2.4-2.9 mi one-way; 560 ft elev gain.

Upper Brooks Lake - Easy hiking along a meadow where **Brooks Lake Creek** flows south between **Upper Brooks Lake** and **Brooks Lake**. Hike northwest around the west shore of **Brooks Lake** and continue north to **Upper Brooks Lake**. The trail crosses the creek at about 2.0 mi. Easy; 3.0 mi one-way; 50 ft elev gain.
Cool Rating: **** **Crowds:** ** **Time:** 2-3 hrs
Directions: W toward Brooks Lake Lodge and immediately N/R 0.3 mi; On the northwest side of the parking loop.

MM: 9.5/0.0 **GPS:** 43.74797/-110.05982 **Elev:** 9564 **Grid:** 14/31 **Land:** NF
End of Highway   **Type:** Highway End
9.5 mi road that begins at **US-26/287** MM 25.9, loops east past **Brooks Lake**, and returns to **US-26/287** MM 32.8. If traveling east, reaching **Brooks Lake** from this direction saves 7.3 mi, but the section of road to **Brooks Lake** is narrow and not recommended for RVs and trailers. **Brooks Lake** is situated in a beautiful valley surrounded by steep volcanic cliffs with 2 National Forest campgrounds, a trailhead, and a private lodge.
Directions: E then S on FR-515/Brooks Lake Rd, past Wind River Lake, 4.5 mi to Brooks Lake; Continue E then S 4.9 mi to US-26/287 MM 32.8.

Buffalo Valley Rd/FR-30050   SW/NE

MM: 0.0/14.1 **GPS:** 43.83831/-110.44330 **Elev:** 6835 **Grid:** 9/29 **Land:** NF
Buffalo Valley Rd/FR-30050   **Type:** Highway Description
14.1 mi route that starts at **US-26/287** MM 3.5 and heads northeast to **Turpin Meadow Recreation Area** and **Turpin Meadow Ranch** before looping south back to **US-26/287** MM 13.0. The recreation area provides campgrounds, trailheads, and stock accommodations for access into the **Teton Wilderness** and to the site of the **Teton-Yellowstone Tornado**. The paved **Buffalo Valley Rd** heads northeast through the **Buffalo Fork Valley**, above the **Buffalo Fork River** and just south of the **Bridger-Teton National Forest**. After 9.9 mi the road passes the **Turpin Meadow Campground**, crosses the **Buffalo Fork River**, and passes the **Turpin Meadow Ranch**. The road then transitions to graveled **FR-30050** before continuing south and climbing out of the valley 4.2 mi back to **US-26/287**. Highlights include: **Box Creek Trail** to the site of the **Teton-Yellowstone Tornado**.
Directions: NE on Buffalo Valley Rd 9.9 mi; S on FR-30050 4.2 mi.
Road Desc: Buffalo Valley Rd is paved, but narrow, rough and bouncy with no shoulders. The speed limit is 35 mph with a residential area at 25 mph. FR-30050 is rough and washboarded gravel.

MM: 0.0/14.1 **GPS:** 43.83831/-110.44330 **Elev:** 6835 **Grid:** 9/29
US-26/287 & US-26 *(see chapter)*   **Type:** Hwy Junction w/Chapter
Directions: SE to Dubois or NW to Moran Jct from MM 3.5

MM: 2.5/11.6 **GPS:** 43.84385/-110.40591 **Elev:** 6905 **Grid:** 9/29
Teton Range Viewpoint   **Type:** Scenic Area
A nice view west, through the **Buffalo Fork Valley**, of the **Buffalo Fork River** and the **Teton Range**.
Cool Rating: *** **Crowds:** * **Time:** 5 min **Directions:** S side of road

MM: 8.7/5.4 **Dist:** 0.7 **GPS:** 43.86031/-110.29453 **Elev:** 7085 **Grid:** 11/29 **Land:** NF
Box Creek Campground: Turpin Meadow Recreation Area   **Type:** Campground
Campground at the **Box Creek Trailhead** *(see next section)* with corrals and stock loading ramps. Sites are on the edge of the forest where some tables are not shaded. *Single loop. Conifer forest. Overgrown grass and under-maintained. Fairly level.*
Crowds: * **[FEE AREA]** **Road Desc:** Gravel, narrow & steep **Directions:** NW on FR-30070 0.7 mi
Campsites: 6 **Shade:** ** **Privacy:** *** **RV Size:** 30' **Other:** GRIZZLIES

MM: 8.7/5.4 **Dist:** 0.7 **GPS:** 43.86126/-110.29493 **Elev:** 7081 **Grid:** 11/28 **Land:** NF
Box Creek Trailhead: Turpin Meadow Recreation Area   **Type:** Trailhead
The **Box Creek Trail** heads north into the **Teton Wilderness** climbing up **Gravel Ridge** and dropping through a tornado-devastated area to **Enos Lake**. The **Teton-Yellowstone Tornado** hit on July 21, 1987 and was the highest altitude tornado ever recorded. It left behind a damage swath 24 mi long by 1.5 mi wide from **Gravel Ridge** all the way into the **Yellowstone River Valley** in **Yellowstone National Park**. The top of **Gravel Ridge** provides good views to the west of **Gravel Mountain** and the tornado area to the northeast. The trail enters the heavy damage in another mile or so. It took years of manual cutting by several organizations to clear the trail of debris, as power equipment is not allowed in wilderness areas. From south of **Enos Lake**, the trail can be completed as a clockwise 20 mi loop by returning on the **Clear Creek Trail** to **Turpin Meadow** and returning to the **Box Creek Campground** along the road. Connecting trails at **Enos Lake** continue farther into the wilderness toward **Yellowstone National Park**. *Gravel Ridge and tornado area: Moderate; 4.6-7.0 mi one-way; 1220 ft elev gain.* **Enos Lake:** *Moderate; 10.0 mi one-way; 1220 ft elev gain; 480 ft elev loss.*
Cool Rating: **** **Crowds:** * **Road Desc:** Gravel, narrow & steep **Directions:** NW on FR-30070 0.7 mi

MM: 9.7/4.4 **Dist:** 0.3 **GPS:** 43.85661/-110.26535 **Elev:** 6936 **Grid:** 11/29 **Land:** NF
Turpin Meadow Campground: Turpin Meadow Recreation Area   **Type:** Campground
Near the **Buffalo Fork River** and next to the **Turpin Meadow Trailhead** with trails into the **Teton Wilderness**, including a loop option with the **Box Creek Trail** *(see previous section)*. This is set up as a horse campground with a hitching post at each site. Corrals are provided at both the campground and trailhead. The north side has better shade and is farther from the horse trailers and corrals. The south side has open grassy sites. *Light conifer forest. Good spacing between sites. Level. 3 pull-thrus.*
Crowds: *** **[FEE AREA]** **Directions:** Just N of bridge; E on FR-30065 0.3 mi.
Campsites: 18 **Shade:** * **Privacy:** * **RV Size:** 40' **Other:** Water GRIZZLIES

MM: 9.8/4.3 **GPS:** 43.85601/-110.27111 **Elev:** 6912 **Grid:** 11/29
Teton Range Viewpoint   **Type:** Scenic Area
A nicely framed view of the **Teton Range** looking straight up the **Buffalo Fork Valley** to the west.
Cool Rating: *** **Crowds:** * **Time:** 5 min **Directions:** Just S of bridge on W side of road

MM: 9.9/4.2 **GPS:** 43.85554/-110.27102 **Elev:** 6915 **Grid:** 11/29
FR-30050   **Type:** Highway Transition
4.2 mi of rough and washboarded gravel road.

MM: 14.1/0.0 **GPS:** 43.81405/-110.26580 **Elev:** 7852 **Grid:** 11/30
US-26/287 & US-26 *(see chapter)*   **Type:** Hwy Junction w/Chapter
Directions: SE to Dubois or NW to Moran Jct from MM 13.0

MM: 14.1/0.0 **GPS:** 43.81405/-110.26580 **Elev:** 7852 **Grid:** 11/30 **Land:** NF
End of Highway   **Type:** Highway End
14.1 mi route that starts at **US-26/287** MM 13.0 and heads north to **Turpin Meadow Recreation Area** and **Turpin Meadow Ranch** before looping southwest back to **US-26/287** MM 3.5. The recreation area provides campgrounds, trailheads, and stock accommodations for access into the **Teton Wilderness** and to the site of the **Teton-Yellowstone Tornado**. **FR-30050** heads north 4.2 mi, descending into the **Buffalo Fork Valley** to the **Turpin Meadow Ranch** before crossing the **Buffalo Fork River** near the **Turpin Meadow Campground**. The road becomes paved and transitions to **Buffalo Valley Rd** before turning southwest through the **Buffalo Fork Valley**, above the **Buffalo Fork River** and just south of the **Bridger-Teton National Forest**. The road becomes paved and continues 9.9 mi, passing **Box Creek Campground** and returning to **US-26/287**. Highlights include: **Box Creek Trail** to the site of the **Teton-Yellowstone Tornado**.
Directions: N on FR-30050 4.2 mi. SW on Buffalo Valley Rd 9.9 mi.

Casper Mountain Rd/Wy-251 — N/S

MM: 0.0/18.4 **GPS:** 42.85009/-106.32395 **Elev:** 5122 **Grid:** 68/54
Casper Mountain Rd/Wy-251 **Type:** Highway Description
18.4 mi series of roads from **Casper** south over **Casper Mountain** (nearly 3,000 ft above Casper) down through the **Red Valley** and up to **Muddy Mountain**. Activities on **Casper Mountain** include camping, hiking, and mountain biking, as well as downhill and cross-country skiing in the winter. Much of **Casper Mountain** is private property; however, **Casper Mountain Park** is a large public access area with 5 campgrounds. Highlights include: **Garden Creek Falls, Bridle Trail**, scenic overlook of **Casper**, **Casper Mountain Park, Crimson Dawn Park and Museum, Muddy Mountain Environmental Education Area**.
Notes: The roads up and down the mountains are steep and winding and few of the campsites accommodate large RVs and trailers. After reaching the top of Casper Mountain from Casper, the road narrows with no center stripe and eventually becomes gravel.
Directions: At the intersection of E 1st St/US-20/26/87 and S Wolcott St/Wy-251, head south 8.9 mi (the first 2 blocks are one-way so stay in the 2 right lanes), where you will first gradually and then steeply climb to the top of Casper Mountain. At a fork with Hogadon Rd are 3 direction and mileage signs to the area attractions. Veer left where the highway transitions to CR-505, narrows with no center stripe, and continues 2 mi to the high point of 8,000 ft at MM 10.9. The pavement ends at MM 11.9 and the road descends into the Red Valley where CR-505 turns west at MM 13.9. At this point a junction with Muddy Mountain Rd (elev 7260) continues south and climbs to the top of Muddy Mountain (elev 8274).

If coming from Wy-220 eastbound or I-25 westbound via Wy-258/SE Wyoming Blvd, the junction with Casper Mountain Rd is at MM 3.0 (42.80624/-106.33027).

MM: 0.0/18.4 **GPS:** 42.85009/-106.32395 **Elev:** 5122 **Grid:** 68/54
Casper **Type:** Town

MM: 3.0/15.4 **GPS:** 42.80614/-106.33019 **Elev:** 5561 **Grid:** 67/55
SE Wyoming Blvd/Wy-258 **Type:** Highway Junction
Starting mile marker for **Casper Mountain Rd/Wy-251** when coming from **I-25** MM 185.4 westbound or **Wy-220** MM 113.4.

MM: 4.9/13.5 **Dist:** 1.0 **GPS:** 42.76701/-106.33233 **GPS2:** 42.76580/-106.33320 **Elev:** 6460 **Grid:** 67/56 **Land:** County
Garden Creek Falls & Bridle Trail **Type:** Waterfall
A 50 ft high waterfall in **Rotary Park** at the base of **Casper Mountain**. This is one of only a few waterfalls in central **Wyoming** and is most spectacular in spring and early summer. The first trail option is just before the bridge that crosses **Garden Creek**. A short 100 yd trail south leads to a midrange view of the falls. Across the bridge is another trail that follows the creek uphill 0.1 mi south to the base of the falls. A more strenuous option is to veer right from the footbridge to the 4.5 mi **Bridle Trail**. This trail loops around the entire park, climbing over 700 ft up switchbacks for good views, and passes through the "split rock" at the top. Much of the trail is adjacent to private property so stay on the trail.

A picnic area is located along a partial loop road south of the parking area. The area looks like a campground but is a day use area. *7 sites. Grills. Fire rings.*
Cool Rating: **** **Crowds:** *** **Time:** 0.5-2 hrs
Directions: S on Garden Creek Rd 0.4 mi; S/L on S Rotary Park Rd 0.6 mi.

MM: 7.2/11.2 **GPS:** 42.76460/-106.32816 **Elev:** 7105 **Grid:** 67/56
Casper Mountain Scenic Overlook **Type:** Scenic Viewpoint
A panoramic view from nearly 2,000 ft above **Casper**.
Cool Rating: ** **Crowds:** * **Time:** 10 min **Directions:** Pullout on N side of hwy

MM: 8.9/9.5 **GPS:** 42.74676/-106.32270 **Elev:** 7786 **Grid:** 68/56
End of Wy-251 **Type:** Highway Transition
Wy-251 ends and transitions to **CR-505/Circle Dr** at a fork with **Hogadon Rd**, where 3 direction and mileage signs direct visitors to the **Casper Mountain** attractions.
Road Desc: The road becomes narrow with no center stripe **Directions:** Keep left at the fork

MM: 9.2/9.2 **GPS:** 42.74174/-106.32140 **Elev:** 7848 **Grid:** 68/56 **Land:** County
Casper Mountain Park (north boundary) **Type:** Park
A county-owned public access area with 5 campgrounds, outdoor recreation, and the **Crimson Dawn Park and Museum**.

MM: 9.7/8.7 **GPS:** 42.73780/-106.31926 **Elev:** 7854 **Grid:** 68/57 **Land:** County
Casper Mountain Trail Center **Type:** Visitor Center
Used in the winter as a base for a vast network of cross-country ski trails that are also used for hiking and mountain biking in the summer. These trails traverse approx 6 mi around the park perimeter as well as many miles of inner trails. A trail map is available at the **Casper Nordic Center** web site. Since the Trail Center gates are often closed, alternate access to the trails in the summer is at the **Skunk Hollow Park** parking area (0.2 mi south) on a road north just past the entrance gate.
Cool Rating: *** **Crowds:** ** **Directions:** E side of road

MM: 9.9/8.5 **GPS:** 42.73802/-106.31661 **Elev:** 7803 **Grid:** 68/57 **Land:** County
Casper Mountain Park Information Sign **Type:** Visitor Information
A sign with visitor information and a map of **Casper Mountain Park**. The sign is located just off the road in a parking area at the entrance for **Skunk Hollow Park**. In the summer the cross-country ski trails are accessed via a road north just past the **Skunk Hollow Park** entrance gate. *Vault toilet.*
Directions: N side of road

MM: 9.9/8.5 **GPS:** 42.73784/-106.31682 **Elev:** 7803 **Grid:** 68/57 **Land:** County
Skunk Hollow Park Campground: Casper Mountain **Type:** Campground
Sites are spread out along a 0.9 mi one-way loop road. *Conifer forest. Good spacing between sites. Not level.*
Crowds: ***** **[FEE AREA]** **Road Desc:** Gravel **Directions:** NE at Skunk Hollow Park on the one-way Strube Loop.
Campsites: 8 **Shade:** **** **Privacy:** *** **RV Size:** 30' **Other:** None

MM: 9.9/8.5 *Dist:* 0.4 *GPS:* 42.74302/-106.31596 *Elev:* 7729 *Grid:* 68/56 *Land:* County
Braille Trail   *Type:* Hiking Trail
A unique self-guided nature trail in **Elkhorn Canyon**, which is set up for both the sighted and the visually impaired. Along the trail are 42 interpretive signs in English with Braille imprints, and rope handrails are provided for guidance. *Easy; 1/3 mi loop; 2 short but steep climbs.*
Cool Rating: ** *Crowds:* * *Time:* 1 hr *Directions:* NE at Skunk Hollow Park on the one-way Strube Loop 0.4 mi.

MM: 9.9/8.5 *GPS:* 42.73770/-106.31645 *Elev:* 7823 *Grid:* 68/57 *Land:* County
Elkhorn Springs Park Campground: Casper Mountain   *Type:* Campground
The campground is located on a hillside just east of the main road. The first 2 sites are the most level but close to the main road. *Conifer forest. One-way, 2 track, half-loop road. Very unlevel.*
Crowds: * *[FEE AREA]* *Notes:* This undesirable campground looks like an afterthought.
Directions: Just to the east of the Skunk Hollow entrance
Campsites: 6 *Shade:* ***** *Privacy:* * *RV Size:* 20' *Other:* None

MM: 10.2/8.2 *Dist:* 0.3 *GPS:* 42.73780/-106.31313 *Elev:* 7980 *Grid:* 68/57 *Land:* County
Tower Hill Park Campground: Casper Mountain   *Type:* Campground
Sites are spread out along a road in a shady forest. The campground is located on a side hill, and no grading has been done to level the sites. *Conifer forest. Good spacing between sites. Unlevel.*
Crowds: ***** *Notes:* There was an old sign that said something about a fee, but I saw nowhere to pay it.
Road Desc: Gravel
Directions: E then N on East End Rd/CR-506 0.3 mi. E on the campground road, which loops east back to the main road.
Campsites: 8 *Shade:* ***** *Privacy:* *** *RV Size:* 30' *Other:* None

MM: 10.2/8.2 *Dist:* 2.3 *GPS:* 42.73574/-106.28357 *GPS2:* 42.73194/-106.28776 *Elev:* 7983 *Grid:* 68/57 *Land:* County
Crimson Dawn Park and Museum   *Type:* Point of Interest
This is the former home of **Neal Forsling** who, after a divorce, moved to **Casper Mountain** in 1929 with her 2 young daughters. Neal wanted to celebrate the **Summer Solstice** and began telling stories of imaginary mystical mountain inhabitants (witches, elves, etc.), which she incorporated into her first **Mid-Summer's Eve Celebration** in June, 1929. With the help of her daughters and others she began building paths through the woods to enchanted places where these inhabitants lived.

Neal later married Jim Forsling, another mountain resident, who later froze to death while returning from town on skis with groceries and supplies. Neal was devastated, and not being able to stay on the mountain alone she began traveling and painting scenery from different parts of the country. She became well known but always returned to her beloved mountain. Before her death in 1977, she donated her mountain land to **Natrona County** for a park. Her log home became a museum and her stories and characters have been passed on to posterity in the form of plaques at each of 19 shrines along the trail. Visitors are welcome to take this 1.0 mi self-guided tour, which travels counterclockwise past a small family cemetery. The mid-summer celebration has become a tradition that is still carried on today. The museum provides a brochure with a more complete story of Neal's life.
Phone: 307-235-1303 *Cool Rating:* *** *Crowds:* ** *Time:* 1-1.5 hrs *Road Desc:* Gravel
Directions: E then N on East End Rd/CR-506 1.9 mi; S/R on Crimson Dawn Rd 1/4 mi; L 0.15 mi to museum parking area.

MM: 10.3/8.1 *GPS:* 42.73314/-106.31288 *Elev:* 7880 *Grid:* 68/57 *Land:* County
Beartrap Meadow Park: Casper Mountain   *Type:* Campground
Primarily a camping and picnic area, but several festivals are also held here. The park provides 3 group shelters, which are reservable through **Natrona County**. This is the most popular campground on **Casper Mountain** and can be rather noisy. *1.0 mi one-way clockwise loop. Conifer forest.*
Crowds: ***** *[FEE AREA]* *Directions:* W side of road
Campsites: 31 *Shade:* ***** *Privacy:* ** *RV Size:* 30' *Other:* Water

MM: 10.3/8.1 *GPS:* 42.73305/-106.31284 *Elev:* 7880 *Grid:* 68/57 *Land:* County
Deerhaven Park Campground: Casper Mountain   *Type:* Campground
Located on a forested hillside across from **Beartrap Meadow Park**. *Conifer forest. Loop road. Decent spacing between sites. Very unlevel.*
Crowds: *** *[FEE AREA]* *Directions:* Road through a small opening in the trees on E side of road.
Campsites: 10 *Shade:* ***** *Privacy:* *** *RV Size:* 20' *Other:* None

MM: 10.7/7.7 *GPS:* 42.72912/-106.30958 *Elev:* 7967 *Grid:* 68/57 *Land:* County
Casper Mountain Park (south boundary)   *Type:* Park

MM: 11.9/6.5 *GPS:* 42.71524/-106.30600 *Elev:* 7693 *Grid:* 68/57
Pavement Ends (southbound)   *Type:* Pavement Change
The deteriorating pavement changes to a rough gravel road.
Road Desc: Gravel, rough spots

MM: 13.9/4.5 *GPS:* 42.69696/-106.31199 *Elev:* 7260 *Grid:* 68/58 *Land:* State
CR-505/Circle Dr   *Type:* Highway Junction
The main road curves and heads west 8.4 mi along a scenic red-cliffed canyon to **Wy-487**. Keep left to continue 4.5 mi south on **Muddy Mountain Rd** to the **Muddy Mountain Environmental Education Area**.
Road Desc: Gravel, rough spots

MM: 18.4/0.0 *GPS:* 42.68002/-106.26376 *Elev:* 8274 *Grid:* 68/58 *Land:* BLM
Muddy Mountain Environmental Education Area   *Type:* Recreation Area
A 2.0 sq mi recreation area for camping, hiking, biking, horseback riding, and OHV usage. A little over half of the area is restricted to non-motorized recreational activities including a short, wheelchair accessible, interpretive hiking trail system. The trailhead parking is just past the entrance where a large sign displays a map and information for the entire trail system. A gazebo serves as an information center with 7 interpretive signs.

The **Aspen Meadow Loop Trail** is an interpretive nature trail through the forest with connecting trails to both campgrounds. *Easy; 0.75 mi loop; Level.* The **Rim Trail** follows the north rim of **Muddy Mountain**, with 2 overlooks into the valley and across to **Casper Mountain**, and ends at the **Rim Campground**. *Easy; 0.4 mi one-way; Level.* The **Lodgepole Pine Trail** is to the south, and along with other trails connects the 2 campgrounds. *Easy; 0.4 mi; Level.* The remainder of the area consists of multi-use trails, which can be used by mountain bikes and OHVs, and are accessed from the 2.2 mi main loop road. A 6.4 mi mountain bike loop starts at the **Rim Campground**, continues east on a side road through a gate, and then immediately southeast on a single track trail. Side roads off **Muddy Mountain Rd** and in the valley between **Muddy Mountain** and **Casper Mountain** provide additional mountain bike and OHV trails.
Cool Rating: *** *Crowds:* *** *Notes:* Some dispersed camping areas off Muddy Mountain Rd.
Road Desc: Gravel, washboard sections. The road up the mountain is so washboarded that it is difficult to go over about 15 mph.
Directions: Where CR-505/Circle Drive Rd turns west at MM 13.9, continue S on Muddy Mountain Rd 4.5 mi.

MM: 18.4/0.0 *Dist:* 0.2 *GPS:* 42.67742/-106.26387 *Elev:* 8240 *Grid:* 68/58 *Land:* BLM
Lodgepole Campground: Muddy Mountain   *Type:* Campground
Just south of the **Aspen Meadow Loop Trail** *(see previous section on the Muddy Mountain Environmental Education Area).* Lodgepole pine forest. Loop road. Back-in sites. Level.
Crowds: *** **[FEE AREA]** *Road Desc:* Gravel *Directions:* At the entrance sign; S 0.2 mi
Campsites: 19 *Shade:* **** *Privacy:* *** *RV Size:* 30' *Other:* Water

MM: 18.4/0.0 *Dist:* 0.3 *GPS:* 42.68061/-106.25855 *Elev:* 8285 *Grid:* 68/58 *Land:* BLM
Rim Campground: Muddy Mountain   *Type:* Campground
Along the north rim of **Muddy Mountain** at the east end of the **Rim Trail** *(see previous section on the Muddy Mountain Environmental Education Area).* Lodgepole pine forest. Pull-through parking areas. Good spacing between sites. Level. Water is available at the entrance to Lodgepole Campground.
Crowds: *** **[FEE AREA]** *Road Desc:* Gravel *Directions:* Continue past the entrance sign 1/4 mi
Campsites: 8 *Shade:* *** *Privacy:* **** *RV Size:* 30' *Other:* Water

MM: 18.4/0.0 *GPS:* 42.68002/-106.26376 *Elev:* 8274 *Grid:* 68/58 *Land:* BLM
End of Highway   *Type:* Highway End

MM: 0.0/20.3 *GPS:* 41.72682/-109.27430 *Elev:* 6525 *Grid:* 25/82
Chilton Rd   *Type:* Highway Description
20.3 mi backcountry route that accesses the **White Mountain Petroglyphs**, **Boar's Tusk**, and the **Killpecker Sand Dunes**. If traveling north on **US-191**, a turnoff to an unnamed road at MM 14.9 creates a 30.5 mi loop starting at **US-191** MM 10.3, passing the **White Mountain Petroglyphs**, and returning to **US-191** MM 32.7. The northwest section of the loop provides good views of the **Boar's Tusk** and **Killpecker Sand Dunes**. Continuing northeast on Chilton Rd leads 1.1 mi to the **Boar's Tusk** turnoff and 7.5 mi to the **Killpecker Sand Dunes Recreation Site** parking area.
Road Desc: Smooth gravel *Directions:* E on CR-4-17/Chilton Rd 1.2 mi; N/L keeping left at the fork at 3.8 mi.

MM: 0.0/20.3 *GPS:* 41.72682/-109.27430 *Elev:* 6525 *Grid:* 25/82
US-191 *(see chapter)*   *Type:* Hwy Junction w/Chapter
Directions: N to Farson or S to Rock Springs from MM 10.3

MM: 13.6/6.7 *Dist:* 1.2 *GPS:* 41.88968/-109.25947 *GPS2:* 41.89116/-109.26522 *Elev:* 7030 *Grid:* 26/78 *Land:* BLM
White Mountain Petroglyphs   *Type:* Petroglyphs
Several hundred incised **Petroglyphs** carved into a 200 ft long soft sandstone cliff on **White Mountain**. This rock art varies in age from 200 to 1000 years and is representative of several different styles. The images include elk, bison, horses, human figures, and hand and foot prints. Many seem to depict hunting, including a warrior on a horse. 2 shallow caves are located along the cliff, one which is at ground level and contains some **Petroglyphs** (bring a flashlight). *Vault toilet at parking area.*
Cool Rating: *** *Crowds:* * *Time:* 1 hr *Road Desc:* Dirt, impassable when wet
Notes: There are a few nice panels of rock art, but also many modern day carvings. Some of the petroglyphs are faint and many are somewhat repetitive.
Directions: W 1.2 mi to parking area; Walk 0.3 mi along a gated 4WD road to the site.

MM: 14.9/5.4 *GPS:* 41.90826/-109.20146 *Elev:* 6636 *Grid:* 26/77 *Land:* BLM
Highway 191 Short Loop (back to US-191)   *Type:* Highway Junction
A 15.6 mi return route to **US-191** northbound, which provides excellent views of the **Boar's Tusk** at MI 4.0 and **Killpecker Sand Dunes** at MI 6.3. This shortcut saves 21.5 mi of driving over returning by the same route.
Directions: At a signed junction; NW 13.5 mi; NW on Old Hwy 191 2.1 mi.
Road Desc: Overall the road is reasonably smooth gravel and hard-packed dirt; however, a few sections are washboarded, rutted, and impassable when wet. The last 0.2 mi is broken/potholed pavement.

MM: 15.9/4.3 *Dist:* 3.7 *GPS:* 41.91736/-109.18533 *GPS2:* 41.96225/-109.19665 *Elev:* 6710 *Grid:* 27/77 *Land:* BLM
Boar's Tusk   *Type:* Geological Feature
A 400 ft high rock formation in the **Red Desert** that is the remainder of a volcanic plug. A volcanic plug, or neck, is the hardened lava in the vent of a volcano, which has been exposed by erosion. A 3.7 mi primitive road leads to the base of the formation; however, it can be adequately viewed from the road, particularly from a pullout 2.0 mi northeast of this road *(see next section)*.
Cool Rating: *** *Crowds:* * *Time:* 1 hr *Directions:* N 3.7 mi
Road Desc: Dirt, rough & impassable when wet, 4WD. The road gets sandy for the last mile or so, which make riding a mountain bike difficult.

MM: 17.9/2.4 *GPS:* 41.93659/-109.15718 *Elev:* 6738 *Grid:* 27/77 *Land:* BLM
Boar's Tusk Overlook   *Type:* Scenic Viewpoint
An elevated view of the **Boar's Tusk** from 2.7 mi southeast. *See previous section.*
Cool Rating: *** *Crowds:* * *Time:* 5 min *Directions:* Pullout on NW side of road

MM: 20.3/0.0 *Dist:* 2.1 *GPS:* 41.96124/-109.08304 *Elev:* 7160 *Grid:* 28/76 *Land:* BLM
Killpecker Sand Dunes   *Type:* Sand Dunes
The sand dunes in this area are known as the **Greater Sand Dunes** and are part of the **Killpecker Dune Field**, the largest active dune field in North America. These dunes stretch 55 mi to the east from the **Green River Basin**, across the **Continental Divide**, and into the **Great Divide Basin**. Approximately 38% of the **Greater Sand Dunes**, including **Boar's Tusk**, are designated an **Area of Critical Environmental Concern** (ACEC) to protect wildlife, including a rare desert elk herd, and geologic and cultural resources. Off-highway vehicles (OHV) are only allowed on the "open play" areas.

The **Sand Dunes Recreation Site** has a huge parking area where camping is allowed. *2 vault toilets.* The dunes are about 1/4 mi from the parking area on narrow sandy access roads. The dunes are most scenic in the early morning and evening.
Cool Rating: *** *Crowds:* *
Directions: At a sharp curve keep left 0.7 mi; Left at fork 0.5 mi; Right at fork 0.9 mi to the Sand Dunes Recreation Site parking area.
Campsites: Dispersed *Shade:* * *Privacy:* * *RV Size:* 40'+ *Other:* None

MM: 20.3/0.0 *GPS:* 41.95023/-109.11792 *Elev:* 6891 *Grid:* 28/76
End of Highway   *Type:* Highway End

Cook Lake Recreation Area and Scenic Drive   S/N

MM: 0.0/26.3 *GPS:* 44.39465/-104.41742 *Elev:* 4960 *Grid:* 95/15 *Land:* NF
Cook Lake Recreation Area and Scenic Drive   *Type:* Highway Description
Access to the **Cook Lake Recreation Area** along a 26.3 mi scenic drive through the **Bear Lodge Mountains** and **Black Hills National Forest** from **US-14 (east)** MM 199.5 (1.0 mi west of **I-90**) north to **Wy-24** MM 30.3. The **Warren Peak Lookout** is at the highest elevation of the drive. Dispersed camping along **FR-838**, **FR-843**, and **FR-830**.
Nearest Town: Sundance 2.6 NE
Road Desc: Paved, steep and winding for the first 7.3 mi from US-14 on the south end. The rest is smooth gravel.
Directions: N on CR-100/Warren Peak Rd/FR-838 12.7 mi;   E/R on FR-843 1.6 mi;   N/L on FR-843 3.7 mi;   NE/L on FR-830 2.7 mi;   N/L on FR-832 4.6 mi;   NE/R on FR-838 1.0 mi to Wy-24 MM 30.3.

MM: 0.0/26.3 *GPS:* 44.39465/-104.41742 *Elev:* 4960 *Grid:* 95/15
US-14 (east) *(see chapter)*   *Type:* Hwy Junction w/Chapter
44.8 mi section of **US-14** from **I-90** MM 185.7 at **Sundance** that loops north and west back to **I-90** MM 154.6 at **Moorcroft**. The primary function of this highway is access to **Wy-24** and **Devils Tower National Monument**. The highway also provides access to the **Warren Peak Lookout** and **Cook Lake Recreation Area**.
Directions: E to Sundance or NW to Devil's Tower from MM 199.5
Notes: US-14 doesn't actually end at I-90 heading east, however the rest of the highway from there simply parallels I-90 through Sundance, 1.7 mi east.

MM: 2.5/23.8 *GPS:* 44.42755/-104.42393 *Elev:* 5470 *Grid:* 95/14 *Land:* NF
Reuter Campground   *Type:* Campground
A nice campground on the south end of the **Bear Lodge Mountains** just inside the National Forest boundary. *Conifer forest. Little understory. Spacious sites. Level.*
Crowds: * *Nearest Town:* Sundance 5.1 SE *[FEE AREA]* *Directions:* S side of road
Campsites: 24 *Shade:* **** *Privacy:* ** *RV Size:* 30' *Other:* 1-877-444-6777:www.recreation.gov,Water

MM: 7.0/19.3 *Dist:* 0.3 *GPS:* 44.47603/-104.44380 *Elev:* 6658 *Grid:* 94/13 *Land:* NF
Warren Peak Lookout   *Type:* Fire Lookout
An active fire lookout with panoramic views of **South Dakota** and **Wyoming**. The tower is generally staffed from June to October depending on weather conditions. When staffed the top deck is accessible. Otherwise a small viewing platform at the top of 4 flights of stairs can be used. *Vault toilet.*
Cool Rating: *** *Crowds:* * *Time:* 30 min *Road Desc:* Gravel, steep & winding *Directions:* N 0.3 mi
Notes: When I was there in July, the flies were so thick I couldn't get out of the truck. I am told that this is not a problem when the wind is blowing, which is normally the case.

MM: 7.3/19.0 *Dist:* 0.2 *GPS:* 44.47813/-104.44970 *Elev:* 6594 *Grid:* 94/13 *Land:* NF
USAF Portable Medium 1 Nuclear Power Plant   *Type:* Historic Site
In operation from 1962-1968, the **PM-1** was the first **U.S. Air Force** nuclear power plant. It furnished electricity and heat to the 731st **Radar Squadron** operations area. It established a new United States continuous power production record for land-based military and civilian nuclear power plants of 4101 hours. The reactor was dismantled and buried in 1969. Some buildings and towers still remain. The short road leads to an interpretive sign and a closed gate.
Cool Rating: ** *Crowds:* * *Time:* 10 min *Road Desc:* Paved, broken & potholed *Directions:* NW 0.2 mi

MM: 11.6/14.7 *GPS:* 44.52484/-104.45325 *Elev:* 5620 *Grid:* 94/12 *Land:* NF
Aspen Tree Canopy over Road   *Type:* Scenic Area
A stand of large aspen trees that form a canopy over the road. Similar to **Aspen Alley** in south-central **Wyoming**.
Cool Rating: *** *Crowds:* * *Time:* Drive through

MM: 18.0/8.3 *Dist:* 1.1 *GPS:* 44.58920/-104.40365 *Elev:* 4760 *Grid:* 95/10 *Land:* NF
Cook Lake Recreation Area   *Type:* Recreation Area
A recreation area around **Cook Lake**, in the **Black Hills National Forest**, which provides camping, picnicking, hiking, and fishing. Along the northeast side of the lake are tables and grills for day use. The lake is stocked with trout, catfish, and sunfish, and a wheelchair accessible pier is provided.

The campground has 2 sections that are separated by the lake and a 1.0 mi road. The first section overlooks the south end of the lake with 6 sites located in a small loop, 4 sites spread along a road, and 8 walk-in tent sites. The second section is above the north end of the lake with 11 sites spread along the outside of the loop road and 4 sites inside the loop. *Conifer forest.*

The **Cook Lake Trail** is an easy 1.0 mi loop around **Cook Lake**. The **Cliff Swallow Trail** is a moderate 3.5 mi loop, which starts in the day use parking area on the north side of the lake and west of the dam. The trail follows **Beaver Creek** for about a mile before climbing 400 ft through the forest to the top of a ridge. Look for cliff swallow nests in the limestone cliff walls. The trail continues 1.5 mi along the ridge, with good views of the lake and valley, before descending back to the parking area.
Cool Rating: *** *Crowds:* ***** *Time:* 1-3 hrs *[FEE AREA]*
Notes: Fills fast on weekends. *Directions:* N 1.1 mi on FR-842
Campsites: 33 *Shade:* *** *Privacy:* ** *RV Size:* 30' *Other:* 1-877-444-6777:www.recreation.gov,Water

MM: 26.3/0.0 *GPS:* 44.65652/-104.36465 *Elev:* 4284 *Grid:* 96/9
Wy-24 *(see chapter)*   *Type:* Hwy Junction w/Chapter
46.3 mi highway from **South Dakota** west and south to **US-14 (east)**, 6 mi south of **Devils Tower**. The primary purpose of this highway is access to **Devils Tower National Monument**. Other highlights include: **Aladdin Tipple Historical Park**, access to **Cook Lake Recreation Area**.
Directions: E to Aladdin or W to Hulett from MM 30.3

MM: 26.3/0.0 *GPS:* 44.65652/-104.36465 *Elev:* 4284 *Grid:* 96/9 *Land:* NF
End of Highway   *Type:* Highway End
Access to the **Cook Lake Recreation Area** along a 26.3 mi scenic drive through the **Bear Lodge Mountains** and **Black Hills National Forest** from **Wy-24** MM 30.3 south to **US-14 (east)** MM 199.5 (1.0 mi west of **I-90**). The **Warren Peak Lookout** is at the highest elevation of the drive. Dispersed camping along **FR-830**, **FR-843**, and **FR-838**.
Nearest Town: Alva 4.9 NW
Directions: SW on FR-838 1.0 mi;   S/L at Cook Lake sign on FR-832 4.6 mi;   SW/R on FR-830 2.7 mi;   W/R on FR-843 3.7 mi; W/R on FR-843 1.6 mi;   S/L on FR-838/Warren Peak Rd/CR-100 12.7 mi to US-14 MM 199.5. (E 0.9 mi to I-90)

CR-406/Lakeshore Drive   N/S

MM: 0.0/5.2 *GPS:* 42.56250/-106.76083 *Elev:* 5668 *Grid:* 61/61
CR-406/Lakeshore Drive   *Type:* Highway Description
5.2 mi road south from **Wy-220** MM 84.7 south along the west side of **Alcova Reservoir** to a paved parking area above the lake. This route provides access to a marina, 3 public campgrounds, 1 private RV park near the marina (requires reservations), and a scenic overlook of the reservoir. The camping along this road is more for boaters, and the campgrounds tend to be pretty full. However, **Okie Beach** has sites away from the lake that are slower to fill. Better overnight camping is located on the east side of the reservoir, south of **Wy-220** MM 86.5 at **Alcova**. *See chapter: Alcova/Pathfinder Reservoir Loop.*
Directions: S on CR-406/Lakeshore Dr from MM 0

MM: 2.3/2.9 *GPS:* 42.53696/-106.76208 *Elev:* 5525 *Grid:* 61/62 *Land:* Bureau of Reclamation
Okie Beach Campground: Alcova Reservoir   *Type:* Campground
A large dispersed camping area below the main road. The area is dirt and runs along about 1/2 mi of the west shore of **Alcova Reservoir**. The sites closer to the road (and farther from the lake) are slower to fill. 4 entrances along a 1/4 mi stretch of the main road provides access. *Scattered small pine trees. Covered and uncovered picnic tables. Fire rings. Not level. Boat ramp.*
Crowds: ***** *[FEE AREA] Directions:* E side of road
Campsites: Dispersed *Shade:* * *Privacy:* * *RV Size:* 40'+ *Other:* None

MM: 2.7/2.5 *GPS:* 42.53200/-106.76300 *Elev:* 5612 *Grid:* 61/62 *Land:* Bureau of Reclamation
Alcova Reservoir Overlook   *Type:* Scenic Viewpoint
A small pullout with several steps that climb to a nice view of **Alcova Reservoir**.
Cool Rating: *** *Crowds:* * *Time:* 15 min *Directions:* SE side of road just past Okie Campground

MM: 4.0/1.2 *GPS:* 42.53138/-106.77852 *Elev:* 5523 *Grid:* 61/62 *Land:* County
RV Dump: Alcova Reservoir   *Type:* RV Dump
RV dump provided by **Natrona County**.
Directions: W side of road. *Across from park, in front of trailer park.*

MM: 4.1/1.1 *GPS:* 42.53056/-106.77820 *Elev:* 5523 *Grid:* 61/62 *Land:* City
Natrona County Park   *Type:* Park
Along the west shore of **Alcova Reservoir** with covered and shaded picnic tables, playground, and a sand volleyball court.
Directions: E side of road

MM: 4.4/0.8 *GPS:* 42.52668/-106.77663 *Elev:* 5520 *Grid:* 61/62 *Land:* Bureau of Reclamation
Westside Campground: Alcova Reservoir   *Type:* Campground
Dirt parking area just off the west lakeshore of **Alcova Reservoir**. *A few short deciduous trees. 6 covered picnic tables. 2 uncovered picnic tables. Not level. Group shelter.*
Crowds: ***** *[FEE AREA] Directions:* E side of road
Campsites: 8 *Shade:* * *Privacy:* * *RV Size:* 40' *Other:* None

MM: 4.9/0.3 *GPS:* 42.51984/-106.77576 *Elev:* 5523 *Grid:* 61/62 *Land:* Bureau of Reclamation
Fremont Campground: Alcova Reservoir   *Type:* Campground
Large dirt parking area along about 1/4 mi of the west shore of **Alcova Reservoir**. *Scattered short trees. Covered and uncovered picnic tables. Not level. Fire rings. Boat ramp.*
Crowds: ***** *[FEE AREA] Directions:* E side near the end of the road
Campsites: Dispersed *Shade:* * *Privacy:* * *RV Size:* 40'+ *Other:* None

MM: 5.2/0.0 *GPS:* 42.51629/-106.77483 *Elev:* 5545 *Grid:* 61/62
End of Highway   *Type:* Highway End

CR-422/Phalow Ln & CR-44/Harmony Ln   E/W

MM: 0.0/10.2 *GPS:* 41.23334/-105.74110 *Elev:* 7213 *Grid:* 76/94
CR-422/Phalow Ln & CR-44/Harmony Ln   *Type:* Highway Description
10.2 mi paved route west from **Wy-230 (Laramie to Colorado)** MM 10.0 with access to 2 small lakes and 2 larger reservoirs. The road reconnects with **Wy-230 (Laramie to Colorado)** at MM 17.8.
Directions: W on CR-422/Phalow Ln 6.9 mi; Continue S on CR-44/Harmony Ln 3.3 mi to Wy-230 MM 17.8.

MM: 4.5/5.7 *Dist:* 1.5 *GPS:* 41.21416/-105.82335 *Elev:* 7243 *Grid:* 75/95 *Land:* Wyoming G & F
Meeboer Lake Public Access Area   *Type:* Public Access Area
Fishing for rainbow trout is the main activity at this lake. Primitive camping in a nice parking area on the west side of the lake. *No trees. Vault toilet. Boat ramp. Windy.*
Crowds: * *Road Desc:* Gravel *Directions:* S on CR-41/Meeboer Rd 1.5 mi
Campsites: Dispersed *Shade:* * *Privacy:* * *RV Size:* 30' *Other:* None

MM: 5.1/5.1 *Dist:* 0.3 *GPS:* 41.23369/-105.83962 *Elev:* 7252 *Grid:* 74/94 *Land:* Wyoming G & F
Gelatt Lake Public Access Area   *Type:* Public Access Area
Fishing for rainbow and cutthroat trout is the main activity at this lake. Primitive camping on the south side of the lake. *No trees. Vault toilet. Boat ramp. Windy. No open fires allowed.*
Crowds: *** *Road Desc:* Gravel *Directions:* N 0.3 mi
Campsites: Dispersed *Shade:* * *Privacy:* * *RV Size:* 30' *Other:* None

MM: 5.5/4.7 *Dist:* 0.3 *GPS:* 41.23376/-105.85359 *Elev:* 7272 *Grid:* 74/94 *Land:* Wyoming G & F
Twin Buttes Reservoir Public Access Area   *Type:* Public Access Area
Fishing for brown and rainbow trout is the main activity at this lake. Primitive camping in 2 areas along the southeast and south ends of the lake. *No trees. Vault toilet. Boat ramp. Windy. No open fires allowed.*
Crowds: *** *Road Desc:* Gravel
Directions: N on CR-44/Big Hollow Rd, then immediately W/L 0.3 mi to first area, and 1.1 to second area.
Campsites: Dispersed *Shade:* * *Privacy:* * *RV Size:* 40'+ *Other:* None

MM: 6.9/3.3 *Dist:* 3.4 *GPS:* 41.23782/-105.90230 *Elev:* 7285 *Grid:* 74/94 *Land:* Wyoming G & F
Lake Hattie Public Access Area   *Type:* Public Access Area
A large reservoir that supports water sports and fishing for brown, cutthroat, rainbow, and lake trout. The lake is popular for windsurfing. A large area for primitive camping is located on the southeast side of the lake. *No trees. Vault toilet. Handicapped accessible boat ramp. Windy.*
Crowds: ** *Road Desc:* Partially paved. Last 0.5 mi is gravel.
Directions: W on CR-424/Hanson Ln 1.9 mi; Continue N on Lake Hattie Rd/CR-45 1.0 mi; Fork R/N 0.5 mi on gravel road.
Campsites: Dispersed *Shade:* * *Privacy:* * *RV Size:* 40'+ *Other:* None

MM: 10.2/0.0 *GPS:* 41.17148/-105.86295 *Elev:* 7315 *Grid:* 74/96
CR-44/Harmony Ln & CR-422/Phalow Ln   *Type:* Highway End
10.2 mi paved route east from **Wy-230 (Laramie to Colorado)** MM 17.8 with access to 2 small lakes and 2 larger reservoirs. The road reconnects with **Wy-230 (Laramie to Colorado)** at MM 10.0.
Directions: N on CR-44/Harmony Ln 3.3 mi; Continue E on CR-422/Phalow Ln 6.9 mi to Wy-230 MM 10.0.

Fossil Butte National Monument S/N

MM: 0.0 *GPS:* 41.81592/-110.71956 *Elev:* 6645 *Grid:* 5/80 *Land:* NPS
Fossil Butte National Monument *Type:* Highway Description
50 million years ago this area was a huge lake in a lush green subtropical forest. Because of profound climate change, what remains today is a semi-arid landscape of flat-topped buttes in a sagebrush desert. The ancient lake sediment hardened and transformed into layers of rocks known as the **Green River Formation**. Trapped between these layers are among the best-preserved fossils in the world. These remarkably detailed fossils include fish, insects, plants, reptiles, birds, and mammals. Paleontologists have unearthed millions of specimens over the past 120 years. The 6.9 mi road through the park includes a visitor center, 2 hiking trails (one that leads to where many of the fossils were unearthed), and a picnic area.
Directions: NW on CR-300 2.3 mi; NW/R on Chicken Creek Rd from MM 2.3.
Notes: There is no camping at the monument and little camping anywhere in the area except private campgrounds in Kemmerer. BLM land is located along US-30 and generally provides a place to park overnight, but watch out for private land.

MM: 0.9 *Dist:* 0.1 *GPS:* 41.82340/-110.73517 *GPS2:* 41.83448/-110.74102 *Elev:* 6670 *Grid:* 5/79 *Land:* NM
Historic Quarry Trail *Type:* Hiking Trail
A hike up **Fossil Butte** where wayside exhibits provide information about geology, area history, and the wildlife and plants of the high desert. The trail also passes a small historic cabin. A steep side trail leads to the site of the **Historic Fossil Quarry**, which was at the deepest part of an ancient lake. Dead fish and animals would sink to a depth with insufficient oxygen to sustain life, which meant there were no scavengers to eat these dead creatures or bacteria to decay them, leaving them entombed and fossilized in the limestone layers. *Loop: Moderate; 2.0 mi loop; 495 ft elev gain.* **Side trail to Historic Fossil Quarry***: Moderate; 0.2 mi one-way; 210 ft elev gain.*
Cool Rating: *** *Crowds:* * *Time:* 1-2 hrs *Notes:* The loop trail is easier hiking counterclockwise.
Directions: N 0.1 mi to large parking area

MM: 2.3 *GPS:* 41.82302/-110.76209 *Elev:* 6629 *Grid:* 4/79
Chicken Creek Rd *Type:* Highway Junction
Road north into **Fossil Butte National Monument**.
Directions: N/R on Chicken Creek Rd 1.2 mi to Visitor Center

MM: 2.5 *GPS:* 41.82467/-110.76329 *Elev:* 6648 *Grid:* 4/79 *Land:* NM
Fossil Butte National Monument sign *Type:* National Monument

MM: 3.5 *GPS:* 41.83670/-110.77112 *Elev:* 6790 *Grid:* 4/79 *Land:* NM
Fossil Butte National Monument Visitor Center *Type:* National Monument
General information, over 80 fossils, 2 video programs, and fossil preparation demonstrations.
Hours: 8am - 7pm (summer); 8am - 4:30pm (offseason) *Cool Rating:* **** *Crowds:* ** *Time:* 1 hr
Directions: Large loop parking area on E side of road

MM: 5.8 *GPS:* 41.86652/-110.78077 *Elev:* 7205 *Grid:* 4/78 *Land:* NM
Chicken Creek Picnic Area *Type:* Picnic Area
A 130 yd walk down a hill to a picnic area with 1 shady table and a table in a gazebo. The other tables are more in the open near some trees that might provide some shade during the later part of the day. The trail to the picnic area is also the south end of the **Fossil Lake Trail**.
Directions: Parking area on E side of road

MM: 5.9 *GPS:* 41.86863/-110.78054 *Elev:* 7287 *Grid:* 4/78 *Land:* NM
Fossil Lake Trail *Type:* Hiking Trail
A hike that winds through sagebrush and an aspen grove at the base of **Cundick Ridge**. Wayside exhibits interpret the wildlife, plants, and geology of this area. The trail ends at the **Chicken Creek Picnic Area**, where a 0.2 mi walk along the road completes the loop. The loop can be done in either direction, but clockwise is easiest. *Easy; 1.3 mi loop; 300 ft elev gain.*
Cool Rating: ** *Crowds:* * *Time:* 45 min *Directions:* Parking pullout on E side of road

MM: 6.9 *GPS:* 41.87518/-110.78410 *Elev:* 7777 *Grid:* 4/78 *Land:* NM
Fossil Butte Overlook *Type:* Scenic Viewpoint
Just past the **Fossil Lake Trail** pullout, the road narrows, changes to washboarded gravel, and climbs steeply 1.0 mi to the top of the ridge for panoramic views of the valley (490 ft elev gain).
Cool Rating: *** *Crowds:* * *Road Desc:* Gravel, rough & washboard, narrow & steep
Notes: Not recommended for trailers and large RVs.

FR-27/Ten Sleep Rd   S/N

MM: 0.0/7.3   *GPS:* 44.16887/-107.24796   *Elev:* 8065   *Grid:* 54/21   *Land:* NF
FR-27/Ten Sleep Rd   *Type:* Highway Description
7.3 mi gravel National Forest road from **US-16** MM 44.1 north to **West Tensleep Lake**, **West Tensleep Trailhead**, and **West Tensleep Falls**. 4 National Forest campgrounds are located along this road, which also offers many dispersed camping opportunities.
Nearest Town: Ten Sleep 17.6 SW   *Directions:* W then N on FR-27/Ten Sleep Rd 7.3 mi

MM: 0.2/7.1   *Dist:* 0.3   *GPS:* 44.16528/-107.25175   *Elev:* 7985   *Grid:* 54/21   *Land:* NF
Boulder Park Campground   *Type:* Campground
2 large loops with a common road down the middle with a few additional sites. The loops are located in a meadow with conifer trees surrounding the perimeter. The east loop is adjacent to **West Tensleep Creek**. This is primarily an RV campground with sites that are reservable up to 30 days in advance. *Little understory. Sites are close together.*
Crowds: ***** *[FEE AREA]* *Directions:* S 1/4 mi
Campsites: 39   *Shade:* ***   *Privacy:* *   *RV Size:* 40'+   *Other:* 1-877-444-6777:www.recreation.gov,Water

MM: 3.0/4.3   *GPS:* 44.20539/-107.23779   *Elev:* 8565   *Grid:* 55/20   *Land:* NF
Island Park Campground   *Type:* Campground
Located just west of a large open park along a short road with an end loop. Some of the sites are near **West Tensleep Creek**. *Conifer forest. Little understory. Somewhat unlevel. 1 pull-thru.*
Crowds: **** *[FEE AREA]* *Directions:* SE side of road
Campsites: 10   *Shade:* ***   *Privacy:* **   *RV Size:* 20'   *Other:* Water

MM: 6.1/1.2   *GPS:* 44.24435/-107.22256   *Elev:* 8901   *Grid:* 55/19   *Land:* NF
Deer Park Campground   *Type:* Campground
Located in a stand of trees on the edge of a large open park. **West Tensleep Creek** flows nearby. *Sites along a short road and loop. Conifer forest. Level.*
Crowds: *** *[FEE AREA]* *Directions:* NW side of road
Campsites: 7   *Shade:* ***   *Privacy:* ***   *RV Size:* 20'   *Other:* Water

MM: 7.1/0.2   *Dist:* 0.2   *GPS:* 44.26242/-107.21222   *Elev:* 9120   *Grid:* 55/18   *Land:* NF
West Tensleep Trailhead   *Type:* Trailhead
The following 2 hikes can be done as long day hikes or overnighters. Both trails start at the north end of the parking area:

The **Lost Twin Lakes** are situated in a glacial cirque in the shadows of **Darton Peak** and **Bighorn Peak**. The trail traverses a valley following **Middle Tensleep Creek** northeast to a small waterfall (1.5 mi), into the **Cloud Peak Wilderness**, and past **Mirror Lake** (3.3 mi). *Moderately strenuous; 6.1 mi one-way; 1300 ft elev gain.*

Hike north past **West Tensleep Lake** to 3 beautiful alpine lakes in the **Cloud Peak Wilderness**: **Lake Helen** (4.0 mi), **Lake Marion** (5.0 mi), and **Mistymoon Lake** (6.0 mi). The trail is rough and difficult to do as a day hike. A shorter option is to hike only to **Lake Helen**. *Strenuous; 6.0 mi one-way; 870 ft elev gain to Lake Helen, 1135 ft to Mistymoon Lake.*
Cool Rating: ****   *Crowds:* ***
Directions: Fork N/R 0.2 mi to West Tensleep Trailhead. Trail starts at N end of parking area.

MM: 7.1/0.2   *Dist:* 0.2   *GPS:* 44.26116/-107.21277   *GPS2:* 44.25139/-107.21272   *Elev:* 9108   *Grid:* 55/18   *Land:* NF
Tensleep Falls   *Type:* Waterfall
A beautiful waterfall on **Middle Tensleep Creek**, which flows through a granite channel before dropping 20 ft over a ledge. After the initial plunge the river rolls steeply down a hill over a boulder field with additional short drops and long cascades. The long length of the cascades offers many different vantage points from the top to the bottom of the falls. The falls are easily accessed along a forested trail above the creek with a short, steep descent to the bottom of the falls. *Easy; 0.9 mi one-way; 110 ft elev loss.*
Cool Rating: ****   *Crowds:* *   *Time:* 1 hr
Directions: Fork N/R 0.2 mi to West Tensleep Trailhead. Trail starts in SE corner of parking area.

MM: 7.3/0.0   *GPS:* 44.25874/-107.21582   *Elev:* 9082   *Grid:* 55/19   *Land:* NF
West Tensleep Lake Campground   *Type:* Campground
A scenic campground on the southeast shore of **West Tensleep Lake**. The campground is located in a valley with **Bald Ridge** to the west and peaks of the **Bighorn Mountains** to the north and east. The area receives considerable activity during the day. *Single loop. Conifer forest. Roomy sites. Little understory. Most sites are level. No pull-thrus.*
Crowds: ***** *[FEE AREA]* *Notes:* No motorized boats on lake. *Directions:* W side of road
Campsites: 10   *Shade:* ***   *Privacy:* **   *RV Size:* 30'   *Other:* 1-877-444-6777:www.recreation.gov,Water

MM: 7.3/0.0   *GPS:* 44.25912/-107.21497   *Elev:* 9085   *Grid:* 55/19
End of Highway   *Type:* Highway End

FR-700/Vedauwoo Glen Rd   SW/NE

MM: 0.0/7.3   **GPS:** 41.15839/-105.40240   **Elev:** 8352   **Grid:** 81/96   **Land:** NF
FR-700/Vedauwoo Glen Rd   **Type:** Highway Description
7.3 mi forest road between **I-80** and **Wy-210/Happy Jack Rd** that passes the **Vedauwoo Recreation Area** (1.1 mi) and **Reynolds Hill Trailhead** (3.6 mi) and provides access to the north entrance of **Curt Gowdy State Park**. This area is very scenic and provides dispersed camping and other recreational opportunities amid sparse pine forest and granite outcroppings. Camping in this area is very popular, particularly on weekends. The closer to **Vedauwoo** the more crowded it gets. This is a very popular area for OHVs.
Road Desc: The first 1.1 mi is paved to Vedauwoo Recreation Area. The rest is gravel, rough, washboarded, and potholed.
Notes: If looking for a place to camp and you don't care about a lake, restrooms, and drinking water, this may be preferable to Curt Gowdy State Park.
Directions: I-80 exit 329; E on Vedauwoo Rd/FR-700 7.3 mi to Wy-210/Happy Jack Rd.

MM: 1.1/6.2   **GPS:** 41.15532/-105.38135   **Elev:** 8230   **Grid:** 81/96   **Land:** NF
Vedauwoo Recreation Area   **Type:** Recreation Area
A 10 sq mi area of towering granite rock formations located in the **Medicine Bow National Forest**. **Vedauwoo** (pronounced VEEda-voo) is an **Arapaho Indian** word meaning "earth born." These oddly shaped jumbled piles of rocks provide an excellent location for camping, picnicking, photography, hiking, mountain biking, and some of the best rock climbing in **Wyoming**. The developed recreation area is situated at the base of a large rock formation called **Turtle Rock**, which is 350 ft high and cut by a box canyon on the south end. While the area offers miles of trails, the 2 most accessible and popular trails are the **Turtle Rock Trail** and **Box Canyon Trail**.

The **Turtle Rock Trail** is a pleasant 2.7 mi hiking and biking loop trail around the base of **Turtle Rock**. The entrance road branches east and west to separate trailhead parking areas, and the road between them serves as part of the loop trail. The trail can be hiked in either direction; however, clockwise seems more popular and the west parking area is larger. Bicyclists might want to ride counterclockwise so hikers can see them coming. The south end of the trail is where the rock formations are visible. On the southwest end the trail passes a beaver pond and some marshy areas. The southeast end of the trail is composed of willow and aspen. The rest of the trail is primarily through light conifer forest. *Easy; 2.7 mi loop; Level.*

The **Box Canyon Trail** heads up the canyon with opportunities to climb up the rocks for excellent views to the north and west. The trail starts from the middle parking area and follows a paved and smooth dirt path 0.3 mi to a bridge. Across the bridge the trail appears to turn right, but instead continue straight west about 25 yds and begins climbing up the rocks. About 40 yds up the rocks keep right to stay on the trail. This turn is not well marked, but the rest of the trail is a bit easier to follow. Keep an eye out for cairns, 2 ramps, and a set of wooden stairs. The trail zigzags up the rocks fairly close to the base of the large rocks to the north. *Moderately easy; 0.6 mi one-way; 220 ft elev gain.*

Picnic tables are located at the **Box Canyon** parking area. Following the road past the east parking area is the **Beaver Ponds Day Use Area** with 2 picnic tables along the road and several scattered through the woods and rocks. The rocks above this area provide some good rock scrambling opportunities.

Near the entrance is a nice campground situated among scattered boulders and pine trees. *2 paved loops. Good spacing between sites. 7 tent-only sites. 12 pull-thrus.* 1/2 mi from the entrance near the trailhead parking is a tent-only campground with many sites.
Cool Rating: *****   **Crowds:** *****   **Time:** 1-4+ hrs   **[FEE AREA]**   **Directions:** N to the entrance station.
Notes: See next section for a free parking area 1/4 mi east.
Campsites: 28   **Shade:** **   **Privacy:** ***   **RV Size:** 40'+   **Other:** Water

MM: 1.4/5.9   **GPS:** 41.15387/-105.37665   **Elev:** 8274   **Grid:** 81/96   **Land:** NF
Vedauwoo Climbing Area   **Type:** Recreation Area
A dirt parking loop that provides access to a granite boulder area that is popular with rock climbers. This is also an alternate free parking area to walk 0.7 mi into the **Vedauwoo Recreation Area**. *Vault toilet. Picnic table.*
Crowds: ^^^^   **Directions:** N side of road.

MM: 3.6/3.7   **Dist:** 0.1   **GPS:** 41.16171/-105.34745   **Elev:** 8963   **Grid:** 81/96   **Land:** NF
Reynolds Hill Trail   **Type:** Hiking Trail
A hiking loop trail through sagebrush, meadows and forest below granite outcrops, which include **Reynolds Hill** and the even taller **Egbert Hill**. Most of the trail is in the open and, surprisingly, provides only a few good views of the rock outcrops. Begin by continuing northwest on **FR-700D** and descend 70 ft to a road junction (MI 0.4). Turn left 0.1 mi and turn left again (MI 0.5). Keep right at a road junction at (MI 0.6). In another 0.2 mi you will reach a crossing point of **Middle Crow Creek** just before a large pine tree (MI 0.8). *At this point you have descended 160 ft.* Keep left to cross the creek and continue north to a bridge across another creek and beaver pond area (MI 0.9). Just past the bridge the trail turns left and heads north through a meadow 0.1 mi to the best view of **Reynolds Hill** (MI 1.0). In another 0.4 mi you will enter a grove of aspen trees. This is the first shade on the trail (MI 1.4). In 0.3 mi take a sharp right at a trail junction to continue the loop (MI 1.7). *At this point you have climbed 240 ft.* This section of the trail passes below **Egbert Hill** to the north. In 0.5 mi keep right at a fork (MI 2.2). Shortly after this point the trail descends steeply into a pine forest and emerges with a view of another rock hill (MI 2.5). In 0.3 mi take a sharp right at a trail junction to continue the loop (MI 2.8). Continue 0.4 mi to a point where the trail appears to end at a rock outcrop (MI 3.2). You must scramble about 60 ft over the rocks where the trail continues. In 0.2 mi you will complete the loop and return to the meadow and bridge. Re-trace the original path back to trailhead. *Moderate; 4.3 mi loop; 160 ft elev loss. 240 ft elev gain.*
Cool Rating: ***   **Crowds:** **   **Time:** 2 hrs   **Directions:** NW on FR-700D 0.1 mi to parking area.

MM: 7.3/0.0   **GPS:** 41.19154/-105.29573   **Elev:** 7759   **Grid:** 82/95   **Land:** NF
End of Highway   **Type:** Highway End
A 7.3 mi forest road southwest to **I-80** passing **Reynolds Hill Trailhead** (3.7 mi) and **Vedauwoo Recreation Area** (6.2 mi). This area is very scenic and provides dispersed camping and other recreational opportunities amid sparse pine forest and granite outcroppings. Camping in this area is very popular, particularly on weekends. The closer to **Vedauwoo** the more crowded it gets. This is a very popular area for OHVs.
Directions: S then SW on FR-700

Fremont Lake Rd/Skyline Drive   SW/NE

MM: 0.0/14.5 *GPS:* 42.86643/-109.85618 *Elev:* 7181 *Grid:* 17/53
Fremont Lake Rd/Skyline Drive   *Type:* Highway Description
14.5 mi paved highway from **US-191** MM 99.3, at the east end of **Pinedale**, northeast through sagebrush flats and foothills, past **Fremont Lake**, then climbing over 1,900 ft to the base of the **Wind River Mountains**. The climb offers great views of **Fremont Lake** and the **Wind River Range**. Along the route are 3 National Forest campgrounds as well as several free primitive camping areas, in particular on the south end of **Fremont Lake**. At the end of the road, the **Elkhart Park Trailheads** provide trails into the **Wind River Mountains** and the **Bridger Wilderness**.
Directions: NE at the curve on the east side of Pinedale

MM: 0.0/14.5 *GPS:* 42.86643/-109.85618 *Elev:* 7181 *Grid:* 17/53
Pinedale   *Type:* Town

MM: 3.2/11.4 *Dist:* 0.4 *GPS:* 42.89748/-109.82065 *Elev:* 7423 *Grid:* 18/53 *Land:* NF
Fremont Lake   *Type:* Lake
A long terminal moraine dammed lake at the end of **Pine Creek Canyon**, a glacial valley formed by ice flowing out of the **Wind River Mountains**. This is **Wyoming**'s second largest natural lake measuring 9 mi long, 1.1 mi wide, and up to 600 ft deep. The lake is considered one of the top ten cleanest in the nation and is the recreational hub and water source for the **Pinedale** area. A marina, lodge, and beach area are located at the south end of the lake. A boat launch is located on the east end near the **Fremont Lake Campground**.
Cool Rating: *** *Crowds:* *** *Directions:* NW/L on Osprey Rd/FR-111 0.2 mi; Keep left 0.2 mi.

MM: 3.2/11.4 *Dist:* 1.3 *GPS:* 42.89983/-109.83808 *Elev:* 7428 *Grid:* 17/52 *Land:* BLM
Dispersed Camping: Fremont Lake   *Type:* Campground
Primitive camping 1/2 mi down the outlet of **Fremont Lake**. Located on a small section of **BLM** land south of the lake. *No trees.*
Crowds: ** *Directions:* NW/L on Osprey Rd/FR-111 0.2 mi; Keep left 0.9 mi; Keep left 0.2 mi.
Campsites: Dispersed *Shade:* * *Privacy:* * *RV Size:* 30' *Other:* None

MM: 3.2/11.4 *Dist:* 3.6 *GPS:* 42.93970/-109.79684 *Elev:* 7480 *Grid:* 18/51 *Land:* NF
Fremont Lake Campground   *Type:* Campground
2 long paved loops that are terraced along a hillside on the eastern shore of **Fremont Lake**. The south end of the campground is primarily aspen forest with dense understory and is fairly level. Farther north the sites are spread out along the road in a mature conifer forest and are not as level. Beyond the north loop are sites along a road with large speed bumps and a tight end loop turnaround. Several sites are along the lakeshore or across the road from the lake with light shrubbery capable of mooring boats at or very close to the camping site. Most of the other sites do not have a view of the lake. *Several pull-thrus. Boat ramp.*
Crowds: ***** *[FEE AREA] Directions:* NW/L on Osprey Rd/FR-111 3.4 mi, keeping right at fork after 0.2 mi.
Notes: The campground is very busy on weekends.
Campsites: 54 *Shade:* **** *Privacy:* **** *RV Size:* 40'+ *Other:* 1-877-444-6777:www.recreation.gov,Water

MM: 6.9/7.6 *Dist:* 1.1 *GPS:* 42.93649/-109.75935 *Elev:* 7620 *Grid:* 19/52 *Land:* NF
Half Moon Lake Campground   *Type:* Campground
Situated in the foothills of the **Wind River Mountains** on the sandy north shore of **Half Moon Lake**. Extremely dense middlestory of willows and other shrubs provide great privacy but block views of the lake and make pitching a tent challenging. Some sites have access to the lakeshore where boats can be moored. *Tightly configured overlapping loop roads. Under-maintained. 1 tent-only site.*
Crowds: ***** *[FEE AREA] Road Desc:* Gravel *Directions:* E/R on FR-114 1.1 mi
Campsites: 18 *Shade:* ***** *Privacy:* ***** *RV Size:* 30' *Other:* None

MM: 11.1/3.5 *GPS:* 42.98535/-109.77535 *Elev:* 8665 *Grid:* 18/50 *Land:* NF
Fremont Lake Scenic Overlook   *Type:* Scenic Viewpoint
A pullout with a great view 1,250 ft above **Fremont Lake**.
Cool Rating: *** *Crowds:* * *Time:* 10 min *Directions:* W side of road

MM: 13.7/0.8 *GPS:* 43.00874/-109.75800 *Elev:* 9320 *Grid:* 19/50 *Land:* NF
Wind River Mountains Scenic Overlook   *Type:* Scenic Viewpoint
A pullout that provides an excellent view of the **Wind River Mountains** along with a sign identifying the peaks. The very north end of **Fremont Lake** is visible from here; however, the views of the lake on the drive back down the mountain are much better. *See previous section.*
Cool Rating: **** *Crowds:* * *Time:* 10 min *Directions:* N side of road

MM: 14.3/0.2 *GPS:* 43.00296/-109.75365 *Elev:* 9344 *Grid:* 19/50 *Land:* NF
U.S. Forest Service Visitor Center   *Type:* Visitor Center
A staffed visitor center at the entrance of **Elkhart Park** with information on the trails into the **Wind River Mountains** and the **Bridger Wilderness**.
Directions: S side of road

MM: 14.4/0.1 *GPS:* 43.00415/-109.75200 *Elev:* 9356 *Grid:* 19/50 *Land:* NF
Elkhart Park Trailheads   *Type:* Trailhead
2 large parking areas that access 2 separate trails into the **Wind River Mountains** and the **Bridger Wilderness**. Both trails offer day hikes as well as connections to other trails for longer overnight hikes. A short distance south of the **Trails End Campground** is the **Pole Creek Trail**, which heads east and offers some moderate day hikes to **Miller Lake** (4.0 mi) and **Photographer's Point** (4.5 mi). The trail connects with the **Highline Trail** at 10.4 mi after a 2,000 ft elevation gain. This trail gets heavy hiking and stock use. Adjacent to the west side of the campground is the strenuous **Pine Creek Trail**, which heads north 2.1 mi dropping 2,000 ft to **Long Lake** and then climbing over 2,000 ft in another 3.9 mi to **Glimpse Lake**. The trail is rocky, steep, and rough, and therefore much less used and not recommended for stock.

The parking areas have toilets and unloading facilities for livestock. Drinking water is available during the summer season. Detailed trail information can be obtained at the **U.S. Forest Service Visitor Center** 0.1 mi west of the lower parking area.
Cool Rating: **** *Crowds:* ***** *Directions:* Pole Creek Trail on E side of road and Pine Creek Trail 0.1 mi N.

MM: 14.5/0.0 *GPS:* 43.00592/-109.75276 *Elev:* 9345 *Grid:* 19/50 *Land:* NF

Trails End Campground   *Type:* Campground

The highest campground in the **Pinedale** area, which is located just north of the very busy **Elkhart Park Trailhead** *(see previous section)*. The lower loop to the left is close to a parking area for the **Pine Creek Trail** and has larger sites, a couple of which accommodate longer RVs. The upper loop to the right is more secluded and best suited for short RVs and tents. *Conifer forest.*

Crowds: ***** *[FEE AREA]* *Directions:* At the end of the road.

Campsites: 8 *Shade:* ***** *Privacy:* ***** *RV Size:* 30' *Other:* Water

MM: 14.5/0.0 *GPS:* 43.00592/-109.75276 *Elev:* 9345 *Grid:* 19/50

End of Highway   *Type:* Highway End

Glendo Park Rd (Glendo State Park)   W/E

MM: 0.0/13.4 *GPS:* 42.50079/-105.02483 *Elev:* 4730 *Grid:* 86/62
Glendo Park Rd (Glendo State Park)   *Type:* Highway Description
13.4 mi road from **Glendo** southeast through **Glendo State Park**.
Directions: I-25 exit 111; E on A St 0.1 mi; S/R on Wy-319/S Yellowstone Hwy 0.2 mi; E/L on C St 1 block; S/R on S Lincoln
Ave/Glendo Park Rd.

MM: 0.0/13.4 *GPS:* 42.50079/-105.02483 *Elev:* 4730 *Grid:* 86/62
Glendo   *Type:* Town

MM: 1.3/12.1 *GPS:* 42.48572/-105.01210 *Elev:* 4662 *Grid:* 86/63 *Land:* State
Glendo State Park - Whiskey Entrance   *Type:* State Park
Glendo State Park is centered around **Glendo Reservoir**, the sixth of 7 reservoirs on the **North Platte River**. This extremely
popular boating lake offers waterskiing, fishing, and other water-based activities. The park provides day use facilities, 12
campgrounds, 6 boat ramps, and a commercial concession, which provides complete marina services, motel units, and fishing
equipment. Although the park is situated on the **Wyoming** plains, much of the area around the lake is lightly forested. The park is
located in one of the state's most historic areas where a large area of aboriginal activity, known as the **Spanish Diggings**, lies just
east of the reservoir. This archaeological area lies between **Manville** to the north, **Guernsey** to the south, the **North Platte River**
to the west, and **US-85** to the east.
Cool Rating: ** *Crowds:* **** *[FEE AREA]* *Directions:* S side of road
Notes: There are no assigned campsites in the park. Camping entails registering at the entrance and driving around to find a site.
The only campground with designated sites is Two Moon Campground, which is the best option if just camping overnight. Only
Sandy Beach Campground takes reservations.

MM: 1.4/12.0 *Dist:* 0.8 *GPS:* 42.48493/-105.01093 *Elev:* 4667 *Grid:* 86/63 *Land:* State
Lakeshore Drive Campgrounds   *Type:* Campground
Approximately 115 sites are spread amongst **Waters Point**, **Colter Bay**, **Custer Cove**, **Soldier Rock**, **Reno Cove**, and **Red Hills**
campgrounds. The campsites are not always well defined and vary insofar as being level and protected from the wind. The sites
closest to the lake are generally occupied first. The pine trees scattered about the area don't offer much shade. The shoreline is
rock and gravel. The campgrounds are near protected bays for tying up boats.
Crowds: ***** *[FEE AREA]* *Notes:* When the area is busy, it is kind of a free-for-all to find a campsite.
Directions: NE on Lakeshore Dr 0.8 mi - 4.1 mi
Campsites: 115 *Shade:* * *Privacy:* * *RV Size:* 40'+ *Other:* Water

MM: 1.4/12.0 *Dist:* 1.4 *GPS:* 42.48097/-104.98837 *Elev:* 4673 *Grid:* 87/63 *Land:* State
Waters Point Campground   *Type:* Campground
See previous description for Lakeshore Drive Campgrounds.
Crowds: ***** *[FEE AREA]* *Directions:* NE on Lakeshore Dr 0.7 mi; SE 0.7 mi.
Campsites: Dispersed *Shade:* * *Privacy:* * *RV Size:* 40'+ *Other:* Water

MM: 1.4/12.0 *Dist:* 1.1 *GPS:* 42.48514/-104.99269 *Elev:* 4662 *Grid:* 87/63 *Land:* State
Colter Bay Campground   *Type:* Campground
See previous description for Lakeshore Drive Campgrounds.
Crowds: ***** *[FEE AREA]* *Directions:* NE on Lakeshore Dr 0.9 mi; SE 0.2 mi.
Campsites: Dispersed *Shade:* * *Privacy:* * *RV Size:* 40'+ *Other:* Water

MM: 1.4/12.0 *Dist:* 1.7 *GPS:* 42.48690/-104.98170 *Elev:* 4670 *Grid:* 87/63 *Land:* State
Custer Cove Campground   *Type:* Campground
See previous description for Lakeshore Drive Campgrounds.
Crowds: ***** *[FEE AREA]* *Directions:* NE on Lakeshore Dr 1.7 mi; SE side of road.
Campsites: Dispersed *Shade:* * *Privacy:* * *RV Size:* 40'+ *Other:* Water

MM: 1.4/12.0 *Dist:* 2.2 *GPS:* 42.49032/-104.97542 *Elev:* 4670 *Grid:* 87/63 *Land:* State
Soldier Rock Campground   *Type:* Campground
*See previous description for Lakeshore Drive Campgrounds. The camping area has sites along the road for about 0.3 mi with no
close access to the shoreline.*
Crowds: ***** *[FEE AREA]* *Directions:* NE on Lakeshore Dr 2.2 mi - 2.5 mi; E side of road.
Campsites: 6 *Shade:* * *Privacy:* * *RV Size:* 40'+ *Other:* Water

MM: 1.4/12.0 *Dist:* 3.0 *GPS:* 42.49647/-104.96779 *Elev:* 4700 *Grid:* 87/63 *Land:* State
Reno Cove Campground   *Type:* Campground
See previous description for Lakeshore Drive Campgrounds. Boat launch area.
Crowds: ***** *[FEE AREA]* *Directions:* NE on Lakeshore Dr 2.7 mi; NE 0.3 mi.
Campsites: 30 *Shade:* * *Privacy:* * *RV Size:* 30' *Other:* Water

MM: 1.4/12.0 *Dist:* 4.1 *GPS:* 42.50346/-104.96639 *Elev:* 4700 *Grid:* 87/62 *Land:* State
Red Hills Campground   *Type:* Campground
*See previous description for Lakeshore Drive Campgrounds. The area above this campground is in the red hills, but the camping
area is below the red hills amid pine and cottonwood trees.*
Crowds: ***** *[FEE AREA]* *Directions:* NE on Lakeshore Dr 3.7 mi; E 0.4 mi.
Campsites: 45 *Shade:* ** *Privacy:* * *RV Size:* 30' *Other:* Water

MM: 2.0/11.4 *GPS:* 42.47814/-105.00180 *Elev:* 4670 *Grid:* 86/63 *Land:* State
Whiskey Gulch Campground   *Type:* Campground
This section covers both **Whiskey Gulch Campground** and **Sagebrush Campground**, which are next to each other along the
south side of the lake in a large bay with good lake access. Level sites are located in grassy areas with large cottonwoods for
shade, although many of the sites are not under the trees. The area has good wind protection including some protected areas for
tying up boats. 100 sites between both campgrounds. *Boat ramp.*
[FEE AREA] *Directions:* NE side of road
Campsites: 100 *Shade:* *** *Privacy:* * *RV Size:* 40'+ *Other:* Water

MM: 2.6/10.8 *GPS:* 42.47350/-104.99302 *Elev:* 4670 *Grid:* 87/63 *Land:* State
Sagebrush Campground   *Type:* Campground
See previous section on Whiskey Gulch Campground.
[FEE AREA] Directions: NE side of road

MM: 3.6/9.8 *GPS:* 42.46848/-104.97542 *Elev:* 4685 *Grid:* 87/63 *Land:* State
Shelter Point Campground   *Type:* Campground
As the name implies, this campground is located on a point in the lake. *Few trees for shade or wind protection.*
Crowds: ***** *[FEE AREA] Directions:* N side of road
Campsites: 20 *Shade:* * *Privacy:* * *RV Size:* 40'+ *Other:* Water

MM: 4.0/9.4 *GPS:* 42.46890/-104.96820 *Elev:* 4756 *Grid:* 87/63 *Land:* State
RV Dump   *Type:* RV Dump
[FEE AREA] Directions: N side of road

MM: 4.4/9.0 *GPS:* 42.46920/-104.95971 *Elev:* 4800 *Grid:* 87/63 *Land:* State
Two Moon Campground   *Type:* Campground
The largest and most traditional campground with well defined and level sites. The campground is located on a bluff above the lake with no access to the water, and therefore generally has available sites when the other campgrounds are full. This is the best option if just camping overnight. *Conifer forest provides shade and wind protection. Spacious sites. Many pull-thrus.*
Crowds: *** *[FEE AREA] Directions:* N side of road
Campsites: 200 *Shade:* ***** *Privacy:* **** *RV Size:* 40'+ *Other:* Water

MM: 5.8/7.6 *GPS:* 42.47616/-104.95070 *Elev:* 4665 *Grid:* 87/63 *Land:* Bureau of Reclamation
Glendo Dam   *Type:* Dam
The sixth of 7 dams on the **North Platte River**. The dam was completed in 1957 and the power plant in 1958. The dam is earth-fill, 167 ft high, and 2,096 ft long.
Time: Drive by *Directions:* Drive across the dam.

MM: 13.4/0.0 *Dist:* 1.3 *GPS:* 42.52197/-104.93714 *Elev:* 4660 *Grid:* 87/62 *Land:* State
Sandy Beach Campground   *Type:* Campground
A large campground with approximately 2 mi of sandy beach. Large cottonwoods are located along the high-water shoreline; however, many sites have no shade. This is a popular area where beach crowds can reach into the thousands.
Crowds: ***** *[FEE AREA] Notes:* No vehicles allowed on beach. *Directions:* W/L on CR-208/Patten Creek Rd 1.3 mi
Campsites: 153 *Shade:* *** *Privacy:* * *RV Size:* 40'+ *Other:* 1-877-996-7275:wyoparks.state.wy.us/reservations,Water

MM: 13.4/0.0 *GPS:* 42.52111/-104.91227 *Elev:* 4782 *Grid:* 88/62
End of Highway   *Type:* Highway End

Grand Teton National Park

History

A bill to create **Grand Teton National Park** was signed by **President Calvin Coolidge** on February 26, 1929. The park was named after the **Grand Teton**, which at 13,770 ft is the tallest peak in the **Teton Range**. The original park contained only the **Teton Range** and the 6 glacial lakes at its base. In 1927, philanthropist **John D. Rockefeller, Jr.** had purchased 36,000 acres of adjacent land in **Jackson Hole** with the intention of donating the land to the National Park. For 15 years the National Park Service refused the land. Wyoming ranchers were in opposition to park expansion, as it was believed that it would destroy the economy and was in violation of the state's rights. After some coercion from **Rockefeller**, in 1943 **President Franklin D. Roosevelt** declared 221,000 acres of public lands as the **Jackson Hole National Monument** in order to protect **Jackson Lake**, the **Snake River**, and **Jackson Hole**'s sagebrush flats. However, the monument still did not include **Rockefeller**'s land. Ongoing battles against the National Monument continued for years, but after **World War II** tourism money increased and local attitudes changed. On September 14, 1950, **President Harry S. Truman** signed a bill to combine the **Rockefeller** lands, the National Park, and National Monument into **Grand Teton National Park** with a combined area of 484 sq mi.

Geography

The **Teton Range** is part of the **Rocky Mountains**, situated just inside **Wyoming**'s western border and is mostly contained in the park. These mountains are unique and stunning, both because of their shape and their abrupt 7,000 ft rise above the valley floor. The pyramid-shaped peaks were carved by glaciers that left U-shaped valleys and moraines, which created glacial lakes. 6 such lakes are located at the eastern base of the range, which from north to south are: **Jackson Lake**, **Leigh Lake**, **String Lake**, **Jenny Lake**, **Bradley Lake**, **Taggart Lake**, and **Phelps Lake**. **Jackson Lake** is the largest and covers 40 sq mi with a maximum depth of 438 ft. Although **Jackson Lake** is a natural lake, before the park was created it had been dammed to raise the water level by 38 ft.

Along with the **Grand Teton** are 8 additional peaks over 12,000 ft with **Mount Owen** being the tallest at 12,928 ft. Near the center of the **Teton Range**, the **Grand Teton**, **Mount Owen**, and **Teewinot Mountain** make up what is collectively known as the **Cathedral Group**, which is generally the focal point of most photographs of the range.

Between the **Teton Range** to the east and the **Gros Ventre Range** to the west is the **Jackson Hole** valley through which the **Snake River** flows. The valley extends from **Jackson Lake** to the north to the town of **Jackson** to the south.

Wildlife

Grand Teton National Park is part of the **Greater Yellowstone Ecosystem**. This is the largest remaining nearly intact ecosystem in the Earth's northern temperate zone and provides habitat for abundant wildlife. **Yellowstone National Park** belongs to the same ecosystem, and therefore both parks have similar wildlife. Over 60 species of mammals live in the park, including deer, elk, pronghorn, moose, coyote, grizzly bear, black bear, bison, beaver, and river otter. Over 300 species of birds have been reported in the park, including bald eagles, ospreys, cranes, herons, pelicans, and swans.

General

The park receives more than 2.5 million visitors per year and provides 5 public campgrounds, none of which take reservations. The campground at **Jenny Lake** is the most popular and is for tents only. The **Signal Mountain Campground** is the next most popular and generally fills by mid-afternoon. The other campgrounds rarely fill.

The following 4 roads provide access to the park (*see the Grand Teton National Park map on page 13*):

US-26/89/191 heads north between **Jackson** and **Moran Jct**. There is no entrance station along this route, which consists primarily of interpretive pullouts with views of the **Teton Range** plus the historic **Cunningham Cabin**.

US-89/191/287 is a continuation of **US-26/89/191** from **Moran Jct** north to **Yellowstone National Park**. An entrance station is located just north of **Moran Jct**, where entrance fees gain access to both **Grand Teton National Park** and **Yellowstone National Park**. This stretch provides access to **Teton Park Rd** and traverses the east side of **Jackson Lake**. **Colter Bay Village** and the **Colter Bay Visitor Center** are about 9.5 mi north of the entrance station.

Teton Park Rd connects between **US-26/89/191** to the south and **US-89/191/287** to the north. This is the primary park road, which parallels the **Teton Range** with close views and access to the glacial lakes. The town of **Moose** and the **Craig Thomas Discovery and Visitor Center** are located at the south end. The **Jenny Lake** area is the most popular area in the park and includes the **Jenny Lake Visitor Center**.

Gros Ventre Rd heads east from **US-26/89/191**, near the south end of the park, and travels across the **Jackson Hole Valley** toward the **Gros Ventre Mountains** with access to the park's largest campground.

Tips For Visiting

• **Upon entering the park read the park newspaper "Teewinot" to understand the park rules and regulations, safety tips, and help plan your time**.
• The best time to photograph the Teton Range is in the morning. By mid-afternoon the glare of the sun makes photography difficult.
• It is best not to bring pets as they are not allowed on any of the trails.
• Gros Ventre is pronounced "gro-vont."

Greys River Rd/FR-10138   N/S

MM: 0.0/82.0 ***GPS:*** 43.16359/-111.01795 ***Elev:*** 5660 ***Grid:*** 1/46 ***Land:*** NF
Greys River Rd/FR-10138   ***Type:*** Highway Description
82 mi side loop road from **US-89** MM 117.7 at **Alpine** returning to **US-89** MM 71.1, 46.6 mi south. The route heads east then south on **Greys River Rd** for 58.4 mi before turning west 23.6 mi on **Smiths Fork Rd** back to **US-89**. This scenic route parallels the **Greys River** in the **Greys River Valley**, between the **Salt River Range** and the **Wyoming Range**, with wildlife viewing and excellent fishing along the way. 5 public campgrounds are located along this route as well as abundant dispersed camping, particularly south of **Forest Park Campground**.
Notes: Given the road conditions, driving the entire length as a scenic drive is not really worth it.
Road Desc: The road becomes gravel after 0.9 mi. The 35 mi road to the Forest Park Campground is fairly smooth gravel; however, the road for the next 33 mi south is narrow, washboarded, and potholed.
Directions: Just S of river bridge in Alpine, SE 58.4 mi on Greys River Rd/FR-10138; W on Smiths Fork Rd/FR-10072 23.6 mi.

MM: 0.0/82.0 ***GPS:*** 43.16359/-111.01795 ***Elev:*** 5660 ***Grid:*** 1/46
US-89 *(see chapter)*   ***Type:*** Hwy Junction w/Chapter
Directions: N to US-26/89 or S to Afton from MM 117.7

MM: 0.0/82.0 ***GPS:*** 43.16359/-111.01795 ***Elev:*** 5660 ***Grid:*** 1/46
Alpine   ***Type:*** Town

MM: 1.4/80.6 ***GPS:*** 43.15129/-110.99644 ***Elev:*** 5700 ***Grid:*** 1/46 ***Land:*** NF
Greys River Rd Information Board   ***Type:*** Visitor Information
A pullout with information on **Greys River Rd**.
Directions: SW side of road 0.6 mi past the National Forest boundary.

MM: 2.5/79.5 ***GPS:*** 43.14411/-110.97783 ***Elev:*** 5706 ***Grid:*** 1/46 ***Land:*** NF
Bridge Campground   ***Type:*** Campground
Located between the road and the **Greys River**. *Conifer forest. Heavy understory. Not level. Best for tents.*
Crowds: * ***Notes:*** Sharp left turn if heading northwest. ***Directions:*** SE side of road
Campsites: 5 ***Shade:*** ***** ***Privacy:*** **** ***RV Size:*** 20' ***Other:*** BEARS

MM: 12.4/69.6 ***GPS:*** 43.09706/-110.84589 ***Elev:*** 6171 ***Grid:*** 3/48 ***Land:*** NPS
Lynx Creek Campground   ***Type:*** Campground
Near the **Greys River** with a few nice sites. *Conifer forest. Heavy understory. Overgrown and under-maintained. Many tables in the sun. Small vault toilet.*
Crowds: * ***Notes:*** Dispersed camping might be preferable to many of these sites. ***Directions:*** W side of road
Campsites: 14 ***Shade:*** ** ***Privacy:*** *** ***RV Size:*** 30' ***Other:*** BEARS

MM: 14.2/67.8 ***GPS:*** 43.07365/-110.83595 ***Elev:*** 6195 ***Grid:*** 3/48 ***Land:*** NF
Murphy Creek Campground   ***Type:*** Campground
Stretches along the **Greys River** with some sites near the river. *Conifer forest. Grass middlestory. Good spacing between most sites. Level. 3 pull-thrus.*
Crowds: *** ***[FEE AREA]*** ***Directions:*** W side of road
Campsites: 11 ***Shade:*** *** ***Privacy:*** *** ***RV Size:*** 40' ***Other:*** Water BEARS

MM: 22.5/59.5 ***GPS:*** 42.97171/-110.76859 ***Elev:*** 6420 ***Grid:*** 4/51 ***Land:*** NF
Moose Flat Campground   ***Type:*** Campground
Stretches along the **Greys River**. *Conifer forest. Dense middlestory. Good spacing between sites. Level. 5 pull-thrus.*
Crowds: *** ***[FEE AREA]*** ***Directions:*** W side of road
Campsites: 10 ***Shade:*** *** ***Privacy:*** ***** ***RV Size:*** 30' ***Other:*** Water BEARS

MM: 34.6/47.4 ***GPS:*** 42.83113/-110.69172 ***Elev:*** 6948 ***Grid:*** 5/54 ***Land:*** NF
Forest Park Campground   ***Type:*** Campground
Across from the **Forest Park Elk Feed Grounds**. *Single loop. Lodgepole pine forest. Grass understory. Level.*
Crowds: *** ***[FEE AREA]*** ***Road Desc:*** South of the campground the road becomes narrow, washboarded, and potholed.
Directions: E side of road
Campsites: 14 ***Shade:*** **** ***Privacy:*** ** ***RV Size:*** 40' ***Other:*** Water BEARS

MM: 58.4/23.6 ***GPS:*** 42.52130/-110.68954 ***Elev:*** 8619 ***Grid:*** 5/62 ***Land:*** NF
Smiths Fork Rd/FR-10072   ***Type:*** Highway Junction
23.6 mi connecting road from **Greys River Rd** west to **US-89**.
Directions: W on Smiths Fork Rd 23.6 mi to US-89.

MM: 82.0/0.0 ***GPS:*** 42.52947/-110.89782 ***Elev:*** 7162 ***Grid:*** 2/62
US-89 *(see chapter)*   ***Type:*** Hwy Junction w/Chapter
Directions: N to Alpine or S to Afton from MM 71.1

MM: 82.0/0.0 ***GPS:*** 42.52947/-110.89782 ***Elev:*** 7162 ***Grid:*** 2/62
End of Highway   ***Type:*** Highway End
82 mi side loop road from **US-89** MM 71.1, returning to **US-89** MM 117.7 at **Alpine**, 46.6 mi north. The route heads east 23.6 mi before turning north then west on **Greys River Rd** for 58.4 mi to **Alpine**. *See Highway Description for details.*
Directions: E on Smiths Fork Rd/FR-10072 23.6 mi; N 50.1 mi then W 8.3 mi on Greys River Rd/FR-10138.

Gros Ventre Rd/FR-30400   W/E

MM: 0.0/19.9   *GPS:* 43.57412/-110.73322   *Elev:* 6404   *Grid:* 5/36
Gros Ventre Rd/FR-30400   *Type:* Highway Description
19.9 mi scenic drive east from **US-26/89/191** MM 161.3 through the **Gros Ventre River** valley (pronounced "gro-vont"). The first half is in **Grand Teton National Park** and then crosses into the **Bridger-Teton National Forest** on **FR-30400**. For this book the route ends at **Crystal Creek Campground**, even though the road actually continues another 17 mi. 4 public campgrounds are located along the route; however, only the National Park campground is close to **US-26/89/191**. Highlights include: **Kelly Warm Spring**, **Gros Ventre Slide Geological Area**, **Red Hills**.
Nearest Town: Jackson 6.8 S
Directions: NE 7.0 mi to Kelly; Continue N 1.1 mi to junction with Antelope Flats Rd; E/R 2.2 mi to National Forest boundary; Continue E on FR-30400 (bumpy, potholed pavement) 3.8 mi; Continue E on FR-30400 (gravel with washboard sections) 5.8 mi.

MM: 0.0/19.9   *GPS:* 43.57412/-110.73322   *Elev:* 6404   *Grid:* 5/36
US-26/89/191 *(see chapter)*   *Type:* Hwy Junction w/Chapter
43.3 mi highway from **Hoback Jct** north to **Moran Jct**. The highway then connects to **US-89/191/287**, using sequential mile markers, and continues 27 mi to **Yellowstone National Park**. The entire length is along the **Centennial Scenic Byway**. Highlights include: **Jackson**, **Jackson Hole and Greater Yellowstone Visitor Center**, **Grand Teton National Park**.
Directions: N to Moran Jct or S to Jackson from MM 161.3

MM: 4.6/15.4   *Dist:* 0.3   *GPS:* 43.61636/-110.66662   *Elev:* 6570   *Grid:* 6/35   *Land:* NPS
Gros Ventre Campground: Grand Teton National Park   *Type:* Campground
The largest campground in **Grand Teton National Park** but farthest from the **Teton Range**. The campground parallels the **Gros Ventre River**; however, the sites are not close to the river. *7 loops. Mature cottonwoods. Flush toilets. Most sites are shaded, but some are wide open. Best option for large RVs. Slowest to fill.*
Crowds: ***** *[FEE AREA] Directions:* SE/R 0.3 mi
Campsites: 360   *Shade:* ***   *Privacy:* *   *RV Size:* 40'+   *Other:* Water,RVDump

MM: 5.0/15.0   *Dist:* 0.4   *GPS:* 43.63092/-110.66416   *GPS2:* 43.63564/-110.69160   *Elev:* 6601   *Grid:* 6/34   *Land:* NPS
Blacktail Butte Trailhead: Grand Teton National Park   *Type:* Trailhead
A prominent butte rising 1100 ft above the **Jackson Hole** valley. Trailheads from opposite sides of the mountain meet at the 7,686 ft summit, offering great views of the **Teton Range** and the surrounding valley. The hike traverses grassland, sagebrush, wildflower meadows, pine and aspen forest, and rock outcroppings. *From US-26/89/191: Moderate; 4.0 mi round-trip; 1085 ft elev gain; From Gros Ventre Rd: Moderate; 5.3 mi round-trip; 1145 ft elev gain.*
Cool Rating: ****   *Crowds:* *   *Time:* 2-3 hrs
Directions: N 0.4 mi on Mormon Row (rough dirt road) to metal gate on left. Don't block the gate.

MM: 7.0/13.0   *GPS:* 43.62551/-110.62438   *Elev:* 6668   *Grid:* 6/34
Kelly   *Type:* Town

MM: 8.1/11.9   *GPS:* 43.64158/-110.62351   *Elev:* 6684   *Grid:* 6/34   *Land:* NPS
Antelope Flats Rd   *Type:* Highway Junction
Turn east/right to continue on **Gros Ventre Rd**. Continuing straight transitions to **Antelope Flats Rd** and continues to **Shadow Mountain**.

MM: 8.5/11.5   *GPS:* 43.63976/-110.61606   *Elev:* 6689   *Grid:* 6/34   *Land:* NPS
Kelly Warm Spring   *Type:* Hot Springs
A slightly warm 30x80 yd pool for swimming. Kayakers like to use the pool to practice their rolls. Across the road is a large parking area with a vault toilet.
Cool Rating: **   *Crowds:* ***   *Directions:* Parking area on N side of road

MM: 10.3/9.6   *GPS:* 43.64108/-110.58402   *Elev:* 6763   *Grid:* 7/34   *Land:* NF
National Park/National Forest Boundary   *Type:* National Forest Boundary
Gros Ventre Rd changes to **FR-30400** and gets rough and potholed.

MM: 12.2/7.8   *GPS:* 43.63324/-110.55701   *Elev:* 7036   *Grid:* 7/34   *Land:* NF
Gros Ventre Slide Overlook   *Type:* Point of Interest
An overlook of the debris left by the **Gros Ventre Slide**. *See next section.*
Cool Rating: ***   *Crowds:* *   *Time:* 5 min   *Road Desc:* Paved, rough & potholed   *Directions:* Pullout on S side of road

MM: 12.7/7.2   *GPS:* 43.63402/-110.54758   *Elev:* 7020   *Grid:* 7/34   *Land:* NF
Gros Ventre Slide Geological Area   *Type:* Geological Feature
In 1925 a huge landslide carried 50 million cubic yards of debris down **Sheep Mountain**. The debris formed a 225 ft high and 1/2 mi wide dam on the **Gros Ventre River**, which created **Lower Slide Lake**. 2 years later a major flood washed out part of this natural dam destroying the town of **Kelly** and lowering the lake level considerably. Detailed interpretive signs are located at the parking area as well as weathered signs along a 1/4 mi trail through the debris and past the terminus of the slide.
Cool Rating: ****   *Crowds:* *   *Time:* 10-60 min   *Road Desc:* Paved, rough & potholed
Directions: Parking area on S side of road

MM: 14.1/5.9   *GPS:* 43.63860/-110.52238   *Elev:* 6995   *Grid:* 8/34   *Land:* NF
Atherton Creek Campground   *Type:* Campground
Located on a hillside below the road on a point into **Lower Slide Lake**. Across the lake is an excellent view of the **Gros Ventre Mountains**; however, the **Gros Ventre Slide Area** is mostly obscured *(see previous section)*. The first loop has a handful of secluded sites surrounded by bushes. The second loop has longer parking areas, but most are in the open. Some sites get light shade from aspen trees. *2 loops. Decent spacing between sites. 2 pull-thrus. Boat ramp.*
Crowds: ***   *[FEE AREA] Road Desc:* Paved, rough & potholed   *Directions:* S side of road
Campsites: 23   *Shade:* **   *Privacy:* ***   *RV Size:* 30'   *Other:* Water BEARS

MM: 17.1/2.8   *GPS:* 43.62125/-110.48015   *Elev:* 7187   *Grid:* 8/34   *Land:* NF

Red Hills   *Type:* Scenic Viewpoint

A colorful view of the **Gros Ventre River** valley and the **Red Hills**. These striking red and partially forested hills are part of a mountain range located between the **Gros Ventre Range** and **Absaroka Range**.

Cool Rating: ***   *Crowds:* *   *Road Desc:* Gravel, washboard sections   *Directions:* Pullout on S side of road

MM: 18.2/1.7   *GPS:* 43.61495/-110.46185   *Elev:* 7095   *Grid:* 8/35   *Land:* NF

Red Hills Trail   *Type:* Hiking Trail

A hike through a small canyon to the top of the **Red Hills** for a great view of the **Teton Range** and the surrounding mountains and valleys. The trail is best hiked in the morning as the colors and views are best at that time, and the shade on the trail is minimal. Walk northeast across a grassy flat to the mouth of the canyon and follow the canyon floor until it veers left and climbs to the overlook. *Moderately strenuous; 3.0 mi round-trip; 1475 ft elev gain.*

Cool Rating: ****   *Crowds:* *   *Road Desc:* Gravel, washboard sections

Directions: N side of road about 90 yds E of the Red Hills Ranch entrance.

MM: 19.6/0.4   *GPS:* 43.61137/-110.43837   *Elev:* 7000   *Grid:* 9/35   *Land:* NF

Red Hills Campground: Gros Ventre Rd   *Type:* Campground

A small campground along the **Gros Ventre River** below the **Red Hills** *(see section above)*. The campground parallels the road, which climbs directly above the campground, generating dust and noise. *Conifer forest. Short road with no turnaround.*

Crowds: * *[FEE AREA]*   *Road Desc:* Gravel, washboard sections   *Directions:* N side of road

Campsites: 5   *Shade:* *****   *Privacy:* ***   *RV Size:* 20'   *Other:* Water BEARS

MM: 19.9/0.0   *GPS:* 43.61037/-110.43141   *Elev:* 7020   *Grid:* 9/35   *Land:* NF

Crystal Creek Campground   *Type:* Campground

A small campground along the **Gros Ventre River** just east of the **Red Hills** *(see section above)*. Across the road is an overflow/group campground with 2 individual sites and 2 group sites. *Conifer forest. Short loop road. All sites are shaded except 1 in the open.*

Crowds: * *[FEE AREA]*   *Road Desc:* Gravel, washboard sections   *Directions:* N side of road

Campsites: 6   *Shade:* ****   *Privacy:* **   *RV Size:* 20'   *Other:* Water BEARS

MM: 19.9/0.0   *GPS:* 43.61037/-110.43141   *Elev:* 7028   *Grid:* 9/35

End of Highway   *Type:* Highway End

Guernsey State Park - Lakeshore Drive/Wy-317   S/N

MM: 0.0/9.5 *GPS:* 42.26970/-104.75873 *Elev:* 4376 *Grid:* 90/68
Guernsey State Park - Lakeshore Drive/Wy-317   *Type:* Highway Description
9.5 mi highway north from **US-26 (I-25 to Nebraska)** into **Guernsey State Park** and along a winding road that follows the east shoreline of **Guernsey Reservoir** with 8 accessible campgrounds. Highlights include: **Guernsey Dam**, **Guernsey Museum**.
Nearest Town: Guernsey 0.6 E *Directions:* NW from MM 0
Notes: Some of the campgrounds and day use areas are marked with mile markers. However, these distances seem to be rounded down to the nearest half-mile, and therefore are not particularly accurate.
Road Desc: The road is paved, but very narrow and winding. The northern section climbs above the reservoir with no guardrails and a sheer drop-off. Trailers and Large RVs accessing Long Canyon Campground should enter through the north entrance.

MM: 0.0/9.5 *GPS:* 42.26970/-104.75873 *Elev:* 4376 *Grid:* 90/68 *Land:* State
US-26 (I-25 to Nebraska) *(see chapter)*   *Type:* Hwy Junction w/Chapter
Directions: E to Guernsey or W to I-25 from MM 14.4

MM: 0.9/8.5 *GPS:* 42.28156/-104.76874 *Elev:* 4523 *Grid:* 90/68
Guernsey State Park - South Entrance   *Type:* State Park
Guernsey State Park is a scenic area centered around **Guernsey Reservoir**, the last of 7 reservoirs on the **North Platte River**. The reservoir is situated in a sandstone canyon amid forested hills and bluffs. The park offers swimming, boating, waterskiing, camping, fishing, hiking, birdwatching, and picnicking. In the 1930s the **Civilian Conservation Corps** (CCC) built projects in the park, including hiking trails, roads, bridges, and buildings. Because of the excellent examples of CCC work the park was designated as a **National Historic Landmark** in 1997. Some believe the **Guernsey Museum** and **The Castle** are the finest examples of CCC work in the United States.

The park is quite popular through the 4th of July weekend after which the reservoir is drained to remove silt deposits and provide water for downstream irrigation demands. This process is known as "the silt run," and by around August 1 the reservoir is filled again. If visiting without a boat most of the points of interest are near the south entrance, including **Guernsey Dam**, the **Guernsey Museum**, **Brimmer Point**, and **The Castle**. Over 12 mi of trails are accessible from **Skyline Drive**. A trail sign is located at the turnoff to **Brimmer Point** or check with park personnel at the entrance station. The camping areas near the water are crowded when the water level is high. The best option for an overnight campground is **Skyline Drive Campground** near the south entrance. *See chapters on Guernsey State Park - Lakeshore Drive/Wy-317 and Guernsey State Park - Skyline Drive.*
Cool Rating: **** *Crowds:* **** [FEE AREA]
Notes: This State Park offers a lot of scenery and attractions in addition to boating, whereas Glendo and Keyhole State Parks are primarily geared towards boating.

MM: 1.0/8.5 *GPS:* 42.28153/-104.76795 *Elev:* 4511 *Grid:* 90/68 *Land:* State
RV Dump   *Type:* RV Dump
[FEE AREA] *Notes:* Requires paying the park entrance fee. *Directions:* E side of road just north of the entrance station

MM: 1.0/8.5 *GPS:* 42.28156/-104.76874 *Elev:* 4523 *Grid:* 90/68
Guernsey State Park - Skyline Drive *(see chapter)*   *Type:* Hwy Junction w/Chapter
Nearest Town: Guernsey 1.6 SE *Directions:* NW just past the south entrance station

MM: 1.6/7.9 *GPS:* 42.28790/-104.76368 *Elev:* 4495 *Grid:* 90/68 *Land:* State
Picnic Shelter and Vault Toilet   *Type:* Picnic Area
A nice grassed area with a picnic shelter and vault toilet located on the south end of the Park Headquarters parking area.
Crowds: * *Directions:* W side of road

MM: 1.7/7.8 *GPS:* 42.28935/-104.76295 *Elev:* 4453 *Grid:* 90/68 *Land:* State
Guernsey Dam   *Type:* Day Use Area
Completed in 1927, this earthen dam is 135 ft high and 560 ft wide. Just to the south of the dam a short road descends to the end of the spillway with a day use area, picnic shelter, and restroom. The reservoir is drained to the river level right after the 4th of July weekend to remove silt deposits and provide water for downstream irrigation demands. This process, known as "the silt run," releases massive amounts of water through the spillway and is quite impressive. The spillway may also be releasing water early in the season during the snowmelt. To the south of the parking area is a power plant. On the north side of the dam is a large parking area with a picnic table. The **Red Cliff Trail** starts across the road and climbs a short distance to provide a view above the dam.
Cool Rating: *** *Crowds:* * *Directions:* Fork N/R 0.2 mi down a steep hill to spillway parking area

MM: 2.2/7.3 *Dist:* 0.3 *GPS:* 42.29466/-104.76301 *Elev:* 4561 *Grid:* 90/68 *Land:* State
Guernsey Museum   *Type:* Museum
The museum was built by the **Civilian Conservation Corps** (CCC) in the 1930s on a hill overlooking **Guernsey Reservoir** to the west. The building is constructed of stone, hand-hewn timber, and hand-forged iron and is known as one of the finest examples of CCC building and architecture in the United States. The archway at the entrance frames **Laramie Peak**, the highest peak in the **Laramie Range**. The museum contains the original 1930s exhibits on the natural and local history of the area, including the native people, emigrant migration, ranching, and the dam and power plant construction.
Hours: 10am - 6pm (May - Labor Day) *Phone:* 307-836-2900 *Cool Rating:* ** *Crowds:* * *Time:* 30-60 min
Directions: E on Museum Rd 0.3 mi to lower parking area (which requires climbing stairs) or 0.9 mi to upper parking area.

MM: 2.2/7.2 *GPS:* 42.29480/-104.76637 *Elev:* 4421 *Grid:* 90/68 *Land:* State
Main Boat Ramp   *Type:* Boat Ramp
[FEE AREA] *Directions:* Boat ramp on W side of road. Parking area on E side of road 0.1 mi south.

MM: 2.7/6.7 *Dist:* 0.1 *GPS:* 42.30069/-104.76182 *Elev:* 4464 *Grid:* 90/67 *Land:* State
Spotted Tail Campground (Upper)   *Type:* Campground
Above and away from the lake on the east side of the road with open sites and few trees. *Decent spacing between sites.*
Crowds: * [FEE AREA] *Directions:* SE side of road
Campsites: 6 *Shade:* * *Privacy:* ** *RV Size:* 20' *Other:* Water

MM: 2.8/6.7 *GPS:* 42.30048/-104.76311 *Elev:* 4430 *Grid:* 90/67 *Land:* State
Spotted Tail Campground (Lower)   *Type:* Campground
Just below the road and above the lake with some access to the water and good views. Pine trees mostly block the campground from the road. *Short cedar and pine trees. Vault toilet across the main road. Not level. Group picnic shelter.*
Crowds: ***** *[FEE AREA] Directions:* NW side of the road
Campsites: 12 *Shade:* * *Privacy:* * *RV Size:* 20' *Other:* Water

MM: 3.1/6.4 *GPS:* 42.30326/-104.76512 *Elev:* 4470 *Grid:* 90/67 *Land:* State
Sitting Bull Day Use Area   *Type:* Day Use Area
2 picnic sites, a handicapped accessible picnic site, and a picnic shelter built by the **Civilian Conservation Corps** (CCC) with 1 table. Nice views of the lake from behind the shelter.
Crowds: ** *[FEE AREA] Directions:* W side of road

MM: 3.1/6.4 *GPS:* 42.30328/-104.76514 *Elev:* 4450 *Grid:* 90/67 *Land:* State
Red Cloud Campground   *Type:* Campground
Just below the road and above the lake with no easy access to the water but good views. The campground is mostly visible from the road *Short cedar and pine trees. Not level. Group picnic shelter. 1 handicapped accessible site.*
Crowds: ***** *[FEE AREA] Directions:* W side of road
Campsites: 5 *Shade:* * *Privacy:* * *RV Size:* 30' *Other:* Water

MM: 3.5/5.9 *GPS:* 42.30907/-104.76489 *Elev:* 4428 *Grid:* 90/67 *Land:* State
Black Canyon Cove Campground   *Type:* Campground
Small parking area just off the road at the end of **Black Canyon Cove**. *Mixed trees line the edge of the cove but don't shade much of the parking area. No toilet.*
Crowds: ***** *[FEE AREA] Directions:* W side of road inside a sharp curve
Campsites: 2 *Shade:* ** *Privacy:* * *RV Size:* 30' *Other:* None

MM: 3.7/5.8 *Dist:* 0.2 *GPS:* 42.30927/-104.76700 *Elev:* 4445 *Grid:* 90/67 *Land:* State
Black Canyon Point Campground   *Type:* Campground
Located on a point into the lake in a scenic canyon area. *Level. No trees. Group picnic shelter. 1 handicapped site.*
Crowds: ***** *[FEE AREA] Road Desc:* Gravel, narrow & steep in spots *Directions:* W 0.2 mi
Campsites: 3 *Shade:* * *Privacy:* * *RV Size:* 40'+ *Other:* None

MM: 4.3/5.2 *GPS:* 42.31568/-104.76361 *Elev:* 4445 *Grid:* 90/67 *Land:* State
Fish Canyon Campground   *Type:* Campground
A 1/2 mi road with 6 widely spaced pull-thru sites along the entrance road and an end loop. Restrooms are located near the entrance, at 1/4 mi along the road, and in the end loop. *Trees in the area provide no shade.*
Crowds: * *[FEE AREA] Directions:* NE side of road
Campsites: 19 *Shade:* * *Privacy:* *** *RV Size:* 40'+ *Other:* Water

MM: 4.3/5.2 *GPS:* 42.31516/-104.76433 *Elev:* 4425 *Grid:* 90/67 *Land:* State
Fish Canyon Cove Campground   *Type:* Campground
A small campground just off the road at the end of **Fish Canyon Cove**. A vault toilet and water is located across the road. *Deciduous trees provide some shade around the edge of the cove.*
Crowds: ***** *[FEE AREA] Directions:* On the inside of the curve on SE side of road
Campsites: 5 *Shade:* ** *Privacy:* * *RV Size:* 30' *Other:* 1-877-996-7275:wyoparks.state.wy.us/reservations,Water

MM: 5.2/4.2 *GPS:* 42.32206/ 104.76896 *Elev:* 4425 *Grid:* 90/67 *Land:* State
Deadman's Cove Campground   *Type:* Campground
A small campground just off a sharp curve in the road and at the end of a small bay. *Deciduous trees provide good shade. No toilet.*
Crowds: ***** *[FEE AREA] Directions:* On the inside of the sharp curve
Notes: The park map reads Deadman's Gulch; however, the road sign reads Deadman's Cove (it is a cove, not a gulch).
Campsites: 3 *Shade:* **** *Privacy:* ** *RV Size:* 30' *Other:* None

MM: 6.9/2.6 *Dist:* 0.1 *GPS:* 42.33133/-104.78157 *Elev:* 4420 *Grid:* 90/67 *Land:* State
Long Canyon Campground   *Type:* Campground
2 separate camping areas on the shore of a large bay. On the east end are 12 reservable RV sites as well as 9 sites spread out along the road. *Mixed trees that don't necessarily shade the sites. Group picnic shelter.* The road continues 0.2 mi west where campsites are spread out for 0.4 mi between the road and the lakeshore. *Large deciduous trees line the road. Vault toilets and water at each end. East end is best for long trailers.*
Crowds: ***** *[FEE AREA] Directions:* NW then SW 0.1 mi. The second camp area is 0.2 mi farther.
Campsites: 35 *Shade:* *** *Privacy:* ** *RV Size:* 40'+ *Other:* 1-877-996-7275:wyoparks.state.wy.us/reservations,Water

MM: 7.0/2.5 *GPS:* 42.33180/-104.77831 *Elev:* 4440 *Grid:* 90/67 *Land:* State
Guernsey State Park - North Entrance   *Type:* State Park
See Guernsey State Park - South Entrance at MM 1.0.
[FEE AREA]

MM: 8.2/1.3 *Dist:* 1.0 *GPS:* 42.34742/-104.76906 *Elev:* 4770 *Grid:* 90/66
Elva Ingram Grave and Trail Ruts   *Type:* Historic Site
On the top of **Emigrant Hill** is the grave of 4 year old **Elva Ingram** who died on the way to **Oregon** on June 23, 1852. South of the grave are visible wagon ruts.
Cool Rating: ** *Crowds:* * *[FEE AREA] Notes:* Respect the surrounding private property.
Road Desc: Gravel, washboard sections, steep & winding. The last 0.3 mi is narrow dirt with no convenient turnaround area.
Directions: NW on Immigrant Hill Rd 0.7 mi; SW 0.3 mi; SE side of road.

MM: 9.5/0.0 *GPS:* 42.33439/-104.73765 *Elev:* 4740 *Grid:* 90/67
Wy-270 (End of Highway)   *Type:* Highway Junction
Return route south 5.3 mi to **US-26 (I-25 to Nebraska)** MM 16.6, 1 mi east of **Guernsey**.
Directions: S on Wy-270 0.8 mi; S/R on Wy-270 4.5 mi.

MM: 0.0/3.7 *GPS:* 42.28156/-104.76874 *Elev:* 4523 *Grid:* 90/68
Guernsey State Park - Skyline Drive   *Type:* Highway Description
3.7 mi road northwest from the south entrance station of **Guernsey State Park** to and along the south side of **Guernsey Reservoir**. The road goes up and down hills before leveling out just before **Sandy Beach**. 7 campgrounds are accessible from this road. Highlights include: **Brimmer Point, The Castle**.
Nearest Town: Guernsey 1.6 SE *Road Desc:* First 2.8 mi paved up to Sandy Beach Campground. The rest is smooth gravel.
Directions: NW just past the south entrance station

MM: 0.4/3.3 *GPS:* 42.28613/-104.77367 *Elev:* 4575 *Grid:* 90/68 *Land:* State
Skyline Drive Campground   *Type:* Campground
A loop road located in a grassy meadow just off the main road and not near the lake. This is the closest campground to **US-26 (I-25 to Nebraska)** and therefore the best option for an overnight stop. *No trees. Parking in the grass off the loop road. Not level.*
Crowds: * *[FEE AREA]* *Directions:* NE side of road
Campsites: 17 *Shade:* * *Privacy:* * *RV Size:* 40'+ *Other:* Water

MM: 2.0/1.7 *Dist:* 0.8 *GPS:* 42.29665/-104.77752 *Elev:* 4450 *Grid:* 90/68 *Land:* State
Newell Bay Campground   *Type:* Campground
The entrance road branches into 2 short roads that lead to 2 camping areas near the water with several hundred feet between them. *Scattered short pine trees.*
Crowds: ***** *[FEE AREA]* *Road Desc:* Gravel, narrow & steep. No turnaround for trailers or large RVs.
Directions: SE 0.6 mi; SE 0.2 mi.
Campsites: 2 *Shade:* * *Privacy:* ***** *RV Size:* 20' *Other:* None

MM: 2.1/1.6 *Dist:* 0.1 *GPS:* 42.30329/-104.78799 *Elev:* 4568 *Grid:* 89/67 *Land:* State
Hiking Trail Sign   *Type:* Hiking Trail
A sign with a map of over 12 miles of trails around this area.
Crowds: * *Road Desc:* Gravel *Directions:* NE 0.1 mi; E side of road

MM: 2.1/1.6 *Dist:* 1.4 *GPS:* 42.30429/-104.76957 *Elev:* 4788 *Grid:* 90/67 *Land:* State
Brimmer Point   *Type:* Scenic Viewpoint
Stone steps lead to a lookout with rock walls and seats. The lookout was built by the **Civilian Conservation Corps** (CCC) on the edge of a sheer cliff. It provides great views of the canyon and **Guernsey Reservoir** below as well as the town of **Guernsey** in the distance. An additional viewing area is located south up a small hill from the parking area. Named for **George Brimmer** who was a **Cheyenne** resident whose influence helped create the park.
Cool Rating: **** *Crowds:* * *Time:* 30 min *Road Desc:* Gravel, steep & winding *Directions:* NE 0.1 mi; E 1.3 mi.
Notes: Not recommended for trailers and large RVs. Hiking trails also lead to the lookout from the trail sign at the Brimmer Point turnoff and from Davis Bay.

MM: 2.1/1.6 *Dist:* 0.8 *GPS:* 42.30621/-104.77996 *Elev:* 4447 *Grid:* 90/67 *Land:* State
Davis Bay Campground   *Type:* Campground
2 sites near **Davis Bay** with no boat access. An additional large site is located across the parking cul-de-sac. *Deciduous trees. Level.*
Crowds: ***** *[FEE AREA]* *Notes:* Not recommended for trailers or large RVs. *Directions:* NE 0.4 mi; E 0.4 mi.
Road Desc: Gravel, steep & winding
Campsites: 3 *Shade:* ***** *Privacy:* **** *RV Size:* 30' *Other:* None

MM: 2.1/1.6 *Dist:* 1.8 *GPS:* 42.32104/-104.78300 *Elev:* 4634 *Grid:* 90/67 *Land:* State
The Castle Day Use Area   *Type:* Picnic and Day Use Area
An elaborate stone picnic shelter called **"The Castle,"** which was built by the **Civilian Conservation Corps** (CCC) in the 1930s. On the lower level is a large fireplace, tables, and grills. 2 arched walkways line up to point at **Laramie Peak**, the highest peak in the **Laramie Range**. A winding stairway leads to an observation deck on top of the shelter, which provides nice views of the canyon and reservoir. A short distance east is a stone walkway to another observation point on the edge of a cliff.

Just to the south is another CCC masterpiece; an elaborate stone latrine that cost over $6,000 to construct, also in the 1930s. It was jokingly named the **"Million Dollar Biffy"** by the CCC workmen because it took so long to build.

An open picnic table and vault toilet is located on the south end of the loop road.
Cool Rating: *** *Crowds:* *** *Road Desc:* Gravel *Directions:* NE 1.8 mi
Notes: These structures are interesting to visit whether picnicking or not.

MM: 2.5/1.2 *Dist:* 0.4 *GPS:* 42.30907/-104.79887 *Elev:* 4423 *Grid:* 89/67 *Land:* State
Sandy Beach Boat Ramp   *Type:* Boat Ramp
[FEE AREA] *Road Desc:* Gravel *Directions:* N 0.4 mi

MM: 2.8/0.9 *GPS:* 42.30585/-104.80164 *Elev:* 4425 *Grid:* 89/67 *Land:* State
Sandy Beach Campground   *Type:* Campground/Day Use Area
The farthest east and first of a series of 4 campgrounds along the southern lakeshore with a sandy beach shoreline. This long campground has a grassy area for tents on the east side and parallel parking areas for RVs, which are very close together. The trees along the lakeshore shade about 1/3 of the sites.
Crowds: ***** *[FEE AREA]* *Directions:* N side of road with entrances at MM 2.8, 3.0, and 3.2
Notes: This is the best campground for large RVs and many sites require reservations from May 15 - Sept 15. Trains pass regularly a short distance south of the campground.
Campsites: 32 *Shade:* * *Privacy:* * *RV Size:* 40'+ *Other:* 1-877-996-7275:wyoparks.state.wy.us/reservations,Water

MM: 3.3/0.4 *GPS:* 42.30637/-104.81040 *Elev:* 4415 *Grid:* 89/67 *Land:* State
Cottonwood Cove Campground   *Type:* Campground
The second of a series of 4 campgrounds along the southern lakeshore with a sandy beach just to the east. *Small loop between 2 larger campgrounds. Large deciduous trees. 3 sites in the open. 4 tent-only sites. 5 reservable sites. Drinking water in the adjacent campgrounds.*
Crowds: ***** *[FEE AREA]* *Notes:* Trains pass regularly a short distance south of the campground.
Directions: N side of road
Campsites: 10 *Shade:* **** *Privacy:* * *RV Size:* 40'+ *Other:* 1-877-996-7275:wyoparks.state.wy.us/reservations,Water

MM: 3.4/0.3 *GPS:* 42.30649/-104.81237 *Elev:* 4440 *Grid:* 89/67 *Land:* State
Sandy Point Campground   *Type:* Campground
The third of a series of 4 campgrounds along the southern lakeshore with a sandy beach just to the east. *Large deciduous trees. Approximately half of the sites are in the open. 27 reservable sites.*
Crowds: ***** *[FEE AREA]* *Notes:* Trains pass regularly a short distance south of the campground.
Directions: N side of road
Campsites: 42 *Shade:* *** *Privacy:* * *RV Size:* 40'+ *Other:* 1-877-996-7275:wyoparks.state.wy.us/reservations,Water

MM: 3.6/0.1 *GPS:* 42.30683/-104.81549 *Elev:* 4430 *Grid:* 89/67 *Land:* State
Sandy Cove Campground   *Type:* Campground
The farthest west and fourth of a series of 4 campgrounds along the southern lakeshore with a sandy beach 0.3 mi to the east. *Large deciduous trees. Approximately half of the sites are in the open. 10 reservable sites.*
Crowds: ***** *[FEE AREA]* *Notes:* Trains pass regularly a short distance south of the campground.
Directions: N side of road
Campsites: 14 *Shade:* *** *Privacy:* * *RV Size:* 40'+ *Other:* 1-877-996-7275:wyoparks.state.wy.us/reservations,Water

MM: 3.7/0.0 *GPS:* 42.30695/-104.81593 *Elev:* 4404 *Grid:* 89/67 *Land:* State
West Sandy Beach Day Use Area   *Type:* Day Use Area
Day use beach area.
Crowds: ** *[FEE AREA]* *Directions:* Day use parking at end of road

I-25   S/N

MM: 0.0 **GPS:** 40.99948/-104.90646 **Elev:** 6098 **Grid:** 88/100
I-25   **Type:** Highway Description
300.1 mi interstate highway through east/central **Wyoming** from **Colorado** north to **I-90** (just past **Buffalo**), which continues northwest to **Montana**. Highlights include: **Pioneer Museum**, **Ayres Park and Natural Bridge**, **National Historic Trails Interpretive Center**, **Hole-in-the-Wall**, **Outlaw Cave**, **Indian Rock Art Cave**.
Nearest Town: Cheyenne 12.7 N **Directions:** N to Cheyenne from MM 0

MM: 7.9 **Dist:** 0.4 **GPS:** 41.10319/-104.85199 **Elev:** 6165 **Grid:** 89/97
Cheyenne Rest Area   **Type:** Rest Area/Visitor Center
Welcome Center with picnic shelters, pet walk area, **RV dump**, and handicapped accessible facilities. On the east side of the rest area along **I-25** stand two ~12 ft high statues on ~12 ft high rock pedestals in a scene called **"The Greeting and the Gift."** This scene depicts a typical meeting and offering of friendship between the **Indian** and **Mountain Man** on the open plains of **Wyoming** during the early 1800s.
Directions: I-25 exit 7; W on W College Dr 0.1 mi; N on Etchepare Cir 0.3 mi.

MM: 8.8 **GPS:** 41.11382/-104.85087 **Elev:** 6133 **Grid:** 89/97
I-80 *(see chapter)*   **Type:** Hwy Junction w/Chapter
403 mi interstate highway through southern **Wyoming** from **Nebraska** west to **Utah**. Highlights include: **Vedauwoo Recreation Area**, **Curt Gowdy State Park**, **Pole Mountain Trails**, **Wyoming Territorial Prison State Historic Site**, **Fort Fred Steele**, **Wyoming Frontier Prison**, **Fort Bridger State Historic Site**, **Bear River State Park**, and much more.
Directions: I-25 exit 8; E to Nebraska or W to Laramie from MM 359.6

MM: 8.8 **Dist:** 2.9 **GPS:** 41.11382/-104.85087 **Elev:** 6133 **Grid:** 89/97
Wy-210/Happy Jack Rd (northbound) *(see chapter)*   **Type:** Hwy Junction w/Chapter
If heading north on **I-25**, this provides easier and shorter access (saves 1.3 mi) to **Wy-210/Happy Jack Rd** than continuing to MM 10.6. *See next section.*
Directions: I-25 exit 8; W on I-80 1.4 mi to exit 357 ramp; Take ramp 0.5 mi; N on Wy-222/Round Top Rd 1.0 mi; W on Wy-210/Happy Jack Rd from MM 3.0.

MM: 10.6 **GPS:** 41.13696/-104.84057 **Elev:** 6078 **Grid:** 89/97
Wy-210/Happy Jack Rd *(see chapter)*   **Type:** Hwy Junction w/Chapter
37.3 mi highway from **I-25** exit 10 in **Cheyenne** west to **I-80** exit 323, 10 mi southeast of **Laramie**. The primary use of this highway is access to the north entrance of **Curt Gowdy State Park** and the **Vedauwoo Recreation Area**.
Directions: I-25 exit 10; W from MM 0

MM: 12.7 **GPS:** 41.16729/-104.84016 **Elev:** 6088 **Grid:** 89/96
Cheyenne   **Type:** Town

MM: 12.7 **Dist:** 0.9 **GPS:** 41.16054/-104.83530 **Elev:** 6160 **Grid:** 89/96
RV Dump: Lake Absarraca - Cheyenne   **Type:** RV Dump
At the entrance to **Lake Absarraca**.
Directions: I-25 exit 12; SE on Central Ave 0.6 mi; W on Kennedy Rd 1/4 mi; N side of road at the Lake Absarraca entrance road next to the golf course.

MM: 17.2 **GPS:** 41.23482/-104.83520 **Elev:** 6210 **Grid:** 89/94
US-85 *(see chapter)*   **Type:** Hwy Junction w/Chapter
239.4 mi highway that begins just north of **Cheyenne** and parallels the **Nebraska** and **South Dakota state lines** north before crossing into **South Dakota** at the end. The highway heads north 76.1 mi to **Torrington** (MM 93.2), joins **US-26 (I-25 to Nebraska)** heading northwest 9.9 mi to **Lingle** (MM 103.1), then continues north for the final 153.5 mi. This is also the southern route to the **Black Hills** of **South Dakota**, which heads east at MM 196.1 on **US-18**. Highlights include: **Hawk Springs State Recreation Area**, **Downar Bird Farm**, **Homesteaders Museum**, **Redwood Water Tank**, **Red Butte**.
Nearest Town: Cheyenne 4.5 S **Directions:** I-25 exit 17; NE to Torrington from MM 17.1

MM: 54.5 **GPS:** 41.75713/-104.82872 **Elev:** 5318 **Grid:** 89/81
Chugwater Rest Area   **Type:** Rest Area
Picnic shelters, pet walk area, **RV dump**, and handicapped accessible facilities.
Directions: I-25 exit 54; E side of hwy.

MM: 54.5 **GPS:** 41.75644/-104.82176 **Elev:** 5296 **Grid:** 89/81
Chugwater   **Type:** Town

MM: 73.0 **Dist:** 5.7 **GPS:** 41.98709/-105.02678 **Elev:** 4978 **Grid:** 86/75 **Land:** Public Lands
Rock Lake   **Type:** Public Access Area
Primitive camping in a small parking area on the northeast end of **Rock Lake**, a small lake south of **Wheatland Reservoir #1**. *No trees. Vault toilet.*
Crowds: * **Nearest Town:** Wheatland 8.3 NE **Road Desc:** Partially paved. Last 0.2 mi is gravel.
Directions: I-25 exit 73; W on Wy-34 3.5 mi; N/R on Grange Rd 2.0 mi; E/L 0.2 mi.
Campsites: Dispersed **Shade:** * **Privacy:** * **RV Size:** 30' **Other:** None

MM: 73.0 **Dist:** 6.8 **GPS:** 42.00224/-105.02649 **Elev:** 4920 **Grid:** 86/75 **Land:** Public Lands
Wheatland Reservoir #1 (northbound)   **Type:** Public Access Area
1.8 mi of dispersed camping along the west and south sides of **Wheatland Reservoir**. The main camping area is at the end of the road on the southeast side of the lake. *Deciduous trees provide some shade. 3 vault toilets. 2 boat ramps.*
Crowds: * **Nearest Town:** Wheatland 7.0 NE
Road Desc: Partially paved. Reservoir Rd is gravel and the first 0.8 is rocky and rough.
Directions: I-25 exit 73; W on Wy-34 3.5 mi; N/R on Grange Rd 3.0 mi; E/L on Reservoir Rd 0.3 mi; Drive counterclockwise around the reservoir up to 2.9 mi. *If continuing north on I-25, see MM 78.9 and reverse the directions.*
Campsites: Dispersed **Shade:** *** **Privacy:** ** **RV Size:** 40' **Other:** None

MM: 78.9 *GPS:* 42.04661/-104.96435 *Elev:* 4770 *Grid:* 87/74
Wheatland   *Type:* Town

MM: 78.9 *Dist:* 7.0 *GPS:* 42.00260/-105.04057 *Elev:* 4920 *Grid:* 86/75 *Land:* Public Lands
Wheatland Reservoir #1 (southbound)   *Type:* Lake
See section above at MM 73.0.
Directions: I-80 exit 78; W on W Mariposa Pkwy 0.8 mi; S/L on Ferguson Rd/Wy-312 0.2 mi; W/R on Palmer Canyon Rd 3.0 mi; S/L on Hightower Rd/Wy-310 3.0 mi; W on Reservoir Rd 0.3 - 2.1 mi. *If continuing south on I-25, see MM 73.0 and reverse the directions.*

MM: 78.9 *Dist:* 0.9 *GPS:* 42.04765/-104.95263 *Elev:* 4750 *Grid:* 87/74 *Land:* City
Wheatland City Park/Lewis Park   *Type:* Park
A large city park that allows camping along the south end. The campground includes 9 closely spaced back-in RV sites plus a separate tent area on the west end. The location is near basketball courts, tennis courts, and a skateboard park. The main park is about 150 yds north. *Cottonwoods. A few tables and grills. Donations appreciated, particularly for electricity use. RV dump 0.1 mi north (see next section).*
Notes: Railroad tracks run along the east end of the park; however, in the couple of hours that I was there, I never saw a train.
Directions: I-25 exit 78; E on W Mariposa Pkwy 0.1 mi; S/R on 16th St 0.1 mi; E/L on Cole St 0.5 mi; N/L on 8th St 0.2 mi.
Campsites: 9 *Shade:* ***** *Privacy:* * *RV Size:* 40'+ *Other:* Electric,RVDump

MM: 78.9 *Dist:* 1.0 *GPS:* 42.04941/-104.95219 *Elev:* 4750 *Grid:* 87/74 *Land:* City
RV Dump: Wheatland City Park/Lewis Park   *Type:* RV Dump
RV dump with non-potable water on the east side of **Wheatland City Park/Lewis Park**. *See previous section for directions.*
Directions: 0.1 mi N of camping turnoff.

MM: 80.1 *GPS:* 42.07434/-104.96485 *Elev:* 4700 *Grid:* 87/73
Wy-160/Grayrocks Rd/Power Plant Rd *(see chapter)*   *Type:* Hwy Junction w/Chapter
30.0 mi route from **I-25** exit 80 at **Wheatland** northeast to **US-26 (I-25 to Nebraska)** MM 27.9 at **Fort Laramie**. Highlights include: **Grayrocks Reservoir, Fort Laramie, Old Bedlam Ruts, Fort Laramie Bridge**.
Nearest Town: Wheatland 1.9 S
Directions: I-25 exit 80; E on Swanson Rd 0.1 mi; Slight left onto Rompoon Rd 0.5 mi; N/L on Wy-320 1.8 mi; E/R on Grayrocks Rd 17.2 mi; N/L on S Guernsey Rd 0.7 mi; E/R on Fort Laramie Rd/CR-54 6.3 mi; Continue NE/L on CR-53/Wy-160 3.4 mi.

MM: 80.9 *Dist:* 4.2 *GPS:* 42.07762/-104.99599 *Elev:* 4735 *Grid:* 87/73
Festo Lake   *Type:* Lake
Primitive camping around the north and east lakeshore of this small lake. A single well-established pull-thru campsite is located on the east side of the lake near some trees. The other possibilities are 2-track paths to the lakeshore. Fishing and non-motorized boating in the lake. *No facilities.*
Crowds: * *Nearest Town:* Wheatland 5 SE *Road Desc:* Partially paved. Ayres Rd is gravel.
Directions: I-25 exit 80; E on Swanson Rd 0.1 mi; N/L on Red Fox Rd 1.0 mi; W/L on W Fairview Rd 2.0 mi; S/L on Ayers Rd 1.1 mi.
Campsites: Dispersed *Shade:* * *Privacy:* * *RV Size:* 30' *Other:* None

MM: 92.4 *GPS:* 42.23303/-105.01450 *Elev:* 4924 *Grid:* 86/69
Dwyer Junction Rest Area   *Type:* Rest Area
A beautifully landscaped rest area with picnic shelters, pet walk area, **RV dump**, and handicapped accessible facilities.
Directions: I-25 exit 92; E to the start of US-26 at the end of the exit ramp; N side of hwy.

MM: 92.4 *GPS:* 42.23303/-105.01450 *Elev:* 4917 *Grid:* 86/69
US-26 (I-25 to Nebraska) *(see chapter)*   *Type:* Hwy Junction w/Chapter
56.2 mi highway southeast from **I-25** exit 92 to **Nebraska**. Highlights include: **Guernsey State Park, Oregon Trail Ruts, Register Cliff, Fort Laramie National Historic Site**.
Nearest Town: Wheatland 12 S; Guernsey 14.2 E *Directions:* I-25 exit 92; E to Guernsey from MM 0

MM: 111.7 *GPS:* 42.50271/-105.02616 *Elev:* 4730 *Grid:* 86/62
Glendo   *Type:* Town

MM: 111.7 *Dist:* 0.2 *GPS:* 42.50079/-105.02483 *Elev:* 4730 *Grid:* 86/62
Glendo Park Rd (Glendo State Park) *(see chapter)*   *Type:* Hwy Junction w/Chapter
13.4 mi road from **Glendo** southeast through **Glendo State Park**.
Directions: I-25 exit 111; E on A St 0.1 mi; S/R on Wy-319/S Yellowstone Hwy 0.2 mi; E/L on C St 1 block; S/R on S Lincoln Ave/Glendo Park Rd.

MM: 111.7 *Dist:* 1.0 *GPS:* 42.51372/-105.02028 *Elev:* 4664 *Grid:* 86/62 *Land:* State
Glendo State Park - Airport Entrance   *Type:* Campground
Alternative entrance into **Glendo State Park** from **Wy-319**. This entrance is 3.1 mi from **Red Hills Campground** and only saves mileage if heading south on **Wy-319** or accessing the northern **Lakeshore Drive** campgrounds. *See chapter: Glendo Park Rd (Glendo State Park).*
[FEE AREA] *Road Desc:* Gravel
Directions: I-25 exit 111; E on A St 0.1 mi; N on Wy-319/N Yellowstone Hwy 0.8 mi; E/R on Lake Shore Dr 0.1 mi.

MM: 111.7 *Dist:* 3.8 *GPS:* 42.55357/-105.03637 *Elev:* 4658 *Grid:* 86/61 *Land:* State
Elkhorn Campground: Glendo State Park   *Type:* Campground
Dispersed camping along the shoreline of **Glendo Reservoir** with cottonwoods for shade and some picnic tables and fire rings. The boat ramp is normally only usable until early July due to receding water levels. The campsite count is approximate as the sites are not well defined.
Crowds: **** **[FEE AREA]**
Directions: I-25 exit 111; E on A St 0.1 mi; N on Wy-319/N Yellowstone Hwy 3.5 mi; NE/R into Glendo SP 0.15 mi; E/R into campground.
Campsites: 20 *Shade:* ** *Privacy:* * *RV Size:* 40' *Other:* Water

MM: 126.5 **Dist:** 0.1 **GPS:** 42.65682/-105.20022 **Elev:** 4766 **Grid:** 84/59
Orin Junction Rest Area   **Type:** Rest Area
Picnic shelters, pet walk area, **RV dump**, and handicapped accessible facilities.
Nearest Town: Orin 0.4 E **Directions:** I-25 exit 126; E 0.1 mi; S side of hwy.

MM: 140.1 **GPS:** 42.75957/-105.38787 **Elev:** 4813 **Grid:** 81/56
Douglas   **Type:** Town

MM: 140.1 **Dist:** 1.0 **GPS:** 42.76294/-105.39175 **Elev:** 4800 **Grid:** 81/56 **Land:** City
Riverside Park   **Type:** Campground
A nice city park on the east bank of the **North Platte River**. Camping is permitted along the parking area for RVs and in the grass for tents. The restrooms/showers are finished in a rustic wood western decor. The park is next to the main street through town so it may not be particularly quiet. No camping in the grass on Mon, Wed, Fri, and Sun as the sprinklers run in the morning. *Trees in the park don't shade the parking area. Tables and grills in the park. Flush toilets. Hot showers.*
Phone: 307-358-9750 **Crowds:** *** **Notes:** These are the best free accommodations that I have run across in Wyoming.
Directions: I-25 exit 140; 0.15 mi to stop light; E on W Yellowstone Hwy 0.8 mi; N/L on Grant St 0.05 mi.
Campsites: Dispersed **Shade:** ** **Privacy:** * **RV Size:** 40' **Other:** Water,Electric,RVDump

MM: 140.1 **Dist:** 1.2 **GPS:** 42.75956/-105.39008 **Elev:** 4804 **Grid:** 81/56 **Land:** City
Pioneer Museum   **Type:** Museum
This 15,900 sq ft facility houses the state's finest displays of pioneer and ranching memorabilia, textiles, **Native American** artifacts and decorative art, an extensive photograph collection, and much more. These displays include a large collection of old guns, tools, **World War** memorabilia, saloon fixtures (including a long wooden bar), historical men's and women's fashions, saddles, carriages, and buggies. Outside is the cabin that was the original museum, 2 school houses, a rebuilt gristmill, and a shelter.
Hours: 8am - 5pm, Mon-Fri (year round); 1pm - 5pm, Sat (summer only) **Phone:** 307-358-9288
Cool Rating: *** **Crowds:** * **Time:** 1-2 hrs
Directions: I-25 exit 140; 0.15 mi to stop light; E on W Yellowstone Hwy 0.9 mi; SW/R at double entrance and *Wyoming State Fair and Pioneer Museum sign* 0.1 mi; Left on W Center St into parking lot (*400 W Center St, Douglas*)

MM: 140.1 **Dist:** 1.3 **GPS:** 42.75900/-105.38753 **Elev:** 4813 **Grid:** 81/56 **Land:** City
Douglas Railroad Interpretive Center   **Type:** Historic Site
A railroad car display located at the historic **Chicago and Northwestern Railroad** depot. This 7 train car collection includes a steam locomotive, dining car, sleeper, baggage car, coach, cattle car, and caboose. Tours are self-guided using plaques and a brochure available from the Chamber of Commerce, which is located at the site. Some of the train cars are open to walk through. The train collection is located in a nice little park with picnic tables. This is the first stop for the **Historic Downtown Douglas Walking Tour** with the tour brochure also available from the Chamber of Commerce office.
Hours: Chamber of Commerce hours: 8am - 8pm, Mon-Fri; 11am - 5pm, Sat-Sun **Phone:** 307-358-2950
Cool Rating: ** **Crowds:** ** **Time:** 20 min
Directions: I-25 exit 140; 0.15 mi to stop light; E on W Yellowstone Hwy 1.1 mi; S/R on Brownfield Rd; Immediate left into parking lot. (*121 Brownfield Rd, Douglas*)

MM: 140.1 **Dist:** 1.4 **GPS:** 42.75934/-105.38433 **Elev:** 4823 **Grid:** 81/56 **Land:** City
Jackalope Square   **Type:** Point of Interest
Douglas is the self-proclaimed "jackalope capital of the world" and features an 8 ft tall jackalope statue at its town square. The jackalope is a mythical creature that is a cross between a jackrabbit and an antelope. *Public restroom. Picnic tables.*
Cool Rating: * **Crowds:** * **Time:** 5 min **Directions:** I-25 exit 140; 0.15 mi to stop light; E on W Yellowstone Hwy 1.2 mi; South side of street (*3rd St and E Center St, Douglas*)

MM: 140.1 **Dist:** 8.2 **GPS:** 42.84090/-105.48784 **Elev:** 4950 **Grid:** 79/54 **Land:** State
Fort Fetterman State Historic Site   **Type:** Historic Site
Located at the junction of the **Oregon Trail** and **Bozeman Trail** on the south bank of the **North Platte River**. The fort was in use from 1867 to 1882 and was established to protect both emigrants and the **Union Pacific Railroad** construction as well as to provide a major supply and starting point for the **U.S. Army**'s operations against the American Indians. The fort was remote, living conditions were difficult, and desertions were common. Today a small museum, restored officer's quarters, and ordinance warehouse contain artifacts and exhibits on the history of the Indians, military, and civilians of **Fort Fetterman** and **Fetterman City**. An interpretive trail leads to a gazebo and overlook of the river to the north. A picnic table is located under the **Werner Memorial Shelter**. A small reservable campground is located on the southeast end, just east of the restored officer's quarters, with no privacy or shade.
Cool Rating: ** **Crowds:** * **Time:** 1 hr **Nearest Town:** Douglas 8 S **[FEE AREA]**
Directions: I-25 exit 140; 0.15 mi to stop light; N/L on S Riverbend Dr/Wy-59 0.1 mi; W/L on Wy-93 7.9 mi.
Campsites: 2 **Shade:** * **Privacy:** * **RV Size:** 40'+ **Other:** 307-684-7629

MM: 140.1 **Dist:** 19.1 **GPS:** 42.85697/-105.66884 **Elev:** 4901 **Grid:** 77/54 **Land:** State
Bixby Public Access Area (northbound)   **Type:** Fishing Area
Public fishing and boating access on the **North Platte River**. Primitive camping is allowed in the gravel parking area with a somewhat secluded site under cottonwoods at the far end. *Vault toilet.*

This route is 7.4 mi farther than staying on I-25 between **Douglas** and **Glenrock** but is convenient and shorter if visiting **Fort Fetterman**.
Crowds: * **Nearest Town:** Glenrock 12.2 NW
Road Desc: Partially paved, smooth. From I-25 at Glenrock, the first 1.4 mi is paved. From I-25 at Douglas, the first 9.9 mi is paved. The 8.4 mi section between Bixby and Wy-93 has some ruts.
Directions: I-25 exit 140; 0.15 mi to stop light; N/L on S Riverbend Dr/Wy-59 0.1 mi; W/L Wy-93 9.6 mi (past Fort Fetterman); W on CR-27/Tank Farm Rd 9.2 mi; S side of road. **To return to I-25 westbound**; Continue W 8.0 mi on CR-27/Tank Farm Rd; SE on US-20/26/87 0.2 mi.
Campsites: Dispersed **Shade:** ** **Privacy:** * **RV Size:** 30' **Other:** None

MM: 151.2 *Dist:* 4.8 *GPS:* 42.73370/-105.61100 *Elev:* 5307 *Grid:* 78/57 *Land:* County
Ayres Park and Natural Bridge   *Type:* Natural Feature
A lush park in a red sandstone canyon that features a 50 ft high and 100 ft long natural bridge with a 90 ft wide x 20 ft high opening cut by **LaPrele Creek**. A short, steep hiking trail leads to the top of the natural bridge. The shady park is grassed with many picnic tables, playground, horseshoes, volleyball area, and reservable group shelters. The large concrete structure near the entrance of the park is an abandoned power plant, which went bankrupt before it was finished. This is a popular spot for weekend trips by **Douglas** residents; however, the park is less crowded during the week.
Hours: 8am - 8pm (Apr - Oct) *Cool Rating:* **** *Crowds:* **** *Time:* 1 hr *Notes:* Gates are closed between 8pm and 8am.
Road Desc: The road near the park entrance is narrow and steep.
Directions: I-25 exit 151; S on CR-13/Natural Bridge Rd 4.8 mi.

MM: 160.9 *Dist:* 8.2 *GPS:* 42.85697/-105.66884 *Elev:* 4901 *Grid:* 77/54 *Land:* State
Bixby Public Access Area (southbound)   *Type:* Fishing Area
Public fishing and boating access on the **North Platte River**. Primitive camping is allowed in the gravel parking area with a somewhat secluded site under cottonwoods at the far end. *Vault toilet.*

This route is 7.4 mi farther than staying on I-25 between **Douglas** and **Glenrock** but is convenient and shorter if visiting **Fort Fetterman**.
Crowds: * *Nearest Town:* Glenrock 12.2 NW
Road Desc: Partially paved, smooth. From I-25 at Glenrock, the first 1.4 mi is paved. From I-25 at Douglas, the first 9.9 mi is paved. The 8.4 mi section between Bixby and Wy-93 has some ruts.
Directions: I-25 exit 160; NW on US-20/26/87 0.2 mi; E/R on CR-27/Tank Farm Rd 8.0 mi; S side of road. *To return to I-25 eastbound;* Continue E 9.2 mi on CR-27/Tank Farm Rd; S/R on Wy-93 9.6 mi (past Fort Fetterman); S/R on S Riverbend Dr/Wy-59 0.1 mi; W/R on W Yellowstone Hwy 0.2 mi.
Campsites: Dispersed *Shade:* ** *Privacy:* * *RV Size:* 30' *Other:* None

MM: 165.9 *GPS:* 42.86135/-105.87222 *Elev:* 5020 *Grid:* 74/53
Glenrock   *Type:* Town

MM: 165.9 *Dist:* 2.5 *GPS:* 42.86123/-105.88266 *Elev:* 5025 *Grid:* 74/53 *Land:* City
Rock in the Glen   *Type:* Historic Site
A 200 yd footpath southwest leads to a rock outcropping that contains some pioneer inscriptions. Most of the inscriptions are on the south side; however, only a few historic inscriptions can be read. The remaining signatures are from the last 20 or 30 years. The parking area is shaded along with a shaded bench at the end of the trail.
Cool Rating: ** *Crowds:* * *Time:* 30 min *Directions:* I-25 exit 165; NE on Deer Creek Rd/Wy-95 2.0 mi; W/L on W Birch St/US 20/26/87 0.5 mi to MM 166; S side of hwy. *If heading west, US 20/26/87 optionally continues to Casper.*

MM: 165.9 *Dist:* 5.2 *GPS:* 42.83586/-105.87350 *Elev:* 5027 *Grid:* 74/54 *Land:* City
Glenrock South Recreation Complex   *Type:* Recreation Area
A recreation complex with a rodeo arena, baseball fields, paintball court, playgrounds, and restrooms. Shady campsites with tables and grills are located next to **Deer Creek**. The campground is just below I-25 so highway noise can be heard.
Crowds: * *Road Desc:* Partially paved. The last 0.9 mi is gravel.
Notes: The city told me that there were 20 campsites. The area in front said "picnicking only," although a trailer was parked in this area. I saw 5 established campsites. There are also grassy areas where you might park. The park was full of little red bugs.
Directions: I-25 exit 165; NE on Deer Creek Rd/Wy-95 2.0 mi; E/R on W Birch St/US-20/26/87 0.4 mi; S/R on Mormon Canyon Rd/CR-18 1.9 mi; W/R 0.9 mi just after crossing under I-25.
Campsites: 5 *Shade:* ***** *Privacy:* * *Other:* Water,Electric,RVDump

MM: 182.5 *Dist:* 2.6 *GPS:* 42.84851/-106.17715 *Elev:* 5062 *Grid:* 70/54 *Land:* State
Edness Wilkins State Park   *Type:* State Park
A day use park featuring a pond with a sandy beach, swimming area, picnic tables, grills, group shelters, playgrounds, launching ramp for canoes and rafts, and 2.8 mi of handicapped accessible hard-surface paths. Huge old cottonwoods along the **North Platte River** provide shade as well providing a natural habitat for a variety of wildlife. The **North Platte River** offers fishing from the bank as well as from a handicapped accessible fishing pier.
Cool Rating: ** *Crowds:* *** *[FEE AREA]*
Directions: I-25 exit 182; N 0.4 mi; E on US-20/26/87 2.2 mi to MM 181.8; N 0.15 mi to entrance station.

MM: 185.4 *Dist:* 5.5 *GPS:* 42.85402/-106.27099 *Elev:* 5157 *Grid:* 68/54
Casper Mountain Rd/Wy-251 *(see chapter)*   *Type:* Hwy Junction w/Chapter
See MM 188.2.
Notes: I-25 exit 188 also accesses Casper Mountain Rd; however, if heading west on I-25 this is a shorter route.
Directions: I-25 exit 185; S on SE Wyoming Blvd/Wy-258 5.5 mi; S on Casper Mountain Rd/Wy-251 from MM 3.0. *See Casper Mountain Rd/Wy-251.*

MM: 188.2 *GPS:* 42.85702/-106.32540 *Elev:* 5106 *Grid:* 68/54
Casper   *Type:* Town

MM: 188.2 *Dist:* 0.5 *GPS:* 42.85009/-106.32395 *Elev:* 5122 *Grid:* 68/54
Casper Mountain Rd/Wy-251 *(see chapter)*   *Type:* Hwy Junction w/Chapter
18.4 mi series of roads from **Casper** south over **Casper Mountain** (nearly 3,000 ft above Casper) down through the **Red Valley** and up to **Muddy Mountain**. Activities on **Casper Mountain** include camping, hiking, and mountain biking, as well as downhill and cross-country skiing in the winter. Much of **Casper Mountain** is private property; however, **Casper Mountain Park** is a large public access area with 5 campgrounds. Highlights include: **Garden Creek Falls**, **Bridle Trail**, scenic overlook of **Casper**, **Casper Mountain Park**, **Crimson Dawn Park and Museum**, **Muddy Mountain Environmental Education Area**.
Notes: The roads up and down the mountains are steep and winding and few of the campsites accommodate large RVs and trailers. After reaching the top of Casper Mountain from Casper, the road narrows with no center stripe and eventually becomes gravel. I-25 exit 185 also accesses Casper Mountain Rd; however, if heading east on I-25, this is a shorter route.
Directions: I-25 exit 188A; S on N Center St/Wy-255 0.5 mi; E/L on E 1st St 1 block; S/R on S Wolcott St/Wy-251 from MM 0. *See Casper Mountain Rd/Wy-251.*

MM: 188.6 *GPS:* 42.85693/-106.33429 *Elev:* 5122 *Grid:* 67/54
Wy-220 *(see chapter)*   *Type:* Hwy Junction w/Chapter
72.6 mi highway from **Casper** southwest to **US-287/Wy-789** and **Rawlins**. The highway transitions to **US-287/Wy-789** at MM 44.3 and the mile markers continue sequentially to **Rawlins**. Highlights include: **Fort Caspar Museum and Historic Site**, **Bessemer Bend National Historic Site**, **Alcova Reservoir**, **Pathfinder Reservoir**, **Independence Rock**, **Devil's Gate**, **Martin's Cove**.
Directions: I-25 exit 188B; SW on N Poplar St/Wy-220 to Alcova from MM 116.9

MM: 188.6 *Dist:* 3.8 *GPS:* 42.83555/-106.37092 *Elev:* 5123 *Grid:* 67/54 *Land:* State
Fort Caspar Museum and Historic Site   *Type:* Historic Site
A reconstructed military post that was active from 1862-1867 and located at a major river crossing on the emigrant, **Pony Express**, and transcontinental telegraph trails. The **Mormons** established a ferry operation at this point in 1847, and **Louis Guinard** established a toll bridge and trading post in 1859-1860. The fort was taken over by the **U.S. Army** primarily to protect emigrants and the telegraph office. It was named in honor of **Lt. Caspar Collins** who was killed while protecting a supply train from an Indian attack. Hostility with the Indians increased over time so the fort was expanded and about 100 soldiers were eventually garrisoned here.

The first stop is the museum, which features exhibits on prehistoric peoples, **Plains Indians**, western **Emigrant Trails**, the frontier army, ranching, the energy industry, and the city of **Casper**. Outside of the museum is a reconstruction of the fort along with a memorial cemetery and a carriage shed with a collection of wagons and other vehicles from the late 19th and early 20th centuries. North of the fort near the **North Platte River** is a replica of the **Mormon Ferry** and a partial reconstruction of the 810 ft **Guinard Bridge**, both with interpretive signs. Directly west of the museum is **Centennial Park**, which was added in 1990 to commemorate the **Wyoming** state centennial. A concrete path leads through the park to picnic shelters, grills, and a playground. Along this path is a series of 16 interpretive signs, called the "**History Walk**," that explain the history of central **Wyoming**. **Fort Caspar Park** is just east of the fort along **Wyoming Blvd SW**.
Cool Rating: *** *Crowds:* ** *Time:* 1-2 hrs *[FEE AREA]*
Notes: A campground is located just west of Centennial Park. This campground is marked with brown signs in several places along the highways, which usually means a public campground. However, this is a crowded private RV park and campground.
Directions: I-25 exit 188B; SW on N Poplar St/Wy-220 0.6 mi; W/R on W 1st St/US-20/26 2.0 mi; S/L on SW Wyoming Blvd/Wy-258 1.0 mi; W/R on Fort Caspar Rd 0.2 mi.

MM: 189.5 *GPS:* 42.86392/-106.40631 *Elev:* 5233 *Grid:* 66/53
Oregon Trail Rd *(see chapter)*   *Type:* Hwy Junction w/Chapter
An interesting alternative route from **US-20/26** (at **Casper**) southwest following the actual **Oregon Trail** 40.4 mi to **Wy-220**. The road passes the historic sites **Emigrant Gap**, **Rock Avenue**, **Willow Springs**, and **Prospect Hill** (a BLM interpretive site) in the same direction that the emigrants traveled. This route from **Casper** is roughly the same distance as taking **Wy-220** but is much slower and bypasses **Alcova Reservoir** and **Pathfinder Reservoir**.
Nearest Town: Casper 4 E
Directions: I-25 exit 189; W on US-20/26 Bypass 2.9 mi; NW/R on US-20/26 0.5 mi; W/L on CR-202/W Zero Rd from MM 0.

MM: 189.5 *GPS:* 42.86725/-106.34527 *Elev:* 5310 *Grid:* 67/53
US-20/26 *(see chapter)*   *Type:* Hwy Junction w/Chapter
96.9 mi highway from **Casper** northwest to **Shoshoni**. Highlights include: **Hell's Half Acre**, **Hole-in-the-Wall**, **Castle Gardens**.
Directions: I-25 exit 189; W on US-20/26 Bypass 2.9 mi; NW/R on US-20/26 to Shoshoni from MM 6.1

MM: 189.5 *Dist:* 0.3 *GPS:* 42.86728/-106.33764 *Elev:* 5290 *Grid:* 67/53 *Land:* BLM
National Historic Trails Interpretive Center   *Type:* Historic Site
A 27,000 sq ft visitor center commemorating the period between 1840 and 1870 when nearly 500,000 people migrated west using the **Oregon-Mormon-California-Pony Express Trails**. The center overlooks the 4 trails and the **North Platte River**. The story is told from thousands of authentic diaries and journals about the journey westward in search of land, wealth, and religious freedom in a raw and wild land that few of the emigrants knew anything about.

Start the experience with the 18-minute multi-media program "**Footsteps to the West**," which is shown in the theatre on a regular basis. The **Inscription Wall** located in the lobby showcases exact replicas of emigrant names carved in rock along the trails. 7 galleries feature hands-on exhibits as well as information on those who lived, worked, and traveled these trails:

Ways of The People - Listen to tribal stories and learn more about **Native American** culture.
The U.S. Looks West - Discover the routes of missionaries, explorers, and mountain men. Many people including **Narcissa Whitman**, **Jim Bridger** and **John C. Fremont**, paved the way for the emigrants who followed.
The Oregon Trail - Ponder the decisions faced by the emigrants. *Features a virtual wagon ride across the **North Platte River**.*
The Mormon Trail - Hear the epic story of the **Martin Handcart Company**, and learn more of why **Mormons** settled in the **Great Salt Lake Valley**. *Features an interactive exhibit pushing a hand-cart.*
The California Trail - Learn about the perils and prosperity of gold fever days.
The Pony Express Trail - Experience the excitement of the brave young riders and learn more about the transportation and communication industries of the 1860s. *Features a virtual stagecoach ride.*
The Trails Today - Learn about America's public lands, state and national historic sites, and recreational opportunities found in **Wyoming**.

These galleries portray daily life on the trails through written, visual, interactive, and authentic life-sized displays, which explain the social and political events that persuaded people to make these journeys of epic proportions. Learn about the people who played a role in America's west, including the native peoples who established the travel routes, explorers, fur trappers, mountain men, missionaries, early farm families in covered wagons, **Mormon** families pushing handcarts toward a new freedom in the **Great Salt Lake Valley**, young **Pony Express** riders, stagecoach drivers, telegraph construction crews, wild and reckless "**Forty-Niners**" in a rush to **California**'s gold fields, and the construction crews building the first transcontinental railroad.
Hours: 8am - 7pm (mid-Apr - mid-Oct); 9am - 4:30pm (winter) *Phone:* 307-261-7700
Cool Rating: **** *Crowds:* *** *Time:* 4 hrs *[FEE AREA]*
Directions: I-25 exit 189; E on Events Dr 0.2 mi; S/R on N Poplar St 0.1 mi; E/L into parking lot (*1501 North Poplar Street, Casper*)

MM: 249.7   *GPS:* 43.65383/-106.62792   *Elev:* 4769   *Grid:* 63/34   *Land:* BLM

Wyoming Backway shortcut from I-25 to US-20/26   *Type:* Scenic Drive

68.1 mi backcountry route from **I-25**, south of **Kaycee**, to **US-20/26** at **Waltman**. This route saves 45 mi over taking the paved highways and is the route to **Hole-in-the-Wall**. 2 backcountry campgrounds are located along this route *(see Wyoming Backway shortcut on US-20/26 MM 50.7).*

Road Desc: The road is smooth gravel except the 2.1 section on CR-111A, which is rougher. The last 9.6 mi is paved. Not recommended when wet.

Directions: I-25 exit 249 to W side of hwy;   S on TTT Rd 0.5 mi (MI 0.5);   SW/R on Lone Bear Rd/CR-51 14.9 mi (MI 15.4);   W/R on Willow Creek Rd/CR-111 5.9 mi (MI 21.3);   W/R on CR-111A 2.1 mi (MI 23.4);   Continue straight on CR-111 to Willow Creek Ranch sign 1.9 mi (MI 25.3);   Keep right to stay on CR-111 6.4 mi (**Hole-in-the-Wall turnoff**) (MI 31.7);   Continue on CR-105 0.6 mi (MI 32.3);   NW/R on CR-110 2.0 mi (MI 34.3);   Continue straight on CR-105 11.1 mi to CR-109 (to BLM campgrounds) (MI 45.4);   Continue straight on CR-105/CR-104 22.7 mi (pavement begins at 13.1 mi) (MI 68.1).

MM: 249.7   *Dist:* 41.6   *GPS:* 43.52958/-106.86484   *Elev:* 5360   *Grid:* 60/37   *Land:* BLM

Hole-in-the-Wall   *Type:* Scenic Area

A gap in the red sandstone escarpment know as the "**Red Wall**," which was used by several outlaw gangs as a hideout from the late 1860s to around 1910. The area was easily defended because it was impossible for lawmen to approach without being seen. The most notable outlaws were **Butch Cassidy and the Sundance Kid** and the **Wild Bunch Gang**. The area itself is colorful, scenic, and remote with access along a 2.6 mi (one-way) hiking trail of county roads and single-track trails. The "hole" is actually a V-shaped section of the **Red Wall** that offers a steep and rocky "trail" allowing a scramble to the top of the butte without encountering a vertical wall. The view from the top is excellent. *See US-20/26 MM 50.7 for details.*

Cool Rating: ****   *Crowds:* *   *Time:* Half to all day

Directions: *See previous section for the road description and follow directions to MI 31.7;*   NE on CR-105 9.7 mi to parking area.

MM: 254.3   *GPS:* 43.71033/-106.63912   *Elev:* 4650   *Grid:* 63/32

Kaycee   *Type:* Town

MM: 254.3   *Dist:* 0.1   *GPS:* 43.71771/-106.64216   *Elev:* 4684   *Grid:* 63/32

Kaycee Rest Area   *Type:* Rest Area

A nice grassed rest area with picnic shelters, pet walk area, and handicapped accessible facilities, plus historical signs about the **Powder River Country** and the **Dull Knife Battle**.

Directions: I-25 exit 254;   W side of hwy.

MM: 254.3   *Dist:* 0.3   *GPS:* 43.71410/-106.64030   *Elev:* 4662   *Grid:* 63/32   *Land:* City

Kaycee Visitor Center   *Type:* Visitor Center

Small information center.

Hours: 9am - 4pm Sun-Fri   *Directions:* I-25 exit 254;   SE 0.1 mi;   S/R on Nolan Ave/Wy-196 0.1 mi;   First right on dirt road across from Barber St 0.05 mi;   N end of parking area.

MM: 254.3   *Dist:* 0.4   *GPS:* 43.71040/-106.64011   *Elev:* 4648   *Grid:* 63/32   *Land:* City

Kaycee Town Park   *Type:* Park

A town park that allows free camping. Only about 3 good RV pullouts are provided, but dispersed camping is available along the edge the loop road as well as a large grassed area for tents and RVs on the south end. *Cottonwoods. Tables and grills. Restrooms. 2 group picnic shelters with grills. Playground.*

Crowds: **   *Directions:* I-25 exit 254;   SE 0.1 mi;   S/R on Nolan Ave/Wy-196 0.3 mi;   W/R on 1st Ave 80 yds.

Campsites: 10   *Shade:* **   *Privacy:* *   *RV Size:* 30'   *Other:* Water

---

MM: 254.3   *Dist:* 25.1   *GPS:* 43.58909/-106.94741   *Elev:* 6064   *Grid:* 59/35   *Land:* BLM

Outlaw Cave   *Type:* Historic Site

A 1/2 mi path drops 660 ft into a remote canyon to **Outlaw Cave**, a favorite hiding place for stolen loot by 19th century outlaws such as **Butch Cassidy** and the **Wild Bunch Gang**. The **Middle Fork Powder River** flows through this canyon and offers blue ribbon trout fishing. The surrounding area is scenic with an escarpment of red sandstone to the east known as the **Red Wall**. A campground is located on the canyon rim; however, a fire in the area has left the trees charred. *Burned trees. Tables. Fire rings. Vault toilet.*

Cool Rating: ****   *Crowds:* *   *Notes:* Hole-in-the-Wall is located only about 6 mi southwest; however, no direct roads provide access. Access is from I-25 MM 249.7 *(see earlier section).*

Road Desc: Partially paved, impassable when wet, high clearance. First 16.7 mi is paved. Only the last 3.4 mi require high clearance.

Directions: I-25 exit 254;   NW on Wy-191 0.9 mi;   S and W on Barnum Rd/Wy-190 15.8 mi;   Keep left at the fork and follow Bar C Rd (which turns south) 5.2 mi;   Keep right to head W on Outlaw Cave Rd 3.0 mi;   N/R 0.2 mi to the campground.   The trail is at the north end of the campground.

Campsites: 5   *Shade:* *   *Privacy:* **   *RV Size:* 20'   *Other:* None

---

MM: 254.3   *Dist:* 25.6   *GPS:* 43.58316/-106.95179   *Elev:* 6227   *Grid:* 59/35   *Land:* BLM

Indian Rock Art Cave   *Type:* Historic Site

A rock overhang with faint **Pictographs** of bear claws, warriors, shields, and 1 large red human figure. The art is somewhat obscured by soot from campfires under the overhang. Walk out over the top of the cave for a good view of the **Red Wall** to the east.

Cool Rating: ***   *Crowds:* *   *Time:* 20 min   *Road Desc:* Dirt, primitive & impassable when wet, high clearance

Directions: *See directions from previous entry on Outlaw Cave.* Continue past the Outlaw Cave turnoff 0.5 mi to a pullout and a footpath that leads 90 yds E to the cave.

MM: 299.3   *GPS:* 44.35426/-106.69906   *Elev:* 4641   *Grid:* 62/16

Buffalo   *Type:* Town

MM: 299.3 *GPS:* 44.35420/-106.68687 *Elev:* 4582 *Grid:* 62/16

US-16 *(see chapter)*   *Type:* Hwy Junction w/Chapter

89.9 mi highway from **Buffalo** southwest to **Worland**. Along this highway is the scenic 45 mi **Cloud Peak Skyway**, which travels through the **Bighorn Mountains** and provides many campgrounds, forest roads with dispersed camping, and recreational opportunities. Highlights include: **Crazy Woman Canyon**, **High Park Lookout**, **Tensleep Canyon**, **West Tensleep Falls**, **Ten Sleep Fish Hatchery**, **Wigwam Rearing Station**, **Medicine Lodge State Archaeological Site**, **Castle Gardens**.

Directions: I-25 exit 299; W on E Hart St 0.6 mi; S/L on N Main St 0.4 mi; W/R to Ten Sleep from MM 92.1

MM: 300.1 *GPS:* 44.36724/-106.68928 *Elev:* 4660 *Grid:* 62/16

I-90 *(see chapter)*   *Type:* Hwy Junction w/Chapter

208.8 mi interstate highway that heads west from **South Dakota** across northeastern **Wyoming** then northwest to **Montana**. Highlights include: **Vore Buffalo Jump**, **Devils Tower National Monument**, **Eagle Butte Coal Mine**, **Dry Creek Petrified Tree Environmental Education Area**, **Fort Phil Kearny** and related historic sites.

Directions: I-25 transitions north to I-90 to Sheridan from MM 56.6 or take I-25 exit 300 E to Gillette from MM 57.2

MM: 300.2 *GPS:* 44.36724/-106.68928 *Elev:* 4660 *Grid:* 62/16

End of Highway   *Type:* Highway End

300 mi interstate highway through east/central **Wyoming** from **I-90** south to **Colorado**. Highlights include: **Outlaw Cave**, **Indian Rock Art Cave**, **Hole-in-the-Wall**, **National Historic Trails Interpretive Center**, **Ayres Park and Natural Bridge**, **Pioneer Museum**.

Nearest Town: Buffalo 1.3 S *Directions:* I-90 exit 56B; S to Casper from MM 300.2

MM: 0.0 **GPS:** 41.24757/-111.04657 **Elev:** 6758 **Grid:** 0/94

I-80   **Type:** Highway Description

403 mi interstate highway through southern **Wyoming** from **Utah** east to **Nebraska**. Highlights include: **Bear River State Park**, **Fossil Butte National Monument**, **Piedmont Charcoal Kilns**, **Fort Bridger State Historic Site**, **Church Butte**, **Expedition Island**, **Flaming Gorge National Recreation Area**, **Western Wyoming Natural History Museum**, **Pilot Butte Wild Horse Tour**, **Reliance Tipple**, **Point of Rocks Stagecoach Station**, **Wyoming Frontier Prison**, **Fort Fred Steele**, **Wyoming Territorial Prison State Historic Site**, **Abraham Lincoln Monument**, **Pole Mountain Trails**, **Curt Gowdy State Park**, **Ames Monument**, **Vedauwoo Recreation Area**.

Nearest Town: Evanston 5.3 E **Directions:** E from the Utah state line from MM 0

MM: 5.3 **GPS:** 41.26554/-110.96113 **Elev:** 6762 **Grid:** 1/93

Evanston   **Type:** Town

MM: 5.3 **GPS:** 41.26218/-110.95332 **Elev:** 6812 **Grid:** 1/93

Mirror Lake Scenic Byway   **Type:** Scenic Byway

78 mi scenic byway from **Evanston** to **Kamas**, **Utah** through the **Uinta Mountains**, which is the only east/west mountain range in the contiguous 48 states. The byway climbs over the 10,700 ft **Bald Mountain Pass** crossing meadows and passing beautiful mountain lakes and high peaks. Several public campgrounds are located along the route in the **Wasatch-Cache National Forest**. If traveling between **Evanston** and **Salt Lake City** this route adds about 34 mi to the drive.

Cool Rating: *** **Crowds:** ** **Directions:** I-80 exit 5; S on Wy-150 23.2 mi to Utah state line; Continue on Ut-150.

MM: 6.3 **Dist:** 0.1 **GPS:** 41.26549/-110.93861 **Elev:** 6800 **Grid:** 2/93 **Land:** State

Bear River State Park   **Type:** State Park

A year-round day use park that features 3 miles of multi-use trails along the **Bear River**. A 1.1 mi paved portion or the trail parallels the entrance road and is part of a 2.1 mi greenbelt trail that connects to **Evanston**. A footbridge across the **Bear River** leads to a 1.7 mi packed gravel trail through a natural area. The trails are used as cross-country ski trails in the winter. Other activities include picnicking and wildlife viewing, which includes a captive herd of bison and elk. A sheltered picnic area and playground are located at the park entrance. Additional sheltered picnic areas are located 1/4 mi farther and at the parking area at the end of the 0.6 mi entrance road. In addition, several individual parking areas with picnic tables and grills are spread along the entrance road.

Cool Rating: **** **Crowds:** ** **Directions:** I-80 exit 6; S on Bear River Dr 0.1 mi; SW/R into park.

MM: 6.3 **Dist:** 0.2 **GPS:** 41.26562/-110.93440 **Elev:** 6807 **Grid:** 2/93

Bear River Welcome Center   **Type:** Rest Area

Welcome Center and rest area with picnic shelters, playground, pet walk area, **RV dump**, and handicapped accessible facilities. On the southwest end of the rest area is an overlook of the buffalo and elk in **Bear River State Park**.

Directions: I-80 exit 6; S on Bear River Dr 0.2 mi.

MM: 18.3 **GPS:** 41.30806/-110.73101 **Elev:** 6922 **Grid:** 5/92

US-189 (see chapter)   **Type:** Hwy Junction w/Chapter

131.5 mi highway from **I-80** exit 18 north to the junctions with **US-189/191**, which heads northwest toward **Jackson**, and **US-191**, which heads east to **Pinedale**. Highlights include: **Names Hill**, **Father DeSmet Monument**.

Nearest Town: Evanston 13 W **Directions:** I-80 exit 18; N to Kemmerer from MM 0

MM: 18.3 **Dist:** 44.6 **GPS:** 41.81592/-110.71956 **Elev:** 6645 **Grid:** 5/80

Fossil Butte National Monument (see chapter)   **Type:** Hwy Junction w/Chapter

50 million years ago this area was a huge lake in a lush green subtropical forest. Because of profound climate change what remains today is a semi-arid landscape of flat-topped buttes in a sagebrush desert. The ancient lake sediment hardened and transformed into layers of rocks known as the **Green River Formation**. Trapped between these layers are among the best-preserved fossils in the world. These remarkably detailed fossils include fish, insects, plants, reptiles, birds, and mammals.

Directions: I-80 exit 18; N on US-189 34.5 mi; W on US-30 10.1 mi; NW on CR-300 from MM 0.

Notes: There is no camping at the monument and little camping anywhere in the area except private campgrounds in Kemmerer. BLM land is located along US-30 and generally provides a place to park overnight, but watch out for private land.

MM: 23.9 **Dist:** 3.4 **GPS:** 41.26897/-110.60321 **Elev:** 6906 **Grid:** 6/93 **Land:** County

Muddy Creek Camp and Crossing   **Type:** Historic Site

A pullout with a historical marker explaining the **Muddy Creek Camp and Crossing**, which was one of the most heavily used camps on the **Overland-Mormon-California-Pony Express Trails**.

Cool Rating: * **Crowds:** * **Time:** 10 min **Road Desc:** Gravel

Directions: I-80 exit 24; S to Piedmont Rd/CR-173; E then S 3.4 mi; W side of road.

MM: 23.9 **Dist:** 7.1 **GPS:** 41.21989/-110.61955 **Elev:** 7047 **Grid:** 6/94 **Land:** County

Piedmont Charcoal Kilns   **Type:** Historic Site

3 beehive-shaped charcoal kilns that measure 30 ft high and 30 ft in diameter. The kilns were built in 1869 by **Moses Byrne** to provide charcoal for smelters in **Utah**. Up the hill from the kilns is the old **Byrne Family Cemetery**, which contains the graves of many young children. The cemetery is interesting, but getting there requires crossing 2 small creeks and wet areas. Continue 0.4 mi southwest past the kilns to several abandoned buildings in the ghost town of **Piedmont**. Please view these building from the road as they are on private property. **Guild Reservoir** is another 0.3 mi southwest.

Cool Rating: *** **Crowds:** * **Time:** 30-60 min **Road Desc:** Gravel

Directions: I-80 exit 24; S to Piedmont Rd/CR-173; E then S 7.1 mi; E side of road.

MM: 34.7 *Dist:* 2.3 *GPS:* 41.31837/-110.38966 *Elev:* 6667 *Grid:* 10/92 *Land:* State

Fort Bridger State Historic Site   *Type:* Historic Site

Fort Bridger was established in 1843 by **Jim Bridger** and **Louis Vasquez** as an emigrant supply stop along the **Oregon-Mormon-California-Pony Express Trails** and served as one of the primary hubs of westward expansion. The fort was controlled by the **Mormons** in the early to mid 1850s; however, a series of conflicts with the **U.S. Army** led to the fort becoming a military outpost in 1858. It remained **U.S. Government** property until 1890 when it was abandoned and the buildings were sold. A very successful ranching operation grew around the fort, which spurred settlement and eventually the town of **Fort Bridger**. After a period of neglect, the fort was restored and in 1933 was dedicated as a **Wyoming Historical Landmark and Museum**. The site contains many original and restored historic buildings, including a reconstructed trading post and a replica of **Jim Bridger**'s original fort. A museum containing artifacts from the various historical time periods is housed in the 1888 stone barracks building. Behind the museum is an interpretive archaeological site. Over Labor Day weekend hundreds of people gather to re-enact the past, which includes authentic demonstrations. *Located at mile 1026 of the* **Oregon Trail***.*

Hours: Grounds: 8am - sunset (year round); Museum: 9am - 5:30pm (May-Sept); Weekends only mid-Mar-Apr and Oct-mid-Nov

Phone: 307-782-3842 *Cool Rating:* *** *Crowds:* ** *Time:* 1-2 hrs *[FEE AREA]*

Notes: One of the most interesting historic forts in Wyoming.

Directions: I-80 exit 34; SE on I-80 Business Loop 2.3 mi; S side of hwy just before Main St in Fort Bridger.

MM: 42.0 *Dist:* 0.1 *GPS:* 41.36430/-110.29932 *Elev:* 6520 *Grid:* 11/91

Lyman Rest Area   *Type:* Rest Area

Picnic shelters, pet walk area, handicapped accessible facilities, and a monument marking the passage of the first **Mormon** pioneers in 1847.

Directions: I-80 exit 41; S on Wy-413 0.1 mi; E side of hwy.

MM: 53.3 *Dist:* 5.5 *GPS:* 41.50522/-110.13724 *Elev:* 6450 *Grid:* 13/87 *Land:* State

Church Butte   *Type:* Point of Interest

Eroded sandstone cliffs named by **Mormon** pioneers for their steeple-like shapes that rise 100 ft above the surrounding area. Religious services were held here. The area around the base of the cliffs is level and hard-packed dirt that could provide overnight camping.

Cool Rating: *** *Crowds:* * *Time:* 30 min *Road Desc:* Gravel, washboard sections

Directions: I-80 exit 53; N on Church Butte Rd 5.4 mi; E/R on CR-233 0.1 mi.

MM: 66.2 *GPS:* 41.54419/-109.91107 *Elev:* 6406 *Grid:* 16/86

US-30 *(see chapter)*   *Type:* Hwy Junction w/Chapter

100 mi highway from **I-80** exit 66 northwest to **Idaho**. Highlights include: **Fossil Butte National Monument**.

Nearest Town: Kemmerer 54.6 NW; Green River 24.5 E *Directions:* I-80 exit 66; NW to Kemmerer from MM 100

MM: 83.0 *GPS:* 41.55540/-109.59076 *Elev:* 6443 *Grid:* 21/86

Wy-372 *(see chapter)*   *Type:* Hwy Junction w/Chapter

48.6 mi highway from **I-80** exit 83 northwest to **US-189** MM 61.3. This is primarily a connecting road to **Wy-28** and **US-189** northbound. 3 BLM campgrounds are located near **Fontenelle Reservoir** 40.4 mi northwest. Highlights include: **Lombard/Mormon Ferry**, **Seedskadee National Wildlife Refuge**.

Nearest Town: Green River 6.5 E *Directions:* I-80 exit 83; NW to US-189 from MM 0

MM: 89.5 *GPS:* 41.52853/-109.46634 *Elev:* 6120 *Grid:* 23/87

Green River (eastbound)   *Type:* Town

MM: 89.5 *Dist:* 0.2 *GPS:* 41.53686/-109.48026 *Elev:* 6169 *Grid:* 22/87

Green River Visitor Information Center   *Type:* Visitor Center

A staffed information center with literature and maps for the surrounding area, including information about the **Pilot Butte Wild Horse Tour** that starts across the street on **Wild Horse Canyon Rd**. *Portable toilets. Picnic table. Water (donation appreciated).*

Directions: I-80 exit 89; SE on Wy-374/W Flaming Gorge Way 0.2 mi; SW side of street.

MM: 89.5 *Dist:* 0.2 *GPS:* 41.53673/-109.47954 *Elev:* 6182 *Grid:* 23/87

Pilot Butte Wild Horse Tour *(see chapter)*   *Type:* Hwy Junction w/Chapter

A 25.8 mi driving tour from **Green River** to **US-191** (11.8 mi north of I-80 at Rock Springs) along the rim of **White Mountain** where wild horses can be seen. 6 interpretive pullouts provide nice views from **White Mountain** and a side road provides access to **Pilot Butte**, which can be climbed on foot.

Directions: I-80 exit 89; SE on Wy-374/W Flaming Gorge Way 0.2 mi; N on Wild Horse Canyon Rd/CR-53/White Mountain Rd from MM 0.

MM: 91.5 *GPS:* 41.52853/-109.46634 *Elev:* 6120 *Grid:* 23/87

Green River (westbound)   *Type:* Town

MM: 91.5 *Dist:* 1.9 *GPS:* 41.52284/-109.47035 *Elev:* 6086 *Grid:* 23/87 *Land:* City

Expedition Island   *Type:* Historic Site

From this point **John Wesley Powell** began his expedition down the **Green River** and **Colorado River** in 1871, which culminated in his trip through the **Grand Canyon**. The island has a shady park with covered picnic tables and a 1/4 mi interpretive loop path around the perimeter. Walking the paved path clockwise, signs explain the history of travel on the **Green River** before and after **Powell**'s celebrated expeditions. In addition, 3 stone monuments dedicated to **Powell** and his expedition are located in the grassed area.

At the south end of the parking area is a footbridge across the **Green River** that leads to the **Greenbelt Pathway**. This paved trail follows the **Green River** 3.4 mi east and south to **FMC Park** and **Scott's Bottom Nature Area**. *See next section.*

Cool Rating: ** *Crowds:* ** *Time:* 1 hr

Directions: I-80 exit 91; S 0.7 mi; N/R on loop to Wy-530/Uinta Dr 0.6 mi; W/R on E 2nd S 0.4 mi; S/L on S 2nd E 0.2 mi.

MM: 91.5 *Dist:* 2.3 *GPS:* 41.51542/-109.45620 *Elev:* 6085 *Grid:* 23/87 *Land:* City
RV Dump: Green River   *Type:* RV Dump
Located at the public works complex. No potable water.
Directions: I-80 exit 91; S 0.7 mi; N/R on loop to Wy-530/Uinta Dr 1.0 mi; E/L on Astle Ave/E Teton Blvd 0.6 mi; E side of hwy.
Continuing 1.8 mi leads to the Scott's Bottom turnoff.

MM: 91.5 *Dist:* 5.9 *GPS:* 41.49307/-109.43927 *Elev:* 6057 *Grid:* 23/88 *Land:* City
Scott's Bottom Nature Area   *Type:* Wildlife Area
A 15 acre section of **FMC Park** located in a wooded area along the **Green River**. A 1/2 mi interpretive trail leads through wildlife habitat and past a series of 10 interpretive signs that correspond to numbered entries in the trail guide available at the trailhead. These signs explain some of the area wildlife and the environment in which they live. The trail makes a partial loop and returns to the starting point. **FMC Park** also provides picnic tables, playground, group shelter, archery range, shooting range, and a paintball complex. The paved **Greenbelt Pathway** that starts at **Expedition Island** ends at the entrance to **FMC Park** *(see section above)*.
Cool Rating: ** *Crowds:* ** *Time:* 1 hr *Road Desc:* Partially paved. The last 0.9 is gravel.
Directions: I-80 exit 91; S 0.7 mi; N/R on loop to Wy-530/Uinta Dr 2.1 mi; SE/L on Upland Way 1.3 mi; S/R on W Teton Blvd 0.9 mi; Keep right at fork onto dirt road 0.7 mi; SW/R 0.2 mi to trailhead.

MM: 91.5 *Dist:* 26.5 *GPS:* 41.24903/-109.59699 *Elev:* 6107 *Grid:* 21/94
Flaming Gorge National Recreation Area - Buckboard Crossing   *Type:* Recreation Area
A **National Recreation Area** centered around the 91 mi long **Flaming Gorge Reservoir**. The **Green River** backs up into a wide canyon in the high sagebrush desert. The majority of the reservoir is located in **Wyoming**, with the remainder in **Utah**, which contains the actual dam in a setting of colorful canyons and National Forest. **Wy-530** runs relatively close to the reservoir in contrast to **US-191**, on the east side, where the primary access road is over 10 mi long. It is 24.0 mi to the primary **Flaming Gorge Reservoir** access point and **Buckboard Crossing Campground**. *2 paved loops. Paved parking areas. Scattered deciduous trees. Picnic shelters. Flush toilets. Showers. Store. Marina. Boat ramp. Boat docks.* 3 additional dispersed camping areas are located to the south: **Buckboard South** (MM 24.7); **Squaw Hollow** (MM 31.4); **Anvil Draw** (MM 37.5).

From **Green River** a 142 mi loop can be made around **Flaming Gorge Reservoir** by heading S on **Wy-530** 46.3 mi to **Manila**; E on **Ut-44** 27.9 mi; N on **US-191** 68.2 mi to **I-80**, just west of **Rock Springs**.
Cool Rating: ** *Crowds:* *** *[FEE AREA]*
Directions: I-80 exit 91; S 0.7 mi; N/R on loop to Wy-530/Uinta Dr 24.0 mi to MM 24.0; E/L 1.8 mi.
Campsites: 68 *Shade:* * *Privacy:* * *RV Size:* 40'+ *Other:* 1-877-444-6777:www.recreation.gov,Water,RVDump

MM: 99.1 *Dist:* 24.0 *GPS:* 41.34975/-109.44604 *Elev:* 6120 *Grid:* 23/91 *Land:* NPS
Flaming Gorge National Recreation Area - Firehole Canyon   *Type:* Recreation Area
A **National Recreation Area** centered around the 91 mi long **Flaming Gorge Reservoir**. The **Green River** backs up into a wide canyon in the high sagebrush desert. The majority of the reservoir is located in **Wyoming**, with the remainder in **Utah**, which contains the actual dam in a setting of colorful canyons and National Forest. **US-191** does not run very close to the reservoir (the primary access road is over 10 mi long) in contrast to **Wy-530** on the west side. It is 23.7 mi to the primary **Flaming Gorge Reservoir** access point and **Firehole Canyon Campground**. *Single paved loop. Paved parking areas. No trees. Shared parking areas. Shared picnic shelters with dividers between tables. Flush toilets. Showers. Beach area. Boat ramp.*

From **I-80** just west of **Rock Springs** a 142 mi loop can be made around **Flaming Gorge Reservoir** by heading S on **US-191** 68.2 mi; W on **Ut-44** 27.9 mi to **Manila**; N on **Wy-530** 46.3 mi to **Green River**.
Cool Rating: ** *Crowds:* *** *[FEE AREA]*
Directions: I-80 exit 99; S on US-191 13.6 mi to MM 513.6; W/R on CR-33/Flaming Gorge Rd 9.8; N/R 0.6 mi.
Campsites: 40 *Shade:* * *Privacy:* * *RV Size:* 40'+ *Other:* 1-877-444-6777:www.recreation.gov,Water,RVDump

MM: 103.8 *Dist:* 0.5 *GPS:* 41.59233/-109.23588 *Elev:* 6456 *Grid:* 26/85 *Land:* City
Western Wyoming Natural History Museum   *Type:* Museum
A museum located in the halls of the **Western Wyoming Community College** in **Rock Springs** with the following displays: **Dinosaur Exhibit** with life-sized dinosaur replicas; **Art Gallery** with displays from regional and national artists; **Fossils** of a monster prehistoric fish, palm leaf, large turtle, and an alligator; **Natural History Museum** focusing on the geology and archaeology of southwestern **Wyoming**; **Fossil Man Displays** with bones, skulls, and tools of early man; **Cave Art** with paintings replicating cave art from France; and a 9 ton replica of the **Easter Island Statue** on the lawn behind the building. A guidebook is available at the front desk. *Donations appreciated.*
Hours: 9am - 10pm *Cool Rating:* *** *Crowds:* ** *Time:* 1 hr
Directions: I-80 exit 103; SE on College Drive 0.5 mi; W/R then right into the north parking lot *(2500 College Dr, Rock Springs)*

MM: 104.8 *GPS:* 41.60772/-109.22943 *Elev:* 6304 *Grid:* 26/85
Rock Springs   *Type:* Town

MM: 104.8 *GPS:* 41.60777/-109.22941 *Elev:* 6304 *Grid:* 26/85
US-191 *(see chapter)*   *Type:* Hwy Junction w/Chapter
109.2 mi highway from **I-80** exit 104 in **Rock Springs** northwest past **Pinedale** to a transition with **US-189/191**, which continues 53.2 mi to **Hoback Jct** (south of **Jackson**) using sequential mile markers. Highlights include: **Reliance Tipple**, **White Mountain Petroglyphs**, **Boar's Tusk**, **Killpecker Sand Dunes**, **Pilot Butte Wild Horse Tour**, **Fremont Lake**, **Green River Lakes**.
Notes: US-191 actually starts at MM 0 at the transition of N Center St and Bridger Ave (1.3 mi south of I-80 exit 104).
Directions: I-80 exit 104; NW to Farson from MM 1.3

MM: 104.8 *Dist:* 5.2 *GPS:* 41.66835/-109.19682 *Elev:* 6515 *Grid:* 27/83 *Land:* City
Reliance Tipple   *Type:* Historic Site
This tipple was used from 1936 - 1955 to sort and grade coal and load it into rail cars. The steel structure replaced a wooden tipple built in 1912 and was one of the largest and most advanced of its kind. The only other coal tipple in the state is the **Aladdin Tipple** in northeastern **Wyoming** *(see Wy-24 MM 40.8)*. A short path with interpretive signs explain the history and operation of the tipple.
Cool Rating: *** *Crowds:* * *Time:* 30 min
Directions: I-80 exit 104; N on US-191 3.2 mi; E on Reliance Rd 1.7 mi; Slight right on South St 0.2 mi.

MM: 104.8   *Dist:* 13.1   *GPS:* 41.74369/-109.32207   *Elev:* 6842   *Grid:* 25/81
Pilot Butte Wild Horse Tour *(see chapter)*   *Type:* Hwy Junction w/Chapter
A 25.8 mi driving tour from **US-191** (11.8 mi north of I-80 at Rock Springs) to **Green River** along the rim of **White Mountain** where wild horses can be seen. 6 interpretive pullouts provide nice views from **White Mountain** and a side road provides access to **Pilot Butte**, which can be climbed.
Directions: I-80 exit 104; N on US-191 13.1 mi; SW on CR-14/Blue Rim Rd.

MM: 130.8   *Dist:* 0.4   *GPS:* 41.67654/-108.79143   *Elev:* 6511   *Grid:* 32/83   *Land:* State
Point of Rocks Stagecoach Station   *Type:* Historic Site
The **Overland Trail** served as a major transportation route from 1862-1869. This trail took a southern route from the **Oregon Trail** and was considered safer from Indian attacks when military strength in the west declined after the start of the **Civil War**. A series of stage stations along this route were built from 10 to 14 mi apart. The **Point of Rocks Stagecoach Station** was one such station and served many additional purposes into the 1870s and beyond. The main structure was built of local sandstone with a sod roof, and was restored by the state of **Wyoming** in 1974. The trail ran between the station and the stables to the south, which remain as a sandstone ruin. Several interpretive signs explain the history of the station and the **Overland Trail**. Just south of **I-80** is an additional historical sign about the **Overland Stage Route**.
Cool Rating: **   *Crowds:* *   *Time:* 30 min
Directions: I-80 exit 130; S to service road and the Overland Stage Route historical sign; W on service road 0.2 mi; S/L on Black Buttes Rd 0.2 mi.

MM: 143.7   *GPS:* 41.64453/-108.54760   *Elev:* 7007   *Grid:* 36/84
Bitter Creek Rest Area (westbound)   *Type:* Rest Area
A natural landscaped rest area with picnic shelters, pet walk area, and handicapped accessible facilities.

MM: 144.5   *GPS:* 41.64201/-108.53201   *Elev:* 6943   *Grid:* 36/84
Bitter Creek Rest Area (eastbound)   *Type:* Rest Area
A natural landscaped rest area with picnic shelters, pet walk area, and handicapped accessible facilities.

MM: 187.2   *GPS:* 41.72834/-107.72852   *Elev:* 7072   *Grid:* 48/82
Wy-789   *Type:* Highway Junction
50.7 mi highway south from I-80 exit 187 to **Wy-70** at **Baggs** *(see Wy-70)* and continuing to **Craig**, **Colorado**.
Nearest Town: Rawlins 25 E

MM: 211.8   *GPS:* 41.78816/-107.23769   *Elev:* 6761   *Grid:* 55/80
Rawlins (eastbound)   *Type:* Town

MM: 211.8   *Dist:* 1.5
Wyoming Frontier Prison (eastbound)   *Type:* Historic Site
See section below at MM 215.6.
Directions: I-80 exit 211; NE on W Spruce St 1.4 mi; NW/L on 5th St 0.1 mi *(500 W Walnut St, Rawlins)*

MM: 211.8   *Dist:* 1.5   *GPS:* 41.78816/-107.23769   *Elev:* 6761   *Grid:* 55/80
US-287/Wy-789 *(see chapter)*   *Type:* Hwy Junction w/Chapter
125 mi highway from **Rawlins**, near **I-80**, northwest to **Lander**. The highway heads north 44.3 mi where the highway and mile markers oddly transition to **Wy-220**, which continues northeast to **Casper**. To continue on **US-287/Wy-789** requires a left turn at a junction where the mile markers start over at MM 0 and the highway heads northwest to **Lander**. Highlights include: **Split Rock**, **Green Mountain**.
Directions: I-80 exit 211; NE on W Spruce St 1.5 mi; N on US-287/Wy-789 from MM 0.2

MM: 214.1   *GPS:* 41.78039/-107.22515   *Elev:* 6765   *Grid:* 55/80
Wy-71   *Type:* Highway Junction
54.8 mi route from **Rawlins** south to **Wy-70** crossing **BLM** and **National Forest** lands and gaining 1,560 ft in elevation. The lone highlight is **Aspen Alley**, which is just north of **Wy-70** *(see Wy-70 MM 32.8)*, so the primary purpose of this route is saving 30 mi over driving the paved highways through **Saratoga** to **Rawlins**. 2 free campgrounds are located along this route: **Teton Reservoir Recreation Site** at 14.6 mi *(see next section)* and **Little Sandstone Campground** at 52.3 mi *(see Wy-70 MM 32.8)*.
Directions: I-80 exit 214; Just N of exit ramp; W then S on Wy-71/CR-401/FR-801 54.8 mi.
Road Desc: First 24.6 mi is paved with some of the pavement being rough and bumpy. The next 30.2 mi is gravel with washboard sections.

MM: 214.1   *Dist:* 15.4   *GPS:* 41.60312/-107.25584   *Elev:* 7050   *Grid:* 54/85   *Land:* BLM
Teton Reservoir Recreation Site   *Type:* Recreation Area
A small reservoir located in a sagebrush landscape, which provides camping, fishing, and floating. *No trees for shade or wind break. Sites are evenly spaced in a loop. Vault toilet. Tables and grills. Fire rings.*

The picnic table across the road overlooking the reservoir is for day use. A vault toilet, 2 tables, and a boat ramp are located at the end of the road 0.2 mi north.
Crowds: *   *Directions:* I-80 exit 214; Just N of exit ramp; W then S on Wy-71/CR-401 14.6 mi; E/L 0.8 mi.
Campsites: 5   *Shade:* *   *Privacy:* *   *RV Size:* 40'+   *Other:* None

MM: 215.6   *Dist:* 2.2   *GPS:* 41.79280/-107.24200   *Elev:* 6848   *Grid:* 54/80
Wyoming Frontier Prison (westbound)   *Type:* Historic Site
The **Old Wyoming State Penitentiary** (sometimes called the "Old Pen") gives visitors a taste of what life was like behind bars from 1901 to 1981. Hour-long guided tours (fee) take place on a regular basis and visit the actual cells, mess hall, prison grounds, and the gallows and gas chamber in the "death house." Just inside the entrance is the prison museum (free).
Hours: 8:30am - 6:30pm (Apr - Oct); 9am - 5pm, Mon-Fri (Nov - Mar)   *Phone:* 307-324-4422
Cool Rating: ***   *Crowds:* **   *Time:* 1 hr *[FEE AREA]*
Notes: The prison can get a bit chilly. They don't take credit cards.
Directions: I-80 exit 215; W on E Cedar St 1.8 mi; NE/R on 3rd St/US-287 0.3 mi; SW/L on W Walnut St 0.1 mi *(500 W Walnut St, Rawlins)*

MM: 215.6 **GPS:** 41.78816/-107.23769 **Elev:** 6761 **Grid:** 55/80
Rawlins (westbound)   **Type:** Town

MM: 215.6 **Dist:** 4.0 **GPS:** 41.78816/-107.23769 **Elev:** 6761 **Grid:** 55/80
US-287/Wy-789 *(see chapter)*   **Type:** Hwy Junction w/Chapter
125 mi highway from **Rawlins**, near **I-80**, northwest to **Lander**. The highway heads north 44.3 mi where the highway and mile markers oddly transition to **Wy-220**, which continues northeast to **Casper**. To continue on **US-287/Wy-789** requires a left turn at a junction where the mile markers start over at MM 0 and the highway heads northwest to **Lander**. Highlights include: **Split Rock**, **Green Mountain**.
Directions: I-80 exit 215; W on E Cedar St 0.6 mi; NW on N Higley Blvd/US-287 Bypass 1.5 mi; N on US-287/Wy-789 from MM 1.9

MM: 219.6 **GPS:** 41.77903/-107.12428 **Elev:** 6595 **Grid:** 56/80
Sinclair   **Type:** Town

MM: 219.6 **GPS:** 41.77903/-107.12428 **Elev:** 6595 **Grid:** 56/80
Seminoe-Alcova Back Country Byway *(see chapter)*   **Type:** Hwy Junction w/Chapter
73.0 mi route from **I-80** exit 219 at **Sinclair** north to **Wy-220** MM 86.5 at **Alcova**. The primary destination along this route is **Seminoe State Park** and **Seminoe Reservoir** along a paved portion of the highway. The route passes through prairie, rolling hills, and over the **Seminoe Mountains**. The distance is 18 mi shorter than taking the highways through **Rawlins**; however, it takes much longer to drive and there are no services along the way. Other highlights include: **White Sand Dunes**, the **Miracle Mile**, **Alcova Reservoir**. This route can be altered at MM 65.9 to incorporate the 2nd and 3rd sections of the **Alcova/Pathfinder Reservoir Loop**, which passes **Fremont Canyon** and **Pathfinder Reservoir** and ends at **Wy-220** MM 80.7.
Notes: The road is suitable for passenger cars but not recommended for large RVs or trailers.
Directions: I-80 exit 219; E on Lincoln Ave 0.2 mi; Left at N 10th St/CR-351 following various county roads 73.0 mi to Alcova.

MM: 228.3 **Dist:** 0.5 **GPS:** 41.75272/-106.95322 **Elev:** 6510 **Grid:** 59/81 **Land:** State
Fort Steele Rest Area   **Type:** Rest Area
A nice grassed rest area with picnic shelters, pet walk area, and handicapped accessible facilities.
Directions: I-80 exit 228; N and E on service road 0.5 mi.

MM: 228.3 **Dist:** 2.1 **GPS:** 41.77682/-106.94616 **GPS2:** 41.77792/-106.94624 **Elev:** 6500 **Grid:** 59/81 **Land:** State
Fort Fred Steele   **Type:** Historic Site
A fort on the west bank of the **North Platte River**, which was established in1868 by soldiers who were sent by the **U.S. Government** to guard the railroad against Indian attacks. The fort was deactivated in 1886 after the Indian threat had passed. Eight years later the fort was sold and turned into a town, but it was destroyed by fire shortly thereafter. Many of the remaining foundations and chimneys are visible, but only a few structures are intact. The restored 1880s **Bridger Tender House** serves as the interpretive center for the fort. Tours of the ruins are self-guided using interpretive signs.
Hours: 9am - 7pm (May-mid-Nov) **Phone:** 307-320-3013 **Cool Rating:** *** **Crowds:** * **Time:** 1 hr **Road Desc:** Paved, bumpy
Directions: I-80 exit 228; N and E on service rd 0.3 mi; N on CR-347 1.8 mi to parking area at the interpretive center. Follow the walking path under the railroad bridge to the fort.

MM: 235.3 **GPS:** 41.74135/-106.83036 **Elev:** 6791 **Grid:** 60/81
Walcott   **Type:** Town

MM: 235.3 **GPS:** 41.74135/-106.83036 **Elev:** 6791 **Grid:** 60/81
Wy-130/Wy-230 (Walcott to Riverside) *(see chapter)*   **Type:** Hwy Junction w/Chapter
38.2 mi highway from **Walcott** south to **Riverside**. Highlights include: **Saratoga National Fish Hatchery**, **Hobo Hot Pool**.
Directions: I-80 exit 235; S to Saratoga from MM 0

MM: 235.3 **GPS:** 41.74135/-106.83036 **Elev:** 6791 **Grid:** 60/81
US-30/287 *(see chapter)*   **Type:** Hwy Junction w/Chapter
93.8 mi highway that loops from **I-80** MM 235.3 at **Walcott**, northeast to **Medicine Bow**, then southeast back to **I-80** MM 313.2 at **Laramie**. At **I-80** in **Laramie** the highway transitions to **US-287 (Laramie to Colorado)** MM 400.9 and continues south to **Colorado**. This highway provides an alternate southern route to **Muddy Mountain**, **Casper Mountain**, and **Wy-220**, but otherwise only serves to access the attractions along the highway and is 16.0 mi longer than staying on **I-80**. Highlights include: **Hanna Cemetery**, **Hanna Memorial Park**, **Fossil Cabin Museum**.
Directions: I-80 exit 235; NE to Hannah from MM 235.2

MM: 267.2 **Dist:** 0.2 **GPS:** 41.63189/-106.28838 **Elev:** 7754 **Grid:** 68/84 **Land:** State
Wick Wildlife Habitat Management Area   **Type:** Wildlife Habitat Mgmt Area
A WHMA located southwest of the **Wagonhound Rest Area** that provides some primitive camping options. Just after the turnoff from CR-402 is a pullout with a **Wick/Beumee WHMA** sign. Just to the south is a primitive camping area in an open field. This area receives highway and rest area noise, including trucks that idle all night in the rest area. Continuing 0.3 mi west is a road that forks left and continues to 2 more primitive campgrounds. The first site at 2.7 mi (41.60922/-106.30989) is a small area in the long grass with no trees. The second site at 2.9 mi (41.60738-106.31322) is located in a small loop next to some cottonwoods.
Crowds: * **Directions:** I-80 exit 267; SW 0.2 mi on CR-402; W/R (before rest area) 0.3 mi; S 2.7 mi.
Notes: None of the camping is very desirable. The WHMA also extends to the north side of I-80.
Road Desc: Gravel, impassable when wet, narrow. The road to the last 2 campgrounds passes a marshy area with no room to pull off or turn around.
Campsites: Dispersed **Shade:** * **Privacy:** * **RV Size:** 20' **Other:** None

MM: 267.2 **Dist:** 0.3 **GPS:** 41.63102/-106.28580 **Elev:** 7754 **Grid:** 68/84
Wagonhound Rest Area   **Type:** Rest Area
Picnic shelters, pet walk area, and handicapped accessible facilities.
Directions: I-80 exit 267; SW 0.3 mi.

MM: 272.1   *GPS:* 41.60811/-106.20394   *Elev:* 7627   *Grid:* 69/85

Foote Creek Rim Wind Energy Project   *Type:* Point of Interest

Over 100 wind turbines are located on **Foote Creek Rim**, a treeless plateau between **Rawlins** and **Laramie**, which is one of the windiest places in the United States. The project began operation in 1999 and generates electricity for over 25,000 homes.

The wind farm can be viewed to the north from **I-80** from about MM 269 or by taking **Wy-13** north. Along **Wy-13** the wind turbines extend 12 mi northeast; however, the closest turbines are within the first 3 mi. If traveling west on **I-80**, an alternative route is to drive north 17.8 mi on **Wy-13** to **US-30/287** and head west past some attractions and back to **I-80** *(see US-30/287 MM 289)*.

Cool Rating: **   *Crowds:* *   *Directions:* I-80 exit 272;   Optionally N on Wy-13 (see description)

MM: 279.9   *Dist:* 5.4   *GPS:* 41.61190/-106.09454   *Elev:* 7358   *Grid:* 71/85   *Land:* State

Diamond Lake Public Access Area   *Type:* Public Access Area

Primitive camping on the west shore of **Diamond Lake**. *No trees. Vault toilet*

Crowds: *   *Road Desc:* Gravel, potholed

Directions: I-80 exit 279;   N on Cooper Cove Rd/CR-15 4.0 mi;   W/L 1.4 mi.

Campsites: Dispersed   *Shade:* *   *Privacy:* *   *RV Size:* 30'   *Other:* None

---

MM: 311.8   *GPS:* 41.30900/-105.61419   *Elev:* 7152   *Grid:* 78/92

Wy-230 (Laramie to Colorado) *(see chapter)*   *Type:* Hwy Junction w/Chapter

42.0 mi highway from the junction with **US-30/287** in **Laramie** southwest to **Colorado**. 4 fishing and camping lakes, including one large reservoir, are located along this route.

Directions: E to Laramie or SW to Colorado from MM 1.3.

MM: 311.8   *GPS:* 41.30892/-105.62925   *Elev:* 7172   *Grid:* 77/92

Wy-130 (Laramie to Wy-230) *(see chapter)*   *Type:* Hwy Junction w/Chapter

68.1 mi highway from **Laramie** west over **Snowy Range Pass** to **Wy-130/Wy-230 (Walcott to Riverside)** (8 mi south of **Saratoga**). Highlights include the many attractions along the 27 mi **Snowy Range Scenic Byway**.

Directions: I-80 exit 311;   W on Snowy Range Rd 0.8 mi;   N then W on Wy-130 from MM 0.

MM: 311.8   *Dist:* 0.3   *GPS:* 41.31076/-105.60988   *Elev:* 7144   *Grid:* 78/92   *Land:* State

Wyoming Territorial Prison State Historic Site   *Type:* Historic Site

From 1872-1902 this prison held some of the most notorious outlaws in the region, including **Butch Cassidy**. The prison was restored in 1989 but retained the original 6 x 8 ft furnished cells, each of which held 2 prisoners. A wooden stockade surrounds the prison and an adjacent broom factory where prisoners were forced to work. The tour of the prison is self-guided with interesting displays and biographies of 19 of the most notorious inmates. Other historic buildings around the prison include the restored **Warden's House** and **Horse Barn Exhibit Hall**, which features rotating displays. Other exhibits include: **Found During Restoration**; **Artifacts Uncovered**; **Warden and Lawman, Innocent or Guilty?**; **Women Inmates of the Wyoming Territorial Prison**; and the **Butch Cassidy exhibit**. To the west of the prison is a re-creation of a **Wyoming Frontier Town** as well as some historic buildings and picnic tables. An **RV dump** is located at the south end of the parking area with a donation requested.

Hours: 9am - 6pm (May-Nov)   *Cool Rating:* ***   *Crowds:* **   *Time:* 2 hrs   *[FEE AREA]*

Directions: I-80 exit 311;   E on Snowy Range Rd 0.3 mi;   W/L side of hwy.

MM: 311.8   *Dist:* 0.5   *GPS:* 41.31016/-105.60418   *Elev:* 7139   *Grid:* 78/92   *Land:* City

Optimist Park & Laramie River Greenbelt Trail   *Type:* Park

A city park with a picnic shelter and portable toilet. The park is a central point and parking area for access to the paved **Laramie River Greenbelt Trail**. Currently about 3.0 mi of the trail runs along the **Laramie River**. The trail system is a work in progress, but currently the total trail distance is 5.2 mi, including 0.9 mi along W Curtis St to the north. The trail for 1/2 mi south and 3/4 mi north of the park is considered a nature trail with wildlife viewing (primarily birds).

Directions: I-80 exit 311;   E on Snowy Range Rd 0.3 mi;   E/R on W Garfield St 0.2 mi;   S/R into parking area.

MM: 313.2   *GPS:* 41.29753/-105.59464   *Elev:* 7162   *Grid:* 78/93

Laramie   *Type:* Town

MM: 313.2   *GPS:* 41.29753/-105.59464   *Elev:* 7162   *Grid:* 78/93

US-287 (Laramie to Colorado) *(see chapter)*   *Type:* Hwy Junction w/Chapter

24.5 mi highway from **I-80** at **Laramie** southeast to **Colorado**. Highlights include: **Fort Sanders**.

Notes: US-287 actually ends 0.9 mi north of I-80 at E Grand Ave at MM 400.

Directions: I-80 exit 313;   S to Colorado from MM 400.9

MM: 313.2   *Dist:* 1.2   *GPS:* 41.29753/-105.59464   *Elev:* 7162   *Grid:* 78/93

US-30/287 *(see chapter)*   *Type:* Hwy Junction w/Chapter

93.8 mi highway that loops from **I-80** MM 313.2 at **Laramie**, northwest to **Medicine Bow**, then southwest back to **I-80** MM 235.3 at **Walcott**. At **I-80** in **Laramie** the highway transitions from **US-287 (Laramie to Colorado)** to **US-30/287** MM 329.4. This highway provides an alternate southern route to **Muddy Mountain**, **Casper Mountain**, and **Wy-220**, but otherwise only serves to access the attractions along the highway and is 16.0 mi longer than staying on **I-80**. Highlights include: **Fossil Cabin Museum, Hanna Cemetery, Hanna Memorial Park**.

Notes: US-30/287 actually ends 0.9 mi north of I-80 at E Grand Ave at MM 328.5.

Directions: I-80 exit 313;   NW to Medicine Bow from MM 329.4

MM: 323.1   *GPS:* 41.24005/-105.43791   *Elev:* 8643   *Grid:* 80/94

Wy-210/Happy Jack Rd *(see chapter)*   *Type:* Hwy Junction w/Chapter

37.3 mi highway from **I-80** exit 323, 10 mi southeast of **Laramie**, east to **I-25** exit 10 in **Cheyenne**. The primary use of this highway is access to the north entrance of **Curt Gowdy State Park**. 2 National Forest campgrounds are located a short distance north of **I-80**.

Nearest Town: Laramie 10 NW   *Directions:* I-80 exit 323;   E 0.1 mi;   N/L from MM 37.8

MM: 323.1 *Dist:* 0.2 *GPS:* 41.23902/-105.43495 *Elev:* 8685 *Grid:* 80/94 *Land:* State
Summit Rest Area & Abraham Lincoln Monument   *Type:* Rest Area/Visitor Center
A big and nice rest area at the highest point along I-80 with picnic shelters, pet walk area, and handicapped accessible facilities.
On the west side of the visitor center stands a 13 ft high bronze bust of **Abraham Lincoln** on a 42 ft pedestal. The old road
through this pass was known as the **Lincoln Highway**. Across from the **Lincoln** statue is a monument to **Henry B. Joy** who was
the first president of the **Lincoln Highway Association** and the president of Packard Motor Cars. Both monuments have been
relocated to this spot. Inside the visitor center are wildlife exhibits and historical displays, plus a viewing room overlooking I-80 with
views to the east, south, and west.
Hours: Visitor center: 9am - 7pm *Cool Rating:* *** *Crowds:* ***** *Time:* 30 min
Directions: I-80 exit 323; E on Happy Jack Rd 0.2 mi.

MM: 323.1 *Dist:* 0.6 *GPS:* 41.23577/-105.42934 *Elev:* 8665 *Grid:* 80/94 *Land:* State
Pole Mountain Trails   *Type:* Trailhead
Over 15 mi of well-maintained and well-marked single track trails through forest and meadows, plus many more miles of dirt roads.
3 fee-based parking areas access these trails: **Summit Trailhead** is 0.4 mi southeast of the **Summit Rest Area** on FR-705 and is
recommended for hikers. **Tie City Trailhead** and **Happy Jack Trailhead** are best for bicycles *(see Wy-210/Happy Jack Rd MM
36.8 and 35.7).* All of these trails have connecting trails so any trailhead can be used. A free option is to park at the rest area.
Maps are provided at the trailheads and at the **Summit Rest Area**. *Also see the map inset on page 11.*

A trail at the **Summit Trailhead** connects to 2 overlapping trails that can be combined to create several different loop options.
Head north/left from the parking area and follow the trail 0.4 mi to a fork in the trail.

The right fork is the **Headquarters Trail**, a National Recreation Trail through pine and aspen forest and open meadows. The trail
travels east traversing the south crest of **Pole Mountain** past an overlook at 1.4 mi (keep right at a trail junction at 1.3 mi) to
another overlook at 2.9 mi. A short distance past the overlook is a junction with the **Browns Landing Trail**, which returns to the
Summit Trail. The trail finishes by descending 480 ft in 0.6 mi to another parking area and trailhead on **FR-707**. *To first overlook:
Moderately easy; 1.4 mi one-way; 225 ft elev gain.* **To second overlook:** *Moderately easy; 2.9 mi one-way; 270 ft elev gain.* **Full
trail:** *Moderate; 3.5 mi one-way; 270 ft elev gain, 480 ft elev loss.*

The left fork is the **Summit Trail**, a wide cross-country ski trail that parallels the **Headquarters Trail** on the north crest of **Pole
Mountain** 1.5 mi before connecting with a 1.3 mi loop. Turning right at the loop 0.15 mi, or left 1.15 mi, intersects the
Headquarters Trail, which can be used as a 1.8 mi return route. *Summit Trail: Moderately easy; 4.3 mi round-trip; 290 ft elev
gain.* **Partial Summit Trail and Headquarters Trail return:** *Moderately easy; 3.7 mi round-trip; 270 ft elev gain.* **Summit Trail
and Headquarters Trail return:** *Moderately easy; 4.4 mi round-trip; 290 ft elev gain.*

The **Happy Jack Trails** and **Tie City Trails** are a maze of cross-country ski trails north of the **Summit Trail** and south of
Wy-210/Happy Jack Rd. The 2 longest trails are the 1.5 mi **Pole Creek Trail**, which is the northern part of the outer loop, and the
1.6 mi **Aspen Trail**, which is the southern part of the outer loop. A 0.6 mi trail completes the 3.7 mi outer loop. The 0.5 mi **Alder
Trail** and 0.0 mi **Middle Aspen Trail** together run west to east to bisect the outer loop. Another 2.2 mi of trails on the east side
create shorter internal loops.
Cool Rating: **** *Crowds:* ** *[FEE AREA]*
Directions: I-80 exit 323; **Tie City Trailhead and Happy Jack Trailhead**: E then N/L on Wy-210/Happy Jack Rd *(see
Wy-210/Happy Jack Rd).* **Summit Trailhead**: E then SE 0.6 mi to parking area.

MM: 323.1 *Dist:* 13.9 *GPS:* 41.18020/-105.23883 *Elev:* 7265 *Grid:* 83/95 *Land:* State
Curt Gowdy State Park   *Type:* State Park
A beautiful park with varied landscapes and 3 small reservoirs. **Granite Reservoir**, near the north entrance, is the largest of the
reservoirs with room for water sports and excellent rainbow trout and kokanee salmon fishing. The west end of the reservoir rises
to lightly forest hills and granite outcrops, which make for fun hiking and climbing as well as providing miles of novice to expert
mountain bike trails. **Crystal Reservoir**, near the south entrance, is situated amid rolling grassy hills with fishing for brown trout,
rainbow trout, and kokanee salmon. It is the smallest reservoir allowing only small boats with under 15 hp motors. **North Crow
Reservoir** is 5 mi northwest of the north entrance *(see section below).*

The campsites are spread out in 18+ separate areas around the lakes. The majority are around **Granite Reservoir** on the north
and south side with a couple farther from the lake to the west. The sites on the north are more exposed but have better boat ramp
access. The sites on the south have more shade. The dozen or so sites around **Crystal Reservoir** are on the west shore with
some trees for shade in several sites.

The camping areas include 35 reservable sites, 15 sites for larger RVs, and 7 tent-only sites. Drinking water is available at
Tumbleweeds, **Granite Point**, and at the north entrance. The **RV dump** is just past the north entrance.
Cool Rating: *** *Crowds:* **** *Nearest Town:* Laramie 24.6 W; Cheyenne 24.8 E *[FEE AREA]*
Directions: I-80 exit 323; NE on Wy-210/Happy Jack Rd 13.9 mi; S on Granite Springs Rd. 0.9 mi.
Campsites: 125 *Shade:* ** *Privacy:* * *RV Size:* 40'+ *Other:* 1-877-996-7275:wyoparks.state.wy.us/reservations,Water,RVDump

MM: 329.3 *Dist:* 1.9 *GPS:* 41.13113/-105.39780 *Elev:* 8285 *Grid:* 81/97 *Land:* State
Ames Monument   *Type:* Historic Site
In 1882, after much planning and great expense, the **Union Pacific Railroad** dedicated a specially designed 60 ft granite pyramid
to honor the **Ames Brothers**. These brothers, one the President of the **Union Pacific Railroad** and the other a Massachusetts
Congressman, were primarily responsible for financing the railway venture. The railway was built; however, use of unscrupulous
financial maneuvers turned out to be, at the time, the biggest scandal in United States history. The placement of the monument
was at the highest point on the transcontinental route. The tracks have since been relocated to the south.
Cool Rating: *** *Crowds:* * *Time:* 15 min *Road Desc:* Gravel, high clearance. Monument Rd is smooth, however the short road
to the monument is rocky and bumpy. Use the 2nd turnoff and be careful in low clearance vehicles.
Directions: I-80 exit 329; SW just past exit ramp; SE/L on Monument Rd/CR-234 1.9 mi to the second turnoff.

MM: 329.3 *GPS:* 41.15839/-105.40240 *Elev:* 8352 *Grid:* 81/96
FR-700/Vedauwoo Glen Rd *(see chapter)*   *Type:* Hwy Junction w/Chapter
7.3 mi forest road between **I-80** and **Wy-210/Happy Jack Rd** that passes the **Vedauwoo Recreation Area** (1.1 mi) and **Reynolds Hill Trailhead** (3.6 mi) and provides access to the north entrance of **Curt Gowdy State Park**. This area is very scenic and provides dispersed camping and other recreational opportunities amid sparse pine forest and granite outcroppings. Camping in this area is very popular, particularly on weekends. The closer to **Vedauwoo** the more crowded it gets. This is a very popular area for OHVs.
Directions: I-80 exit 329; E on Vedauwoo Rd/FR-700 7.3 mi to Wy-210/Happy Jack Rd.
Notes: If looking for a place to camp and you don't care about a lake, restrooms, and drinking water, this may be preferable to Curt Gowdy State Park.

MM: 335.1 *Dist:* 7.0 *GPS:* 41.15111/-105.19681 *Elev:* 7018 *Grid:* 84/96 *Land:* State
Curt Gowdy State Park - South Entrance   *Type:* State Park
This entrance enters near the south end of **Crystal Reservoir**. *See Curt Gowdy State Park - North Entrance at MM 323.1.*
[FEE AREA] *Directions:* I-80 exit 335; NE on Buford Rd/CR-30 6.9 mi; N/L 0.1 mi to entrance station.
Road Desc: First 2.5 mi is through sparse forest and rock formations on rough, deteriorated pavement and potholed gravel. The remainder is smooth gravel.

MM: 358.0 *GPS:* 41.11672/-104.88648 *Elev:* 6274 *Grid:* 88/97
Wy-210/Happy Jack Rd (westbound) *(see chapter)*   *Type:* Hwy Junction w/Chapter
If heading west on **I-80**, this provides easier and shorter access (saves 1.5 mi) to **Wy-210/Happy Jack Rd** than via **I-25**.
Directions: I-80 exit 357; N on Wy-222/Round Top Rd 1.0 mi; W on Wy-210/Happy Jack Rd from MM 3.0.

MM: 359.6 *GPS:* 41.11382/-104.85087 *Elev:* 6133 *Grid:* 89/97
I-25 *(see chapter)*   *Type:* Hwy Junction w/Chapter
300.1 mi interstate highway through east/central **Wyoming** from **Colorado** north to **I-90** (just past **Buffalo**), which continues northwest to **Montana**. Highlights include: **Pioneer Museum, Ayres Park and Natural Bridge, National Historic Trails Interpretive Center, Hole-in-the-Wall, Outlaw Cave, Indian Rock Art Cave**.
Directions: I-80 exit 359; N to Wheatland or S to Colorado.

MM: 362.0 *GPS:* 41.11897/-104.80494 *Elev:* 6083 *Grid:* 89/97
Cheyenne   *Type:* Town

MM: 401.5 *GPS:* 41.17670/-104.07580 *Elev:* 5057 *Grid:* 100/96
Pine Bluffs   *Type:* Town

MM: 401.5 *GPS:* 41.17501/-104.07570 *Elev:* 5110 *Grid:* 100/96
Pine Bluffs Rest Area   *Type:* Rest Area
A nice **Welcome Center** amid pine treed bluffs with picnic shelters, playground, pet walk area, and handicapped accessible facilities. A 1/4 mi walking path starts on the west side and leads around the south end of the bluff to a covered **University of Wyoming** archeological dig site called **Windows of the Past**, where the actual excavation can be observed from a viewing platform. On the north side of the rest area is a short interpretive loop trail. Another trail climbs 0.6 mi to the top of the west bluff where a couple more miles of trails lead to 3 observation areas and past several stone teepee rings. All of the trails start at the top of the stairs across from the visitor center. A free brochure with a trail map is available from the visitor center.
Hours: Windows of the Past: 9am - 5pm (summer) *Directions:* I-80 exit 401; S side of hwy.
Notes: One of the area wildlife species is the prairie rattlesnake, so be careful.

MM: 402.8 *Dist:* 1.7 *GPS:* 41.18228/-104.05382 *Elev:* 5045 *Grid:* 100/95
Our Lady of Peace Shrine   *Type:* Point of Interest
A 30 ft tall concrete sculpture of the **Virgin Mary**, which is the largest concrete sculpture in Wyoming and one of the largest in the United States. Located on the east end of **Pine Bluffs** just 160 yds northwest of **I-80**.
Directions: Continue NE on I-80 0.25 mi to Nebraska Exit 1; Take the exit 0.25 mi; NW 0.4 mi; SW on US-30 0.5 mi; S 0.25 mi.

MM: 402.8 *GPS:* 41.18080/-104.05335 *Elev:* 5053 *Grid:* 100/95
End of Highway - Nebraska State Line   *Type:* Highway End
403 mi interstate highway through southern **Wyoming** from **Nebraska** west to **Utah**. Highlights include: **Vedauwoo Recreation Area, Ames Monument, Curt Gowdy State Park, Pole Mountain Trails, Abraham Lincoln Monument, Wyoming Territorial Prison State Historic Site, Fort Fred Steele, Wyoming Frontier Prison, Point of Rocks Stagecoach Station, Reliance Tipple, Pilot Butte Wild Horse Tour, Western Wyoming Natural History Museum, Flaming Gorge National Recreation Area, Expedition Island, Church Butte, Fort Bridger State Historic Site, Piedmont Charcoal Kilns, Fossil Butte National Monument, Bear River State Park**.
Nearest Town: Pine Bluffs 1.3 W *Directions:* W from the Nebraska state line from MM 402.8

MM: 0.0 *GPS:* 45.00004/-107.29837 *Elev:* 4297 *Grid:* 54/0
I-90   *Type:* Highway Description
208.8 mi interstate highway that heads southeast from **Montana** to **South Dakota** across northeastern **Wyoming**. The highway heads south 56 mi to a transition with **I-25**, which continues south, and then turns east 150 mi. Highlights include: **Fort Phil Kearny** and related historic sites, **Dry Creek Petrified Tree Environmental Education Area**, **Eagle Butte Coal Mine**, **Devils Tower National Monument**, **Vore Buffalo Jump**.
Nearest Town: Ranchester 10.5 S *Directions:* SE from the Montana state line from MM 0
Notes: It is 2.5 mi between MM 14 and MM 15.

MM: 0.0 *GPS:* 45.00004/-107.29837 *Elev:* 4297 *Grid:* 54/0
Montana State Line   *Type:* State Line
Nearest Town: Ranchester 10.5 S

MM: 9.9 *GPS:* 44.90885/-107.16341 *Elev:* 3762 *Grid:* 56/2
Ranchester   *Type:* Town

MM: 9.9 *GPS:* 44.91575/-107.15160 *Elev:* 3847 *Grid:* 56/2
US-14 *(see chapter)*   *Type:* Hwy Junction w/Chapter
80.5 mi highway from **Ranchester** southwest to **Greybull**. A large portion of the highway is through National Forest along the **Bighorn Scenic Byway** with 10 public campgrounds. Highlights include: **Tongue River Canyon**, **Dayton Bell Tower**, **Shell Falls**, **Red Gulch Dinosaur Tracksite**, **Medicine Lodge State Archaeological Site**, **Devil's Kitchen Geological Site**.
Directions: I-90 exit 9; SW to Dayton from MM 89.8

MM: 9.9 *Dist:* 1.4 *GPS:* 44.90445/-107.16342 *Elev:* 3760 *Grid:* 56/2 *Land:* State
Connor Battlefield State Park and Historic Site   *Type:* State Park
A grassy park on the south-central side of **Ranchester**, which is situated inside a large bend in the **Tongue River**. The park is located at the site of an attack of 200 troops on **Chief Black Bear's Arapaho Indian** village in 1865. The attack was led by **General Patrick E. Connor** who led part of the **Powder River Expedition** into this area as part of a broad military program to protect the **Bozeman Trail**, as well as other trails into the **Montana** mining fields, from the **Plains Indians**. A monument and interpretive sign commemorate this battle.

The park provides camping that accommodates large RVs. Large cottonwoods shade the park, although the sites on the east end are in the open. *3 pull-thrus.*
Cool Rating: * *Crowds:* ** *[FEE AREA]* *Notes:* A train goes by every hour blowing the horn several times.
Directions: I-90 exit 9; SW on US-14 0.8 mi; S/L on Gillette St 0.4 mi; E/L 0.2 mi.
Campsites: 20 *Shade:* **** *Privacy:* ** *RV Size:* 40'+ *Other:* Water

MM: 23.2 *GPS:* 44.80681/-106.95586 *Elev:* 3750 *Grid:* 59/5
Sheridan   *Type:* Town

MM: 23.2 *Dist:* 0.2 *GPS:* 44.80540/-106.93236 *Elev:* 3895 *Grid:* 59/5
Sheridan Visitor Center and Rest Area   *Type:* Rest Area/Visitor Center
Welcome Center with picnic shelters, playground, pet walk area, **RV dump**, and handicapped accessible facilities.
Directions: I-90 exit 23; E 0.2 mi; N side of hwy.

MM: 23.2 *Dist:* 1.8 *GPS:* 44.80197/-106.96580 *Elev:* 3843 *Grid:* 58/5 *Land:* State
Trail End State Historic Site   *Type:* Historic Site
A 13,748 sq ft mansion that was completed in 1913 and is the only known example of **Flemish Revival Architecture** in **Wyoming**. The mansion was built by the highly successful cattle rancher **John B. Kendrick**, who was elected **Governor** of **Wyoming** in 1914 and a **U.S. Senator** 2 years later. After his entry into politics, **Trail End** was used as a summer home until his death in 1933. His wife Eula lived at **Trail End** until her death in 1961. The house stood empty for 7 years until it was purchased for historical preservation in 1968. Exhibits and displays throughout the home utilize primarily original artifacts and provide information on daily life, entertainment, interior design, changing technology, and early twentieth century ranching on the northern plains. The mansion sits on 3.8 acres of beautifully groomed grounds.
Hours: 1pm - 4pm (Mar 1 - May 31); 10am - 5pm (Memorial Day and Labor Day Weekends); 9am - 6pm (June 1 - Aug 31); 1pm - 4pm (Sept 1 - Dec 14); closed (Dec 15 - Feb 28) *Cool Rating:* ** *Crowds:* * *Time:* 1-2 hrs *[FEE AREA]*
Directions: I-90 exit 23; W on E 5th St/Wy-336 1.4 mi; S/L on Clarendon Ave 0.4 mi (5 blocks). Park on Victoria St on the N side of the grounds (*400 Clarendon Avenue, Sheridan*) *If coming through town northbound on Main St;* Turn E/L on W 5th St 0.5 mi and follow directions above from Clarendon Ave.

MM: 33.6 *GPS:* 44.66553/-106.87981 *Elev:* 4281 *Grid:* 60/8
Wy-193/US-87 (southbound) *(see chapter)*   *Type:* Hwy Junction w/Chapter
14.0 mi side trip from **I-90** MM 33.6 south back to **I-90** MM 44.7. After 6.1 mi **US-87** MM 38.9 transitions to **Wy-193** MM 106.2 (the mile markers change direction) and continues 7.9 mi to **I-90** exit 44. Highlights include: **Wyoming State Bird Farm**, **Story Fish Hatchery**, **Wagon Box Fight Historic Site**, **Fort Phil Kearny**, **Fetterman Massacre Monument and Battlefield**.
Nearest Town: Sheridan 8.2 N
Directions: I-90 exit 33; W on Meade Creek Rd/Wy-343 1.1 mi; S on US-87 from MM 34.

MM: 44.7 *GPS:* 44.51933/-106.80052 *Elev:* 4700 *Grid:* 61/12
Wy-193/US-87 (northbound) *(see chapter)*   *Type:* Hwy Junction w/Chapter
14.0 mi side trip from **I-90** MM 44.7 north back to **I-90** MM 33.6. After 7.9 mi **Wy-193** MM 106.2 transitions to **US-87** MM 38.9 and continues 5.0 mi to MM 34.0 (the mile markers change direction), which returns 1.1 mi to **I-90** exit 33. Continuing north on **US-87** leads 12.8 mi to **Sheridan** and back to **I-90** exit 20. Highlights include: **Fetterman Massacre Monument and Battlefield**, **Fort Phil Kearny**, **Wagon Box Fight Historic Site**, **Story Fish Hatchery**, **Wyoming State Bird Farm**.
Nearest Town: Buffalo 13 S; Sheridan 21.2 N *Directions:* I-90 exit 44; NW on Piney Creek Rd from MM 0

MM: 47.7 *Dist:* 1.3 *GPS:* 44.47768/-106.77182 *Elev:* 4750 *Grid:* 61/13 *Land:* County
Father DeSmet Monument   *Type:* Historical Marker
A stone monument dedicated to Belgian Jesuit missionary **Father Pierre Jeane DeSmet**. He maintained friendships with both the Indians and whites, and therefore was trusted with peacemaking roles at **Fort Laramie**. The monument is located on the west side of **Lake DeSmet**.
Cool Rating: * *Crowds:* * *Time:* 5 min
Directions: I-90 exit 47; E on CR-262/Shell Creek Rd 1.3 mi to the intersection with Monument Rd. *Optionally;* Continue SE on Monument Rd 2.4 mi to the turnoff to Lake DeSmet Recreation Area and another 0.8 mi back to I-90 southbound. This road is paved, but in very bad shape.

MM: 51.4 *Dist:* 1.5 *GPS:* 44.45100/-106.74452 *Elev:* 4666 *Grid:* 62/14 *Land:* County
Lake DeSmet Recreation Area   *Type:* Recreation Area
Lake DeSmet is a deep natural lake that was formed when coal burned underground leading to a collapse that filled with water. The lake is known for its fishing, boating, and swimming.

Upon entering the recreation area, 2 roads to the left access the primary camping areas. The first road leads to a large camping area with 19 sites in grassy areas separated by shrubs and trees. The sites are not level with the west side of the loop being worse than the east side. The second road is about 100 ft past the entrance and leads to a smaller camping area with 9 sites separated by taller shrubs and trees. Heading either direction follows a loop road that overlooks the lake and leads to additional scattered campsites. A boat ramp is located 0.1 mi southeast of the smaller campground.

Additional dispersed camping is located across the bay from the boat ramp, and can be accessed by continuing east 0.4 mi on **Lake DeSmet Rd**.
Crowds: ** *[FEE AREA]*
Directions: I-90 exit 51; NE a short distance then continue NW/L on Monument Rd 0.6 mi; E/R on Lake Desmet Rd 0.6 mi; L/NE on Mikesell-Potts Rd 0.3 mi. *From the turnoff to Lake DeSmet Rd;* Continuing NW on Monument Rd 2.4 mi leads to the Father DeSmet Monument *(see previous section)*. This road is paved, but in very bad shape.
Campsites: 28 *Shade:* * *Privacy:* *** *RV Size:* 40'+ *Other:* Water

MM: 56.4 *Dist:* 1.5 *GPS:* 44.35426/-106.69906 *Elev:* 4641 *Grid:* 62/16
Buffalo (eastbound)   *Type:* Town
Directions: I-90 exit 56; S on Wy-196 1.5 mi.

MM: 56.8 *GPS:* 44.36724/-106.68928 *Elev:* 4660 *Grid:* 62/16
I-25 *(see chapter)*   *Type:* Hwy Junction w/Chapter
300 mi interstate highway through east/central **Wyoming** from **I-90** south to **Colorado**. Highlights include: **Outlaw Cave**, **Indian Rock Art Cave**, **Hole-in-the-Wall**, **National Historic Trails Interpretive Center**, **Ayres Park and Natural Bridge**, **Pioneer Museum**.
Nearest Town: Buffalo 1.3 S *Directions:* I-90 exit 56B; S to Casper from MM 300.2

MM: 58.7 *GPS:* 44.35838/-106.65782 *Elev:* 4523 *Grid:* 63/16
US-16 *(see chapter)*   *Type:* Hwy Junction w/Chapter
89.9 mi highway from **Buffalo** southwest to **Worland**. Along this highway is the scenic 45 mi **Cloud Peak Skyway**, which travels through the **Bighorn Mountains** and provides many campgrounds, forest roads with dispersed camping, and recreational opportunities. Highlights include: **Crazy Woman Canyon**, **High Park Lookout**, **Tensleep Canyon**, **West Tensleep Falls**, **Ten Sleep Fish Hatchery**, **Wigwam Rearing Station**, **Medicine Lodge State Archaeological Site**, **Castle Gardens**.
Directions: I-90 exit 58; W on E Hart St 2.5 mi; S/L on N Main St 0.4 mi; W/R to Ten Sleep from MM 92.1

MM: 58.7 *Dist:* 2.0 *GPS:* 44.35426/-106.69906 *Elev:* 4641 *Grid:* 62/16
Buffalo (westbound)   *Type:* Town
Directions: I-90 exit 58; SW on US-16 2.0 mi.

MM: 66.0 *Dist:* 6.4 *GPS:* 44.35028/-106.52859 *Elev:* 4517 *Grid:* 65/16 *Land:* BLM
Dry Creek Petrified Tree Environmental Education Area   *Type:* Natural Feature
An easy 3/4 mi counterclockwise loop through 60 million year old petrified metasequoia trees that originally grew in a swamp environment. The trail leads to 8 stations with interpretive signs explaining the geology, history, and the surrounding environment. The petrified trees consist of a few stumps, several broken up trunks, and 1 large intact trunk at station 8, which was excavated to show greater detail. The loop parking area provides a well maintained vault toilet and picnic table with no shade. No signs prevent camping in the parking area.
Cool Rating: *** *Crowds:* * *Time:* 1 hr
Notes: Because of lack of use the path is overgrown with high grass in spots and is somewhat difficult to follow. The area has no shade so a morning or evening visit is preferable.
Road Desc: First 5.8 mi is paved but bumpy with a lot of patched road damage. Last 0.6 mi is gravel.
Directions: I-90 exit 65; E then N on Tipperary Rd 5.8 mi; W/L 0.6 mi.

MM: 88.7 *Dist:* 0.1 *GPS:* 44.21360/-106.15859 *Elev:* 3957 *Grid:* 70/20
Powder River Rest Area   *Type:* Rest Area
A nice grassed rest area with picnic shelters, pet walk area, and handicapped accessible facilities. Located on the east side is an open circular picnic area with 7 tables that get partial day shade, and a sign about energy production in the **Powder River Basin**.
Directions: I-90 exit 88; N 0.1 mi.

MM: 124.3 *Dist:* 4.7 *GPS:* 44.36057/-105.52711 *GPS2:* 44.38721/-105.51655 *Elev:* 4340 *Grid:* 79/16
Eagle Butte Coal Mine   *Type:* Point of Interest
A pullout above the **Eagle Butte Coal Mine** with displays of a huge dump truck tire and excavation shovel. An elevated platform allows views from above the fence; however, the actual coal excavation is 3/4 mi away and cannot be seen from here. If time permits it is recommended to take the free guided tour for an up close look at the mine operations *(see section below on the Eagle Butte Coal Mine Tour at MM 126.4)*.
Cool Rating: ** *Crowds:* * *Time:* 15 min
Directions: I-90 exit 124; NE on Skyline Dr 0.2 mi; N on US-14/16 4.5 mi; E side of hwy.

MM: 126.4   *GPS:* 44.27952/-105.49408   *Elev:* 4540   *Grid:* 79/18
Gillette   *Type:* Town

MM: 126.4   *Dist:* 0.1   *GPS:* 44.27783/-105.49486   *Elev:* 4540   *Grid:* 79/18
Gillette Visitor Center   *Type:* Visitor Center
A small visitor center that is the start the **Eagle Butte Coal Mine** tour. *See next section.*
Directions: I-90 exit 126; S on S Douglas Hwy 0.05 mi; N end of Flying J parking lot on W side of hwy.

MM: 126.4   *Dist:* 0.1   *GPS:* 44.27783/-105.49486   *Elev:* 4540   *Grid:* 79/18
Eagle Butte Coal Mine Tour   *Type:* Point of Interest
An interesting guided tour of the **Eagle Butte Coal Mine**, which is provided free by **Foundation Coal West, Inc**. The tours offer the chance to see a working open pit coal mine up close, including haul trucks dumping coal into the hoppers and trains getting loaded with coal to be distributed across the nation. The entire process creates a "moving hole" as the newly dug dirt fills in the previous hole after the coal is extracted. At a later time the land is reclaimed with native grasses, plants, and trees.

Wyoming is the leading coal producer in the nation producing 40% of the nation's coal and providing fuel for over 15 percent of the nation's electrical energy. The coal seam being mined is 120 ft thick and buried under 250 ft of dirt. The coal seam contains trillions of tons of coal; however, most is too deep to be economically mined. The first coal was shipped from this mine in 1978. The coal in the **Powder River Basin** area is low in sulfur and is used in power plants in approximately 36 states.
Hours: Tours: 9am and 11am, Mon-Fri (June - Aug); Overflow tour: 2pm   *Phone:* 1-800-544-6136; 307-686-0040
Cool Rating: ****   *Crowds:* *****   *Time:* 2 hrs
Notes: This is a popular tour and fills up fast. Tour reservations are on a first come, first served basis so it is best to call several days ahead. An overflow tour is sometimes run at 2 pm.
Directions: I-90 exit 126; S on S Douglas Hwy 0.05 mi; N end of Flying J parking lot on W side of hwy.

MM: 153.4   *Dist:* 0.3   *GPS:* 44.27557/-104.97416   *Elev:* 4154   *Grid:* 87/18
Moorcroft Rest Area   *Type:* Rest Area
A large grassed rest area that looks more like a park with picnic shelters, playground, pet walk area, and handicapped accessible facilities. Large cottonwood trees provide shade, even in some sections of the parking area.
Directions: I-90 exit 153; Just NE of ramps; W/L 0.3 mi.

MM: 154.7   *GPS:* 44.26352/-104.95033   *Elev:* 4225   *Grid:* 87/18
Moorcroft   *Type:* Town

MM: 154.7   *GPS:* 44.26352/-104.95033   *Elev:* 4225   *Grid:* 87/18
US-14 (east) *(see chapter)*   *Type:* Hwy Junction w/Chapter
44.8 mi section of **US-14** from **I-90** MM 154.6 at **Moorcroft** that loops north and east back to **I-90** MM 185.7 at **Sundance**. The primary function of this highway is access to **Wy-24** and **Devils Tower National Monument**. The highway also provides access to **Keyhole State Park**.
Notes: US-14 doesn't actually end at I-90 heading east, however the rest of the highway from there simply parallels I-90 through Sundance, 1.7 mi east.
Directions: I-90 exit 154; S 0.2 mi; W/R on E Converse St 0.2 mi; N/R on US-14/N Yellowstone Ave from MM 154.6.

MM: 165.7   *Dist:* 5.6   *GPS:* 44.28134/-104.72477   *Elev:* 4303   *Grid:* 90/18
Keyhole State Park via CR-205/CR-180 *(see chapter)*   *Type:* Hwy Junction w/Chapter
A State Park centered around **Keyhole Reservoir** on the western edge of the **Black Hills**. The park offers fishing, water sports, camping, picnicking, hiking, and birdwatching. Wildlife includes pronghorn and deer plus over 200 species of birds, including bald eagles, ospreys, white pelicans, and wild turkeys. 2 roads provide access to the park with the primary recreation area located on the east side straight north from **I-90**. This area contains the **Keyhole Marina**, **Keyhole Motel**, park headquarters, and 8 campgrounds. The other access is to the west between the 2 main bodies of water near the town of **Pine Haven**. This area has 2 less developed campgrounds, both with boat ramps. The park is located on the grassy plains but has stands of conifer trees in most of the camping and day use areas on the east side. The park can be accessed from **I-90** or **US-14 (east)**.
Nearest Town: Moorcroft 11 W
Directions: I-90 exit 165; N on Pine Ridge Rd/CR-205 5.1 mi; Continue 0.5 mi on McKean Rd/CR-180.

MM: 185.7   *GPS:* 44.39208/-104.39800   *Elev:* 4880   *Grid:* 95/15
US-14 (east) *(see chapter)*   *Type:* Hwy Junction w/Chapter
44.8 mi section of **US-14** from **I-90** MM 185.7 at **Sundance** that loops north and west back to **I-90** MM 154.6 at **Moorcroft**. The primary function of this highway is access to **Wy-24** and **Devils Tower National Monument**. The highway also provides access to the **Warren Peak Lookout** and **Cook Lake Recreation Area**.
Directions: I-90 exit 185; E to Sundance or W to Devils Tower from MM 200.5
Notes: US-14 doesn't actually end at I-90 heading east, however the rest of the highway from there simply parallels I-90 through Sundance, 1.7 mi east.

MM: 185.7   *GPS:* 44.39465/-104.41742   *Elev:* 4960   *Grid:* 95/15
Cook Lake Recreation Area and Scenic Drive *(see chapter)*   *Type:* Hwy Junction w/Chapter
Access to the **Cook Lake Recreation Area** along a 26.3 mi scenic drive through the **Bear Lodge Mountains** and **Black Hills National Forest** from **US-14 (east)** MM 199.5 (1.0 mi west of **I-90**) north to **Wy-24** MM 30.3. The **Warren Peak Lookout** is at the highest elevation of the drive. Dispersed camping along **FR-838**, **FR-843**, and **FR-830**.
Nearest Town: Sundance 2.6 NE
Directions: I-90 exit 185; W on US-14 0.9 mi; N on CR-100/Warren Peak Rd from MM 0.

MM: 185.7   *Dist:* 3.5   *GPS:* 44.42755/-104.42393   *Elev:* 5470   *Grid:* 95/14   *Land:* NF
Reuter Campground   *Type:* Campground
A nice campground on the south end of the **Bear Lodge Mountains** just inside the National Forest boundary. *Conifer forest. Little understory. Spacious sites. Level.*
Crowds: *   *Nearest Town:* Sundance 5.1 SE   *[FEE AREA]*
Directions: W on US-14 1.0 mi; N/R on CR-100/Warren Peak Rd 2.5 mi; S side of road.
Campsites: 24   *Shade:* ****   *Privacy:* **   *RV Size:* 30'   *Other:* 1-877-444-6777:www.recreation.gov,Water

MM: 187.5 **Dist:** 0.6 **GPS:** 44.40639/-104.37501 **Elev:** 4735 **Grid:** 95/15
Sundance   **Type:** Town
Directions: I-90 exit 187; NW 0.6 mi.

MM: 189.0 **GPS:** 44.41417/-104.34112 **Elev:** 4602 **Grid:** 96/15
Sundance Rest Area   **Type:** Rest Area/Visitor Center
Welcome Center with picnic shelters, pet walk area, **RV dump**, and handicapped accessible facilities.
Directions: I-90 exit 189; SE side of hwy.

MM: 189.0 **Dist:** 2.5 **GPS:** 44.44286/-104.34734 **Elev:** 4811 **Grid:** 96/14 **Land:** NF
Sundance Campground   **Type:** Campground
The campground is located at the base of the **Bear Lodge Mountains** and is primarily a horse camp and trailhead for the
Sundance Trail System. The campground includes 7 sites for tents and short RVs, plus 3 sites for large RVs. Large RVs can also
use the tent sites by parking on the road in front of the site. *No trees.*
Crowds: * *[FEE AREA]*
Directions: I-90 exit 189; Just N to US-14/Cleveland St; W/L 0.4 mi; N/R on CR-123/Government Valley Rd 2.1 mi.
Campsites: 10 **Shade:** * **Privacy:** * **RV Size:** 40'+ **Other:** 1-877-444-6777;www.recreation.gov,Water

MM: 199.3 **Dist:** 2.8 **GPS:** 44.53612/-104.15736 **Elev:** 3862 **Grid:** 98/12
Vore Buffalo Jump (eastbound)   **Type:** Historic Site
The **Vore** site is a natural sinkhole that was used as a bison trap from around 1500 to 1800 A.D. This is one of the most important
archaeological sites of the late-prehistoric **Plains Indians**. Bison were driven over the edge of the sink hole as a method for the
Native American tribes to procure the large quantities of meat and hides needed to survive the harsh prairie winters. The site
features enormous quantities of bone and stone artifacts, which are perfectly preserved in discrete, precisely datable layers, held in
place within a natural bowl. This site was discovered during the construction of **I-90** in the early 1970s and is currently under
development by the **Vore Buffalo Jump Foundation**. Visitors can walk around the edge of the sinkhole where interpretive signs
explain the site. *Donations are welcome.*
Cool Rating: *** **Crowds:** * **Time:** 30 min **Directions:** I-90 exit 199; Just north to Old Hwy-14; E 2.8 mi.

MM: 199.3 **Dist:** 15.5 **GPS:** 44.57994/-104.19338 **Elev:** 3787 **Grid:** 98/11
Cook Lake Recreation Area (eastbound)   **Type:** Recreation Area
Alternate access to the **Cook Lake Recreation Area** that saves 16.1 mi over the route from MM 185.7. *See Cook Lake Recreation
Area and Scenic Drive MM 18.0/8.3.*
Cool Rating: *** **Crowds:** ***** *[FEE AREA]*
Directions: I-90 exit 199; N on Wy-111 4.1 mi; W/L on CR-144/Farrall Rd/FR-843 10.3 mi; N on FR-842 1.1 mi.

MM: 205.9 **GPS:** 44.54195/-104.08103 **GPS2:** 44.34434/-104.20043 **Elev:** 3584 **Grid:** 100/11 **Land:** NF
Sand Creek Canyon Scenic Drive   **Type:** Scenic Drive
A 54.6 mi drive between **I-90** and **US-85** through **Sand Creek Canyon**, also referred to as **Grand Canyon**. The red-walled canyon
is not magnificent, but the drive is nice if already heading this way and time permits. The road travels through the bottom of the
canyon climbing 2,300 ft from **I-90** to **US-85**.

Sand Creek Campground is 1.9 mi south on **Sand Creek Rd/FR-863** *(see next section)*.
Cool Rating: ** **Crowds:** * **Time:** 2 hrs **Road Desc:** Partially paved, narrow. Wy-585 is paved and the rest is gravel.
Directions: I-90 exit 205; S on Sand Creek Rd/FR-863/Grand Canyon Rd 23.3 mi; N on Moskee Rd 2.0 mi; W on Berglund
Rd/FR-872/Reynolds Rd 1.9 mi; W on Clark Rd/CR-247 5.0 mi; SE on Wy-585 22.4 mi.

MM: 205.9 **Dist:** 1.9 **GPS:** 44.51581/-104.08247 **Elev:** 3627 **Grid:** 100/12 **Land:** Wyoming G & F
Sand Creek Campground   **Type:** Campground
Primitive camping in 4 designated areas along **Sand Creek** 1.9-2.9 mi from **I-90**. **Sand Creek** is a blue ribbon trout stream. The
campgrounds tend to fill to capacity on holidays.
Crowds: **** **Directions:** I-90 exit 205; S on Sand Creek Rd/FR-863 1.9 mi; W side of road.
Campsites: Dispersed **Shade:** * **Privacy:** ** **RV Size:** 30' **Other:** None

MM: 205.9 **Dist:** 3.9
Vore Buffalo Jump (westbound)   **Type:** Historic Site
See MM 199.3.
Cool Rating: *** **Crowds:** * **Directions:** I-90 exit 205; Just north to Old Hwy-14; W 3.9 mi.

MM: 207.1 **GPS:** 44.54254/-104.05667 **Elev:** 3550 **Grid:** 100/11
End of Highway - South Dakota State Line   **Type:** Highway End
208.8 mi interstate highway that heads west from **South Dakota** across northeastern **Wyoming** then northwest to **Montana**.
Highlights include: **Vore Buffalo Jump**, **Devils Tower National Monument**, **Eagle Butte Coal Mine**, **Dry Creek Petrified Tree
Environmental Education Area**, **Fort Phil Kearny** and related historic sites.
Nearest Town: Sundance 19.6 W **Directions:** W from the South Dakota state line from MM 207.1

Jenny Lake Loop Rd: Grand Teton National Park | Loop

MM: 0.0 *GPS:* 43.79020/-110.70211 *Elev:* 6968 *Grid:* 5/30 *Land:* NPS
Jenny Lake Loop Rd: Grand Teton National Park   *Type:* Highway Description
A 4.0 mi loop road in **Grand Teton National Park** starting at **Teton Park Rd** MM 10.8/10.0. The first 1.5 mi is 2-way providing access to the **String Lake** area, which includes hiking trails, a picnic area, and a swimming/floating area. The last 2.5 mi is one-way passing an interpretive overlook of **Jenny Lake** and returning to **Teton Park Rd** MM 8.5/12.3. Highlights include: **String Lake**, **Leigh Lake**, **Jenny Lake**.
Directions: NW on Jenny Lake Loop Rd 1.5 mi; Continue straight on one-way loop road 2.5 mi.
Notes: The one-way section is paved and narrow and mostly in the trees with no views.

MM: 0.8 *GPS:* 43.78979/-110.71369 *Elev:* 6933 *Grid:* 5/30 *Land:* NPS
Cathedral Group Turnout   *Type:* Scenic Viewpoint
Interpretive signs and a unique view of the **Cathedral Group**, which is comprised of **Grand Teton**, **Teewinot Mountain**, and **Mount Owen**.
Cool Rating: **** *Crowds:* ** *Time:* 10 min *Directions:* NW side of road.

MM: 1.5 *GPS:* 43.78486/-110.72779 *Elev:* 6884 *Grid:* 5/30 *Land:* NPS
String Lake Trail   *Type:* Hiking Trail
See next section on String Lake for a description of the lake. A loop trail that circles **String Lake** crossing the outlet and inlet streams on footbridges. On the west side of the lake the trail diverges from the lake and climbs 200 ft up the base of **Rockchuck Peak** providing overlooks of the lake. This loop trail intersects several other trails so keep right at all trail junctions to stay on the loop. *Moderately easy; 3.6 mi loop; 200 ft elev gain.*

The **Jenny Lake Loop Trail** can also be started from this trailhead. *See earlier section on Jenny Lake and Trails.*
Cool Rating: **** *Crowds:* ** *Time:* 2 hrs *Directions:* NW/R 70 yds; SW side of road.

MM: 1.5 *Dist:* 0.3 *GPS:* 43.78727/-110.72969 *Elev:* 6884 *Grid:* 5/30 *Land:* NPS
String Lake   *Type:* Lake
A long, narrow, shallow and warm lake at the base of the middle **Teton Range**. The north end of the lake begins at the outflow of **Leigh Lake** and the south end flows into **Jenny Lake** via a 1/2 mi long creek. On the northwest side of the lake is a small wetland area, which is prime moose habitat. The lake is popular for canoeing, kayaking, and floating, with a swimming area on the east shore near the picnic area. A canoe launch is located just before the parking area.
Cool Rating: *** *Crowds:* **** *Directions:* NW/R to parking area at end of road 0.3 mi.

MM: 1.5 *Dist:* 0.3 *GPS:* 43.78843/-110.73088 *Elev:* 6884 *Grid:* 5/30 *Land:* NPS
String Lake Picnic Area   *Type:* Picnic Area
A large, nice and shady picnic area with tables on the north and west end of the parking area. *Flush and vault toilets. Drinking water.*
Directions: NW/R to parking area at end of road 0.3 mi.

MM: 1.5 *Dist:* 0.3 *GPS:* 43.78843/-110.73088 *Elev:* 6884 *Grid:* 5/30 *Land:* NPS
Leigh Lake Trail   *Type:* Hiking Trail
A smooth trail along the east shores of **String Lake** and **Leigh Lake**. The trail heads northeast 0.8 mi along the east shore of **String Lake** to the junction with the **String Lake Trail**. A short distance farther is a junction to either the **Leigh Lake** portage or the east shore beach and **Bearpaw Lake**. Take the left fork 0.1 mi north to the south tip of **Leigh Lake**. Taking the fork to the right continues 1.4 mi to the sandy beach on the east shore of **Leigh Lake** and 2.8 mi to **Bearpaw Lake**. *Easy; Leigh Lake south shore: 0.9 mi; Leigh Lake east shore beach: 2.2 mi; Bearpaw Lake: 3.7 mi; Level.*
Cool Rating: **** *Crowds:* *** *Time:* 45 min-3 hrs
Directions: NW/R to parking area at end of road 0.3 mi; A paved path on the north end of the parking area leads 100 yds to the trailhead.

MM: 3.0 *GPS:* 43.76771/-110.71748 *Elev:* 6837 *Grid:* 5/31 *Land:* NPS
Jenny Lake Overlook   *Type:* Scenic Viewpoint
Interpretive overlook on the east shore of **Jenny Lake**, which is situated directly below the highest peaks of the **Teton Range**. The overlook provides excellent photo opportunities as well as access to the lakeshore where the **Jenny Lake Loop Trail** passes by. *See section on Jenny Lake and Trails in chapter: Teton Park Rd MM 7.9/12.9.*
Cool Rating: **** *Crowds:* ***** *Time:* 30 min *Directions:* W side of road.
Road Desc: The one-way section is paved and narrow and most is in the trees with no views.

MM: 4.0 *GPS:* 43.76073/-110.71180 *Elev:* 6834 *Grid:* 5/31 *Land:* NPS
End of Highway   *Type:* Highway End

Keyhole State Park via CR-205/CR-180   S/N

MM: 0.0/7.0 *GPS:* 44.28134/-104.72477 *Elev:* 4303 *Grid:* 90/18
Keyhole State Park via CR-205/CR-180   *Type:* Highway Description
A State Park centered around **Keyhole Reservoir** on the western edge of the **Black Hills**. The park offers fishing, water sports, camping, picnicking, hiking, and birdwatching. Wildlife includes pronghorn and deer plus over 200 species of birds, including bald eagles, ospreys, white pelicans, and wild turkeys. 2 roads provide access to the park with the primary recreation area located on the east side straight north from **I-90**. This area contains the **Keyhole Marina**, **Keyhole Motel**, park headquarters, and 8 campgrounds. The other access is to the west between the 2 main bodies of water near the town of **Pine Haven**. This area has 2 less developed campgrounds, both with boat ramps. The park is located on the grassy plains but has stands of conifer trees in most of the camping and day use areas on the east side. The park can be accessed from **I-90** or **US-14 (east)**.
Nearest Town: Moorcroft 11 W
Directions: I-90 exit 165; N on Pine Ridge Rd/CR-205 5.1 mi; Continue 0.5 mi on McKean Rd/CR-180.

MM: 3.6/3.4 *Dist:* 7.0 *GPS:* 44.36547/-104.80020 *Elev:* 4150 *Grid:* 89/16 *Land:* State
Coulter Bay Campground   *Type:* Campground
One of the 2 campgrounds at the west access near Pine Haven. This area contains a combination of gently rolling grassland and rocky bluffs overlooking the lake and is best suited for tents. The first area on the west side has 3 reservable sites that can be used by anybody if they are not reserved. The second area on the northwest side has 9 good-sized walk-in tent sites along the rock cliffs among trees with sand tent pads, fire rings, and picnic tables. RVs can park in the cul-de-sac parking area. The restroom is not close. The third area is a single site located at the end of the **"Bear's Claw"** (a point into the lake) on the northeast side. One overflow RV site is located at the boat ramp parking area. *Double lane boat launch at the northeastern point of the peninsula.*
Crowds: ***** *[FEE AREA]*
Directions: W on CR-93/Old Sundance Rd 4.0 mi; N on Pine Haven Rd 2.1 mi; E/R on Hays Blvd 0.7 mi; Keep left at fork 0.2 mi to the turnoff to the reservable sites; Continue another 0.2 mi to the turnoff to the main camping area; Continue another 0.4 mi to the turnoff to Bears Claw.
Campsites: 14 *Shade:* ** *Privacy:* * *RV Size:* 40'+ *Other:* None

MM: 3.6/3.4 *Dist:* 7.8 *GPS:* 44.36727/-104.83163 *Elev:* 4113 *Grid:* 89/16 *Land:* State
Wind Creek Campground   *Type:* Campground
One of the 2 campgrounds at the west access near Pine Haven. Undeveloped and poorly defined campsites along the road and near the lakeshore. *Most of the campsites are in or near some pine trees. Tables. Fire rings. Boat ramp.*
Crowds: ***** *[FEE AREA]* *Road Desc:* Last 1.7 mi is gravel.
Directions: W on CR-93/Old Sundance Rd 4.0 mi; N on Pine Haven Rd 1.5 mi; W/L on Lakeview Dr 2.3 mi.
Campsites: 16 *Shade:* ** *Privacy:* * *RV Size:* 40'+ *Other:* None

MM: 5.6/1.4 *GPS:* 44.35595/-104.75075 *Elev:* 4164 *Grid:* 90/16 *Land:* State
RV Dump   *Type:* RV Dump
For registered campers only.
[FEE AREA] *Directions:* W side of road

MM: 5.6/1.4 *Dist:* 0.9 *GPS:* 44.36090/-104.76494 *Elev:* 4142 *Grid:* 90/16 *Land:* State
Arch Rock Campground   *Type:* Campground
Located in a stand of conifers near the western tip of **Cottonwood Bay**. *Gravel parking areas. 1 handicapped accessible site. 1 pull-thru. Overflow parking for extra vehicles.*
Crowds: **** *[FEE AREA]* *Directions:* NW/L 0.1 mi to fee booth; Continue 0.8 mi; NE/R into campground.
Campsites: 13 *Shade:* **** *Privacy:* ** *RV Size:* 30' *Other:* None

MM: 5.6/1.4 *Dist:* 1.1 *GPS:* 44.36411/-104.76805 *Elev:* 4144 *Grid:* 90/16 *Land:* State
Tatanka Campground   *Type:* Campground
Located in a stand of conifers on the west side of **Cottonwood Bay**. This is the only reservable campground in the park, and all but 2 sites are reservable. *Gravel parking areas. 2 handicapped accessible sites. 18 tent sites. 2 group sites. Overflow parking for extra vehicles. Reservable group shelter.*
Crowds: ***** *[FEE AREA]* *Directions:* NW/L 0.1 mi to fee booth; Continue 1.0 mi; NE/R into campground.
Campsites: 49 *Shade:* ***** *Privacy:* * *RV Size:* 40'+ *Other:* 1-877-996-7275:wyoparks.state.wy.us/reservations,Water

MM: 5.6/1.4 *Dist:* 2.0 *GPS:* 44.36903/-104.78482 *Elev:* 4109 *Grid:* 90/16 *Land:* State
Pat's Point Campground   *Type:* Campground
Located on a short peninsula with easy access to the reservoir. Some sites have a gravel pad while others are on the grass. *Few trees. Reservable group shelter. Boat ramp.*
Crowds: ***** *[FEE AREA]* *Directions:* NW/L 0.1 mi to fee booth; Continue 1.1 mi; SW/L 0.8 mi.
Campsites: 34 *Shade:* * *Privacy:* * *RV Size:* 40'+ *Other:* Water

MM: 5.6/1.4 *Dist:* 1.3 *GPS:* 44.36586/-104.76957 *Elev:* 4144 *Grid:* 90/16 *Land:* State
Pronghorn Campground   *Type:* Campground
Located in a stand of conifers on the west side of **Cottonwood Bay**. *Gravel parking areas. 2 handicapped accessible sites. A few pull-thrus. Overflow parking for extra vehicles. Playground.*
Crowds: ***** *[FEE AREA]* *Directions:* NW/L 0.1 mi to fee booth; Continue 1.2 mi; NE/R into campground.
Campsites: 33 *Shade:* ***** *Privacy:* * *RV Size:* 40'+ *Other:* Water

MM: 5.6/1.4 *Dist:* 1.6 *GPS:* 44.36961/-104.77557 *Elev:* 4110 *Grid:* 90/16 *Land:* State
Beach Area Campground   *Type:* Campground
Undeveloped sites in a stand of conifers close to the reservoir. The parking is located in a large unshaded parking area. The campground is best suited for tents. *Tables. Fire rings. Ground not level. No tent pad.*
Crowds: ***** *[FEE AREA]* *Directions:* NW/L 0.1 mi to fee booth; Continue 1.4 mi; W/L 0.1 mi.
Campsites: 6 *Shade:* *** *Privacy:* ** *RV Size:* 30' *Other:* Water

MM: 6.2/0.8 *Dist:* 0.2 *GPS:* 44.36273/-104.75569 *Elev:* 4140 *Grid:* 90/16 *Land:* State
Homestead Campground   *Type:* Campground
The campground is made up of 3 sections in a stand of conifers near the eastern tip of **Cottonwood Bay**. *Gravel parking areas. Several pull-thrus.*
Crowds: **** *[FEE AREA]* *Directions:* W/L 0.2 mi
Campsites: 40 *Shade:* *** *Privacy:* ** *RV Size:* 40'+ *Other:* Water

MM: 7.0/0.0 *Dist:* 0.8 *GPS:* 44.37551/-104.76810 *Elev:* 4193 *Grid:* 90/16 *Land:* State
Cottonwood Campground   *Type:* Campground
Undeveloped sites near the inlet of **Cottonwood Bay** on the east side. The sites are in stands of conifers. *Tables. Fire rings. Playground. Reservable group shelter.*
Crowds: *** *[FEE AREA]* *Directions:* W/L 0.8 mi keeping left at the fork.
Campsites: 35 *Shade:* **** *Privacy:* ** *RV Size:* 40'+ *Other:* Water

MM: 7.0/0.0 *Dist:* 0.9 *GPS:* 44.37883/-104.76878 *Elev:* 4123 *Grid:* 90/16 *Land:* State
Rocky Point Campground   *Type:* Campground
Undeveloped sites near the dam, which are mostly in the open with easy access to the lake. *Tables. Fire rings.*
Crowds: **** *[FEE AREA]* *Directions:* W/L 0.9 mi keeping right at the fork.
Campsites: 22 *Shade:* ** *Privacy:* ** *RV Size:* 40'+ *Other:* Water

MM: 7.0/0.0 *GPS:* 44.37560/-104.75387 *Elev:* 4239 *Grid:* 90/16
End of Highway   *Type:* Highway End
Nearest Town: Moorcroft 18 SW

MM: 0.0/40.4 *GPS:* 42.86392/-106.40631 *Elev:* 5233 *Grid:* 66/53
Oregon Trail Rd *Type:* Highway Description
An interesting alternative route from **US-20/26** (at **Casper**) southwest following the actual **Oregon Trail** 40.4 mi to **Wy-220**. The road passes the historic sites **Emigrant Gap**, **Rock Avenue**, **Willow Springs**, and **Prospect Hill** (a BLM interpretive site) in the same direction that the emigrants traveled. This route from **Casper** is roughly the same distance as taking **Wy-220** but is much slower and bypasses **Alcova Reservoir** and **Pathfinder Reservoir**.
Nearest Town: Casper 4 E
Road Desc: The first 6.0 mi from US-20/26 on the north end is paved. The rest is packed dirt to Wy-220 and is impassible when wet.
Directions: W on W Zero Rd/CR-202 5.5 mi; S/L on N Ten Mile Rd/CR-206 0.5 mi; W/R on Poison Spider Rd 3.0 mi; W/R on CR-306 0.05 mi; SW/L on CR-206 1.8 mi; S on CR-319/Oregon Trail Rd 29.5 mi. Connects with Wy-220 13.7 mi W of Alcova Reservoir.

MM: 7.6/32.8 *GPS:* 42.84428/-106.53890 *Elev:* 5587 *Grid:* 64/54 *Land:* BLM
Emigrant Gap *Type:* Historic Site
Many emigrant pioneers passed through this gap in **Emigrant Ridge**. From **Casper** the **Oregon Trail** briefly divided into 3 routes of which the northern route passed through **Emigrant Gap**. The trail diverged to various **North Platte River** crossings via the ferries and bridges around **Casper**. This route was especially favored by those using the **Mormon Ferry**. Passing through the gap the emigrants had a sweeping view to the west, the scene of their next week's journey. **Emigrant Gap** signified the departure from the **North Platte River Valley** and the beginning of the ascent into the **Rocky Mountains**. The site is marked by a **BLM** interpretive sign on the northwest side of the road.
Cool Rating: * *Crowds:* * *Time:* 5 min
Directions: W on W Zero Rd/CR-202 5.5 mi; S/L on N Ten Mile Rd/CR-206 0.5 mi; W/R on Poison Spider Rd/CR-206 1.6 mi. A sign identifies the site.

MM: 10.9/29.5 *GPS:* 42.82155/-106.59292 *Elev:* 5442 *Grid:* 64/54
CR-319/Oregon Trail Rd *Type:* Highway Junction
The actual start of **Oregon Trail Rd**.
Directions: From Emigrant Gap continue SW on Poison Spider Rd 1.4 mi; W/R on CR-306 0.05 mi; SW/L on CR-206 1.8 mi.

MM: 11.9/28.5 *Dist:* 5.3 *GPS:* 42.80622/-106.59365 *GPS2:* 42.77322/-106.53147 *Elev:* 5183 *Grid:* 64/55 *Land:* BLM
Bessemer Bend National Historic Site *Type:* Historic Site
The famous landmark **Red Buttes** stand above this bend in the **North Platte River**, which the emigrants followed for nearly 500 mi on their journey west. At this low-water crossing the river turns south and became impassable without a ferry or bridge, which weren't established until 1847. Even after safer means of crossing were established, some emigrants who didn't want to pay the tolls or wait in line still chose to cross here. This included the **Martin Handcart Company** and **Willie Handcart Company** who had many members perish when a blizzard blew in after they had crossed at this point. Interpretive signs along a short loop trail explain the history of the area. *Picnic tables. Restroom.*
Cool Rating: ** *Crowds:* * *Time:* 30 min *Nearest Town:* Casper 10.2 NE
Directions: From the Oregon Trail Rd turnoff; S on CR-319/Oregon Trail Rd 1.0 mi; E then S on Bessemer Bend Rd/CR-308 3.0 mi; E/L to continue on Bessemer Bend Rd/CR-308 2.3 mi just before the river bridge. *Road Desc:* Gravel

---

MM: 18.1/22.3 *GPS:* 42.73613/-106.66103 *GPS2:* 42.73623/-106.66144 *Elev:* 5570 *Grid:* 63/57 *Land:* State
Avenue of Rocks (Devil's Backbone) *Type:* Historic Site
A well-known landmark where a jagged rock ridge juts out of the otherwise rolling prairie. This unique geographical feature is also known as **Devil's Backbone**. Many emigrant signatures once existed here; however, most have been lost to development and natural causes. A few can still be found in the area. One in particular is **"W.H. Stephens**, July 5, 49" and can be found by walking 40 yds along the northeast base of the ridge to a rock outcrop where the name is at chest level *(see GPS2)*. This name also appears at **Independence Rock** and reads; **"W.H. Stephens** July 6, 49."
Cool Rating: ** *Crowds:* * *Time:* 15 min
Notes: If venturing out to find pioneer inscriptions, watch out for rattlesnakes.
Directions: W side of road just north of where the rock ridge crosses the road.

MM: 19.9/20.5 *GPS:* 42.71944/-106.68448 *Elev:* 5554 *Grid:* 62/57 *Land:* State
William Clayton's Slough (Poison Springs) *Type:* Historic Site
An area of alkali swamp located in a dry stretch between the **North Platte River** and the **Sweetwater River** where, according to **William Clayton**, the water was "nauseous in the extreme." He described the area as "one of the most horrid, swampy, stinking places" he ever saw. The soil in this area has high concentrations of alkali making the little water that was there being mostly undrinkable.
Cool Rating: * *Crowds:* * *Time:* Drive by

MM: 23.6/16.8 *GPS:* 42.68768/-106.74190 *Elev:* 5876 *Grid:* 62/58 *Land:* Private
Willow Springs (east end) *Type:* Historic Site
The north end of a 2.9 mi stretch that provided the first cool, drinkable water west of **Casper**. It therefore became one of the more popular emigrant campsites between the **North Platte River** and **Independence Rock**. The area was so popular that there was little food for the animals, which led many emigrants to camp outside of the springs area for better grass.
Cool Rating: * *Crowds:* * *Time:* Drive by

MM: 26.4/14.0 *GPS:* 42.67469/-106.79303 *Elev:* 6156 *Grid:* 61/58 *Land:* Private
Willow Springs (west end) *Type:* Historic Site
The south end of a 2.9 mi stretch that provided the first cool, drinkable water west of **Casper**. It therefore became one of the more popular emigrant campsites between the **North Platte River** and **Independence Rock**. This end is at the base of **Prospect Hill**. Just north of the road is an interpretive sign about **Willow Springs** and a metal post marking the **Willow Springs Pony Express Station**.
Cool Rating: * *Crowds:* * *Time:* 10 min *Directions:* N side of road

MM: 27.9/12.5 *Dist:* 0.2 *GPS:* 42.66025/-106.81012 *Elev:* 6570 *Grid:* 61/58 *Land:* BLM
Prospect Hill   *Type:* Historic Site
For the emigrants the next mile southwest from **Willow Springs** began a trying 400 ft climb to **Prospect Hill** (now known as **Ryan Hill**). The top of the hill provided a good view into the **Sweetwater Valley** where the famous landmarks **Independence Rock**, **Devil's Gate**, and **Split Rock** lay ahead, and beyond that the forbidding **Rocky Mountains**.

A short road north leads to a circle drive with 4 interpretive signs about the journey along the trail and what lay ahead for the emigrants. A short footpath leads northwest to well-defined wagon ruts along the trail (identified by a white marker).
Cool Rating: ** *Crowds:* * *Time:* 20 min *Directions:* NW 0.2 mi

MM: 40.4/0.0 *GPS:* 42.56673/-106.99060 *Elev:* 5926 *Grid:* 58/61
End of Highway   *Type:* Highway End
An interesting alternative route from **Wy-220** northeast to **Casper** following the actual **Oregon Trail** 40.4 mi to **US-20/26**. The road passes the historic sites **Prospect Hill** (a BLM interpretive site), **Willow Springs**, **Rock Avenue**, and **Emigrant Gap** in the opposite direction that the emigrants traveled. The route to **Casper** is roughly the same distance as taking **Wy-220** but is much slower and bypasses **Alcova Reservoir** and **Pathfinder Reservoir**.
Nearest Town: Alcova 13.7 E
Directions: N on CR-319/Oregon Trail Rd 29.5 mi; NE/R on CR-206 1.8 mi; E/R on CR-306 0.05 mi; NE/L on Poison Spider Rd 3.0 mi; N/L on N Ten Mile Rd/CR-206 0.5 mi; E/R on W Zero Rd/CR-202 5.5 mi. Connects to US-20/26 just W of Casper.

Pilot Butte Wild Horse Tour

MM: 0.0/25.8 *GPS:* 41.53673/-109.47954 *Elev:* 6182 *Grid:* 23/87
Pilot Butte Wild Horse Tour *Type:* Highway Description
Most **Wild Horses** in **Wyoming** are located in the southwestern quarter of the state. The **BLM** office in **Rock Springs** is the headquarters for the **Wild Horse Program** in **Wyoming**. The appropriate management level for wild horses in **Wyoming** is approximately 6,000. Some 2,500 of these horses are in the **Rock Springs** district and some can be seen on this driving tour. This is a large area where horses are seldom seen close up so be sure to take binoculars or a spotting scope. 6 interpretive pullouts provide nice views from **White Mountain**. A side road provides access to **Pilot Butte**, which can be climbed on foot.

The tour is 25.8 mi from **Green River** to **US-191** (11.8 mi north of I-80 at Rock Springs). The road traverses the rim of **White Mountain**, paralleling **I-80** until about the halfway point then paralleling **US-191**. To make this a 52.9 mi loop starting in **Green River** return via **US-191** and **I-80** from **Rock Springs**.
Notes: Watch for wild horses along US-191 to and from Rock Springs.
Directions: I-80 exit 89; 0.2 mi SE of I-80 exit 89; N on Wild Horse Canyon Rd/CR-53/White Mountain Rd 23.6 mi; E on CR-14/Blue Rim Rd 2.2 mi; *To return to Green River:* S on US-191 11.8 mi; W on I-80 15.3 mi.

MM: 0.0/25.8 *GPS:* 41.53686/-109.48026 *Elev:* 6169 *Grid:* 22/87
Green River Visitor Information Center *Type:* Visitor Center
A staffed information center with literature and maps for the surrounding area, including information about the **Pilot Butte Wild Horse Tour** that starts across the street on **Wild Horse Canyon Rd**. *Portable toilets. Picnic table. Water (donation appreciated).*
Directions: On the SW side of W Flaming Gorge Way across from Wild Horse Canyon Rd.

MM: 4.7/21.0 *GPS:* 41.55343/-109.39628 *Elev:* 7344 *Grid:* 24/86 *Land:* BLM
Interpretive Pullout #1 *Type:* Point of Interest
The road climbs 1,160 ft in elevation from **Green River** to this first pullout, which provides a view overlooking the valley and the city of **Green River**. 2 interpretive signs provide information about the city of **Green River** and the **Trona Patch**, which is a rare mineral found in the **Green River Basin** used to make common household products.
Cool Rating: ** *Crowds:* * *Directions:* S side of road

MM: 6.1/19.7 *GPS:* 41.56035/-109.37302 *Elev:* 7404 *Grid:* 24/86 *Land:* BLM
Interpretive Pullout #2 *Type:* Point of Interest
A view of **Wilkins Peak** and an interpretive sign explaining that the peak is the sediment of the ancient **Lake Gosiute**, which is explained by a second sign.
Cool Rating: ** *Crowds:* * *Directions:* SE side of road

MM: 7.1/18.7 *GPS:* 41.56803/-109.35725 *Elev:* 7467 *Grid:* 24/86 *Land:* BLM
Interpretive Pullout #3 *Type:* Point of Interest
2 signs about the **Lincoln Highway** and the historical importance of the east/west transportation corridor where **I-80** is now located. This is the best panoramic view of the valley below.
Cool Rating: *** *Crowds:* * *Directions:* SE side of road

MM: 9.1/16.7 *GPS:* 41.57970/-109.32328 *Elev:* 7578 *Grid:* 25/85 *Land:* Private
Radio Towers on top of White Mountain *Type:* Point of Interest
The high point of **White Mountain** at 7,614 ft elevation where radio towers are located for a number of regional users.
Directions: SE side of road

MM: 13.0/12.8 *GPS:* 41.63209/-109.30801 *Elev:* 7520 *Grid:* 25/84 *Land:* BLM
Interpretive Pullout #4 *Type:* Point of Interest
2 interpretive signs about the **White Mountain Wild Horse Herd** and **Pilot Butte**.
Cool Rating: ** *Crowds:* * *Directions:* W side of road

MM: 13.0/12.8 *Dist:* 2.3 *GPS:* 41.63244/-109.30808 *GPS2:* 41.64374/-109.34509 *Elev:* 7589 *Grid:* 25/84 *Land:* BLM
Pilot Butte (northbound) *Type:* Geological Feature
A 2.3 mi primitive road to the base of **Pilot Butte**, which at 7,937 ft it is the second highest point in the region. This flat-top butte was named by early travelers as a sign that they were close to the **Green River**. The top of the butte can be accessed by a short, steep trail that leads to a steel ladder to the top. From the bottom of the butte it is about 250 yds to the ladder, but the climb is straight uphill gaining 235 ft in this short distance (31% grade). Reaching the top is rewarded with an expansive view to the east. Hiking west another 0.2 mi climbs another 100 ft to a point with views to the west, northwest, and southwest. Be careful descending down the butte as the rocks and dirt are very loose.
Cool Rating: **** *Crowds:* * *Time:* 1.5 hrs *Directions:* NW 2.3 mi on primitive road
Road Desc: Dirt, primitive, deeply rutted & impassable when wet, high clearance

MM: 13.4/12.4 *Dist:* 2.3 *GPS:* 41.63777/-109.30706 *Elev:* 7589 *Grid:* 25/84
Pilot Butte (southbound) *Type:* Geological Feature
Another road that joins with the road to **Pilot Butte**. *See previous section.*
Directions: W 2.3 mi on primitive road

MM: 14.8/10.9 *GPS:* 41.65445/-109.29523 *Elev:* 7488 *Grid:* 25/84 *Land:* BLM
Interpretive Pullout #5 *Type:* Point of Interest
A view of **Rock Springs** plus 2 interpretive signs about the history of **Rock Springs** and the checkerboard pattern of private and BLM lands that make up the area.
Cool Rating: ** *Crowds:* * *Directions:* SE side of road

MM: 19.8/6.0 *GPS:* 41.72072/-109.31817 *Elev:* 7508 *Grid:* 25/82 *Land:* BLM
Interpretive Pullout #6 *Type:* Point of Interest
2 signs about the 3 surrounding mountain ranges and the **Red Desert**. Provides a panoramic vista from 670 ft above the highway below with distant views of the **Boar's Tusk**, **Killpecker Sand Dunes**, and the **Lucite Hills**.
Cool Rating: *** *Crowds:* * *Directions:* N side of road

MM: 22.4/3.4   *GPS:* 41.73350/-109.36196   *Elev:* 7329   *Grid:* 24/82   *Land:* BLM
Eskridge Draw Monument   *Type:* Point of Interest
The draw was named in honor of 2 young brothers, Edward and Richard Eskridge, who both died after a car accident. Richard was killed in the accident and Edward was later found about 3 mi down this draw. This tragedy led to the founding of the **Rock Springs Motorized and Rescue Unit**.
Directions: SW side of road

MM: 23.5/2.2   *GPS:* 41.74907/-109.36204   *Elev:* 7108   *Grid:* 24/81
Junction of CR-53/White Mountain Rd & CR-14/Blue Rim Rd   *Type:* Highway Junction
If coming from **Green River**, **CR-14/Blue Rim Rd** heads east to **US-191**. If coming from **US-191**, **CR-53/White Mountain Rd** heads south to **Green River**.

MM: 25.0/0.7   *GPS:* 41.74310/-109.33539   *Elev:* 7030   *Grid:* 25/81
Wild Horse Scenic Tour sign   *Type:* Visitor Information
Introductory sign for the **Pilot Butte Wild Horse Tour**.

MM: 25.8/0.0   *GPS:* 41.74369/-109.32207   *Elev:* 6842   *Grid:* 25/81
End of Highway   *Type:* Highway End
Most **Wild Horses** in **Wyoming** are located in the southwestern quarter of the state. The **BLM** office in **Rock Springs** is the headquarters for the **Wild Horse Program** in **Wyoming**. The appropriate management level for wild horses in **Wyoming** is approximately 6,000. Some 2,500 of these horses are in the **Rock Springs** district and some can be seen on this driving tour. This is a large area where horses are seldom seen close up so be sure to take binoculars or a spotting scope. 6 interpretive pullouts provide nice views from **White Mountain**. A side road provides access to **Pilot Butte**, which can be climbed on foot.

The tour is 25.8 mi from **US-191** (11.8 mi north of I-80 at Rock Springs) to **Green River**. The road traverses the rim of **White Mountain**, paralleling **US-191** until about the halfway point then paralleling **I-80**. To make this a 52.9 mi loop starting at **I-80** in **Rock Springs**, head north 11.8 mi on **US-191** and return from **Green River** via **I-80**.
Directions: From US-191 MM 13.1; SW on CR-14/Blue Rim Rd 2.2 mi; S on CR-53/White Mountain Rd 23.6 mi; *To return to Rock Springs:* E on I-80 15.3 mi.

Seminoe-Alcova Back Country Byway   S/N

MM: 0.0/73.0   *GPS:* 41.77903/-107.12428   *Elev:* 6595   *Grid:* 56/80

Seminoe-Alcova Back Country Byway   *Type:* Highway Description

73.0 mi route from **I-80** exit 219 at **Sinclair** north to **Wy-220** MM 86.5 at **Alcova**. The primary destination along this route is **Seminoe State Park** and **Seminoe Reservoir** along a paved portion of the highway. The route passes through prairie, rolling hills, and over the **Seminoe Mountains**. The distance is 18 mi shorter than taking the highways through **Rawlins**; however, it takes much longer to drive and there are no services along the way. Other highlights include: **White Sand Dunes**, the **Miracle Mile**, **Alcova Reservoir**. This route can be altered at MM 65.9 to incorporate the 2nd and 3rd sections of the **Alcova/Pathfinder Reservoir Loop**, which passes **Fremont Canyon** and **Pathfinder Reservoir** and ends at **Wy-220** MM 80.7.

Notes: The road is suitable for passenger cars but not recommended for large RVs or trailers.

Road Desc: The first 31.5 mi from I-80 and the last 14.4 mi to Wy-220 are paved. The rest is gravel that is washboarded in spots. The section through the Seminoe Mountains is steep and washboarded.

Directions: I-80 exit 219; E on Lincoln Ave 0.2 mi; Left at N 10th St/CR-351 following various county roads 73.0 mi to Alcova.

MM: 0.0/73.0   *GPS:* 41.77903/-107.12428   *Elev:* 6595   *Grid:* 56/80

Sinclair   *Type:* Town

MM: 8.0/65.0   *Dist:* 0.3   *GPS:* 41.86160/-107.05626   *Elev:* 6408   *Grid:* 57/78   *Land:* BLM

Dugway Recreation Site   *Type:* Recreation Area

Next to the **North Platte River** with a day use area, primitive float launch, and group campsite. This is a good starting point for float trips. *No trees. Understory is native grass and sagebrush.1 pull-thru. Tables. Fire rings.*

Crowds: **   *Directions:* SE 1/4 mi

Campsites: 5   *Shade:* *   *Privacy:* *   *RV Size:* 40'+   *Other:* None

---

MM: 25.8/47.2   *GPS:* 42.07437/-106.92323   *Elev:* 6560   *Grid:* 59/73   *Land:* State

Seminoe State Park (northbound)   *Type:* State Park

Located at the southern end of the **Seminoe Mountains**, this park is centered around **Seminoe Reservoir**, the first of 7 reservoirs on the **North Platte River**. The reservoir offers a full range of water-based activities and is known for both trout and walleye fishing. The park includes a day use area with 2 picnic shelters and a large beach, 2 full-service campgrounds, and 1 primitive campground.

Cool Rating: **   *Crowds:* ****   [FEE AREA]   *Directions:* E on access roads to the lakeshore.

MM: 25.9/47.1   *Dist:* 2.5   *GPS:* 42.06995/-106.88083   *Elev:* 6385   *Grid:* 60/73   *Land:* State

Sand Mountain Day Use Area: Seminoe State Park   *Type:* State Park

Located on the southwest shore of **Seminoe Reservoir** with 2 picnic shelters, a large sand beach, and a boat ramp.

Cool Rating: **   *Crowds:* ***   [FEE AREA]   *Directions:* E 2.5 mi

---

MM: 27.8/45.2   *Dist:* 0.7   *GPS:* 42.10152/-106.93640   *Elev:* 6540   *Grid:* 59/72   *Land:* BLM

White Sand Dunes   *Type:* Sand Dunes

A 100 ft high white sand dune west of **Seminoe Reservoir**.

Cool Rating: ***   *Crowds:* *   *Directions:* NE 0.7 mi

MM: 31.4/41.6   *Dist:* 1.0   *GPS:* 42.12330/-106.89180   *Elev:* 6400   *Grid:* 59/72   *Land:* State

Sunshine Beach Campground: Seminoe State Park   *Type:* Campground

Located on the west shore of **Seminoe Reservoir** off a shoreline with both rocky areas and sandy coves. The campground provides a few developed sites and 2 picnic shelters. The entrance road descends 300 ft from the road to the lakeshore.

Crowds: ***   [FEE AREA]   *Road Desc:* Gravel, rough, steep   *Directions:* E 1.0 mi

Campsites: Dispersed   *Shade:* *   *Privacy:* *   *RV Size:* 30'   *Other:* None

---

MM: 31.5/41.5   *GPS:* 42.12287/-106.91134   *Elev:* 6715   *Grid:* 59/72

Pavement Ends (northbound)   *Type:* Pavement Change

The road turns to gravel with washboard sections.

MM: 32.4/40.6   *Dist:* 0.6   *GPS:* 42.13190/-106.89918   *Elev:* 6430   *Grid:* 59/72   *Land:* State

South Red Hills Campground: Seminoe State Park   *Type:* Campground

A 2-tiered campground located in a bay on the northwest shore of **Seminoe Reservoir**. The upper level has a view of the lake. The lower level offers some protection from the wind. *No trees. Some picnic shelters. Playground. Boat ramp.*

Crowds: ***   [FEE AREA]   *Road Desc:* Gravel, washboard sections   *Directions:* E 0.6 mi

Campsites: 22   *Shade:* *   *Privacy:* *   *RV Size:* 40'+   *Other:* Water

---

MM: 32.6/40.4   *Dist:* 0.7   *GPS:* 42.13573/-106.89270   *Elev:* 6422   *Grid:* 59/72   *Land:* State

North Red Hills Campground: Seminoe State Park   *Type:* Campground

Located on the northwest shore of **Seminoe Reservoir**. The shoreline is steep and covered with rock in most areas. *A few shade trees. A few picnic shelters. Playground. Not level. Exposed to the wind. Boat launch.*

Crowds: ***   [FEE AREA]   *Road Desc:* Gravel, washboard sections   *Directions:* E 0.7 mi

Campsites: 30   *Shade:* *   *Privacy:* *   *RV Size:* 40'+   *Other:* Water,RVDump

---

MM: 32.6/40.4   *GPS:* 42.13656/-106.90653   *Elev:* 6581   *Grid:* 59/72   *Land:* State

Seminoe State Park (southbound)   *Type:* State Park

Located at the southern end of the **Seminoe Mountains**, this park is centered around **Seminoe Reservoir**, the first of 7 reservoirs on the **North Platte River**. The reservoir offers a full range of water-based activities and is known for both trout and walleye fishing. The park includes a day use area with 2 picnic shelters and a large beach, 2 full-service campgrounds, and 1 primitive campground.

Cool Rating: **   *Crowds:* ****   [FEE AREA]   *Directions:* E on access roads to the lakeshore.

MM: 33.5/39.5 *GPS:* 42.14526/-106.89756 *Elev:* 6770 *Grid:* 59/71
Seminoe Reservoir Overlook   *Type:* Scenic Viewpoint
South facing overlook 375 ft above **Seminoe Reservoir** and **Seminoe State Park** with 3 interpretive signs about the dam and reservoir, the state park, and the surrounding lands.
Cool Rating: *** *Crowds:* * *Time:* 10 min *Road Desc:* Gravel, washboard sections, steep & winding
Directions: Pullout on E side of road

MM: 34.3/38.7 *GPS:* 42.15195/-106.90768 *Elev:* 6698 *Grid:* 59/71
Seminoe Dam Overlook   *Type:* Scenic Viewpoint
An overlook 330 ft above the **Seminoe Dam**. The dam is a concrete arch structure built into a canyon in the **Seminoe Mountains** measuring 295 ft high and 530 ft long. This is the first of 7 dams on the **North Platte River**, which was completed in 1939.
Cool Rating: *** *Crowds:* * *Time:* 10 min *Road Desc:* Gravel, washboard sections, steep & winding
Directions: Pullout on N side of road

MM: 35.1/37.9 *GPS:* 42.15229/-106.91938 *Elev:* 6760 *Grid:* 59/71
Cutoff Road (south)   *Type:* Highway Junction
A 2.0 mi 2-track dirt road that traverses the mountainside with a gradual elevation loss and gain. This route avoids the nearly 400 ft elevation loss and gain into and out of a canyon along a 2.3 mi winding, washboarded section of the main road. There is plenty of room to pull off the road for oncoming vehicles.
Road Desc: Dirt, impassable when wet, narrow *Directions:* SW then NW 2.0 mi

MM: 37.5/35.5 *GPS:* 42.16422/-106.94295 *Elev:* 6846 *Grid:* 59/71
Cutoff Road (north)   *Type:* Highway Junction
See previous section.
Directions: W then SE 2.0 mi

MM: 42.5/30.5 *GPS:* 42.20634/-106.87749 *Elev:* 5903 *Grid:* 60/70 *Land:* BLM
Miracle Mile   *Type:* Public Access Area
Blue ribbon trout fishing along a 5.5 mi section of the **North Platte River** from just below **Kortes Dam** (to the south) to the **Pathfinder Wildlife Refuge** (to the north). To the north and south of **Seminoe Rd** are side roads that provide public access along both sides of the river with several primitive camp areas. *Few trees. Several vault toilets.*
Crowds: ** *Notes:* Kortes Reservoir is the second of 7 reservoirs on the North Platte River. *Road Desc:* Gravel
Directions: This turnoff is 0.1 mi SW of the river with sites both SE and N up to 1.7 mi.
Campsites: Dispersed *Shade:* * *Privacy:* * *RV Size:* 40' *Other:* None

MM: 42.6/30.4 *GPS:* 42.20818/-106.87650 *Elev:* 5881 *Grid:* 60/70
North Platte River   *Type:* River

MM: 43.1/29.9 *GPS:* 42.21060/-106.86864 *Elev:* 5938 *Grid:* 60/70 *Land:* BLM
Miracle Mile   *Type:* Public Access Area
See Miracle Mile at MM 42.4.
Crowds: ** *Road Desc:* Gravel
Directions: This turnoff is 0.5 mi E of the river with sites both S and N up to 1.5 mi. The road S toward Kortes Dam is paved.
Campsites: Dispersed *Shade:* * *Privacy:* * *RV Size:* 40' *Other:* None

MM: 47.3/25.7 *GPS:* 42.24405/-106.80029 *Elev:* 6186 *Grid:* 61/69
Mileage Signs   *Type:* Point of Reference
Mileage signs at a fork in the road. Keep right if heading south.

MM: 58.6/14.4 *GPS:* 42.38539/-106.73831 *Elev:* 6600 *Grid:* 62/65
Pavement Ends (southbound)   *Type:* Pavement Change
The road turns to gravel with washboard sections.

MM: 66.0/7.0 *GPS:* 42.48322/-106.74944 *Elev:* 6043 *Grid:* 61/63
Alcova/Pathfinder Reservoir Loop *(see chapter)*   *Type:* Hwy Junction w/Chapter
A 13 mi section of the **Alcova/Pathfinder Reservoir Loop** that ends at **Wy-220** MM 80.7, 5.8 mi west of **Alcova**. The route passes **Fremont Canyon** and **Pathfinder Reservoir**, and is a good alternative if ultimately heading southwest on **Wy-220**. Highlights include: **Fremont Canyon Bridge and Overlook**, **Pathfinder Dam Overlook**, **Pathfinder Interpretive Center and Trail**.
Road Desc: Paved *Directions:* W on CR-408/Fremont Canyon Rd from MM 7.0 of the Alcova/Pathfinder Reservoir Loop
Notes: **Fremont Canyon** and the **Pathfinder Dam Overlook** are worth seeing even as an out and back.

MM: 67.9/5.1 *Dist:* 1.2 *GPS:* 42.52152/-106.74319 *Elev:* 5560 *Grid:* 62/62 *Land:* Bureau of Reclamation
Cottonwood Creek Campground: Alcova Reservoir   *Type:* Campground
A fairly large campground on the south shore of **Alcova Reservoir**. Dispersed sites are located near the lake, and better defined sites are up a hill above the pay station. Dozens of sites are scattered about the area in several loops. Some of the upper sites have a nice view of the lake. The camping areas near the lake fill fast, but the upper sites are less used. *Most of the sites are not level. Few sites have tables, but most have fire rings.*
Crowds: *** **[FEE AREA]** *Road Desc:* Gravel
Directions: NW 1.2 mi to pay station; Continue straight to sites around the reservoir or turn right for sites above.
Campsites: Dispersed *Shade:* * *Privacy:* ** *RV Size:* 40' *Other:* None

MM: 67.9/5.1 *Dist:* 1.3 *GPS:* 42.52114/-106.74165 *Elev:* 5613 *Grid:* 62/62 *Land:* Bureau of Reclamation
Cottonwood Creek Dinosaur Trail   *Type:* Historic Site
In 1991 numerous dinosaur bones and the skeleton of a medium-sized dinosaur were discovered by 5th grade field science students in the sandstone ledges of the **Morrison Formation** south of **Alcova Reservoir**. A 0.3 mi round-trip hiking trail provides access to the site for further research and educational purposes and includes interpretive signs about the geology and fossils. The trail climbs steeply to a fine view of **Alcova Reservoir** and the surrounding area. The trail loops at the top and returns by the same route.
Cool Rating: * *Crowds:* * *Time:* 30 min *Road Desc:* Gravel
Notes: The trail is very steep and the footing is not good. Unless you are a geologist, the climb is more worth it for the scenic view than the geological information on the signs.
Directions: NW 1.2 mi to pay station; Just before the pay station at Cottonwood Creek Campground NE/R 0.05 mi; S/R 0.1 mi.

MM: 69.9/3.1 *Dist:* 0.7 *GPS:* 42.53183/-106.71240 *Elev:* 5510 *Grid:* 62/62 *Land:* Bureau of Reclamation
Black Beach Campground: Alcova Reservoir   *Type:* Campground
Located on a point at the east end of **Alcova Reservoir** with nice views of the red hills along the shoreline. *Sheltered picnic tables. No trees.*
Crowds: **** *[FEE AREA]* *Road Desc:* Gravel *Directions:* NW on Black Beach Rd. 0.7 mi
Campsites: 14 *Shade:* * *Privacy:* * *RV Size:* 40'+ *Other:* None

MM: 73.0/0.0 *GPS:* 42.56102/-106.72524 *Elev:* 5377 *Grid:* 62/61
Alcova   *Type:* Town

MM: 73.0/0.0 *GPS:* 42.56102/-106.72524 *Elev:* 5377 *Grid:* 62/61
End of Highway   *Type:* Highway End
73.0 mi route from **Wy-220** MM 86.5 at **Alcova** south to **I-80** exit 219 at **Sinclair**. The route passes through prairie, rolling hills, and over the **Seminoe Mountains**. The distance is 18 mi shorter than taking the highways through **Rawlins**; however, it takes much longer to drive and there are no services along the way. Highlights include: **Alcova Reservoir**, the **Miracle Mile**, **Seminoe State Park** and **Seminoe Reservoir**, **White Sand Dunes**.
Directions: S on CR-407 following various county roads 73.0 mi to Sinclair. W/R on Lincoln Ave 0.2 mi to I-80 exit 219.

Sugarloaf Recreation Area/FR-346   S/N

MM: 0.0 **GPS:** 41.34810/-106.29027 **Elev:** 10715 **Grid:** 68/91 **Land:** NF
Sugarloaf Recreation Area/FR-346   **Type:** Highway Description
A recreation area near the top of **Snowy Range Pass** with parking areas at **Libby Lake** and **Lewis Lake**. Picnic areas are located at each lake and **Sugarloaf Campground** is located across from **Libby Lake**. A trailhead at **Lewis Lake** provides access to several hiking trails that lead to alpine lakes and **Medicine Bow Peak**. The area provides beautiful views of the **Snowy Range**, **Medicine Bow Peak**, **Browns Peak**, and the surrounding valleys. The scenery in this area is the most magnificent along the scenic byway.
Road Desc: Gravel **Directions:** From Wy-130 MM 38.7; NW on FR-346 90 yds to self-pay fee station.

MM: 0.7 **GPS:** 41.35421/-106.29566 **Elev:** 10781 **Grid:** 68/91 **Land:** NF
Libby Lake Picnic Ground   **Type:** Picnic Area
Unshaded picnic tables overlooking **Libby Lake** with a backdrop of **Medicine Bow Peak**. *Vault toilet.*
Directions: N side of road

MM: 0.8 **GPS:** 41.35480/-106.29424 **Elev:** 10800 **Grid:** 68/91 **Land:** NF
Sugarloaf Campground   **Type:** Campground
Wyoming's highest campground with beautiful views of the **Snowy Range**. The campground is just across the road from **Libby Lake**. *Sparse conifer forest. Spacious sites. Level.*
Crowds: ***** **[FEE AREA]** **Notes:** Gets very cold and may not open until July. Closes shortly after Labor Day.
Directions: S side of road
Campsites: 16 **Shade:** ** **Privacy:** *** **RV Size:** 30' **Other:** 1-877-444-6777:www.recreation.gov,Water

MM: 1.0 **GPS:** 41.35818/-106.29445 **Elev:** 10780 **Grid:** 68/91 **Land:** NF
Lewis Lake   **Type:** Lake
A beautiful alpine lake in a valley below **Medicine Bow Peak**. The parking area is primarily used to access 2 popular trailheads and is generally full. *Picnic tables. Vault toilet. Water. Trash cans.*
Cool Rating: **** **Crowds:** ***** **Directions:** End of road

MM: 1.0 **GPS:** 41.35814/-106.29476 **GPS2:** 41.36042/-106.31747 **Elev:** 10773 **Grid:** 68/91 **Land:** NF
Medicine Bow Peak Trail from Lewis Lake   **Type:** Hiking Trail
Starting at **Lewis Lake**, this is the shortest trail to the top of **Medicine Bow Peak** (12,013 ft). The trail heads west 0.9 mi along the northern base of **Sugarloaf Mountain** across an alpine environment consisting of meadows, boulders, and small lakes. After climbing 300 ft the trail reaches the junction with the **Lakes Trail** from the south. Turn right and follow a very steep trail 0.8 mi to the **Medicine Bow Peak summit**. The trail climbs 900 ft over scattered boulders, along switchbacks, and over and around lingering snowdrifts. *Strenuous; 1.7 mi one-way; 1200 ft elev gain.*
Cool Rating: ***** **Crowds:** *** **Time:** 2-3 hrs
Notes: It is best to be off the trail by 3 pm to avoid afternoon thunderstorms. Exercise extreme caution climbing to the top of Medicine Bow Peak.
Directions: End of road at the Lewis Lake parking area. Trailhead on west side.

MM: 1.0 **GPS:** 41.35877/-106.29453 **Elev:** 10770 **Grid:** 68/91 **Land:** NF
Gap Lakes Trail   **Type:** Hiking Trail
A trail north to **South Gap Lake** and **North Gap Lake** through a beautiful alpine valley between **Medicine Bow Peak** to the west and **Browns Peak** to the east. From the **Lewis Lake** parking area the trail heads north 1/4 mi to a junction with the **Lost Lake Trail** (MI 0.25), *which heads 1.75 mi northeast to **Lost Lake** (see Brooklyn Lake Rd/FR-317 MM 1.9). Continue 0.65 mi gradually climbing 200 ft to **South Gap Lake** (MI 0.9). Following the trail another 0.1 mi climbs slightly to a good view of the lake (MI 1.0). Continue along the east shore 0.2 mi (MI 1.3) before crossing a boulder field and climbing to the top of the ridge between **South Gap Lake** and **North Gap Lake**, which is also a saddle between **Medicine Bow Peak** and **Browns Peak** (MI 1.4). Descend 0.1 mi to a **North Gap Lake** sign above the lake (MI 1.5). *Moderate; 1.5 mi one-way; 260 ft elev gain.*

Trail options beyond North Gap Lake to Deep Lake:
Continuing to and along the southeast lakeshore 0.15 mi leads to the **Shelf Lakes Trail** (MI 1.65), *which heads 1.1 mi northeast to **Shelf Lakes**. The trail then descends through meadows and patches of forest to the **Quealy Lake Trail** (MI 2.8), *which heads west 0.4 mi to deep **Reservoir Lake** and another 2.35 mi to **Quealy Lake**. Continuing northeast 0.2 mi the trail passes the west shore of **Cutthroat Lake** (MI 3.0), which is 240 ft below **North Gap Lake**. In another 0.5 mi the **Deep Lake Trail** (MI 3.5) heads north 0.5 mi to **Deep Lake** (MI 4.0), which is 180 ft below **Cutthroat Lake**. *Moderately strenuous; 4.0 mi one-way (to Deep Lake); 530 ft elev loss.*

Continuing 0.7 mi past the **Deep Lake** junction connects to the **Sheep Lake Trail**, just southwest of **Sheep Lake**, which continues north to **Sand Lake** or east to **Brooklyn Lake** with the possibility of completing an 11.25 mi loop *(see section on Sheep Lake Trail in chapter: Brooklyn Lake Rd/FR-317 MM 1.9).*
Cool Rating: ***** **Crowds:** *** **Time:** 2+ hrs
Directions: NW on FR-346 1.0 mi to the Lewis Lake parking area. Trailhead on north end.

Teton Park Rd: Grand Teton National Park | S/N

MM: 0.0/20.8 **GPS:** 43.65090/-110.70767 **Elev:** 6509 **Grid:** 5/34
Teton Park Rd: Grand Teton National Park   **Type:** Highway Description
20.8 mi road north through the main section of **Grand Teton National Park**, which traverses the central-eastern base of the **Teton Range** and offers the closest access and views. Highlights include: the **Craig Thomas Discovery and Visitor Center**, **Chapel of the Transfiguration and Menor's Ferry Historic District**, **Jenny Lake**, **Hidden Falls**, **Inspiration Point**, **Signal Mountain**, **Jackson Lake**.
Nearest Town: Moose 0.5 W; Jackson 12.3 S **Directions:** NW from MM 0

MM: 0.0/20.8 **GPS:** 43.65090/-110.70767 **Elev:** 6509 **Grid:** 5/34
US-26/89/191 (see chapter)   **Type:** Hwy Junction w/Chapter
43.3 mi highway from **Hoback Jct** north to **Moran Jct**. The highway then connects to **US-89/191/287**, using sequential mile markers, and continues 27 mi to **Yellowstone National Park**. The entire length is along the **Centennial Scenic Byway**. Highlights include: **Jackson**, **Jackson Hole and Greater Yellowstone Visitor Center**, **Grand Teton National Park**.
Directions: N to Moran Jct or S to Jackson from MM 166.8

MM: 0.5/20.3 **GPS:** 43.65635/-110.71891 **Elev:** 6455 **Grid:** 5/34
Moose   **Type:** Town

MM: 0.5/20.3 **GPS:** 43.65469/-110.71668 **Elev:** 6450 **Grid:** 5/34 **Land:** NPS
Craig Thomas Discovery and Visitor Center   **Type:** Visitor Center
A state of the art visitor center that opened in 2007 and includes: **interactive exhibits** including endangered species, wildlife, and mountaineering; **video river** of large video screens built into the floor displaying park scenery; **3-D relief map** that serves as a focal point for orientation and interpretive programs; **20 minute ranger talks** on a variety of topics; **30 ft windows** facing the **Teton Range**. The site also provides a large theater, general information, maps, activity schedules, backcountry camping and boat permits, guided walks and talks, and a large bookstore. The park newspaper **"Teewinot"** is available, which contains considerable information on the park. The park headquarters and a post office are located across the road. A paved bike path connects this visitor center to the **Jenny Lake Visitor Center**.
Hours: 8am - 7pm (June - Sept); 8am - 5pm (offseason) **Phone:** 307-739-3399 **Crowds:** ***** **Directions:** SW side of road

MM: 0.7/20.1 **GPS:** 43.65635/-110.71891 **Elev:** 6455 **Grid:** 5/34
Wy-390/Moose-Wilson Rd (see chapter)   **Type:** Hwy Junction w/Chapter
14.7 mi road from **Teton Park Rd** in **Grand Teton National Park**, at **Moose**, south to **Wy-22**, 1.4 mi east of **Wilson**. The mile markers don't start for **Wy-390** until leaving **Grand Teton National Park** at the **Granite Canyon Entrance**, so set the trip odometer to zero at **Teton Park Rd** and use the mile markers in parenthesis. Highlights include: **Death Canyon Trailhead**, **Laurance S. Rockefeller Preserve**, **Granite Canyon Trailhead**, **Teton Village**.
Notes: RVs and trailers are prohibited. **Directions:** S to Wy-22, 1.4 mi E of Wilson, from MM 14.7

MM: 1.0/19.8 **GPS:** 43.66026/-110.72161 **Elev:** 6465 **Grid:** 5/34 **Land:** NPS
Grand Teton National Park - Moose Entrance   **Type:** National Park
Pay the National Park entrance fee that covers both **Grand Teton National Park** and **Yellowstone National Park**. *See chapter: Grand Teton National Park.*
[FEE AREA]

MM: 1.2/19.6 **Dist:** 0.5 **GPS:** 43.65963/-110.71464 **Elev:** 6464 **Grid:** 5/34 **Land:** NPS
Chapel of the Transfiguration & Menor's Ferry Historic District   **Type:** Historic Site
The **Chapel of the Transfiguration** is a log church built in 1925 that features a large window behind the altar framing the **Grand Teton** and adjacent peaks. The bell in the front is from a church in **New York** and was cast in 1842. The chapel is located on land donated by **Maude Noble** and is still a functioning **Episcopal Church**. Detailed literature about the chapel is provided at the site.

Menor's Ferry trail is 0.3 mi long and offers a glimpse of pioneer life around the turn of the 19th century. Visit **Bill Menor's Cabin** and store, a replica of **Menor's Ferry** that crossed the **Snake River**, the **transportation shed** with a collection of wagons and coaches, and **Maude Noble's Cabin**. A self-guided tour brochure is available at the trailhead.
Cool Rating: *** **Crowds:** *** **Time:** 1 hr
Directions: SE 0.5 mi to parking lot. Chapel on NW side and Historic District on the SE side.

MM: 2.2/18.6 **GPS:** 43.67711/-110.72466 **Elev:** 6609 **Grid:** 5/33 **Land:** NPS
Windy Point Turnout   **Type:** Scenic Viewpoint
A pullout facing the plains to the east, away from the **Teton Range**, with 3 interpretive signs about the glacial landscape of the plains, the effect of pollution on the park, and the plains wildlife and wildflowers. About 10 mi southeast a reddish stripe is visible on **Sheep Mountain** where the **Gros Ventre Slide** occurred in 1925 *(see Gros Ventre Rd MM 12.7)*. The turnout also provides a view of the **Teton Range** from the south end looking north.
Cool Rating: ** **Crowds:** ** **Time:** 10 min **Directions:** NE side of road

MM: 3.4/17.4   *GPS:* 43.69280/-110.73264   *Elev:* 6628   *Grid:* 5/33   *Land:* NPS

Taggart Lake Trailhead   *Type:* Trailhead

Taggart Lake is a glacially created lake at the mouth of **Avalanche Canyon** below the primary southern peaks of the **Teton Range**. The hike is around the perimeter of the glacial terminal moraine that formed the lake. The loop trail can be hiked in either direction so the mileages are shown for both. The trail is described hiking counterclockwise.

At 1/3 mi the trail crosses a bridge over **Taggart Creek** (MI 0.3/3.5), which cascades beautifully over boulders and downed trees. The trail climbs gradually gaining 250 ft over the next 0.9 mi, passing the **Bradley Lake Trail** loop junction (MI 1.1/2.7) before entering an interesting alley of young pine trees (MI 1.2/2.6). In 1/2 mi the trail passes the other end of the **Bradley Lake Trail** and reaches **Taggart Lake**, where a large flat boulder protrudes into the lake and tends to attract a crowd (1.7/2.1). Continuing 0.1 mi along the east shore of the lake reaches a footbridge across a narrow channel before climbing 130 ft in 0.2 mi to the high point of the trail (MI 2.0/1.8). Don't forget to look back at the views from above **Taggart Lake**. The trail descends steeply 270 ft in 0.4 mi to the base of the moraine and then follows a gradual descent along **Beaver Creek** back to the trailhead.

Hiking counterclockwise (as described above) offers a gradual ascent to **Taggart Lake** (250 ft in 3/4 mi) and allows the options of returning by the same route or hiking the **Bradley Lake Trail** loop. To complete the loop requires an additional climb of 130 ft in 0.2 mi after the lake. Alternatively, hiking clockwise requires a very gradual 140 ft climb in 1.4 mi, followed by a single steep climb of 270 ft in 0.4 mi. It is mostly downhill from this point and the next 0.2 mi offer nice views from above **Taggart Lake**. *Moderately easy; 3.8 mi loop; 410 ft elev gain.*

The hike can be extended 1.9 mi by taking the loop to **Bradley Lake**, another glacially created lake at the mouth of **Garnet Canyon**, 120 ft above **Taggart Lake**. The loop trail starts at 1.1 mi along the **Taggart Lake Trail**, loops past **Bradley Lake**, and returns to **Taggart Lake**. It is 1.0 mi to **Bradley Lake**, climbing 230 ft over a moraine before dropping 100 ft to the lakeshore. The loop continues 1.5 mi, climbing 130 ft over the moraine (providing a good view of **Taggart Lake**) before dropping 250 ft to **Taggart Lake**. *Taggart Lake and Bradley Lake loops combined: Moderate; 5.7 mi round-trip; 790 ft cumulative elev gain.*

Cool Rating: ****   *Crowds:* **   *Time:* 2-3 hrs   *Notes:* I prefer hiking the Taggart Lake loop clockwise.

Directions: Parking area on W side of road

MM: 3.8/17.0   *GPS:* 43.69722/-110.73001   *Elev:* 6628   *Grid:* 5/33   *Land:* NPS

Cottonwood Creek Picnic Area   *Type:* Picnic Area

Provides access to **Cottonwood Creek** with 4 picnic tables that are close together and out in the open. On the south end of the parking area is an interpretive sign about the **Beaver Creek Fire** and the regeneration of the forest. *Vault toilet.*

Directions: SE side of road

Notes: Not a particularly nice picnic area, but there are no other picnic sites in the Moose/Jenny Lake area. A very nice picnic area is located at String Lake 8.7 mi north.

MM: 5.0/15.8   *GPS:* 43.71300/-110.72803   *Elev:* 6709   *Grid:* 5/32   *Land:* NPS

Teton Glacier Turnout   *Type:* Scenic Viewpoint

Interpretive sign and view of the **Teton Glacier**, which is the largest glacier in the park. It is located just below and northeast of the **Grand Teton**.

Cool Rating: ***   *Crowds:* **   *Time:* 10 min   *Directions:* W side of road

---

MM: 7.9/12.9   *Dist:* 0.2   *GPS:* 43.75348/-110.72090   *Elev:* 6803   *Grid:* 5/31   *Land:* NPS

Jenny Lake Campground   *Type:* Campground

A very popular tent-only campground near the east shore of **Jenny Lake** with great views of the **Teton Range**. *Sparse conifer forest. Flush toilets. 10 walk-in sites. 14 ft vehicle length limit. Fills by 11 am.*

Crowds: *****   *[FEE AREA]*   *Directions:* W 0.1 mi; W/R 0.1 mi.

Campsites: 50   *Shade:* ***   *Privacy:* *   *RV Size:* Tent   *Other:* Water   GRIZZLIES

MM: 7.9/12.9   *Dist:* 0.3   *GPS:* 43.75130/-110.72133   *Elev:* 6794   *Grid:* 5/31   *Land:* NPS

Jenny Lake Visitor Center   *Type:* Visitor Center

General park information, geology exhibits, relief map of the park, activity schedules, guided walks and talks, maps, and a bookstore. A boat ride across **Jenny Lake** starts southwest of the visitor center, where payment is taken at the dock *(see next section)*. A paved bike path connects this visitor center to the **Craig Thomas Discovery and Visitor Center**. *No picnic area.*

Hours: 8am - 7pm (June - Sept); 8am - 4:30pm (offseason)   *Directions:* W 0.3 mi

---

MM: 7.9/12.9   *Dist:* 0.3   *GPS:* 43.75156/-110.72578   *Elev:* 6787   *Grid:* 5/31   *Land:* NPS

Jenny Lake and Trails   *Type:* Trailhead

Jenny Lake is situated in a glacial moraine at the end of **Cascade Canyon** and is the second largest lake in **Grand Teton National Park**. The lake is situated at the base of the middle section of the **Teton Range** directly below the **Grand Teton**, which is part of the **Cathedral Group** along with **Teewinot Mountain** and **Mount Owen**.

The 6.6 mi **Jenny Lake Loop Trail** circles the perimeter of **Jenny Lake**. It also providing a 2.5 mi trail to **Hidden Falls** and the attractions beyond. Start at the boat dock and hike clockwise 2.5 mi to **Hidden Falls**, a 200 ft cascade from which the final 100 ft drop can be seen from the viewing area (43.7649/-110.75076). Continue past the falls and climb 0.4 mi to **Inspiration Point** (43.76698/-110.74832), located at the mouth of **Cascade Canyon** with a spectacular view east to the **Gros Ventre Mountains** from 440 ft above **Jenny Lake**. The trail continues 3.6 mi through **Cascade Canyon** below the towering **Teewinot Mountain**, **Mount Owen**, and **Grand Teton**, where even a partial hike is worthwhile. At this point the trail forks to either the **North Fork** or **South Fork Cascade Canyon**. Keep right to follow the **North Fork** 2.7 mi to **Lake Solitude**, a glacial lake located in a cirque at the end of the canyon.

For the aforementioned hiking destinations, follow either the **Jenny Lake Loop Trail** clockwise 2.5 mi from the boat dock to **Hidden Falls** or take the shuttle boat across **Jenny Lake**. The following one-way distances will be reduced by 2.0 mi by taking the shuttle boat (which charges a fee). *Jenny Lake Loop Trail: Moderately easy; 6.6 mi loop; Level. **Hidden Falls**: Moderate; 2.5 mi one-way; 175 ft elev gain. **Inspiration Point**: Moderate; 2.9 mi one-way; 440 ft elev gain. **Cascade Canyon**: Moderately strenuous; 6.5 mi one-way; 1060 ft elev gain. **Lake Solitude**: Strenuous; 9.2 mi one-way; 2250 ft elev gain.*

Cool Rating: *****   *Crowds:* *****   *Time:* 1-10 hrs

Directions: W 0.3 mi to 2nd parking area. Take paved path SW to the boat dock and bridge.

MM: 9.4/11.4 *GPS:* 43.77318/-110.71191 *Elev:* 6882 *Grid:* 5/31 *Land:* NPS
Cascade Canyon Turnout   *Type:* Scenic Viewpoint
A view into **Cascade Canyon** with an interpretive sign.
Cool Rating: *** *Crowds:* ** *Time:* 10 min *Directions:* W side of road

MM: 10.8/10.0 *GPS:* 43.79020/-110.70211 *Elev:* 6968 *Grid:* 5/30
Jenny Lake Loop Rd: Grand Teton National Park *(see chapter)*   *Type:* Hwy Junction w/Chapter
A 4.0 mi loop road that provides access to 3 glacial lakes. The first 1.5 mi is 2-way providing access to the **String Lake** area, which includes hiking trails, a picnic area, and a swimming/floating area. The last 2.5 mi is one-way passing an interpretive overlook of **Jenny Lake** and returning to **Teton Park Rd** MM 8.5/12.3. Highlights include: **String Lake**, **Leigh Lake**, **Jenny Lake**.
Directions: NW on Jenny Lake Loop Rd 1.5 mi; Continue straight on one-way loop road 2.5 mi.
Notes: The one-way section is paved and narrow and mostly in the trees with no views.

MM: 11.2/9.6 *GPS:* 43.79375/-110.69640 *Elev:* 6989 *Grid:* 5/30 *Land:* NPS
Mountain View Turnout   *Type:* Scenic Viewpoint
A view of the **Teton Range** with an interpretive sign about their formation and identifying the peaks.
Cool Rating: *** *Crowds:* ** *Time:* 10 min *Directions:* N side of road

MM: 14.4/6.4 *GPS:* 43.80330/-110.64155 *Elev:* 6888 *Grid:* 6/30 *Land:* NPS
Mount Moran Turnout   *Type:* Scenic Viewpoint
Interpretive sign and view of the 12,605 ft **Mount Moran**.
Cool Rating: *** *Crowds:* ** *Time:* 10 min *Directions:* NW side of road

MM: 15.1/5.7 *GPS:* 43.80740/-110.62852 *Elev:* 6892 *Grid:* 6/30 *Land:* NPS
Potholes Turnout   *Type:* Scenic Viewpoint
Kettles (or potholes) are depressions that are often filled with water from massive chunks of ice left behind by retreating glaciers. The purpose of this turnout is unclear as the potholes are actually about 1.5 mi to the south. The turnout has no interpretive signs and the loop doesn't even provide parking spaces. Information and a view of the potholes is located at the **Jackson Point Overlook** on **Signal Mountain**. *See next section on Signal Mountain Rd.*
Cool Rating: * *Crowds:* * *Directions:* SE side of road

MM: 16.7/4.1 *Dist:* 4.7 *GPS:* 43.82675/-110.61475 *GPS2:* 43.84926/-110.56710 *Elev:* 6901 *Grid:* 6/29 *Land:* NPS
Signal Mountain Rd   *Type:* Scenic Viewpoint
A 4.7 mi road that climbs 800 ft to the top of **Signal Mountain** for panoramic views of the **Snake River** winding through the **Jackson Hole** valley and the mountain ranges beyond. *Vault toilet. Picnic table.*

The **Jackson Point Overlook** is at mile 4.0 (43.846632/-110.574123), where a 200 yd trail leads to an overlook of the same valley as previously described plus part of the **Teton Range** above the south end of **Jackson Lake**. 2 interpretive signs are located at the end of the trail, one about the valley landscape (including the potholes) and the other about **William H. Jackson**'s early photographs of the **Teton Range**.
Cool Rating: **** *Crowds:* *** *Time:* 1 hr *Notes:* No RVs or trailers. *Directions:* NE on Signal Mountain Rd 4.7 mi
Road Desc: Paved, narrow, steep & winding

MM: 17.8/3.0 *Dist:* 0.1 *GPS:* 43.84195/-110.61235 *Elev:* 6818 *Grid:* 6/29 *Land:* NPS
Signal Mountain Campground   *Type:* Campground
Located on a hill above the southeast shore of **Jackson Lake** with a fine view of the **Teton Range** across the lake. Some sites have a partial view of the lake. Just north of the campground is **Signal Mountain Lodge** and marina with a store, restaurant, and fuel. *Conifer forest. Many sites are in the open. Small sites. Amphitheater. Fills by late morning.*

The **Signal Mountain Trail** starts at the east end of the campground and leads to the **Jackson Point Overlook** on **Signal Mountain**. This can also be reached by a 4.7 mi paved road to the top *(see Teton Park Rd MM 16.7). Moderate; 5.7 mi round-trip; 750 ft elev gain.*
Crowds: ***** [FEE AREA] *Directions:* W 0.1 mi
Campsites: 81 *Shade:* *** *Privacy:* * *RV Size:* 30' *Other:* Water,RVDump BEARS

MM: 18.4/2.4 *Dist:* 0.1 *GPS:* 43.84544/-110.60284 *Elev:* 6814 *Grid:* 6/29 *Land:* NPS
Chapel of the Sacred Heart   *Type:* Historic Site
A small log **Catholic Church** built in 1935. Services are held on weekends.
Hours: Mass: 5:30pm, Sat-Sun *Cool Rating:* * *Crowds:* * *Time:* 10 min *Directions:* N and left 0.1 mi

MM: 18.4/2.4 *Dist:* 0.1 *GPS:* 43.84577/-110.60057 *Elev:* 6807 *Grid:* 6/29 *Land:* NPS
Picnic Area and Jackson Lake Access   *Type:* Picnic Area
Close access to the southeast shore of **Jackson Lake** with 2 picnic tables in the open.
Directions: N and right 0.1 mi

MM: 18.8/2.0 *GPS:* 43.84855/-110.59416 *Elev:* 6793 *Grid:* 7/29 *Land:* NPS
Teton View across Jackson Lake   *Type:* Scenic Viewpoint
A long pullout with a nice view of the **Teton Range** across **Jackson Lake**.
Cool Rating: *** *Crowds:* ** *Time:* 10 min *Directions:* W side of road

MM: 19.5/1.3 *GPS:* 43.85694/-110.58927 *Elev:* 6791 *Grid:* 7/29 *Land:* NPS

Jackson Lake Dam Overlook   *Type:* Dam

An overlook of the **Jackson Lake Dam** and water release into the **Snake River**. **Jackson Lake** is a natural glacier created lake; however, the lake was dammed twice before the existing dam was built in 1916. This raised the lake level 39 ft in order to provide water to **Idaho** farmers downstream. This is the largest lake in **Grand Teton National Park**. A set of concrete steps descends toward the dam water release and provides access to the south bank of the **Snake River**.

Across the road is a 180 yd path along the lakeshore that leads to 3 points of interest:
1) The old dam release gate hoist equipment and a sign explaining its usage
2) A gazebo with 4 signs explaining the history of the dam construction and the recreational and irrigation use of the water
3) An overlook of **Jackson Lake**, with a bench, at the end of the trail.

Cool Rating: *** *Crowds:* *** *Time:* 30 min

Directions: Parking area on E side of road, just south of the dam. Another large parking area is located on the W side of road.

MM: 19.8/1.0 *Dist:* 0.3 *GPS:* 43.85848/-110.58675 *Elev:* 6744 *Grid:* 7/29 *Land:* NPS

Picnic Area and Snake River Access below Jackson Lake Dam   *Type:* Picnic and Day Use Area

A parking area just below the **Jackson Lake Dam** on the north bank of the **Snake River**. A shady picnic area is located 0.1 mi along the access road. *Vault toilet*

Crowds: *** *Road Desc:* Gravel *Directions:* Just N of the Jackson Lake Dam; SE 1/4 mi.

MM: 20.8/0.0 *GPS:* 43.86610/-110.57058 *Elev:* 6762 *Grid:* 7/28

US-89/191/287 *(see chapter)*   *Type:* Hwy Junction w/Chapter

27 mi highway from **Moran Jct** north through **Grand Teton National Park** to the south entrance of **Yellowstone National Park**. Highlights include: **Oxbow Bend**, views of **Jackson Lake** and the **Teton Range**.

Directions: N to Yellowstone or SE to Moran Jct from MM 4.0/23.0

Notes: There are no mile markers along this highway, so some rivers and creeks have been included as points of reference. The official mile markers are provided as well as the mileages starting at zero in both directions.

MM: 20.8/0.0 *GPS:* 43.86610/-110.57058 *Elev:* 6762 *Grid:* 7/28

End of Highway   *Type:* Highway End

20.8 mi road south through the main section of **Grand Teton National Park**, which traverses the central-eastern base of the **Teton Range** and offers the closest access and views. Highlights include: **Jackson Lake, Signal Mountain, Jenny Lake, Hidden Falls, Inspiration Point, Chapel of the Transfiguration and Menor's Ferry Historic District, Craig Thomas Discovery and Visitor Center**.

Nearest Town: Moose 20.4 S, Jackson 33.2 S *Directions:* S from MM 20.8

Trail Lake Rd/CR-411   NE/SW

MM: 0.0/9.1 *GPS:* 43.51340/-109.56840 *Elev:* 6842 *Grid:* 21/37
Trail Lake Rd/CR-411   *Type:* Highway Description
9.1 mi gravel road south through the **Whiskey Basin Wildlife Habitat Management Area** and ending at the **Torrey Creek Trailhead**. Along the route are 3 lakes, 5 campgrounds, and 2 spectacular **Petroglyphs**. The WHMA provides **Bighorn Sheep** winter and spring habitat, and the trailhead provides hiking into the **Wind River Range**.
Road Desc: Gravel road that gets rough, rocky, and rutted at the WHMA boundary at MM 5.9.
Directions: S and immediately left at the fork

MM: 2.2/6.9 *GPS:* 43.48654/-109.58633 *Elev:* 7281 *Grid:* 21/38 *Land:* Wyoming G & F
Whiskey Basin Wildlife Habitat Management Area   *Type:* Wildlife Habitat Mgmt Area
This area provides crucial winter range for a herd of about 1200 **Bighorn Sheep**, the largest herd in the world, that summer in the **Wind River Mountains**. In the summer months the area provides camping, hiking, fishing, and **Petroglyph** viewing. For more information on the bighorn sheep, visit the **National Bighorn Sheep Interpretive Center** is in **Dubois** *(see US-26/287 MM 54.8)*. The WHMA boundary begins a short 0.6 mi section with an observation area *(see next section)*. The road then crosses 3.5 mi of private land before re-entering the WHMA.
Cool Rating: **** *Crowds:* ***

MM: 2.3/6.7 *GPS:* 43.48439/-109.58625 *Elev:* 7312 *Grid:* 21/38 *Land:* Wyoming G & F
Bighorn Sheep Observation Parking Area   *Type:* Wildlife Habitat Mgmt Area
A parking area for observing bighorn sheep on the slopes of **Whiskey Mountain** and the **BLM Ridge Wintering Site** to the southwest. The breeding season lasts from late November through December and is the best time to see the larger rams. The ewes can be seen from November through early May. Bring binoculars and/or a spotting scope. A large sign board plus 3 interpretive signs provide a map of the area, explains the WHMA, provides information on the **Bighorn Sheep**, and shows other large mammals in the area.
Cool Rating: **** *Crowds:* ** *Directions:* E side of road
Notes: The Cool Rating is based on the Bighorn Sheep being present in the winter and spring, otherwise it is a **.

MM: 2.8/6.3 *GPS:* 43.48272/-109.57970 *Elev:* 7379 *Grid:* 21/38 *Land:* Wyoming G & F
Whiskey Basin Wildlife Habitat Management Area Boundary   *Type:* Wildlife Habitat Mgmt Area
The road leaves the WHMA and enters private land for the next 3.5 mi. Be respectful of private property.

MM: 5.9/3.2 *GPS:* 43.44991/-109.54486 *Elev:* 7529 *Grid:* 22/39 *Land:* Wyoming G & F
Whiskey Basin Wildlife Habitat Management Area Boundary   *Type:* Wildlife Habitat Mgmt Area
The road re-enters the WHMA from private land.

MM: 6.1/3.0 *Dist:* 0.2 *GPS:* 43.44984/-109.54265 *Elev:* 7430 *Grid:* 22/39 *Land:* Wyoming G & F
Ring Lake Campground   *Type:* Campground
A long open parking area on the south shore of **Ring Lake**. The campground includes 7 established sites, but 10 units could probably fit. *Stone fire rings. Vault toilet. Primitive boat ramp.*
Crowds: *** *Directions:* NW then E/R 0.2 mi
Campsites: Dispersed *Shade:* * *Privacy:* * *RV Size:* 40' *Other:* None

MM: 6.4/2.7 *GPS:* 43.44361/-109.53998 *Elev:* 7450 *Grid:* 22/39 *Land:* Wyoming G & F
Torrey Creek Campground   *Type:* Campground
A 0.15 mi road with an end loop along a strip of land between the north end of **Trail Lake** and the outflow of **Ring Lake** with 4 areas:
  1) A wide open site is just off the entrance road to the left
  2) A short road down a hill to the right leads to the most private site with a few trees
  3) 2 sites just before the end loop
  4) 2 sites on the end loop.
Stone fire rings. No toilet.
Crowds: ** *Directions:* E side of road
Campsites: 6 *Shade:* * *Privacy:* ** *RV Size:* 30' *Other:* None

MM: 6.4/2.7 *GPS:* 43.44376/-109.54000 *Elev:* 7474 *Grid:* 22/39 *Land:* Wyoming G & F
Trail Lake Rd Petroglyphs   *Type:* Petroglyphs
Some of the oldest **Petroglyphs** in **Wyoming** are located on the sides of large glacial boulders along the road. The most interesting are 2 elaborate and well defined panels depicting large humanlike figures. A few smaller **Petroglyphs** of animals are also scattered around the area. The first panel has figures about 2 ft tall and is about 60 yds west of and 30 ft above the road (43.443809/-109.540715). The second panel is quite ornate with figures about 4 ft tall and is about 100 yds west of and 100 ft above the road (43.443321/-109.541095). Reaching this panel requires climbing up a steep hill along a narrow dirt path with loose sections. Both panels can be seen from the road; the first from about 17 yds before the **Torrey Creek Campground** turnoff; the second from about 30 yds past the turnoff. Please help protect these irreplaceable treasures.
Cool Rating: ***** *Crowds:* ** *Time:* 30 min
Directions: Petroglyphs on W side of road across from the Torrey Creek Campground entrance. Park at the campground.

MM: 6.5/2.5 *GPS:* 43.44190/-109.54043 *Elev:* 7463 *Grid:* 22/39 *Land:* Wyoming G & F
Petroglyphs   *Type:* Petroglyphs
Petroglyphs depicting humans and animals on some fallen boulders near the west side of the road.
Cool Rating: *** *Crowds:* * *Time:* 10 min *Directions:* Small pullout on W side of road

MM: 6.8/2.3 *GPS:* 43.43791/-109.54066 *Elev:* 7457 *Grid:* 22/39 *Land:* Wyoming G & F
Trail Lake Boat Ramp   *Type:* Boat Ramp
Gravel boat ramp on the southwest end of **Trail Lake** near **Trail Lake Campground**.
Directions: Parking pullout on W side of road

MM: 6.9/2.2   *GPS:* 43.43730/-109.54060   *Elev:* 7448   *Grid:* 22/39   *Land:* Wyoming G & F

Trail Lake Campground   *Type:* Campground

Circular parking area on the southwest shore of **Trail Lake** with room for 3 or 4 vehicles. *Stone fire rings. Vault toilet.*

Crowds: *****   *Directions:* SE 100 yds.

Campsites: Dispersed   *Shade:* *   *Privacy:* *   *RV Size:* 30'   *Other:* None

---

MM: 6.9/2.1   *GPS:* 43.43634/-109.54138   *Elev:* 7441   *Grid:* 22/39   *Land:* Wyoming G & F

Moose and Beaver Area   *Type:* Wildlife Area

Torrey Creek flows out of **Trail Lake** and meanders near the road for the next 1.6 mi. Willows grow along the banks providing food and shelter for moose. Beavers can also be seen here, particularly around dawn and dusk.

MM: 8.5/0.6   *GPS:* 43.42535/-109.56532   *Elev:* 7492   *Grid:* 21/39   *Land:* Wyoming G & F

Trail Meadow Campground   *Type:* Campground

Campsites along a short road with a site in the open, one next to the trees, and an unlevel site in an end loop with a stone fire ring. *No toilet.*

Crowds: *   *Directions:* S side of road

Campsites: 3   *Shade:* **   *Privacy:* **   *RV Size:* 30'   *Other:* None

---

MM: 9.1/0.0   *GPS:* 43.42572/-109.57335   *Elev:* 7600   *Grid:* 21/39   *Land:* Wyoming G & F

Torrey Creek Trailhead   *Type:* Trailhead

Trails through an impressive granite canyon into the **Wind River Mountains** and the **Fitzpatrick Wilderness**. The most reasonable day hike is to **Lake Louise**, a beautiful lake surrounded by granite cliffs. Keep left at the **Whiskey Mountain Trail** and right at the **Glacier Trail**. *Moderate; 2.3 mi one-way; 800 ft elev gain.* Other long and strenuous hikes include: **Bomber Lake Trail** to **Bomber Falls**: *4.7 mi one-way; 1650 ft elev gain.* **Whiskey Mountain Trail** to **Ross Lake**: *6.0 mi one-way, 2850 ft elev gain, 900 ft elev loss.* **Glacier Trail** to **Dinwoody Glacier**: *22.1 mi one-way; 5300 ft elev gain.* At the parking area are 2 picnic tables and a vault toilet.

Cool Rating: ****   *Crowds:* *****   *Directions:* Keep right at the fork to an end of road loop parking area

---

MM: 9.1/0.0   *GPS:* 43.42564/-109.57223   *Elev:* 7568   *Grid:* 21/39   *Land:* Wyoming G & F

Glacier Trail Campground   *Type:* Campground

Located at the end of the road in a large open loop just east of the **Torrey Creek Trailhead**. 3 sites are located on the south end of the loop plus a short road leads to another site near an outfitters corral. Inside the loop is room for several RVs and trailers; however, there is only 1 established site. *Stone fire rings. Vault toilet at trailhead.*

Crowds: ***   *Directions:* Keep left at the fork just before the end of the road

Campsites: Dispersed   *Shade:* *   *Privacy:* ***   *RV Size:* 30'   *Other:* None

---

MM: 9.1/0.0   *GPS:* 43.42632/-109.57221   *Elev:* 7604   *Grid:* 21/39   *Land:* Wyoming G & F

End of Highway   *Type:* Highway End

Union Pass Rd

MM: 0.0/44.6 *GPS:* 43.26002/-110.01643 *Elev:* 7750 *Grid:* 15/43
Union Pass Rd   *Type:* Highway Description
44.6 mi route on National Forest and county roads that connect **Wy-352/FR-10091**, in the **Upper Green River Valley**, north to **US-26/287** by climbing over the 9,643 ft **Union Pass**. This drive offers nice scenery and a chance to see wildlife and wildflowers. The area is popular for ATVs and provides many dispersed camping opportunities. The north side of the pass offers great views across the valley to the northeast. Using this route and **Wy-352/FR-10091** between **US-191** and **US-26/287** saves 74 mi over driving the paved roads.
Nearest Town: Pinedale 34 SE *Directions:* NW on Union Pass Rd from MM 0
Notes: This is a seasonal road and is typically open from July through September. I would only recommend this route for recreational purposes or travel between Wy-352 & US-26/287, as the road is fairly slow and the scenery is not that spectacular.
Road Desc: The first 17 mi from the south is extremely washboarded as is the section between the Union Pass summit and Warm Springs Creek Rd.

MM: 12.2/32.4 *GPS:* 43.40003/-110.06779 *Elev:* 8883 *Grid:* 14/40 *Land:* NF
Mosquito Lake   *Type:* Lake
A small lake in the sagebrush hills where **Trumpeter Swans** are sometimes seen.
Cool Rating: * *Crowds:* * *Directions:* E side of road

MM: 24.2/20.4 *GPS:* 43.46032/-109.95515 *Elev:* 8840 *Grid:* 16/38 *Land:* NF
Fish Creek   *Type:* Creek

MM: 30.3/14.2 *Dist:* 1.5 *GPS:* 43.47858/-109.87866 *GPS2:* 43.48260/-109.89637 *Elev:* 9240 *Grid:* 17/38 *Land:* NF
Lake of the Woods   *Type:* Lake
A small fishing lake.
Cool Rating: * *Crowds:* * *Road Desc:* Dirt, primitive, deeply rutted & impassable when wet, high clearance
Directions: NW on FR-696 1.5 mi

MM: 30.6/14.0 *GPS:* 43.48003/-109.87473 *GPS2:* 43.48086/-109.87493 *Elev:* 9211 *Grid:* 17/38
Union Pass National Historic Site   *Type:* Historic Site
A 120 yd trail climbs north to a ring of 10 plaques describing the history, flora, and fauna of **Union Pass** as well as the surrounding geology. One plaque points out **Three Waters Mountain**, located about 7.5 mi southeast, which is 1 of only 2 places in North America where a single raindrop of water might travel to 3 different watersheds and end up in the **Gulf of Mexico**, **Gulf of California**, or the **Pacific Ocean**.
Cool Rating: ** *Crowds:* * *Time:* 20 min
Notes: This site is easy to miss. There used to be a sign marking this spot, but as of my visit all that remains are 2 postholes. The pullout is just west of a sign where the forest changes from **Bridger-Teton National Forest** to **Shoshone National Forest**. Each plaques is also marked with "tripods" of wooden posts that can be seen up the hill on the north side of the road.
Directions: N side of road in a visitor information board pullout, just west of the National Forest boundary sign.

MM: 34.5/10.1 *GPS:* 43.52187/-109.84206 *Elev:* 9643 *Grid:* 17/37 *Land:* NF
Union Pass Summit   *Type:* Pass
Union Pass was a major mountain crossing for Indians and early mountain men on their way to and from the northwest.

MM: 39.2/5.3 *GPS:* 43.56603/-109.81541 *Elev:* 8372 *Grid:* 18/36 *Land:* NF
Warm Springs Creek Rd/FR-532   *Type:* Highway Junction
A National Forest road that winds through the mountains 17.3 mi to **US-26/287** MM 38.2. The National Forest boundary is 1.0 mi west and a primitive campground is 0.6 mi farther *(see next section)*. The road roughly parallels **Warm Springs Creek** for 9.5 mi before crossing the creek and heading north.
Road Desc: Gravel, rough spots *Directions:* W on Warm Springs Creek Rd

MM: 39.2/5.3 *Dist:* 1.6 *GPS:* 43.56700/-109.84606 *Elev:* 8371 *Grid:* 17/36 *Land:* NF
Warm Springs Creek Campground   *Type:* Campground
Primitive camping next to **Warm Springs Creek**. Additional dispersed camping can be found in the area, including along a road across from the campground, which accommodates small campers and tents. *Mixed forest. Stone fire rings. 1 bear-proof box. Vault toilet.*
Crowds: ***** *Road Desc:* Gravel
Directions: W on Warm Springs Rd/FR-532 1.6 mi; E side of road down a hill just before bridge.
Campsites: 5 *Shade:* ***** *Privacy:* *** *RV Size:* 30' *Other:* BEARS

MM: 44.6/0.0 *GPS:* 43.59980/-109.78564 *Elev:* 7288 *Grid:* 18/35
End of Highway   *Type:* Highway End
44.6 mi route on National Forest and county roads that connect **US-26/287** south to **Wy-352/FR-10091**, in the **Upper Green River Valley**, by climbing over the 9,643 ft **Union Pass**. This drive offers nice scenery and a chance to see wildlife and wildflowers. The area is popular for ATVs and provides many dispersed camping opportunities. The north side of the pass offers great views across the valley to the northeast. This is the best route from **US-26/287** to the **Green River Lakes** area as it would be over 100 mi farther by taking the paved highways. Combined with **Wy-352/FR-10091**, this also saves 74 mi between **US-26/287** and **US-191**.
Nearest Town: Dubois 9.5 SE *Directions:* SW on Union Pass Rd from MM 44.6

MM: 0.0 *GPS:* 44.48897/-108.05540 *Elev:* 3792 *Grid:* 43/13
US-14 *Type:* Highway Description
80.5 mi highway from **Greybull** northeast to **Ranchester**. A large portion of the highway is through National Forest along the **Bighorn Scenic Byway** with 10 public campgrounds. Highlights include: **Devil's Kitchen Geological Site**, **Red Gulch Dinosaur Tracksite**, **Medicine Lodge State Archaeological Site**, **Shell Falls**, **Dayton Bell Tower**, **Tongue River Canyon**.
Directions: E to Shell from MM 0
Notes: There are 2 junctions with US-14A (at Burgess Jct) depending on the direction traveled. These 2 junctions are 1/4 mi apart, but the mile markers jump from 47.8 to 57.1, gaining 9.4 mi. The attractions along US-14A near Burgess Jct are listed twice, both from MM 47.8 (heading north) and MM 57.1 (heading south). Many National Forest side roads with dispersed camping are located along US-14.

MM: 0.0 *GPS:* 44.48897/-108.05540 *Elev:* 3792 *Grid:* 43/13
US-20/Wy-789 & US-16/20/Wy-789 & US-14/16/20/Wy-789 *(see chapter)* *Type:* Hwy Junction w/Chapter
157 mi highway from **Shoshoni** north to **Montana**. Highlights include: **Boysen State Park**, **Wind River Canyon**, **Hot Springs State Park**, **Medicine Lodge State Archaeological Site**, **Devil's Kitchen Geological Site**, **Museum of Flight and Aerial Firefighting**.
Directions: N on US-14/16/20/Wy-789 to Lovell or S on US-16/20/Wy-789 to Worland from MM 204.1

MM: 0.0 *GPS:* 44.48897/-108.05540 *Elev:* 3792 *Grid:* 43/13
Greybull *Type:* Town

MM: 0.6 *GPS:* 44.48841/-108.04457 *Elev:* 3825 *Grid:* 43/13
East Bridge Rest Area and Boat Ramp *Type:* Rest Area
Restroom and a couple of picnic tables in the open. A road leads under the highway bridge to a boat ramp on the **Bighorn River**.
Directions: N side of hwy on the east end of the bridge.

MM: 0.7 *Dist:* 7.1 *GPS:* 44.53373/-107.96993 *Elev:* 4050 *Grid:* 44/12 *Land:* BLM
Devil's Kitchen Geological Site (eastbound) *Type:* Scenic Area
A colorful badlands area of red and gray weathered hills and eroded cliffs. This geology is part of the **Cloverly Formation**, a 100+ million year-old sequence of sediments containing important dinosaur remains. The cliffs drop off from the north at the road level, where an overlook offers picturesque views into the badlands below. From the overlook the cliff extends along a narrow ridge about 100 yds into the badlands offering the best views of these fascinating formations. This ridge has steep drop-offs, so proceed with caution and do not take small children. For a different perspective, a 3/4 mi dirt road descends into the badlands 0.4 mi west of the overlook.
Cool Rating: ***** *Crowds:* * *Time:* 30-60+ min
Notes: Heavy truck traffic on CR-33 so keep your distance to avoid flying rocks.
Road Desc: Partially paved. The final short roads to the site are primitive and impassable when wet.
Directions: N on Division St 0.1 mi; Continue left on Sandy Row 0.2 mi; Continue right on Rimrock Rd 0.3 mi; NW/L on Rimrock Rd/CR-27 2.0 mi (pavement ends about halfway); E/R on CR-33 3.1 mi; Keep right at fork to stay on CR-33 1.2 mi; S on dirt road 0.2 mi to overlook.

MM: 6.8 *GPS:* 44.52040/-107.93490 *Elev:* 3991 *Grid:* 45/12
Lower Shell Schoolhouse *Type:* Historic Site
A stone schoolhouse built in 1903, which was one of the first non-log community buildings in the **Bighorn Basin**.
Cool Rating: ** *Crowds:* * *Time:* 10 min *Directions:* N side of hwy

MM: 7.4 *Dist:* 3.8
Devil's Kitchen Geological Site (westbound) *Type:* Scenic Area
See MM 0.7 above.
Cool Rating: ***** *Crowds:* * *Time:* 30-60+ min *Road Desc:* Partially paved
Directions: N on CR-29/Davis Rd 1.2 mi; W on CR-33 2.4 mi; S on dirt road 0.2 mi to overlook.

MM: 10.5 *GPS:* 44.51984/-107.86159 *Elev:* 4183 *Grid:* 46/12 *Land:* BLM
Red Gulch/Alkali National Back Country Byway *Type:* Highway Junction
35 mi backcountry route across **BLM** land from **US-14**, west of **Shell**, to **Wy-31** at **Hyattville**. This is wide open and barren land with hills, gullies, and ridges along the western edge of the **Bighorn Mountains**. The **Red Gulch Dinosaur Tracksite** is located 5.2 mi along this route *(see next section)*. Beyond that, this is primarily a shortcut to the **Medicine Lodge State Archaeological Site** and **Hyattville**. It is approximately 61 mi on the paved highways to **Hyattville**, so this route can cut off 26 mi, or 37 mi if visiting the dinosaur tracksite.
Crowds: * *Road Desc:* Gravel, impassable when wet
Directions: S then SE on Red Gulch Rd/BLM-1109 20.3 mi; S on Alkali Rd/ BLM-1111 14.4 mi to the turnoff to Medicine Lodge; S 0.3 mi to Wy-31.

MM: 10.5 *Dist:* 5.3 *GPS:* 44.46253/-107.81554 *Elev:* 4516 *Grid:* 46/13 *Land:* BLM
Red Gulch Dinosaur Tracksite *Type:* Historic Site
This tracksite area contains hundreds of rare **Middle Jurassic** age (160+ million years old) **Dinosaur Tracks** embedded in oolitic limestone. The area is very nice with restrooms, sheltered picnic tables, and a boardwalk to the tracksite with interpretive signs. Visitors are allowed to walk on the tracksite and examine the **Dinosaur Tracks**. Random 3-toed tracks can be seen in various places; however, looking carefully reveals sets of tracks that fit together to define the walking path of a dinosaur.

The site is along the **Red Gulch/Alkali National Back Country Byway**, which travels 35 mi to **Hyattville**. *See previous section.*
Cool Rating: **** *Crowds:* * *Time:* 30-60 min *Road Desc:* Gravel, impassable when wet
Directions: S then SE on Red Gulch Rd/BLM-1109 5.2 mi; S/R 0.1 mi.

MM: 10.5 **Dist:** 40.1 **GPS:** 44.29815/-107.54190 **Elev:** 4890 **Grid:** 50/18 **Land:** State
Medicine Lodge State Archaeological Site   **Type:** Petroglyphs
In 1973 this site was the scene of one of the most significant archaeological excavations in North America. For 2 years scientists unearthed evidence of over 10,000 years of human habitation from depths up to 26 ft. These findings document the entire history of human occupation in the **Bighorn Basin**. The dig site (which has been filled in) is located below a 750 ft long cliff that is covered with hundreds of **Petroglyphs** and **Pictographs**. Along the base of the cliff are interpretive signs explaining the rock art and the excavation. *See US-20/Wy-789 MM 185.0 for a complete description.*
Hours: Visitor Center: 8am - 5pm, Mon-Fri; 9am - 8pm, Sat-Sun
Cool Rating: **** **Crowds:** ** **Time:** 1-3 hrs **Nearest Town:** Hyattville 6.2 SW
Road Desc: Partially paved, mostly gravel. Only the 3.7 mi on Cold Springs Rd is paved.
Directions: S then SE on Red Gulch Rd/BLM-1109 20.3 mi; S on Alkali Rd/ BLM-1111 14.4 mi; E/L on Cold Springs Rd/CR-268 3.2 mi; Take sharp curve N/L 0.5 mi; Where road curves E/R continue straight 1.7 mi to the park.

MM: 15.3 **GPS:** 44.53540/-107.78002 **Elev:** 4215 **Grid:** 47/12
Shell   **Type:** Town

MM: 17.0 **GPS:** 44.54929/-107.75316 **Elev:** 4324 **Grid:** 47/11 **Land:** NF
Bighorn Scenic Byway (southwest end)   **Type:** Scenic Byway
A scenic 55 mi section of **US-14** between **Shell** and **Dayton** that climbs over the crest of the **Bighorn Mountains** from the **Bighorn Basin** to the **Powder River Basin**. The high point is at **Granite Pass** at 9,035 ft. The majority of the route is through the **Bighorn National Forest**.
Cool Rating: *** **Crowds:** ***

MM: 18.2 **GPS:** 44.55828/-107.73360 **GPS2:** 44.54920/-107.72800 **Elev:** 4353 **Grid:** 47/11
Chimney Rock   **Type:** Geological Feature
A red sandstone pillar about 1/2 mi south of the highway at the west end of **Shell Canyon**.
Cool Rating: ** **Crowds:** * **Time:** Drive by

MM: 20.1 **GPS:** 44.57321/-107.70396 **Elev:** 4432 **Grid:** 48/11 **Land:** NF
Bighorn National Forest   **Type:** National Forest Boundary

MM: 26.5 **GPS:** 44.58656/-107.61522 **Elev:** 6270 **Grid:** 49/10 **Land:** NF
Shell Falls   **Type:** Waterfall
A waterfall on **Shell Creek** that plunges 120 ft into **Shell Canyon**. Directly in front of the falls is an easily accessible viewing platform. Along the canyon rim is a short paved interpretive loop trail that offers additional views of the falls, river, canyon, and geological and scenic features of the surrounding area.
Cool Rating: ***** **Crowds:** *** **Time:** 15-60 min **Directions:** N side of hwy

MM: 31.3 **Dist:** 0.3 **GPS:** 44.57005/-107.52995 **Elev:** 7632 **Grid:** 50/11 **Land:** NF
Cabin Creek Meadows Campground   **Type:** Campground
An oddly configured campground in a sagebrush meadow with few trees. At 0.2 mi there is a single site at the campground entrance. Continuing 120 yds are 4 sites in a small loop. 1/4 mi farther begins a 0.2 mi section with 11 sites that are close together. Another small loop with 5 sites is located the end of the road. *Not level. Outhouse-like vault toilets. Not very nice.*
Crowds: ** **[FEE AREA]** **Road Desc:** Gravel **Directions:** E on FR-17 0.05 mi; E/L on FR-251 1/4 mi.
Campsites: 21 **Shade:** ** **Privacy:** * **RV Size:** 40' **Other:** 1-877-444-6777:www.recreation.gov,Water

MM: 31.3 **Dist:** 0.2 **GPS:** 44.56820/-107.53500 **Elev:** 7497 **Grid:** 50/11 **Land:** NF
Cabin Creek Campground   **Type:** Campground
Just off the highway with open sites in a small loop. *Stands of aspen that don't shade the camping areas. Highway noise.*
Crowds: * **[FEE AREA]** **Road Desc:** Gravel **Directions:** E then S FR-17 0.1 mi; W/R 0.1 mi.
Campsites: 4 **Shade:** * **Privacy:** * **RV Size:** 20' **Other:** Water

MM: 31.3 **Dist:** 1.6 **GPS:** 44.55213/-107.51867 **Elev:** 7558 **Grid:** 50/11 **Land:** NF
Shell Creek Campground   **Type:** Campground
Located at the base of a sagebrush hill below the main road. The campground road parallels **Shell Creek** with a small loop on each end. *Mixed forest that doesn't shade most sites. No understory for privacy. Decent spacing between sites along the road. 2 tent-only sites. 2 pull-thrus.*
Crowds: *** **[FEE AREA]** **Road Desc:** Gravel **Directions:** E then SE on FR 17 1.6 mi
Campsites: 15 **Shade:** * **Privacy:** ** **RV Size:** 40' **Other:** 1-877-444-6777:www.recreation.gov,Water

MM: 31.3 **Dist:** 2.7 **GPS:** 44.54560/-107.49904 **Elev:** 7683 **Grid:** 51/11 **Land:** NF
Ranger Creek Campground   **Type:** Campground
Near **Shell Creek** with 3 separate groups of sites:
1) On the west side of the road, keeping right at a fork are sites 1-4, which are down a hill near the creek with little parking space and no room to turn around an RV. Site 5 sits by itself in the open at the top of this hill.
2) Keeping left at the fork, 3 additional sites are grouped together in the trees.
3) On the east side of the road are 2 forested sites.
Conifer forest. Sites are close together. Some leveling required. Campground is best for tents. Reservable group site.
Crowds: *** **[FEE AREA]** **Road Desc:** Gravel. There are huge bumps in the campground road.
Directions: E then SE on FR 17 2.7 mi
Campsites: 10 **Shade:** **** **Privacy:** * **RV Size:** 20' **Other:** Water

MM: 38.0 **GPS:** 44.63983/-107.50325 **Elev:** 9035 **Grid:** 51/9 **Land:** NF
Granite Pass Summit   **Type:** Pass

MM: 38.2 **GPS:** 44.64411/-107.50320 **Elev:** 8971 **Grid:** 51/9
FR-10/Hunt Mountain Rd   **Type:** Highway Junction
A 22.5 mi backcountry route that traverses the crest of the **Bighorn Mountains** across high mountain meadows. The route heads northwest from **US-14** to **US-14A** MM 85.7, 14.2 mi west of Burgess Jct. Best as an OHV route.
Cool Rating: ** **Crowds:** * **Road Desc:** Dirt, rough & impassable when wet, narrow, high clearance
Directions: W then NW on FR-10/Hunt Mountain Rd

MM: 38.4   *GPS:* 44.64517/-107.50221   *Elev:* 8950   *Grid:* 51/9   *Land:* NF

Interpretive Pullout: Mother Nature's Dam Builders   *Type:* Point of Interest

A sign about beavers in the **Bighorn National Forest**.

Cool Rating: *   *Crowds:* *   *Time:* 5 min   *Directions:* E side of hwy just N of FR-10.

MM: 42.6   *Dist:* 2.8   *GPS:* 44.71536/-107.45083   *Elev:* 8359   *Grid:* 51/7   *Land:* NF

Tie Flume Campground   *Type:* Campground

The campground is composed of 2 sections near the **South Tongue River**. The first loop is away from the river and is heavily wooded. The second section is along a road with an end loop. This section is more sparsely wooded with the river flowing nearby, but not along the campground. The campground and surrounding area gets considerable OHV usage so it can get rather noisy. *Conifer forest. Roomy sites. Fairly level. 1 tent-only site. 2 pull-thrus.*

Crowds: *****   *[FEE AREA]*   *Road Desc:* Gravel

Notes: Dispersed camping is not allowed within 1/4 mi of FR-26; however, dispersed camping can be found within these restrictions on side roads beyond Dead Swede Campground.

Directions: E on FR-26 2.6 mi; Keep left at the fork onto FR-16 0.2 mi.

Campsites: 25   *Shade:* ****   *Privacy:* *   *RV Size:* 40'+   *Other:* 1-877-444-6777:www.recreation.gov,Water

---

MM: 42.6   *Dist:* 3.2   *GPS:* 44.70825/-107.45449   *Elev:* 8450   *Grid:* 51/7   *Land:* NF

Interpretive Pullout: Majesty of Nature   *Type:* Point of Interest

A sign about a microburst that lasted 15 minutes and blew down over 1,100 acres of trees along an 8 mi path near this point in 1991.

Cool Rating: *   *Crowds:* *   *Time:* 5 min   *Road Desc:* Gravel

Directions: E on FR-26 3.2 mi keeping right at the fork at 2.6 mi; E side of road.

MM: 42.6   *Dist:* 4.5   *GPS:* 44.68957/-107.44865   *Elev:* 8449   *Grid:* 51/8   *Land:* NF

Dead Swede Campground   *Type:* Campground/Picnic Area

The campground is composed of 2 sections that are not close together. The first loop is up a hill from the second and away from the river. The second section is along the **South Tongue River** on a long road with an end loop. The campground is popular with fishermen. *Conifer forest. Roomy sites. Some leveling required. 4 tent-only sites. No pull-thrus.*

A picnic area is to the left at the campground entrance with 6 sites and a toilet.

Crowds: ***   *[FEE AREA]*   *Road Desc:* Gravel   *Directions:* E on FR-26 4.5 mi keeping right at the fork at 2.6 mi.

Notes: Dispersed camping is not allowed within 1/4 mi of FR-26; however, dispersed camping can be found within these restrictions on side roads beyond this campground.

Campsites: 22   *Shade:* *****   *Privacy:* *   *RV Size:* 30'   *Other:* 1-877-444-6777:www.recreation.gov,Water BEARS

MM: 42.8   *Dist:* 0.2   *GPS:* 44.70508/-107.50047   *Elev:* 8458   *Grid:* 51/7   *Land:* NF

Owen Creek Campground   *Type:* Campground

Located in a sparse forest on the edge of a meadow with **Owen Creek** flowing through the campground. *One site in the middle of the end loop turnaround. The trees have been cut down in the first 4 sites. Some parking areas are very short. Not a very nice campground.*

Crowds: ***   *[FEE AREA]*   *Notes:* Dispersed camping areas are located farther along FR-236.   *Road Desc:* Gravel

Directions: SW on FR-236 0.2 mi

Campsites: 8   *Shade:* **   *Privacy:* *   *RV Size:* 30'   *Other:* 1-877-444-6777:www.recreation.gov,Water

---

MM: 47.7   *GPS:* 44.77005/-107.51805   *Elev:* 8088   *Grid:* 51/6

US-14A (northbound) *(see chapter)*   *Type:* Hwy Junction w/Chapter

98.9 mi highway west from **Burgess Jct** to **Lovell**, then southwest to **Cody**. The first 27 mi follow the **Medicine Wheel Passage**, a scenic high elevation route (over 9,000 ft) with excellent views into the **Bighorn Basin**. Highlights include: **Porcupine Falls**, **Bucking Mule Falls, Medicine Wheel National Historic Landmark, Bighorn Canyon National Recreation Area, Heart Mountain Relocation Center**.

Directions: W to Lovell from MM 98.9

MM: 47.7   *GPS:* 44.77005/-107.51805   *Elev:* 8088   *Grid:* 51/6

Mile Marker Discrepancy (northbound)   *Type:* MM Discrepancy

Heading north the mile markers jump from MM 47.7 to MM 57.1 (gaining 9.4 mi) in the 1/4 mi between the south and north junctions with **US-14A** at **Burgess Jct**.

MM: 47.7   *GPS:* 44.77005/-107.51805   *Elev:* 8088   *Grid:* 51/6

Burgess Jct (northbound)   *Type:* Highway Junction

A named highway junction with no services.

MM: 47.7   *Dist:* 1.3   *GPS:* 44.78122/-107.53402   *Elev:* 7837   *Grid:* 50/6   *Land:* NF

North Tongue Campground (northbound)   *Type:* Campground

Composed of 2 sections across the road from the **North Tongue River**. The lower section is adjacent to a creek with 3 sites. The upper section climbs up a forested hillside with 9 sites, including 2 pull-thrus. *Conifer forest. Level. Lantern pole.*

Crowds: ***   *[FEE AREA]*   *Road Desc:* Gravel   *Directions:* W on US-14A 0.2 mi; N on FR-15 1.1 mi.

Notes: Dispersed camping along FR-15.

Campsites: 12   *Shade:* *****   *Privacy:* *   *RV Size:* 30'   *Other:* 1-877-444-6777:www.recreation.gov,Water BEARS

MM: 47.7   *Dist:* 2.0   *GPS:* 44.78443/-107.52822   *Elev:* 7796   *Grid:* 50/5   *Land:* NF

Burgess Picnic Area (northbound)   *Type:* Picnic Area

A very nice picnic area along the **North Tongue River** with 5 sites. This is also a popular fishing access point.

Road Desc: Gravel

Directions: W on US-14A 0.2 mi; N on FR-15 1.3 mi (the turnoff is just past North Tongue Campground); E/R on FR-162 0.5 mi.

MM: 57.1   *GPS:* 44.77312/-107.51642   *Elev:* 8054   *Grid:* 51/6

Mile Marker Discrepancy (southbound)   *Type:* MM Discrepancy

Heading south the mile markers jump from MM 57.1 to MM 47.7 (losing 9.4 mi) in the 1/4 mi between the north and south junctions with **US-14A** at **Burgess Jct**.

MM: 57.1 **GPS:** 44.77312/-107.51642 **Elev:** 8054 **Grid:** 51/6
US-14A (southbound) *(see chapter)*   **Type:** Hwy Junction w/Chapter
98.9 mi highway west from **Burgess Jct** to **Lovell**, then southwest to **Cody**. The first 27 mi follow the **Medicine Wheel Passage**, a scenic high elevation route (over 9,000 ft) with excellent views into the **Bighorn Basin**. Highlights include: **Porcupine Falls**, **Bucking Mule Falls**, **Medicine Wheel National Historic Landmark**, **Bighorn Canyon National Recreation Area**, **Heart Mountain Relocation Center**.
Directions: W to Lovell from MM 98.9

MM: 57.1 **GPS:** 44.77312/-107.51642 **Elev:** 8054 **Grid:** 51/6
Burgess Jct (southbound)   **Type:** Highway Junction
A named highway junction with no services.

MM: 57.1 **Dist:** 1.5
North Tongue Campground (southbound)   **Type:** Campground
See MM 47.7.
Directions: W on US-14A 0.4 mi (from the point where the highway forks right); N on FR-15 1.1 mi.

MM: 57.1 **Dist:** 2.2
Burgess Picnic Area (southbound)   **Type:** Picnic Area
See MM 47.7.
Directions: W on US-14A 0.4 mi (from the point where the highway forks right); N on FR-15 1.3 mi (the turnoff is just past North Tongue Campground); E/R on FR-162 0.5 mi.

MM: 57.2 **GPS:** 44.77399/-107.51506 **Elev:** 8045 **Grid:** 51/6 **Land:** NF
RV Dump: Bighorn National Forest   **Type:** RV Dump
A National Forest **RV dump** with 3 stations. *Donations accepted.*
Directions: Just NE of junction of US-14 & US-14A; NW side of hwy.

MM: 58.4 **GPS:** 44.78610/-107.49583 **Elev:** 7970 **Grid:** 51/5 **Land:** NF
Burgess Jct Visitor Center   **Type:** Visitor Center
General information, maps, books, and gifts, as well as short films on area topics and exhibits about activities and history in the **Bighorn Mountains** region. Just southwest of the parking area is a 0.4 mi self-guided interpretive nature trail "A Traveler's Preview of the Bighorns."
Hours: 8am - 5:30pm **Directions:** NW side of hwy

MM: 60.9 **GPS:** 44.77005/-107.46907 **Elev:** 7682 **Grid:** 51/6 **Land:** NF
Prune Creek Campground   **Type:** Campground
The campground is composed of 2 sections separated by **Prune Creek**, which flows into the **South Tongue River**. The west section is a loop with 13 sites near a bend in the river. A few sites are near the river. The east section parallels the highway with 7 sites along a road with 3 small loops. This section is not near the river, but 3 sites are near **Prune Creek**. *Conifer forest. Grass understory. Roomy sites. Level. Lantern pole. No pull-thrus. Highway noise.*
Crowds: ***** **[FEE AREA]** **Directions:** SW side of hwy
Campsites: 21 **Shade:** ***** **Privacy:** ** **RV Size:** 40'+ **Other:** 1-877-444-6777:www.recreation.gov,Water

MM: 62.4 **Dist:** 0.3 **GPS:** 44.75949/-107.43977 **Elev:** 7983 **Grid:** 52/6 **Land:** NF
Sibley Lake Campground   **Type:** Campground
Composed of 2 loops above and just west of **Sibley Lake**. The west loop has 15 RV sites with parallel parking areas, electricity, no privacy, and little shade. The east loop has better shade, no electricity, and little privacy. Neither loop has a view of the lake. *Conifer forest. Grass understory. Good spacing between sites. 1 tent-only site. No pull-thrus. Fills fast.*
Crowds: ***** **[FEE AREA]** **Directions:** SE 0.3 mi
Campsites: 25 **Shade:** *** **Privacy:** * **RV Size:** 40'+ **Other:** 1-877-444-6777:www.recreation.gov,Water,Electric

MM: 62.4 **Dist:** 0.5 **GPS:** 44.75869/-107.43784 **Elev:** 7961 **Grid:** 52/6 **Land:** NF
Sibley Lake Picnic Areas   **Type:** Picnic and Day Use Area
Just past the turnoff, turning left leads to a picnic area below **Sibley Dam** with tables across **Prune Creek**. **Sibley Lake** is reached by continuing 0.2 mi past the campground to a large parking area at the end of the road. Off the parking area is a boat ramp, a handicapped accessible dock and fishing pier, and a second picnic area. This picnic area is nicer and more accessible than the first, but is more crowded.
Crowds: ***** **Directions:** At the Sibley Lake Campground turnoff; SE 0.5 mi

MM: 72.2 **GPS:** 44.80499/-107.33216 **Elev:** 6692 **Grid:** 53/5 **Land:** NF
Fallen City   **Type:** Point of Interest
An interpretive pullout with a view of a massive tumbled boulder field across the canyon which gives the appearance of the toppled buildings of a "fallen city."
Cool Rating: ** **Crowds:** * **Time:** 5 min **Directions:** S side of hwy

MM: 72.9 **GPS:** 44.80497/-107.31928 **Elev:** 6500 **Grid:** 53/5 **Land:** NF
Sand Turn Overlook   **Type:** Scenic Viewpoint
Located on a sharp curve with nice views to the northeast of the valley toward **Dayton** plus an interpretive sign about "**The Buffalo Tongue**," an 1,800 ft limestone slab on the hillside.
Cool Rating: ** **Crowds:** * **Time:** 10 min **Directions:** E side of hwy

MM: 75.4 **GPS:** 44.82792/-107.32841 **Elev:** 5722 **Grid:** 53/4 **Land:** NF
Hogback Overlook   **Type:** Geological Feature
An overlook of the ridges below called "hogbacks," with an interpretive sign explaining this geological formation.
Cool Rating: * **Crowds:** * **Time:** 5 min **Directions:** Elevated overlook inside of a sharp curve.

MM: 76.6 **GPS:** 44.82151/-107.32198 **Elev:** 5388 **Grid:** 53/4 **Land:** NF
Bighorn National Forest   **Type:** National Forest Boundary

MM: 76.9   *GPS:* 44.82165/-107.32204   *Elev:* 5380   *Grid:* 53/4   *Land:* NF
Syncline Thrust Fault   *Type:* Geological Feature
Across the road is a thrust fault/syncline formation exposed by the road cut.
Cool Rating: *   *Crowds:* *   *Time:* 5 min   *Directions:* NW side of hwy

MM: 81.0   *GPS:* 44.84942/-107.28514   *Elev:* 4227   *Grid:* 54/4   *Land:* NF
Bighorn Scenic Byway (northeast end)   *Type:* Scenic Byway
A scenic 55 mi section of **US-14** between **Shell** and **Dayton** that climbs over the crest of the **Bighorn Mountains** from the **Bighorn Basin** to the **Powder River Basin**. The high point is at **Granite Pass** at 9,035 ft. The majority of the route is through the **Bighorn National Forest**.
Cool Rating: ***   *Crowds:* ***

MM: 83.3   *GPS:* 44.87523/-107.26268   *Elev:* 3920   *Grid:* 54/3
Dayton   *Type:* Town

MM: 83.4   *Dist:* 0.1   *GPS:* 44.87776/-107.26070   *Elev:* 3907   *Grid:* 54/3   *Land:* City
Dayton Bell Tower   *Type:* Historic Site
Built in 1910 as a fire watch and later used to watch for enemy aircraft after the attack on **Pearl Harbor**. The bell tower is now located in the **Scott Bicentennial Park**, a nice shady city park.
Cool Rating: **   *Crowds:* *   *Time:* 20 min
Directions: On the north side of Dayton; E on 2nd Ave 0.1 mi; N/L into the park.

MM: 83.6   *Dist:* 4.8   *GPS:* 44.85001/-107.30404   *GPS2:* 44.84706/-107.32952   *Elev:* 4211   *Grid:* 54/4   *Land:* Wyoming G & F
Tongue River Recreation Area & Amsden Wildlife Habitat Management Area   *Type:* Recreation Area
2 primitive camping areas on the southern boundary of the **Amsden Wildlife Habitat Management Area** near the **Tongue River**. The first area is just inside the WHMA boundary (MI 3.2) with a few small camps on both sides and just off the road. Continuing a short distance the road enters the spectacular **Tongue River Canyon**, where the road narrows with steep drop-offs to the river. At MI 4.2 is the best view of the **Needles Eye Arch**, located on the top of a narrow, eroded butte. At MI 4.8 the road ends at a parking area that provides fishing access and the trailhead for the **Tongue River Trail**. This trail continues through the canyon for about 2 mi to a good turnaround point for a day hike, although the trail continues another 7 mi. The gravel parking area is located above the river and 1,500 ft below towering eroded cliffs and the **Needles Eye Arch**, where 5 undeveloped campsites are situated around the edges. The camping area is very nice but rather busy with day use activity. *Deciduous trees. Vault toilet. Stone fire rings.*
Cool Rating: ****   *Crowds:* *   *Notes:* No large RVs or trailers.   *Road Desc:* Gravel, rough spots, narrow
Directions: On the north end of Dayton; W on CR-92/Tongue River Rd 3.2 mi to first camping area; Continue 1.6 mi to the end of the road.
Campsites: Dispersed   *Shade:* ***   *Privacy:* *   *RV Size:* 30'   *Other:* None

MM: 85.6   *GPS:* 44.89620/-107.23040   *Elev:* 3896   *Grid:* 55/3
Sawyer Expedition Bozeman Trail   *Type:* Historical Marker
In 1865, **Colonel James Sawyer**'s wagon train and road building expedition of 82 wagons fought the **Arapaho Indians** at this point on the **Bozeman Trail**. The battle lasted 13 days until they were rescued by **General Patrick E. Connor** and his **Powder River Expedition**. The Indian attack was in retaliation for the attack on the **Arapaho Indian** village 2 days earlier by **General Patrick E. Connor** *(see next section)*. Also at the pullout is a historical sign about the **Bingham Post Office and Stage Station** plus a stone **Bozeman Trail** marker.
Cool Rating: *   *Crowds:* *   *Time:* 5 min   *Directions:* N side of hwy

MM: 89.0   *Dist:* 0.6   *GPS:* 44.90445/-107.16342   *Elev:* 3760   *Grid:* 56/2   *Land:* State
Connor Battlefield State Park and Historic Site   *Type:* State Park
A grassy park on the south-central side of **Ranchester**, which is situated inside a large bend in the **Tongue River**. The park is located at the site of an attack of 200 troops on **Chief Black Bear**'s **Arapaho Indian** village in 1865. The attack was led by **General Patrick E. Connor** who led part of the **Powder River Expedition** into this area as part of a broad military program to protect the **Bozeman Trail**, as well as other trails into the **Montana** mining fields, from the **Plains Indians**. A monument and interpretive sign commemorate this battle.

The park provides camping that accommodates large RVs. Large cottonwoods shade the park, although the sites on the east end are in the open. *3 pull-thrus.*
Cool Rating: *   *Crowds:* **   [FEE AREA]   *Notes:* A train goes by every hour blowing the horn several times.
Directions: S on Gillette St 0.4 mi; E/L 0.2 mi.
Campsites: 20   *Shade:* ****   *Privacy:* **   *RV Size:* 40'+   *Other:* Water

MM: 89.0   *GPS:* 44.90885/-107.16341   *Elev:* 3762   *Grid:* 56/2
Ranchester   *Type:* Town

MM: 89.8   *GPS:* 44.91575/-107.15160   *Elev:* 3847   *Grid:* 56/2
I-90 *(see chapter)*   *Type:* Hwy Junction w/Chapter
208.8 mi interstate highway that heads southeast from **Montana** to **South Dakota** across northeastern **Wyoming**. The highway heads south 56 mi to a transition with **I-25**, which continues south, and then turns east 150 mi. Highlights include: **Fort Phil Kearny** and related historic sites, **Dry Creek Petrified Tree Environmental Education Area**, **Eagle Butte Coal Mine**, **Devils Tower National Monument**, **Vore Buffalo Jump**.
Directions: NW to Montana or SE to Sheridan from MM 9.9

MM: 89.8   *GPS:* 44.91575/-107.15160   *Elev:* 3847   *Grid:* 56/2
End of Highway   *Type:* Highway End
80.5 mi highway from **Ranchester** southwest to **Greybull**. A large portion of the highway is through National Forest along the **Bighorn Scenic Byway** with 10 public campgrounds. Highlights include: **Tongue River Canyon**, **Dayton Bell Tower**, **Shell Falls**, **Red Gulch Dinosaur Tracksite**, **Medicine Lodge State Archaeological Site**, **Devil's Kitchen Geological Site**.
Directions: I-90 exit 9; SW to Dayton from MM 89.8

US-14 (east)   W/E

MM: 154.6 *GPS:* 44.26352/-104.95033 *Elev:* 4225 *Grid:* 87/18
US-14 (east)   *Type:* Highway Description
44.8 mi section of **US-14** from **I-90** MM 154.6 at **Moorcroft** that loops north and east back to **I-90** MM 185.7 at **Sundance**. The primary function of this highway is access to **Wy-24** and **Devils Tower National Monument**. The highway also provides access to **Keyhole State Park**.
Notes: US-14 doesn't actually end at I-90 heading east, however the rest of the highway from there simply parallels I-90 through Sundance, 1.7 mi east.
Directions: I-90 exit 154; S 0.2 mi; W/R on E Converse St 0.2 mi; N/R on US-14/N Yellowstone Ave from MM 154.6.

MM: 154.6 *GPS:* 44.26352/-104.95033 *Elev:* 4225 *Grid:* 87/18
Moorcroft   *Type:* Town

MM: 154.7 *GPS:* 44.26640/-104.94379 *Elev:* 4302 *Grid:* 87/18
I-90 *(see chapter)*   *Type:* Hwy Junction w/Chapter
208.8 mi interstate highway that heads west from **South Dakota** across northeastern **Wyoming** then northwest to **Montana**. Highlights include: **Vore Buffalo Jump**, **Devils Tower National Monument**, **Eagle Butte Coal Mine**, **Dry Creek Petrified Tree Environmental Education Area**, **Fort Phil Kearny** and related historic sites.
Directions: At E Converse St in Moorcroft; E/L 0.2 mi; N/L 0.2 mi to I-90; E to South Dakota or W to Gillette from MM 154.6.

MM: 159.7 *Dist:* 7.2 *GPS:* 44.32258/-104.91409 *Elev:* 4147 *Grid:* 88/17
Keyhole State Park   *Type:* State Park
See chapter on Keyhole State Park via CR-205/CR-180 MM 3.6. **US-14 (east)** is closest to the west access near **Pine Haven** and can be reached by taking **Wy-113** 5.1 mi east to **Pine Haven Rd** and heading north. To reach the east access continue another 3.9 mi east to **Pine Ridge Rd/CR-205** and head north 2.0 mi to the east entrance.
Directions: **West access**: E on Wy-113 5.1 mi (MM 15.1); N on Pine Haven Rd 2.1 mi to Pine Haven. **East access**: E on Wy-113/CR-93 9.0 mi; N on Pine Creek Rd/CR-205 from MM 3.6.

MM: 181.2 *GPS:* 44.50255/-104.69047 *Elev:* 4184 *Grid:* 91/12
Wy-24 *(see chapter)*   *Type:* Hwy Junction w/Chapter
46.3 mi highway from **US-14 (east)**, 6 mi south of **Devils Tower**, north and east to **South Dakota**. The primary purpose of this highway is access to **Devils Tower National Monument**. Other highlights include: access to **Cook Lake Recreation Area**, **Aladdin Tipple Historical Park**.
Nearest Town: Hulett 15.5 N *Directions:* N to Devils Tower from MM 0

MM: 184.7 *GPS:* 44.46568/-104.64441 *Elev:* 4613 *Grid:* 92/13
Devils Tower Scenic Overlook   *Type:* Scenic Viewpoint
A distant view of **Devils Tower** 9 mi northwest across green rolling hills.
Cool Rating: *** *Crowds:* * *Time:* 10 min *Directions:* E side of hwy

MM: 199.5 *GPS:* 44.39465/-104.41742 *Elev:* 4960 *Grid:* 95/15
Cook Lake Recreation Area and Scenic Drive *(see chapter)*   *Type:* Hwy Junction w/Chapter
Access to the **Cook Lake Recreation Area** along a 26.3 mi scenic drive through the **Bear Lodge Mountains** and **Black Hills National Forest** from **US-14 (east)** MM 199.5 (1.0 mi west of **I-90**) north to **Wy-24** MM 30.3. The **Warren Peak Lookout** is at the highest elevation of the drive. Dispersed camping along **FR-838**, **FR-843**, and **FR-830**.
Nearest Town: Sundance 2.6 NE *Directions:* N on Warren Peak Rd/FR-838 from MM 0

MM: 200.4 *Dist:* 1.7 *GPS:* 44.40639/-104.37501 *Elev:* 4735 *Grid:* 95/15
Sundance   *Type:* Town
Directions: E on US-14 1.7 mi

MM: 200.4 *GPS:* 44.39208/-104.39800 *Elev:* 4880 *Grid:* 95/15
I-90 *(see chapter)*   *Type:* Hwy Junction w/Chapter
208.8 mi interstate highway that heads west from **South Dakota** across northeastern **Wyoming** then northwest to **Montana**. Highlights include: **Vore Buffalo Jump**, **Devils Tower National Monument**, **Eagle Butte Coal Mine**, **Dry Creek Petrified Tree Environmental Education Area**, **Fort Phil Kearny** and related historic sites.
Directions: E to South Dakota or W to Moorcroft from MM 185.7

MM: 200.4 *GPS:* 44.39208/-104.39800 *Elev:* 4880 *Grid:* 95/15
End of Highway   *Type:* Highway End
44.8 mi section of **US-14** from **I-90** MM 185.7 at **Sundance** that loops north and west back to **I-90** MM 154.6 at **Moorcroft**. The primary function of this highway is access to **Wy-24** and **Devils Tower National Monument**. The highway also provides access to the **Warren Peak Lookout** and **Cook Lake Recreation Area**.
Directions: I-90 exit 185; E on US-14 from MM 200.5

MM: 0.0 *GPS:* 44.48973/-110.00129 *Elev:* 6946 *Grid:* 15/13
US-14/16/20   *Type:* Highway Description
100.1 mi highway east from the east entrance of **Yellowstone National Park** to either a transition east to **Greybull** or a junction north to **Lovell**. The **Buffalo Bill Cody Scenic Byway** runs 27.4 mi from the east entrance of **Yellowstone National Park** to the east boundary of the **Shoshone National Forest**. Highlights include: interesting volcanic rock formations, **Firefighters Memorial and Trail**, **Holy City**, **Buffalo Bill Dam and Visitor Center**, **Old West Miniature Village and Museum**, **Buffalo Bill Historical Center**.
Nearest Town: Pahaska 2 E *Directions:* E to Cody from MM 0
Notes: No dispersed camping on this route. If heading to Yellowstone be aware that the last 2 campgrounds are for hard-sided RVs only. Only 2 very small towns west of Cody.

MM: 0.0 *GPS:* 44.48859/-110.00382 *Elev:* 6946 *Grid:* 15/13
Yellowstone - East Entrance to Fishing Bridge *(see chapter)*   *Type:* Hwy Transition w/Chapter
25.8 mi highway from the east entrance of **Yellowstone National Park**, via **US-14/16/20**, west to **Fishing Bridge**. There is hiking and **Yellowstone Lake** access but very little thermal activity. Highlights include: **Lake Butte Overlook**, **Steamboat Point**, **Fishing Bridge**.
Nearest Town: Pahaska 2 E; Fishing Bridge 25.1 W *[FEE AREA]* *Directions:* W to Fishing Bridge from MM 0

MM: 0.0 *GPS:* 44.48973/-110.00129 *Elev:* 6946 *Grid:* 15/13 *Land:* NF
Buffalo Bill Cody Scenic Byway (eastbound)   *Type:* Scenic Byway
A 27.4 mi scenic byway from the east entrance of **Yellowstone National Park** to the east boundary of the **Shoshone National Forest**. The highway follows the **North Fork Shoshone River** through the beautiful **Wapiti Valley** with opportunities to view a number of wildlife species, including deer, elk, moose, black bear, and grizzly bear. The river and its tributaries offer blue ribbon trout fishing. Along the highway are many interesting rock formations that were created from volcanic lava flows 50 million years ago. Several of these have been named and can be viewed from pullouts.
Cool Rating: **** *Crowds:* *** *Nearest Town:* Pahaska 2 E

MM: 2.0 *GPS:* 44.50201/-109.96344 *Elev:* 6670 *Grid:* 16/12
Pahaska   *Type:* Town
Home of the **Pahaska Teepee**, **Buffalo Bill**'s original 1904 hunting lodge, which is on the **National Register of Historic Places**. This is now a restaurant and lodge with cabins, fuel, gift shop, and a convenience store.

MM: 3.0 *GPS:* 44.49648/-109.94733 *Elev:* 6648 *Grid:* 16/13 *Land:* NF
Three Mile Campground   *Type:* Campground
2 loops in a figure 8 configuration along the **North Fork Shoshone River** with a few sites overlooking the river. *Conifer forest. 5 pull-thrus. Lantern poles.*
Crowds: *** *[FEE AREA]* *Notes:* Because of grizzly activity, hard-sided campers only. *Directions:* SW side of hwy
Road Desc: Gravel
Campsites: 21 *Shade:* *** *Privacy:* * *RV Size:* 40' *Other:* Water GRIZZLIES

MM: 3.2 *GPS:* 44.49541/-109.94486 *Elev:* 6617 *Grid:* 16/13 *Land:* NF
Interpretive Pullout: Grizzly Bears   *Type:* Point of Interest
3 interesting signs about grizzly bears and a monument dedicated to **Cody Peak** and the **Buffalo Bill Cody Scenic Byway**.
Cool Rating: ** *Crowds:* * *Time:* 10 min *Directions:* SW side of hwy

MM: 3.9 *GPS:* 44.49224/-109.92983 *Elev:* 6585 *Grid:* 16/13 *Land:* NF
Sleeping Giant Picnic Area   *Type:* Picnic Area
Near the **North Fork Shoshone River**. *Vault toilet.*
Road Desc: Gravel *Directions:* SW side of hwy

MM: 6.8 *GPS:* 44.47229/-109.88832 *Elev:* 6470 *Grid:* 17/13 *Land:* NF
Eagle Creek Campground   *Type:* Campground
Stretched along the **North Fork Shoshone River** with 2 separate sections. The west section is a loop with 7 sites. The east section is a long road with 13 sites and an end loop turnaround. The south end of the loop and the far east end of the road are close to the river. *Conifer forest. Good middlestory. Roomy sites. Several pull-thrus.*
[FEE AREA] *Notes:* Due to grizzly activity, hard-sided campers only. *Road Desc:* Gravel *Directions:* S side of hwy
Campsites: 20 *Shade:* **** *Privacy:* ** *RV Size:* 40' *Other:* Water GRIZZLIES

MM: 11.2 *GPS:* 44.45405/-109.81464 *Elev:* 6359 *Grid:* 18/14 *Land:* NF
Chimney Rock   *Type:* Geological Feature
A tall rectangular shaped rock formation at the edge of a cliff, resembling a chimney.
Cool Rating: * *Crowds:* * *Time:* 5 min *Directions:* Pullout on N side of hwy

MM: 12.6 *GPS:* 44.45264/-109.78990 *GPS2:* 44.45414/-109.79067 *Elev:* 6286 *Grid:* 18/14 *Land:* NF
Window Rock Arch   *Type:* Geological Feature
A small rock window on the north side of the highway near the west end and at the top of the rock cliffs.
Cool Rating: * *Time:* Drive by

MM: 14.4 *Dist:* 0.1 *GPS:* 44.45384/-109.75928 *Elev:* 6217 *Grid:* 19/14 *Land:* NF
Newton Creek Campground   *Type:* Campground
Stretched along the **North Fork Shoshone River** on 2 separate roads with end loops that are divided by **Newton Creek**. Sites on the east end are more open and closer to the river. *Conifer forest. Little understory. Roomy sites.*
Crowds: *** *[FEE AREA]* *Road Desc:* Gravel *Directions:* SW then SE 0.1 mi
Campsites: 31 *Shade:* ***** *Privacy:* * *RV Size:* 30' *Other:* Water GRIZZLIES

MM: 14.7 *GPS:* 44.45324/-109.75290 *Elev:* 6230 *Grid:* 19/14 *Land:* NF
Newton Springs Picnic Area   *Type:* Picnic Area
Picnic tables in a stand of conifers between the parking area and the road.
Directions: N side of hwy

MM: 15.2 **GPS:** 44.45813/-109.74756 **Elev:** 6193 **Grid:** 19/14 **Land:** NF
Firefighters Memorial   *Type:* Historical Marker
A memorial to honor 15 firefighters who were killed and 39 others who were injured during the **Blackwater Fire** in August 1937. This tragedy happened when a sudden gale-force wind whipped up the fire, which raced up the mountainside where the men were working. This also marks the beginning of the **Firefighters Memorial Trail** *(see next section)*. The trailhead parking is just below and north of the memorial. Below the memorial is a picnic area and a marshy pond with benches.
Cool Rating: ** **Crowds:** * **Time:** 10-20 min **Directions:** E side of hwy

MM: 15.3 **GPS:** 44.45878/-109.74694 **Elev:** 6175 **Grid:** 19/14 **Land:** NF
Firefighters Memorial Trail   *Type:* Hiking Trail
A hiking trail to the **Firefighters Monument** near where the **Blackwater Fire** originated in August 1937. Signs marking important locations are located along the trail. The hike starts out heading east across a bridge over the river and then turns south following a jeep road for 1.8 mi. At the end of the road the trail crosses **Blackwater Creek** and continues another 1.2 mi to a fork in the trail and the creek. Keep left and cross both creeks and travel another 2.0 mi to the monument. *Moderately strenuous; 5.0 mi one-way; 2180 ft elev gain.* The trail continues steeply to another monument on **Post Point**. *0.5 mi, 650 ft elev gain.*
Cool Rating: **** **Crowds:** * **Time:** 4-5 hrs **Directions:** SE 70 yds; SW/R into parking area.

MM: 16.6 **Dist:** 0.1 **GPS:** 44.45598/-109.72843 **Elev:** 6133 **Grid:** 19/14 **Land:** NF
Rex Hale Campground   *Type:* Campground
A wide open campground along the north side of the **North Fork Shoshone River**. The forested base of the **Absaroka Mountains** are south across the river. *Long single loop. Scattered juniper trees. Grass understory. 8 sites with water and electricity. Lantern poles. No pull-thrus. Best for RVs.*
Crowds: *** **[FEE AREA]** **Road Desc:** Partially paved **Directions:** S 0.1 mi
Campsites: 30 **Shade:** * **Privacy:** * **RV Size:** 40' **Other:** 1-877-444-6777:www.recreation.gov,Water,Electric GRIZZLIES

MM: 19.9 **Dist:** 0.1 **GPS:** 44.46251/-109.66845 **Elev:** 6008 **Grid:** 20/13 **Land:** NF
Clearwater Campground   *Type:* Campground
An oddly configured campground along the north side of the **North Fork Shoshone River**. The forested base of the **Absaroka Mountains** are south across the river. *Cottonwoods and conifers. 11 tent-only sites in an open area and 4 closely spaced RV sites with no privacy. Best for tents.*
Crowds: *** **[FEE AREA]** **Road Desc:** Gravel **Directions:** S 0.1 mi
Campsites: 15 **Shade:** ** **Privacy:** * **RV Size:** 30' **Other:** Water GRIZZLIES

MM: 22.2 **Dist:** 0.1 **GPS:** 44.46482/-109.62688 **Elev:** 5960 **Grid:** 20/13 **Land:** NF
Elk Fork Campground   *Type:* Campground
Adjacent to **Elk Fork Creek** along a short road ending at the **Elk Fork Trailhead**, which has horse facilities and long trails into the **Washakie Wilderness** and **Teton Wilderness**. *Cottonwoods and junipers. Roomy. Paved parking areas. 3 pull-thrus. Highway noise.*
Crowds: *** **[FEE AREA]** **Road Desc:** Gravel **Directions:** SW 0.1 mi
Campsites: 13 **Shade:** ** **Privacy:** * **RV Size:** 40' **Other:** GRIZZLIES

MM: 22.3 **Dist:** 0.1 **GPS:** 44.46439/-109.62423 **Elev:** 5945 **Grid:** 20/13 **Land:** NF
Wapiti Campground   *Type:* Campground
Located between the highway and the **North Fork Shoshone River** with ancient mudflow cliffs of the **Absaroka Volcanic Field** north across the river. *2 loops. Cottonwood and juniper trees. Generally roomy sites. Dense middlestory. No pull-thrus. 20 electric sites in east loop. Highway noise.*
Crowds: ***** **[FEE AREA]** **Road Desc:** Gravel **Directions:** N 0.1 mi
Campsites: 40 **Shade:** **** **Privacy:** **** **RV Size:** 40' **Other:** 1-877-444-6777:www.recreation.gov,Water,Electric GRIZZLIES

MM: 22.7 **GPS:** 44.46314/-109.61525 **Elev:** 5927 **Grid:** 21/13 **Land:** NF
Wapiti Wayside Visitor Center and Ranger Station   *Type:* Visitor Center
A small visitor center with maps, books, and interpretive displays, plus information on camping, recreation, local bear sightings, and other general information.

Located behind the visitor center is the **Wapiti Ranger Station**, which was built in 1903 and used continuously since that time. This is the oldest **U.S. Forest Service Ranger Station** in the United States and was placed on the **National Register of Historic Places** in 1966.
Directions: N side of hwy

MM: 23.1 **GPS:** 44.46145/-109.60762 **Elev:** 5917 **Grid:** 21/13 **Land:** NF
Big Game Campground   *Type:* Campground
Located between the highway and a bend in the **North Fork Shoshone River**; however, the sites are not close to the river. *Single loop. Cottonwoods. Good spacing between sites. Dense middlestory. Level. 2 pull-thrus. Highway noise.*
Crowds: *** **[FEE AREA]** **Road Desc:** Gravel **Directions:** NE side of hwy
Campsites: 16 **Shade:** ***** **Privacy:** ***** **RV Size:** 40' **Other:** 1-877-444-6777:www.recreation.gov,Water GRIZZLIES

MM: 24.2 **Dist:** 0.1 **GPS:** 44.46385/-109.58690 **Elev:** 5870 **Grid:** 21/13 **Land:** NF
Forest Creek Picnic Area   *Type:* Picnic Area
Located on the inside of a bend in the **North Fork Shoshone River** with a few trees.
Road Desc: Gravel **Directions:** N 0.1 mi

MM: 25.1 **GPS:** 44.46023/-109.56912 **Elev:** 5832 **Grid:** 21/14 **Land:** NF
Holy City & Goose Rock   *Type:* Geological Feature
A parking area to view **Holy City**, a volcanic rock formation to the northwest that resembles the silhouette of the ancient city of **Jerusalem**. Also directly north is **Goose Rock**, another famous landmark. A 0.2 mi trail heading west along the river leads to a view into a short canyon below the **Holy City** rocks. This can also be seen by driving west 0.2 mi and parking on the north side of the highway.
Cool Rating: *** **Crowds:** ** **Time:** 5-20 min **Directions:** NE side of hwy

MM: 27.4 *GPS:* 44.46036/-109.52581 *Elev:* 5795 *Grid:* 22/14 *Land:* NF
Informational Pullout   *Type:* Visitor Information
A large pullout just inside the **Shoshone National Forest** boundary with area information.
Directions: NW side of hwy

MM: 27.4 *GPS:* 44.46052/-109.52518 *Elev:* 5798 *Grid:* 22/14 *Land:* NF
Buffalo Bill Cody Scenic Byway (westbound)   *Type:* Scenic Byway
A 27.4 mi scenic byway from the east entrance of **Yellowstone National Park** to the east boundary of the **Shoshone National Forest**. The highway follows the **North Fork Shoshone River** through the beautiful **Wapiti Valley** with opportunities to view a number of wildlife species, including deer, elk, moose, black bear, and grizzly bear. The river and its tributaries offer blue ribbon trout fishing. Along the highway are many interesting rock formations that were created from volcanic lava flows 50 million years ago. Several of these have been named and can be viewed from pullouts.
Cool Rating: **** *Crowds:* ***

MM: 29.0 *GPS:* 44.46251/-109.49349 *Elev:* 5755 *Grid:* 22/13
Chinese Wall   *Type:* Geological Feature
An unusual sharp volcanic rock ridge to the north.
Cool Rating: ** *Time:* Drive by

MM: 31.8 *GPS:* 44.46591/-109.44130 *Elev:* 5625 *Grid:* 23/13
Wapiti   *Type:* Town

MM: 37.3 *Dist:* 0.1 *GPS:* 44.48618/-109.33118 *Elev:* 5413 *Grid:* 25/13 *Land:* State
North Fork Campground: Buffalo Bill State Park   *Type:* Campground
The campground is composed of 2 grassed loops just west of **Buffalo Bill Reservoir** near the **North Fork Shoshone River**. The upper loop is larger with *14 reservable sites and 5 tent-only sites* and is more exposed to wind. The lower loop has 15 sites on the west side of a large grove of cottonwoods, which provide some wind protection. *Scattered deciduous trees. Roomy sites. Paved road and parking areas. All pull-thrus. 1 group site.*
Crowds: *** *[FEE AREA]* *Directions:* S 0.1 mi; W to fee station.
Campsites: 61 *Shade:* * *Privacy:* * *RV Size:* 40'+ *Other:* 307-587-9227,Water,RVDump

MM: 42.0 *Dist:* 0.1 *GPS:* 44.50395/-109.24452 *Elev:* 5447 *Grid:* 26/12 *Land:* State
North Shore Bay Campground: Buffalo Bill State Park   *Type:* Campground
3 half-loops on short peninsulas between the highway and the north shore of **Buffalo Bill Reservoir**. *A few scattered trees. Roomy sites. 7 reservable sites in loop 1. 3 tent-only sites in loop 2. Many pull-thrus. Paved roads and parking areas. Drinking water at* **RV dump**. *Highway noise.*
Crowds: *** *[FEE AREA]* *Directions:* S 0.1 mi to fee station
Campsites: 32 *Shade:* * *Privacy:* * *RV Size:* 40'+ *Other:* 307-587-9227,Water,RVDump

MM: 44.7 *GPS:* 44.50064/-109.18879 *GPS2:* 44.50154/-109.18326 *Elev:* 5423 *Grid:* 27/13 *Land:* Bureau of Reclamation
Buffalo Bill Dam and Visitor Center   *Type:* Dam
A 353 ft high dam located in a steep and narrow canyon on the **Shoshone River** in **Buffalo Bill State Park**. The dam was finished in 1910 and named after **Colonel William F. Cody (Buffalo Bill)**. The original height of the dam was 325 ft, which at the time made it the highest dam in the world. The dam was raised an additional 25 ft during an 8 year project that began in 1933. The visitor center is located adjacent to the top of the dam and offers views across the reservoir and of the massive concrete structure descending to the river below. Inside the visitor center are historical displays and videos about the construction and use of the dam and reservoir as well as a gift shop and restrooms. An audio tour is available for a small fee. A free shuttle is provided for the 1/4 mi trip between the parking area and the visitor center. Located at the shuttle waiting area is a series of informative signs about the surrounding area as well as displays of historic dam equipment.
Hours: 8am - 6pm, Mon-Sat; 10am - 6pm, Sun (May-Sept); Weekday hours extend to 8pm June - August; Dam overlook open year-round *Phone:* 307-527-6076 *Cool Rating:* **** *Crowds:* *** *Time:* 1-2 hrs
Directions: S side of hwy just west of the tunnel.

MM: 49.4 *GPS:* 44.51360/-109.10503 *Elev:* 5075 *Grid:* 28/12 *Land:* City
Colter's Hell   *Type:* Historic Site
When **Lewis and Clark Expedition** member **John Colter** returned to the mountains in 1807 with a fur-trading party, he discovered bubbling mudpots and steaming geysers along the **Shoshone River** in what is now the west end of **Cody**. People found his stories unbelievable and jokingly called it "**Colter's Hell.**" This is now an extinct geyser basin; however, a pullout and a 1/2 mi walking trail with interpretive signs commemorates Colter's discovery.
Cool Rating: ** *Crowds:* * *Time:* 30 min *Directions:* Long paved pullout on N side of hwy

MM: 49.6 *GPS:* 44.51425/-109.10035 *Elev:* 5060 *Grid:* 28/12 *Land:* City
Tecumseh's Trading Post   *Type:* Museum
A western store that houses the **Old West Miniature Village and Museum**, where thousands of miniature figures trace the history of **Wyoming** and **Montana** from the 1600s to the late 1890s. **Jerry Fick** spent his lifetime collecting and making the figures. Portrayals are historically accurate although not necessarily to scale. The perimeter of the room contains thousands of western, fur trade, and Indian artifacts, plus full-sized wildlife mounts. *Donations appreciated.*
Hours: 8am - 8pm *Phone:* 307-587-5362 *Cool Rating:* *** *Crowds:* ** *Time:* 45 min
Directions: S side of hwy *(142 W Yellowstone Ave, Cody)*

MM: 51.5 *GPS:* 44.52493/-109.07203 *Elev:* 5011 *Grid:* 28/12 *Land:* City
Buffalo Bill Historical Center   *Type:* Museum
Widely regarded as the finest western museum in America. The museum contains the boyhood home of **Buffalo Bill**, 2 sculpture gardens, and 5 separate museums:

Buffalo Bill Museum - History and memorabilia of **Colonel William F. Cody**.
Whitney Gallery of Western Art - A wonderful collection of masterworks of western artists and sculptors.
Plains Indian Museum - The largest museum in the complex containing items from the 7 Indian tribes of **Wyoming**.
Draper Museum of Natural History - Exhibits on the **Greater Yellowstone Ecosystem** and the integral role of humans.
Cody Firearms Museum - One of the most comprehensive collections of American firearms in the world containing more than 5000 firearms.
Hours: 8am - 8pm (May); 7am - 8pm (June - Sept); 8am - 5pm (Sept & Oct) *Phone:* 307-587-4771
Cool Rating: **** *Crowds:* ***** *Time:* 3-4 hrs
Directions: W side of the intersection of 8th St/US-14/16/20 & Beck Ave (just south of the large curve) *(720 Sheridan Avenue, Cody)*

MM: 51.8 *GPS:* 44.52602/-109.06784 *Elev:* 5012 *Grid:* 28/12 *Land:* City
Cody City Park   *Type:* Park
A nice park with good shade, picnic tables, and a public restroom.
Directions: SW corner of Sheridan Ave/US-14/16/20 & 8th St

MM: 52.0 *GPS:* 44.52574/-109.06399 *Elev:* 5008 *Grid:* 28/12 *Land:* City
Cody Gunfighters   *Type:* Entertainment
A 45 minute gunfight re-enactment featuring actors garbed as real and fictional heroes and desperadoes. Donations are accepted for charity. Fun for the kids.
Hours: 6pm, Mon-Sat (June - Sept) *Cool Rating:* ** *Crowds:* ***** *Time:* 1 hr
Notes: The show is more comedy than real gunfight re-enactments.
Directions: Just south of the intersection of Sheridan Ave/US-14/16/20 & 12th St in front of the Irma Hotel. The best parking is to the south.

MM: 52.4 *GPS:* 44.52606/-109.05633 *Elev:* 4996 *Grid:* 29/12
Cody   *Type:* Town

MM: 52.4 *GPS:* 44.52606/-109.05633 *Elev:* 4996 *Grid:* 29/12
US-14A *(see chapter)*   *Type:* Hwy Junction w/Chapter
98.9 mi highway northeast from **Cody** to **Lovell**, then east to **Burgess Jct**. The last 27 mi follow the **Medicine Wheel Passage**, a scenic high elevation route (over 9,000 ft) with excellent views into the **Bighorn Basin**. Highlights include: **Heart Mountain Relocation Center, Bighorn Canyon National Recreation Area, Medicine Wheel National Historic Landmark, Porcupine Falls, Bucking Mule Falls**.
Directions: NE to Powell from MM 0

MM: 52.4 *Dist:* 0.4 *GPS:* 44.52606/-109.05633 *Elev:* 4996 *Grid:* 29/12
Wy-120 (north) *(see chapter)*   *Type:* Hwy Junction w/Chapter
37.8 mi section of **Wy-120** from **Cody** north to **Montana**. The highway provides 2 scenic routes to the northeast entrance of **Yellowstone National Park**. Route 1 connects to **Wy-296 (Chief Joseph Scenic Highway)**, which climbs over the spectacular **Dead Indian Pass** and connects to **US-212**. Route 2 travels into **Montana** and loops back into **Wyoming** on **US-212** over the even more spectacular **Beartooth Pass**.
Directions: N on US-14A/Wy-120 0.4 mi; W/L on Wy-120 from MM 100.

MM: 53.9 *GPS:* 44.51287/-109.03942 *Elev:* 5089 *Grid:* 29/12 *Land:* City
RV Dump: Cody   *Type:* RV Dump
A municipal **RV dump** with no potable water.
Directions: N on 26th St 50 yds; W/L into parking lot. *Just west of the airport and north of the Vietnam Memorial Park.*

MM: 54.6 *GPS:* 44.51160/-109.02610 *Elev:* 5086 *Grid:* 29/12
Wy-120 (south) *(see chapter)*   *Type:* Hwy Junction w/Chapter
81.6 mi section of **Wy-120** from **Cody** southeast to **Thermopolis**. Highlights include: **Gooseberry Badlands Scenic Area, Legend Rock Petroglyphs**.
Directions: S to Thermopolis from MM 81.2

MM: 87.4 *GPS:* 44.50572/-108.39170 *Elev:* 4448 *Grid:* 38/12
Emblem   *Type:* Town

MM: 100.8 *GPS:* 44.50929/-108.13325 *Elev:* 3994 *Grid:* 42/12
US-14/16/20/Wy-789 & US-310/Wy-789   *Type:* Highway Junction
109 mi highway south to **Shoshoni** or 48 mi north past **Lovell** to **Montana**. Highlights include: **Museum of Flight and Aerial Firefighting, Devil's Kitchen Geological Site, Medicine Lodge State Archaeological Site, Hot Springs State Park, Wind River Canyon, Boysen State Park**. *See chapter: US-20/Wy-789 & US-16/20/Wy-789 & US-14/16/20/Wy-789 & US-310/Wy-789.*
Directions: E on US-14/16/20/Wy-789 to Greybull or N on US-310/Wy-789 to Lovell from MM 209.

MM: 100.8 *GPS:* 44.50929/-108.13325 *Elev:* 3994 *Grid:* 42/12
End of Highway   *Type:* Highway End
100.1 mi highway west from a transition with **US-14/16/20/Wy-789**, west of **Greybull**, to the east entrance of **Yellowstone National Park**. The **Buffalo Bill Cody Scenic Byway** runs 27.4 mi from the east boundary of the **Shoshone National Forest** to the east entrance of **Yellowstone National Park**. Highlights include: **Buffalo Bill Historical Center, Old West Miniature Village and Museum, Buffalo Bill Dam and Visitor Center, Holy City, Firefighters Memorial and Trail**, interesting volcanic rock formations.
Nearest Town: Greybull 5 SE *Directions:* W to Cody from MM 100.8

MM: 0.0 *GPS:* 44.52606/-109.05633 *Elev:* 4996 *Grid:* 29/12
US-14A   *Type:* Highway Description
98.9 mi highway northeast from **Cody** to **Lovell**, then east to **Burgess Jct**. The last 27 mi follow the **Medicine Wheel Passage**, a scenic high elevation route (over 9,000 ft) with excellent views into the **Bighorn Basin**. Highlights include: **Heart Mountain Relocation Center, Bighorn Canyon National Recreation Area, Medicine Wheel National Historic Landmark, Porcupine Falls, Bucking Mule Falls**.
Directions: NE to Powell from MM 0
Notes: A short section between MM 43.5 and 46.7 connects via US-310/Wy-789 from mile markers 239.3 to 236.1. The US-14A theoretical mile markers are used for reference and the US-310/Wy-789 markers are noted in the directions. A 19 mi section between Bighorn Lake (MM 59) and the Medicine Wheel turnoff (MM 78.1) is EXTREMELY steep with 10% grades.

MM: 0.0 *GPS:* 44.52606/-109.05633 *Elev:* 4996 *Grid:* 29/12
US-14/16/20 *(see chapter)*   *Type:* Hwy Junction w/Chapter
100.1 mi highway west from a transition with **US-14/16/20/Wy-789**, west of **Greybull**, to the east entrance of **Yellowstone National Park**. The **Buffalo Bill Cody Scenic Byway** runs 27.4 mi from the east boundary of the **Shoshone National Forest** to the east entrance of **Yellowstone National Park**. Highlights include: **Buffalo Bill Historical Center, Old West Miniature Village and Museum, Buffalo Bill Dam and Visitor Center, Holy City, Firefighters Memorial and Trail**, interesting volcanic rock formations.
Directions: E to Greybull or W to Yellowstone National Park from MM 52.4
Notes: No dispersed camping on this route. If heading to Yellowstone be aware that the last 2 campgrounds are for hard-sided RVs only. Only 2 very small towns west of Cody.

MM: 0.0 *GPS:* 44.52606/-109.05633 *Elev:* 4996 *Grid:* 29/12
Cody   *Type:* Town

MM: 0.4 *GPS:* 44.53234/-109.05600 *Elev:* 4978 *Grid:* 29/12
Wy-120 *(see chapter)*   *Type:* Hwy Junction w/Chapter
118.7 mi highway that runs diagonally from **Thermopolis** northwest to **Cody** and continues to **Montana**. From **Cody, US-14/16/20** heads straight east to the east entrance of **Yellowstone National Park**. Continuing north from **Cody** the highway provides 2 scenic routes to the northeast entrance of **Yellowstone National Park**. Route 1 connects to **Wy-296 (Chief Joseph Scenic Highway)**, which climbs over the spectacular **Dead Indian Pass** and connects to **US-212**. Route 2 travels into **Montana** and loops back into **Wyoming** on **US-212** over the even more spectacular **Beartooth Pass**. Highlights include: **Legend Rock Petroglyphs, Gooseberry Badlands Scenic Area**, attractions in **Cody** *(see US-14/16/20 MM 52.4)*.
Directions: NW to Montana or SE to Thermopolis from MM 100

MM: 13.1 *Dist:* 0.6 *GPS:* 44.67054/-108.94967 *Elev:* 4705 *Grid:* 30/8
Heart Mountain Relocation Center   *Type:* Historic Site
After the **Japanese** bombing of **Pearl Harbor** in 1941, approximately 110,000 people of Japanese ancestry were relocated to Internment camps based on **President Franklin D. Roosevelt's** executive order. This was 1 of 10 such camps and housed over 10,000 people. The site includes a monument in recognition of those who were interred at this camp and subsequently lost their lives fighting for the United States in **World War II**. Another monument is dedicated to all who were interred during the 3 years the camp was active. A 0.1 mi loop path features interpretive signs about life at the camp. A video about the history of the camp is available for viewing at the free **Homesteader Museum** in **Powell** *(see MM 24.1 below)*.
Cool Rating: *** *Crowds:* * *Time:* 30 min *Directions:* NW on CR-19 0.6 mi; SW/L on Lane 15 70 yds.

MM: 18.1 *GPS:* 44.71622/-108.86479 *Elev:* 4554 *Grid:* 31/7
Ralston   *Type:* Town

MM: 18.8 *GPS:* 44.72268/-108.85486 *GPS2:* 44.72121/-108.85563 *Elev:* 4500 *Grid:* 31/7 *Land:* City
Ralston Bridges   *Type:* Point of Interest
This unusual bit of civil engineering has a railroad bridge crossing over a highway bridge crossing over **Alkali Creek**, all in different directions. This was once featured in **"Ripley's Believe It or Not."** There is no longer a road to the highway bridge. The site can be viewed from the pullout or accessed by walking 175 yds southwest down a gravel road.
Cool Rating: ** *Crowds:* * *Time:* 5 - 20 min
Directions: Parking area on SE side of hwy just before the west end of the canal bridge.

MM: 24.0 *GPS:* 44.75180/-108.75630 *Elev:* 4391 *Grid:* 33/6
Powell   *Type:* Town

MM: 24.1 *Dist:* 0.1 *GPS:* 44.75254/-108.75622 *Elev:* 4391 *Grid:* 33/6 *Land:* City
Homesteader Museum   *Type:* Museum
The museum celebrates 46 years of homesteading from 1906-1952 and the **Shoshone Reclamation Project** of 1908-1954. Exhibits include early-day farm implements, home furnishings, a pioneer kitchen, antique toys, medical equipment, military gear, fossils, **Powell** town site history, an original homestead house, and the red **Burlington Northern** caboose. A video documentary explains the history of the **Heart Mountain Relocation Center** 11 mi southwest of town *(see MM 13.1 above)*.
Cool Rating: ** *Crowds:* * *Time:* 30 min
Directions: N on S Clark St 1 block to E 1st St; SE corner *(133 South Clark St, Powell)*

MM: 24.9 *GPS:* 44.75603/-108.74180 *Elev:* 4367 *Grid:* 33/6 *Land:* City
Homesteader Park and Rest Area   *Type:* Rest Area
A rest area with informational signs about the history of the **Powell** area and the role that water projects played in irrigating this sagebrush prairie. The rest area is part of a nice park with covered picnic shelters and a playground. The park allows RV camping along the road and tent camping in the grass. The road is configured with 5 back-in sites and 5 long parallel parking areas that could each fit 2 vehicles.
Crowds: *** *Directions:* E end of Powell on N side of hwy
Campsites: 20 *Shade:* * *Privacy:* * *RV Size:* 40'+ *Other:* Water,RVDump

MM: 35.0 **GPS:** 44.77345/-108.57246 **Elev:** 4063 **Grid:** 35/6
Sidon Canal   **Type:** Historical Marker
In 1900 several hundred **Mormons** migrated from **Utah** and **Idaho** to **Wyoming**'s **Bighorn Basin**, where they built a 37 mi long canal and community. The canal is located behind the sign and the trees.
Cool Rating: * **Crowds:** * **Time:** 5 min **Directions:** NW side of hwy

MM: 38.8 **GPS:** 44.79636/-108.50709 **Elev:** 4028 **Grid:** 36/5
Byron   **Type:** Town

MM: 39.2 **GPS:** 44.79615/-108.50017 **Elev:** 4023 **Grid:** 36/5 **Land:** City
Byron Sessions Statue   **Type:** Historical Marker
In 1900 the president of the **Mormon Church** appointed **Byron Sessions** to oversee the construction of the **Sidon Canal**, which would bring water to 17,715 acres in the **Shoshone Valley**. The 37 mi canal was completed in the spring of 1904. A statue of **Byron Sessions** holding his survey map stands atop a grassy hill. Along the walking path is an interpretive sign with the **Byron Sessions** story as well as a plaque and memorial to the **Byron** war veterans.
Cool Rating: ** **Crowds:** * **Time:** 15 min
Directions: SW corner of US-14A and S Mountain View St at the east end of Byron.

MM: 43.5 **GPS:** 44.84287/-108.44141 **Elev:** 3905 **Grid:** 37/4
US-310/Wy-789 (west end)   **Type:** Highway Transition
If heading east: Turn south/right to begin a 3.2 mi section of shared highway between **US-14A** and **US-310/Wy-789**. For consistency, the next 3 sections continue the **US-14A** mile markers; however, the actual mile markers are those for **US-310/Wy-789** from MM 239.3 to MM 236.1, and are referenced in the directions for each section.

If heading west: Turn west/left to continue on **US-14A** from MM 43.5.
Directions: SE to Lovell or W to Powell from MM 43.5

MM: 43.6 **GPS:** 44.84163/-108.43953 **Elev:** 3906 **Grid:** 37/4 **Land:** City
Mormon Colonists Monument   **Type:** Historical Marker
A rock monument in honor of the accomplishments of the **Mormon** colonists who in 1900 established towns in the **Bighorn Basin**.
Cool Rating: * **Crowds:** * **Time:** 5 min
Directions: US-310/Wy-789 MM 239.1; SW side of hwy; 0.1 mi SE of the junction of US-14A and US-310/Wy-789.

MM: 46.0 **GPS:** 44.83749/-108.38925 **Elev:** 3836 **Grid:** 38/4
Lovell   **Type:** Town

MM: 46.4 **Dist:** 0.4 **GPS:** 44.84114/-108.38317 **Elev:** 3822 **Grid:** 38/4 **Land:** City
Lovell Camper Park   **Type:** Campground
A shady and free camping park on the northeast end of **Lovell**. *Deciduous trees. Dirt and gravel sites. Level. Tables. Grills. Flush toilets. Showers. Water refill station. Several pull-thrus. 3-day limit.*
Crowds: ***
Directions: US-310/Wy-789 MM 236.4; On the east end of Lovell; N on Pennsylvania Ave 0.2 mi; E/R on E 2nd St 0.1 mi; N/L on Quebec Ave 0.05 mi; W side of street. **To return to US-14A eastbound**: S on Quebec Ave 0.05 mi; E on E 2nd St 0.3 mi.
Campsites: 9 **Shade:** ***** **Privacy:** * **RV Size:** 40'+ **Other:** Water,RVDump

MM: 46.7 **GPS:** 44.83698/-108.37915 **Elev:** 3818 **Grid:** 38/4
US-310/Wy-789 (east end)   **Type:** Highway Transition
If heading east: Turn north/left to continue on **US-14A** from MM 46.7.

If heading west: Turn west/right to begin a 3.2 mi section of shared highway between **US-14A** and **US-310/Wy-789**. For consistency, the next 3 sections continue the **US-14A** mile markers; however, the actual mile markers are those for **US-310/Wy-789** from MM 236.1 to MM 239.3, and are referenced in the directions for each section.
Directions: NE to Burgess Jct or W to Powell from MM 46.7

MM: 46.8 **GPS:** 44.83828/-108.37824 **Elev:** 3817 **Grid:** 38/4
Bighorn Canyon National Recreation Area Visitor Center   **Type:** Visitor Center
A visitor center with information and maps for the **Bighorn Canyon National Recreation Area**. The center also includes exhibits on the park history, natural features, and recreational opportunities. A video highlights park activities. Behind the building is a short nature trail around a pond. Several picnic tables are located in the grassed areas on the perimeter of the parking lot.
Hours: 8am - 6pm (Memorial Day - Labor Day); 8:30am - 5pm (offseason) **Cool Rating:** ** **Crowds:** ** **Time:** 30 min
Directions: 0.1 mi NE of the junction with US-310/Wy-789; SE side of hwy.

MM: 49.2 **GPS:** 44.84063/-108.33153 **Elev:** 3795 **Grid:** 39/4
Wy-37 (Bighorn Canyon National Recreation Area) *(see chapter)*   **Type:** Hwy Junction w/Chapter
16.2 mi highway north to the **Bighorn Canyon National Recreation Area**, which is partially in **Montana**. This is not a through highway, so the return is by the same route. The mile markers for **Wy-37** end at MM 9.0, so they are also shown as starting at zero from the fee station to allow the trip odometer to be reset. Highlights include: **Sykes Mountain Trail**, **Mouth of the Canyon Trail**, **Devil Canyon Overlook**.
Nearest Town: Lovell 2.8 W **Directions:** N to Bighorn Canyon National Recreation Area from MM 0

MM: 55.5 **Dist:** 1.0 **GPS:** 44.84349/-108.19875 **Elev:** 3660 **Grid:** 41/4 **Land:** State
Yellowtail Wildlife Habitat Management Area: Kane Ponds   **Type:** Wildlife Habitat Mgmt Area
Primitive camping in 3 parking areas on the east side of the road. At 1.0 mi is a small dirt parking area just off the main road near a medium-sized tree. At 2.0 mi is a large open area 40 yds from the road near a grove of large trees. At 2.5 mi is a large area that is overgrown with weeds. *No toilet.*
Crowds: * **Notes:** This is not very desirable camping. **Directions:** S on CR-20 just E of the railroad tracks.
Road Desc: Gravel
Campsites: Dispersed **Shade:** *** **Privacy:** ** **RV Size:** 30' **Other:** None

MM: 59.2 *Dist:* 0.3 *GPS:* 44.83064/-108.15894 *Elev:* 3675 *Grid:* 41/4 *Land:* State
Yellowtail Wildlife Habitat Management Area: Mason-Lovell Ranch   *Type:* Wildlife Habitat Mgmt Area
Primitive camping in a parking area across the road from the historic **Mason-Lovell Ranch** (1883-1902). An interpretive sign
identifies and describes the buildings. Visitors can walk around the ranch, but watch out for rattlesnakes. *No toilet.*
Crowds: * *Road Desc:* Gravel
Directions: *At ML Ranch Historic Site sign; W 0.2 mi; SW/L at intersection 0.1 mi.*
Campsites: Dispersed *Shade:* * *Privacy:* * *RV Size:* 30' *Other:* None

MM: 60.1 *Dist:* 3.2 *GPS:* 44.78333/-108.16377 *Elev:* 3662 *Grid:* 41/5 *Land:* State
Yellowtail Wildlife Habitat Management Area - Crystal Creek Rd   *Type:* Wildlife Habitat Mgmt Area
Following the directions below leads to a fork in the road. Heading left leads 0.4 mi to the **Bighorn River** with many camping
possibilities but no established sites. Heading right follows the cliff line, east of the river, 1.6 mi to a parking area next to the river.
The road continues 2.0 mi to the **Mason-Lovell Ranch** *(see previous section). No toilet.*
Crowds: * *Directions:* SW on Crystal Creek Rd/BLM-1129 3.1 mi; NW/R 0.1 mi to fork.
Notes: Rather out of the way for mediocre camping.
Road Desc: Gravel, high clearance. The entrance road is wide, smooth gravel. The road into the WHMA is narrow, rutted dirt and
impassable when wet.
Campsites: Dispersed *Shade:* * *Privacy:* * *RV Size:* 30' *Other:* None

MM: 68.6 *GPS:* 44.79783/-107.98755 *Elev:* 5700 *Grid:* 44/5
The Original Dayton-Kane Highway   *Type:* Historical Marker
A sign explaining the history of the original highway through this area.
Cool Rating: * *Crowds:* * *Time:* 5 min *Directions:* N side of hwy at the junction with Old US-14A.

MM: 68.6 *Dist:* 2.1 *GPS:* 44.80481/-107.96884 *Elev:* 6600 *Grid:* 44/5 *Land:* BLM
Five Springs Falls Campground   *Type:* Campground/Picnic Area
A small tent campground in the shadow of vertical rock cliffs near **Five Springs Creek**. **Five Springs Falls** is northeast of the
campground *(see next section). Mixed forest. Level tent pads.*
Crowds: * *[FEE AREA] Road Desc:* Paved, broken & potholed, steep w/switchbacks. Road climbs 900 ft.
Notes: 1 site at the northeast part of the parking area has room for a pickup camper or small RV.
Directions: N 2.1 mi on Old US Hwy-14A.
Campsites: 9 *Shade:* **** *Privacy:* *** *RV Size:* Tent *Other:* None

MM: 68.6 *Dist:* 2.1 *GPS:* 44.80506/-107.96826 *GPS2:* 44.80561/-107.96762 *Elev:* 6613 *Grid:* 44/5 *Land:* NF
Five Springs Falls   *Type:* Waterfall
Five Springs Creek drops 100 ft over a cliff in a vertical granite walled canyon. A full view of the falls is not possible from the trail;
however, a few openings in the trees offer some good views. From the northeast side of **Five Springs Falls Campground** a short
shady trail leads northeast along **Five Springs Creek** to the falls.
Cool Rating: *** *Crowds:* * *Time:* 20 min
Directions: See previous section for directions to Five Springs Falls Campground.

MM: 68.7 *Dist:* 0.2 *GPS:* 44.79529/-107.98567 *Elev:* 5693 *Grid:* 44/5 *Land:* BLM
Dispersed Camping: US-14A   *Type:* Campground
Primitive camping in some small groves of trees and in the open. Another site is located 0.1 mi down the road. *Stone fire rings.*
Crowds: * *Road Desc:* Dirt *Directions:* S 0.2 mi
Campsites: Dispersed *Shade:* ** *Privacy:* *** *Other:* None

MM: 71.0 *GPS:* 44.78903/-107.97083 *Elev:* 6540 *Grid:* 44/5
Reconstruction Finally   *Type:* Historical Marker
A sign explaining the reconstruction of 52 mi of **US-14A** from 1967 to 1983. The pullout offers a good view into the valley, although
there is a chain link fence in the way.
Cool Rating: * *Crowds:* * *Time:* 5 min *Directions:* W side of hwy

MM: 71.7 *GPS:* 44.79543/-107.96231 *Elev:* 6916 *Grid:* 44/5 *Land:* NF
Medicine Wheel Passage (east end)   *Type:* Scenic Byway
Named for the **Medicine Wheel National Historic Landmark** along the way, this 27 mi section of **US-14A** runs from the western
edge of the **Bighorn National Forest** to **Burgess Jct**. This is one of the highest routes in the state with a high point of 9,446 ft
and a long and incredibly steep 10% grade just west of the **Medicine Wheel National Historic Landmark**.
Cool Rating: *** *Crowds:* ** *Notes:* Many side National Forest roads with dispersed camping.

MM: 74.3 *GPS:* 44.78938/-107.93174 *Elev:* 7875 *Grid:* 45/5 *Land:* NF
Bighorn Basin Overlook   *Type:* Scenic Viewpoint
A panoramic view into the **Bighorn Basin** which is surrounded by 6 mountain ranges. The overlook has interpretive signs about
the history, creation, geology, cities, natural features, and attractions in the **Bighorn Basin**.
Cool Rating: *** *Crowds:* * *Time:* 10 min *Directions:* S side of hwy

MM: 76.0 *GPS:* 44.79607/-107.91056 *Elev:* 8425 *Grid:* 45/5
Crystal Creek Rest Area   *Type:* Rest Area
A large dirt pullout with no facilities except a vault toilet.
Directions: NW side of hwy

MM: 78.1 **Dist:** 1.7 **GPS:** 44.81965/-107.89827 **GPS2:** 44.82617/-107.92155 **Elev:** 9625 **Grid:** 45/5 **Land:** NPS
Medicine Wheel National Historic Landmark   **Type:** Historic Site
On top of **Medicine Mountain** is the **Medicine Wheel**, an 80 ft diameter "spoke and wheel" alignment of rocks, with 28 spokes radiating from a central cairn and 6 smaller cairns evenly spaced around the perimeter. The original purpose of the **Medicine Wheel** is unknown, although scientists and archeologists believe that it was created between 1200 and 1700 A.D. by **Native Americans**. For many traditional Indian people the **Medicine Wheel** is considered to be the altar for **Medicine Mountain**, a site of great spiritual significance. **Native American** interpreters are present at the site during the tourist season from 8am - 6pm. Reaching the site requires walking 1.2 mi along a dirt road. A restroom is located just northeast of the site. *Moderately easy; 1.2 mi one-way; 100 ft elev loss, 100 ft elev gain.*
Cool Rating: **** **Crowds:** ** **Time:** 1-1.5 hrs **Road Desc:** Gravel, short but steep
Directions: NW then NE 1.7 mi to parking area

MM: 78.5 **Dist:** 1.7 **GPS:** 44.83049/-107.85911 **Elev:** 8803 **Grid:** 46/4 **Land:** NF
Porcupine Campground   **Type:** Campground
A very nice campground that is convenient to **Porcupine Falls** and **Bucking Mule Falls**. *Single loop. Conifer forest. Roomy sites. 2 tent-only sites. Level. Lantern poles. 1 pull-thru.*
Crowds: *** **[FEE AREA] Road Desc:** Gravel, potholed
Directions: N on FR-13 1.7 mi. **To Porcupine Falls and Bucking Mule Falls**: continue on FR-13 0.5 mi (keeping right at fork); N/L 1.4 mi on FR-133; NW/L on FR-14 4.4 mi to the turnoff to Porcupine Falls *(see sections below)*.
Campsites: 16 **Shade:** *** **Privacy:** *** **RV Size:** 30' **Other:** Water

MM: 78.8 **Dist:** 0.1 **GPS:** 44.80640/-107.85920 **Elev:** 9080 **Grid:** 46/5 **Land:** NF
Bald Mountain Campground   **Type:** Campground
A high elevation campground in a stand of conifers on the edge of a large meadow where **Bald Mountain Creek** flows. The campsites are spread out along a 1/4 mi road. *Some sites have shared parking areas. 1 pull-thru. Lantern pole.*
Crowds: ** **[FEE AREA] Road Desc:** Gravel **Directions:** S 0.1 mi
Notes: There were 3 moose along the creek on my visit. Abundant dispersed camping is available along FR-14 on the route to Porcupine Falls and Bucking Mule Falls *(see sections below)*.
Campsites: 15 **Shade:** ** **Privacy:** ** **RV Size:** 30' **Other:** 1-877-444-6777:www.recreation.gov,Water

MM: 79.7 **GPS:** 44.80917/-107.84161 **Elev:** 9268 **Grid:** 46/5
Gold Fever and Medicine Wheel   **Type:** Historical Marker
Signs with historical information about gold mining in the area in the late 1800s and the **Medicine Wheel** to the northwest.
Cool Rating: * **Crowds:** * **Time:** 5 min **Directions:** NE side of hwy

MM: 80.5 **Dist:** 7.7 **GPS:** 44.85781/-107.91255 **GPS2:** 44.85593/-107.91547 **Elev:** 8414 **Grid:** 45/4 **Land:** NF
Porcupine Falls   **Type:** Waterfall
A stunning 192 ft waterfall on **Porcupine Creek** that drops through a chasm in a sheer granite cliff into a large pool. To the right of the falls is another small cascade that flows out of a small cave in the side of the cliff. The waterfall, pool, canyon, and river are spectacular. The trail to the falls is an old mining road that is extremely steep with loose dirt and rocks. An old mining camp is located near the trailhead. *Moderately strenuous; 1/2 mi one-way; 450 ft elev loss.*
Cool Rating: ***** **Crowds:** *** **Time:** 1-1.5 hr **Notes:** Abundant dispersed camping is available along FR-14.
Road Desc: Gravel. The last 0.3 mi to the trailhead is bumpy and rutted.
Directions: NE on FR-11/Sheep Mountain Rd 3.0 mi; Continue straight on FR-14 4.4 mi; SW/L on FR-146 0.3 mi to trailhead parking.

MM: 80.5 **Dist:** 9.8 **GPS:** 44.88442/-107.90615 **GPS2:** 44.89444/-107.92698 **Elev:** 8320 **Grid:** 45/3 **Land:** NF
Bucking Mule Falls   **Type:** Waterfall
A 500 ft waterfall on **Bucking Mule Creek**, which flows through a chasm over a sheer granite cliff. The falls are viewed from about 400 yds across the rugged **Devil Canyon**. A nice hike through forest leads to the overlook. The trail drops 1.1 mi to a bridge over **Big Teepee Creek** and then levels off. At 2.0 mi is a trail junction. Continue straight the last 1/4 mi to the overlook. *Moderate; 2.25 mi one-way; 300 ft elev loss. Vault toilet at trailhead.*
Cool Rating: **** **Crowds:** * **Time:** 2-3 hrs **Road Desc:** Gravel
Notes: The waterfall is spectacular; however, it is too far away to get a true appreciation. The overlook is on a point with steep drop-offs and no railing. Abundant dispersed camping is available on FR-14 as well as adjacent to the trailhead.
Directions: NE on FR-11/Sheep Mountain Rd 3.0 mi; Continue straight on FR-14 6.8 mi to the end of the road at the trailhead parking. This is 2.4 mi past Porcupine Falls.

MM: 84.5 **GPS:** 44.75882/-107.77738 **Elev:** 9446 **Grid:** 47/6 **Land:** NF
Bighorn Basin Observation Point   **Type:** Scenic Viewpoint
The high point along the **Medicine Wheel Passage** with expansive views of the **Bighorn Basin**. A multi-use non-motorized vehicle trail starts at the overlook and heads south through a hilltop meadow.
Cool Rating: ** **Crowds:** * **Time:** 5 min **Directions:** S side of hwy

MM: 85.7 **GPS:** 44.76339/-107.75514 **Elev:** 9242 **Grid:** 47/6
FR-10/Hunt Mountain Rd   **Type:** Highway Junction
A 22.5 mi backcountry route that traverses the crest of the **Bighorn Mountains** across high mountain meadows. The route heads southeast from **US-14A** to **US-14** MM 38.2, just north of the **Granite Pass** summit and 9.5 mi south of Burgess Jct . Best as an OHV route.
Cool Rating: ** **Crowds:** * **Road Desc:** Dirt, rough & impassable when wet, narrow, high clearance
Directions: S then SE on FR-10/Hunt Mountain Rd

MM: 98.6 **Dist:** 1.1 **GPS:** 44.78122/-107.53402 **Elev:** 7837 **Grid:** 50/6 **Land:** NF
North Tongue Campground   **Type:** Campground
Composed of 2 sections across the road from the **North Tongue River**. The lower section is adjacent to a creek with 3 sites. The upper section climbs up a forested hillside with 9 sites, including 2 pull-thrus. *Conifer forest. Level. Lantern pole.*
Crowds: *** **[FEE AREA] Notes:** Dispersed camping along FR-15. **Road Desc:** Gravel **Directions:** N on FR-15 1.1 mi
Campsites: 12 **Shade:** ***** **Privacy:** * **RV Size:** 30' **Other:** 1-877-444-6777:www.recreation.gov,Water BEARS

MM: 98.6 *Dist:* 1.8 *GPS:* 44.78443/-107.52822 *Elev:* 7796 *Grid:* 50/5 *Land:* NF
Burgess Picnic Area   *Type:* Picnic Area
A very nice picnic area along the **North Tongue River** with 5 sites. This is also a popular fishing access point.
Road Desc: Gravel
Directions: N on FR-15 1.3 mi (the turnoff is just past North Tongue Campground); E/R on FR-162 0.5 mi.

MM: 98.7 *GPS:* 44.76960/-107.52243 *Elev:* 8085 *Grid:* 50/6 *Land:* NF
Medicine Wheel Passage (west end)   *Type:* Scenic Byway
Named for the **Medicine Wheel National Historic Landmark** along the way, this 27 mi section of **US-14A** runs from the western edge of the **Bighorn National Forest** to **Burgess Jct**. This is one of the highest routes in the state with a high point of 9,446 ft and a long and incredibly steep 10% grade just west of the **Medicine Wheel National Historic Landmark**.
Cool Rating: *** *Crowds:* ** *Notes:* Many side National Forest roads with dispersed camping.

MM: 98.9 *GPS:* 44.77005/-107.51805 *Elev:* 8088 *Grid:* 51/6
Burgess Jct   *Type:* Highway Junction
A named highway junction with no services.

MM: 98.9 *GPS:* 44.77005/-107.51805 *Elev:* 8088 *Grid:* 51/6
US-14 *(see chapter)*   *Type:* Hwy Junction w/Chapter
80.5 mi highway from **Greybull** northeast to **Ranchester**. A large portion of the highway is through National Forest along the **Bighorn Scenic Byway** with 10 public campgrounds. Highlights include: **Devil's Kitchen Geological Site**, **Red Gulch Dinosaur Tracksite**, **Medicine Lodge State Archaeological Site**, **Shell Falls**, **Dayton Bell Tower**, **Tongue River Canyon**.
Directions: NE to Dayton from MM 57.1 or SW to Greybull from MM 47.7

MM: 98.9 *GPS:* 44.77005/-107.51805 *Elev:* 8088 *Grid:* 51/6
End of Highway   *Type:* Highway End
98.9 mi highway west from **Burgess Jct** to **Lovell**, then southwest to **Cody**. The first 27 mi follow the **Medicine Wheel Passage**, a scenic high elevation route (over 9,000 ft) with excellent views into the **Bighorn Basin**. Highlights include: **Porcupine Falls**, **Bucking Mule Falls**, **Medicine Wheel National Historic Landmark**, **Bighorn Canyon National Recreation Area**, **Heart Mountain Relocation Center**.
Nearest Town: Dayton 26.3 NE *Directions:* W to Lovell from MM 98.9

US-16   SW/NE

MM: 0.0 **GPS:** 44.01685/-107.95575 **Elev:** 4063 **Grid:** 44/25
US-16   **Type:** Highway Description
89.9 mi highway from **Worland** northeast to **Buffalo**. Along this highway is the scenic 45 mi **Cloud Peak Skyway**, which travels through the **Bighorn Mountains** and provides many campgrounds, forest roads with dispersed camping, and recreational opportunities. Highlights include: **Castle Gardens**, **Medicine Lodge State Archaeological Site**, **Tensleep Canyon**, **Wigwam Rearing Station**, **Ten Sleep Fish Hatchery**, **West Tensleep Falls**, **High Park Lookout**, **Crazy Woman Canyon**.
Directions: E to Ten Sleep from MM 0
Notes: The mile markers jump from MM 71 to MM 75 in 1.8 mi, gaining 2.2 mi. Dispersed camping opportunities on most forest roads in the Bighorn National Forest.

MM: 0.0 **GPS:** 44.01685/-107.95575 **Elev:** 4063 **Grid:** 44/25
US-20/Wy-789 & US-16/20/Wy-789 & US-14/16/20/Wy-789 *(see chapter)*   **Type:** Hwy Junction w/Chapter
157 mi highway from **Shoshoni** north to **Montana**. Highlights include: **Boysen State Park**, **Wind River Canyon**, **Hot Springs State Park**, **Medicine Lodge State Archaeological Site**, **Devil's Kitchen Geological Site**, **Museum of Flight and Aerial Firefighting**.
Directions: N on US-16/20/Wy-789 to Greybull or S on US-20/Wy-789 to Thermopolis from MM 165.7

MM: 0.0 **GPS:** 44.01685/-107.95575 **Elev:** 4063 **Grid:** 44/25
Worland   **Type:** Town

MM: 0.0 **GPS:** 44.01685/-107.95575 **Elev:** 4063 **Grid:** 44/25 **Land:** City
Trail of the Whispering Giants & Pioneer Square   **Type:** Point of Interest
The 36th wood carving in the **Trail of the Whispering Giants** by **Peter Toth**. This 15 ft statue honors the first Americans who still live in **Wyoming**; the **Shoshone**, **Arapaho**, and **Sioux Indians**. The carving is one of 67 in the United States and Canada and was given to **Wyoming** in 1980.

Across the street to the west is **Pioneer Square**, a nice park with metal sculptures depicting pioneer settlers. *Public restroom.*
Cool Rating: ** **Crowds:** * **Time:** 20 min
Directions: NE & NW corners of the intersection of N 10th St/US-16 and Big Horn Ave/US-20 in front of the court house.

MM: 0.1 **Dist:** 0.3 **GPS:** 44.01273/-107.95344 **Elev:** 4071 **Grid:** 44/25 **Land:** City
Washakie Museum   **Type:** Museum
The museum houses a **Colby Mammoth Kill Site** display of the earliest mammoth kill site in North America. The actual site is located a short distance east of town near a historical marker at MM 4.5. The museum also contains displays on early settlers of the west in the "**Time Traveler's Room**," which contains a covered wagon, sheep wagon, and sod house, as well as Indian displays and a large collection of important historical photographs of the early settlement of the **Bighorn Basin**.
Cool Rating: ** **Crowds:** * **Time:** 1 hr *[FEE AREA]*
Directions: S on N 12th St 0.3 mi (4 blocks); NW corner across from park *(1115 Obie Sue Ave, Worland)*

MM: 1.3 **GPS:** 44.01891/-107.93250 **Elev:** 4105 **Grid:** 45/25 **Land:** City
Worland City Park   **Type:** Park
A nice park with picnic shelters, restroom, and a basketball court.
Directions: E end of Worland on NW side of hwy at N Hillcrest Dr.

MM: 4.5 **GPS:** 44.02399/-107.86712 **Elev:** 4315 **Grid:** 46/24
Colby Mammoth Kill Site   **Type:** Historical Marker
Approximately 400 yds south of this sign was an arroyo used by humans to trap and kill young mammoths 11,000 year ago. Materials from this site can be seen at the **Washakie Museum** in **Worland** *(see section above at MM 0.1)*.
Cool Rating: * **Crowds:** * **Time:** 5 min **Directions:** S side of hwy

MM: 17.0 **Dist:** 7.9 **GPS:** 43.93948/-107.54593 **GPS2:** 43.93246/-107.57294 **Elev:** 5013 **Grid:** 50/27 **Land:** BLM
The Honeycombs - From US-16   **Type:** Geological Feature
An expansive and scenic badlands area of red, brown, grey, and gold colors. The gold color is created from vegetation on the hillsides. This area is best viewed from a hilltop which is accessed by a very primitive 2-track path, which is best traveled on foot, OHV, or Jeep. The entire trail is in the open with no shade.

Travel southwest on the primitive road climbing 120 ft in 0.9 mi. The road then turns right and climbs another 100 ft in 0.7 mi to a good place to park a vehicle. The last 0.1 mi climbs another 50 ft, is on a side hill, and is so deeply rutted that it is advisable to walk it. The road is blocked off at this point, but you can optionally continue 0.5 mi on foot and climb 175 ft to the top of **North Butte** for even better views. **To viewpoint**: *Moderate; 1.7 mi one-way; 270 ft elev gain.* **To top of North Butte**: *Moderately strenuous; 2.2 mi one-way; 450 ft elev gain..*
Cool Rating: ***** **Crowds:** * **Road Desc:** Gravel. There are some ruts in the road, but it is fairly smooth.
Notes: You will pass the edge of the badlands on Blue Bank Rd, but the views are not that spectacular from the road. Another 2-track path is located 1.4 mi south on BLM-1411 (0.3 mi south of BLM-1435) that connects to the same route described above.
Directions: S 1.2 mi; E/L on Old Ten Sleep Hwy 0.4 mi; SE/R on BLM-1411/Blue Bank Rd 6.3 mi; Trail is on the SW side of road and is easy to miss.

MM: 24.4 *Dist:* 6.3 *GPS:* 43.95558/-107.51778 *Elev:* 5036 *Grid:* 51/26 *Land:* BLM

Castle Gardens (north)   *Type:* Scenic Area

A 0.4 mi road loops through a small valley below eroded sandstone cliffs that form hoodoos, castles, and other interesting shapes. You can climb to the top of the cliffs using paths above the lower campsite. This is the second **Castle Gardens** in **Wyoming**, the other being 70 mi south.

The area includes 2 campsites that are spaced 0.1 mi apart offering excellent privacy. However, the vault toilet is near one of the sites and therefore far from the other. The site at the top of the loop is large and open. The other site has a pullout where a medium-sized RV can be parked plus a walk-in tent site up a small hill. *Scattered pinion pines. Picnic tables. Fire rings. Vault toilet.*
Cool Rating: **** *Crowds:* * *Time:* 1 hr
Notes: If one of the campsites is not open, there are a couple of other places in the area to pull off.
Road Desc: The first 1.3 mi is on the Old Tensleep Highway, which is potholed pavement. The rest is smooth gravel.
Directions: S 0.3 mi; W/R on Old Tensleep Highway 1.0 mi; S/L on BLM-1435/Two Mile Hill Rd 4.3 mi; Keep right at the fork in the road 0.7 mi.
Campsites: 2 *Shade:* * *Privacy:* ***** *RV Size:* 40' *Other:* None

MM: 24.4 *Dist:* 11.6 *GPS:* 43.93948/-107.54593 *GPS2:* 43.93246/-107.57294 *Elev:* 5013 *Grid:* 50/27 *Land:* BLM

The Honeycombs - From Castle Gardens   *Type:* Geological Feature

If visiting **Castle Gardens**, this a shorter route to **The Honeycombs**. *See MM 17 above.*
Cool Rating: ***** *Crowds:* * *Road Desc:* Gravel. There are some ruts in the roads, but they are fairly smooth.
Directions: From Castle Gardens; N 0.7 mi; SE 4.2 mi on BLM-1435/Two Mile Hill Rd; N/R on BLM-1411/Blue Bank Rd 1.1 mi; Trail is on the SW side of road and is easy to miss.

MM: 25.9 *Dist:* 24.4 *GPS:* 44.29815/-107.54190 *Elev:* 4890 *Grid:* 50/18 *Land:* State

Medicine Lodge State Archaeological Site   *Type:* Petroglyphs

In 1973 this site was the scene of one of the most significant archaeological excavations in North America. For 2 years scientists unearthed evidence of over 10,000 years of human habitation from depths up to 26 ft. These findings document the entire history of human occupation in the **Bighorn Basin**. The dig site (which has been filled in) is located below a 750 ft long cliff that is covered with hundreds of **Petroglyphs** and **Pictographs**. Along the base of the cliff are interpretive signs explaining the rock art and the excavation. *See US-20/Wy-789 MM 185.0 for a complete description.*

A turnoff to **Renner Wildlife Management Area** and **Renner Reservoir** is located 11.8 mi along this route, 6.4 mi south of **Hyattville**, and 2.2 mi north of the junction with **CR-83**. This road heads east 3.0 mi to a cul-de-sac parking area at the edge of the reservoir. There is a vault toilet and camping is allowed. The dirt road looks like a ranch road but eventually runs through a nice canyon to the reservoir, which cannot be seen from the road. The road through the canyon is rather narrow with a couple of dispersed campsites in the canyon along the road at 1.8 mi.
Hours: Visitor Center: 8am - 5pm, Mon-Fri; 9am - 8pm, Sat-Sun
Cool Rating: **** *Crowds:* ** *Time:* 1-3 hrs *Nearest Town:* Hyattville 6.2 SW
Road Desc: Partially paved, mostly gravel. Lower Norwood Rd and Cold Springs Rd are paved. The rest is smooth gravel.
Directions: (0.5 mi W of Ten Sleep) N on CR-47/Lower Norwood Rd 8.5 mi; NE/R on CR-83/Buffalo Creek Rd 1.1 mi; N/L on CR-54/CR-49 9.1 mi through Hyattville; Where the road curves W/L to Wy-31, turn right on Alkali Rd 0.3 mi; E/R on Cold Springs Rd/CR-268 3.2 mi; Take sharp curve N/L 0.5 mi; Where road curves E/R, keep left to continue straight 1.7 mi to the park.

MM: 26.6 *GPS:* 44.03404/-107.44856 *Elev:* 4424 *Grid:* 51/24

Ten Sleep   *Type:* Town

MM: 26.8 *GPS:* 44.03390/-107.44507 *Elev:* 4429 *Grid:* 52/24 *Land:* City

Ten Sleep City Park   *Type:* Park

A nice green park with sheltered and open picnic tables, a playground, and a restroom.
Directions: E end of town on S side of hwy

MM: 31.2 *Dist:* 0.2 *GPS:* 44.06567/-107.38026 *Elev:* 4753 *Grid:* 52/23 *Land:* Wyoming G & F

Wigwam Rearing Station   *Type:* Fish Hatchery

A fish rearing station near the mouth of the **Tensleep Canyon**. This is not a fish hatchery as it does not have the capabilities to hatch eggs. Instead the station receives various species of fish after they reach a size of at least 2 in long (called fingerlings) and raises them to a size that is most beneficial for a particular fishery. The station also contains captive broodstocks of **Eagle Lake Rainbow Trout** and **Snake River Cutthroat Trout**, which provide eggs and milt (sperm) to another fish hatchery. 2 springs and a well provide approximately 1400 gallons of water per minute at a constant temperature of 50° F, providing for year-round growth of the fish. The water from the adjacent **Tensleep Creek** also provides water for the **Snake River Cutthroat Trout broodstock** held in a pond at the east end of the facility. A single raceway may hold from 20,000 to 50,000 fish. Several signs at the entrance explain the workings of the rearing station.
Cool Rating: ** *Crowds:* * *Time:* 30 min *Road Desc:* Gravel *Directions:* NW 0.2 mi
Notes: Just before the bridge over Tensleep Creek is a parking area and picnic table along the river.

MM: 31.6 *GPS:* 44.06791/-107.36886 *Elev:* 4827 *Grid:* 53/23 *Land:* Wyoming G & F

Wigwam Rearing Station Access Area   *Type:* Public Access Area

Primitive camping just below the highway next to **Tensleep Creek**. *Cottonwoods. Vault toilet. Stone fire rings.*
Crowds: * *Directions:* N side of hwy on a curve. The area is down a hill and the road is easy to miss.
Campsites: Dispersed *Shade:* **** *Privacy:* ** *RV Size:* 30' *Other:* None

MM: 34.0 *Dist:* 0.9 *GPS:* 44.08065/-107.31472 *Elev:* 5333 *Grid:* 53/23 *Land:* NF

Leigh Creek Campground   *Type:* Campground

A low elevation campground in **Tensleep Canyon** adjacent to **Tensleep Creek**. The sites are along a short road and a loop on the west end. The 4 sites in the loop are in heavy brush with excellent shade and privacy and are best for tents and pickup campers. The remaining sites have less privacy and less shade. The sites on the east are better for RVs. A few sites back up to the creek. *Deciduous trees.*
Crowds: ** *[FEE AREA]* *Directions:* E on Wy-435 0.9 mi
Campsites: 11 *Shade:* *** *Privacy:* *** *RV Size:* 30' *Other:* Water

MM: 34.0 *Dist:* 1.1 *GPS:* 44.08250/-107.31000 *Elev:* 5392 *Grid:* 53/23 *Land:* NF
Ten Sleep Fish Hatchery   *Type:* Fish Hatchery
Constructed in 1939 in **Tensleep Canyon**, this fish hatchery raises various trout species with the primary focus on the
Yellowstone Cutthroat Trout. The public is welcome and the tour of the facility is self-guided with 4 stations:
    1) **Information kiosk** with general information and a self-guided tour brochure
    2) **Main hatchery building** with the incubator room (closed to public) and indoor rearing tanks
    3) **Outdoor raceways** to raise growing fish
    4) **Yellowstone Cutthroat Trout information** describing the challenges for this indigenous fish species.
Hours: 8am - 5pm *Cool Rating:* *** *Crowds:* * *Time:* 30 min *Directions:* E on Wy-435 1.1 mi

MM: 34.0 *Dist:* 1.3 *GPS:* 44.08414/-107.30842 *Elev:* 5421 *Grid:* 53/23 *Land:* NF
Tensleep Creek Campground   *Type:* Campground
A low elevation campground in **Tensleep Canyon** near the mouth of **Leigh Canyon** and adjacent to **Tensleep Creek**. *Deciduous*
trees. Heavy understory and middlestory.
Crowds: ** *[FEE AREA] Directions:* E on Wy-435 1.3 mi
Campsites: 5 *Shade:* *** *Privacy:* ***** *RV Size:* 30' *Other:* Water

MM: 34.0 *GPS:* 44.07690/-107.33008 *Elev:* 5191 *Grid:* 53/23 *Land:* NF
Bighorn National Forest   *Type:* National Forest Boundary

MM: 35.0 *GPS:* 44.08206/-107.31362 *Elev:* 5475 *Grid:* 53/23 *Land:* NF
Cloud Peak Skyway (eastbound)   *Type:* Scenic Byway
A 45 mi scenic byway that travels through the southern section of the **Bighorn National Forest**. This is the least grade across the
Bighorn Mountains and provides the only view of **Cloud Peak**, the highest peak in the **Bighorn Mountains**. The high elevation
point of the drive is **Powder River Pass** at 9,663 ft.
Cool Rating: *** *Crowds:* ***
Directions: The route begins 10 mi east of **Ten Sleep** and ends 10 mi west of **Buffalo**.

MM: 36.2 *GPS:* 44.09048/-107.29759 *GPS2:* 44.08488/-107.30401 *Elev:* 5825 *Grid:* 54/23
Leigh Creek Monument   *Type:* Historical Marker
A monument to **Gilbert E. Leigh** is located to the southwest across the canyon on the top edge of the left canyon cliff. Binoculars
are required to see the monument. A sign explains the story behind the monument. An additional sign provides information about
Tensleep Canyon.
Cool Rating: ** *Crowds:* * *Time:* 10 min *Directions:* Pullout on SE side of hwy

MM: 44.1 *GPS:* 44.16887/-107.24796 *Elev:* 8065 *Grid:* 54/21
FR-27/Ten Sleep Rd *(see chapter)*   *Type:* Hwy Junction w/Chapter
7.3 mi gravel National Forest road from **US-16** MM 44.1 north to **West Tensleep Lake**, **West Tensleep Trailhead**, and **West
Tensleep Falls**. 4 National Forest campgrounds are located along this road, which also offers many dispersed camping
opportunities.
Nearest Town: Ten Sleep 17.6 SW *Directions:* W then N on FR-27/Ten Sleep Rd 7.3 mi

MM: 45.1 *Dist:* 0.2 *GPS:* 44.18198/-107.23779 *Elev:* 8360 *Grid:* 55/20 *Land:* NF
Willow Park Group Picnic Area   *Type:* Picnic Area
A reservable group picnic area for up to 150 people. Overnight camping is allowed, although RVs and trailers are limited to the
parking area. *Drinking water. Vault toilets. Trash collection. Extended serving tables. Playground.*
[FEE AREA] Road Desc: Gravel *Directions:* N 0.2 mi

MM: 45.4 *Dist:* 0.9 *GPS:* 44.16725/-107.23249 *Elev:* 8557 *Grid:* 55/21 *Land:* NF
Lake Point Picnic Area   *Type:* Picnic Area
10 individual picnic sites in a scenic area above the southwest shore of **Meadowlark Lake**. The first 6 sites are in a loop 80 ft
above the lake. A single site will be passed before an end of road cul-de-sac with 3 more sites 30 ft above the dam. *Vault toilet in*
first loop.
Crowds: *** *Directions:* SW on FR-438 0.1 mi; Left on FR-437 3/4 mi to first 6 sites or 0.9 mi to last 4 sites.
Notes: This is one of the nicest picnic areas in Wyoming. Not recommended for RVs or trailers.
Road Desc: Gravel, rough, narrow & steep

MM: 46.4 *Dist:* 0.1 *GPS:* 44.18004/-107.22034 *Elev:* 8490 *Grid:* 55/21 *Land:* NF
North Cove Boat Ramp   *Type:* Boat Ramp
Boat ramp on the north shore of **Meadowlark Lake**.
Directions: SW 0.1 mi

MM: 46.4 *Dist:* 0.8 *GPS:* 44.19169/-107.21160 *Elev:* 8680 *Grid:* 55/20 *Land:* NF
Sitting Bull Campground   *Type:* Campground
A large scenic campground near **Meadowlark Lake** and **Lake Creek**, in the forest on the edge of a large mountain meadow. *Large*
loop road as well as a road along the meadow with a small end loop. Dense mixed forest. Lantern posts. No pull-thrus.
Crowds: ***** *[FEE AREA] Road Desc:* Gravel *Directions:* NE on FR-432 0.8 mi
Campsites: 42 *Shade:* ***** *Privacy:* * *RV Size:* 40'+ *Other:* 1-877-444-6777:www.recreation.gov,Water

MM: 46.7 *Dist:* 0.1 *GPS:* 44.17685/-107.21422 *Elev:* 8554 *Grid:* 55/21 *Land:* NF
Lakeview Campground and Picnic Area   *Type:* Campground/Picnic Area
A scenic campground above the northeast shore of **Meadowlark Lake**, composed of 2 separate sections. The upper section is for
RVs with 6 sites in a side loop (plus a campground host) and 4 unlevel sites lined up at the end of the road, all with views of the
lake. The lower section is down a hill near the lake with 9 tent-only sites on the left side of a cul-de-sac. Across from the tent area
is a picnic area in the forest. *Conifer forest. Highway noise in RV section.*
Crowds: ***** *[FEE AREA] Directions:* W on FR-424 0.1 mi. 0.2 mi farther to tent and picnic area.
Campsites: 20 *Shade:* ***** *Privacy:* ** *RV Size:* 30' *Other:* 1-877-444-6777:www.recreation.gov,Water

MM: 47.3 *GPS:* 44.17015/-107.21253 *Elev:* 8580 *Grid:* 55/21 *Land:* NF
Firefighters Memorial   *Type:* Historical Marker
A pullout above **Meadowlark Lake** with a memorial to firefighters who died in the **Shoshone Forest Fire** in 1937 plus a sign about Company 841 of the **Civilian Conservation Corps** (CCC) who built the **Meadowlark Lake Dam** in 1936.
Cool Rating: * *Crowds:* * *Time:* 5 min *Directions:* W side of hwy

MM: 48.6 *Dist:* 0.2 *GPS:* 44.15625/-107.19084 *Elev:* 8894 *Grid:* 55/21 *Land:* NF
St. Christopher's in the Bighorns Episcopal Chapel   *Type:* Chapel
An outdoor Episcopal chapel with Sunday services.
Hours: 11 am Sun (July & Aug) *Road Desc:* Gravel *Directions:* SW on FR-429 0.15 mi; Right into parking area.

MM: 48.6 *Dist:* 1.3 *GPS:* 44.15118/-107.20162 *GPS2:* 44.14961/-107.20231 *Elev:* 9241 *Grid:* 55/21 *Land:* NF
High Park Lookout   *Type:* Fire Lookout
Nice views of the **Cloud Peak Wilderness** from the deck of an unused fire lookout. An interpretive sign at the parking area explains manned fire lookouts. Accessing the lookout requires a short but steep hike. *Moderately easy; 1/4 mi one-way; 200 ft elev gain.*
Cool Rating: *** *Crowds:* * *Time:* 30-60 min *Road Desc:* Gravel
Notes: The parking area is not big enough to easily turn a trailer around.
Directions: SW on FR-429 1.3 mi, keeping right after 0.9 mi.

MM: 53.3 *GPS:* 44.16092/-107.11007 *Elev:* 9410 *Grid:* 56/21 *Land:* NF
RV Dump: Bighorn National Forest   *Type:* RV Dump
A National Forest **RV dump** with 3 stations. *Donations accepted.*
Directions: S side of hwy

MM: 55.3 *GPS:* 44.14983/-107.07967 *Elev:* 9663 *Grid:* 57/21 *Land:* NF
Powder River Pass   *Type:* Pass
A large pullout with an informational sign at the high elevation point on **US-16**.
Directions: S side of hwy

MM: 62.4 *Dist:* 0.3 *GPS:* 44.14678/-106.95352 *Elev:* 8208 *Grid:* 59/21 *Land:* NF
Lost Cabin Campground   *Type:* Campground
A shady campground on a 1/2 mi loop road. *Mixed forest. No understory. Roomy sites. 1 tent-only site. 9 pull-thrus. Slower to fill than other campgrounds.*
Crowds: *** *[FEE AREA]* *Road Desc:* Gravel *Directions:* N 0.3 mi
Campsites: 18 *Shade:* ***** *Privacy:* ** *RV Size:* 40'+ *Other:* 1-877-444-6777:www.recreation.gov,Water

MM: 63.4 *GPS:* 44.15066/-106.93301 *Elev:* 7955 *Grid:* 59/21
Hazelton Rd   *Type:* Highway Junction
A 72.3 mi series of county roads that end at **CR-105/Buffalo Creek Rd**, 22.7 mi north of **US-20/26**. This route provides access to **Hole-in-the-Wall**. It also saves about 90 miles to **US-20/26**; however, long sections of the road are so bad it will probably take at least as long to drive it.

Doyle Campground (MI 6.2) and 3 free BLM campgrounds are located along this route: **Middle Fork Powder River Campground** (MI 49.4), **Grave Springs Campground** (MI 61.5) *(see US-20/26 MM 50.7)*, and **Buffalo Creek Campground** (MI 63.4) *(see US-20/26 MM 50.7)*. **Dullknife Reservoir** is at (MI 11.0).

The turnoff to **Hole-in-the-Wall** on **CR-84/CR-110/Thirty Three Mile Rd** is at (MI 55.7). Follow this road southeast 12 mi to **CR-105/Buffalo Creek Rd**. Turn left 2.5 mi and proceed to the gate *(see US-20/26 MM 50.7)*.
Road Desc: Pavement for 3.6 mi. Gravel for 26.3 mi where it turns to rough dirt. At about 48 mi the road gets very rocky and rough for many miles. One of the worst roads that I have ever driven on.
Directions: S on CR-3/CR-74/CR-81/CR-109 72.3 mi; To US-20/26: S on CR-105/Buffalo Creek Rd 22.7 mi.

MM: 63.4 *Dist:* 6.5 *GPS:* 44.07315/ 106.98864 *Elev:* 8140 *Grid:* 58/23 *Land:* NF
Doyle Campground   *Type:* Campground
A quiet campground far from the highway near **Doyle Creek**. The first 6 sites are on the edge of the forest, have longer parking areas, and are not well shaded. *Large single loop. Dense lodgepole pine forest. Good spacing between sites. 1 long pull-thru with 2 sites. Unlevel.*
Crowds: ** *[FEE AREA]* *Road Desc:* Gravel *Directions:* S on CR-3/Hazelton Rd 6.2 mi; SE/L 0.3 mi.
Notes: There are dispersed camping areas along the forest road past the campground.
Campsites: 19 *Shade:* **** *Privacy:* *** *RV Size:* 30' *Other:* Water

MM: 64.5 *Dist:* 4.2 *GPS:* 44.16257/-106.91786 *Elev:* 7833 *Grid:* 59/21 *Land:* NF
Crazy Woman Canyon   *Type:* Scenic Drive
A 13.3 mi backcountry route from **US-16** east to **Wy-196** (which connects to **I-25**) through **Crazy Woman Canyon**. At the turnoff from **US-16** a narrow forest road descends steeply into the canyon for about 4 mi. The road parallels **Crazy Woman Creek** for only about 1.5 mi through the bottom of the canyon. A short section passes below high canyon walls and past giant boulders that have tumbled from above. The final 7.8 mi is a wider gravel county road through a valley at the base of the **Bighorn Mountains** with good views to the west. Dispersed camping opportunities are minimal along this route except perhaps a few areas on the descent into the canyon.
Cool Rating: *** *Crowds:* * *Time:* 1-2 hrs *Road Desc:* Gravel, narrow, steep & winding, high clearance
Notes: No trailers or RVs.
Directions: E on FR-33/CR-14 13.3 mi to Wy-196; **To continue to I-25 north**: N on Wy-196 3.4 mi; E/R on Buffalo Sussex Cutoff Rd 1.0 mi to I-25 exit 291. **To continue to I-25 south**: S on Wy-196 23.4 mi; E/L on Reno Rd 0.6 mi to I-25 exit 265.

MM: 64.9 **Dist:** 0.3 **GPS:** 44.16665/-106.91997 **Elev:** 7730 **Grid:** 59/21 **Land:** NF
Crazy Woman Campground   **Type:** Campground
Camping along a short road adjacent to **Crazy Woman Creek** with an end loop turnaround. *Light conifer forest. First 3 sites are close together and badly unlevel; second 3 sites have a little better spacing and are a bit more level. Not a very nice campground.*
Crowds: *** **[FEE AREA]** **Road Desc:** Gravel **Directions:** W 0.3 mi
Campsites: 6 **Shade:** ** **Privacy:** * **RV Size:** 20' **Other:** Water

MM: 70.0
Mile Marker Discrepancy (northbound)   **Type:** MM Discrepancy
Between mile marker 70 and mile marker 80 there are only 8 mile markers. This means that the mileages will jump 1 mile at MM 73 and at MM 77. The mile markers noted in the book will be referenced as best as possible traveling northbound. The attractions between MM 72 and MM 80 are clearly marked with highway signs, so keep in mind that the mile markers may be off.
Notes: I believe that the missing mile marker is MM 77 but am sure the other is MM 73.

MM: 71.9 **Dist:** 0.1 **GPS:** 44.24941/-106.94126 **Elev:** 8096 **Grid:** 59/19 **Land:** NF
Loaf Mountain Overlook   **Type:** Scenic Viewpoint
A view of mountain peaks in the **Cloud Peak Wilderness**. 2 signs identify the peaks and explain timber management.
Cool Rating: * **Crowds:** * **Time:** 10 min **Directions:** NE 0.1 mi
Notes: Because of mile marker discrepancies this is MM 74.1 if heading south (0.9 mi south of MM 75 and 0.9 mi north of MM 71).

MM: 75.6 **Dist:** 0.1 **GPS:** 44.27735/-106.94833 **Elev:** 7655 **Grid:** 59/18 **Land:** NF
South Fork Campground   **Type:** Campground
Along the **South Fork Clear Creek** in a small valley below rock outcrops. Across the creek are 5 tent-only sites with parking off the end loop. *Mixed forest. Little understory. Small sites. No pull-thrus.*
Crowds: ***** **[FEE AREA]** **Notes:** Not recommended for large RVs or trailers. **Directions:** SE 0.1 mi
Campsites: 15 **Shade:** ***** **Privacy:** * **RV Size:** 30' **Other:** 1-877-444-6777:www.recreation.gov,Water

MM: 76.0 **Dist:** 0.4 **GPS:** 44.28290/-106.94353 **Elev:** 7760 **Grid:** 59/18 **Land:** NF
Tie Hack Campground   **Type:** Campground
Just off the 1.5 mi road to **Tie Hack Reservoir**. *Large initial loop and a small loop on south end with 4 sites. Conifer forest. Grass understory. Good spacing between sites. Lantern pole.*
Crowds: *** **[FEE AREA]** **Road Desc:** Gravel **Directions:** E on FR-21 1/4 mi; S/R 0.1 mi.
Campsites: 20 **Shade:** **** **Privacy:** *** **RV Size:** 40'+ **Other:** 1-877-444-6777:www.recreation.gov,Water

MM: 76.0 **Dist:** 1.5 **GPS:** 44.28790/-106.92373 **Elev:** 7500 **Grid:** 59/18 **Land:** NF
Tie Hack Reservoir   **Type:** Lake
A small reservoir with fishing, non-motorized boat use, and a picnic area.
Crowds: ** **Road Desc:** Gravel **Directions:** E on FR-21 1.5 mi

MM: 76.4 **Dist:** 2.0 **GPS:** 44.28122/-106.98495 **Elev:** 8093 **Grid:** 58/18 **Land:** NF
Circle Park Campground   **Type:** Campground
Located in a stand of trees at the edge of a meadow where the surrounding forest burned in 1988. Moose are often seen in the area. Best for tents and pickup campers. *Mixed forest. Good spacing between sites. Not level. 3 tent-only sites. No pull-thrus.*
Crowds: *** **[FEE AREA]** **Notes:** Dispersed camping along FR-20. **Road Desc:** Gravel **Directions:** W on FR-20 2.0 mi
Campsites: 10 **Shade:** ***** **Privacy:** **** **RV Size:** 20' **Other:** Water

MM: 76.4 **Dist:** 2.4 **GPS:** 44.27663/-106.98496 **Elev:** 8165 **Grid:** 58/18 **Land:** NF
Circle Park Trailhead   **Type:** Trailhead
A hike into the **Cloud Peak Wilderness** in the **Bighorn Mountains** past several small lakes. The largest of the lakes along the trail is **Sherd Lake**, which is 1.7 mi from the trailhead and offers a short out and back option. Turning left starts a clockwise loop that passes **Her Lake** (5.1 mi), **Otter Lake** (6.1) and **Rainy Lake** (6.4). Two 0.2 mi side trails access the largest lake, **Trigger Lake** (4.1 mi), and **Old Crow Lake** (5.4 mi). *Moderately strenuous; 9.4 mi loop; 1235 ft elev gain at Rainy Lake.*
Cool Rating: *** **Crowds:** *** **Time:** 2-4 hrs **Road Desc:** Gravel **Directions:** W on FR-20 2.0 mi; S/L 0.4 mi.
Notes: Dispersed camping along FR-20.

MM: 76.9 **Dist:** 0.4 **GPS:** 44.29708/-106.95153 **Elev:** 7650 **Grid:** 59/18 **Land:** NF
Hettinger Picnic Area   **Type:** Picnic Area
A group picnic area that takes reservations.
[FEE AREA] **Road Desc:** Gravel **Directions:** NW on FR-374 0.4 mi

MM: 78.4 **Dist:** 0.3 **GPS:** 44.30130/-106.94722 **Elev:** 7411 **Grid:** 59/17 **Land:** NF
Middle Fork Campground   **Type:** Campground
Along the **Middle Fork Clear Creek** at the mouth of a small valley. The first 2 sites are separated by the creek, are close together, have no shade, and 1 is a pull-thru. The first site across the bridge sits by itself with good privacy. The remaining sites are along a short road with a turnaround at the end. *Conifer forest. Roomy sites. Level. Lantern poles.*
Crowds: *** **[FEE AREA]** **Notes:** Fishing parking is located just outside the campground. **Road Desc:** Gravel
Directions: SW on FR-373 1/4 mi
Campsites: 10 **Shade:** **** **Privacy:** * **RV Size:** 30' **Other:** 1-877-444-6777:www.recreation.gov,Water

MM: 80.0
Mile Marker Discrepancy (southbound)   **Type:** MM Discrepancy
Between mile marker 80 and mile marker 70 there are only 8 mile markers. This means that the mileages will jump 1 mile at MM 77 and at MM 73. The mile markers noted in the book will be referenced as best as possible traveling northbound. The attractions between MM 80 and MM 72 are clearly marked with highway signs, so keep in mind that the mile markers may be off.
Notes: I believe that the missing mile marker is MM 77 but am sure the other is MM 73.

MM: 82.0 **GPS:** 44.32214/-106.88980 **Elev:** 7070 **Grid:** 59/17 **Land:** NF
National Forest Informational Signs   **Type:** Visitor Information
A loop pullout with 3 large signs: *Climb into Bighorn Country, Along the Cloud Peak Skyway, The Adventure that Lies Ahead.*
Directions: N side of hwy

MM: 82.2 *GPS:* 44.32200/-106.88699 *Elev:* 7000 *Grid:* 60/17 *Land:* NF
Cloud Peak Skyway (westbound)   *Type:* Scenic Byway
A 45 mi scenic byway that travels through the southern section of the **Bighorn National Forest**. This is the least grade across the **Bighorn Mountains** and provides the only view of **Cloud Peak**, the highest peak in the **Bighorn Mountains**. The high elevation point of the drive is **Powder River Pass** at 9,663 ft.
Cool Rating: *** *Crowds:* ***
Directions: The route begins 10 mi west of **Buffalo** and ends 10 mi east of **Ten Sleep**.

MM: 85.9 *Dist:* 0.2 *GPS:* 44.33054/-106.81401 *Elev:* 5654 *Grid:* 61/17 *Land:* BLM
Mosier Gulch Recreation Area   *Type:* Recreation Area
A recreation area near **Clear Creek** at the foothills of the **Big Horn Mountains**. Includes a picnic area with 1 very nice shady site and 3 other sites that are not nearly as shady or nice. *Vault toilet.*
Crowds: * *Notes:* If heading east the turn into the picnic area is very sharp. *Road Desc:* Gravel, bumpy
Directions: SE 0.2 mi

MM: 92.1 *GPS:* 44.34824/-106.69923 *Elev:* 4645 *Grid:* 62/16
Buffalo   *Type:* Town

MM: 92.1 *Dist:* 1.0 *GPS:* 44.35420/-106.68687 *Elev:* 4582 *Grid:* 62/16
I-25 *(see chapter)*   *Type:* Hwy Junction w/Chapter
300 mi interstate highway through east/central **Wyoming** from **I-90** south to **Colorado**. Highlights include: **Outlaw Cave, Indian Rock Art Cave, Hole-in-the-Wall, National Historic Trails Interpretive Center, Ayres Park and Natural Bridge, Pioneer Museum**.
Directions: N/L on N Main St 0.4 mi; E/R on E Hart St 0.6 mi; I-25 heads N to I-90 or S to Casper from MM 299.3

MM: 92.1 *Dist:* 2.5 *GPS:* 44.35838/-106.65782 *Elev:* 4523 *Grid:* 63/16
I-90 *(see chapter)*   *Type:* Hwy Junction w/Chapter
208.8 mi interstate highway that heads west from **South Dakota** across northeastern **Wyoming** then northwest to **Montana**. Highlights include: **Vore Buffalo Jump, Devils Tower National Monument, Eagle Butte Coal Mine, Dry Creek Petrified Tree Environmental Education Area, Fort Phil Kearny** and related historic sites.
Directions: N/L on N Main St 0.4 mi; E/R on E Hart St 2.5 mi; I-90 heads NW to Sheridan or E to Gillette from MM 58.6.

MM: 92.1 *GPS:* 44.34824/-106.69923 *Elev:* 4645 *Grid:* 62/16
End of Highway   *Type:* Highway End
89.9 mi highway from **Buffalo** southwest to **Worland**. Along this highway is the scenic 45 mi **Cloud Peak Skyway**, which travels through the **Bighorn Mountains** and provides many campgrounds, forest roads with dispersed camping, and recreational opportunities. Highlights include: **Crazy Woman Canyon, High Park Lookout, Tensleep Canyon, West Tensleep Falls, Ten Sleep Fish Hatchery, Wigwam Rearing Station, Medicine Lodge State Archaeological Site, Castle Gardens**.
Directions: W to Ten Sleep from MM 92.1

US-189   S/N

MM: 0.0 *GPS:* 41.30806/-110.73101 *Elev:* 6922 *Grid:* 5/92
US-189   *Type:* Highway Description
131.5 mi highway from **I-80** exit 18 north to the junctions with **US-189/191**, which heads northwest toward **Jackson**, and **US-191**, which heads east to **Pinedale**. Highlights include: **Names Hill, Father DeSmet Monument**.
Nearest Town: Evanston 13 W *Directions:* I-80 exit 18; N to Kemmerer from MM 0

MM: 0.0 *GPS:* 41.30806/-110.73101 *Elev:* 6922 *Grid:* 5/92
I-80 *(see chapter)*   *Type:* Hwy Junction w/Chapter
403 mi interstate highway through southern **Wyoming** from **Utah** east to **Nebraska**. Highlights include: **Bear River State Park, Fort Bridger State Historic Site, Wyoming Frontier Prison, Fort Fred Steele, Wyoming Territorial Prison State Historic Site, Pole Mountain Trails, Curt Gowdy State Park, Vedauwoo Recreation Area**, and much more.
Directions: W to Evanston or E to Rock Springs from MM 18.3

MM: 34.5 *GPS:* 41.77124/-110.55310 *Elev:* 7071 *Grid:* 7/81
US-30 *(see chapter)*   *Type:* Hwy Junction w/Chapter
100 mi highway from **Idaho** southeast to **I-80** exit 66. Highlights include: **Fossil Butte National Monument**.
Directions: NW to Cokeville or SE to I-80 from MM 54.6

MM: 36.9 *GPS:* 41.79308/-110.53719 *Elev:* 6944 *Grid:* 7/80
Kemmerer   *Type:* Town

MM: 38.1 *Dist:* 0.5 *GPS:* 41.81568/-110.53433 *Elev:* 6937 *Grid:* 7/80 *Land:* City
Kemmerer Tent Park   *Type:* Campground
A small tent-only campground in a loop right off the highway. Not even small self-contained units are allowed. *Cottonwoods. Vault toilet. Water and restrooms are available at City Hall (south of the campground) during business hours (8am - 5pm).*
Crowds: ** *[FEE AREA] Directions:* NW 0.5 mi on Wy-233; E/R into south end of campground.
Campsites: 5 *Shade:* **** *Privacy:* * *RV Size:* Tent *Other:* None

MM: 61.3 *GPS:* 41.96807/-110.21309 *Elev:* 6895 *Grid:* 12/76
Wy-372 *(see chapter)*   *Type:* Hwy Junction w/Chapter
48.6 mi highway from **US-189** MM 61.3 southeast to **I-80** exit 83. This is primarily a connecting road to **Wy-28** and **I-80** eastbound. 3 BLM campgrounds are located near **Fontenelle Reservoir** 8.2 mi east. Highlights include: **Seedskadee National Wildlife Refuge, Lombard/Mormon Ferry**.
Nearest Town: Kemmerer 24 SW *Directions:* SE to I-80 from MM 48.6

MM: 61.3 *Dist:* 9.0 *GPS:* 41.98115/-110.04703 *Elev:* 6380 *Grid:* 14/75 *Land:* BLM
Slate Creek Campground   *Type:* Campground
A large dispersed camping area on the inside of a bend on the west side of the **Green River**. A handful of designated sites provide tables, fire rings, and grills; however, the area is huge with plenty of dispersed camping outside of the established sites. The campground is popular for ATVs. *Scattered cottonwoods. Native grass understory. Stone fire rings. Primitive float ramp. The campground is big enough to provide some distance between sites. Approximately 30 sites.*
Crowds: *** *Notes:* ATVs may be running around the campground at all hours of the day and evening. *Road Desc:* Gravel
Directions: E on Wy-372 8.2 mi; Continue NE on Fontenelle Townsite Rd/CR-311 0.8 mi.
Campsites: Dispersed *Shade:* ** *Privacy:* ** *RV Size:* 40'+ *Other:* None

MM: 61.3 *Dist:* 13.5 *GPS:* 42.02476/-110.06113 *Elev:* 6404 *Grid:* 14/74 *Land:* BLM
Tailrace Campground   *Type:* Campground
A small campground along the **Green River** just below the spillway from **Fontenelle Dam**. A couple of sites have tables, fire rings, and grills. *Cottonwoods. Stone fire rings. Primitive float ramp. Approximately 10 sites.*
Crowds: * *Road Desc:* Gravel
Directions: E on Wy-372 8.2 mi; Continue NE on Fontenelle Townsite Rd/CR-311 0.9 mi (past Slate Creek Campground); Just across the river bridge N/L on County Line Rd/CR-52; Follow signs 4.4 mi to campground.
Campsites: Dispersed *Shade:* *** *Privacy:* ** *RV Size:* 40' *Other:* None

MM: 66.5 *Dist:* 5.7 *GPS:* 42.02070/-110.04963 *Elev:* 6400 *Grid:* 14/74 *Land:* BLM
Weeping Rock Campground   *Type:* Campground
Below **Fontenelle Dam** southwest of a bend in the **Green River**. A handful of designated sites provide tables, fire rings, and grills. *Scattered cottonwoods. Native grass understory. Stone fire rings. Primitive float ramp. Approximately 20 sites.*
Crowds: ** *Road Desc:* Gravel
Directions: E on Fontenelle Dam Rd/CR-313 4.0 mi; S/R on Fontenelle North Rd/CR-316 0.3 mi; E/L 1.4 mi.
Campsites: Dispersed *Shade:* ** *Privacy:* ** *RV Size:* 40'+ *Other:* None

MM: 70.0 *Dist:* 0.9 *GPS:* 42.07328/-110.15252 *Elev:* 6525 *Grid:* 13/73 *Land:* BLM
Fontenelle Creek Campground   *Type:* Campground/Picnic Area
A large campground near the east shore of **Fontenelle Reservoir**. *2 paved loops. No trees. Sheltered tables. No fire rings. Flush toilets and running water. Picnic area. Boat ramp.*
Crowds: * *[FEE AREA] Directions:* E 0.5 mi; Right 0.4 mi.
Campsites: 55 *Shade:* * *Privacy:* * *RV Size:* 40'+ *Other:* Water,RVDump

MM: 79.2 *GPS:* 42.17668/-110.18725 *Elev:* 6543 *Grid:* 12/71
Names Hill   *Type:* Historic Site
A popular emigrant campsite near the crossing of the **Green River** on the **Sublette Cutoff** trail. This is 1 of 3 locations along the **Oregon-Mormon-California Trails** where pioneers carved their names into rock (the others being **Register Cliff** and **Independence Rock**). The most famous inscription is that of legendary mountain man **Jim Bridger** from 1844. The carving is fenced in along with a sign paying tribute to the man. A ferry was operated near here.
Cool Rating: *** *Crowds:* * *Time:* 15 min *Directions:* Large pullout on W side of hwy
Notes: I have read that an inscription from 1827 and Indian petroglyphs are located here; however, with all of the modern day graffiti I could not find them.

MM: 109.4 *Dist:* 12.8 *GPS:* 42.60560/-109.85672 *Elev:* 6860 *Grid:* 17/60 *Land:* BLM
New Fork River Campground   *Type:* Campground
On **Wy-351** MM 12.8. A large gravel parking area on the west bank of the **New Fork River**. *A few trees that provide little shade. Tables. Vault toilet. Boat launch.*
Crowds: *** *Nearest Town:* Marbleton 15.2 SW *Directions:* E on Wy-351 12.8 mi; N side of hwy just before bridge.
Campsites: 5 *Shade:* * *Privacy:* * *RV Size:* 40' *Other:* None

MM: 127.8 *Dist:* 2.3 *GPS:* 42.86746/-110.04314 *Elev:* 7289 *Grid:* 14/53
Father DeSmet's Prairie Mass Monument   *Type:* Historic Site
A shrine dedicated on July 5, 1925 in memory of **Father Pierre Jeane DeSmet** who performed **Wyoming's** first mass on July 5, 1840. The monument is a replica of an altar with a cross enclosed in a cobblestone structure with an A-frame roof (which resembles a small chapel). The structure faces northwest from a bluff overlooking the **Green River Rendezvous Site**, which is located in the **Upper Green River Valley** at the confluence of **Horse Creek** and the **Green River**. Trappers, traders, and Indians met trade wagons from the east at this site in the 1820s and 1830s *(see next section)*.

On the north side of the junction with **CR-188** is a pullout with a historical sign explaining **"The Prairie of the Mass."**
Cool Rating: ** *Crowds:* * *Time:* 30 min *Road Desc:* Gravel
Directions: NE on CR-188/DeSmet Rd 2.3 mi; NW/L side of road.

MM: 129.8 *GPS:* 42.86640/-110.07137 *Elev:* 7195 *Grid:* 14/53
Green River Rendezvous Historical Marker   *Type:* Historical Marker
A historical marker that explains the **Green River Rendezvous**, which took place near this point from 1824 to 1840 at the confluence of **Horse Creek** and the **Green River**. On the north end of the parking area is a large rock with a plaque commemorating 2 women missionaries who were the first white women in **Wyoming** and the first women over the **Oregon Trail** in 1836.
Cool Rating: * *Crowds:* * *Time:* 10 min *Directions:* E side of hwy

MM: 131.5 *GPS:* 42.89041/-110.06952 *Elev:* 7233 *Grid:* 14/53
US-189/191 *(see chapter)*   *Type:* Hwy Junction w/Chapter
53.1 mi highway northwest to **Hoback Jct** from the transition with **US-191** and junction with **US-189**. The mile markers continue sequentially from **US-191**. Highlights include: **Hoback Canyon**, **Granite Falls**, **Granite Hot Springs**, **Stinking Springs**.
Nearest Town: Daniel 1.9 S; Pinedale 10.9 E *Directions:* NW to Hoback Jct from MM 110.5

MM: 131.5 *GPS:* 42.89041/-110.06952 *Elev:* 7233 *Grid:* 14/53
US-191 *(see chapter)*   *Type:* Hwy Junction w/Chapter
109.2 mi highway that transitions from **US-189/191**, using sequential mile markers, and continues southeast to **I-80** exit 104 in **Rock Springs**. Highlights include: **Green River Lakes**, **Fremont Lake**, **Killpecker Sand Dunes**, **Boar's Tusk**, **White Mountain Petroglyphs**, **Pilot Butte Wild Horse Tour**, **Reliance Tipple**.
Nearest Town: Daniel 1.9 S, Pinedale 10.9 E *Directions:* E to Pinedale then S to Rock Springs from MM 110.5

MM: 131.5 *GPS:* 42.89041/-110.06952 *Elev:* 7233 *Grid:* 14/53
End of Highway   *Type:* Highway End
131.5 mi highway from the transition of **US-189/191** to **US-191**, south to **I-80** exit 18. Highlights include: **Father DeSmet Monument**, **Names Hill**.
Nearest Town: Daniel 1.9 S; Pinedale 10.9 E *Directions:* S to Daniel from MM 131.5

MM: 110.5 *GPS:* 42.89041/-110.06952 *Elev:* 7233 *Grid:* 14/53
US-189/191 *Type:* Highway Description
53.1 mi highway northwest to **Hoback Jct** from the transition with **US-191** and junction with **US-189**. The entire length is along the **Centennial Scenic Byway**. The mile markers continue sequentially from **US-191**. Highlights include: **Hoback Canyon, Granite Falls, Granite Hot Springs, Stinking Springs**.
Nearest Town: Daniel 1.9 S; Pinedale 10.9 E *Directions:* NW to Hoback Jct from MM 110.5

MM: 110.5 *GPS:* 42.89041/-110.06952 *Elev:* 7233 *Grid:* 14/53
US-191 *(see chapter)* *Type:* Hwy Transition w/Chapter
109.2 mi highway that transitions from **US-189/191**, using sequential mile markers, and continues southeast to **I-80** exit 104 in **Rock Springs**. Highlights include: **Green River Lakes, Fremont Lake, Killpecker Sand Dunes, Boar's Tusk, White Mountain Petroglyphs, Pilot Butte Wild Horse Tour, Reliance Tipple**.
Nearest Town: Daniel 1.9 S, Pinedale 10.9 E *Directions:* E to Pinedale then S to Rock Springs from MM 110.5

MM: 110.5 *GPS:* 42.89041/-110.06952 *Elev:* 7233 *Grid:* 14/53
US-189 *(see chapter)* *Type:* Hwy Junction w/Chapter
131.5 mi highway from the transition of **US-189/191** to **US-191**, south to **I-80** exit 18. Highlights include: **Father DeSmet Monument, Names Hill**.
Nearest Town: Daniel 1.9 S; Pinedale 10.9 E *Directions:* S to Daniel from MM 131.5

MM: 114.1 *Dist:* 2.4 *GPS:* 42.92827/-110.12604 *Elev:* 7355 *Grid:* 13/52 *Land:* State
Daniel Fish Hatchery *Type:* Fish Hatchery
A fish hatchery that was completed in 1923 and expanded in 1966 and 1999. This facility is used for incubation and rearing of various species of trout, splake, grayling, and kokanee salmon. Offspring from these broods are used for restoration efforts as well as for stocking throughout the state. Due to the cold water the growth of fish can be slowed, which provides small fish for helicopter, horse packing, backpacking, and ATV stocking.
Hours: 8am - 5pm *Cool Rating:* ** *Crowds:* * *Time:* 30 min *Road Desc:* Gravel *Directions:* W on CR-150/Pape Rd 2.4 mi

MM: 114.1 *Dist:* 3.5 *GPS:* 42.94410/-110.13158 *Elev:* 7357 *Grid:* 13/51 *Land:* State
Daniel Public Access Area *Type:* Public Access Area
Primitive camping in a gravel fishing access parking area along the **Green River**. *No trees. Some stone fire rings. Vault toilet.*
Crowds: ** *Road Desc:* Gravel *Directions:* W on CR-150/Pape Rd 3.5 mi; W side of road.
Campsites: Dispersed *Shade:* * *Privacy:* * *RV Size:* 40' *Other:* None

MM: 117.5 *GPS:* 42.98718/-110.09265 *Elev:* 7465 *Grid:* 14/50
CR-149/40 Rod Rd to Wy-352 *Type:* Highway Junction
Cutoff road to **Wy-352/FR-10091** and **Green River Lakes**. If traveling south this saves 15.0 mi. *See Wy-352/FR-10091.*
Directions: E 4.9 mi

MM: 120.1 *GPS:* 43.01816/-110.11814 *Elev:* 7472 *Grid:* 13/50 *Land:* BLM
Warren Bridge Campground *Type:* Campground/Day Use Area
An open sagebrush campground just off the highway on the south bank of the **Green River**. The first loop is a day use area with 9 sites with tables and grills. *Single loop. No trees. Level. All pull-thrus. RV dump is free with camping fee, or a small fee otherwise.*
Crowds: * *Nearest Town:* Pinedale 20.3 SE *[FEE AREA] Directions:* SW side of hwy
Campsites: 16 *Shade:* * *Privacy:* * *RV Size:* 40'+ *Other:* Water,RVDump

MM: 120.3 *Dist:* 8.4 *GPS:* 43.02857/-110.10613 *Elev:* 7614 *Grid:* 14/49 *Land:* BLM
Warren Bridge Public Fishing Area *Type:* Public Access Area
At least 27 river access and camping areas along an 8.4 mi road that follows the **Green River**. The land is jointly administered by the **BLM** and **Wyoming Game and Fish**. Side roads lead to 13 well-established parking areas with vault toilets, tables, and fire rings at MM 1.0, 1.5, 3.5, 4.9, 5.0, 5.6, 6.0, 6.4, 8.2, and 8.4. Additional primitive sites are located on these same roads as well as other side roads. Many of the side roads descend steeply to the river. *Few trees.*
Crowds: ** *Nearest Town:* Pinedale 20.5 SE *Road Desc:* Gravel. Side roads are dirt and rock.
Notes: No trailers allowed because of steep narrow access roads that descend up to 170 ft to the river.
Directions: NE on BLM-5201 8.4 mi to the end of road and last parking area.
Campsites: Dispersed *Shade:* * *Privacy:* * *RV Size:* 30' *Other:* None

MM: 128.0 *GPS:* 43.11945/-110.17964 *Elev:* 7846 *Grid:* 13/47
Astorian Campsite Historical Marker *Type:* Historical Marker
In 1811 the first white men came through this area. At this location 61 **Astorians** camped for 5 days while they traded and pow-wowed with the Snake Indians, killed buffalo, and cured meat.
Cool Rating: * *Crowds:* * *Time:* 5 min *Directions:* NE side of hwy

MM: 147.5 *GPS:* 43.24565/-110.47651 *Elev:* 6425 *Grid:* 8/44
Hoback Canyon (heading northwest) *Type:* Canyon
The **Hoback River** flows through this 10 mi scenic canyon that varies from forested hills to steep rocky cliffs. At this point a pullout with a historical marker provides information about the history of navigation through the canyon.

MM: 150.7 *GPS:* 43.27017/-110.51703 *Elev:* 6340 *Grid:* 8/43 *Land:* NF
Kozy Campground *Type:* Campground
Located between the highway and the **Hoback River** in **Hoback Canyon** with scenic views. Tends to be an overnight stop that fills toward evening. *Scattered conifers. Good spacing between sites. Highway noise. Paved road and parking areas. Level. 1 pull-thru.*
Crowds: ***** *[FEE AREA] Directions:* N side of hwy
Campsites: 8 *Shade:* * *Privacy:* ** *RV Size:* 30' *Other:* Water

MM: 152.1   *Dist:* 8.6   *GPS:* 43.35963/-110.44669   *Elev:* 6850   *Grid:* 9/41   *Land:* NF
Granite Creek Campground   *Type:* Campground
A scenic campground along **Granite Creek** with some sites that overlook the creek and others with good views of the mountains. Close to **Granite Falls** and **Granite Hot Springs** *(see next sections). 3 loops. Conifer forest. Little understory. Roomy sites. Flush and vault toilets. 6 pull-thrus. Amphitheater with weekend programs.*
Crowds: *****   *[FEE AREA]*   *Road Desc:* Gravel, rough & washboard   *Directions:* NE on Granite Rd/FR-30500 8.6 mi
Campsites: 51   *Shade:* *****   *Privacy:* ***   *RV Size:* 30'   *Other:* Water

MM: 152.1   *Dist:* 8.9   *GPS:* 43.36419/-110.44539   *GPS2:* 43.36765/-110.43328   *Elev:* 9150   *Grid:* 9/41   *Land:* NF
The Open Door   *Type:* Natural Feature
Located on the mountain peak to the east ~2,100 ft above **Granite Falls** is a "shield" shaped void in the rock face known as **The Open Door**.
Cool Rating: **   *Crowds:* *   *Road Desc:* Gravel, rough & washboard   *Directions:* NE on Granite Rd/FR-30500 8.9 mi

MM: 152.1   *Dist:* 8.9   *GPS:* 43.36419/-110.44539   *GPS2:* 43.36542/-110.44363   *Elev:* 6900   *Grid:* 9/41   *Land:* NF
Granite Falls   *Type:* Waterfall
A 20 ft high and 70 ft wide waterfall on **Granite Creek**. Short trails lead from the parking area to the base and the top of the falls.
Cool Rating: ****   *Crowds:* ***   *Time:* 30 min   *Road Desc:* Gravel, rough & washboard
Notes: The falls are popular, so it is difficult to get a picture without people in it.
Directions: NE on Granite Rd/FR-30500 8.9 mi

MM: 152.1   *Dist:* 9.2   *GPS:* 43.36771/-110.44604   *GPS2:* 43.36975/-110.44560   *Elev:* 7005   *Grid:* 9/41   *Land:* NF
Granite Hot Springs   *Type:* Hot Springs
A hot springs pool built by the **Civilian Conservation Corps** (CCC) in 1933. The concrete pool is ~50 ft in diameter, 6-7 ft deep, and surrounded by a deck. The water temperature ranges from 93° F in the summer to 112° F in the winter.
Cool Rating: ***   *Crowds:* *****   *[FEE AREA]*
Directions: NE on Granite Rd/FR-30500 9.2 mi to parking area; 200 yd path leads to pool.

MM: 155.5   *GPS:* 43.28166/-110.59355   *Elev:* 6190   *Grid:* 7/43   *Land:* NF
Hoback Campground and Picnic Area   *Type:* Campground/Picnic Area
Located between the highway and the **Hoback River** in **Hoback Canyon**. The campsites are spread out along the road and around an end loop. Some sites have river access and 1 site overlooks the river. *Light conifer forest that only shades a few sites. Good spacing between sites. Light highway noise. Paved road and parking areas. Level. 1 pull-thru.*

A minimal picnic area is located at the campground entrance.
Crowds: *****   *[FEE AREA]*   *Directions:* S side of hwy
Campsites: 14   *Shade:* **   *Privacy:* ***   *RV Size:* 40'   *Other:* Water BEARS

MM: 157.8   *GPS:* 43.28881/-110.63417   *Elev:* 6127   *Grid:* 6/43   *Land:* NF
Stinking Springs   *Type:* Thermal Area
At the west end of **Hoback Canyon** is a hot spring that discharges milky-blue, sulfur-smelling water into the **Hoback River**. The water enters the river just above the water line from a steep rocky bank on the opposite side. The water forms a long bluish strip along the edge of the river that contrasts with the normal water color. To view the spring, take the trail down to the river and walk east along the bank a short distance. No road signs mark this location or explain this thermal feature.
Cool Rating: **   *Crowds:* *   *Time:* 15 min   *Directions:* Gravel pullout on N side of hwy

MM: 158.0   *GPS:* 43.28853/-110.63762   *Elev:* 6110   *Grid:* 6/43
Hoback Canyon (heading southeast)   *Type:* Canyon
The **Hoback River** flows through this 10 mi scenic canyon that varies from forested hills to steep rocky cliffs.

MM: 163.6   *GPS:* 43.32292/-110.73040   *Elev:* 5940   *Grid:* 5/42
Hoback Jct   *Type:* Town

MM: 163.6   *GPS:* 43.32292/-110.73040   *Elev:* 5940   *Grid:* 5/42
US-26/89/191 *(see chapter)*   *Type:* Hwy Junction w/Chapter
43.3 mi highway from **Hoback Jct** north to **Moran Jct**. The highway then connects to **US-89/191/287**, using sequential mile markers, and continues 27 mi to **Yellowstone National Park**. The entire length is along the **Centennial Scenic Byway**. Highlights include: **Jackson, Jackson Hole and Greater Yellowstone Visitor Center, Grand Teton National Park**.
Notes: The highway section between Hoback Jct and Jackson might be referred to as US-26/89/189/191.
Directions: N to Jackson from MM 141.3

MM: 163.6   *Dist:* 1.0   *GPS:* 43.32292/-110.73040   *Elev:* 5940   *Grid:* 5/42
US-26/89 *(see chapter)*   *Type:* Hwy Junction w/Chapter
23 mi highway from **Hoback Jct** southwest to **Alpine Jct** through the **Snake River Canyon**. The mile markers continue sequentially from **US-26/89/191** at **Hoback Jct**. No highlights along this route, but there are 4 National Forest campgrounds.
Nearest Town: Jackson 13.2 N   *Notes:* Camping in designated campgrounds only.   *Directions:* SW to Alpine from MM 141.3

MM: 163.6   *GPS:* 43.32292/-110.73040   *Elev:* 5940   *Grid:* 5/42
End of Highway   *Type:* Highway End
53.1 mi highway southeast from **Hoback Jct** to the transition with **US-191** and junction with **US-189**. The entire length is along the **Centennial Scenic Byway**. The mile markers continue sequentially to **US-191**. Highlights include: **Hoback Canyon, Stinking Springs, Granite Falls, Granite Hot Springs**.
Nearest Town: Jackson 13.2 N   *Directions:* SE to Pinedale from MM 163.6

US-191 S/N

MM: 1.3 **GPS:** 41.60777/-109.22931 **Elev:** 6304 **Grid:** 26/85
US-191 **Type:** Highway Description
109.2 mi highway from **I-80** exit 104 in **Rock Springs** northwest past **Pinedale** to a transition with **US-189/191**, which continues
53.2 mi to **Hoback Jct** (south of **Jackson**) using sequential mile markers. Highlights include: **Reliance Tipple**, **White Mountain Petroglyphs**, **Boar's Tusk**, **Killpecker Sand Dunes**, **Pilot Butte Wild Horse Tour**, **Fremont Lake**, **Green River Lakes**.
Notes: US-191 actually starts at MM 0 at the transition of N Center St and Bridger Ave (1.3 mi south of I-80 exit 104).
Directions: N to Farson from MM 1.3

MM: 1.3 **GPS:** 41.60777/-109.22931 **Elev:** 6304 **Grid:** 26/85
I-80 (see chapter) **Type:** Hwy Junction w/Chapter
403 mi interstate highway through southern **Wyoming** from **Utah** east to **Nebraska**. Highlights include: **Bear River State Park**,
Fort Bridger State Historic Site, **Wyoming Frontier Prison**, **Fort Fred Steele**, **Wyoming Territorial Prison State Historic Site**, **Pole Mountain Trails**, **Curt Gowdy State Park**, **Vedauwoo Recreation Area**, and much more.
Directions: W to Rock Springs or E to Rawlins from MM 104.8

MM: 1.3 **GPS:** 41.60772/-109.22943 **Elev:** 6304 **Grid:** 26/85
Rock Springs **Type:** Town

MM: 2.4 **Dist:** 0.9 **GPS:** 41.63030/-109.21898 **Elev:** 6384 **Grid:** 26/84
Wild Horse Corrals **Type:** Wildlife Area
Corrals used to hold and process **Wild Horses** gathered from around the area. These horses are held for adoption through the
1972 **Wild Horse and Burrow Act**. See chapter: Pilot Butte Wild Horse Tour.
Cool Rating: ** **Crowds:** * **Time:** 20 min **Directions:** NE on Lionkol Rd 0.9 mi

MM: 4.5 **Dist:** 2.0 **GPS:** 41.66835/-109.19682 **Elev:** 6515 **Grid:** 27/83 **Land:** City
Reliance Tipple **Type:** Historic Site
This tipple was used from 1936 - 1955 to sort and grade coal and load it into rail cars. The steel structure replaced a wooden tipple
built in 1912 and was one of the largest and most advanced of its kind. The only other coal tipple in the state is the **Aladdin Tipple**
in northeastern **Wyoming** (see Wy-24 MM 40.8). A short path with interpretive signs explain the history and operation of the tipple.
Cool Rating: *** **Crowds:** * **Time:** 30 min **Directions:** NE on Reliance Rd 1.75 mi; Slight right on South St 0.2 mi.

MM: 10.3 **GPS:** 41.72682/-109.27430 **Elev:** 6525 **Grid:** 25/82
Chilton Rd (northbound) (see chapter) **Type:** Hwy Junction w/Chapter
20.3 mi backcountry route that accesses the **White Mountain Petroglyphs**, **Boar's Tusk**, and the **Killpecker Sand Dunes**. If
traveling north on **US-191**, a turnoff to an unnamed road at MM 14.9 creates a 30.5 mi loop starting at **US-191** MM 10.3, passing
the **White Mountain Petroglyphs**, and returning to **US-191** MM 32.7. The northwest section of the loop provides good views of
the **Boar's Tusk** and **Killpecker Sand Dunes**. Continuing northeast on Chilton Rd leads 1.1 mi to the **Boar's Tusk** turnoff and 7.5
mi to the **Killpecker Sand Dunes Recreation Site** parking area.
Directions: E on CR-4-17/Chilton Rd 1.2 mi; N/L keeping left at the fork at 3.8 mi.

MM: 13.1 **GPS:** 41.74369/-109.32207 **Elev:** 6842 **Grid:** 25/81
Pilot Butte Wild Horse Tour (see chapter) **Type:** Hwy Junction w/Chapter
A 25.8 mi driving tour from **US-191** (11.8 mi north of I-80 at Rock Springs) to **Green River** along the rim of **White Mountain** where
wild horses can be seen. 6 interpretive pullouts provide nice views from **White Mountain** and a side road provides access to **Pilot
Butte**, which can be climbed.
Notes: Watch for wild horses along US-191 to and from Rock Springs. **Directions:** SW on CR-14/Blue Rim Rd from MM 25.8

MM: 32.7 **GPS:** 42.00015/-109.41706 **Elev:** 6605 **Grid:** 23/75
Chilton Rd (southbound) (see chapter) **Type:** Hwy Junction w/Chapter
A backcountry route that accesses the **White Mountain Petroglyphs**, **Boar's Tusk**, and the **Killpecker Sand Dunes**. If traveling
south on **US-191**, a 30.5 mi loop starts at MM 32.7, passes the **White Mountain Petroglyphs**, and returns to **US-191** MM 10.3. A
round-trip to the **Boar's Tusk** turnoff and **Killpecker Sand Dunes Recreation Site** adds an additional 2-15 mi; however, the main
loop already provides excellent views of the **Killpecker Sand Dunes** at MI 9.6 and **Boar's Tusk** at MI 11.6.
Directions: E then S on Old Hwy 191 2.1 mi; E 13.5 mi to CR-4-17/Chilton Rd MM 14.9.

MM: 33.8 **GPS:** 42.01437/-109.42519 **Elev:** 6574 **Grid:** 23/75
Roadside Table **Type:** Picnic Area
A long pullout with a single picnic table under a scraggly cottonwood on the north side. A much nicer option is **Bicentennial Park**,
2.8 mi north (see next section).
Directions: SW side of hwy

MM: 36.6 **GPS:** 42.05384/-109.43804 **Elev:** 6614 **Grid:** 23/74 **Land:** City
Bicentennial Park **Type:** Park
A beautiful shady park in **Eden** with 14 picnic tables, grills, a playground, and portable toilets.
Crowds: * **Directions:** E side of hwy

MM: 40.5 **GPS:** 42.10859/-109.44899 **Elev:** 6595 **Grid:** 23/72
Farson **Type:** Town

MM: 40.5 **GPS:** 42.10859/-109.44899 **Elev:** 6595 **Grid:** 23/72
Wy-28 (Farson to US-287) (see chapter) **Type:** Hwy Junction w/Chapter
66.3 mi highway from **Farson** northeast to **US-287/Wy-789**, 8.4 mi southeast of **Lander**. Highlights include: **South Pass** and
related historic markers, **Carissa Mine**, **South Pass City State Historic Site**, **Miner's Delight**, **Atlantic City**, **Red Canyon**.
Directions: NE to Lander from MM 0

MM: 40.5   *GPS:* 42.10859/-109.44899   *Elev:* 6595   *Grid:* 23/72
Wy-28 (Wy-372 to Farson) *(see chapter)*   *Type:* Hwy Junction w/Chapter
28.3 mi highway from **Farson** southwest to **Wy-372**. This is a continuation of **Wy-28** from the northeast; however, the mile markers change from 0.0 to 128.3 at the intersection with **US-191**. Highlights include: **Simpson's Hollow**, **Pilot Butte Emigrant Trails Interpretive Site**, **Lombard/Mormon Ferry**.
Directions: SW to Wy-372 from MM 128.3

MM: 40.5   *Dist:* 0.2   *GPS:* 42.10797/-109.45322   *Elev:* 6586   *Grid:* 23/72
Little Sandy Crossing   *Type:* Historical Marker
A fording and camping location on the **Big Sandy River** for emigrants taking the southern route of the **Oregon Trail** toward **Fort Bridger**. A monument recounts a conversation from 1847 between **Jim Bridger** and **Brigham Young** about the route and the ability to sustain a large population in the **Great Salt Lake Valley**.
Cool Rating: *   *Crowds:* *   *Time:* 5 min   *Directions:* W on Wy-28 0.2 mi; N side of hwy.

MM: 40.5   *GPS:* 42.10893/-109.44937   *Elev:* 6595   *Grid:* 23/72
Big Sandy Pony Express Station   *Type:* Historical Marker
The **Big Sandy Pony Express Station** stood a short distance south of this pullout. The station was burned by Indians in 1862. The pullout includes a steel silhouette of a **Pony Express** rider and 3 stone markers:
    1) **Big Sandy Station** marker giving the exact dates and location of the original station
    2) Marker dedicated to the **Pony Express** riders
    3) Marker titled "East meets West"
Cool Rating: *   *Crowds:* *   *Time:* 5 min   *Directions:* NW corner of US-191 and Wy-28

MM: 48.6   *GPS:* 42.22138/-109.46928   *Elev:* 6712   *Grid:* 23/69
Monument to the Pioneers   *Type:* Historical Marker
A stone monument that reads: "To all pioneers who passed this way to win and hold the west. Route of the Sublette Cutoff from Big Sandy to Bear River traversed after 1834 by emigrants to **Oregon** and **California**."
Cool Rating: *   *Crowds:* *   *Time:* 5 min   *Directions:* W side of hwy in a long pullout

MM: 49.6   *Dist:* 1.2   *GPS:* 42.24213/-109.44220   *Elev:* 6800   *Grid:* 23/69   *Land:* Bureau of Reclamation
Big Sandy Recreation Area   *Type:* Recreation Area
4 camping areas along the shores of **Big Sandy Reservoir** plus 1 area below the dam.

West Shore - Loop road with 1 large site down a hill under trees plus 3 other sites with no shade. A boat ramp is located just north. *Tables. Fire rings with grates. Vault toilet.*
South Shore - 2 large pullout areas that accommodate the largest rigs. *1 fire ring with grate.*
Southeast Shore - Dispersed camping near the lakeshore. *No facilities.*
Below Dam - Sagebrush area with 2 sites. *Fire rings with grates (1 under a shelter). Vault toilet.*
East Shore - 4 well-established sites along the shore. Open range with cows wandering through camp. *Tables. Fire rings with grates. Vault toilet.*
Crowds: **   *Road Desc:* Gravel
Directions: E on Big Sandy Reservoir Rd 1.2 mi; **West shore** camping and boat ramp - N/L 1.3 mi; **South shore** - Straight 0.5 mi; **Southeast shore** - Straight and N across dam 1.2 mi and to the left; **Below dam** - Straight and N across dam 1.2 mi; E/R then S 0.3 mi; **Northeast shore** - Straight and N across dam 1.3 mi; Fork left 0.2 mi; Fork left 0.1 mi.
Campsites: 12   *Shade:* *   *Privacy:* *   *RV Size:* 40'+   *Other:* None

MM: 76.8   *Dist:* 11.3   *GPS:* 42.60560/-109.85672   *Elev:* 6860   *Grid:* 17/60   *Land:* BLM
New Fork River Campground   *Type:* Campground
On **Wy-351** MM 12.8. A large gravel parking area on the west bank of the **New Fork River**. *A few trees that provide little shade. Tables. Vault toilet. Boat launch.*
Crowds: ***   *Nearest Town:* Boulder 22.6 NE   *Directions:* W on Wy-351 11.3 mi; N side of hwy just past bridge.
Campsites: 5   *Shade:* *   *Privacy:* *   *RV Size:* 40'   *Other:* None

MM: 87.8   *GPS:* 42.74607/-109.72065   *Elev:* 7014   *Grid:* 19/56
Boulder   *Type:* Town

MM: 87.8   *Dist:* 9.1   *GPS:* 42.81914/-109.71593   *Elev:* 7195   *Grid:* 19/55   *Land:* BLM
Stokes Crossing Campground   *Type:* Campground
Stokes Crossing is a historic crossing site on **Boulder Creek** located 1.25 mi south of **Boulder Lake**. Only remnants of the historic crossing structure remain across the creek. The campground is located amid sagebrush hills with a stand of conifers for shade. *Large grassy parking area. 2 tables and fire rings. Grill. Vault toilet.*
Road Desc: Wy-353 is paved. Boulder Lake Rd is gravel. The last 1.9 mi is dirt and impassable when wet.
Directions: NE on Wy-353 2.4 mi to Boulder Lake sign; N/L on Boulder Lake Rd/CR-23-125 4.8 mi; NW/L 1.9 mi.
Campsites: 4   *Shade:* ***   *RV Size:* 20'   *Other:* None

MM: 87.8 *Dist:* 9.7 *GPS:* 42.83412/-109.68445 *Elev:* 7295 *Grid:* 20/54 *Land:* BLM
Boulder Lake   *Type:* Lake
A long terminal moraine dammed lake at the end of **Boulder Canyon**, a glacial valley formed by ice flowing out of the **Wind River Mountains**. The lake measures 4.3 mi long, 0.7 mi wide, and up to 250 ft deep. The surrounding terrain is primarily sagebrush and boulder covered hills. Fishing and hiking into the **Wind River Mountains** and **Bridger Wilderness** would be the primary activities here. Several treeless dispersed camping areas are located on the southwest end of the lake. Vault toilets are located in the parking areas at the boat ramp and near the dam.

Continuing 0.7, 1.0, and 1.1 mi north on **Boulder Lake Rd** past the **Boulder Dam Rd** are additional dispersed campsites that are reached by heading west and north on primitive roads to the lakeshore. The last area leads to 2 separate parking areas.
Cool Rating: * *Crowds:* * *Road Desc:* Wy-353 is paved and the rest is gravel.
Notes: Unless boating or looking for a free campsite, this lake doesn't have much to offer. I couldn't even find a picnic table for lunch.
Directions: NE on Wy-353 2.4 mi to Boulder Lake sign; N/L on Boulder Lake Rd/CR-23-125 5.9 mi; NW/L on Boulder Dam Rd 0.7 mi; N 0.7 mi to boat ramp parking area (42.8341/-109.684) OR continue straight 1.3 to parking area near the dam (42.8356/-109.704).
Campsites: Dispersed *Shade:* * *Privacy:* * *RV Size:* 30' *Other:* None

MM: 87.8 *Dist:* 12.6 *GPS:* 42.85572/-109.61945 *Elev:* 7310 *Grid:* 21/54 *Land:* NF
Boulder Lake Trailhead   *Type:* Trailhead
The lowest trailhead into the **Bridger Wilderness** and **Wind River Mountains** and as such requires a longer and less spectacular hike to reach the high country. However, this trail is popular with stock parties. The **Boulder Canyon Trail** traverses **Boulder Canyon** 9.5 mi, gaining 2,400 ft in elevation, to the **Highline Trail** at **Lake Vera**.
Crowds: * *Road Desc:* Wy-353 is paved and the rest is gravel.
Directions: NE on Wy-353 2.4 mi to Boulder Lake sign; N/L on Boulder Lake Rd/CR-23-125 10.2 mi.

MM: 87.8 *Dist:* 12.7 *GPS:* 42.85674/-109.61731 *Elev:* 7298 *Grid:* 21/54 *Land:* NF
Boulder Lake Campground   *Type:* Campground
Located at the base of the **Wind River Mountains** on the northeast end of **Boulder Lake** just across **Boulder Creek**. 0.1 mi southwest of the campground is trailhead parking, dispersed camping, and a primitive boat launch. *Single loop. Mixed forest. Grass understory and dense middlestory. Level. Several sites are overgrown. Trees do not provide shade to all sites.*
Crowds: * *Road Desc:* Wy-353 is paved and the rest is gravel. Campground loop road is rough and potholed.
Directions: NE on Wy-353 2.4 mi to Boulder Lake sign; N/L on Boulder Lake Rd/CR-23-125 10.3 mi.
Campsites: 21 *Shade:* **** *Privacy:* **** *RV Size:* 30' *Other:* None

MM: 87.8 *Dist:* 14.8 *GPS:* 42.82102/-109.55835 *Elev:* 8215 *Grid:* 21/54 *Land:* BLM
Scab Creek Trailhead   *Type:* Trailhead
Parking and horse facilities for the **Scab Creek Trail** into the **Bridger Wilderness** and **Wind River Mountains**. The trail heads northeast 11.3 mi to the **Fremont Trail** gaining 2,450 ft in elevation and passing **Little Divide Lake** (6.2 mi), **Lightning Lakes** (7.2 mi), and **Dream Lake** and the **Highline Trail** (10.5 mi). The hikes are long and best suited for horses.
Crowds: * *Road Desc:* Wy-353 is paved and the rest is gravel.
Directions: NE on Wy-353 6.5 mi; NE/L on CR-23-122/Scab Creek Rd 1.4 mi; Slight left at Scab Creek Access Rd/BLM-5423 6.9 mi.

MM: 87.8 *Dist:* 15.1 *GPS:* 42.82077/-109.55265 *Elev:* 8200 *Grid:* 21/54 *Land:* BLM
Scab Creek Campground   *Type:* Campground
Situated in the high foothills of the **Wind River Mountains** above **Boulder Lake**. The **Scab Creek Trailhead** is near the campground entrance *(see previous section)*. *Mature mixed forest. Single loop. Some pull-thrus. Quiet.*
Crowds: * *[FEE AREA] Road Desc:* Wy-353 is paved and the rest is gravel.
Directions: NE on Wy-353 6.5 mi; NE/L on CR-23-122/Scab Creek Rd 1.4 mi; Slight left at Scab Creek Access Rd/BLM-5423 7.2 mi.
Campsites: 9 *Shade:* ***** *Privacy:* **** *RV Size:* 30' *Other:* None

MM: 88.8 *Dist:* 8.0 *GPS:* 42.84173/-109.70181 *Elev:* 7300 *Grid:* 19/54 *Land:* BLM
Boulder Lake North Campground   *Type:* Campground
Located in a stand of trees amid sagebrush and boulders. *5 tables. Grill. Vault toilet. Primitive boat launch.*
Crowds: * *Road Desc:* Gravel
Directions: E then N on Burnt Lake Rd/BLM 5106 7.1 mi; Keep right on Boulder Lake Dam Rd 0.5 mi; NE/L 0.4 mi (keep right at the 2 forks).
Campsites: 5 *Shade:* * *Privacy:* * *RV Size:* 40' *Other:* None

MM: 99.3 *GPS:* 42.86643/-109.85618 *Elev:* 7181 *Grid:* 17/53
Fremont Lake Rd/Skyline Drive *(see chapter)*   *Type:* Hwy Junction w/Chapter
14.5 mi paved highway from **US-191** MM 99.3, at the east end of **Pinedale**, northeast through sagebrush flats and foothills, past **Fremont Lake**, then climbing over 1,900 ft to the base of the **Wind River Mountains**. The climb offers great views of **Fremont Lake** and the **Wind River Range**. Along the route are 3 National Forest campgrounds as well as several free primitive camping areas, in particular on the south end of **Fremont Lake**. At the end of the road, the **Elkhart Park Trailheads** provide trails into the **Wind River Mountains** and the **Bridger Wilderness**.
Directions: NE at the curve on the east side of Pinedale

MM: 99.6 *GPS:* 42.86643/-109.85618 *Elev:* 7181 *Grid:* 17/53
Pinedale   *Type:* Town

MM: 100.0   *Dist:* 6.9   *GPS:* 42.95894/-109.85784   *Elev:* 7580   *Grid:* 17/51   *Land:* Wyoming G & F
Soda Lake Wildlife Habitat Management Area   *Type:* Wildlife Habitat Mgmt Area
Primitive camping amid sagebrush covered hills with a good view of the **Wind River Mountains** to the northeast. 10 campsites are scattered around the perimeter of **Soda Lake**. An additional site and other dispersed camping is located east of the lake near a forest at the base of a 700 ft mountain that separates this area from **Fremont Lake**. *Vault toilets. Stone fire rings.*
Crowds: *   *Road Desc:* Gravel, rough   *Directions:* N on Willow Lake Rd/CR-119 6.8 mi;   E/R 0.1 mi.
Campsites: Dispersed   *Shade:* *   *Privacy:* *   *RV Size:* 40'+   *Other:* None

MM: 100.0   *Dist:* 10.7   *GPS:* 42.99107/-109.90027   *Elev:* 7718   *Grid:* 16/50   *Land:* NF
Willow Lake Campground   *Type:* Campground
Willow Lake is a long terminal moraine dammed lake at the end of a glacial valley formed by ice flowing out of the **Wind River Mountains**. The lake is situated amid sagebrush covered hills and measures 4.5 mi long, 0.8 mi wide, and up to 280 ft deep. The southwest end of the lake has a sandy beach and a small campground with 5 sites in a main loop and an additional site to the west. *A few trees along the shoreline that don't provide much shade. Tables. Fire rings with grates. Primitive boat ramp.*
Crowds: *   *Notes:* Dispersed camping is available outside of the established campground.   *Road Desc:* Gravel, rough
Directions: N on Willow Lake Rd/CR 119 10.7 mi
Campsites: 6   *Shade:* *   *Privacy:* *   *RV Size:* 40'   *Other:* None

MM: 105.5   *GPS:* 42.88084/-109.97460   *Elev:* 7262   *Grid:* 15/53
Wy-352/FR-10091 *(see chapter)*   *Type:* Hwy Junction w/Chapter
43.9 mi route north from **US-191** ending at the **Green River Lakes** area. **Wy-352** is paved and heads north 25.3 mi before becoming gravel at the **Bridger-Teton National Forest** boundary. At this point the road transitions to **FR-10091** and loops east then south to the **Green River Lakes Trailhead** at the end of the road. The mile markers for **Wy-352** end at MM 25.3, so they are also shown as starting at zero from **FR-10091** to allow the trip odometer to be reset. Along the way are 4 public campgrounds as well as numerous dispersed camping options after entering the National Forest. This route also connects to the 44.6 mi road over **Union Pass** that connects to **US-26/287** 8 mi northwest of **Dubois**. Highlights include: **New Fork Lake**, **Kendall Warm Springs**, **Green River Lakes area**, **Clear Creek Falls**, **Clear Creek Natural Bridge**, **Porcupine Falls**, **Slide Lake**.
Nearest Town: Pinedale 5.9 E   *Directions:* N from MM 0
Notes: If the wind isn't blowing the evening mosquitoes are awful in the National Forest area along this route.

MM: 105.5   *Dist:* 0.4   *GPS:* 42.87964/-109.97457   *GPS2:* 42.88006/-109.98186   *Elev:* 7348   *Grid:* 15/53
Trappers Point   *Type:* Historic Site
A historical marker on the top of a hill overlooking the **Upper Green River Valley**. The valley was a rendezvous site in the 1830s where trappers, traders, and Indians met trade wagons from the east. The sign lists the primary figures in these historical meetings *(see the related section on Father DeSmet's Prairie Mass Monument in chapter: US-189 MM 127.8)*. The hill also offers a good view of the **Wind River Mountains** to the northwest. This site is on the **National Register of Historic Places**, not for the rendezvous site below, but because it is the site of the earliest known mass kill and processing of pronghorn in North America.
Cool Rating: *   *Crowds:* *   *Time:* 20 min   *Road Desc:* Dirt, high clearance
Directions: S on Green River Rd 0.1 mi;   W/R on a 2-track road 0.3 to 0.4 mi depending on the ground clearance of your vehicle. From the first parking area, it is a 50 ft climb to the overlook.

MM: 110.5   *GPS:* 42.89041/-110.06952   *Elev:* 7233   *Grid:* 14/53
US-189 *(see chapter)*   *Type:* Hwy Junction w/Chapter
131.5 mi highway from the transition of **US-189/191** to **US-191**, south to **I-80** exit 18. Highlights include: **Father DeSmet Monument**, **Names Hill**.
Nearest Town: Daniel 1.9 S; Pinedale 10.9 E   *Directions:* S to Daniel from MM 131.5

MM: 110.5   *GPS:* 42.89041/-110.06952   *Elev:* 7233   *Grid:* 14/53
US-189/191 *(see chapter)*   *Type:* Hwy Junction w/Chapter
53.1 mi highway northwest to **Hoback Jct** from the transition with **US-191** and junction with **US-189**. The mile markers continue sequentially from **US-191**. Highlights include: **Hoback Canyon**, **Granite Falls**, **Granite Hot Springs**, **Stinking Springs**.
Nearest Town: Daniel 1.9 S; Pinedale 10.9 E   *Directions:* NW to Hoback Jct from MM 110.5

MM: 110.5   *GPS:* 42.89041/-110.06952   *Elev:* 7233   *Grid:* 14/53
End of Highway   *Type:* Highway End
109.2 mi highway that transitions from **US-189/191**, using sequential mile markers, and continues southeast to **I-80** exit 104 in **Rock Springs**. Highlights include: **Green River Lakes**, **Fremont Lake**, **Killpecker Sand Dunes**, **Boar's Tusk**, **White Mountain Petroglyphs**, **Pilot Butte Wild Horse Tour**, **Reliance Tipple**.
Nearest Town: Daniel 1.9 S, Pinedale 10.9 E   *Directions:* E to Pinedale then S to Rock Springs from MM 110.5

US-20/26   E/W

MM: 3.2 **GPS:** 42.86725/-106.34527 **Elev:** 5310 **Grid:** 67/53
US-20/26   **Type:** Highway Description
96.9 mi highway from **Casper** northwest to **Shoshoni**. Highlights include: **Hell's Half Acre**, **Hole-in-the-Wall**, **Castle Gardens**.
Directions: I-25 exit 189; W on US-20/26 Bypass 2.9 mi; NW/R on US-20/26 to Shoshoni from MM 6.1

MM: 3.2 **GPS:** 42.86725/-106.34527 **Elev:** 5310 **Grid:** 67/53
I-25 (see chapter)   **Type:** Hwy Junction w/Chapter
300.1 mi interstate highway through east/central **Wyoming** from **Colorado** north to **I-90** (just past **Buffalo**), which continues
northwest to **Montana**. Highlights include: **Pioneer Museum**, **Ayres Park and Natural Bridge**, **National Historic Trails
Interpretive Center**, **Hole-in-the-Wall**, **Outlaw Cave**, **Indian Rock Art Cave**.
Directions: N to Buffalo or E to Glenrock from MM 189.5

MM: 3.2 **GPS:** 42.86725/-106.34527 **Elev:** 5310 **Grid:** 67/53
Casper   **Type:** Town

MM: 6.1 **GPS:** 42.86068/-106.40069 **Elev:** 5230 **Grid:** 66/53
Connection to I-25 or US-20/26/87   **Type:** Highway Transition
If heading southeast on **US-20/26**, turn left 2.9 mi to reach **I-25** or continue straight 4.2 mi through **Casper** to a transition with
US-20/26/87, which continues east to **Glenrock** with access to **Edness Wilkins State Park** at MM 181.8.

MM: 6.4 **GPS:** 42.86392/-106.40631 **Elev:** 5233 **Grid:** 66/53
Oregon Trail Rd (see chapter)   **Type:** Hwy Junction w/Chapter
An interesting alternative route from **US-20/26** (at **Casper**) southwest following the actual **Oregon Trail** 40.4 mi to **Wy-220**. The
road passes the historic sites **Emigrant Gap**, **Rock Avenue**, **Willow Springs**, and **Prospect Hill** (a BLM interpretive site) in the
same direction that the emigrants traveled. This route from **Casper** is roughly the same distance as taking **Wy-220** but is much
slower and bypasses **Alcova Reservoir** and **Pathfinder Reservoir**.
Nearest Town: Casper 4 E **Directions:** W on W Zero Rd from MM 0

MM: 25.4 **Dist:** 1.1 **GPS:** 43.01474/-106.71206 **Elev:** 5512 **Grid:** 62/50 **Land:** BLM
Goldeneye Wildlife and Recreation Area   **Type:** Recreation Area
A treeless day use area near the south shore of **Goldeneye Reservoir** with a large parking area, picnic tables, vault toilet, and a
boat ramp. The lake supports fishing for trout and walleye. Camping is allowed in the parking area.
Cool Rating: * **Crowds:** * **Road Desc:** Gravel **Directions:** NE 1.1 mi
Campsites: Dispersed **Shade:** * **Privacy:** * **RV Size:** 40'+ **Other:** None

MM: 30.4 **GPS:** 43.02968/-106.80921 **Elev:** 5605 **Grid:** 61/49
Natrona   **Type:** Town

MM: 45.2 **GPS:** 43.04725/-107.09244 **Elev:** 6035 **Grid:** 57/49 **Land:** County
Hell's Half Acre   **Type:** Scenic Area
Just south of the highway is a spectacular 150 ft deep, 320 acre badlands canyon of colorful eroded rock formations. The parking
area is just off the highway, where the northwest end of the canyon can be viewed with no obstructions. The rest of the canyon
perimeter is surrounded by an 8 ft chain link fence which restricts access and obstructs the views. Hiking into the canyon is not
allowed.
Cool Rating: ***** **Crowds:** ** **Time:** 5 - 30 min **Directions:** SW side of hwy
Notes: Historical notes: There used to be a restaurant and small motel at the top of the canyon. These were removed in 2010 and
replaced with the perimeter fence. The canyon was used in 1997 as the fictional planet of Klendathu in the movie Starship
Troopers.

MM: 50.7 **GPS:** 43.07026/-107.19596 **Elev:** 6050 **Grid:** 55/48
Waltman   **Type:** Town

MM: 50.7 **GPS:** 43.07026/-107.19596 **Elev:** 6051 **Grid:** 55/48 **Land:** BLM
Wyoming Backway shortcut from US-20/26 to I-25   **Type:** Scenic Drive
A 68.1 mi backcountry route from **US-20/26**, at **Waltman**, to **I-25** south of **Kaycee**. This route saves 45 mi over taking the paved
highways. This is the route to **Hole-in-the-Wall** with access to 2 backcountry campgrounds (see next 3 sections).
Road Desc: The first 9.6 mi is paved. The rest is smooth gravel except the 2.1 section on CR-111A, which is rougher. Not
recommended when wet.
Directions: N on CR-104/Arminto Rd and CR-105/Buffalo Creek Rd 35.8 mi (MI 35.8); Keep left at the fork with CR-110 and
continue 0.6 mi to the **Hole-in-the-Wall turnoff** (MI 36.4); The road transitions to CR-111/Willow Creek Rd; Continue 8.3 mi (MI
44.7); E/L on CR-111A 2.1 mi (MI 46.8); E/L on CR-111/Willow Creek Rd 5.9 mi (MI 52.7); NE/L on CR-51/Lone Bear Rd 14.9 mi
(MI 67.6); N/L on TTT Rd 0.5 mi to I-25 exit 249 (MI 68.1).

MM: 50.7 **Dist:** 31.8 **GPS:** 43.43784/-107.22349 **Elev:** 8118 **Grid:** 55/39 **Land:** BLM
Buffalo Creek Campground   **Type:** Campground
A camping loop near **Buffalo Creek** in the forested foothills at the southern end of the **Bighorn Mountains**. There is a site in the
open at the entrance, a site with a long parking spur at the end of the loop, and 2 more sites in the loop with short parking areas.
Single loop. Sparse conifer forest. Tables. Fire rings. Vault toilet.
Crowds: * **Road Desc:** The first 9.6 mi is paved. CR-105 is smooth gravel. CR-109 has rough spots & impassable when wet.
Directions: N on CR-104/Arminto Rd and CR-105/Buffalo Creek Rd 22.7 mi; NW/L on CR-109/Bighorn Mountain Rd 8.9 mi; W/L
0.2 mi.
Campsites: 4 **Shade:** *** **Privacy:** *** **RV Size:** 30' **Other:** None

MM: 50.7 *Dist:* 33.7 *GPS:* 43.46383/-107.22846 *Elev:* 8251 *Grid:* 55/38 *Land:* BLM
Grave Springs Campground   *Type:* Campground
In the forested foothills at the southern end of the **Bighorn Mountains**. As you enter, a road to the left ends in a loop with 4 sites. Continuing straight there are 3 unlevel sites on the left side of the road. To the right is a turnaround loop with 2 tables. At the end of the road are 2 sites with unlevel parking areas. *Sparse conifer forest. Tables. Fire rings. Vault toilet.*
Crowds: * *Road Desc:* The first 9.6 mi is paved. CR-105 is smooth gravel. CR-109 has rough spots & impassable when wet.
Directions: N on CR-104/Arminto Rd and CR-105/Buffalo Creek Rd 22.7 mi; NW/L on CR-109/Bighorn Mountain Rd 10.7 mi; NW/L 0.2 mi.
Campsites: 10 *Shade:* *** *Privacy:* *** *RV Size:* 30' *Other:* None

MM: 50.7 *Dist:* 46.3 *GPS:* 43.52958/-106.86484 *GPS2:* 43.54671/-106.82935 *Elev:* 5360 *Grid:* 60/37 *Land:* BLM
Hole-in-the-Wall   *Type:* Scenic Area
A gap in the red sandstone escarpment know as the "**Red Wall**," which was used by several outlaw gangs as a hideout from the late 1860s to around 1910. The area was easily defended because it was impossible for lawmen to approach without being seen. The most notable outlaws were **Butch Cassidy and the Sundance Kid** and the **Wild Bunch Gang**. The area itself is colorful, scenic, and remote with access along a 2.6 mi (one-way) hiking trail of county roads and single-track paths. The "hole" is actually a V-shaped section of the **Red Wall** that offers a steep and rocky route to the top of the butte without encountering a vertical wall. The view from the top is excellent.

The access road starts at a steel gate and travels 9.7 mi through the sagebrush prairie along a primitive 2-track road to the parking area. The first 7 miles are along private property, including an old ranch building at (MI 6), so stay on the road. At (MI 7) CR-105 ends and changes to BLM-6214. At (MI 9.3) is a fenced in area with a historical sign about the **Hole-in-the-Wall Fight**. The parking area is at (MI 9.7).

The trail is well marked with narrow, flat, brown markers; however, many are broken or knocked down so pay attention to these directions. From the parking area the trail drops steeply 120 ft to a wet marshy area (MI 0.2). The trail gets lost a bit here, but a little jog to the right will get you across the water. A short steep climb out of the ravine gets you back on the well worn trail to a gate (MI 0.3). The trail continues 0.4 mi through a shallow valley (keep left at the fork at MI 0.4) climbing 150 ft to a dirt road (MI 0.7). This is the high point of the trail until climbing up the **Red Wall**. Continue past this road a short distance to another road and turn left. In another 0.1 mi you will reach the closest destination from the parking area to get a good distant view of the **Hole-in-the-Wall** (MI 0.8) The road from the top descends 140 ft in 0.5 mi to a NOT well-marked single-track trail to the right (MI 1.2). Keep a close eye out as this is easy to miss. There are visible trail markers up the hill, but when I was there they were knocked down. Turn right and continue 0.2 mi through a ravine (MI 1.4). The trail levels off and continues 0.5 mi to where the trail will start to climb (MI 1.9). The trail then climbs 240 ft in 0.7 miles up into the "hole". The trail is reasonably well established up to this point, where a large boulder provides some shade (MI 2.6). Past this point it is basically a scramble across rocks and a side hill to climb the last 120 ft to the top. On the return route, keep left at the 2 forks in the trail. *2.6 mi one-way; 160 ft elev loss; 430 ft elev gain (part way up Red Wall) or 550 ft (top of Red Wall).*
Cool Rating: ^^^^ *Crowds:* ^ *Time:* Half to all day
Notes: This is a primitive area with no services, so take adequate water, food and fuel. Pack out trash and respect private property. The final 9.7 mi can be traveled in a vehicle with good ground clearance, but 4WD would be necessary if the road gets wet. An OHV is ideal. This destination is far out of the way and requires a significant effort.
Road Desc: The 2-track primitive road is impassable when wet and has 4 livestock gates that must be opened and closed. The tire ruts are wider than an ATV, which makes navigation difficult.
Directions: See "Wyoming Backway shortcut" 3 sections earlier for the road description and follow directions to MI 36.4; NE on CR-105/BLM-6214/Buffalo Creek Rd 9.7 mi to parking area.

MM: 53.2 *GPS:* 43.07482/-107.24496 *Elev:* 6120 *Grid:* 54/48
Waltman Rest Area   *Type:* Rest Area
Sheltered picnic tables.
Directions: N side of hwy

MM: 78.5 *Dist:* 20.9 *GPS:* 42.93109/-107.61748 *Elev:* 6131 *Grid:* 49/52 *Land:* BLM
Castle Gardens   *Type:* Scenic Area
Cliffs and outcroppings of colorful eroded sandstone that resemble the towers of a castle. The cliffs and hills form a small valley of rock outcrops and boulders in colorful soil dotted with juniper and pine trees. Along the northern cliffs is a fenced in area with **Petroglyphs** that are done in the regional **Castle Gardens Shield Style**, the oldest recognizable example of shields and shield-bearing warrior figures. After viewing the **Petroglyphs** spend some time walking around this beautiful area, which is particularly nice in the evening. Although no official campsites are provided, you can camp along the road or in the parking area. This is the second **Castle Gardens** in **Wyoming**, the other being off **US-16** about 70 mi north.
Cool Rating: ***** *Crowds:* * *Time:* 1-2 hrs
Road Desc: Gravel, impassable when wet. The BLM road is dirt and not as well-maintained.
Directions: S on CR-460/Buck Camp Rd 0.9 mi; Keep right at fork in road onto CR-459/Castle Gardens Rd 14.1 mi; E/L at BLM sign on BLM-2107 5.9 mi. *If continuing south on Wy-789, see Wy-789 MM 103.8 and reverse directions.*

MM: 79.3 *GPS:* 43.16179/-107.72677 *Elev:* 5440 *Grid:* 48/46
Moneta   *Type:* Town

MM: 99.7 *GPS:* 43.23523/-108.10337 *Elev:* 4845 *Grid:* 42/44 *Land:* City
Shoshoni Picnic Area   *Type:* Picnic Area
2 picnic shelter with 2 tables each in a grassed area. *Restrooms.*
Directions: E end of Shoshoni; S side of hwy.

MM: 100.0 *GPS:* 43.23552/-108.11071 *Elev:* 4841 *Grid:* 42/44
Shoshoni   *Type:* Town

MM: 100.0 *Dist:* 0.4 *GPS:* 43.23361/-108.11710 *Elev:* 4826 *Grid:* 42/44 *Land:* City
Shoshoni City Park   *Type:* Park
A city park with a few shade trees, sheltered picnic tables, a restroom, and a playground. The north end of the **Wyoming Heritage Trail** starts just south of the park. Camping is permitted at the southwest end of the park.
Crowds: *
Directions: On the west end of Shoshoni; Continue W 0.3 mi on US-26/Wy-789/W 2nd St; S on Maple St 2 blocks.
Campsites: Dispersed *Shade:* * *Privacy:* * *RV Size:* 40' *Other:* Water

MM: 100.4 *GPS:* 43.23552/-108.11071 *Elev:* 4841 *Grid:* 42/44
US-20/Wy-789 & US-16/20/Wy-789 & US-14/16/20/Wy-789 *(see chapter)*   *Type:* Hwy Junction w/Chapter
157 mi highway from **Shoshoni** north to **Montana**. Highlights include: **Boysen State Park**, **Wind River Canyon**, **Hot Springs State Park**, **Medicine Lodge State Archaeological Site**, **Devil's Kitchen Geological Site**, **Museum of Flight and Aerial Firefighting**.
Directions: N to Thermopolis from MM 100

MM: 100.4 *GPS:* 43.23552/-108.11071 *Elev:* 4841 *Grid:* 42/44
Wy-789 & US-26/Wy-789 *(see chapter)*   *Type:* Hwy Transition w/Chapter
46.2 mi highway from **Shoshoni** southwest to **Lander**. The highway heads southwest from **Shoshoni** as **US-26/Wy-789**. After 22.1 mi **US-26** heads northwest and the highway continues 24.1 mi to **Lander** as **Wy-789**. Highlights include: **Wyoming Heritage Trail**, access to **Castle Gardens**.
Directions: Continue straight to head SW to Riverton from MM 127.3

MM: 100.0 *GPS:* 43.23552/-108.11071 *Elev:* 4841 *Grid:* 42/44
End of Highway   *Type:* Highway End
96.9 mi highway from **Shoshoni** southeast to **Casper**. Highlights include: **Castle Gardens**, **Hole-in-the-Wall**, **Hell's Half Acre**.
Directions: SE to Casper from MM 100

US-20/Wy-789 & US-16/20/Wy-789 & US-14/16/20/Wy-789 & US-310/Wy-789   S/N

MM: 100.0 **GPS:** 43.23552/-108.11071 **Elev:** 4841 **Grid:** 42/44
US-20/Wy-789 & US-16/20/Wy-789 & US-14/16/20/Wy-789 & US-310/Wy-789   *Type:* Highway Description
157 mi highway from **Shoshoni** north to **Montana**. The common highway that anchors the mile markers is **Wy-789**, which combines with **US-20** at **Shoshoni** (**US-20/Wy-789**) and heads north past **Thermopolis**. The highway combines with **US-16** at **Worland** (**US-16/20/Wy-789**) and **US-14** at **Greybull** (**US-14/16/20/Wy-789**). From **Greybull** the highway turns west where **Wy-789** diverges from **US-14/16/20** (which continues west to **Cody**) and joins **US-310** (**US-310/Wy-789**) heading northwest to **Lovell** and **Montana**. Highlights include: **Boysen State Park**, **Wind River Canyon**, **Hot Springs State Park**, **Medicine Lodge State Archaeological Site**, **Devil's Kitchen Geological Site**, **Museum of Flight and Aerial Firefighting**.
Directions: N to Thermopolis from MM 100

MM: 100.0 **GPS:** 43.23552/-108.11071 **Elev:** 4841 **Grid:** 42/44
US-20/26 *(see chapter)*   *Type:* Hwy Junction w/Chapter
96.9 mi highway from **Shoshoni** southeast to **Casper**. Highlights include: **Castle Gardens**, **Hole-in-the-Wall**, **Hell's Half Acre**.
Directions: SE to Casper from MM 100

MM: 100.0 **GPS:** 43.23552/-108.11071 **Elev:** 4841 **Grid:** 42/44
Wy-789 & US-26/Wy-789 *(see chapter)*   *Type:* Hwy Junction w/Chapter
46.2 mi highway from **Shoshoni** southwest to **Lander**. The highway heads southwest from **Shoshoni** as **US-26/Wy-789**. After 22.1 mi **US-26** heads northwest and the highway continues 24.1 mi to **Lander** as **Wy-789**. Highlights include: **Wyoming Heritage Trail**, access to **Castle Gardens**.
Directions: SW to Riverton from MM 127.3

MM: 100.0 **GPS:** 43.23552/-108.11071 **Elev:** 4841 **Grid:** 42/44
Shoshoni   *Type:* Town

MM: 106.2 **Dist:** 1.6 **GPS:** 43.32980/-108.15205 **Elev:** 4735 **Grid:** 41/42 **Land:** State
Tough Creek Campground: Boysen State Park   *Type:* Campground
Located on a peninsula on the east side of **Boysen Reservoir**. *Cottonwoods. Group shelter. Level. Playground. Boat ramp with large parking area.*
Crowds: *** *[FEE AREA]* *Directions:* W 1.6 mi
Campsites: 65 *Shade:* * *Privacy:* * *RV Size:* 40'+ *Other:* Water

MM: 113.1 **GPS:** 43.40284/-108.16585 **Elev:** 4815 **Grid:** 41/40 **Land:** State
RV Dump: Boysen State Park   *Type:* RV Dump
Directions: At the Boysen State Park Headquarters turnoff, NE 100 yds

MM: 113.1 **Dist:** 0.2 **GPS:** 43.40264/-108.16731 **Elev:** 4803 **Grid:** 41/40 **Land:** State
Boysen State Park Headquarters   *Type:* Visitor Center
Information for **Boysen State Park** as well as other **Wyoming State Parks**.
Directions: NE 0.2 mi

MM: 113.3 **Dist:** 0.1 **GPS:** 43.40338/-108.16995 **Elev:** 4760 **Grid:** 41/40 **Land:** State
Brannon Campground: Boysen State Park   *Type:* Campground
Located on the northeast end of **Boysen Reservoir** just off the highway. RV camping is around the perimeter of a large grassy area with tables. Tenting is only allowed in the grass on the weekends due to the watering schedule. The campground sits at the base of a 120 ft tall hill which blocks the view and access to the lake. However, a day use picnic and beach area are located just northwest of the campground near the highway entrance. A boat ramp and full service marina are located just southeast. *Scattered shade trees. A few tables are sheltered. Playground.*
Crowds: * *[FEE AREA]* *Directions:* SW side of hwy
Campsites: 25 *Shade:* * *Privacy:* * *RV Size:* 40'+ *Other:* Water

MM: 113.3 **Dist:** 0.4 **GPS:** 43.39989/-108.16694 **Elev:** 4755 **Grid:** 41/40 **Land:** State
Tamarask Campground: Boysen State Park   *Type:* Campground
Located on the northeast end of **Boysen Reservoir** just south of **Brannon Campground** and the marina. Several camping areas are scattered 0.7 mi along the road in large pullouts, on short roads, and in loops. Most sites provide close access to the lake. This area is best suited for RVs. *Scattered trees. Playground.*
Crowds: *** *[FEE AREA]* *Directions:* SW 0.4 mi
Campsites: 40 *Shade:* * *Privacy:* * *RV Size:* 40'+ *Other:* Water

MM: 113.8 **GPS:** 43.41121/-108.17467 **Elev:** 4780 **Grid:** 41/40
Boysen Dam Overlook   *Type:* Point of Interest
Boysen Reservoir was created by this 1,100 ft long and 230 ft high earthen dam on the **Wind River** in **Wind River Canyon**. The dam was completed in 1952 and is located on the north end of the reservoir. A large gravel pullout overlooks the dam and includes interpretive signs about the dam, the **Wind River Canyon** and its geology, and the bighorn sheep that were released into the **Wind River Canyon** in 1995. Some of these bighorn sheep are often visible near the dam.
Cool Rating: ** *Crowds:* * *Time:* 10 min *Directions:* W side of hwy

MM: 115.4 **GPS:** 43.43450/-108.17674 **Elev:** 4633 **Grid:** 41/39 **Land:** State
Upper Wind River Campground: Boysen State Park   *Type:* Campground
Located north of **Boysen Dam** just below the highway and above the **Wind River**. *Large cottonwoods. Grassy sites. Roomy sites. Playground. Horseshoe pits. Road noise.*
Crowds: ** *[FEE AREA]* *Directions:* W side of hwy
Campsites: 50 *Shade:* *** *Privacy:* ** *RV Size:* 40'+ *Other:* 307-876-2796,Water

MM: 116.0 *GPS:* 43.44095/-108.17143 *Elev:* 4630 *Grid:* 41/39 *Land:* State
Lower Wind River Campground: Boysen State Park   *Type:* Campground
Just below the highway and above the **Wind River** a short distance south of the first tunnel into the **Wind River Canyon**. *2 loops.*
Large cottonwoods. More shade in the north loop. Grassy sites. Roomy sites. Playground. Reservable group shelter. Road and
tunnel noise.
Crowds: ** **[FEE AREA]** *Directions:* W side of hwy
Campsites: 50 *Shade:* *** *Privacy:* ** *RV Size:* 40'+ *Other:* 307-876-2796,Water

MM: 116.1 *GPS:* 43.44350/-108.16999 *Elev:* 4664 *Grid:* 41/39
Wind River Canyon (south end)   *Type:* Scenic Drive
A scenic canyon that cuts 11.9 mi through the **Owl Creek Mountains**. The canyon starts to the south at the first of 3 tunnels and
ends to the north at **Wedding of the Waters**. The canyon is 1.3 - 2.0 mi wide with walls that reach 2,400 ft in height. The road
through the canyon provides many pullouts and 2 picnic areas.
Cool Rating: *** *Crowds:* * *Time:* Drive through

MM: 119.8 *GPS:* 43.49284/-108.15924 *Elev:* 4515 *Grid:* 41/38
Picnic Area: Wind River Canyon   *Type:* Picnic Area
A nice picnic area with 2 sheltered tables along the **Wind River** in **Wind River Canyon**. The shelters are down a small hill and are
not visible from the road when heading north.
Crowds: *** *Directions:* W side of hwy just north of a business area.

MM: 127.5 *GPS:* 43.58154/-108.21341 *Elev:* 4371 *Grid:* 41/35
Picnic Area: Wind River Canyon   *Type:* Picnic Area
2 covered picnic tables at each end of a long pullout above the **Wind River** at the north end of **Wind River Canyon**.
Crowds: * *Directions:* W side of hwy

MM: 127.6 *GPS:* 43.58346/-108.21388 *Elev:* 4376 *Grid:* 41/35
Wind River Canyon (north end)   *Type:* Scenic Drive
A scenic canyon that cuts 11.9 mi through the **Owl Creek Mountains**. The canyon starts to the north at **Wedding of the Waters**
and ends to the south at the third of 3 tunnels. The canyon is 1.3 - 2.0 mi wide with walls that reach 2,400 ft in height. The road
through the canyon provides many pullouts and 2 picnic areas.
Cool Rating: *** *Crowds:* * *Time:* Drive through

MM: 128.0 *Dist:* 0.1 *GPS:* 43.58896/-108.21493 *Elev:* 4364 *Grid:* 41/35
Wedding of the Waters   *Type:* Point of Interest
The **Wind River** flows past this point on its way to the **Yellowstone River** in **Montana**. Early explorers arriving at the river in
Montana named it the **Bighorn River** after the **Bighorn Sheep** found along the river. Other explorers who found the river from the
south in **Wyoming** named it the **Wind River**. In time people realized that there was only one river with 2 well-established names.
To avoid confusion it was decided to have the river change names at a point 1/2 mi south of this site. This point is known as
Wedding of the Waters and is one of the few places where a river changes its name midstream. To the south the canyon was
named the **Wind River Canyon**, while the canyon to the north retained the name **Bighorn Canyon**. 2 signs provide information
about **Wedding of the Waters** as well as the importance of this part of the river for wildlife. This stretch of the river is a blue ribbon
trout fishery. A restroom and float launch are located at the site.
Cool Rating: ** *Crowds:* ** *Time:* 10 min *Directions:* W 0.1 mi to parking area.

MM: 132.5 *GPS:* 43.64610/-108.21200 *Elev:* 4330 *Grid:* 41/34
Thermopolis   *Type:* Town

MM: 132.5 *GPS:* 43.64610/-108.21200 *Elev:* 4330 *Grid:* 41/34
Wy-120 *(see chapter)*   *Type:* Hwy Junction w/Chapter
118.7 mi highway that runs diagonally from **Thermopolis** northwest to **Cody** and continues to **Montana**. From **Cody**, **US-14/16/20**
heads straight east to the east entrance of **Yellowstone National Park**. Continuing north from **Cody** the highway provides 2
scenic routes to the northeast entrance of **Yellowstone National Park**. Route 1 connects to **Wy-296 (Chief Joseph Scenic
Highway)**, which climbs over the spectacular **Dead Indian Pass** and connects to **US-212**. Route 2 travels into **Montana** and loops
back into **Wyoming** on **US-212** over the even more spectacular **Beartooth Pass**. Highlights include: **Legend Rock Petroglyphs**,
Gooseberry Badlands Scenic Area, attractions in **Cody** *(see US-14/16/20 MM 52.4)*.
Directions: NW to Cody from MM 0

MM: 133.0   *Dist:* 0.5   *GPS:* 43.65054/-108.19744   *GPS2:* 43.65492/-108.19638   *Elev:* 4340   *Grid:* 41/34   *Land:* State
Hot Springs State Park   *Type:* State Park
This popular state park contains the world's largest mineral hot spring. **Big Spring**, on the north end of the park, discharges over 3 million gallons of mineral water every day at a constant temperature of 135° F. The water is channeled into cooling pools and then piped into public pools at 104° F. The remaining water flows over the **Rainbow Terrace** *(see GPS2)* into the **Bighorn River**. This colorful cliff of travertine can be seen by crossing a suspension footbridge across the **Bighorn River**, known as the **Swinging Bridge** *(see GPS2)*. The original bridge was built in 1916, condemned in 1984, removed in 1991, and replaced in 1992. Crossing the bridge is an interesting experience in itself.

Just south of the terrace is the **State Bath House**, a hot mineral pool for soaking free of charge. The bath house has a changing room with showers. The soaking time in the pool is limited to 30 min for safety reasons. On both the east and west side of the bath house are fee-based swimming pools, hot tubs, and water slides.

West of the bath house is the **Teepee Fountain** at the end of **Teepee St** (43.6522/-108.19988). This structure was created in 1903 by piping the hot mineral water through a vertical pipe built into a rock pyramid. As the water cools travertine is deposited on the existing surface, which has grown over time to around 25 ft high and 25 ft in diameter.

Some additional thermal features are located on the north end of the park past the picnic area on **Big Spring Dr**. The most interesting is **White Sulphur Spring**. Continuing up and around the hill is a roaming herd of bison, the historic **Smokey Row Cemetery**, and good views of the park.
Hours: Bath House: 8am - 5:30pm, Mon-Sat; noon - 5:30pm, Sundays and summer holidays; Open year-round except winter holidays   *Phone:* 307-864-3765   *Cool Rating:* ****   *Crowds:* ***   *Time:* 1-4 hrs
Directions: On the NE end of town, just before a wide curve to the NE; E on E Park St 0.5 mi.

MM: 133.6   *GPS:* 43.65528/-108.19870   *Elev:* 4360   *Grid:* 41/34
Hot Springs State Park Scenic Overlook   *Type:* Scenic Viewpoint
A half-loop road with a view of **Hot Springs State Park** and the colorful **Rainbow Terrace**. The **Teepee Fountain** can be seen to the south. Another small turnout is located 100 yds northeast with a sign about the hot springs. *See previous section.*
Cool Rating: ****   *Crowds:* *   *Time:* 10 min   *Directions:* SE side of hwy

MM: 156.6   *Dist:* 23.2   *GPS:* 44.00640/-108.47500   *Elev:* 5044   *Grid:* 37/25   *Land:* BLM
Gooseberry Badlands Scenic Area   *Type:* Scenic Area
Named for **Gooseberry Creek** south of the site, this overlook provides a panoramic view of colorful eroded badlands. A 1.5 mi loop trail leads through these interesting rock formations.

Camping is allowed in the parking area or along BLM roads 0.8 mi to the east and 1.3 mi to the west of the overlook. Both roads head north, and the road to the west is in better condition than the road to the east.
Cool Rating: *****   *Crowds:* *   *Time:* 1 hr   *Nearest Town:* Worland 32.3 NE, Meeteetse 26.3 NW
Directions: W on Wy-431 23.2 mi to parking area on N side of hwy at MM 23.2.
Campsites: Dispersed   *Shade:* *   *Privacy:* *   *RV Size:* 30'   *Other:* None

MM: 165.7   *GPS:* 44.01685/-107.95575   *Elev:* 4063   *Grid:* 44/25
Worland   *Type:* Town

MM: 165.7   *GPS:* 44.01685/-107.95575   *Elev:* 4063   *Grid:* 44/25
US-16 *(see chapter)*   *Type:* Hwy Junction w/Chapter
89.9 mi highway from **Worland** northeast to **Buffalo**. Along this highway is the scenic 45 mi **Cloud Peak Skyway**, which travels through the **Bighorn Mountains** and provides many campgrounds, forest roads with dispersed camping, and recreational opportunities. Highlights include: **Castle Gardens, Medicine Lodge State Archaeological Site, Tensleep Canyon, Wigwam Rearing Station, Ten Sleep Fish Hatchery, West Tensleep Falls, High Park Lookout, Crazy Woman Canyon**.
Directions: E to Ten Sleep from MM 0

MM: 185.0   *Dist:* 0.3   *GPS:* 44.26923/-107.96385   *Elev:* 3890   *Grid:* 44/18
Manderson   *Type:* Town
Directions: NE on Wy-31 0.3 mi

MM: 185.0   *GPS:* 44.26608/-107.96880   *Elev:* 3897   *Grid:* 44/18
Wy-31   *Type:* Highway Junction
22.1 mi highway from **Manderson** to **Hyattville**, which provides access to **Medicine Lodge State Archaeological Site**. *See next section.*
Directions: N then E to Hyattville from MM 0

MM: 185.0　*Dist:* 27.2　*GPS:* 44.29815/-107.54190　*Elev:* 4890　*Grid:* 50/18　*Land:* State
Medicine Lodge State Archaeological Site　　　*Type:* Petroglyphs
In 1973 this site was the scene of one of the most significant archaeological excavations in North America. For 2 years scientists unearthed evidence of over 10,000 years of human habitation from depths up to 26 ft. These findings document the entire history of human occupation in the **Bighorn Basin**. The dig site (which has been filled in) is located below a 750 ft long cliff that is covered with hundreds of **Petroglyphs** and **Pictographs**. Along the base of the cliff are interpretive signs explaining the rock art and the excavation. Across the parking area is a small unstaffed visitor center with information on the dig site, rock art, flora and fauna, and general information.

Just southwest of the visitor center is the 1.0 mi **Deer Path Interpretive Hiking Trail**. This loop trail was developed as an Eagle Scout project and follows actual deer trails up a hill (180 ft elev gain) and along a ridge with good views of the surrounding area. Along the trail are lettered signs at 24 different plant species, which correspond to descriptions in a trail guide available at the visitor center. In addition, the **Medicine Lodge Nature Trail** is a short and easy walk that starts at the petroglyph cliff and visits 10 stations around the park, which are listed in a trail guide available at the visitor center. This is a beautiful park with grassy campsites and a group camping area that accommodates a large number of people. 3 of the regular campsites are reservable.

The park is located within the 19 sq mi **Medicine Lodge Wildlife Habitat Management Area**, which provides abundant wildlife viewing. To access this area drive through the park to the north end where a narrow dirt road continues north through a canyon that parallels **Dry Medicine Lodge Creek**. This road is only suitable for OHVs, mountain bikes, and hiking.

Accessed by this road is a large rock arch located 4.3 mi up **Dry Medicine Lodge Canyon** near the mouth of **Sheep Springs Canyon**. Follow the road 3.0 mi where the route continues on an old abandoned roadbed through the canyon while the main road climbs out of the canyon. Hike 1.3 mi along this brush-filled path to the arch on the west canyon wall.
Hours: Visitor Center: 8am - 5pm, Mon-Fri; 9am - 8pm, Sat-Sun
Cool Rating: ****　*Crowds:* **　*Time:* 1-3 hrs　*Nearest Town:* Hyattville 6.2 SW　*[FEE AREA]*
Notes: The only fee is for camping.　*Road Desc:* All but last 1.7 mi is paved.
Directions: N then E on Wy-31 21.5 mi;　N on Alkali Rd 0.3 mi;　E/R on Cold Springs Rd/CR-268 3.2 mi;　Take sharp curve N/L 0.5 mi;　Where road curves E/R, continue straight 1.7 mi to the park.　*If continuing north to US-14;　See Red Gulch/Alkali National Back Country Byway on US-14 MM 10.5* for a much shorter, cross-country route and reverse the directions.　*If continuing south to US-16;　See chapter: US-16 MM 26.5* and reverse the directions.
Campsites: 30　*Shade:* ****　*Privacy:* ***　*RV Size:* 40'　*Other:* 1-877-996-7275:wyoparks.state.wy.us/reservations,Water BEARS

MM: 196.5　*GPS:* 44.38123/-108.03895　*Elev:* 3876　*Grid:* 43/15
Basin　　　*Type:* Town

MM: 196.5　*GPS:* 44.38185/-108.03823　*Elev:* 3873　*Grid:* 43/15　*Land:* City
RV Dump: Overland Express Mart - Basin　　　*Type:* RV Dump
The **RV dump** requires obtaining a key from inside the store. It is free, but buying some gas or something is appreciated.
Directions: NE corner of intersection with C St;　Directly behind store.

MM: 204.1　*GPS:* 44.48897/-108.05540　*Elev:* 3792　*Grid:* 43/13
Greybull　　　*Type:* Town

MM: 204.1　*GPS:* 44.48897/-108.05540　*Elev:* 3792　*Grid:* 43/13
US-14 *(see chapter)*　　　*Type:* Hwy Junction w/Chapter
80.5 mi highway from **Greybull** northeast to **Ranchester**. A large portion of the highway is through National Forest along the **Bighorn Scenic Byway** with 10 public campgrounds. Highlights include: **Devil's Kitchen Geological Site**, **Red Gulch Dinosaur Tracksite**, **Medicine Lodge State Archaeological Site**, **Shell Falls**, **Dayton Bell Tower**, **Tongue River Canyon**.
Directions: E to Shell from MM 0

MM: 204.1　*Dist:* 7.9　*GPS:* 44.53373/-107.96993　*Elev:* 4050　*Grid:* 44/12　*Land:* BLM
Devil's Kitchen Geological Site　　　*Type:* Scenic Area
A colorful badlands area of red and gray weathered hills and eroded cliffs. This geology is part of the **Cloverly Formation**, a 100+ million year-old sequence of sediments containing important dinosaur remains. The cliffs drop off from the north at the road level, where an overlook offers picturesque views into the badlands below. From the overlook the cliff extends along a narrow ridge about 100 yds into the badlands offering the best views of these fascinating formations. This ridge has steep drop-offs, so proceed with caution and do not take small children. For a different perspective, a 3/4 mi dirt road descends into the badlands 0.4 mi west of the overlook.
Cool Rating: *****　*Crowds:* *　*Time:* 30-60+ min
Notes: Heavy truck traffic on CR-33 so keep your distance to avoid flying rocks.
Road Desc: Partially paved. The final short roads to the site are primitive and impassable when wet.
Directions: E on US-14 0.8 mi;　N on Division St 0.1 mi;　Continue left on Sandy Row 0.2 mi;　Continue right on Rimrock Rd 0.3 mi;　NW/L on Rimrock Rd/CR-27 2.0 mi (pavement ends about halfway);　E/R on CR-33 3.1 mi;　Keep right at fork to stay on CR-33 1.2 mi;　S on dirt road 0.2 mi to overlook.

MM: 206.6　*GPS:* 44.50928/-108.08418　*Elev:* 3920　*Grid:* 42/12
Greybull Rest Area　　　*Type:* Rest Area
Picnic shelters and a **"Pre-historic Wildlife"** sign about dinosaur discoveries in the **Bighorn Basin**.
Directions: N 70 yds then left

MM: 206.6　*Dist:* 0.1　*GPS:* 44.50902/-108.08128　*Elev:* 3906　*Grid:* 42/12

Museum of Flight and Aerial Firefighting　　*Type:* Museum

Contains some of the last remaining examples of **World War II** bombers and transport aircraft as well as aerial firefighting planes. Guided tours are available on a limited basis. The tour guide explains the use of each airplane and allows visitors into a few of them. The tour is free, but a donation is appreciated (and probably expected). If the tours are not running or time is limited, a few of the airplanes can be seen through the fence.

Hours: 10am - 4pm, Fri, Sat, Sun, & Wed (summer); Possible early closing due to extreme heat in aircraft　*Phone:* 307-765-4322

Cool Rating: ***　*Crowds:* *　*Time:* 30 min

Directions: N 70 yds then E/R 0.1 mi to a small cabin. *At the South Bighorn County Airport.*

Notes: The future of the museum depends on finding volunteers to run the tours.

MM: 209.0　*GPS:* 44.50929/-108.13325　*Elev:* 3994　*Grid:* 42/12

US-14/16/20 *(see chapter)*　　*Type:* Hwy Transition w/Chapter

100.1 mi highway west from a transition with **US-14/16/20/Wy-789**, west of **Greybull**, to the east entrance of **Yellowstone National Park**. The **Buffalo Bill Cody Scenic Byway** runs 27.4 mi from the east boundary of the **Shoshone National Forest** to the east entrance of **Yellowstone National Park**. Highlights include: **Buffalo Bill Historical Center**, **Old West Miniature Village and Museum**, **Buffalo Bill Dam and Visitor Center**, **Holy City**, **Firefighters Memorial and Trail**, interesting volcanic rock formations.

Nearest Town: Greybull 5 SE　*Directions:* W to Cody from MM 100.8

Notes: No dispersed camping on this route. If heading to Yellowstone be aware that the last 2 campgrounds are for hard-sided RVs only. Only 2 very small towns west of Cody.

MM: 236.1　*GPS:* 44.83698/-108.37915　*Elev:* 3817　*Grid:* 38/4

US-14A (east) *(see chapter)*　　*Type:* Hwy Junction w/Chapter

52.2 mi section of **US-14A** from **Lovell** east to **Burgess Jct**. The last 27 mi follow the **Medicine Wheel Passage**, a scenic high elevation route (over 9,000 ft) with excellent views into the **Bighorn Basin**. Highlights include: **Bighorn Canyon National Recreation Area**, **Medicine Wheel National Historic Landmark**, **Porcupine Falls**, **Bucking Mule Falls**.

Directions: NE on US-14A from MM 46.7

MM: 236.4　*Dist:* 0.6　*GPS:* 44.84114/-108.38317　*Elev:* 3822　*Grid:* 38/4　*Land:* City

Lovell Camper Park　　*Type:* Campground

A shady and free camping park on the northeast end of **Lovell**. *Deciduous trees. Dirt and gravel sites. Level. Tables. Grills. Flush toilets. Showers. Water refill station. Several pull-thrus. 3-day limit.*

Crowds: ***

Directions: On the east end of Lovell; N on Pennsylvania Ave 0.2 mi; E/R on E 2nd St 0.1 mi; N/L on Quebec Ave 0.05 mi; W side of street.

Campsites: 9　*Shade:* *****　*Privacy:* *　*RV Size:* 40'+　*Other:* Water,RVDump

MM: 236.6　*GPS:* 44.83749/-108.38925　*Elev:* 3836　*Grid:* 38/4

Lovell　　*Type:* Town

MM: 239.1　*GPS:* 44.84163/-108.43953　*Elev:* 3906　*Grid:* 37/4　*Land:* City

Mormon Colonists Monument　　*Type:* Historical Marker

A rock monument in honor of the accomplishments of the **Mormon** colonists who in 1900 established towns in the **Bighorn Basin**.

Cool Rating: *　*Crowds:* *　*Time:* 5 min　*Directions:* SW side of hwy; 0.1 mi SE of the intersection with US-14A.

MM: 239.3　*GPS:* 44.84287/-108.44141　*Elev:* 3905　*Grid:* 37/4

US-14A (southwest) *(see chapter)*　　*Type:* Hwy Junction w/Chapter

43.5 mi section of **US-14A** from **Lovell** southwest to **Cody**. Highlights include: **Heart Mountain Relocation Center**.

Directions: W on US-14A from MM 43.5

MM: 242.8　*GPS:* 44.88345/-108.46930　*Elev:* 3992　*Grid:* 37/3

Cowley　　*Type:* Town

MM: 254.8　*GPS:* 44.96925/-108.62134　*Elev:* 4216　*Grid:* 35/1

Frannie　　*Type:* Town

MM: 257.0　*GPS:* 45.00033/-108.62252　*Elev:* 4265　*Grid:* 35/0

US-310/Wy-789 & US-14/16/20/Wy-789 & US-16/20/Wy-789 & US-20/Wy-789　　*Type:* Highway End

157 mi highway from **Montana** south to **Shoshoni**. The common highway that anchors the mile markers is **Wy-789**, which combines with **US-310** (**US-310/Wy-789**) heading southeast past **Lovell** to a junction with **US-14/16/20**, which heads west to **Cody**. At this junction **US-310** drops off and **Wy-789** converges with **US-14/16/20** (**US-14/16/20/Wy-789**) heading east. **US-14** drops off at **Greybull** (**US-16/20/Wy-789**) and **US-16** drops off at **Worland** (**US-20/Wy-789**). The highway continues south past **Thermopolis** to **Shoshoni**. Highlights include: **Museum of Flight and Aerial Firefighting**, **Devil's Kitchen Geological Site**, **Medicine Lodge State Archaeological Site**, **Hot Springs State Park**, **Wind River Canyon**, **Boysen State Park**.

Nearest Town: Frannie 2.2 S, Lovell 20.4 SE　*Directions:* S to Lovell from MM 257

US-212 (Beartooth Scenic Byway)   W/E

MM: 0.0/43.6 *GPS:* 45.00451/-110.01040 *Elev:* 7355 *Grid:* 15/0
US-212 (Beartooth Scenic Byway)   *Type:* Highway Description
43.6 mi highway east from the northeast entrance of **Yellowstone National Park**, briefly into **Montana**, across far northern **Wyoming**, and back into **Montana** on **Beartooth Pass**. This is a remote section of highway with only a single small town, **Cooke City, Montana**, and only a single highway junction to **Wy-296**, another remote highway with no towns. A return route through **Montana** back to **Wyoming** is detailed at the end of this chapter. The first 8.7 mi are through **Montana** before crossing back into **Wyoming** where the highway has no mile markers. Since the mile markers are inconsistent or non-existent, the mileages are provided starting from zero at each end. Some rivers and creeks have been included as points of reference. Highlights include: **Crazy Creek Falls, Lake Creek Falls, Clay Butte Fire Lookout, Beartooth Falls, Beartooth Pass.**
Nearest Town: Cooke City, MT 4.1 NE *Directions:* NE then SE from the northeast entrance of Yellowstone from MM 0
Notes: Disregard any mile markers on the Montana section of US-212.

MM: 0.0/43.6 *GPS:* 45.00451/-110.01040 *Elev:* 7355 *Grid:* 15/0
Yellowstone - Northeast Entrance to Tower-Roosevelt *(see chapter)*   *Type:* Hwy Junction w/Chapter
28.2 mi highway from the northeast entrance of **Yellowstone National Park**, via **US-212** in **Montana**, southwest to **Tower-Roosevelt**. A few minor points of interest along the way.
Nearest Town: Cooke City, MT 4.1 NE *Directions:* SW to Tower-Roosevelt from MM 0

MM: 4.1/39.6 *GPS:* 45.01973/-109.93369 *Elev:* 7580 *Grid:* 16/0
Cooke City, Montana   *Type:* Town

MM: 5.0/38.6 *GPS:* 45.02372/-109.91730 *Elev:* 7788 *Grid:* 16/-1 *Land:* NF
Soda Butte Campground: Montana   *Type:* Campground
A long, spread-out campground near **Soda Butte Creek** in 2 sections with end loops. The east section has 21 sites spread along the road. The west section toward the end of the road has 6 sites with better spacing but less shade and is closer to the highway. *Light conifer forest. 5 vault toilets. Good spacing between most sites. Parking areas not level.*
Crowds: *** *[FEE AREA]* *Road Desc:* Gravel *Directions:* 0.9 mi NE of Cooke City, MT; S side of hwy
Campsites: 27 *Shade:* ** *Privacy:* **** *RV Size:* 30' *Other:* Water GRIZZLIES

MM: 6.1/37.5 *Dist:* 0.1 *GPS:* 45.02691/-109.89509 *Elev:* 8044 *Grid:* 17/-1 *Land:* NF
Colter Campground: Montana   *Type:* Campground
The campground is composed of 2 sections. The first section is on the entrance road with 3 sites plus the camp host. Just beyond is a loop with 8 sites. The road continues with 6 private sites spread out along a 0.4 mi road with an end loop turnaround. *Patchy conifer forest, part of which is regenerating from fire. Many sites in the open.*
Crowds: *** *[FEE AREA]* *Directions:* 2.1 mi NE of Cooke City, MT; NE 0.1 mi
Campsites: 18 *Shade:* ** *Privacy:* *** *RV Size:* 30' *Other:* Water GRIZZLIES

MM: 7.5/36.2 *GPS:* 45.01858/-109.87291 *Elev:* 8040 *Grid:* 17/0 *Land:* NF
Chief Joseph Campground: Montana   *Type:* Campground
A small campground with 3 sites along the road and 3 in an end loop. The campground is close to the highway, but is blocked by thick forest. *Conifer forest. Good spacing between sites. Parking areas not level.*
Crowds: *** *[FEE AREA]* *Notes:* For reference, the official mile marker 7 is at the campground entrance.
Directions: 1.3 mi NW of the Montana State Line; SW side of hwy
Campsites: 6 *Shade:* *** *Privacy:* **** *RV Size:* 30' *Other:* Water GRIZZLIES

MM: 8.7/34.9 *GPS:* 45.00319/-109.85931 *Elev:* 7811 *Grid:* 17/0 *Land:* NF
Montana State Line (west)   *Type:* State Line

MM: 9.8/33.8 *Elev:* 7492
Index Creek   *Type:* Point of Reference
No sign, but there are guardrails and a rocky creek bed.

MM: 10.7/32.9 *Elev:* 7220
Fox Creek   *Type:* Point of Reference
No sign, but there are guardrails and a rocky creek bed.

MM: 11.4/32.3 *Dist:* 0.1 *GPS:* 44.97416/-109.83360 *Elev:* 7066 *Grid:* 17/1 *Land:* NF
Fox Creek Campground   *Type:* Campground
Some sites along the **Clarks Fork Yellowstone River**. *2 loops. Conifer forest. Roomy sites. Level. Expensive.*
Crowds: *** *[FEE AREA]* *Directions:* NE 0.1 mi
Campsites: 34 *Shade:* **** *Privacy:* **** *RV Size:* 40' *Other:* Water,Electric GRIZZLIES

MM: 13.2/30.4 *Elev:* 6930
Clarks Fork Yellowstone River   *Type:* River
No sign, but there are guardrails and a cobblestone river bed.

MM: 15.2/28.5 *Dist:* 0.1 *GPS:* 44.94296/-109.77349 *GPS2:* 44.94413/-109.77380 *Elev:* 6943 *Grid:* 18/1 *Land:* NF
Crazy Creek Falls   *Type:* Waterfall
An impressive cascade on **Crazy Creek** that thunders down the mountainside over granite slabs and boulders. Follow the **Crazy Lakes Trail** 0.1 mi north from the parking area to the base of the falls. Continuing another 0.15 mi and turning west about 100 yds leads to the top of the falls.
Cool Rating: **** *Crowds:* * *Time:* 30 min
Directions: Half-loop parking area on north side of hwy just west of the Crazy Creek Campground entrance. The campground also provides a trail to the falls.

MM: 15.2/28.4 *GPS:* 44.94237/-109.77279 *Elev:* 6920 *Grid:* 18/1 *Land:* NF
Crazy Creek Campground   *Type:* Campground
Near **Crazy Creek** and the **North Fork Yellowstone River**. A 250 yd trail leads to **Crazy Creek Falls** just northwest of the campground *(see previous section)*. Conifer forest on the edge of a meadow. Grass understory. Roomy private sites along the entrance road. End loop has less privacy. 2 pull-thrus.
Crowds: *** *[FEE AREA]* *Directions:* S side of hwy
Campsites: 15 *Shade:* ***** *Privacy:* *** *RV Size:* 30' *Other:* Water GRIZZLIES

MM: 16.8/26.8 *GPS:* 44.93221/-109.74513 *Elev:* 6943 *Grid:* 19/2 *Land:* NF
Index and Pilot Peaks Scenic Overlook   *Type:* Scenic Viewpoint
A half-loop pullout with a view northwest of **Index Peak** and **Pilot Peak**. A short path from the parking area leads to additional viewpoints.
Cool Rating: *** *Crowds:* * *Time:* 10 min *Notes:* The pullout is marked with a "Scenic Overlook" sign.
Directions: Pullout on the SW side of hwy

MM: 17.8/25.9 *GPS:* 44.93001/-109.72608 *Elev:* 7115 *Grid:* 19/2
Wy-296 (Chief Joseph Scenic Highway) *(see chapter)*   *Type:* Hwy Junction w/Chapter
46.2 mi highway from **US-212** southeast to **Wy-120**. The highway follows the route of the historic pursuit of **Chief Joseph** and the **Nez Perce Indians** by the **United States 7th Cavalry** in 1877. This is one of the most scenic highways in **Wyoming**. Highlights include: **Sunlight Gorge**, overlooks from **Dead Indian Pass**.
Nearest Town: Cooke City, MT 13.8 NW *Notes:* No towns or services. *Directions:* SE to Wy-120 from MM 0

MM: 17.8/25.9 *Dist:* 1.2 *GPS:* 44.92096/-109.70723 *Elev:* 6930 *Grid:* 19/2 *Land:* NF
Lake Creek Campground   *Type:* Campground
Located on a hillside near **Lake Creek**, which flows near the west side of the campground and is closest to the site at the end. *Dense conifer forest. Roomy sites. Not level. 2 sites close to highway.*
Crowds: ** *[FEE AREA]* *Notes:* A cattle grate on the highway clangs loudly as vehicles pass by.
Directions: SE on Wy-296 1.2 mi; NE side of hwy
Campsites: 6 *Shade:* ***** *Privacy:* **** *RV Size:* 20' *Other:* GRIZZLIES

MM: 19.0/24.6 *Dist:* 0.1 *GPS:* 44.92815/-109.70265 *GPS2:* 44.93001/-109.70329 *Elev:* 7450 *Grid:* 19/2 *Land:* NF
Lake Creek Falls and Historic Bridge   *Type:* Waterfall
Just north of the highway is the historic **Lake Creek Bridge** overlooking **Lake Creek Falls**. This beautiful waterfall plunges and cascades through a narrow, steep-walled granite channel. The bridge was constructed by the **Civilian Conservation Corps** (CCC) as part of the original road across the **Beartooth Plateau**. The bridge was in use from 1932 to 1974.
Cool Rating: **** *Crowds:* ** *Time:* 30 min
Directions: Park in a long pullout on the SW side of hwy just east of a long bridge on a curve. The falls are N 200 yds along a dirt path.

MM: 19.5/24.1 *GPS:* 44.92479/-109.69498 *Elev:* 7572 *Grid:* 19/2 *Land:* NF
Clarks Fork Overlook   *Type:* Scenic Viewpoint
A scenic view of the **Clarks Fork Yellowstone River** canyon. The river is **Wyoming**'s only designated **Wild and Scenic River**. Also visible is the aftermath of the 400,000 acre 1988 **Clover Mist Fire**, which originated in **Yellowstone National Park**. *Vault toilet.*
Cool Rating: ** *Crowds:* * *Time:* 5 min *Directions:* Large half-loop pullout on S side of hwy

MM: 24.5/19.1 *GPS:* 44.93260/-109.63853 *Elev:* 8755 *Grid:* 20/2 *Land:* NF
Pilot Index Overlook   *Type:* Scenic Viewpoint
A scenic overlook with panoramic views of the **Clarks Fork River Valley**, plus **Pilot Peak** and **Index Peak** of the **Absaroka Mountains** 12 mi west.
Cool Rating: *** *Crowds:* * *Time:* 10 min
Directions: Off a sharp west-facing curve in the hwy towards the bottom of Beartooth Pass; NW into loop parking area.

MM: 25.4/18.2 *Dist:* 2.6 *GPS:* 44.93711/-109.62223 *GPS2:* 44.94453/-109.62649 *Elev:* 9810 *Grid:* 20/2 *Land:* NF
Clay Butte Fire Lookout   *Type:* Fire Lookout
A forest road climbs 800 ft to an abandoned fire lookout, which is now staffed by volunteers and provides 360 degree panoramic views of the surrounding mountains and the **Beartooth Plateau**. Inside the lower section of the lookout are interpretive displays about the surrounding area and the 1988 wildfires.
Cool Rating: **** *Crowds:* * *Time:* 1 hr *Notes:* No trailers or RVs. *Road Desc:* Gravel, steep & winding
Directions: N on FR-2501 2.6 mi (the road has a large gravel entrance)

MM: 26.4/17.2 *GPS:* 44.93872/-109.60426 *GPS2:* 44.93685/-109.60243 *Elev:* 8862 *Grid:* 21/2 *Land:* NF
Beartooth Falls   *Type:* Waterfall
A 100 ft waterfall on **Beartooth Creek**. The falls are across the canyon about 300 yds southeast and are viewed from the edge of the road. The road past the falls viewpoint traverses a canyon with a mountain on one side and a guardrail on the other. Parking is in a small pullout on the mountain side. Read the directions carefully as the pullout is easy to miss.
Cool Rating: *** *Crowds:* * *Time:* 15 min
Notes: If you miss the pullout, turn around at the Clay Butte Lookout or the Beartooth Lake Campground.
Directions: Small pullout on a curve on the N (mountain) side of the hwy. Walk SW about 60 yds and cross the road. *Heading west* you will cross Beartooth Creek, pass through a cut in the mountain, and encounter a guardrail to the left. The pullout is 0.1 mi farther. *Heading east* you will encounter a steep cut in the mountainside. Shortly after the guardrail starts on the right. The pullout is 0.2 mi farther.

MM: 26.7/16.9 *Elev:* 8910
Beartooth Creek   *Type:* Point of Reference
The creek is wide and rocky on the outlet of **Beartooth Lake**. A nice rock and steel railed bridge crosses the creek.

MM: 26.9/16.7 *Dist:* 0.5 *GPS:* 44.94417/-109.58899 *Elev:* 8938 *Grid:* 21/1 *Land:* NF
Beartooth Lake Campground and Picnic Area   *Type:* Campground/Picnic Area
Near the east shore of **Beartooth Lake** at the base of **Beartooth Butte**. A picnic area and boat ramp are located at the entrance of the campground. *3 loops with no view of the lake. Loop C has 4 sites and is best for tents. Conifer forest. Roomy sites. 4 pull-thrus.*
Crowds: ***** *[FEE AREA]* *Road Desc:* Gravel *Directions:* NE 0.5 mi
Campsites: 21 *Shade:* **** *Privacy:* ** *RV Size:* 30' *Other:* Water GRIZZLIES

MM: 30.0/13.7 *Dist:* 0.2 *GPS:* 44.94069/-109.53799 *Elev:* 9530 *Grid:* 22/2 *Land:* NF
Island Lake Campground   *Type:* Campground
A high elevation campground south of **Island Lake** with good views of the **Beartooth Mountains**. The **Island Lake Trailhead** trails start from the north end of the campground *(see next section). 3 loops. Conifer forest on the edge of an alpine meadow. Loop C has a view of the lake. Most sites are roomy. 2 tent-only sites.*
Hours: Open around July 1 - Sept 15 *Crowds:* ***** *[FEE AREA]* *Directions:* N 0.2 mi
Campsites: 20 *Shade:* **** *Privacy:* *** *RV Size:* 30' *Other:* Water GRIZZLIES

MM: 30.0/13.7 *Dist:* 0.3 *GPS:* 44.94141/-109.53605 *Elev:* 9558 *Grid:* 22/2 *Land:* NF
Island Lake Trailhead   *Type:* Trailhead
The **Island Lake Trailhead** starts at the north end of the campground with day hikes north to 4 high mountain lakes as well as longer hikes to many other lakes.
1) **Island Lake** is just north of the campground, where the trail follows the west shore 1.0 mi to the north end. *Easy; 1.0 mi one-way; Level.*
2) **Night Lake** is 1/4 mi north of **Island Lake**, where the trail follows the west shore 1/2 mi to the north end. *Moderately easy; 1.75 mi one-way; Level.*
3) About 1.0 mi past **Night Lake** is a trail junction, where continuing straight leads 1.1 mi to **Becker Lake**, a long narrow lake in a rocky mountain valley. *Moderate; 3.75 mi one-way; 190 ft elev gain.*
4) Taking the left trail leads 0.3 mi to another trail junction, where turning left leads to **Beauty Lake**, situated in a rocky, forested bowl. *Moderate; 3.75 mi one-way; 180 ft elev gain, 260 ft elev loss.*
Cool Rating: **** *Crowds:* *****
Directions: N 0.2 mi; NE/R 0.1 mi to trailhead parking. Another parking area is at the boat ramp past the campground.

MM: 31.6/12.0 *Elev:* 9665
Long Lake   *Type:* Point of Reference
A nice rock and steel railed bridge crossing the marshy outlet of **Long Lake**.

MM: 37.3/6.3 *Dist:* 0.1 *GPS:* 44.96898/-109.47134 *Elev:* 10950 *Grid:* 23/1 *Land:* NF
Beartooth Pass Summit   *Type:* Pass
US-212 over **Beartooth Pass** is the highest paved primary road in **Wyoming**. From the summit south into **Wyoming** offers spectacular views and high mountain lakes.
Cool Rating: ***** *Crowds:* ** *Directions:* W 0.1 mi to parking area

MM: 43.6/0.0 *Dist:* 48.5 *GPS:* 45.00527/-109.40962 *Elev:* 10228 *Grid:* 23/0
Beartooth Pass to Wy-120 to Cody   *Type:* Highway Junction
US-212 enters **Montana** with no return route to **Wyoming** until reaching **Red Lodge, Montana** 23.6 mi north. This is part of a 48.5 mi route returning to **Wyoming** on **Wy-120**, which heads south to **Cody**. *See Wy-120 MM 137.5.*
Directions: Continue NE on US-212 23.6 mi to Red Lodge, MT; E on Mt-308 14.4 mi; S on Mt-72 10.5 mi to the Wyoming state line.

MM: 43.6/0.0 *GPS:* 45.00527/-109.40962 *Elev:* 10226 *Grid:* 23/0
End of Highway - Montana State Line   *Type:* Highway End
43.6 mi highway west from **Montana** on **Beartooth Pass**, across far northern **Wyoming**, and briefly through **Montana** to the northeast entrance of **Yellowstone National Park**. This is a remote section of highway with only a single small town, **Cooke City, Montana**, and only a single highway junction to **Wy-296**, another remote highway with no towns. The route to **Beartooth Pass** from the north is from the end of **Wy-120**. The majority of the route is through **Wyoming**, but the last 8.7 mi are through **Montana**. Since the mile markers are inconsistent or non-existent, the mileages are provided starting from zero at each end. Some rivers and creeks have been included as points of reference. Highlights include: **Beartooth Pass, Beartooth Falls, Clay Butte Fire Lookout, Lake Creek Falls, Crazy Creek Falls**.
Nearest Town: Red Lodge, MT 23.6 N *Directions:* SW from the Montana state line from MM 43.6

US-26 (I-25 to Nebraska)   W/E

MM: 0.0 *GPS:* 42.23303/-105.01450 *Elev:* 4917 *Grid:* 86/69
US-26 (I-25 to Nebraska)   *Type:* Highway Description
56.2 mi highway southeast from **I-25** exit 92 to **Nebraska**. Highlights include: **Guernsey State Park**, **Oregon Trail Ruts**, **Register Cliff**, **Fort Laramie National Historic Site**.
Nearest Town: Wheatland 12 S; Guernsey 14.2 E *Directions:* I-25 exit 92; E to Guernsey from MM 0

MM: 0.5 *GPS:* 42.23303/-105.01450 *Elev:* 4924 *Grid:* 86/69
Dwyer Junction Rest Area   *Type:* Rest Area
A beautifully landscaped rest area with picnic shelters, pet walk area, **RV dump**, and handicapped accessible facilities.
Directions: N side of hwy just before the I-25 entrance ramps.

MM: 14.4 *GPS:* 42.26970/-104.75873 *Elev:* 4376 *Grid:* 90/68
Guernsey State Park - Lakeshore Drive/Wy-317 *(see chapter)*   *Type:* Hwy Junction w/Chapter
9.5 mi highway north from **US-26 (I-25 to Nebraska)** into **Guernsey State Park** and along a winding road that follows the east shoreline of **Guernsey Reservoir** with 8 accessible campgrounds. Highlights include: **Guernsey Dam**, **Guernsey Museum**.
Nearest Town: Guernsey 0.6 E *Directions:* NW from MM 0
Notes: Some of the campgrounds and day use areas are marked with mile markers. However, these distances seem to be rounded down to the nearest half-mile, and therefore are not particularly accurate.

MM: 14.4 *Dist:* 0.9 *GPS:* 42.28156/-104.76874 *Elev:* 4523 *Grid:* 90/68
Guernsey State Park - South Entrance   *Type:* State Park
Guernsey State Park is a scenic area centered around **Guernsey Reservoir**, the last of 7 reservoirs on the **North Platte River**. The reservoir is situated in a sandstone canyon amid forested hills and bluffs. The park offers swimming, boating, waterskiing, camping, fishing, hiking, birdwatching, and picnicking. In the 1930s the **Civilian Conservation Corps** (CCC) built projects in the park, including hiking trails, roads, bridges, and buildings. Because of the excellent examples of CCC work the park was designated as a **National Historic Landmark** in 1997. Some believe the **Guernsey Museum** and **The Castle** are the finest examples of CCC work in the United States.

The park is quite popular through the 4th of July weekend after which the reservoir is drained to remove silt deposits and provide water for downstream irrigation demands. This process is known as "the silt run," and by around August 1 the reservoir is filled again. If visiting without a boat most of the points of interest are near the south entrance, including **Guernsey Dam**, the **Guernsey Museum**, **Brimmer Point**, and **The Castle**. Over 12 mi of trails are accessible from **Skyline Drive**. A trail sign is located at the turnoff to **Brimmer Point** or check with park personnel at the entrance station. The camping areas near the water are crowded when the water level is high. The best option for an overnight campground is **Skyline Drive Campground** near the south entrance. *See chapters on Guernsey State Park - Lakeshore Drive/Wy-317 and Guernsey State Park - Skyline Drive.*
Cool Rating: **** *Crowds:* **** *[FEE AREA]* *Directions:* NW on Wy-317 0.9 mi
Notes: This State Park offers a lot of scenery and attractions in addition to boating, whereas Glendo and Keyhole State Parks are primarily geared towards boating.

MM: 15.1 *GPS:* 42.26982/-104.74159 *Elev:* 4355 *Grid:* 90/68
Guernsey   *Type:* Town

MM: 15.3 *Dist:* 0.1 *GPS:* 42.26892/-104.74139 *Elev:* 4353 *Grid:* 90/68 *Land:* City
Guernsey Visitor Center and Museum   *Type:* Visitor Center
Visitor information and a small museum.
Hours: 9am - 7pm, Mon-Sat; noon - 4pm; Sun (Memorial Day - Labor Day) *Phone:* 307-836-2715
Directions: Toward the east end of town; S on S Wyoming Ave 1 block *(90 S Wyoming Ave)*

MM: 15.3 *Dist:* 0.9 *GPS:* 42.25668/-104.74276 *Elev:* 4329 *Grid:* 90/69 *Land:* City
Larson Park   *Type:* Campground
Camping in a municipal park with water, electricity, and a bathhouse. The park is next to a 9-hole golf course. 16 RV sites and plenty of tent space. *Some cottonwoods for shade.*
Crowds: *** *[FEE AREA]* *Notes:* The park is between the Oregon Trail Ruts and Register Cliff.
Directions: S on S Wyoming Ave 0.9 mi
Campsites: 16 *Shade:* ** *Privacy:* * *RV Size:* 40'+ *Other:* 307-836-2255,Water,Electric

MM: 15.3 *Dist:* 1.5 *GPS:* 42.25705/-104.74920 *Elev:* 4380 *Grid:* 90/69 *Land:* State
Oregon Trail Ruts   *Type:* Historic Site
Among the best preserved wagon ruts along the overland trail routes. Thousands of wagon wheels cut 5 ft deep ruts into solid rock as oxen strained to pull heavy wagons up the steep hillside out of the **North Platte River Valley**. A 1/3 mi concrete loop path starts at the northwest end of the parking area and affords a gradual climb counterclockwise to the trail ruts. The short and steep walk down passes several historical interpretive signs. Since almost all of the signs and information are on the east side of the loop trail, a more direct route is to start from the southeast end of the parking area. However, this climbs steeply with a 50 ft elevation gain in about 150 yds. This site was designated as a **National Historic Landmark** in 1975. A restroom is located in the parking area.
Cool Rating: **** *Crowds:* ** *Time:* 30 min *Directions:* S on S Wyoming Ave 0.8 mi; W 0.5 mi; S 0.2 mi.
Notes: The white monument just northwest of the entrance is the grave of Lucindy Rollins 1849-1934.

MM: 15.3 **Dist:** 3.0 **GPS:** 42.24739/-104.71215 **Elev:** 4335 **Grid:** 91/69 **Land:** State
Register Cliff   *Type:* Historic Site
The first of 3 famous landmarks where emigrants left inscriptions. A long soft sandstone cliff provided an excellent setting for carving names at this favored stopping point along the emigrant trails. A short trail at the base of the cliff leads past an interpretive sign to a fenced area where the most historically significant inscriptions have been preserved. Most of these were carved by emigrants during the 1840s and 1850s, although some were carved by trappers and traders as far back as 1829. A small trading post, which turned into a **Pony Express** stop and then into a stage station was also located here. A fenced-in pioneer cemetery is located off the northwest corner of the parking area next to a vault toilet. A **Pony Express** marker is located on the north side of the entrance road. *Located at mile 658 of the* **Oregon Trail**.
Cool Rating: *** *Crowds:* ** *Time:* 30 min
Notes: While there are thousands of inscriptions along the cliff face, I only located maybe a dozen from the 1800s with dates that are legible. The top of Independence Rock is far more impressive.
Directions: S on S Wyoming Ave/S Guernsey Rd 2.6 mi; E 0.4 mi to parking area. *S Guernsey Rd continues south 9.5 mi to the turnoff to Grayrocks Reservoir (see Wy-160/Grayrocks Rd/Power Plant Rd).*

MM: 16.6 **GPS:** 42.26491/-104.71951 **Elev:** 4384 **Grid:** 90/68
Wy-270   *Type:* Highway Junction
An alternate route to the north entrance of **Guernsey State Park**. If heading northeast to **Lusk**, this highway north combined with **US-18/20** east is 19.4 mi shorter than continuing southeast on **US-26 (I-25 to Nebraska)** and north on **US-85**.
Directions: **To Guernsey State Park north entrance**: N 4.5 mi to stop sign; W/L 0.8 mi; W/L on Lakeshore Dr 2.5 mi. **To Lusk**: N 4.5 mi to stop sign; W/L then N 34.9 mi to US-18/20; E/R 9.1 mi.

MM: 17.7 **GPS:** 42.26131/-104.69754 **Elev:** 4420 **Grid:** 91/68
Guernsey Rest Area & North Platte Valley Overlook   *Type:* Rest Area
A nice grassed rest area with covered picnic shelters. On the south side behind the restrooms is the **North Platte Valley Overlook** with 10 plaques and viewfinders pointing out historic sites that are visible from this point.
Cool Rating: ** *Crowds:* * *Time:* 15 min *Directions:* SW side of hwy

MM: 23.8 **GPS:** 42.24658/-104.58320 **Elev:** 4309 **Grid:** 92/69
Cheyenne-Black Hills Trail Monument   *Type:* Historical Marker
A stone monument that explains that the **Cheyenne-Black Hills Trail** passed near this point between 1876 and 1887. The road to the Dakota gold camps was constructed in violation of the **Fort Laramie Treaty** of 1868.
Cool Rating: * *Crowds:* * *Directions:* Pullout on NE side of hwy

MM: 27.9 **GPS:** 42.21292/-104.51935 **Elev:** 4240 **Grid:** 93/70
Wy-160/Grayrocks Rd/Power Plant Rd *(see chapter)*   *Type:* Hwy Junction w/Chapter
30.0 mi route from **US-26 (I-25 to Nebraska)** MM 27.9 at **Fort Laramie** southwest to **I-25** exit 80 at **Wheatland**. Highlights include: **Fort Laramie Bridge**, **Old Bedlam Ruts**, **Fort Laramie**, **Grayrocks Reservoir**.
Directions: W on Wy-160/CR-53/Grayrocks Rd from MM 0

MM: 27.9 **GPS:** 42.21292/-104.51935 **Elev:** 4240 **Grid:** 93/70
Fort Laramie   *Type:* Town

MM: 27.9 **Dist:** 0.2 **GPS:** 42.21041/-104.51800 **Elev:** 4232 **Grid:** 93/70 **Land:** City
Fort Laramie City Park   *Type:* Park
A city park that allows camping along the edge of a 0.1 mi long road on the south and west side of the park. *Cottonwoods near parking areas. Picnic shelters with grills. Playground. Donations appreciated.*
Crowds: * *Directions:* S on Laramie Ave 0.2 mi; W/R on dirt road on south side of park.
Notes: Sprinklers run in early morning. 2 blocks north of the park trains pass frequently blowing their horns. Hard-sided campers and ear plugs are recommended.
Campsites: Dispersed *Shade:* *** *Privacy:* ** *RV Size:* 40'+ *Other:* Water

MM: 38.3 **GPS:** 42.13698/-104.34746 **Elev:** 4173 **Grid:** 96/72 **Land:** City
Whipple Park   *Type:* Park
A nice park with 6 picnic tables under 3 shelters, restroom, playground, and a swimming pool.
Directions: 1 block W of the intersection of US-26/W 4th St and US-85/Main St; N on Freimuth Ave into parking area.

MM: 38.4 **GPS:** 42.13690/-104.34553 **Elev:** 4172 **Grid:** 96/72
Lingle   *Type:* Town

MM: 38.4 **GPS:** 42.13690/-104.34553 **Elev:** 4172 **Grid:** 96/72
US-85 *(see chapter)*   *Type:* Hwy Junction w/Chapter
153.5 mi section of **US-85** that starts at **Lingle** and parallels the **South Dakota state line** north before crossing into **South Dakota** at the end. Highlights include: **Redwood Water Tank**, **Red Butte**.
Directions: N to Lusk from MM 103.1

MM: 48.3 **GPS:** 42.06270/-104.18439 **Elev:** 4103 **Grid:** 98/73
Torrington   *Type:* Town

MM: 48.3 **GPS:** 42.06270/-104.18439 **Elev:** 4103 **Grid:** 98/73
US-85 *(see chapter)*   *Type:* Hwy Junction w/Chapter
76.1 mi section of **US-85** that starts at **Torrington** and parallels the **Nebraska state line** south to **I-25** exit 17. Highlights include: **Homesteaders Museum**, **Downar Bird Farm**, **Hawk Springs State Recreation Area**.
Directions: S to Cheyenne from MM 93.2

MM: 48.3 *Dist:* 0.8 *GPS:* 42.05785/-104.19024 *Elev:* 4086 *Grid:* 98/74 *Land:* City

Pioneer Park   *Type:* Park

A nice park that provides a public campground, which is located at the south end and includes designated parking areas plus an open area for RVs and tents. The campground is far enough away from the park to alleviate most noise, and nothing exists south of the campground except trees and the **North Platte River**. *Scraggly cottonwoods provide little shade. Ground is mowed weeds. 8 picnic tables. Donations appreciated, particularly for electricity use.*

Phone: 307-532-5666 *Crowds:* **

Directions: S on Main St/US-85 0.4 mi; W/R on W 14th Ave 0.3 mi; S/L on D St 0.1 mi.

Campsites: 12 *Shade:* * *Privacy:* * *RV Size:* 40' *Other:* Electric,RVDump

---

MM: 48.3 *Dist:* 1.0 *GPS:* 42.04791/-104.18392 *Elev:* 4085 *Grid:* 98/74 *Land:* City

Homesteaders Museum   *Type:* Museum

A museum located inside the historic **Union Pacific Depot**, which contains written records, photographs, and memorabilia of the ranching and homesteading history from 1882 through **World War II**. Other exhibits include the historic **Trout Cabin** built in 1910 and a **Union Pacific Gallery**. This area was populated by mass migration when the **U.S. Government** offered free land with a homesteading act.

Hours: 9:30am - 4pm, Mon - Wed; 9:30am - 7pm, Thurs & Fri; 12pm - 6pm, Saturday; (June 1 - Aug 28); 9:30am - 4pm, Mon-Fri (offseason) *Phone:* 307-754-9481 *Cool Rating:* ** *Crowds:* * *Time:* 1 hr *Directions:* S on Main St/US-85 1.0 mi; E side of hwy *(495 S Main St, Torrington)*

MM: 56.3 *GPS:* 42.00285/-104.05234 *Elev:* 4044 *Grid:* 100/75

End of Highway - Nebraska State Line   *Type:* Highway End

56.2 mi highway northwest from **Nebraska** to **I-25** exit 92. Highlights include: **Fort Laramie National Historic Site**, **Register Cliff**, **Oregon Trail Ruts**, **Guernsey State Park**.

Nearest Town: Torrington 8.2 NW *Directions:* NW to Torrington from MM 56.3

US-26/287 & US-26   NW/SE

MM: 0.0 *GPS:* 43.84002/-110.50993 *Elev:* 6733 *Grid:* 8/29
US-26/287 & US-26   *Type:* Highway Description
133.7 mi highway from **Moran Jct** southeast to **Riverton**. **US-287 (Lander to US-26)** splits off south at MM 98.8 and the highway continues southeast as **US-26**. Heading southeast to **Dubois** is along the **Centennial Scenic Byway**. Highlights include: **Breccia Cliffs**, **Wind River Lake**, **Pinnacle Buttes**, **Brooks Lake Creek Falls**, **Brooks Lake**, **Dubois Recreation Area Scenic Overlook**, colorful badlands, **Trail Lake Rd Petroglyphs**.
Nearest Town: Moose 18.3 SW; Dubois 55.6 SE *Directions:* SE to Dubois from MM 0

MM: 0.0 *GPS:* 43.84002/-110.50993 *Elev:* 6733 *Grid:* 8/29
US-89/191/287 *(see chapter)*   *Type:* Hwy Junction w/Chapter
27 mi highway from **Moran Jct** north through **Grand Teton National Park** to the south entrance of **Yellowstone National Park**. Highlights include: **Oxbow Bend**, views of **Jackson Lake** and the **Teton Range**.
Directions: N to Yellowstone NP from MM 0

MM: 0.0 *GPS:* 43.84002/-110.50993 *Elev:* 6733 *Grid:* 8/29
US-26/89/191 *(see chapter)*   *Type:* Hwy Junction w/Chapter
43.3 mi highway from **Moran Jct** south to **Hoback Jct**, where the highway transitions to **US-26/89** using sequential mile markers. The entire length is along the **Centennial Scenic Byway**. Highlights include: **Grand Teton National Park**, **Jackson Hole and Greater Yellowstone Visitor Center**, **Jackson**.
Directions: S to Jackson from MM 184.6

MM: 0.0 *GPS:* 43.84002/-110.50993 *Elev:* 6733 *Grid:* 8/29
Moran Jct   *Type:* Highway Junction
A named highway junction with no services.
Nearest Town: Moose 18.3 SW; Dubois 55.6 SE

MM: 2.1 *GPS:* 43.83909/-110.47013 *Elev:* 6820 *Grid:* 8/29 *Land:* NPS
Grand Teton National Park (east boundary)   *Type:* National Park
A pullout with a **Grand Teton National Park** sign, but no entrance station.
Directions: N side of hwy

MM: 3.5 *GPS:* 43.83831/-110.44330 *Elev:* 6835 *Grid:* 9/29
Buffalo Valley Rd/FR-30050 *(see chapter)*   *Type:* Hwy Junction w/Chapter
14.1 mi route that starts at **US-26/287** MM 3.5 and heads northeast to **Turpin Meadow Recreation Area** and **Turpin Meadow Ranch** before looping south back to **US-26/287** MM 13.0. The recreation area provides campgrounds, trailheads, and stock accommodations for access into the **Teton Wilderness** and to the site of the **Teton-Yellowstone Tornado**. Highlights include: **Box Creek Trail** to the site of the **Teton-Yellowstone Tornado**.
Directions: NE on Buffalo Valley Rd 9.9 mi; S on FR-30050 4.2 mi.

MM: 4.6 *GPS:* 43.83244/-110.42282 *Elev:* 6788 *Grid:* 9/29 *Land:* NF
Bridger-Teton National Forest   *Type:* National Forest Boundary

MM: 8.2 *Dist:* 0.1 *GPS:* 43.82451/-110.35538 *Elev:* 6875 *Grid:* 10/29 *Land:* NF
Hatchet Campground   *Type:* Campground
A small campground located just west of the **Black Rock Ranger Station**. This is the last public campground to the west before reaching **Grand Teton National Park**. *Conifer forest. 2 pull-thrus. Under-maintained.*
Crowds: * *[FEE AREA] Directions:* SW 70 yds
Campsites: 8 *Shade:* ** *Privacy:* * *RV Size:* 40' *Other:* Water GRIZZLIES

MM: 8.3 *GPS:* 43.82434/-110.35240 *Elev:* 6882 *Grid:* 10/29 *Land:* NF
Black Rock Ranger Station   *Type:* Visitor Center
Directions: S side of hwy

MM: 13.0 *GPS:* 43.81370/-110.26630 *Elev:* 7855 *Grid:* 11/30 *Land:* NF
Four Mile Meadows Picnic Area   *Type:* Picnic Area
A half-loop pullout with 3 picnic tables.
Crowds: * *Directions:* S side of hwy

MM: 13.0 *GPS:* 43.81405/-110.26580 *Elev:* 7852 *Grid:* 11/30
Buffalo Valley Rd/FR-30050 *(see chapter)*   *Type:* Hwy Junction w/Chapter
14.1 mi route that starts at **US-26/287** MM 13.0 and heads north to **Turpin Meadow Recreation Area** and **Turpin Meadow Ranch** before looping southwest back to **US-26/287** MM 3.5. The recreation area provides campgrounds, trailheads, and stock accommodations for access into the **Teton Wilderness** and to the site of the **Teton-Yellowstone Tornado**. Highlights include: **Box Creek Trail** to the site of the **Teton-Yellowstone Tornado**.
Directions: N on FR-30050 4.2 mi. SW on Buffalo Valley Rd 9.9 mi.

MM: 16.9 *Dist:* 0.1 *GPS:* 43.82120/-110.19388 *Elev:* 8695 *Grid:* 12/29 *Land:* NF
Togwotee Overlook   *Type:* Scenic Viewpoint
A nice distant view of the **Teton Range** to the west across the valley.
Cool Rating: *** *Crowds:* * *Time:* 10 min *Directions:* N 0.1 mi to large parking area

MM: 21.8 **GPS:** 43.77489/-110.11807 **Elev:** 9005 **Grid:** 13/31 **Land:** NF

Breccia Cliffs & Lost Lake   **Type:** Geological Feature

Eroded volcanic cliffs that rise 2,200 ft to the northeast. These cliffs are part of the southernmost portion of the **Absaroka Range**, which were formed by volcanic eruptions and sculpted by erosion and glaciation. The cliffs can be viewed from a dirt pullout on the southwest side of the highway or from a forest road on the other side 100 yds northwest.

For a better view of the **Breccia Cliffs**, the forest road leads 0.4 mi southeast to a closed 4WD road that heads north 1.2 mi to **Lost Lake**. This trail can be reached by continuing on the forest road by vehicle or by walking. Hike north 0.8 mi and keep right 0.4 mi to the lake. *Moderate; 1.2 mi one-way; 430 ft elev gain.*

Cool Rating: **** **Crowds:** *

Directions: Pullout on SW side of hwy or parking along the forest road on the NE side of hwy. A small Lost Lake sign is located at the forest road turnoff.

MM: 25.3 **GPS:** 43.75294/-110.06843 **Elev:** 9550 **Grid:** 14/31 **Land:** NF

Togwotee Pass   **Type:** Pass

This pass was named after a sub-chief under **Chief Washakie**, of the **Sheepeater** tribe, who led a **U.S. Government** exploratory expedition over this pass in 1873. The pass rises over the **Continental Divide** in the **Absaroka Mountains** between the sagebrush plains to the east and the forested valley to the west.

Cool Rating: * **Crowds:** * **Directions:** Pullout on W side of hwy

MM: 25.9 **GPS:** 43.74797/-110.05982 **Elev:** 9564 **Grid:** 14/31

Brooks Lake Rd/FR-515 (eastbound) *(see chapter)*   **Type:** Hwy Junction w/Chapter

9.5 mi road that begins at **US-26/287** MM 25.9, loops east past **Brooks Lake**, and returns to **US-26/287** MM 32.8. If traveling east, reaching **Brooks Lake** from this direction saves 7.3 mi, but the section of road to **Brooks Lake** is narrow and not recommended for RVs and trailers. **Brooks Lake** is situated in a beautiful valley surrounded by steep volcanic cliffs with 2 National Forest campgrounds, a trailhead, and a private lodge.

Directions: E then S on FR-515/Brooks Lake Rd past Wind River Lake from MM 9.5

MM: 25.9 **Dist:** 0.1 **GPS:** 43.74740/-110.05902 **Elev:** 9550 **Grid:** 14/31 **Land:** NF

Wind River Lake and Picnic Area   **Type:** Picnic & Scenic area

At the summit of **Togwotee Pass** next to **Wind River Lake**. Eroded, castle-like volcanic cliffs rise to the north 1,500 ft above this small lake, providing a nice photo opportunity. A handicapped accessible picnic site is next to the parking area and 2 private sites are up a hill overlooking the lake. Vault toilet.

Cool Rating: **** **Crowds:** *** **Time:** 15 min **Directions:** E 0.1 mi to parking area

MM: 30.9 **GPS:** 43.72049/-109.99252 **Elev:** 8590 **Grid:** 15/32 **Land:** NF

Pinnacle Buttes Viewpoint   **Type:** Scenic Viewpoint

Pinnacle Butte rises 2,900 ft to the northeast where it is grouped with other eroded volcanic cliffs and spires collectively known as the **Pinnacle Buttes**. These cliffs are part of the southernmost portion of the **Absaroka Range**, which were formed by volcanic eruptions and sculpted by erosion and glaciation.

Cool Rating: *** **Crowds:** * **Time:** 5 min **Directions:** Pullout on S side of hwy

MM: 32.3 **Dist:** 0.2 **GPS:** 43.70643/ 109.97060 **GPS2:** 43.70390/ 109.96749 **Elev:** 8310 **Grid:** 15/32 **Land:** NF

Brooks Lake Creek Falls   **Type:** Waterfall

A beautiful waterfall on **Brooks Lake Creek** that drops a short distance and then cascades through 2 tiers into a steep-sided gorge. A 1/4 mi trail leads to the first overlook above the falls. Continuing another 90 yds south provides a straight-on view from above. A picnic table is located at the trailhead parking area. *Easy; 0.3 mi one-way; Level.*

Cool Rating: **** **Crowds:** ** **Time:** 30 min **Road Desc:** Gravel

Directions: South 0.2 mi to parking area at the Falls Campground entrance.

MM: 32.3 **Dist:** 0.2 **GPS:** 43.70650/-109.97044 **Elev:** 8367 **Grid:** 15/32 **Land:** NF

Falls Campground   **Type:** Campground

A nice campground just west of **Brooks Lake Creek**, which meanders and drops over **Brooks Lake Creek Falls** *(see next section)* just south of Loop B. The **Pinnacle Buttes** are also visible northeast of the campground *(see previous section)*. The campground was renovated and modernized in 2008, including the addition of electricity in 20 sites in Loop A. Loop B has better shade and includes walk-in tent sites. All sites are handicapped accessible. *2 loops. Conifer forest. Good spacing between sites. Level. Several pull-thrus.*

Crowds: *** **[FEE AREA]** **Road Desc:** Gravel **Directions:** S 0.2 mi

Campsites: 54 **Shade:** *** **Privacy:** *** **RV Size:** 30' **Other:** Water,Electric

MM: 32.8 **GPS:** 43.70587/-109.96506 **Elev:** 8359 **Grid:** 16/32

Brooks Lake Rd/FR-515 (westbound) *(see chapter)*   **Type:** Hwy Junction w/Chapter

9.5 mi road that begins at **US-26/287** MM 32.8, loops north and west past **Brooks Lake**, and returns to **US-26/287** MM 25.9. If continuing west on **US-26/287**, completing the loop west past **Brooks Lake** saves 7.3 mi, but the road narrows and is not recommended for RVs and trailers. **Brooks Lake** is situated in a beautiful valley surrounded by steep volcanic cliffs with 2 National Forest campgrounds, a trailhead, and a private lodge.

Directions: N on FR-515 from MM 0

MM: 37.6 **GPS:** 43.64677/-109.92620 **Elev:** 7760 **Grid:** 16/34 **Land:** NF

Tie Hack Monument   **Type:** Historical Marker

A 14 ft tall limestone monument in memory of the **Tie Hacks**, the men who hand hewed railroad ties for building and maintaining the **Chicago and Northwestern Railroad** railway. From 1914 to 1947 the **Wyoming Tie and Timber Company** ran tie-cutting operations about 1.5 mi west of the monument. Mostly Scandinavian immigrants populated the logging camps and worked year-round. In the spring the ties were carried or floated down man-made flumes to the **Wind River**, which carried them nearly 100 mi to **Riverton**. A 0.1 mi half-loop path leads up a hill to the monument. Vault toilet *at east end of path.*

Cool Rating: * **Crowds:** * **Time:** 10 min **Directions:** SW side of hwy

MM: 38.2 **Dist:** 0.4 **GPS:** 43.63803/-109.91990 **Elev:** 7700 **Grid:** 16/34 **Land:** NF
Sheridan Creek Campground   **Type:** Campground
Primitive camping in a large open area. *Light conifer forest on the perimeter. Stone fire rings. Bear-proof boxes. Vault toilet.*
Crowds: *** **Road Desc:** Gravel **Directions:** SW on FR-532/Warm Springs Rd 0.4 mi
Campsites: Dispersed **Shade:** * **Privacy:** * **RV Size:** 40'+ **Other:** GRIZZLIES

MM: 40.7 **GPS:** 43.63005/-109.87061 **Elev:** 7620 **Grid:** 17/34
Shoshone National Forest   **Type:** National Forest Boundary

MM: 46.1 **GPS:** 43.59980/-109.78564 **Elev:** 7288 **Grid:** 18/35
Union Pass Rd *(see chapter)*   **Type:** Hwy Junction w/Chapter
44.6 mi route on National Forest and county roads that connect **US-26/287** south to **Wy-352/FR-10091**, in the **Upper Green River Valley**, by climbing over the 9,643 ft **Union Pass**. This drive offers nice scenery and a chance to see wildlife and wildflowers. The area is popular for ATVs and provides many dispersed camping opportunities. The north side of the pass offers great views across the valley to the northeast. This is the best route from **US-26/287** to the **Green River Lakes** area as it would be over 100 mi farther by taking the paved highways. Combined with **Wy-352/FR-10091**, this also saves 74 mi between **US-26/287** and **US-191**.
Nearest Town: Dubois 9.5 SE **Directions:** SW on Union Pass Rd from MM 44.6
Notes: This is a seasonal road and is typically open from July through September. I would only recommend this route for recreational purposes or travel between Wy-352 & US-26/287, as the road is fairly slow and the scenery is not that spectacular.

MM: 46.2 **GPS:** 43.59912/-109.78497 **Elev:** 7290 **Grid:** 18/35
Union Pass Monument   **Type:** Historical Marker
A memorial to the **Astorians** who passed over **Union Pass** on their way to the **Columbia River** in 1811.
Cool Rating: * **Crowds:** * **Time:** 5 min **Directions:** S side of hwy

MM: 54.4 **Dist:** 1.2 **GPS:** 43.54813/-109.64905 **Elev:** 7485 **Grid:** 20/36 **Land:** City
Dubois Recreation Area Scenic Overlook   **Type:** Scenic Viewpoint
A road climbs 600 ft to a flat-top butte that provides colorful panoramic views in all directions. To the north are red-hued badlands and the **Absaroka Mountains**. To the south is the town of **Dubois**, the **Wind River Valley**, and the **Wind River Mountains**.
Cool Rating: **** **Crowds:** * **Time:** 20 min **Notes:** No large RVs or trailers. **Road Desc:** Gravel, narrow & steep
Directions: NE at the Recreation Area Scenic Overlook sign 1.2 mi

MM: 54.8 **GPS:** 43.53690/-109.64454 **Elev:** 6942 **Grid:** 20/37
National Bighorn Sheep Interpretive Center   **Type:** Visitor Center
A visitor center dedicated to educating the public about the biological needs of the **Rocky Mountain Bighorn Sheep** and to encouraging the active stewardship of wildlife and wildlands. The "Grand Slam" diorama displays full-sized mounts of the 4 types of wild sheep found in North America. Learn about these sheep with hands-on displays. Additional information about **Bighorn Sheep** is located around the outside of the building. The **Whiskey Basin Wildlife Habitat Management Area**, 8 mi southeast, is home to the largest herd of **Bighorn Sheep** in the world *(see Trail Lake Rd at MM 59.3)*.
Cool Rating: ** **Crowds:** * **[FEE AREA]** **Notes:** A nice shady park with picnic tables is located next to the center.
Directions: SW on Bighorn Ln 200 ft *(907 West Ramshorn, Dubois)*

MM: 55.5 **Dist:** 10.5 **GPS:** 43.66544/-109.63623 **Elev:** 7680 **Grid:** 20/33 **Land:** NF
Horse Creek Campground   **Type:** Campground
Along **Horse Creek** in the foothills of the **Absaroka Mountains**. *Light conifer forest. Good spacing. Level.*
Crowds: *** **[FEE AREA]** **Notes:** Sites near road get dust from passing traffic. **Directions:** N on Horse Creek Rd 10.5 mi
Road Desc: Partially paved, rough spots. First 3.8 mi is paved.
Campsites: 9 **Shade:** ** **Privacy:** *** **RV Size:** 40' **Other:** Water

MM: 55.6 **GPS:** 43.53368/-109.63091 **Elev:** 6936 **Grid:** 20/37
Dubois   **Type:** Town

MM: 57.8 **GPS:** 43.48201/-109.50074 **Elev:** 6920 **Grid:** 22/38
Colorful Badlands Area (heading southeast)   **Type:** Scenic Area
The next 4.8 mi southeast from **Dubois** pass colorful badlands on the northeast side of the highway.
Cool Rating: ***

MM: 59.3 **GPS:** 43.51340/-109.56840 **Elev:** 6842 **Grid:** 21/37
Trail Lake Rd/CR-411 *(see chapter)*   **Type:** Hwy Junction w/Chapter
9.1 mi gravel road south through the **Whiskey Basin Wildlife Habitat Management Area** and ending at the **Torrey Creek Trailhead**. Along the route are 3 lakes, 5 campgrounds, and 2 spectacular **Petroglyphs**. The WHMA provides **Bighorn Sheep** winter and spring habitat, and the trailhead provides hiking into the **Wind River Range**.
Directions: S and immediately left at the fork

MM: 59.3 **Dist:** 1.3 **GPS:** 43.49912/-109.58494 **Elev:** 6920 **Grid:** 21/38 **Land:** Wyoming G & F
Dubois State Fish Hatchery   **Type:** Fish Hatchery
The fish hatchery was originally constructed in the early 1930s. Hatchery operations were abandoned in 1937 and a new facility was constructed in 1940. The concrete raceways and 2 dirt rearing ponds support rainbow, cutthroat, and brown trout. The incubators handle several million eggs each year. Visitors are welcome.
Hours: 8am - 5pm **Phone:** 307-455-2431 **Cool Rating:** ** **Crowds:** * **Time:** 30 min **Road Desc:** Gravel
Directions: S and immediately right at the fork to head SW on Fish Hatchery Rd 1.3 mi

MM: 63.6 **GPS:** 43.48201/-109.50074 **Elev:** 6574 **Grid:** 22/38
Colorful Badlands Area (heading northwest)   **Type:** Scenic Area
The next 4.8 mi northwest to **Dubois** pass colorful badlands on the northeast side of the highway.
Cool Rating: ***

MM: 90.0 **GPS:** 43.27338/-109.11618 **Elev:** 5958 **Grid:** 28/43
Crowheart Butte Historical Marker   **Type:** Historical Marker
Crowheart Butte is 2.5 mi northeast of the pullout. The site was named for **Chief Washakie**, the Shoshone Indian chief who displayed a Crow Indian heart on his lance after a victory in a battle against the Crow Indians.
Cool Rating: * **Crowds:** * **Time:** 5 min **Directions:** Pullout on SW side of hwy

MM: 96.4 *GPS:* 43.22962/-109.00825 *Elev:* 5745 *Grid:* 29/44
Diversion Dam Rest Area *Type:* Rest Area
A nice grassed rest area with covered picnic shelters.
Directions: SW side of hwy

MM: 98.8 *GPS:* 43.21335/-108.96864 *Elev:* 5664 *Grid:* 30/45
US-287 (Lander to US-26) *(see chapter)* *Type:* Hwy Junction w/Chapter
31.6 mi highway southeast from **US-26** to **Lander**. Highlights include: **Sacajawea's Grave**.
Nearest Town: Fort Washakie 15.9 S *Directions:* SE to Lander from MM 31.6

MM: 114.6 *GPS:* 43.15571/-108.69511 *Elev:* 5428 *Grid:* 34/46
Wy-134 & Wy-133 *(see chapter)* *Type:* Hwy Junction w/Chapter
28.3 mi on 2 highways from **US-26** north and east to **US-26/Wy-789**, which heads northeast to **Shoshoni**. If traveling east between **Dubois** and **Shoshoni**, this route is 4.7 mi shorter than continuing through **Riverton** and offers 3 primitive campgrounds on the north side of **Ocean Lake**.
Nearest Town: Riverton 19.1 SE *Directions:* N on Wy-133 4.1 mi; E on Wy-134 24.2 mi.

MM: 115.5 *Dist:* 3.0 *GPS:* 43.17126/-108.64450 *Elev:* 5251 *Grid:* 34/46 *Land:* Bureau of Reclamation
Ocean Lake Wildlife Habitat Management Area - Lindholm *Type:* Wildlife Habitat Mgmt Area
Primitive camping 260 yds west of the southwest shore of **Ocean Lake**. The area has no established campsites or parking areas. It is located at the junction of **Long Point Rd** and the road to **Long Point Campground**, which is 1.8 mi farther and a better camping option *(see next section). Some trees. Vault toilet.*
Crowds: * *Nearest Town:* Kinnear 3.3 SW
Directions: N on Kinnear Spur Rd 0.8 mi; E/R on Angler Rd 1.0 mi; N/L on Gabes Rd 0.5 mi; E/R on Long Point Rd 0.7 mi;
Campsites: Dispersed *Shade:* * *Privacy:* * *RV Size:* 30' *Other:* None

MM: 115.5 *Dist:* 3.2 *GPS:* 43.16581/-108.63795 *Elev:* 5244 *Grid:* 35/46 *Land:* Bureau of Reclamation
Ocean Lake Wildlife Habitat Management Area - South Cove *Type:* Wildlife Habitat Mgmt Area
Lake access and a treeless primitive camping on the southwest shore of **Ocean Lake**. The access road heads south 0.2 mi to a lake access area. *Vault toilet. Primitive boat ramp.* The road then curves right 1/4 mi, paralleling the lakeshore and passing a half-loop pullout (with a grill) before reaching a large parking area. *Group shelter. Vault toilet. Handicapped accessible picnic shelter and fishing pier.*
Crowds: * *Nearest Town:* Kinnear 3.2 SW
Directions: N on Kinnear Spur Rd 0.8 mi; E/R on Angler Rd 2.0 mi; N/L 0.4 mi.
Campsites: Dispersed *Shade:* * *Privacy:* * *RV Size:* 30' *Other:* None

MM: 115.5 *Dist:* 4.9 *GPS:* 43.17598/-108.61642 *Elev:* 5243 *Grid:* 35/46 *Land:* Bureau of Reclamation
Ocean Lake Wildlife Habitat Management Area - Long Point *Type:* Wildlife Habitat Mgmt Area
Lake access and an established campground on a long and narrow peninsula that extends almost to the center of the west side of **Ocean Lake**. *No trees. 9 sheltered tables with grills. Stone fire rings. Vault toilet. Boat ramp.*
Crowds: ** *Nearest Town:* Kinnear 5.2 SW
Directions: N on Kinnear Spur Rd 0.8 mi; E/R on Angler Rd 1.0 mi; N/L on Gabes Rd 0.5 mi; E/R on Long Point Rd 0.7 mi; NE past Lindholm Campground 1.9 mi.
Campsites: Dispersed *Shade:* * *Privacy:* * *RV Size:* 30' *Other:* None

MM: 133.7 *GPS:* 43.02463/-108.38063 *Elev:* 4952 *Grid:* 38/49
Riverton *Type:* Town

MM: 133.7 *GPS:* 43.02463/-108.38063 *Elev:* 4952 *Grid:* 38/49
Wy-789 & US-26/Wy-789 *(see chapter)* *Type:* Hwy Junction w/Chapter
46.2 mi highway from **Lander** northeast to **Shoshoni**. The highway heads northeast from **Lander** as **Wy-789** continuing the mile markers from **US-287/Wy-789**. After 24.1 mi the highway combines with **US-26** and continues northeast 22.1 mi to **Shoshoni** as **US-26/Wy-789**. Highlights include: access to **Castle Gardens**, **Wyoming Heritage Trail**.
Directions: N to Shoshoni or S to Lander from MM 105.2

MM: 133.7 *GPS:* 43.02463/-108.38063 *Elev:* 4952 *Grid:* 38/49
US-26 & US-26/287 *Type:* Highway End
133.7 mi highway from **Riverton** northwest to **Moran Jct**. **US-26** merges with **US-287 (Lander to US-26)** at MM 98.8 and continues northwest as **US-26/287**. This is a primary access route to **Grand Teton National Park** and **Yellowstone National Park**. Heading northwest between **Dubois** and **Moran Jct** is along the **Centennial Scenic Byway**. Highlights include: **Trail Lake Rd Petroglyphs**, colorful badlands, **Dubois Recreation Area Scenic Overlook**, **Brooks Lake**, **Brooks Lake Creek Falls**, **Pinnacle Buttes**, **Wind River Lake**, **Breccia Cliffs**.
Directions: NW to Dubois from MM 133.7

MM: 118.3 *GPS:* 43.17220/-111.01850 *Elev:* 5660 *Grid:* 1/46
US-26/89   *Type:* Highway Description
23 mi highway from **US-89** at **Alpine Jct** northeast to **Hoback Jct** through the **Snake River Canyon**. The mile markers continue sequentially from **US-89** at **Alpine Jct**. No highlights along this route, but there are 4 National Forest campgrounds.
Nearest Town: Alpine 0.6 S *Notes:* Camping in designated campgrounds only. *Directions:* NE to Hoback Jct from MM 118.3

MM: 118.3 *GPS:* 43.17220/-111.01850 *Elev:* 5660 *Grid:* 1/46
US-89 *(see chapter)*   *Type:* Hwy Junction w/Chapter
62.4 mi highway from **US-26/89** at **Alpine Jct**, roughly paralleling the **Idaho** state line south to **Idaho**. The mile markers continue sequentially from **US-26/89**. Highlights include: **Intermittent Spring**, the **World's Largest Elk Antler Arch**.
Nearest Town: Alpine 0.6 S *Directions:* S to Alpine from MM 118.3

MM: 118.3 *Dist:* 2.1 *GPS:* 43.19708/-111.04099 *Elev:* 5694 *Grid:* 0/45 *Land:* NF
Alpine Campground   *Type:* Campground
Composed of 2 loops on the southeast side of the **Palisades Reservoir** just east of the **Idaho** state line. The second loop is considered an overflow area. The campground is popular for whitewater rafters from the **Snake River Canyon**. *Mixed forest. Heavy understory. Roomy sites. Tent pads. Some highway noise.*
Crowds: *** *Nearest Town:* Alpine 2.7 SE *[FEE AREA]* *Directions:* NW on US-26 2.1 mi; SW side of hwy.
Campsites: 22 *Shade:* **** *Privacy:* **** *RV Size:* 30' *Other:* 1-877-444-6777:www.recreation.gov,Water

MM: 124.8 *GPS:* 43.19834/-110.90341 *Elev:* 5820 *Grid:* 2/45 *Land:* NF
Wolf Creek Campground   *Type:* Campground
Just above the highway on a hill at the southern base of the **Snake River Range**. *3 loops. 2 loops close to highway. No shade. Good spacing between sites. 8 pull-thrus in lower loops.*
Crowds: * *[FEE AREA]* *Directions:* N side of hwy
Campsites: 20 *Shade:* * *Privacy:* ** *RV Size:* 40'+ *Other:* Water BEARS

MM: 128.6 *GPS:* 43.20514/-110.83453 *Elev:* 5800 *Grid:* 3/45 *Land:* NF
Station Creek Campground   *Type:* Campground
Located on a ridge above the **Snake River**, but with no direct access to the river. The campground consists of 2 sections. The right section has wider and shorter parking areas and less understory for privacy. *Conifer forest. Roomy sites. Highway noise.*
Crowds: ***** *[FEE AREA]* *Notes:* A group camp is located on the north side of the highway. *Directions:* S side of hwy
Campsites: 15 *Shade:* ***** *Privacy:* *** *RV Size:* 40' *Other:* 1-877-444-6777:www.recreation.gov,Water BEARS

MM: 129.3 *GPS:* 43.20740/-110.82082 *Elev:* 5775 *Grid:* 3/45
West Table Boat Ramp and Picnic Area   *Type:* Boat Ramp
A large area along the **Snake River** with a boat ramp, float launch, and picnic area on the west end.
Notes: The picnic area is rather buggy and not particularly inviting. *Directions:* SE side of hwy

MM: 130.1 *GPS:* 43.21287/-110.80766 *Elev:* 5810 *Grid:* 4/45 *Land:* NF
East Table Creek Campground   *Type:* Campground
Located between the highway and the **Snake River** with some sites overlooking the river. The campground provides carry-down access for rafts and kayaks. *Single loop. Conifer forest. Good spacing between sites except those close to river. 5 pull-thrus.*
Crowds: *** *[FEE AREA]* *Notes:* Overflow parking across the highway. *Directions:* S side of hwy
Campsites: 17 *Shade:* *** *Privacy:* *** *RV Size:* 30' *Other:* Water BEARS

MM: 141.3 *GPS:* 43.32292/-110.73040 *Elev:* 5940 *Grid:* 5/42
Hoback Jct   *Type:* Town

MM: 141.3 *GPS:* 43.32292/-110.73040 *Elev:* 5940 *Grid:* 5/42
US-26/89/191 *(see chapter)*   *Type:* Hwy Junction w/Chapter
43.3 mi highway from **Hoback Jct** north to **Moran Jct**. The highway then connects to **US-89/191/287**, using sequential mile markers, and continues 27 mi to **Yellowstone National Park**. The entire length is along the **Centennial Scenic Byway**. Highlights include: **Jackson**, **Jackson Hole and Greater Yellowstone Visitor Center**, **Grand Teton National Park**.
Notes: The highway section between Hoback Jct and Jackson might be referred to as US-26/89/189/191.
Directions: N to Jackson from MM 141.3

MM: 141.3 *GPS:* 43.32292/-110.73040 *Elev:* 5940 *Grid:* 5/42
US-189/191 *(see chapter)*   *Type:* Hwy Junction w/Chapter
53.1 mi highway southeast from **Hoback Jct** to the transition with **US-191** and junction with **US-189**. The mile markers continue sequentially to **US-191**. Highlights include: **Hoback Canyon**, **Stinking Springs**, **Granite Falls**, **Granite Hot Springs**.
Nearest Town: Jackson 13.2 N *Directions:* SE to Pinedale from MM 163.6

MM: 141.3 *GPS:* 43.32292/-110.73040 *Elev:* 5940 *Grid:* 5/42
End of Highway   *Type:* Highway End
23 mi highway from **Hoback Jct** southwest to **Alpine Jct** through the **Snake River Canyon**. The mile markers continue sequentially from **US-26/89/191** at **Hoback Jct**. No highlights along this route, but there are 4 National Forest campgrounds.
Nearest Town: Jackson 13.2 N *Directions:* SW to Alpine from MM 141.3

MM: 141.3 *GPS:* 43.32292/-110.73040 *Elev:* 5940 *Grid:* 5/42
US-26/89/191   *Type:* Highway Description
43.3 mi highway from **Hoback Jct** north to **Moran Jct**. The highway then connects to **US-89/191/287**, using sequential mile markers, and continues 27 mi to **Yellowstone National Park**. The entire length is along the **Centennial Scenic Byway**. Highlights include: **Jackson** (the only town between Hoback Jct and Yellowstone), **Jackson Hole and Greater Yellowstone Visitor Center**, **Grand Teton National Park**.
Notes: The highway section between Hoback Jct and Jackson might be referred to as US-26/89/189/191.
Directions: N to Jackson from MM 141.3

MM: 141.3 *GPS:* 43.32292/-110.73040 *Elev:* 5940 *Grid:* 5/42
US-26/89 *(see chapter)*   *Type:* Hwy Junction w/Chapter
23 mi highway from **Hoback Jct** southwest to **Alpine Jct** through the **Snake River Canyon**. The mile markers continue sequentially from **US-26/89/191** at Hoback Jct. No highlights along this route, but there are 4 National Forest campgrounds.
Nearest Town: Jackson 13.2 N *Notes:* Camping in designated campgrounds only. *Directions:* SW to Alpine from MM 141.3

MM: 141.3 *GPS:* 43.32292/-110.73040 *Elev:* 5940 *Grid:* 5/42
US-189/191 *(see chapter)*   *Type:* Hwy Junction w/Chapter
53.1 mi highway southeast from **Hoback Jct** to the transition with **US-191** and junction with **US-189**. The mile markers continue sequentially to **US-191**. Highlights include: **Hoback Canyon**, **Stinking Springs**, **Granite Falls**, **Granite Hot Springs**.
Nearest Town: Jackson 13.2 N *Directions:* SE to Pinedale from MM 163.6

MM: 141.3 *GPS:* 43.32292/-110.73040 *Elev:* 5940 *Grid:* 5/42
Hoback Jct   *Type:* Town

MM: 153.1 *GPS:* 43.47349/-110.78848 *Elev:* 6160 *Grid:* 4/38
Wy-22 *(see chapter)*   *Type:* Hwy Junction w/Chapter
17.7 mi highway from **Jackson** west over **Teton Pass** and northwest to **Idaho**. The highway transitions to **Id-33** in **Idaho**, which is the route to **Cave Falls** and **Bechler Falls** in **Yellowstone National Park**, **Upper Mesa Falls** and **Lower Mesa Falls** in **Idaho**, and ending at the west entrance of **Yellowstone National Park**. Other highlights include: hiking and biking around **Teton Pass**.
Directions: NW to Wilson from MM 0

MM: 154.1 *Dist:* 0.9 *GPS:* 43.47252/-110.76116 *Elev:* 6245 *Grid:* 4/38 *Land:* City
Snow King Mountain   *Type:* Scenic Area
Hike, bike, or take the chairlift up 1,670 ft to the top of **Snow King Mountain** for great views of the **Teton Range**, **Jackson**, and **Jackson Hole**. A short nature trail is located on the top of the mountain. Other activities include an alpine slide and horseback riding.
Hours: Chairlift: 9am - 6pm (May 24 - June 20 & Aug 18 - Sept 7); 9am - 8pm (June 21 - Aug 17) *Phone:* 307-733-5200
[FEE AREA]
Directions: (0.4 mi W of the town square) S on Flat Creek Dr 0.4 mi; E/L on W Snow King Ave 0.4 mi; S/R on S Cache Dr 0.1 mi (past ball field); Left into parking area.

MM: 154.4 *GPS:* 43.47960/-110.76504 *Elev:* 6226 *Grid:* 4/38
Truck Route (northbound)   *Type:* Highway Junction
Take the truck route north on N Millward St to avoid congestion in the center of **Jackson**.

MM: 154.5 *GPS:* 43.47958/-110.76236 *Elev:* 6239 *Grid:* 4/38
Jackson   *Type:* Town
The town square is located on the northeast corner in the center of town at the intersection of Broadway and N Cache Dr. This shady park has elk antler arches at all 4 corners, benches, and a cowboy statue in the middle. The square is the center of a popular area with bars, restaurants, shops, and art galleries.
Crowds: *****
Notes: This area is quite congested and can be avoided by taking the truck route *(see sections above and below)*.

MM: 154.5 *Dist:* 8.2 *GPS:* 43.51385/-110.66113 *Elev:* 7055 *Grid:* 6/37 *Land:* NF
Curtis Canyon Campground   *Type:* Campground
East of **Jackson** on the side of a mountain. One site has a good view of the **Teton Range**, but the rest are in the trees. The **Curtis Canyon Overlook** provides a nice view of the **Teton Range** and is located on the north side of the road just before the campground. *Conifer forest. Grass understory. Small sites. 2 tent-only sites. 2 pull-thrus.*
Crowds: *** *Nearest Town:* Jackson 8.2 SW *[FEE AREA]* *Road Desc:* Gravel. Last 2.6 mi are narrow, rough and rocky.
Directions: At the intersection of W Broadway Ave and N Cache Dr, at the center of town; E on E Broadway Ave 1.0 mi; NE/L on Elk Refuge Rd 3.6 mi; N/L to stay on National Elk Refuge Rd 1.0 mi; E/R on Sheep Creek Rd 2.6 mi.
Campsites: 12 *Shade:* ***** *Privacy:* * *RV Size:* 20' *Other:* Water BEARS

MM: 154.8 *GPS:* 43.48337/-110.76238 *Elev:* 6219 *Grid:* 4/38
Truck Route (southbound)   *Type:* Highway Junction
Take the truck route west on Mercill Ave to avoid congestion in the center of **Jackson**.

MM: 154.9 *GPS:* 43.48596/-110.76197 *Elev:* 6215 *Grid:* 4/38
Jackson Hole and Greater Yellowstone Visitor Center   *Type:* Visitor Center
This sod-roofed visitor center is located in the heart of the **Greater Yellowstone Ecosystem** and is staffed by representatives from multiple government agencies and private organizations. Inside are wildlife dioramas and museum displays highlighting the local flora, fauna, and geology of this ecosystem, as well as an extensive book and gift store. On the outside is a wildlife observation deck with an overlook of the **National Elk Refuge**. A large open space with a picnic area is located on the north side of the visitor center.
Hours: 8am - 7pm (Memorial Day - Sept 30); 9am - 5pm (offseason) *Cool Rating:* *** *Crowds:* *****
Directions: E side of hwy (4 blocks north of Broadway) *(532 N Cache Dr, Jackson)*

MM: 158.8   **GPS:** 43.53851/-110.73660   **Elev:** 6363   **Grid:** 5/37   **Land:** NPS
Grand Teton National Park (south boundary)   **Type:** National Park
A **Grand Teton National Park** entrance sign with no pullout or entrance station. The entrance fee is charged when entering through the **Moose Entrance** or the **Buffalo Entrance**. *See chapter: Grand Teton National Park.*

MM: 161.3   **GPS:** 43.57412/-110.73322   **Elev:** 6404   **Grid:** 5/36
Gros Ventre Rd/FR-30400 *(see chapter)*   **Type:** Hwy Junction w/Chapter
19.9 mi scenic drive east from **US-26/89/191** MM 161.3 through the **Gros Ventre River** valley (pronounced "gro-vont"). The first half is in **Grand Teton National Park** and then crosses into the **Bridger-Teton National Forest** on **FR-30400**. For this book the route ends at **Crystal Creek Campground**, even though the road actually continues another 17 mi. 4 public campgrounds are located along the route; however, only the National Park campground is close to **US-26/89/191**. Highlights include: **Kelly Warm Spring**, **Gros Ventre Slide Geological Area**, **Red Hills**.
Nearest Town: Jackson 6.8 S   *Directions:* E on Gros Ventre Rd from MM 0

MM: 165.5   **GPS:** 43.63349/-110.71720   **Elev:** 6504   **Grid:** 5/34   **Land:** NPS
Albright View Turnout   **Type:** Scenic Viewpoint
The farthest south of 6 designated pullouts offering panoramic views of the **Teton Range**. An interpretive sign provides information on the creation and expansion of **Grand Teton National Park** with the help of the **Superintendent of Yellowstone National Park**, **Horace Albright** and philanthropist **John D. Rockefeller, Jr.**, who kept the park idea alive and helped make it become a reality in the face of opposition. The next 3 pullouts to the north provide better views of the **Teton Range**.
Cool Rating: ***   *Crowds:* *   *Time:* 10 min   *Directions:* W side of hwy

---

MM: 166.8   **GPS:** 43.65090/-110.70767   **Elev:** 6509   **Grid:** 5/34
Teton Park Rd: Grand Teton National Park *(see chapter)*   **Type:** Hwy Junction w/Chapter
20.8 mi road north through the main section of **Grand Teton National Park**, which traverses the central-eastern base of the **Teton Range** and offers the closest access and views. Highlights include: the **Craig Thomas Discovery and Visitor Center**, **Chapel of the Transfiguration and Menor's Ferry Historic District**, **Jenny Lake**, **Hidden Falls**, **Inspiration Point**, **Signal Mountain**, **Jackson Lake**.
Nearest Town: Moose 0.5 W; Jackson 12.3 S   *Directions:* NW from MM 0
Notes: If traveling north and taking Teton Park Rd, several scenic overlooks will be missed. An alternative is to continue to the Teton View Overlook, Snake River Overlook, and perhaps Cunningham Cabin before returning to Teton Park Rd.

MM: 167.7   **GPS:** 43.66140/-110.69788   **GPS2:** 43.63564/-110.69160   **Elev:** 6541   **Grid:** 5/33   **Land:** NPS
Blacktail Butte Trailhead: Grand Teton National Park   **Type:** Trailhead
A prominent butte rising 1100 ft above the **Jackson Hole** valley. Trailheads from opposite sides of the mountain meet at the 7,686 ft summit, offering great views of the **Teton Range** and the surrounding valley. The hike traverses grassland, sagebrush, wildflower meadows, pine and aspen forest, and rock outcroppings. *From US-26/89/191: Moderate; 4.0 mi round-trip; 1085 ft elev gain; From Gros Ventre Rd: Moderate; 5.3 mi round-trip; 1145 ft elev gain.*
Cool Rating: ****   *Crowds:* *   *Time:* 2-3 hrs   *Directions:* Parking area on SE side of hwy

---

MM: 168.0   **Dist:** 1.6   **GPS:** 43.66519/-110.66460   **Elev:** 6614   **Grid:** 6/33   **Land:** NPS
Mormon Row   **Type:** Historic Site
A row of well-preserved homes and barns of early settlers, which have stood for nearly a century. Just north of the intersection of **Antelope Flats Rd** and **Mormon Row** is a parking area with a brochure describing the history of **Mormon Row** and identifying 7 buildings. Several buildings are located in this area, 3 of which are described in the brochure. Heading south 0.6 mi on **Mormon Row** are several more buildings, 4 from the brochure. The surrounding open fields are home to herds of grazing bison in the summer, which are often seen close to or on the road. **Mormon Row** continues south 2.8 mi to **Gros Ventre Rd**, just northeast of **Gros Ventre Campground**.
Cool Rating: **   *Crowds:* *   *Time:* 30-60 min   *Directions:* E on Antelope Flats Rd 1.6 mi
Road Desc: Partially paved. Antelope Flats Rd is paved. Mormon Row is washboarded gravel.

MM: 168.0   **Dist:** 5.7   **GPS:** 43.64162/-110.62339   **Elev:** 6684   **Grid:** 6/34   **Land:** NPS
Gros Ventre Rd (southbound) *(see chapter)*   **Type:** Hwy Junction w/Chapter
If heading south, this is a shortcut to **Gros Ventre Rd** MM 8.1 just west of **Kelly Warm Spring** *(see Gros Ventre Rd)*. The route saves 9.1 mi and ends 3.5 mi northeast of **Gros Ventre Campground** and 4.0 mi west of the **Gros Ventre Slide Area**.
Directions: E on Antelope Flats Rd 3.3 mi; S/R 2.4 mi; E/L on Gros Ventre Rd from MM 8.1.

MM: 168.0   **Dist:** 9.1   **GPS:** 43.71128/-110.58614   **Elev:** 8251   **Grid:** 7/32   **Land:** NF
Shadow Mountain   **Type:** Scenic Area & Bicycle Trail
Shadow Mountain is in the **Bridger-Teton National Forest** just outside **Grand Teton National Park**. The name comes from being in the shadow of the **Teton Range**. A parking area is located at the eastern base of the mountain (43.7039/-110.62214) from which a road climbs 1,410 ft to the top, offering spectacular vistas of both the **Teton Range** to the west and the **Gros Ventre Range** to the southeast. The road continues in a loop; however, the surface deteriorates to where returning by the same route is advisable. Completing the loop is popular with mountain bikers, as is a singletrack trail down the west side of the mountain. This trail can be found opposite a junction with a road heading east (43.711308/-110.58598) to the summit. This fun trail winds through the trees, with a few technical sections, 2.4 mi to the bottom and 1.2 mi south back to the parking area. The area offers abundant dispersed camping opportunities at the base, on the way up, and at the top of the mountain.
Cool Rating: ****   *Crowds:* **
Notes: The road to the top is not recommended for RVs or trailers; however, camping at the base of the mountain accommodates large rigs.
Road Desc: The first 4.7 mi is paved. The gravel road up the mountain is narrow, steep & winding
Directions: E on Antelope Flats Rd (past Mormon Row) 3.2 mi; N on Shadow Mountain Rd 1.5 mi to a parking area; Keep left to continue NE 0.8 mi to a parking/camping area with a National Forest information board; SE/R on FR-30340 3.6 mi to top.
Campsites: Dispersed   *Shade:* **   *Privacy:* *****   *RV Size:* 30'   *Other:* None

MM: 168.1 **Dist:** 0.2 **GPS:** 43.66665/-110.69697 **Elev:** 6526 **Grid:** 5/33 **Land:** NPS
Blacktail Ponds Overlook   **Type:** Scenic Viewpoint
This area is situated at the transition of 3 different plant communities. The overlook is situated in the sagebrush flats between the coniferous forest of **Blacktail Butte** and the willow and cottonwood-lined wetlands of the **Snake River** flood plain. The wetlands provide excellent wildlife viewing, and a sign explains how beaver activity helped create this environment. From the south, this is the second of 6 designated pullouts and offers a beautiful panoramic view of the **Teton Range** with wetlands (instead of sagebrush) in the foreground.
Cool Rating: **** **Crowds:** ** **Time:** 10 min **Directions:** NW 0.2 mi to parking area.

MM: 170.2 **GPS:** 43.69080/-110.67291 **Elev:** 6633 **Grid:** 5/33 **Land:** NPS
Glacier View Turnout   **Type:** Scenic Viewpoint
From the south, this is the third of 6 designated pullouts offering panoramic views of the **Teton Range**. The view is not quite as centered as the **Teton View Turnout**, but is at an angle that allows a view of the **Teton Glacier**, the largest glacier in the park. An interpretive sign explains how glaciers sculpted the **Teton Range**.
Cool Rating: **** **Crowds:** ** **Time:** 10 min **Directions:** Large pullout on W side of hwy

MM: 170.8 **Dist:** 1.0 **GPS:** 43.71153/-110.67054 **Elev:** 6547 **Grid:** 5/32 **Land:** NPS
Schwabacher Landing   **Type:** River Access Point
Off-road parking on the banks of the **Snake River**. Beautiful, centered views of the **Teton Range** with the **Snake River** in the foreground.
Cool Rating: **** **Crowds:** * **Road Desc:** Gravel **Directions:** NW on Schwabacher Landing Rd 1.0 mi

MM: 172.2 **GPS:** 43.71786/-110.66038 **Elev:** 6730 **Grid:** 6/32 **Land:** NPS
Teton View Turnout   **Type:** Scenic Viewpoint
From the south, this is the fourth of 6 designated pullouts offering panoramic views of the **Teton Range**. This is the best view centered directly in front of the **Cathedral Group**, which includes the **Grand Teton**, with no trees obstructing the view.
Cool Rating: **** **Crowds:** ** **Time:** 10 min **Directions:** Large pullout on W side of hwy

MM: 175.1 **GPS:** 43.75184/-110.62532 **Elev:** 6904 **Grid:** 6/31 **Land:** NPS
Snake River Overlook   **Type:** Scenic Viewpoint
From the south, this is the fifth of 6 designated pullouts offering panoramic views of the **Teton Range**. This is one of the premier viewpoints with the **Snake River** in the foreground below. **Ansel Adams'** famous shot of the **Teton Range** was taken here. Interpretive signs identify the **Teton** peaks and provide information about the **Snake River** and the **Greater Yellowstone Ecosystem**.
Cool Rating: **** **Crowds:** *** **Time:** 20 min **Directions:** Large parking area on NW side of hwy

MM: 175.8 **Dist:** 0.8 **GPS:** 43.76055/-110.62698 **Elev:** 6625 **Grid:** 6/31 **Land:** NPS
Deadman's Bar   **Type:** River Access Point
A primary access point on the **Snake River** where many float trips launch.
Crowds: *** **Notes:** Not recommended for large RVs and trailers. **Directions:** N then NW on Deadman's Bar Rd 0.8
Road Desc: The road descends 200 ft with one steep section. The first 1/4 mi is paved, then gravel.

MM: 179.3 **Dist:** 0.4 **GPS:** 43.77767/-110.55768 **GPS2:** 43.77860/-110.55827 **Elev:** 6750 **Grid:** 7/31 **Land:** NPS
Cunningham Cabin   **Type:** Historic Site
Established as the **Bar Flying U Ranch** by J. Pierce Cunningham in the 1880s. This is one the best and few remaining homestead cabins in **Jackson Hole** and is on the **National Register of Historic Places**. An informational booklet at the trailhead provides more detailed information about the site, including a self-guided 1/2 mi trail around the grounds.
Cool Rating: ** **Crowds:** ** **Time:** 30 min **Directions:** N 0.4 mi

MM: 182.3 **GPS:** 43.81081/-110.52705 **Elev:** 6745 **Grid:** 8/30 **Land:** NPS
Elk Ranch Flats Turnout   **Type:** Scenic Viewpoint
The farthest north of 6 designated pullouts offering panoramic views of the **Teton Range**. This is the most distant view and much better views are provided by the pullouts to the south.
Cool Rating: ** **Crowds:** * **Time:** 5 min **Directions:** Large pullout on W side of hwy

MM: 184.6 **GPS:** 43.84002/-110.50993 **Elev:** 6733 **Grid:** 8/29
Moran Jct   **Type:** Highway Junction
A named highway junction with no services.
Nearest Town: Moose 18.3 SW

MM: 184.6 **GPS:** 43.84002/-110.50993 **Elev:** 6733 **Grid:** 8/29
US-89/191/287 (see chapter)   **Type:** Hwy Transition w/Chapter
27 mi highway from **Moran Jct** north through **Grand Teton National Park** to the south entrance of **Yellowstone National Park**. Highlights include: **Oxbow Bend**, views of **Jackson Lake** and the **Teton Range**.
Directions: N to Yellowstone NP from MM 184.6 (0)

MM: 184.6 **GPS:** 43.84002/-110.50993 **Elev:** 6733 **Grid:** 8/29
US-26/287 & US-26 (see chapter)   **Type:** Hwy Junction w/Chapter
133.7 mi highway from **Moran Jct** southeast to **Riverton**. **US-287 (Lander to US-26)** splits off south at MM 98.8 and the highway continues southeast as **US-26**. Heading southeast to **Dubois** is along the **Centennial Scenic Byway**. Highlights include: **Breccia Cliffs**, **Wind River Lake**, **Pinnacle Buttes**, **Brooks Lake Creek Falls**, **Brooks Lake**, **Dubois Recreation Area Scenic Overlook**, colorful badlands, **Trail Lake Rd Petroglyphs**.
Nearest Town: Moose 18.3 SW; Dubois 55.6 SE **Directions:** SE to Dubois from MM 0

MM: 184.6 **GPS:** 43.84002/-110.50993 **Elev:** 6733 **Grid:** 8/29
End of Highway   **Type:** Highway End
43.3 mi highway from **Moran Jct** south to **Hoback Jct**, where the highway transitions to **US-26/89** using sequential mile markers. The entire length is along the **Centennial Scenic Byway**. Highlights include: **Grand Teton National Park**, **Jackson Hole and Greater Yellowstone Visitor Center**, **Jackson**.
Directions: S to Jackson from MM 184.6

US-287 (Lander to US-26)   S/N

MM: 0.0 **GPS:** 42.83107/-108.72393 **Elev:** 5384 **Grid:** 33/54
US-287 (Lander to US-26)   **Type:** Highway Description
31.6 mi highway northwest from **Lander** to **US-26**. The highway transitions from **US-287/Wy-789**; however, the mile markers start at MM 0. Highlights include: **Sacajawea's Grave**.
Directions: NW to Fort Washaki from MM 0

MM: 0.0 **GPS:** 42.83107/-108.72393 **Elev:** 5384 **Grid:** 33/54
US-287/Wy-789 *(see chapter)*   **Type:** Hwy Junction w/Chapter
125 mi highway from **Lander** southeast to **Rawlins** near **I-80**. Highlights include: **Green Mountain**, **Split Rock**.
Directions: Continue straight, SE to Rawlins from MM 81

MM: 0.0 **GPS:** 42.83107/-108.72393 **Elev:** 5384 **Grid:** 33/54
Wy-789 & US-26/Wy-789 *(see chapter)*   **Type:** Hwy Junction w/Chapter
46.2 mi highway from **Lander** northeast to **Shoshoni**. The highway heads northeast from **Lander** as **Wy-789** continuing the mile markers from **US-287/Wy-789**. After 24.1 mi the highway combines with **US-26** and continues northeast 22.1 mi to **Shoshoni** as **US-26/Wy-789**. Highlights include: access to **Castle Gardens**, **Wyoming Heritage Trail**.
Directions: NE to Riverton from MM 81.1

MM: 0.0 **GPS:** 42.83107/-108.72393 **Elev:** 5384 **Grid:** 33/54
Lander   **Type:** Town

MM: 0.0 **Dist:** 0.2 **GPS:** 42.82858/-108.72577 **Elev:** 5404 **Grid:** 33/54 **Land:** City
RV Dump: Lander   **Type:** RV Dump
Located next to the **Lander Public Works Building**.
Directions: SW on Buena Vista Dr 0.2 mi; NW side of street.

MM: 0.4 **Dist:** 0.9 **GPS:** 42.82152/-108.73706 **Elev:** 5405 **Grid:** 33/54 **Land:** City
Lander City Park   **Type:** Park
Free camping on the southeast side of **Lander City Park**. Tent camping is allowed in the grassed areas south of the baseball field. RV camping is allowed across the street in a large gravel parking area as well as along the street for the next 0.1 mi. A river serves as a noise barrier on the southeast side, but there may be park and street noise. *Cottonwoods. Tables. 2 restrooms with flush toilets.*
Crowds: ***
Directions: SW on S 3rd St to Fremont St 0.6 mi; Continue past baseball fields 1/4 mi. *If heading to Sinks Canyon State Park, head west on Fremont St, which turns into Wy-131 (see Wy-131/FR-300).*
Campsites: Dispersed **Shade:** *** **Privacy:** * **RV Size:** 40'+ **Other:** Water

MM: 0.6 **GPS:** 42.83397/-108.73519 **Elev:** 5358 **Grid:** 33/54
Wy-131/FR-300/Louis Lake Rd *(see chapter)*   **Type:** Hwy Junction w/Chapter
36.5 mi route from **US-287 (Lander to US-26)** in **Lander** south to **Wy-28**. The road traverses **Sinks Canyon** and climbs 4,240 ft above the city of **Lander** along the southeastern end of the **Wind River Mountains**. 7 public campgrounds are located along this route plus many dispersed camping opportunities. Highlights include: **Sinks Canyon State Park**, **Popo Agie Falls**, trailheads into the **Wind River Mountains**, **Blue Ridge Fire Lookout**, **Louis Lake**.
Directions: S to Wy-28 from MM 0
Notes: The last 5 mi of this route, north of Wy-28, offers abundant dispersed camping. This route driven counterclockwise with connections to Wy-28 northeast and US-287/Wy-789 northwest creates a 70 mi scenic loop route from Lander. A nice, inexpensive self-guided tour booklet fully documents this loop and is available at the Sinks Canyon State Park visitor center. This route is not recommended solely as a shortcut between Lander and Wy-28 as it is an extremely slow drive.

MM: 1.5 **GPS:** 42.84098/-108.74575 **Elev:** 5356 **Grid:** 33/54 **Land:** County
Fremont County Pioneer Museum   **Type:** Museum
A museum with exhibits, photographs, artifacts, and memorabilia that explore the history of the **Fremont County** area.
Hours: 10am - 6pm Tues - Sat **Cool Rating:** ** **Crowds:** * **Time:** 1 hr
Directions: W side of hwy (1443 Main St, Lander)

MM: 14.8 **Dist:** 2.1 **GPS:** 42.98576/-108.91189 **Elev:** 5676 **Grid:** 31/50 **Land:** City
Shoshone Episcopal Mission Boarding School   **Type:** Historic Site
A boarding school for Shoshone Indian girls, which was in session from 1890-1945. The school was founded by the **Reverend John Roberts** and built on land donated by **Chief Washakie**. A sign summarizes the history of the school.
Cool Rating: * **Crowds:** * **Time:** 15 min
Directions: SW on Trout Creek Rd 2.1 mi; S side of road just before Cemetery Ln.

MM: 14.8 **Dist:** 2.7 **GPS:** 42.99286/-108.91550 **GPS2:** 42.99266/-108.91442 **Elev:** 5715 **Grid:** 31/50 **Land:** City
Sacajawea's Grave (northbound)   **Type:** Historic Site
Sacajawea was a Shoshone Indian woman who served as a guide, interpreter, and translator to the **Lewis and Clark Expedition** in 1805. Although there is disagreement among scholars as to where **Sacajawea** is buried, many believe her gravesite is in **Fort Washakie**. This gravesite is located on the south-central side of the **Fort Washakie Cemetery** and is marked by a large granite headstone between her 2 sons. About 90 yds west of the grave is a nice monument to **Sacajawea** with a statue, 2 interpretive signs, 2 benches, and 2 flagpoles. The monument is located inside the south end of a loop road at the west end of the cemetery.
Cool Rating: *** **Crowds:** * **Time:** 30 min
Directions: SW on Trout Creek Rd 2.2 mi; N/R on Cemetery Ln 0.5 mi; W side of road. Drive in and follow the road 1/4 mi to the monument at the southwest end of the cemetery. The grave is 90 yds east.

MM: 15.7 **GPS:** 43.00379/-108.87922 **Elev:** 5570 **Grid:** 31/50
Fort Washakie   **Type:** Town

MM: 15.7 **Dist:** 2.5
Sacajawea's Grave & Shoshone Episcopal Mission Boarding School (southbound)   **Type:** Historic Site
See Sacajawea's Grave and Shoshone Episcopal Mission Boarding School at MM 14.8 above.
Cool Rating: *** **Crowds:** *
Directions: W on North Fork Rd 0.7 mi; Keep left on South Fork Rd 1.5 mi; S/L on Cemetery Ln 0.3 mi; W side of road; Drive in and follow the road 1/4 mi to the monument at the southwest end of the cemetery. The grave is 90 yds east.

The Shoshone Episcopal Mission Boarding School is 0.6 mi farther by continuing S on Cemetery Ln 0.5 mi to Trout Creek Rd. Turn left 100 yds where the school is on the right.

MM: 31.6 **GPS:** 43.21335/-108.96864 **Elev:** 5664 **Grid:** 30/45
US-26/287 & US-26 *(see chapter)*   **Type:** Hwy Junction w/Chapter
133.7 mi highway from **Riverton** northwest to **Moran Jct**. **US-26** merges with **US-287 (Lander to US-26)** at MM 98.8 and continues northwest as **US-26/287**. This is a primary access route to **Grand Teton National Park** and **Yellowstone National Park**. Heading northwest between **Dubois** and **Moran Jct** is along the **Centennial Scenic Byway**. Highlights include: **Trail Lake Rd Petroglyphs**, colorful badlands, **Dubois Recreation Area Scenic Overlook**, **Brooks Lake**, **Brooks Lake Creek Falls**, **Pinnacle Buttes**, **Wind River Lake**, **Breccia Cliffs**.
Directions: NW to Dubois or SE to Riverton from MM 98.8

MM: 31.6 **GPS:** 43.21335/-108.96864 **Elev:** 5664 **Grid:** 30/45
End of Highway   **Type:** Highway End
31.6 mi highway southeast from **US-26** to **Lander**. Highlights include: **Sacajawea's Grave**.
Nearest Town: Fort Washakie 15.9 S **Directions:** SE to Lander from MM 31.6

US-287 (Laramie to Colorado)   SE/NW

MM: 400.9 **GPS:** 41.29753/-105.59464 **Elev:** 7162 **Grid:** 78/93
US-287 (Laramie to Colorado)   **Type:** Highway Description
24.5 mi highway from **I-80** at **Laramie** southeast to **Colorado**. Highlights include: **Fort Sanders**.
Notes: US-287 actually ends 0.9 mi north of I-80 at E Grand Ave at MM 400.
Directions: I-80 exit 313; S to Colorado from MM 400.9

MM: 400.9 **GPS:** 41.29753/-105.59464 **Elev:** 7162 **Grid:** 78/93
US-30/287 *(see chapter)*   **Type:** Hwy Transition w/Chapter
93.8 mi highway that loops from **I-80** MM 313.2 at **Laramie**, northwest to **Medicine Bow**, then southwest back to **I-80** MM 235.3 at **Walcott**. At **I-80** in **Laramie** the highway transitions from **US-287 (Laramie to Colorado)** to **US-30/287** MM 329.4. This highway provides an alternate southern route to **Muddy Mountain**, **Casper Mountain**, and **Wy-220**, but otherwise only serves to access the attractions along the highway and is 16.0 mi longer than staying on **I-80**. Highlights include: **Fossil Cabin Museum**, **Hanna Cemetery**, **Hanna Memorial Park**.
Notes: US-30/287 actually ends 0.9 mi north of I-80 at E Grand Ave at MM 328.5.
Directions: I-80 exit 313; NW to Medicine Bow from MM 329.4

MM: 400.9 **GPS:** 41.29753/-105.59464 **Elev:** 7162 **Grid:** 78/93
I-80 *(see chapter)*   **Type:** Hwy Junction w/Chapter
403 mi interstate highway through southern **Wyoming** from **Nebraska** west to **Utah**. Highlights include: **Vedauwoo Recreation Area**, **Curt Gowdy State Park**, **Pole Mountain Trails**, **Wyoming Territorial Prison State Historic Site**, **Fort Fred Steele**, **Wyoming Frontier Prison**, **Fort Bridger State Historic Site**, **Bear River State Park**, and much more.
Directions: W to Rawlins or E to Cheyenne.

MM: 400.9 **GPS:** 41.29753/-105.59464 **Elev:** 7162 **Grid:** 78/93
Laramie   **Type:** Town

MM: 402.4 **Dist:** 0.9 **GPS:** 41.27137/-105.59817 **Elev:** 7187 **Grid:** 78/93 **Land:** State
Fort Sanders (southbound)   **Type:** Historic Site
The last remains of **Fort Sanders**. This wooden fort was originally named **Fort John Buford** but was later renamed in honor of **Brigadier General William P. Sanders**. The fort was established September 5, 1866 to protect travelers from Indian attacks along the nearby **Overland Trail**. It was later tasked with protecting the workers of the **Union Pacific Railroad**. The fort was abandoned May 18, 1882. A monument (erected in June 1914) and the shell of the guardhouse are located inside a chain link fence on a dirt street in a neighborhood on the southern outskirts of **Laramie**.
Cool Rating: * **Crowds:** * **Time:** 10 min **Notes:** The turnoff is just before the large cement plant to the west.
Directions: W on Huron St 0.4 mi; S/L on Fort Sanders Rd 0.4 mi; E/L on S Kiowa St 0.1 mi. **To continue south on US-287**: Return to Fort Sanders Rd; S/L on Fort Sanders Rd 0.65 mi.

MM: 403.4 **Dist:** 0.8 **GPS:** 41.27137/-105.59817 **Elev:** 7187 **Grid:** 78/93 **Land:** State
Fort Sanders (northbound)   **Type:** Historic Site
See previous section.
Cool Rating: * **Crowds:** * **Time:** 10 min **Notes:** The turnoff is just after the large cement plant to the west.
Directions: W on CR-22 0.1 mi; Continue N/R on Fort Sanders Rd 0.55 mi; E/R on S Kiowa St 0.1 mi. **To continue north on US-287**: Return to Fort Sanders Rd; N/R on Fort Sanders Rd 0.4 mi; E on Huron St 0.4 mi;

MM: 425.4 **GPS:** 40.99784/-105.41275 **Elev:** 7555 **Grid:** 81/100
End of Highway - Colorado State Line   **Type:** Highway End
24.5 mi highway from **Colorado** to **I-80** at **Laramie**. Highlights include: **Fort Sanders**.
Nearest Town: Laramie 24.5 NW **Directions:** N to Laramie from MM 425.4

US-287/Wy-789

MM: 0.0 *GPS:* 41.78816/-107.23769 *Elev:* 6761 *Grid:* 55/80
US-287/Wy-789   *Type:* Highway Description
125 mi highway from **Rawlins**, near **I-80**, northwest to **Lander**. The highway heads north 44.3 mi where the highway and mile markers oddly transition to **Wy-220**, which continues northeast to **Casper**. To continue on **US-287/Wy-789** requires a left turn at a junction where the mile markers start over at MM 0 and the highway heads northwest to **Lander**. Highlights include: **Split Rock**, **Green Mountain**.
Directions: No direct connection to I-80. See I-80 MM 211.8 and MM 215.6 for directions.

MM: 0.0 *GPS:* 41.78816/-107.23769 *Elev:* 6761 *Grid:* 55/80
I-80 *(see chapter)*   *Type:* Hwy Junction w/Chapter
403 mi interstate highway through southern **Wyoming** from **Utah** east to **Nebraska**. Highlights include: **Bear River State Park**, **Fort Bridger State Historic Site**, **Wyoming Frontier Prison**, **Fort Fred Steele**, **Wyoming Territorial Prison State Historic Site**, **Pole Mountain Trails**, **Curt Gowdy State Park**, **Vedauwoo Recreation Area**, and much more.
Directions: No direct connection to I-80. Follow the signs to head E to Laramie or W to Rock Springs.

MM: 0.0 *GPS:* 41.78816/-107.23769 *Elev:* 6761 *Grid:* 55/80
Rawlins   *Type:* Town

MM: 1.9 *GPS:* 41.81191/-107.22691 *Elev:* 6836 *Grid:* 55/80
N Higley Blvd/US-287 bypass to I-80 (southbound)   *Type:* Highway Junction
If heading south and then east on I-80, this cutoff road leads to the I-80 business loop west of the I-80 entrance ramp.
Directions: SE on N Higley Blvd/US-287 Bypass 1.5 mi; E on E Cedar St 0.6 mi to I-80 exit 215

MM: 44.3 *GPS:* 42.36282/-107.44393 *Elev:* 6272 *Grid:* 52/66
US-287/Wy-789 (northbound)   *Type:* Highway Junction
If heading north from **Rawlins**, turn left to continue on **US-287/Wy-789**. The mile markers start over at zero and the highway heads northwest to **Lander**.
Directions: Turn left to continue NW to Lander from MM 0

MM: 44.3 *GPS:* 42.36282/-107.44393 *Elev:* 6272 *Grid:* 52/66
Wy-220 (northbound) *(see chapter)*   *Type:* Hwy Junction w/Chapter
If heading north from **Rawlins**, continue straight to transition to **Wy-220** and continue 72.9 mi northeast to **Casper**. The mile markers continue sequentially. Highlights include: **Martin's Cove**, **Devil's Gate**, **Independence Rock**, **Pathfinder Reservoir**, **Alcova Reservoir**, **Bessemer Bend National Historic Site**, **Fort Caspar Museum and Historic Site**.
Nearest Town: Rawlins 44.3 S *Directions:* Continue straight NE on Wy-220 to Casper.

MM: 0.0 *GPS:* 42.36282/-107.44393 *Elev:* 6272 *Grid:* 52/66
US-287/Wy-789 (heading southeast)   *Type:* Highway Junction
If heading southeast from **Lander**, turn right to continue on **US-287/Wy-789** to **Rawlins**. The mile markers count down from MM 44.3.
Directions: S to Rawlins from MM 44.3

MM: 0.0 *GPS:* 42.36282/-107.44393 *Elev:* 6272 *Grid:* 52/66
Wy-220 (heading southeast) *(see chapter)*   *Type:* Hwy Junction w/Chapter
If heading southeast, turn left onto **Wy-220** and continue northeast 72.9 mi to **Casper** from MM 44.3. Highlights include: **Martin's Cove**, **Devil's Gate**, **Independence Rock**, **Pathfinder Reservoir**, **Alcova Reservoir**, **Bessemer Bend National Historic Site**, **Fort Caspar Museum and Historic Site**.
Nearest Town: Rawlins 44.3 S *Directions:* NE to Casper from MM 44.3

MM: 8.2 *GPS:* 42.45298/-107.54587 *Elev:* 6304 *Grid:* 50/64 *Land:* BLM
Split Rock Historic Site   *Type:* Historic Site
Split Rock is the third of 3 distinctive granite landmarks in the **Sweetwater Valley**, the other 2 being **Independence Rock** and **Devil's Gate** 16 mi east. This notch in the **Rattlesnake Range** rises nearly 1,000 ft and was visible from the east for an entire day, guiding travelers along the **Oregon-Mormon-California Trails** toward **South Pass** more than 75 mi west. Emigrants often camped in this area along the **Sweetwater River** where good grass and water was available for stock.

This historic site is located on the south side of **Split Rock**. A short trail leads to a viewpoint with interpretive panels regarding the area and its history. This site is the closest point from the road to **Split Rock**; however, the view is at an angle where the notch cannot actually be seen. Another 3.5 mi northwest is a turnout with a historical marker for **Split Rock**, which offers a good view of the notch from the west *(see next section)*. The historic site is situated among an outcropping of smooth rocks with a vault toilet and 3 picnic tables without shade.
Cool Rating: *** *Crowds:* * *Time:* 20 min *Directions:* NE side of hwy

MM: 11.5 *GPS:* 42.47279/-107.60415 *Elev:* 6181 *Grid:* 49/63
Split Rock Historical Marker   *Type:* Historical Marker
A long pullout with a stone monument and viewing area for **Split Rock**, which provides a straight-on view of the notch in the mountain. *See previous section for a description of Split Rock.*
Cool Rating: *** *Crowds:* * *Time:* 10 min *Directions:* NE side of hwy

MM: 16.9 *Dist:* 6.2 *GPS:* 42.39995/-107.70159 *Elev:* 6807 *Grid:* 48/65 *Land:* County
Green Mountain   *Type:* Recreation Area
A 9,100 ft forested mountain that rises 2,650 ft above the surrounding sagebrush plains. The mountain is on BLM lands and includes 2 developed campgrounds *(see next sections)*, a remote picnic area, abundant dispersed camping, and many side roads for OHVs and mountain bikes. A 6.2 mi road leads south to a 15.8 mi loop road. The loop climbs 2,180 ft to a road junction at the top of the mountain near the halfway point. This junction is adjacent to the edge of the mountain and provides expansive views to the southwest. Just northwest of here is a large, flat and open area where **Wild Horses** may be seen.

From this junction, a primitive forest road heads east 3.0 mi to **Wild Horse Point**. This area is developed with 6 picnic tables, a vault toilet, and a short 0.1 mi trail to an overlook with expansive views to the east. The road is narrow and has a short rough section at 2.0 mi. This is a good destination for an OHV or mountain bike. There is abundant dispersed camping along the first 2.0 mi, including a large tree-lined meadow for the last 0.2 mi.
Cool Rating: ** *Crowds:* *
Notes: If just passing by, the long trip up Green Mountain may not be worth it. If just trying to reach the top of Green Mountain keep right at the fork and return the same way. The road is much better on the west side.
Road Desc: Gravel. The right fork of the loop is a wide, smooth gravel road. The left fork is more narrow and rough, with 14% grades and impassable when wet.
Directions: S on BLM-2411 6.2 mi; Keep left to Cottonwood Campground or right to Green Mountain Park Campground and the top of the mountain.

MM: 16.9 *Dist:* 8.7 *GPS:* 42.37205/-107.72816 *Elev:* 7860 *Grid:* 48/66 *Land:* County
Green Mountain Park Campground: Green Mountain   *Type:* Campground
This under-maintained campground is located part of the way up **Green Mountain** a short distance after the forest begins. It is a strange configuration of walk-in tent sites. The center of the campground is a cabled-off area of long grass and sagebrush with 2 tables. The cows get into this area and leave a mess. A creek flows along the east side of the campground with what appears to be 7 picnic sites on the other side. These sites might possibly be used for camping; however, there is very little room to pitch a tent. To the south, beyond the vault toilet, are 6 more walk-in sites. The campground caretaker said that there are 13 sites. The most useful parts of the campground are the large level areas at each end where RVs can be parked. *Tables. Vault toilet. Some fire rings with grates.*
Crowds: * *Road Desc:* Gravel *Directions:* S on BLM-2411 6.2 mi; Keep right at fork 2.5 mi.
Notes: Dispersed camping or paying the fee at Cottonwood Campground is probably a better option. In 2 weekend visits here, I have not seen anybody camped here.
Campsites: 13 *Shade:* * *Privacy:* * *RV Size:* 30' *Other:* None

MM: 16.9 *Dist:* 9.5 *GPS:* 42.36470/-107.68354 *Elev:* 7760 *Grid:* 48/66 *Land:* BLM
Cottonwood Campground: Green Mountain   *Type:* Campground
The campground is about halfway up **Green Mountain** in a small valley. The sites are stretched out along a 0.7 mi road that loops back to the main road. *Several walk-in sites. Good spacing between sites.*
Crowds: *** *[FEE AREA]* *Road Desc:* Gravel *Directions:* S on BLM-2411 6.2 mi; Keep left at fork 3.3 mi.
Campsites: 17 *Shade:* *** *Privacy:* **** *RV Size:* 30' *Other:* Water

MM: 32.5 *GPS:* 42.51754/-108.00871 *Elev:* 6430 *Grid:* 44/62
Ice Slough   *Type:* Historical Marker
A historical sign that partially reads "Ice Slough is a small stream that flows into the Sweetwater River five miles east of here. In front of this point is a slough (i.e. a marsh or shallow un-drained depression). The Slough gave the name to the stream east of here. In the "Ice Slough" the marshes soils and plants insulated the previous winter's ice and it melted slowly throughout the summer. Under the marshes a thick mat of ice could be found late into June or early July. Westward bound immigrants would stop their wagons here for the purpose of breaking out chunks of ice to use in their drinks and to preserve meat."
Cool Rating: * *Crowds:* * *Directions:* N side of hwy.

MM: 41.2 *GPS:* 42.54125/-108.17116 *Elev:* 6590 *Grid:* 41/61
Sweetwater Valley Historical Marker   *Type:* Historical Marker
The **Sweetwater Valley** was the mid-section of the 2000 mi long **Oregon Trail**. This sign explains what the valley meant to the emigrants traveling this route.
Cool Rating: * *Crowds:* * *Time:* 5 min *Directions:* N side of hwy

MM: 41.8 *Dist:* 0.1 *GPS:* 42.54022/-108.18265 *Elev:* 6545 *Grid:* 41/61 *Land:* Private
Mormon Handcart Historic Site: Willie Center Sixth Crossing   *Type:* Historic Site
A historic site run by the **Mormon Church**, which was an emigrant campsite before the ill-fated crossing of **Rocky Ridge** by the **Willie Handcart Company** *(see Atlantic City Rd/CR-237 MM 2.9/5.3)*. This was the sixth crossing point of the **Sweetwater River**. The welcome center contains some displays and is staffed by members of the **Mormon Church** who tell the history of the handcart companies.
Cool Rating: ** *Crowds:* ** *Directions:* S 0.1 mi

MM: 42.0 *GPS:* 42.54425/-108.18815 *Elev:* 6562 *Grid:* 41/61
Sweetwater Station Rest Area   *Type:* Rest Area
A nice grassed rest area with picnic shelters and **Oregon Trail** historical markers about the **Sweetwater Valley**.
Directions: N side of hwy

MM: 42.1 *GPS:* 42.54320/-108.18949 *Elev:* 6562 *Grid:* 41/61
Wy-135/136 *(see chapter)*   *Type:* Hwy Junction w/Chapter
35.6 mi highway from **US-287/Wy-789** northwest to **Wy-789**, just south of **Riverton**. **Wy-135** transitions to **Wy-136** for the last mile. The landscape is prairie and badlands with no towns or services along the way. This highway saves 24.5 mi over driving through **Lander**. Highlights include: **Badlands Scenic Overlook**.
Nearest Town: Jeffrey City 18.9 E; Lander 39 NW *Directions:* N to Riverton from MM 34.6

MM: 42.1   *Dist:* 4.2
Carmody Lake (westbound)   *Type:* Campground
A slightly shorter route to **Carmody Lake** if heading west *(see next section)*. There is additional dispersed camping about 6 mi north of the **Carmody Lake** turnoff on **Wy-135** *(see chapter)*.
Crowds: *   *Road Desc:* Dirt, primitive & impassable when wet, narrow
Directions: N on Wy-135 1.1 mi; W/L on unmarked dirt road 3.1 mi.

MM: 46.9   *Dist:* 2.6   *GPS:* 42.56930/-108.22869   *Elev:* 6630   *Grid:* 40/61   *Land:* BLM
Carmody Lake (eastbound)   *Type:* Campground
Primitive camping near a shallow lake on the sagebrush plains. *No facilities. No trees.*
Crowds: *   *Road Desc:* Dirt, primitive & impassable when wet, narrow
Directions: NE on BLM-2302 0.9 mi; SE/R on unmarked dirt road 1.7 mi.
Campsites: Dispersed   *Shade:* *   *Privacy:* *****   *RV Size:* 30'   *Other:* None

MM: 46.9   *Dist:* 23.3   *GPS:* 42.57678/-108.26335   *GPS2:* 42.43970/-108.62318   *Elev:* 6687   *Grid:* 40/61   *Land:* LDS
Willie Handcart Company Tragedy Memorial   *Type:* Historic Site
See Atlantic City Rd/CR-237 MM 2.9/5.3 for the description. This backcountry route saves ~33 mi over the main route via **Atlantic City**. Camping options along the route include 2 small reservoirs, **Antelope Springs Reservoir** (MI 0.8) and **Silver Creek Reservoir** (2 roads at MI 8.8 and MI 9.9). The **Sage Creek Campground** at MI 11.1 is under lease by the LDS church and set up as a large group camp for Mormon handcart treks over **Rocky Ridge** to the **Willie Handcart Company Tragedy Memorial** site.
Cool Rating: **   *Crowds:* *   *Time:* 30-60 min
Notes: The site is crowded during the handcart treks in July and early August.
Road Desc: Gravel, rough spots & impassable when wet, high clearance. The 2.1 mi section between BLM-23-2 and CR-475 is recommended for 4wd; however, high clearance vehicles should be ok.
Directions: SW on Hudson-Atlantic City Rd/BLM-2302 20.4 mi; SW 2.1 mi on primitive road; W on Lewiston Rd/CR-475 0.8 mi.
Campsites: Dispersed   *Shade:* *   *Privacy:* *   *RV Size:* 30'   *Other:* None

MM: 48.5   *GPS:* 42.58533/-108.29037   *Elev:* 6726   *Grid:* 39/60
Interpretive Pullout: Beaver Rim and the Wind River Range   *Type:* Point of Interest
A sign about the **Wind River Range** and a nice view from the edge of the **Beaver Rim** across the valley to the northwest. The **Wind River Range** runs roughly parallel to the highway heading northwest and can be seen in the distance. These mountains are part of the **Rocky Mountains** and include 53 granite peaks over 13,000 ft.
Cool Rating: ***   *Crowds:* *   *Time:* 5 min   *Directions:* N side of hwy

MM: 72.9   *GPS:* 42.72881/-108.64653   *Elev:* 5546   *Grid:* 34/57
Wy-28 (Farson to US-287) *(see chapter)*   *Type:* Hwy Junction w/Chapter
66.3 mi highway from **US-287/Wy-789**, 8.4 mi southeast of **Lander**, southwest to **Farson**. Highlights include: **Red Canyon**, **Miner's Delight**, **Atlantic City**, **Carissa Mine**, **South Pass City State Historic Site**, **South Pass** and related historic markers.
Nearest Town: Lander 8.4 NW   *Directions:* SW to Farson from MM 68.2

MM: 79.3   *GPS:* 42.81058/-108.70360   *Elev:* 5377   *Grid:* 34/55
Mortimore Ln   *Type:* Highway Junction
If heading to **Sinks Canyon State Park**, this 2.6 mi cutoff road connects to **Wy-131** without driving through **Lander**.
Directions: W on Mortimore Ln 2.6 mi; SW on Wy-131 from MM 2.3

MM: 81.1   *GPS:* 42.83107/-108.72393   *Elev:* 5384   *Grid:* 33/54
Lander   *Type:* Town

MM: 81.1   *GPS:* 42.83107/-108.72393   *Elev:* 5384   *Grid:* 33/54
US-287 (Lander to US-26) *(see chapter)*   *Type:* Hwy Transition w/Chapter
31.6 mi highway northwest from **Lander** to **US-26**. The highway transitions from **US-287/Wy-789**; however, the mile markers start at MM 0. Highlights include: **Sacajawea's Grave**.
Directions: Continue straight through Lander and NW to Fort Washaki from MM 0

MM: 81.1   *GPS:* 42.83107/-108.72393   *Elev:* 5384   *Grid:* 33/54
Wy-789 & US-26/Wy-789 *(see chapter)*   *Type:* Hwy Junction w/Chapter
46.2 mi highway from **Lander** northeast to **Shoshoni**. The highway heads northeast from **Lander** as **Wy-789** continuing the mile markers from **US-287/Wy-789**. After 24.1 mi the highway combines with **US-26** and continues northeast 22.1 mi to **Shoshoni** as **US-26/Wy-789**. Highlights include: access to **Castle Gardens**, **Wyoming Heritage Trail**.
Directions: NE to Riverton from MM 81.1

MM: 81.1   *GPS:* 42.83107/-108.72393   *Elev:* 5384   *Grid:* 33/54
End of Highway   *Type:* Highway End
125 mi highway from **Lander** southeast to **Rawlins** near **I-80**. After 81.1 mi (at MM 0) is an odd junction with **Wy-220** eastbound. Turn right to continue south on **US-287/Wy-789** to **Rawlins**. At this point the mile markers count down from MM 44.3. Highlights include: **Green Mountain**, **Split Rock**.
Directions: SE to Rawlins from MM 81.1

MM: 0.0 *GPS:* 42.21346/-111.04714 *Elev:* 6074 *Grid:* 0/70
US-30   *Type:* Highway Description
100 mi highway from **Idaho** southeast to **I-80** exit 66. Highlights include: **Fossil Butte National Monument**.
Nearest Town: Cokeville 10.6 SE *Directions:* SE to Cokeville from MM 0

MM: 0.0 *GPS:* 42.21346/-111.04714 *Elev:* 6074 *Grid:* 0/70
Idaho State Line   *Type:* State Line
Nearest Town: Cokeville 10.6 SE

MM: 0.2 *GPS:* 42.21314/-111.04256 *Elev:* 6112 *Grid:* 0/70
Wy-89   *Type:* Highway Junction
10.3 mi highway north along the **Idaho** state line to **US-89**.
Directions: N on Wy-89

MM: 10.6 *GPS:* 42.08549/-110.95380 *Elev:* 6195 *Grid:* 1/73
Cokeville   *Type:* Town

MM: 10.6 *Dist:* 0.5 *GPS:* 42.08503/-110.95906 *Elev:* 6195 *Grid:* 1/73 *Land:* City
Cokeville City Park   *Type:* Park
A cottonwood lined city park with a picnic shelter, restroom, and playground. RV camping is allowed on the east, south, and west side of the park, or across the street to the east in a concrete parking area. Due to the sprinkler system, no tent camping is allowed in the park; however, a grassed area with a table and grill is located next to the concrete RV parking. Railroad tracks are located on the west side of the park, and trains pass regularly blowing their horns.
Crowds: * *Directions:* W on E Main St/Wy-231 0.5 mi; S on Park St into parking area.
Campsites: Dispersed *Shade:* ** *Privacy:* * *RV Size:* 40'+ *Other:* None

MM: 44.5 *GPS:* 41.81592/-110.71956 *Elev:* 6645 *Grid:* 5/80
Fossil Butte National Monument *(see chapter)*   *Type:* Hwy Junction w/Chapter
50 million years ago this area was a huge lake in a lush green subtropical forest. Because of profound climate change what remains today is a semi-arid landscape of flat-topped buttes in a sagebrush desert. The ancient lake sediment hardened and transformed into layers of rocks known as the **Green River Formation**. Trapped between these layers are among the best-preserved fossils in the world. These remarkably detailed fossils include fish, insects, plants, reptiles, birds, and mammals.
Directions: NW on CR-300 2.3 mi; NW/R on Chicken Creek Rd from MM 2.3.
Notes: There is no camping at the monument and little camping anywhere in the area except private campgrounds in Kemmerer. BLM land is located along US-30 and generally provides a place to park overnight, but watch out for private land.

MM: 54.6 *GPS:* 41.77124/-110.55310 *Elev:* 7070 *Grid:* 7/81
US-189 *(see chapter)*   *Type:* Hwy Junction w/Chapter
131.5 mi highway from **I-80** exit 18 north to the junctions with **US-189/191**, which heads northwest toward **Jackson**, and **US-191**, which heads east to **Pinedale**. Highlights include: **Names Hill**, **Father DeSmet Monument**.
Directions: N to Kemmerer or S to Evanston from MM 34.5

MM: 54.6 *Dist:* 2.3 *GPS:* 41.79308/-110.53719 *Elev:* 6944 *Grid:* 7/80
Kemmerer   *Type:* Town
Directions: N on US-189 2.3 mi

MM: 54.6 *Dist:* 4.1 *GPS:* 41.81568/-110.53433 *Elev:* 6937 *Grid:* 7/80 *Land:* City
Kemmerer Tent Park   *Type:* Campground
A small tent-only campground in a loop right off the highway. Not even small self-contained units are allowed. *Cottonwoods. Vault toilet. Water and restrooms are available at City Hall (south of the campground) during business hours (8am - 5pm).*
Crowds: ** *[FEE AREA]*
Directions: N on US-189 through Kemmerer 3.6 mi to MM 38.1; NW/L 0.5 mi on Wy-233; E/R into south end of campground.
Campsites: 5 *Shade:* **** *Privacy:* * *RV Size:* Tent *Other:* None

MM: 100.0 *GPS:* 41.54419/-109.91107 *Elev:* 6406 *Grid:* 16/86
I-80 *(see chapter)*   *Type:* Hwy Junction w/Chapter
403 mi interstate highway through southern **Wyoming** from **Utah** east to **Nebraska**. Highlights include: **Bear River State Park**, **Fort Bridger State Historic Site**, **Wyoming Frontier Prison**, **Fort Fred Steele**, **Wyoming Territorial Prison State Historic Site**, **Pole Mountain Trails**, **Curt Gowdy State Park**, **Vedauwoo Recreation Area**, and much more.
Directions: W to Evanston or E to Rock Springs from MM 66.2

MM: 100.0 *GPS:* 41.54419/-109.91107 *Elev:* 6406 *Grid:* 16/86
End of Highway   *Type:* Highway End
100 mi highway from **I-80** exit 66 northwest to **Idaho**. Highlights include: **Fossil Butte National Monument**.
Nearest Town: Kemmerer 54.6 NW; Green River 24.5 E *Directions:* I-80 exit 66; NW to Kemmerer from MM 100

MM: 235.2 *GPS:* 41.74135/-106.83036 *Elev:* 6791 *Grid:* 60/81
US-30/287   *Type:* Highway Description
93.8 mi highway that loops from **I-80** MM 235.3 at **Walcott**, northeast to **Medicine Bow**, then southeast back to **I-80** MM 313.2 at **Laramie**. At **I-80** in **Laramie** the highway transitions to **US-287 (Laramie to Colorado)** MM 400.9 and continues south to **Colorado**. This highway provides an alternate southern route to **Muddy Mountain**, **Casper Mountain**, and **Wy-220**, but otherwise only serves to access the attractions along the highway and is 16.0 mi longer than staying on **I-80**. Highlights include: **Hanna Cemetery**, **Hanna Memorial Park**, **Fossil Cabin Museum**.
Notes: US-30/287 actually ends 0.9 mi north of I-80 at E Grand Ave at MM 328.5.
Directions: I-80 exit 235; NE to Hannah from MM 235.2

MM: 235.2 *GPS:* 41.74135/-106.83036 *Elev:* 6791 *Grid:* 60/81
I-80 *(see chapter)*   *Type:* Hwy Junction w/Chapter
Directions: W to Rawlins or E to Laramie from MM 235.3

MM: 235.2 *GPS:* 41.74135/-106.83036 *Elev:* 6791 *Grid:* 60/81
Walcott   *Type:* Town

MM: 252.7 *Dist:* 2.9 *GPS:* 41.85629/-106.58484 *Elev:* 6929 *Grid:* 64/79 *Land:* City
Hanna Cemetery   *Type:* Point of Interest
A **Miner's Memorial** is located at this interesting cemetery, which is located in a square with benches and a large stone monument that reads, *"Those who lost their lives. Dedicated to all coal miners in the Hanna and Carbon area who lost their lives in mining accidents."* The cemetery itself is very unique set in native grass, red gravel roads, and graves landscaped in gravel, some with iron and decorative chain fences.
Cool Rating: ** *Crowds:* * *Time:* 30 min *Road Desc:* Partially paved. The last 1.6 mi is gravel.
Directions: NW on Wy-72 1.1 mi; SW on S Tipperary St 0.2 mi to curve in road; N/R on gravel road 1.3 mi; Keep left at fork 1/4 mi.

MM: 252.7 *Dist:* 1.4 *GPS:* 41.87021/-106.56387 *Elev:* 6805 *Grid:* 64/78
Hanna   *Type:* Town
Directions: NW on Wy-72 1.4 mi

MM: 252.7 *Dist:* 2.4 *GPS:* 41.87333/-106.54612 *Elev:* 6805 *Grid:* 64/78 *Land:* City
Hanna Memorial Park   *Type:* Point of Interest
A park with baseball fields, several picnic shelters, and the following points of interest:

Miner's Memorial - A stone monument that reads *"Dedicated to all coal miners in the Carbon - Hanna area. In memory of those who lost their lives in mining accidents."* There were 2 major accidents with 171 men killed in 1903 and 58 killed in 1908. The monument also lists the names of those killed.
Hanna VFW War Memorial - Cobblestone monuments to the 20th century American wars, plus a U.S. Army tank.
Rotary Snowplow Locomotive - Used to clear snow from the railroad track using a large circular set of blades on the front end. Only 3 of these still exist in the world.
Cool Rating: ** *Crowds:* * *Time:* 30 min *Directions:* NW on Wy-72 1.4 mi; E/R on 2nd St 1.0 mi.

MM: 271.7 *GPS:* 41.89565/-106.20470 *Elev:* 6568 *Grid:* 69/78
Wy-487 to Casper Mountain and Wy-220   *Type:* Highway Junction
Wy-487 leads 72.2 mi highway north to **Wy-220**. **Muddy Mountain** and **Casper Mountain** can also be accessed on this route at MM 64.3 *(see Wy-220 MM 97.3)*. A rest area is located at MM 45.1.
Directions: N on Wy-487

MM: 271.9 *GPS:* 41.89565/-106.20470 *Elev:* 6570 *Grid:* 69/78
Medicine Bow   *Type:* Town

MM: 271.9 *Dist:* 2.0 *GPS:* 41.87361/-106.21367 *Elev:* 6564 *Grid:* 69/78 *Land:* Wyoming G & F
East Allen Lake - East Shore   *Type:* Public Access Area
A secondary parking area, camping area, and access point on the east shore of this small lake. *No trees. Vault toilet.*
Crowds: * *Road Desc:* Gravel
Directions: At the town of Medicine Bow; S on CR-1/Medicine Bow McFadden Rd 0.8 mi; SW/R on BLM-3157 1.2 mi.
Campsites: Dispersed *Shade:* * *Privacy:* * *Other:* None

MM: 271.9 *Dist:* 3.5 *GPS:* 41.87021/-106.22210 *Elev:* 6548 *Grid:* 69/78 *Land:* Wyoming G & F
East Allen Lake - South Shore   *Type:* Public Access Area
A parking area, camping area, and primary access point on the south shore of this small lake. *No trees. Vault toilet. Boat ramp.*
Crowds: *
Directions: At the town of Medicine Bow; S on CR-1/Medicine Bow McFadden Rd 2.1 mi; W/R on BLM-3158 1.4 mi.
Campsites: Dispersed *Shade:* * *Privacy:* * *Other:* None

MM: 279.0 *GPS:* 41.86498/-106.07335 *Elev:* 6785 *Grid:* 71/78 *Land:* Private
Fossil Cabin Museum   *Type:* Historic Site
A museum built in 1933 and constructed entirely of dinosaur bone fragments that were excavated from the nearby **Como Bluffs** dig site. When the museum is open it houses a collection of dinosaur bones, petrified sea life, fossils, and other objects of interest. The dig site on **Como Ridge**, behind the museum, unearthed many dinosaur skeletons between 1880 and 1890, including the giant **Diplodocus**. At 72 ft long, 22 ft high, and weighing between 50 and 70 tons, this was the largest dinosaur discovery at the time. This huge skeleton now stands in the **New York Museum of Natural History**. A **Wyoming** historical sign about the "Dinosaur Graveyard" is located on the east end of a long pullout. The **Como Bluffs** are on the **National Register of Historic Places**.
Cool Rating: ** *Crowds:* * *Time:* 30 min *Notes:* There is a good chance that the Fossil Cabin will be closed.
Directions: N side of hwy

MM: 289.0 *GPS:* 41.75207/-105.97547 *Elev:* 6900 *Grid:* 73/81
Wy-13 *Type:* Highway Junction
17.8 mi highway southwest to **I-80**. The **Foote Creek Rim Wind Energy Project** runs roughly parallel along the northwest side of this highway *(see I-80 MM 272.1)*.
Directions: SW on Wy-13

MM: 289.8 *GPS:* 41.74129/-105.97543 *Elev:* 6898 *Grid:* 73/81
Rock River *Type:* Town

MM: 289.8 *GPS:* 41.74136/-105.97574 *Elev:* 6898 *Grid:* 73/81 *Land:* City
Rock River City Park *Type:* Park
A nice city park with 2 picnic shelters, playground, basketball court, sand volleyball pit, and portable toilets.

MM: 328.2 *GPS:* 41.31480/-105.59319 *Elev:* 7160 *Grid:* 78/92
Laramie *Type:* Town

MM: 328.2 *GPS:* 41.31480/-105.59319 *Elev:* 7160 *Grid:* 78/92
Wy-230 (Laramie to Colorado) *(see chapter)* *Type:* Hwy Junction w/Chapter
42.0 mi highway from the junction with **US-30/287** in **Laramie** southwest to **Colorado**. 4 fishing and camping lakes, including one large reservoir, are located along this route.
Directions: W from the intersection of N 3rd St/US-30/287 and Clarke St from MM 0
Notes: Intersects a north/south section of I-80 at MM 1.3.

MM: 329.4 *GPS:* 41.74135/-106.83036 *Elev:* 6791 *Grid:* 60/81
US-287 (Laramie to Colorado) *(see chapter)* *Type:* Hwy Transition w/Chapter
The highway transitions to **US-287 (Laramie to Colorado)** at **I-80** and continues 24.5 mi southeast to **Colorado**. Highlights include: **Fort Sanders**.
Notes: US-287 actually ends 0.9 mi north of I-80 at E Grand Ave at MM 400. *Directions:* S to Colorado from MM 400.9

MM: 329.4 *GPS:* 41.29753/-105.59464 *Elev:* 7162 *Grid:* 78/93
I-80 *(see chapter)* *Type:* Hwy Junction w/Chapter
Directions: W to Rawlins or E to Cheyenne from MM 313.2

MM: 329.4 *GPS:* 41.29753/-105.59464 *Elev:* 7162 *Grid:* 78/93
End of Highway *Type:* Highway End
93.8 mi highway that loops from **I-80** MM 313.2 at **Laramie**, northwest to **Medicine Bow**, then southwest back to **I-80** MM 235.3 at **Walcott**. At **I-80** in **Laramie** the highway transitions from **US-287 (Laramie to Colorado)** to **US-30/287** MM 329.4. This highway provides an alternate southern route to **Muddy Mountain**, **Casper Mountain**, and **Wy-220**, but otherwise only serves to access the attractions along the highway and is 16.0 mi longer than staying on **I-80**. Highlights include: **Fossil Cabin Museum**, **Hanna Cemetery**, **Hanna Memorial Park**.
Directions: I-80 exit 313; NW to Medicine Bow from MM 329.4

US-85   S/N

MM: 17.1 *GPS:* 41.23482/-104.83520 *Elev:* 6210 *Grid:* 89/94
US-85   *Type:* Highway Description
239.4 mi highway that begins just north of **Cheyenne** and parallels the **Nebraska** and **South Dakota state lines** north before crossing into **South Dakota** at the end. The highway heads north 76.1 mi to **Torrington** (MM 93.2), joins **US-26 (I-25 to Nebraska)** heading northwest 9.9 mi to **Lingle** (MM 103.1), then continues north for the final 153.5 mi. This is also the southern route to the **Black Hills** of **South Dakota**, which heads east at MM 196.1 on **US-18**. Highlights include: **Hawk Springs State Recreation Area, Downar Bird Farm, Homesteaders Museum, Redwood Water Tank, Red Butte**.
Nearest Town: Cheyenne 4.5 S *Directions:* I-25 exit 17; NE to Torrington from MM 17.1

MM: 17.1 *GPS:* 41.23482/-104.83520 *Elev:* 6210 *Grid:* 89/94
I-25 *(see chapter)*   *Type:* Hwy Junction w/Chapter
300.1 mi interstate highway through east/central **Wyoming** from **Colorado** north to **I-90** (just past **Buffalo**), which continues northwest to **Montana**. Highlights include: **Pioneer Museum, Ayres Park and Natural Bridge, National Historic Trails Interpretive Center, Hole-in-the-Wall, Outlaw Cave, Indian Rock Art Cave**.
Directions: N to Wheatland or S to Cheyenne from MM 17.2

MM: 53.8 *GPS:* 41.53711/-104.32344 *Elev:* 4983 *Grid:* 96/87
Meriden Rest Area   *Type:* Rest Area
Sheltered picnic tables.
Directions: SE side of hwy

MM: 67.4 *Dist:* 3.6 *GPS:* 41.71267/-104.19702 *Elev:* 4490 *Grid:* 98/82 *Land:* State
Hawk Springs State Recreation Area   *Type:* Recreation Area
A campground and boat ramp are located on the west side of the medium-sized **Hawk Springs Reservoir**. A blue heron rookery (breeding place) is located at the south end of the reservoir and is only accessible by boat. *Cottonwoods shade 12 sites along the lakeshore. 12 sites in an unshaded end loop. Fills on weekends.*
Crowds: ***** *[FEE AREA]* *Road Desc:* Gravel *Directions:* E on RD-22/CR-225 3.6 mi
Campsites: 24 *Shade:* *** *Privacy:* * *RV Size:* 40'+ *Other:* Water

MM: 72.6 *GPS:* 41.78414/-104.26590 *Elev:* 4386 *Grid:* 97/80 *Land:* City
Roadside Table   *Type:* Picnic Area
Small, under-maintained park in **Hawk Springs** with several picnic tables under a shelter.
Notes: Nicer picnic options are the Meriden Rest Area 19 mi south and Pioneer Park 20 mi north. *Directions:* E side of hwy

MM: 72.7 *GPS:* 41.78614/-104.26641 *Elev:* 4390 *Grid:* 97/80
Hawk Springs   *Type:* Town

MM: 77.5 *Dist:* 0.1 *GPS:* 41.85653/-104.26762 *Elev:* 4265 *Grid:* 97/79 *Land:* Wyoming G & F
Downar Bird Farm   *Type:* Game Farm
Wyoming Game and Fish raises thousands of ring-necked pheasants at this facility each year to be released for hunting. An interesting place for children and visitors are welcome.
Phone: 307-532-3449 *Cool Rating:* ** *Crowds:* * *Time:* 30 min *Directions:* W 0.05 mi; N into bird farm.

MM: 77.5 *Dist:* 3.0 *GPS:* 41.86164/-104.31121 *GPS2:* 41.89241/-104.28690 *Elev:* 4295 *Grid:* 96/78 *Land:* State
Springer Wildlife Habitat Management Area (northbound)   *Type:* Wildlife Habitat Mgmt Area
2 primitive camping areas. The south area is on a peninsula through the middle of **Bump Sullivan Reservoir** in a large parking area. *No toilet or fire rings. Close to railroad tracks.* The north area is along a long road ending at the northwest end of **Goshen Hole Reservoir**. A boat ramp is at the end of the road. *Vault toilet. Fire rings.*
Crowds: * *Directions:* W 2.5 mi to junction; **To south camp**: Straight 0.5 mi; **To north camp**: N/R 1.5 mi; E/R 1.4 mi.
Campsites: Dispersed *Shade:* * *Privacy:* ** *RV Size:* 30' *Other:* None

MM: 79.0 *GPS:* 41.87740/-104.26728 *Elev:* 4280 *Grid:* 97/78 *Land:* State
Springer Wildlife Habitat Management Area   *Type:* Wildlife Habitat Mgmt Area
Parking area on the west side of the highway where camping is permitted. *No facilities.*
Crowds: *

MM: 81.5 *Dist:* 5.4 *GPS:* 41.89241/-104.28690 *GPS2:* 41.86164/-104.31121 *Elev:* 4271 *Grid:* 97/78 *Land:* State
Springer Wildlife Habitat Management Area (southbound)   *Type:* Wildlife Habitat Mgmt Area
See section above at MM 77.5.
Directions: W on Wy-152 2.0 mi; S/L on Wy-152 0.9 mi; At a curve in the road, fork left to continue straight on RD-133 1.1 mi; **To north camp**: E/L 1.4 mi. **To south camp**: Continue S 1.5 mi; W/R 0.5 mi.

MM: 92.2 *GPS:* 42.04791/-104.18392 *Elev:* 4085 *Grid:* 98/74 *Land:* City
Homesteaders Museum   *Type:* Museum
A museum located inside the historic **Union Pacific Depot**, which contains written records, photographs, and memorabilia of the ranching and homesteading history from 1882 through **World War II**. Other exhibits include the historic **Trout Cabin** built in 1910 and a **Union Pacific Gallery**. This area was populated by mass migration when the **U.S. Government** offered free land with a homesteading act.
Hours: 9:30am - 4pm, Mon - Wed; 9:30am - 7pm, Thurs & Fri; 12pm - 6pm, Saturday; (June 1 - Aug 28); 9:30am - 4pm, Mon-Fri (offseason) *Phone:* 307-754-9481 *Cool Rating:* ** *Crowds:* * *Time:* 1 hr *Directions:* E side of hwy *(495 S Main St, Torrington)*

MM: 92.9 *Dist:* 0.4 *GPS:* 42.05785/-104.19024 *Elev:* 4086 *Grid:* 98/74 *Land:* City
Pioneer Park   *Type:* Park
A nice park that provides a public campground, which is located at the south end and includes designated parking areas plus an open area for RVs and tents. The campground is far enough away from the park to alleviate most noise, and nothing exists south of the campground except trees and the **North Platte River**. *Scraggly cottonwoods provide little shade. Ground is mowed weeds. 8 picnic tables. Donations appreciated, particularly for electricity use.*
Phone: 307-532-5666 *Crowds:* ** *Directions:* W on W 14th Ave 0.3 mi; S/L on D St 0.1 mi.
Campsites: 12 *Shade:* * *Privacy:* * *RV Size:* 40' *Other:* Electric,RVDump

MM: 93.2　*GPS:* 42.06270/-104.18439　*Elev:* 4103　*Grid:* 98/73
Torrington　　*Type:* Town

MM: 93.2　*GPS:* 42.06270/-104.18439　*Elev:* 4103　*Grid:* 98/73
US-26 (I-25 to Nebraska) *(see chapter)*　　*Type:* Hwy Junction w/Chapter
56.2 mi highway northwest from **Nebraska** to **I-25** exit 92. Highlights include: **Fort Laramie National Historic Site**, **Register Cliff**, **Oregon Trail Ruts**, **Guernsey State Park**.
Directions: SE to Nebraska or NW to Lingle from MM 48.3

MM: 103.1　*GPS:* 42.13690/-104.34553　*Elev:* 4172　*Grid:* 96/72
Lingle　　*Type:* Town

MM: 103.1　*GPS:* 42.13698/-104.34746　*Elev:* 4173　*Grid:* 96/72　*Land:* City
Whipple Park　　*Type:* Park
A nice park with 6 picnic tables under 3 shelters, restroom, playground, and a swimming pool.
Directions: 1 block W at the intersection of US-85/Main St and US-26/W 4th St;　N on Freimuth Ave into parking area.

MM: 103.1　*GPS:* 42.13688/-104.34552　*Elev:* 4172　*Grid:* 96/72
US-26 (I-25 to Nebraska) *(see chapter)*　　*Type:* Hwy Junction w/Chapter
56.2 mi highway northwest from **Nebraska** to **I-25** exit 92. Highlights include: **Fort Laramie National Historic Site**, **Register Cliff**, **Oregon Trail Ruts**, **Guernsey State Park**.
Directions: SE to Torrington or NW to Guernsey from MM 38.4

MM: 129.0　*Dist:* 15.2　*GPS:* 42.62613/-104.53129　*Elev:* 5422　*Grid:* 93/59
Featherlegs Monument and Grave & Rawhide Buttes (northbound)　　*Type:* Historical Marker
A 26.7 mi side trip off **US-85** through rolling green, rocky, semi-forested hills, past the monument and grave of **Mother Featherlegs Shepherd**, a prostitute who died in 1879. The **Rawhide Buttes** are about 3 mi southeast of the monument. The route also passes the **Lusk Rest Area** and **George Lathrop Monument** on **US-18/20** just east of **Silver Springs Rd**. This route is 6.4 mi farther and will add about 45 min over staying on **US-85**, but is more scenic and interesting.
Cool Rating: **　*Crowds:* *　*Time:* 45 min　*Road Desc:* Gravel　*Directions:* NW on Harris Ranch Rd 8.6 mi;　W/L on County Line Rd 0.5 mi;　N/R on Silver Springs Rd/CR-54 6.1 mi (past Rawhide Buttes to the east);　E side of road. **To return to US-85 heading north**: Continue N 9.7 mi;　E on US-18/20 1.8 mi passing the Lusk Rest Area/George Lathrop Monument.

MM: 139.0　*GPS:* 42.61014/-104.43085　*Elev:* 4960　*Grid:* 95/60
Rawhide Buttes Historical Marker　　*Type:* Historical Marker
The **Rawhide Buttes** are located 4 mi to the west and just south. This marker that tells the story of how they were named after a man that was skinned alive for shooting an Indian in 1849.
Cool Rating: *　*Crowds:* *　*Directions:* W side of hwy

MM: 149.3　*Dist:* 1.6　*GPS:* 42.74805/-104.48227　*Elev:* 5085　*Grid:* 94/56
Lusk Rest Area　　*Type:* Rest Area
A very nice rest area that was **Wyoming's** first in the national **Highway Beautification Act** of 1965. In 1998 it was selected as **Wyoming's** first 21st century rest area upgrade and was re-opened in November 2000 with passive solar and geothermal elements to create maximum energy efficiency. The rest area includes picnic shelters, a nice playground, and an **RV dump**. On the west side of the rest area is the **George Lathrop Monument**.
Directions: W on US-18/20 1.6 mi to MM 39.3;　S side of hwy.

MM: 149.3　*Dist:* 1.7　*GPS:* 42.74760/-104.48332　*Elev:* 5086　*Grid:* 94/56
George Lathrop Monument　　*Type:* Historical Marker
The grave and a monument in memory of **George Lathrop** (1830-1915), a pioneer of the west, Indian fighter, and veteran stage driver. The monument also marks the location of the **Cheyenne and Black Hills Stage Road**.
Cool Rating: *　*Crowds:* *　*Time:* 10 min　*Directions:* W on US-18/20 1.6 mi to MM 39.3;　West end of the Lusk Rest Area.

MM: 149.3　*Dist:* 11.5
Featherlegs Monument and Grave & Rawhide Buttes (southbound)　　*Type:* Historical Marker
See MM 129 above.
Time: 45 min　*Road Desc:* Gravel　*Directions:* W on US-18/20 1.8 mi to MM 39.1 (just past Lusk Rest Area);　S/L on Silver Springs Rd/CR-54 9.7 mi. **To return to US-85 heading south**: Continue S 6.1 mi (past Rawhide Buttes to the east);　E/L on County Line Rd 0.5 mi;　SE/R on Harris Ranch Rd 8.6 mi.

MM: 149.8　*GPS:* 42.76261/-104.45214　*Elev:* 5019　*Grid:* 94/56
Lusk　　*Type:* Town

MM: 149.8　*Dist:* 0.5　*GPS:* 42.76283/-104.44276　*Elev:* 5000　*Grid:* 94/56　*Land:* City
Redwood Water Tank　　*Type:* Historic Site
This water tank was built in 1886 to supply water for the railroad steam engines. The water was furnished from a windmill powered well. The original site was several hundred ft west of the current location. The tank is one of 6 still standing in the United States.
Cool Rating: **　*Crowds:* *　*Time:* 15 min
Directions: E on E 3rd St/US-20 0.3 mi (just past bridge);　N on unnamed street past railroad tracks 0.1 mi;　SE/R on E Railroad Ave 0.1 mi;　Veer R on 5th Ave 150 ft.

MM: 159.4　*GPS:* 42.89430/-104.40869　*Elev:* 5012　*Grid:* 95/53
Roadside Table　　*Type:* Picnic Area
A single unsheltered picnic table on the edge of a large paved parking area.
Directions: E side of hwy

MM: 163.4 **Dist:** 3.1 **GPS:** 42.93910/-104.36957 **GPS2:** 42.93027/-104.34309 **Elev:** 4465 **Grid:** 95/52 **Land:** Private
Fort Hat Creek Stage Station   **Type:** Historic Site
After gold was discovered in the **Black Hills** in 1874, the **U.S. Army** established this fort in 1875 on the banks of **Sage Creek**. However, the fort was named **Fort Hat Creek** because the soldiers thought they were on **Hat Creek** in **Nebraska**. In 1876 the fort became a stage stop on the **Cheyenne to Deadwood Stage Route** and was known as the **Hat Creek Station**. Still standing from the 1880s is a 2-story multi-purpose log building, which replaced the original buildings that had burned. A historical marker is located off the road at the south entrance. Observe from the road as this is on private land.

A historical sign about **Fort Hat Creek** is located in a large pullout on the southeast side of the highway, directly south of the turnoff from **US-85**.
Cool Rating: ** **Crowds:** * **Time:** 20 min **Road Desc:** Gravel, rough
Directions: E on Hat Creek Rd 2.0 mi; SW on Stage Rd 1.1 mi; NW side of road.

MM: 196.2 **GPS:** 43.37990/-104.22165 **Elev:** 3770 **Grid:** 98/41
Mule Creek Jct Rest Area   **Type:** Rest Area
A nice xeriscaped rest area with sheltered picnic tables.
Directions: At the NE corner at the intersection of US-85 & US-18.

MM: 229.3 **Dist:** 1.0 **GPS:** 43.85004/-104.20174 **Elev:** 4340 **Grid:** 98/29
Newcastle   **Type:** Town
Directions: W on US-16 1.0 mi

MM: 235.0 **GPS:** 43.92213/-104.18151 **Elev:** 5165 **Grid:** 98/27
Black Hills Scenic Overlook   **Type:** Scenic Viewpoint
A large pullout with interpretive signs and views to the east of the **Black Hills**.
Cool Rating: ** **Crowds:** * **Time:** 5 min **Directions:** E side of hwy

MM: 242.2 **GPS:** 44.01382/-104.16813 **Elev:** 5528 **Grid:** 98/25
Red Butte   **Type:** Geological Feature
A red sandstone butte that is a local landmark. It is best viewed from the south. To get a photo, a very small pullout is located on the east side of the highway exactly at MM 242.
Cool Rating: ** **Time:** Drive by **Directions:** SE side of hwy

MM: 247.3 **Dist:** 6.0 **GPS:** 44.07592/-104.05014 **Elev:** 6155 **Grid:** 100/23 **Land:** NF
Beaver Creek Campground   **Type:** Campground
Beaver Creek flows on the west side of this remote campground just across the **South Dakota** state line. *Conifer forest. Level. Grass understory. Good spacing between sites.*
Crowds: ** **[FEE AREA]** **Road Desc:** Gravel. Gets steep and winding at FR-111.
Directions: E on Mallo Rd/CR-4/FR-810 4.4 mi; E/R on FR-111 0.5 mi; Keep left at ranch 1.1 mi.
Campsites: 8 **Shade:** *** **Privacy:** *** **RV Size:** 40' **Other:** Water

MM: 247.6 **GPS:** 44.08076/-104.13610 **GPS2:** 44.34434/-104.20043 **Elev:** 5880 **Grid:** 99/23 **Land:** NF
Sand Creek Canyon Scenic Drive   **Type:** Scenic Drive
A 54.6 mi drive between **US-85** and **I-90** through **Sand Creek Canyon**, also referred to as **Grand Canyon**. The red-walled canyon is not magnificent, but the drive is nice if already heading this way and time permits. The road travels through the bottom of the canyon descending 2,300 ft from **US-85** to **I-90**. **Sand Creek Campground** is 20.4 mi north on **FR-863**, 2.9 mi south of **I-90** *(see I-90 MM 205.9).*
Cool Rating: ** **Crowds:** * **Time:** 2 hrs **Road Desc:** Wy-585 is paved and the rest is narrow gravel.
Directions: NW on Wy-585 22.4 mi; E on Clark Rd/CR-247 5.0 mi; N on Reynolds Rd/FR-872/Berglund Rd 1.9 mi; S on Moskee Rd 2.0 mi; NE on FR-863/Grand Canyon Rd/Sand Creek Rd 23.3 mi.

MM: 256.6 **GPS:** 44.17388/-104.05473 **Elev:** 6333 **Grid:** 100/21
End of Highway - South Dakota State Line   **Type:** Highway End
239.4 mi highway that begins at the **South Dakota** state line and parallels the **South Dakota** and **Nebraska state lines** before ending at **I-25** just north of **Cheyenne**. The highway heads south 153.5 mi to **Lingle** (MM 103.1), joins **US-26 (I-25 to Nebraska)** heading southeast 9.9 mi to **Torrington** (MM 93.2), then continues south for the final 76.1 mi. Highlights include: **Red Butte, Redwood Water Tank, Homesteaders Museum, Downar Bird Farm, Hawk Springs State Recreation Area**.
Nearest Town: Newcastle 26.4 S **Directions:** SW from the South Dakota state line to Newcastle from MM 256.6

MM: 55.9 **GPS:** 42.40050/-111.04744 **Elev:** 6258 **Grid:** 0/65
US-89 **Type:** Highway Description
62.4 mi highway from **Idaho**, roughly paralleling the **Idaho** state line north to **US-26/89** at **Alpine Jct**. The mile markers for **US-89** continue sequentially 93.3 mi to **Yellowstone National Park** as **US-26/89**, **US-26/89/191**, and **US-89/191/287**. Highlights include: the **World's Largest Elk Antler Arch**, **Intermittent Spring**.
Nearest Town: Geneva, Id 3.6 S **Directions:** N from the Idaho state line from MM 55.9

MM: 65.2 **Dist:** 0.3 **GPS:** 42.48876/-110.96189 **Elev:** 6760 **Grid:** 1/63 **Land:** NF
Allred Flat Campground **Type:** Campground
At the base of **Salt River Pass** along **Little White Creek**, which has been dammed by beavers across the highway. *Single loop. Mixed forest. Heavy understory. Good spacing between sites. Partially level. 10 pull-thrus.*
Crowds: * [FEE AREA] **Road Desc:** Gravel **Directions:** NW 0.3 mi
Campsites: 32 **Shade:** ***** **Privacy:** ***** **RV Size:** 40' **Other:** Water

MM: 69.0 **GPS:** 42.50607/-110.90825 **Elev:** 7615 **Grid:** 2/62 **Land:** NF
Salt River Pass **Type:** Pass
A large pullout at the summit of **Salt River Pass** with a view of the **Salt River Range** to the east plus 3 signs about **Periodic Spring** (**Intermittent Spring**), **Greys River Rd**, and the **Lander Cutoff**, all of which are accessed north on **US-89** *(see Greys River Rd, Lander Cutoff Monument, and Intermittent Spring below)*.
Cool Rating: ** **Crowds:** ** **Directions:** Large pullout on E side of hwy

MM: 71.1 **GPS:** 42.52947/-110.89782 **Elev:** 7162 **Grid:** 2/62 **Land:** NF
Smiths Fork Rd/FR-10072 **Type:** Highway Junction
Dispersed camping within a few miles along this road. This is also the south access to **Greys River Rd** *(see next section)*.
Road Desc: Gravel **Directions:** SE on Smiths Fork Rd/FR-10072
Campsites: Dispersed **Shade:** **** **Privacy:** ***** **RV Size:** 30' **Other:** None

MM: 71.1 **GPS:** 42.52947/-110.89782 **Elev:** 7162 **Grid:** 2/62
Greys River Rd/FR-10138 *(see chapter)* **Type:** Hwy Junction w/Chapter
82 mi side loop gravel road from **US-89** MM 71.1, returning to **US-89** MM 117.7 at **Alpine**, 46.6 mi north. This scenic route parallels the **Greys River** in the **Greys River Valley** and provides wildlife viewing, fishing, and camping.
Road Desc: A 33 mi section is narrow, washboarded, and potholed. **Directions:** SE on Smiths Fork Rd/FR-10072 from MM 82

MM: 72.2 **GPS:** 42.54417/-110.89351 **Elev:** 6930 **Grid:** 2/61
Lander Cutoff Monument **Type:** Historical Marker
A monument on the west end of the **Lander Cutoff**, which was a shortcut between **South Pass** and the **Snake River** country for those traveling the **Oregon Trail** to the **Pacific Northwest**. The route saved considerable distance but was much more difficult to travel than the original route. *A historical marker is located at the other end of the Lander Cutoff on Wy 28 MM 37.4, 103 mi east. See this section for a complete description.*
Cool Rating: * **Crowds:** * **Time:** 5 min **Directions:** E side of hwy

MM: 77.2 **Dist:** 6.2 **GPS:** 42.63928/ 110.81684 **Elev:** 7493 **Grid:** 3/59 **Land:** NF
Cottonwood Lake Campground **Type:** Campground
Located in a beautiful mountain setting near **Cottonwood Lake**. The campground consists of 2 sections that are separated by **North Fork Creek**. One section has 7 sites set up for horses with hitching rails, corrals, and trailheads for the **Trail Fork Trail** and **North Fork Cottonwood Trail**. The non-horse section has 5 tent-only sites and 2 pull-thrus. *Conifer forest.*
Crowds: *** [FEE AREA] **Road Desc:** Gravel **Directions:** E on CR-153/FR-10208 6.2 mi
Campsites: 18 **Shade:** ***** **Privacy:** *** **RV Size:** 30' **Other:** Water

MM: 85.1 **GPS:** 42.72537/-110.93350 **Elev:** 6235 **Grid:** 2/57
Afton **Type:** Town

MM: 85.2 **GPS:** 42.72431/-110.93354 **Elev:** 6234 **Grid:** 2/57 **Land:** City
World's Largest Elk Antler Arch **Type:** Point of Interest
Over 3000 elk antlers have created an 18 ft high arch over **US-89/N Washington St**.
Cool Rating: ** **Crowds:** * **Time:** 10 min **Directions:** Between 4th Ave and 5th Ave in Afton.

MM: 85.5 **GPS:** 42.72995/-110.93370 **Elev:** 6230 **Grid:** 2/57 **Land:** City
City of Afton Information Center **Type:** Visitor Center
Visitor information and a free **RV dump**.
Directions: NW corner of US-89/N Washington St and 2nd Ave.

MM: 85.5 **Dist:** 1.5 **GPS:** 42.72519/-110.90656 **Elev:** 6415 **Grid:** 2/57 **Land:** NF
Swift Creek Campground **Type:** Campground
Along **Swift Creek** at the mouth of **Swift Creek Canyon**. *Thick conifer forest. Thick middlestory. Most sites are roomy, but a couple are tight. Not level. Under-maintained. Tightly configured interior road.*
Crowds: * [FEE AREA] **Road Desc:** Last 1/4 mi is gravel. **Directions:** E on 2nd Ave/Swift Creek Canyon Rd 1.5 mi
Campsites: 10 **Shade:** ***** **Privacy:** **** **RV Size:** 20' **Other:** Water

MM: 85.5 *Dist:* 5.1 *GPS:* 42.74948/-110.85944 *GPS2:* 42.74501/-110.84913 *Elev:* 6954 *Grid:* 3/56 *Land:* NF
Intermittent Spring   *Type:* Natural Feature
Also known as **Periodic Spring**, this spring flows intermittently through a scenic, steep walled canyon on 4 min to 25 min intervals. This is the largest of only 3 intermittent springs known in the world. The intermittent flow starts in late summer through the fall when groundwater tables are lower. An easy 0.6 mi hike leads to a view of the spring and a steep, rough trail leads to the spring itself. A vault toilet and picnic tables are located at the parking area plus a picnic table near the spring.
Cool Rating: **** *Crowds:* * *Time:* 1 hr
Notes: This feature is not completely natural. There are some inner mechanical workings, including metal doors that close when the flow is low. One door was actually missing when I was there and the water flow never completely stopped.
Road Desc: Partially paved, rough spots, narrow & winding. The first 1.25 mi is paved and the rest is gravel.
Directions: E on E 2nd Ave/Swift Creek Canyon Rd 5.1 mi to parking area; Hike 0.6 mi E and cross a bridge.

MM: 97.3 *Dist:* 0.3 *GPS:* 42.88202/-110.99802 *Elev:* 5933 *Grid:* 1/53 *Land:* Wyoming G & F
Upper Salt River Public Access Area   *Type:* Public Access Area
A gravel parking area that provides camping and fishing access to the **Salt River**. One of the sites is situated in some aspen trees. *Stone fire rings. Vault toilet.*
Crowds: ** *Road Desc:* Gravel *Directions:* SW on Strawberry Creek Rd 0.3 mi
Campsites: Dispersed *Shade:* * *Privacy:* * *RV Size:* 40' *Other:* None

MM: 97.6 *GPS:* 42.88658/-110.99252 *Elev:* 5978 *Grid:* 1/53
Star Valley Rest Area   *Type:* Rest Area
A nice rest area with covered picnic shelters.
Directions: E side of hwy

MM: 100.0 *GPS:* 42.92051/-111.00238 *Elev:* 5903 *Grid:* 1/52
Thayne   *Type:* Town

MM: 104.4 *Dist:* 5.6 *GPS:* 43.00497/-111.10237 *Elev:* 5855 *Grid:* -1/50 *Land:* NF
Tin Cup Campground   *Type:* Campground
Located just across the **Idaho** state line on **Tin Cup Creek**, in the midst of an extensive trail system. *Conifer forest.*
Crowds: ** *Nearest Town:* Freedom 4.1 SE *[FEE AREA]*
Directions: W on Wy-239 1.6 mi; N/R on County Line Rd 0.9 mi; W/L on Id-34 3.1 mi.
Campsites: 5 *Shade:* ***** *Privacy:* *** *RV Size:* 30' *Other:* None

MM: 112.0 *Dist:* 1.5 *GPS:* 43.09521/-111.04303 *Elev:* 5665 *Grid:* 0/48 *Land:* Wyoming G & F
Lower Salt River Public Access Area   *Type:* Public Access Area
A gravel parking area that provides camping and fishing access to the **Salt River**. *Vault toilet.*
Crowds: ** *Road Desc:* Gravel *Directions:* W on CR-105 1.0 mi; W/L 0.5 mi to parking area.
Campsites: Dispersed *Shade:* * *Privacy:* * *RV Size:* 30' *Other:* None

MM: 117.7 *GPS:* 43.16359/-111.01795 *Elev:* 5660 *Grid:* 1/46
Alpine   *Type:* Town

MM: 117.7 *GPS:* 43.16359/-111.01795 *Elev:* 5660 *Grid:* 1/46
Greys River Rd/FR-10138 *(see chapter)*   *Type:* Hwy Junction w/Chapter
82 mi side loop gravel road from **US-89** MM 117.7 at **Alpine** returning to **US-89** MM 71.1, 46.6 mi south. This scenic route parallels the **Greys River** in the **Greys River Valley** and provides wildlife viewing, fishing, and camping.
Road Desc: A 33 mi section is narrow, washboarded, and potholed.
Directions: Just before the Snake River bridge in Alpine, SE on Greys River Rd from MM 0

MM: 118.3 *GPS:* 43.17220/-111.01850 *Elev:* 5660 *Grid:* 1/46
US-26/89 *(see chapter)*   *Type:* Hwy Junction w/Chapter
23 mi highway from **US-89** at **Alpine Jct** northeast to **Hoback Jct** through the **Snake River Canyon**. The mile markers continue sequentially from **US-89** at **Alpine Jct**. No highlights along this route, but there are 4 National Forest campgrounds.
Nearest Town: Alpine 0.6 S *Notes:* Camping in designated campgrounds only. *Directions:* NE to Hoback Jct from MM 118.3

MM: 118.3 *Dist:* 2.1 *GPS:* 43.19708/-111.04099 *Elev:* 5694 *Grid:* 0/45 *Land:* NF
Alpine Campground   *Type:* Campground
Composed of 2 loops on the southeast side of the **Palisades Reservoir** just east of the **Idaho** state line. The second loop is considered an overflow area. The campground is popular for whitewater rafters from the **Snake River Canyon**. *Mixed forest. Heavy understory. Roomy sites. Tent pads. Some highway noise.*
Crowds: *** *Nearest Town:* Alpine 2.7 SE *[FEE AREA]* *Directions:* NW on US-26 2.1 mi; SW side of hwy.
Campsites: 22 *Shade:* **** *Privacy:* **** *RV Size:* 30' *Other:* 1-877-444-6777:www.recreation.gov,Water

MM: 118.3 *GPS:* 43.17220/-111.01850 *Elev:* 5660 *Grid:* 1/46
End of Highway   *Type:* Highway End
62.4 mi highway from **US-26/89** at **Alpine Jct**, roughly paralleling the **Idaho** state line south to **Idaho**. The mile markers continue sequentially from **US-26/89**. Highlights include: **Intermittent Spring**, the **World's Largest Elk Antler Arch**.
Nearest Town: Alpine 0.6 S *Directions:* S to Alpine from MM 118.3

MM: 184.6 (0.0/27.0) *GPS:* 43.84002/-110.50993 *Elev:* 6733 *Grid:* 8/29
US-89/191/287 *Type:* Highway Description
27 mi highway from **Moran Jct** north through **Grand Teton National Park** to the south entrance of **Yellowstone National Park**. The mile markers continue sequentially from **US-26/89/191** *(see notes)*. Highlights include: **Oxbow Bend**, views of **Jackson Lake** and the **Teton Range**.
Directions: N to Yellowstone NP from MM 184.6 (0)
Notes: There are no mile markers along this highway, so some rivers and creeks have been included as points of reference. The official mile markers are provided as well as the mileages starting at zero in both directions.

MM: 184.6 (0.0/27.0) *GPS:* 43.84002/-110.50993 *Elev:* 6733 *Grid:* 8/29
US-26/89/191 *(see chapter)* *Type:* Hwy Junction w/Chapter
43.3 mi highway from **Moran Jct** south to **Hoback Jct**, where the highway transitions to **US-26/89** using sequential mile markers. The entire length is along the **Centennial Scenic Byway**. Highlights include: **Grand Teton National Park, Jackson Hole** and **Greater Yellowstone Visitor Center, Jackson**.
Directions: S to Jackson from MM 184.6

MM: 184.6 (0.0/27.0) *GPS:* 43.84002/-110.50993 *Elev:* 6733 *Grid:* 8/29
US-26/287 & US-26 *(see chapter)* *Type:* Hwy Junction w/Chapter
133.7 mi highway from **Moran Jct** southeast to **Riverton**. **US-287 (Lander to US-26)** splits off south at MM 98.8 and the highway continues southeast as **US-26**. Heading southeast to **Dubois** is along the **Centennial Scenic Byway**. Highlights include: **Breccia Cliffs, Wind River Lake, Pinnacle Buttes, Brooks Lake Creek Falls, Brooks Lake, Dubois Recreation Area Scenic Overlook**, colorful badlands, **Trail Lake Rd Petroglyphs**.
Nearest Town: Moose 18.3 SW; Dubois 55.6 SE *Directions:* SE to Dubois from MM 0

MM: 184.6 (0.0/27.0) *GPS:* 43.84002/-110.50993 *Elev:* 6733 *Grid:* 8/29
Moran Jct *Type:* Highway Junction
A named highway junction with no services.
Nearest Town: Moose 18.3 SW

MM: 184.9 (0.3/26.7) *GPS:* 43.84398/-110.51216 *Elev:* 6739 *Grid:* 8/29 *Land:* NPS
Grand Teton National Park - Buffalo Entrance *Type:* National Park
Pay the National Park entrance fee, which covers both **Grand Teton National Park** and **Yellowstone National Park**. *See chapter: Grand Teton National Park.*
[FEE AREA]

MM: 185.8 (1.2/25.8) *Dist:* 8.1 *GPS:* 43.93936/-110.44286 *Elev:* 7020 *Grid:* 9/27 *Land:* NF
Pacific Creek Campground *Type:* Campground
Near **Pacific Creek** just outside **Grand Teton National Park** in the **Bridger-Teton National Forest**. The **Pacific Creek Trailhead** into the **Teton Wilderness** starts from the campground. *Light conifer forest. Tables. Fire rings with grates.*
Crowds: ^^^ **[FEE AREA]** *Directions:* NE on Pacific Creek Rd 2.2 mi; 2nd left to stay on Pacific Creek Rd 5.9 mi.
Notes: Dispersed camping along the 2 mi of forest road into the campground
Road Desc: Partially paved. Last 5.9 mi is gravel.
Campsites: 7 *Shade:* ** *Privacy:* ** *RV Size:* 40' *Other:* Water GRIZZLIES

MM: 187.4 (2.8/24.2) *GPS:* 43.86618/-110.54758 *Elev:* 6760 *Grid:* 7/28 *Land:* NPS
Oxbow Bend *Type:* Scenic Viewpoint
What was originally a bend in the **Snake River** became a calm backwater when the river cut a new channel to the south. An interpretive sign explains how the oxbow was formed and how it provides a rich habitat many types of animals, including moose, beaver, otters, great blue herons, and pelicans. **Mount Moran** dominates the background to the west and reflects vividly in the water when calm.
Cool Rating: *** *Crowds:* *** *Time:* 10-30 min *Directions:* Pullout on S side of hwy

MM: 188.0 (3.5/23.5) *Dist:* 1.0 *GPS:* 43.85654/-110.55326 *Elev:* 6735 *Grid:* 7/29 *Land:* NPS
Snake River Access at Oxbow Bend *Type:* Hiking Trail
A short road leads to the bank of the **Snake River** on the south side of **Oxbow Bend**.
Cool Rating: *** *Crowds:* ** *Time:* 30 min *Notes:* Not recommended for RVs or trailers. *Road Desc:* Gravel, narrow
Directions: S on unnamed road 1.0 mi

MM: 188.6 (4.0/23.0) *GPS:* 43.86610/-110.57058 *Elev:* 6762 *Grid:* 7/28
Teton Park Rd: Grand Teton National Park *(see chapter)* *Type:* Hwy Junction w/Chapter
20.8 mi road south through the main section of **Grand Teton National Park**, which traverses the central-eastern base of the **Teton Range** and offers the closest access and views. Highlights include: **Jackson Lake, Signal Mountain, Jenny Lake, Hidden Falls, Inspiration Point, Chapel of the Transfiguration and Menor's Ferry Historic District, Craig Thomas Discovery and Visitor Center**.
Nearest Town: Moose 20.4 S, Jackson 33.2 S *Directions:* S from MM 20.8

MM: 188.6 (4.0/23.0) *Dist:* 3.0 *GPS:* 43.84195/-110.61235 *Elev:* 6818 *Grid:* 6/29 *Land:* NPS
Signal Mountain Campground *Type:* Campground
Located on a hill above the southeast shore of **Jackson Lake** with a fine view of the **Teton Range** across the lake. Some sites have a partial view of the lake. Just north of the campground is **Signal Mountain Lodge** and marina with a store, restaurant, and fuel. *Conifer forest. Many sites are in the open. Small sites. Amphitheater. Fills by late morning.*

The **Signal Mountain Trail** starts at the east end of the campground and leads to the **Jackson Point Overlook** on **Signal Mountain**. This can also be reached by a 4.7 mi paved road to the top *(see Teton Park Rd MM 16.7)*. *Moderate; 5.7 mi round-trip; 750 ft elev gain.*
Crowds: ***** **[FEE AREA]** *Directions:* SW on Teton Park Rd 3.0 mi; W 0.1 mi.
Campsites: 81 *Shade:* *** *Privacy:* * *RV Size:* 30' *Other:* Water,RVDump BEARS

MM: 189.1 (4.5/22.5)   *GPS:* 43.87300/-110.57368   *Elev:* 6845   *Grid:* 7/28   *Land:* NPS
Willow Flats Overlook   *Type:* Scenic Viewpoint
A view of the **Teton Range** from the northern end. An interpretive sign explains the formation of the **Teton Range** and identifies the **Teton** peaks. Below the overlook is **Willow Flats**, a moist, flat plain that supports abundant wildlife, which is explained by a second interpretive sign.
Cool Rating: ***   *Crowds:* ***   *Time:* 10 min   *Directions:* Pullout on W side of hwy

MM: 190.5 (6.0/21.0)   *Dist:* 0.9   *GPS:* 43.89820/-110.56101   *GPS2:* 43.90684/-110.55566   *Elev:* 7020   *Grid:* 7/28   *Land:* NPS
Grand View Point Trail   *Type:* Hiking Trail
A steep climb to **Grand View Point**, which provides nice views of the **Teton Range** and **Jackson Lake** to the west; **Two Ocean Lake** and **Emma Matilda Lake** to the east; and **Gros Ventre Range**, **Blacktail Butte**, and the **Jackson Hole** valley to the south. *Moderate; 1.1 mi one-way; 550 ft elev gain.*
Cool Rating: ****   *Crowds:* **   *Time:* 1.5 hr   *Road Desc:* Gravel, rough   *Directions:* E/R on unmarked road 0.9 mi

MM: 194.1 (9.5/17.5)   *Dist:* 0.7   *GPS:* 43.90576/-110.63979   *Elev:* 6832   *Grid:* 6/27   *Land:* NPS
Colter Bay Village and Campground: Grand Teton National Park   *Type:* Town & Campground
Located on the east side of **Jackson Lake** with a visitor center, grocery store, 2 restaurants, laundry, showers, gift shops, service station, log and tent cabins, and a full service marina. Behind the visitor center is an easy 2.0 mi trail on a peninsula, across a dike, and on an island in **Jackson Lake**. On the north side is a huge campground. *15 loops. Conifer forest. 2 tent-only loops. 9 walk-in sites. 11 group sites. Generators permitted in some loops. Rarely fills.*
Crowds: *****   *[FEE AREA]*   *Directions:* SW on Colter Bay Village Rd 0.7 mi
Campsites: 350   *Shade:* *****   *Privacy:* ***   *RV Size:* 40'+   *Other:* Water,RVDump   BEARS

MM: 194.1 (9.5/17.5)   *Dist:* 0.9   *GPS:* 43.90325/-110.64353   *Elev:* 6800   *Grid:* 6/27   *Land:* NPS
Colter Bay Visitor Center & Indian Arts Museum   *Type:* Visitor Center
A visitor center with information, audiovisual programs, permits, and a bookstore. Also houses the **Indian Arts Museum**, which contains a fine collection of Indian artifacts as well as craft demonstrations by tribal members and ranger-led museum tours.
Hours: 8am - 7pm (Summer); 8am - 5pm (offseason)   *Phone:* 307-739-3594   *Crowds:* ***
Directions: SW on Colter Bay Village Rd 0.9 mi; NW/R into parking area.

MM: 196.0 (11.4/15.6)   *GPS:* 43.93711/-110.62999   *Elev:* 6952   *Grid:* 6/27   *Land:* NPS
Sargent's Bay Picnic Area   *Type:* Picnic Area
A half-loop pullout with 4 shaded picnic tables.
Directions: NW side of hwy

MM: 198.3 (13.7/13.3)   *GPS:* 43.96749/-110.63937   *Elev:* 6849   *Grid:* 6/26   *Land:* NPS
Arizona Island Picnic Area   *Type:* Picnic Area
A half-loop pullout in a meadow with 2 picnic tables and a few conifer trees, but little shade.
Directions: SW side of hwy

MM: 199.4 (14.8/12.2)   *GPS:* 43.97719/-110.65607   *Elev:* 6804   *Grid:* 6/26   *Land:* NPS
Lake View Picnic Area   *Type:* Picnic Area
A loop road in a conifer forest on the northeast shore of **Jackson Lake**. *8 picnic tables with several near the lake.*
Directions: SW side of hwy

MM: 199.8 (15.2/11.8)   *GPS:* 43.98137/-110.66179   *Elev:* 6787   *Grid:* 6/25   *Land:* NPS
Interpretive Pullout: Waterfalls Canyon Fire   *Type:* Point of Interest
A long pullout along **Jackson Lake** with an interpretive sign about the 1974 **Waterfalls Canyon** fire that burned the forest across the lake. The sign explains how fire benefits the ecosystem.
Cool Rating: *   *Crowds:* **   *Time:* 5 min   *Directions:* SW side of hwy

MM: 201.4 (16.8/10.2)   *GPS:* 44.00036/-110.67737   *Elev:* 6795   *Grid:* 5/25   *Land:* NPS
Northern Teton Range Overlook   *Type:* Scenic Viewpoint
A long pullout with a view across the northern tip of **Jackson Lake** and the northern end of the **Teton Range**. *1 picnic table in the open.*
Cool Rating: **   *Crowds:* *   *Time:* 5 min   *Directions:* W side of hwy

MM: 202.0 (17.5/9.5)   *GPS:* 44.00680/-110.68449   *Elev:* 6822   *Grid:* 5/25   *Land:* NPS
Lizard Creek Campground: Grand Teton National Park   *Type:* Campground
Located on the northeast end of **Jackson Lake** with an upper and lower loop. The upper loop accommodates larger RVs and allows the use of generators. The lower loop is closest to the lake and is best for tents, vans, and pickup campers. *Conifer forest. 20 tent-only sites. Flush toilets. Rarely fills.*
Crowds: ****   *[FEE AREA]*   *Directions:* S side of hwy
Campsites: 60   *Shade:* *****   *Privacy:* ****   *RV Size:* 30'   *Other:* Water   GRIZZLIES

MM: 205.0 (20.4/6.6)   *GPS:* 44.04329/-110.69324   *Elev:* 7359   *Grid:* 5/24   *Land:* NPS
Grand Teton National Park (north boundary)   *Type:* National Park
A pullout with a **Grand Teton National Park** entrance sign and a vault toilet. *See chapter: Grand Teton National Park.*
Directions: NW side of hwy

MM: 205.0 (20.4/6.6)   *GPS:* 44.04329/-110.69324   *Elev:* 7359   *Grid:* 5/24   *Land:* NF
John D. Rockefeller, Jr. Memorial Parkway (northbound)   *Type:* Scenic Drive
A 6.8 mi section of highway between **Yellowstone National Park** and **Grand Teton National Park** in recognition of **John D. Rockefeller, Jr.**'s work in establishing or expanding several national parks, including **Grand Teton National Park**.

MM: 205.5 (20.9/6.1)   *GPS:* 44.05220/-110.69050   *Elev:* 7310   *Grid:* 5/24   *Land:* NF
Interpretive Pullout: Forest Fires   *Type:* Point of Interest
2 signs about forest fires.
Cool Rating: *   *Crowds:* *   *Time:* 5 min   *Directions:* E side of hwy

MM: 209.1 (24.5/2.5)
Snake River   *Type:* River

MM: 209.6 (25.0/2.0) **Dist:** 0.1 **GPS:** 44.10727/-110.66703 **Elev:** 6857 **Grid:** 6/22 **Land:** NF

Flagg Ranch Information Station   **Type:** Visitor Center

A staffed visitor center with National Park, National Forest, and area information. The visitor center is located in the **Flagg Ranch Lodge** parking lot, which has a gas station. *3 picnic tables with no shade.*

Hours: 8am - 5pm (June 6 - Sept 4) **Phone:** 307-543-2372 **Notes:** The campground to the south is a private resort.

Directions: W then immediately N/R; N 130 yds; Left into the Flagg Ranch Lodge parking lot; Information Station is S 50 yds.

MM: 209.6 (25.0/2.0) **Dist:** 1.5 **GPS:** 44.10670/-110.66547 **GPS2:** 44.10421/-110.68727 **Elev:** 6860 **Grid:** 6/22 **Land:** NF

Grassy Lake Rd   **Type:** Campground

A road that accesses 16 well-maintained campsites in 8 camping areas on or near the **Snake River**. The first area is just above the river with 4 sites (MI 1.5). The second and third areas have 2 sites each near the river (MI 2.1 and 2.7). The forth area has 2 sites on a hill above the river (MI 2.9). The last 4 areas have 1 site each and are not on the river (MI 3.5, 5.4, 6.9, 7.5). *Conifer forest. Vault toilet. Bear-proof box. Trash.*

Crowds: **** **Notes:** Camping only in designated campsites. **Road Desc:** Gravel, narrow

Directions: W then immediately N/R on Grassy Lake Rd; Follow the road north, then west around the large parking lot 0.3 mi; Continue 1.2 mi to first campsite.

Campsites: 16 **Shade:** *** **Privacy:** *** **RV Size:** 30' **Other:** GRIZZLIES

MM: 211.5 (26.9/0.1) **GPS:** 44.13268/-110.66480 **Elev:** 6885 **Grid:** 6/22

Yellowstone National Park Boundary Pullout   **Type:** Visitor Information

Located on the west side of the highway is a long pullout with **Grand Teton National Park** information on a signboard as well as an interpretive sign about the **John D. Rockefeller, Jr. Memorial Parkway** *(see next section)*. On the east side of the highway is a long pullout just before the **Yellowstone National Park** sign.

MM: 211.6 (27.0/0.0) **GPS:** 44.13331/-110.66521 **Elev:** 6885 **Grid:** 6/22 **Land:** NF

John D. Rockefeller, Jr. Memorial Parkway (southbound)   **Type:** Scenic Drive

A 6.8 mi section of highway between **Yellowstone National Park** and **Grand Teton National Park** in recognition of **John D. Rockefeller, Jr.**'s work in establishing or expanding several national parks, including **Grand Teton National Park**.

MM: 211.6 (27.0/0.0) **GPS:** 44.13331/-110.66521 **Elev:** 6885 **Grid:** 6/22

Yellowstone - South Entrance to West Thumb *(see chapter)*   **Type:** Hwy Transition w/Chapter

21.2 mi highway from the south entrance of **Yellowstone National Park**, via **US-89/191/287**, north to **West Thumb**. Highlights include: **Moose Falls**, **Lewis Falls**.

Nearest Town: Grant Village 20.4 N **[FEE AREA]** **Directions:** N to West Thumb from MM 0

MM: 211.6 (27.0/0.0) **GPS:** 44.13331/-110.66521 **Elev:** 6885 **Grid:** 6/22

End of Highway   **Type:** Highway End

27 mi highway from the south entrance of **Yellowstone National Park** south through **Grand Teton National Park** to **Moran Jct**. Highlights include: views of **Jackson Lake** and the **Teton Range**, **Oxbow Bend**.

Nearest Town: Grant Village 20.4 N **Directions:** S to Grand Teton NP from MM 211.6 (27)

Wy-110/Devils Tower Rd (Devils Tower National Monument) E/W

MM: 0.0/3.4 *GPS:* 44.58218/-104.69560 *Elev:* 3941 *Grid:* 91/10
Wy-110/Devils Tower Rd (Devils Tower National Monument)   *Type:* Highway Description
3.4 mi road west into **Devils Tower National Monument** ending at **Devils Tower** and the visitor center parking area.
Directions: W from MM 0

MM: 0.0/3.4 *GPS:* 44.58218/-104.69560 *Elev:* 3941 *Grid:* 91/10
Wy-24 *(see chapter)*   *Type:* Hwy Junction w/Chapter
46.3 mi highway from **US-14 (east)**, 6 mi south of **Devils Tower**, north and east to **South Dakota**. The primary purpose of this highway is access to **Devils Tower National Monument**. Other highlights include: access to **Cook Lake Recreation Area**, **Aladdin Tipple Historical Park**.
Directions: N to Hulett or S to US-14 from MM 6

MM: 0.6/2.8 *GPS:* 44.58924/-104.70050 *Elev:* 3855 *Grid:* 91/10 *Land:* NM
Devils Tower National Monument Entrance Station   *Type:* National Monument
[FEE AREA]

MM: 1.1/2.3 *GPS:* 44.58582/-104.70791 *Elev:* 3879 *Grid:* 91/10 *Land:* NM
Prairie Dog Town   *Type:* Wildlife Area
A large black-tailed prairie dog town just off the road. 3 pullouts on the southeast side of the road allow visitors to observe the prairie dogs.
Cool Rating: ** *Crowds:* ** *Time:* 10 min *Directions:* SE side of road.

MM: 1.5/1.9 *Dist:* 0.4 *GPS:* 44.58191/-104.70774 *Elev:* 3863 *Grid:* 91/10 *Land:* NM
Belle Fourche Campground   *Type:* Campground
Just southwest of the **Belle Fourche River** with a good view of **Devils Tower**. Cottonwood trees don't shade all sites. *2 loops. Native grass understory. Level. 3 group sites. 1 handicapped accessible site. All pull-thrus. Flush toilets.*
Crowds: ***** *[FEE AREA]* *Directions:* S then E 0.4 mi
Campsites: 30 *Shade:* *** *Privacy:* ** *RV Size:* 40' *Other:* Water

---

MM: 2.8/0.6 *Dist:* 0.3 *GPS:* 44.59873/-104.72389 *Elev:* 4201 *Grid:* 90/10 *Land:* NM
Joyner Ridge Trail   *Type:* Hiking Trail
An interpretive trail that traverses the 3 different life zones of the area. The trail starts to the left with a sign that gives an overview of the trail and heads into zone 1, a **ridge-top forest**. At about 0.7 mi is a bench with a fine view of **Devils Tower**. The trail then descends 140 ft into a canyon past sandstone cliffs and across a meadow. At 1.0 mi is a connecting trail to the left to the **Red Beds Trail**. Just past this junction is zone 2, **the ravine**, a shady and moist thicket of deciduous trees and shrubs, which is cooler and darker than on top. The trail gradually climbs out of the canyon 0.4 mi to zone 3, **the prairie**, where the trail continues through a meadow of tall grass back to the parking area. This is an excellent sunset hike. *Moderately easy; 1.7 mi loop; 190 ft elev loss.*
Cool Rating: *** *Crowds:* * *Time:* 1 hr *Road Desc:* Gravel, narrow *Directions:* N 1/4 mi

---

MM: 3.4/0.0 *GPS:* 44.59082/-104.72022 *Elev:* 4250 *Grid:* 90/10 *Land:* NM
Devils Tower   *Type:* National Monument
Devils Tower National Monument was designated the United States first national monument in 1906. **Devils Tower** is a spectacular rock formation that rises 1,267 ft above the **Belle Fourche River** with a flat top 600 ft above the base and about the size of a football field. The tower is composed of igneous (volcanic) rock that was sculpted by millions of years of erosion that continues today. The most unusual feature is the polygonal columns that make up the sides of the tower. **Devils Tower** is a rock climbing mecca, which was first climbed in 1937. The area itself is beautiful with green and red rolling hills, patches of forest, and **Devils Tower**.

The **Tower Trail** is a shady and pleasant paved trail through a ponderosa pine forest around the base of **Devils Tower**. This popular trail provides close up views of **Devils Tower** and the **talus** fields at the base. Interpretive signs provide information about the tower, plants, and wildlife. Benches are provided along the trail. *Easy; 1.3 mi loop; Level. 45-60 min.*

The staffed visitor center contains a bookstore and exhibits on the history and geology of **Devils Tower**.
Hours: Visitor Center: 8am - 8pm (Memorial Day - Labor Day); 9am - 4pm (mid Mar - Memorial Day) *Phone:* 307-467-5283
Cool Rating: ***** *Crowds:* ***** *Time:* 1-2 hrs *Directions:* End of road at parking area
Notes: The motorcycle rally in Sturgis, South Dakota takes place in early August and thousands of motorcyclists visit Devils Tower. The Wednesday of the rally week is usually the busiest day at the park.

MM: 3.4/0.0 *GPS:* 44.59027/-104.71956 *Elev:* 4261 *Grid:* 90/10 *Land:* NM
Red Beds Trail   *Type:* Hiking Trail
A loop trail that descends down the hill below **Devils Tower** to a red sandstone formation named the **Red Beds**. The trail branches left from the paved path to **Devils Tower** after about 60 yds and travels in a clockwise direction. The hike starts through a pine forest that eventually offers good views of the **Red Beds**, the valley floor, and the distant hills. At 0.6 mi begins a steep descent toward the **Red Beds**. At 1.2 mi the trail leaves the forest and comes to a junction with a 3/4 mi trail that connects to the **Joyner Ridge Trail** *(see earlier section)*. Continuing 0.2 mi enters an area of red dirt and a 0.2 mi walk through the **Red Beds**, emerging to an overlook of the **Belle Fourche River**, the entrance station, and the valley below. The trail continues with excellent views of the river valley and gradually climbs through the forest back to the parking area. *Moderately easy; 3.0 mi loop; 330 ft elev loss.*
Cool Rating: **** *Crowds:* * *Time:* 1.5 to 2 hrs *Directions:* SE end of parking area.

MM: 0.0 **GPS:** 43.64610/-108.21200 **Elev:** 4330 **Grid:** 41/34
Wy-120   **Type:** Highway Description
118.7 mi highway that runs diagonally from **Thermopolis** northwest to **Cody** and continues to **Montana**. From **Cody**, **US-14/16/20** heads straight east to the east entrance of **Yellowstone National Park**. Continuing north from **Cody** the highway provides 2 scenic routes to the northeast entrance of **Yellowstone National Park**. Route 1 connects to **Wy-296 (Chief Joseph Scenic Highway)**, which climbs over the spectacular **Dead Indian Pass** and connects to **US-212**. Route 2 travels into **Montana** and loops back into **Wyoming** on **US-212** over the even more spectacular **Beartooth Pass**. Highlights include: **Legend Rock Petroglyphs**, **Gooseberry Badlands Scenic Area**, attractions in **Cody** (see US-14/16/20 MM 52.4).
Directions: NW to Cody from MM 0
Notes: The highway winds 2.6 mi northwest through Cody on US-14/16/20 and US-14A before connecting back to Wy-120. During this jog through Cody the mile markers jump from MM 81.2 to MM 100 gaining 18.8 mi.

MM: 0.0 **GPS:** 43.64610/-108.21200 **Elev:** 4330 **Grid:** 41/34
US-20/Wy-789 & US-16/20/Wy-789 & US-14/16/20/Wy-789 (see chapter)   **Type:** Hwy Junction w/Chapter
157 mi highway from **Shoshoni** north to **Montana**. Highlights include: **Boysen State Park**, **Wind River Canyon**, **Hot Springs State Park**, **Medicine Lodge State Archaeological Site**, **Devil's Kitchen Geological Site**, **Museum of Flight and Aerial Firefighting**.
Directions: N to Worland or S to Shoshoni from MM 132.5

MM: 0.0 **GPS:** 43.64610/-108.21200 **Elev:** 4330 **Grid:** 41/34
Thermopolis   **Type:** Town

MM: 20.2 **Dist:** 8.1 **GPS:** 43.79845/-108.60310 **GPS2:** 43.79921/-108.59706 **Elev:** 5379 **Grid:** 35/30 **Land:** BLM
Legend Rock Petroglyphs   **Type:** Petroglyphs
A 300 yd long cliff face contains an impressive collection of nearly 300 **Petroglyphs** depicting bison, elk, humans, and even a rabbit. This rock art ranges from 100 to 11,000 years old, but most are classified as the **Dinwoody** tradition, which is only seen in the **Bighorn Basin** and **Wind River Basin** west of the **Bighorn River**. **Dinwoody Petroglyphs** are always pecked and are often of large humanlike figures with headdresses, an unusual amount of fingers or toes, have a pattern of interior lines in the torso, and are sometimes upside down. This site is considered one of the oldest and best examples of the **Dinwoody** rock art. Picnic table. Vault toilet.
Cool Rating: ***** **Crowds:** * **Time:** 1 hr **Road Desc:** Gravel
Notes: The site is protected by a locked gate. A key can be obtained at Hot Springs State Park in Thermopolis. Leave the key in the drop-box on the way out. The site is accessible without a key by parking at the gate and walking 0.3 mi to the site. Beware of rattlesnakes.
Directions: At the Hamilton Dome sign; W on CR-10/Upper Cottonwood Creek Rd 5.3 mi; W/R on BLM-1305 2.3 mi; Just after cattle guard; S/L 0.2 mi to gate; Continue 0.3 mi to parking area.

MM: 32.3 **Dist:** 7.0 **GPS:** 44.00640/-108.47500 **Elev:** 5044 **Grid:** 37/25 **Land:** BLM
Gooseberry Badlands Scenic Area   **Type:** Scenic Area
Named for **Gooseberry Creek** south of the site, this overlook provides a panoramic view of colorful eroded badlands. A 1.5 mi loop trail leads through these interesting rock formations.

Camping is allowed in the parking area or along BLM roads 0.8 mi to the east and 1.3 mi to the west of the overlook. Both roads head north, and the road to the west is in better condition than the road to the east.
Cool Rating: ***** **Crowds:** * **Time:** 1 hr **Nearest Town:** Worland 32.3 NE, Meeteetse 26.3 NW
Directions: E on Wy-431 7.0 mi to parking area on N side of hwy at MM 23.2.
Campsites: Dispersed **Shade:** * **Privacy:** * **RV Size:** 30' **Other:** None

MM: 37.1 **GPS:** 44.01297/-108.67133 **Elev:** 5546 **Grid:** 34/25
Gooseberry Creek Rest Area   **Type:** Rest Area
Sheltered picnic tables.
Directions: NE side of hwy

MM: 51.6 **GPS:** 44.15686/-108.87030 **Elev:** 5760 **Grid:** 31/21
Meeteetse   **Type:** Town

MM: 81.2
Mile Marker Discrepancy (northbound)   **Type:** MM Discrepancy
From the junction with **US-14/16/20** the highway winds 2.6 mi northwest through **Cody** and reconnects with **Wy-120**. The mile markers gain 18.8 mi and continue north from MM 100.0.
Directions: **To continue N on Wy-120:** W/L on US-14/16/20 2.2 mi; N on US-14A/16th St 0.4 mi; W/L then N on Wy-120 from MM 100.0.

MM: 81.2 **GPS:** 44.51159/-109.02610 **Elev:** 5086 **Grid:** 29/12
US-14/16/20 (see chapter)   **Type:** Hwy Junction w/Chapter
100.1 mi highway west from a transition with **US-14/16/20/Wy-789**, west of **Greybull**, to the east entrance of **Yellowstone National Park**. The **Buffalo Bill Cody Scenic Byway** runs 27.4 mi from the east boundary of the **Shoshone National Forest** to the east entrance of **Yellowstone National Park**. Highlights include: **Buffalo Bill Historical Center**, **Old West Miniature Village and Museum**, **Buffalo Bill Dam and Visitor Center**, **Holy City**, **Firefighters Memorial and Trail**, interesting volcanic rock formations.
Directions: W to Cody or E to Greybull from MM 54.6
Notes: No dispersed camping on this route. If heading to Yellowstone be aware that the last 2 campgrounds are for hard-sided RVs only. Only 2 very small towns west of Cody.

MM: 100.0   *GPS:* 44.53234/-109.05600   *Elev:* 4978   *Grid:* 29/12
US-14A *(see chapter)*   *Type:* Hwy Junction w/Chapter
98.9 mi highway northeast from **Cody** to **Lovell**, then east to **Burgess Jct**. The last 27 mi follow the **Medicine Wheel Passage**, a scenic high elevation route (over 9,000 ft) with excellent views into the **Bighorn Basin**. Highlights include: **Heart Mountain Relocation Center, Bighorn Canyon National Recreation Area, Medicine Wheel National Historic Landmark, Porcupine Falls, Bucking Mule Falls**.
Directions: S to Cody or NE to Powell from MM 0.4

MM: 100.0
Mile Marker Discrepancy (southbound)   *Type:* MM Discrepancy
From the junction with **US-14A** the highway winds 2.6 mi southeast through **Cody** and reconnects with **Wy-120**. The mile markers lose 18.8 mi and continue south from MM 81.2.
Directions: **To continue S on Wy-120**: S on US-14A/16th St 0.4 mi; E/L on US-14/16/20 2.2 mi; S/R on Wy-120 from MM 81.2.

MM: 100.0   *GPS:* 44.53234/-109.05600   *Elev:* 4978   *Grid:* 29/12
Cody   *Type:* Town

MM: 116.5   *GPS:* 44.72716/-109.21737   *Elev:* 4983   *Grid:* 26/7
Wy-296 (Chief Joseph Scenic Highway) *(see chapter)*   *Type:* Hwy Junction w/Chapter
46.2 mi highway from **Wy-120** northwest to **US-212**. The highway follows the route of the historic pursuit of **Chief Joseph** and the **Nez Perce Indians** by the **United States 7th Cavalry** in 1877. This is one of the most scenic highways in **Wyoming**. Highlights include: overlooks from **Dead Indian Pass, Sunlight Gorge**.
Nearest Town: Cody 16.5 SE   *Notes:* No towns or services.   *Directions:* NW to US-212 from MM 46.2

MM: 118.1   *Dist:* 5.6   *GPS:* 44.78760/-109.25608   *Elev:* 4825   *Grid:* 26/5   *Land:* BLM
Hogan Reservoir   *Type:* Lake
Camping and the **Bald Ridge Trailhead** on the north shore of **Hogan Reservoir**. Fishing in the reservoir as well as a 0.3 mi trail southeast to **Luce Reservoir**, which contains **Kamloops Rainbow Trout**. The strenuous **Bald Ridge Trail** starts at the campground and winds 5 mi climbing 3,500 ft to **Bald Ridge**. *No Trees. Vault toilet. Tables. Fire rings with grates. Horse trailer parking. Horse stanchions and hitching rails.*
Crowds: *   *Road Desc:* Gravel   *Directions:* NW on CR-7RP 4.6 mi; NW/L 1.0 mi.
Campsites: 5   *Shade:* *   *Privacy:* *   *RV Size:* 40'   *Other:* None

MM: 137.5   *Dist:* 48.5   *GPS:* 44.99959/-109.05453   *Elev:* 4051   *Grid:* 29/0
US-212 to Beartooth Pass to Yellowstone National Park   *Type:* Pass
A connecting route through **Montana** to **US-212**, which climbs over the spectacular **Beartooth Pass** crossing back into **Wyoming**. **US-212** continues through northwestern **Wyoming** and briefly back into **Montana** before entering **Yellowstone National Park** at the northeast entrance. *See US-212 MM 43.6.*
Directions: N on Mt-72 10.5 mi; W on Mt-308 14.4 mi; S over Beartooth Pass to Wyoming on US-212 23.6 mi.

MM: 137.5   *GPS:* 44.99959/-109.05453   *Elev:* 4051   *Grid:* 29/0
End of Highway - Montana State Line   *Type:* Highway End
118.7 mi highway from **Montana** southeast through **Cody** to **Thermopolis**. Highlights include: Attractions in **Cody** *(see US-14/16/20 MM 52.4)*, **Gooseberry Badlands Scenic Area, Legend Rock Petroglyphs**.
Directions: S to Cody from MM 137.5

MM: 0.0 *GPS:* 41.30892/-105.62925 *Elev:* 7172 *Grid:* 77/92
Wy-130 (Laramie to Wy-230)　　*Type:* Highway Description
68.1 mi highway from **Laramie** west over **Snowy Range Pass** to **Wy-130/Wy-230 (Walcott to Riverside)** (8 mi south of
Saratoga). **Wy-130** actually continues 28.2 mi north to **Walcott**; however, this section uses the mile markers from **Wy-230** and is
included in the chapter on **Wy-130/Wy-230 (Walcott to Riverside)**. Highlights include the many attractions along the 27 mi **Snowy
Range Scenic Byway**.
Directions: I-80 exit 311; W on Snowy Range Rd 0.8 mi; N then W on Wy-130 from MM 0.
Notes: The mile markers are not particularly accurate along this route. The distance between MM 27 and MM 28 is 1.3 mi, and
MM 42 to MM 43 is 0.6 mi. Several forest access roads are located between MM 46 and MM 53.

MM: 0.0 *GPS:* 41.30892/-105.62925 *Elev:* 7172 *Grid:* 77/92
Wy-230 (Laramie to Colorado) *(see chapter)*　　*Type:* Hwy Junction w/Chapter
42.0 mi highway from the junction with **US-30/287** in **Laramie** southwest to **Colorado**. 4 fishing and camping lakes, including one
large reservoir, are located along this route.
Notes: Intersects a north/south section of I-80 at MM 1.3. *Directions:* E to Laramie or SW to Colorado from MM 2.1

MM: 0.0 *GPS:* 41.30892/-105.62925 *Elev:* 7172 *Grid:* 77/92
I-80 *(see chapter)*　　*Type:* Hwy Junction w/Chapter
403 mi interstate highway through southern **Wyoming** from **Utah** east to **Nebraska**.
Directions: E on Snowy Range Rd 0.8 mi to I-80; E to Nebraska or W to Rawlins from MM 311.8.

MM: 0.0 *GPS:* 41.30892/-105.62925 *Elev:* 7172 *Grid:* 77/92
Laramie　　*Type:* Town

MM: 9.6 *GPS:* 41.31128/-105.80136 *Elev:* 7439 *Grid:* 75/92
Overland Trail Historical Marker　　*Type:* Historical Marker
A historical marker and sign about the history of the **Overland Trail**, which was a primary transportation route from 1862-1868 until
the completion of the **Transcontinental Railroad** in 1869.
Cool Rating: * *Crowds:* * *Time:* 5 min *Directions:* N side of hwy

MM: 27.4 *GPS:* 41.29718/-106.13633 *Elev:* 8005 *Grid:* 70/93 *Land:* City
Nici Self Historical Museum　　*Type:* Museum
A local museum containing exhibits on the history of the **Centennial Valley**. The museum building is the **1907 Hahn's Peak and
Pacific Railroad** depot, which contains historic artifacts. Outside the building is a 1944 **Union Pacific Railroad** caboose, farm and
ranch equipment, a beehive burner containing displays of lumbering tools, a barn, and a one-room schoolhouse.
Cool Rating: ** *Crowds:* ** *Notes:* My favorite is an old snow cat with a body made of plywood. *Directions:* S side of hwy

MM: 27.7 *GPS:* 41.29740/-106.13976 *Elev:* 8041 *Grid:* 70/93
Centennial　　*Type:* Town

MM: 28.8 *GPS:* 41.31187/-106.15095 *Elev:* 8458 *Grid:* 70/92 *Land:* NF
Snowy Range Scenic Byway (east end)　　*Type:* Scenic Byway
This scenic route took 6 years to construct in the 1920s and was known as the "**Great Skyroad**." It was widened and improved in
the 1980s and designated the second **National Forest Scenic Byway** in the United States. It crosses 27 mi of the **Medicine Bow
National Forest**, rising from 8,000 ft on the valley floor to 10,847 ft at **Snowy Range Pass**, where nearby **Medicine Bow Peak**
towers to 12,013 ft with year-round glaciers. This elevation change includes all of the major life zones in the **Rocky Mountain**
west. Wildflowers carpet the alpine meadows throughout the summer.

Along the byway are popular recreational activities, including interpretive areas, camping, picnicking, fishing, and hiking (including
trails to **Medicine Bow Peak**). The area offers excellent fishing in the many alpine lakes and numerous streams for rainbow,
brook, and cutthroat trout.

Many species of wildlife can be seen, including yellow-bellied marmots, pikas, beaver, blue grouse, deer, moose, and Rocky
Mountain bighorn sheep near **Medicine Bow Peak**. Near the summit is an old-growth spruce-fir forest that is home to the pine
marten, red-backed vole, ruby-crowned kinglet, northern three-toed woodpecker, and boreal owl to name a few.
Hours: Generally open from Memorial Day - mid-Nov *Cool Rating:* **** *Crowds:* *** *Time:* Varies

MM: 28.8 *GPS:* 41.31297/-106.15304 *Elev:* 8460 *Grid:* 70/92 *Land:* NF
Centennial Visitor Center　　*Type:* Visitor Center
General information on the **Snowy Range**, including maps, trail maps, brochures, permits, books, and schedules for interpretive
programs. Behind the building is a short trail through the forest that parallels the highway. *Easy; 0.4 mi one-way; 100 ft elev gain.*
Hours: 9am - 5pm (Late May - Sept); Closed Mondays *Phone:* 307-742-6023 *Directions:* NE side of hwy
Notes: This has been closed to build a larger building. It is planned to be re-opened in 2013.

MM: 29.3 *Dist:* 0.1 *GPS:* 41.31810/-106.16115 *Elev:* 8581 *Grid:* 70/92 *Land:* NF
Aspen Campground　　*Type:* Campground
A shared circular parking area for walk-in tent sites. Small campers can be parked in the parking area with no shade or privacy.
Spacious sites. Tables and fire rings in the trees. Near highway.
Crowds: * *[FEE AREA]* *Directions:* NW on Barber Lake Rd/FR-351 0.1 mi
Campsites: 8 *Shade:* ***** *Privacy:* **** *RV Size:* 20' *Other:* Water

MM: 29.3 *Dist:* 0.2 *GPS:* 41.31913/-106.16393 *Elev:* 8604 *Grid:* 70/92 *Land:* NF
Fir Picnic Ground　　*Type:* Picnic Area
4 picnic sites with good shade. Vault toilet.
Directions: NW on Barber Lake Rd/FR-351 1/4 mi

MM: 29.3 **Dist:** 0.3 **GPS:** 41.31959/-106.16556 **Elev:** 8630 **Grid:** 70/92 **Land:** NF
Pine Campground   **Type:** Campground
Campsites along a one-way half-loop road with **Libby Creek** flowing along the northwest side and **Willow Campground** across the creek. *Mixed forest. Angled back-in sites. Sites at the end are the most private.*
Crowds: *** [FEE AREA] **Directions:** NW on Barber Lake Rd/FR-351 0.3 mi
Campsites: 6 **Shade:** **** **Privacy:** **** **RV Size:** 20' **Other:** Water

MM: 29.3 **Dist:** 1.0 **GPS:** 41.32104/-106.16770 **Elev:** 8640 **Grid:** 70/92 **Land:** NF
Willow Campground   **Type:** Campground
Along a narrow dirt road that parallels **Libby Creek** with a cul-de-sac at the end. Provides direct access to the **Corner Mountain Trails** *(see section below). Mixed forest. Good spacing between sites. Some sites are next to the creek.*
Crowds: **** [FEE AREA] **Notes:** Fills first because it is farthest from traffic and takes reservations.
Road Desc: Gravel. Barber Lake Rd is paved. **Directions:** NW on Barber Lake Rd/FR-351 3/4 mi; E/R 1/4 mi.
Campsites: 16 **Shade:** ***** **Privacy:** **** **RV Size:** 30' **Other:** 1-877-444-6777:www.recreation.gov,Water

MM: 29.3 **Dist:** 1.0 **GPS:** 41.32376/-106.17586 **Elev:** 8756 **Grid:** 70/92 **Land:** NF
Barber Lake Picnic Ground   **Type:** Picnic Area
10 picnic sites across from **Barber Lake**, which is a small kids-only fishing lake. This is also parking for the **Corner Mountain Trails** which start 0.15 mi north on the east side of the road.
[FEE AREA] **Directions:** NW on Barber Lake Rd/FR-351 1.0 mi; W side of road on the hairpin curve.

MM: 29.5 **GPS:** 41.31953/-106.15730 **Elev:** 8550 **Grid:** 70/92 **Land:** NF
Spruce Campground   **Type:** Campground
Just off the highway near **Libby Creek**. Site1 has a long parking area below the highway and site 2 is a pull-thru. The other 6 sites are on the inside and outside of a small loop with little privacy *Mixed forest. Highway noise.*
Crowds: **** [FEE AREA] **Directions:** W side of hwy (0.3 mi N of Barber Lake Rd)
Campsites: 8 **Shade:** **** **Privacy:** * **RV Size:** 30' **Other:** Water

MM: 29.9 **GPS:** 41.32413/-106.15772 **Elev:** 8500 **Grid:** 70/92 **Land:** NF
Corner Mountain Trails   **Type:** Hiking/Biking Trail
Hiking and biking on approximately 5 mi of cross-country ski trails located between the junction of **Wy-130** and **Barber Lake Rd** at the base of **Corner Mountain**. The trail is comprised of 2 interconnected loops along rolling terrain with some short, steep sections. *Directions:* Keep right at 0.1 mi and ride 1.7 mi, with a several very steep uphill sections, to a trail junction. From here the trail descends and finishes the ~2.5 mi **Corner Mountain Loop**. Continuing straight on the **Camp Loop** will descend to the **Willow Campground**. Follow a mixture of trails to the **Spruce Campground** where the highway leads 0.3 mi back to the trailhead for a 3.9 mi loop. See the trail map inset on the Snowy Range map on page 12. *Moderate; 200 to 300 ft elev gain.*
Cool Rating: *** **Crowds:** * [FEE AREA] **Directions:** Parking on SW side of hwy (0.6 mi N of Barber Lake Rd).
Notes: There are several section that may be too steep to ride, plus rocks, roots, and several downed trees. Not a great biking trail and not much to see for a hiking trail. The trails can also be accessed from the 4 campgrounds and the **Barber Lake Picnic Ground** along **Barber Lake Rd**.

MM: 30.9 **GPS:** 41.33855/-106.16461 **GPS2:** 41.35180/-106.16363 **Elev:** 8790 **Grid:** 70/91 **Land:** NF
Little Laramie Trails   **Type:** Hiking/Biking Trail
Hiking and biking on cross-country ski trails located north of **Wy-130** along both sides of **FR-101/Sand Lake Rd**. 3 interconnected loops are comprised of approximately 5.6 mi of trails plus 0.9 mi of **FR-101** from **Wy-130** to the north trailhead. The outer trails, **Lodgepole Loop** to the west and **River Trail** to the east, are closed forest roads that are steep and rocky. **Meadow Loop** is located in the middle with sections near the creek along a more diverse terrain of wet areas, pine forest, and meadows. Access to the trails is from either the lower trailhead along **Wy-130** (fee) or the upper dirt parking area 1.0 mi north on **FR-101** (free). It is a 310 ft elevation gain from the bottom trailhead to the top.

Planning a route on these trails is tricky, as only the **Meadow Loop** has reasonable uphill rides. The trails are on a mountainside, so they are primarily either uphill or downhill. Consult the trail map inset on the Snowy Range map on page 12 for different combinations of trails. The **Meadow Loop** is best for hiking and starts on the east side of **FR-101** 0.1 mi north of **Wy-130**.

Following are directions for a fun 6.5 mi ride: From the upper trailhead, take the trail southeast 0.6 mi to the **River Trail** *(muddy in spots and may require some walking)* (MI 0.6). Ride the **River Trail** downhill south 1.8 mi to the south trailhead parking (MI 2.4). Exit the trailhead parking and take the road west 1/4 mi to **FR-101** (MI 2.7). Ride north up **FR-101** 0.9 mi to the **Lodgepole Loop** junction on the left (MI 3.6). Ride the **Lodgepole Loop** downhill south 1.1 mi (MI 4.7). Cross the road and just south to the **Meadow Loop** junction and ride the **Meadow Loop** uphill 1.6 mi back to **FR-101** (MI 6.3). Return 0.2 mi north to the trailhead parking (MI 6.5). *Moderate; 560 ft elev loss and gain.*
Cool Rating: *** **Crowds:** * [FEE AREA]
Directions: To fee area trailhead: NE side of hwy. **To free trailhead parking**: Continue NW 1/4 mi on Wy-130; N on FR-101/Sand Lake Rd 1.0 mi; E/R 0.1 mi to parking area *(see GPS2, elev 9100)*.

MM: 31.2 **Dist:** 1.6 **GPS:** 41.36004/-106.17028 **Elev:** 9190 **Grid:** 70/91 **Land:** NF
North Fork Campground   **Type:** Campground
A large RV-friendly campground composed of 2 sections. The north section is a teardrop loop with 31 reservable sites. The teardrop shape makes a second pass difficult in a large RV or trailer. To the south is a 0.4 mi road through the woods with 29 sites. This road parallels the **North Fork Little Laramie River**, which flows behind the campsites on the west side. The road connects to **FR-330**. The **North Fork Trail** starts at the end of the loop and heads 5.0 mi to **Brooklyn Lake**. The **Little Laramie Trails** are 1/2 mi south of the campground *(see previous section). No pull-thrus. Better privacy in south section. Level.*
Crowds: **** [FEE AREA] **Road Desc:** Gravel, washboard sections **Directions:** NE on FR-101/Sand Lake Rd 1.6 mi
Notes: There is abundant dispersed camping along FR-101 and a couple sites along FR-330. Many dead trees have been removed from the campground.
Campsites: 60 **Shade:** ** **Privacy:** ** **RV Size:** 40' **Other:** 1-877-444-6777:www.recreation.gov,Water

MM: 33.7 **Dist:** 1.0 **GPS:** 41.34150/-106.20661 **GPS2:** 41.34020/-106.20871 **Elev:** 9377 **Grid:** 69/91 **Land:** NF

Libby Creek Falls **Type:** Waterfall

A long beautiful cascade on **Libby Creek**. There is no official trail to the falls, so reaching them requires scrambling down a steep hill with a 125 ft elevation loss. From the roadside parking, cross the road to the **Barber Lake Trail**. Follow the trail west for 0.1 mi to a rock cairn on the south side. Scramble straight south down the hill 0.1 mi. Alternatively, and perhaps easier, from the parking area scramble at an angle down the hill due southwest 0.2 mi. There is no path, so you must listen for the falls to guide the way.

Cool Rating: **** **Crowds:** *

Directions: SE on Barber Lake Rd 1.0 mi passing 2 hairpin curves to a less-sharp curve heading SE. Park on the inside of the curve on the E side of the road.

MM: 34.0 **GPS:** 41.34853/-106.21686 **Elev:** 9820 **Grid:** 69/91 **Land:** NF

Greenrock Trailhead and Picnic Ground **Type:** Picnic Area and Trailhead

Fee area with 9 picnic sites, a vault toilet, and the trailhead for 2 trails:

Libby Creek Trail - A counterclockwise loop trail that descends into **Libby Creek Canyon** along the impressively cascading **Libby Creek** (which is more of a river than a creek). From the picnic area, the trail heads southwest, then southeast 0.3 mi to the start of the counterclockwise loop (MI 0.3). The trail climbs 150 ft (MI 0.7) and then traverses the ridgeline of **Libby Creek Canyon** climbing another 80 ft (MI 1.5) before a 300 ft descent into the canyon (MI 2.1). The next mile parallels **Libby Creek** and descends another 280 ft (MI 3.1). The creek is not visible directly from the trail, but instead requires short side trails for access, including a medium sized waterfall at MI 2.7. The trail climbs 150 ft out of the canyon back to the **Barber Lake Trail** (MI 3.5), which heads northwest 0.7 mi, gaining 180 ft, back to the parking area. *Moderate; 4.2 mi loop; 230 ft elev gain, 580 ft elev loss, 330 ft elev gain.*

Alternatively, at MI 2.9 (about 0.1 mi on the ascent out of the canyon) is a trail to the northeast that also connects to the **Barber Lake Trail**. Just east of this trail junction is a rock cairn that marks **Libby Creek Falls** 0.1 mi south down a steep hill with no trail *(see previous section)*.

Barber Lake Trail - An advanced mountain bike trail that drops to **Barber Lake** via a combination of ski trails, forest roads, and single-track trails. Requires a shuttle vehicle in the **Barber Lake** area. *Easy with difficult sections over large rocks and roots; 3.1 mi one-way; 1100 ft elev loss.* About 0.9 mi along the **Barber Lake Trail** is a rock cairn that marks **Libby Creek Falls** 0.1 mi south down a steep hill with no trail *(see previous section)*.

Cool Rating: **** **Crowds:** * **Time:** 2-3 hrs **[FEE AREA]** **Directions:** S side of hwy

---

MM: 35.3 **GPS:** 41.35706/-106.23280 **Elev:** 10150 **Grid:** 69/91

Brooklyn Lake Rd/FR-317 *(see chapter)* **Type:** Hwy Junction w/Chapter

1.9 mi road north from **Wy-130** to **Brooklyn Lake** with access to scenic hiking trails around **Browns Peak** and 2 campgrounds.

Notes: The road is gravel with washboard sections and somewhat narrow. It is usually open around July 1.

MM: 38.0 **GPS:** 41.35109/-106.28005 **Elev:** 10580 **Grid:** 68/91 **Land:** NF

FR-332/Towner Lake Rd **Type:** Highway Junction

A 2.9 mi forest road that connects to **Brooklyn Lake Rd/FR-317**. A few dispersed camping areas are located along this route, although signs state camping must be 500 ft from the road.

Road Desc: Dirt, rough & potholed, narrow **Directions:** N then NE on FR-332/Towner Lake Rd 2.9 mi

Notes: I saw no opportunities to get 500 ft from the road but plenty of people camping.

MM: 38.7 **GPS:** 41.34810/-106.29027 **Elev:** 10715 **Grid:** 68/91

Sugarloaf Recreation Area/FR-346 *(see chapter)* **Type:** Hwy Junction w/Chapter

A recreation area near the top of **Snowy Range Pass** with parking areas at **Libby Lake** and **Lewis Lake**. Picnic areas are located at each lake and **Sugarloaf Campground** is located across from **Libby Lake**. A trailhead at **Lewis Lake** provides access to several hiking trails that lead to alpine lakes and **Medicine Bow Peak**. The area provides beautiful views of the **Snowy Range**, **Medicine Bow Peak**, **Browns Peak**, and the surrounding valleys. The scenery in this area is the most magnificent along the scenic byway.

Cool Rating: ***** **Crowds:** ***** **Time:** varies **[FEE AREA]**

Directions: From Wy-130 MM 38.7; NW on FR-346 90 yds to self-pay fee station.

MM: 38.8 **Dist:** 4.5 **GPS:** 41.34603/-106.29124 **GPS2:** 41.32531/-106.24006 **Elev:** 10065 **Grid:** 68/91 **Land:** NF

Bear Lake & Silver Run Lake **Type:** Lake

Primitive forest roads on the south side of **Wy-130** that head away from the **Snowy Range**, across **Libby Flats**, through meadows and pockets of trees, dropping 650 ft to 2 subalpine lakes popular with fisherman: **Bear Lake** (3.6 mi) and the larger **Silver Run Lake** (4.5 mi).

Cool Rating: ** **Crowds:** ** **Road Desc:** Dirt, primitive & impassable when wet, 4WD

Directions: Parking area on SE side of hwy; S on FR-336 1.0 mi; Keep left on FR-396 2.0 mi; Left fork 0.6 mi to Bear Lake; Right fork 1.5 mi to Silver Run Lake.

MM: 39.2 **GPS:** 41.34264/-106.29905 **Elev:** 10847 **Grid:** 68/91 **Land:** NF

Libby Observation Point **Type:** Scenic Viewpoint

A stone observation platform at the summit of **Snowy Range Pass**, which provides panoramic views of the surrounding mountain ranges all the way to northern **Colorado**. Off the path to the observation platform is a short interpretive loop trail with information about the plants and animals living at this high elevation. *Vault toilet.*

Cool Rating: *** **Crowds:** *** **Time:** 20 min **Directions:** SE side of hwy

MM: 39.6 *GPS:* 41.34168/-106.30467 *Elev:* 10813 *Grid:* 68/91 *Land:* NF
Medicine Bow Peak Overlook & Miner's Cabin Trail   *Type:* Historic Site
This overlook is at the summit of **Snowy Range Pass** and provides a good view to the west of the **Snowy Range** and **Medicine Bow Peak**. Below the parking area a short loop trail descends through sub-alpine meadows and patches of forest past mining ruins and a historic cabin. Interpretive signs along the trail explain the area and its wildlife. Turn left after about 100 yds to walk the loop clockwise and pass the remains of the **Red Mask Mine**, which was constructed in the 1920s. The mine was thought to contain rich veins of gold, silver, and copper; however, only small amounts were ever extracted. The collapsed hoisting tower, rusted boiler, and shafthouse are all that remain. A cabin that was used by the miners is located about halfway along the trail at its lowest point. The **Miner's Cabin** is located near a water source and in the trees to help protect it from the harsh elements. Near the cabin, a junction with the **Tipple Trail** heads 2.2 mi south to **Wy-130** near **Lake Marie** *(see Tipple Trail at MM 41.7). Easy; 0.7 mi loop; 100 ft elev loss.*
Cool Rating: *** *Crowds:* ** *Time:* 45 min *Directions:* W side of hwy

MM: 40.9 *Dist:* 0.3 *GPS:* 41.33786/-106.32220 *Elev:* 10568 *Grid:* 68/92 *Land:* NF
Mirror Lake and Lake Marie Parking and Picnic Area   *Type:* Scenic Area
2 of the most beautiful lakes in **Wyoming** with steep mountain backdrops reflected in the dark blue water. **Mirror Lake** is north of the entrance road. **Lake Marie** is south and is accessed by a short trail between the 2 lakes. An alternate trailhead to **Medicine Bow Peak** *(see next section)* starts at the north end of the **Mirror Lake Picnic Area**, which has 6 sites plus a group site.
Cool Rating: **** *Crowds:* ***** *Time:* 1+ hrs *Directions:* NW side of hwy. Parking is W 0.3 mi.

MM: 40.9 *Dist:* 0.4 *GPS:* 41.33861/-106.32319 *GPS2:* 41.35823/-106.30892 *Elev:* 10604 *Grid:* 68/91 *Land:* NF
Lakes Trail w/option to Medicine Bow Peak   *Type:* Hiking Trail
A trail from the **Mirror Lake Picnic Area** that meets the trail from **Lewis Lake** at the base of **Medicine Bow Peak**, with the option of climbing the steep 0.8 mi trail to the summit of **Medicine Bow Peak** (12,013 ft). This beautiful and popular trail heads north following the east shore of the long, large, and deep **Lookout Lake** before climbing 500 ft to the gap between **Medicine Bow Peak** and **Sugarloaf Mountain**. An interesting feature upon reaching the lake at 0.1 mi is a 400 yd stretch of giant boulders along the southeastern lakeshore. The rocks completely block the view but are fun to climb on. The sheer rock cliff behind **Lookout Lake** is known as the **Disaster Wall**. In 1955 a United Airlines flight from **Denver** veered off course and crashed into this cliff, killing all 66 aboard. Wreckage can still be seen in the area. A memorial stone and plaque were placed near the crash site in August 2001. The 0.8 mi hike to **Medicine Bow Peak summit** consists of a steep 900 ft climb over scattered boulders, along switchbacks and over and around lingering snowdrifts. *Junction with the Lewis Lake Trail at the base of Medicine Bow Peak: Moderate; 1.7 mi one-way; 500 ft elev gain. Top of Medicine Bow Peak: Strenuous; 2.5 mi one-way; 1400 ft elev gain.*

For a short hike, head north 0.3 mi and climb 50 ft to a good viewpoint of **Lookout Lake**. Continue 0.2 mi to the end of the lake where the trail begins climbing 450 ft to the base of **Medicine Bow Peak**. *Easy; 0.3-0.5 mi one-way; 50 ft elev gain.*
Cool Rating: ***** *Crowds:* *** *Time:* 30 min - 4 hrs
Notes: It is best to be off the trail by 3 pm to avoid afternoon thunderstorms. Exercise extreme caution climbing to the top of Medicine Bow Peak.
Directions: W 0.4 mi to the upper parking at Mirror Lake Picnic Area. *See next section for additional parking.*

MM: 41.1 *GPS:* 41.33546/-106.32044 *Elev:* 10524 *Grid:* 68/92 *Land:* NF
Lake Marie Parking   *Type:* Parking Area
The closest parking for **Lake Marie** and alternative parking for **Mirror Lake** *(see section above).*
Directions: NW side of hwy

MM: 41.5 *GPS:* 41.33165/-106.32555 *GPS2:* 41.36042/-106.31747 *Elev:* 10488 *Grid:* 68/92 *Land:* NF
Lake Marie West Trailhead to Medicine Bow Peak   *Type:* Hiking Trail
The longest and steepest trail to the top of **Medicine Bow Peak** (12,013 ft), which crosses a broad ridgeline on the west side of the **Snowy Range**. In the first mile the trail makes a steep initial ascent of 900 ft to an elevation of 11,400 ft offering nice views to the east and south. The trail then levels out for the next mile to the junction with the **Dipper Lake Trail**, where the final mile climbs steeply 600 ft up switchbacks to the summit of **Medicine Bow Peak**. Return by the same route or make a loop by descending 0.8 mi down the east side and taking the **Lakes Trail** south 1.7 mi past **Lookout Lake** *(see earlier section on Lakes Trail w/option to Medicine Bow Peak). Strenuous; 3.0 mi one-way, 5.5 mi loop; 1500 ft elev gain.*
Cool Rating: ***** *Crowds:* ** *Time:* 4+ hrs *Directions:* Parking area on W side of hwy
Notes: It is best to be off the trail by 3 pm to avoid afternoon thunderstorms. Exercise extreme caution climbing to the top of Medicine Bow Peak. The **Lake Marie Falls Trail** and **Tipple Trail** start across the highway from the north and south end of the parking loop respectively *(see following sections).* Follow the trail 0.1 mi for a view above **Lake Marie**.

MM: 41.5 *GPS:* 41.33175/-106.32501 *GPS2:* 41.33218/-106.32477 *Elev:* 10486 *Grid:* 68/92 *Land:* NF
Lake Marie Falls   *Type:* Waterfall
A short loop trail that follows the outlet of **Lake Marie** as it cascades into a pool and continues down **French Creek Canyon**. The trail includes somewhat steep rock steps and a bridge over the creek. *Easy; 1/4 mi loop; 50 ft elev loss.*
Cool Rating: *** *Crowds:* *** *Time:* 30 min *Directions:* Parking area on W side of hwy at the Lake Marie West trailhead. Trail starts across the hwy from the north side of the parking area.

MM: 41.7 *GPS:* 41.32999/-106.32382 *GPS2:* 41.33817/-106.30573 *Elev:* 10505 *Grid:* 68/92 *Land:* NF
Tipple Trail   *Type:* Hiking Trail
A hike northeast through the forest and meadows to the **Miner's Cabin** at the junction with the **Miner's Cabin Trail** *(see earlier section on Medicine Bow Peak Overlook & Miner's Cabin Trail).* It is 0.1 mi to the edge of **French Creek Canyon** where you can walk a short distance to the left to view the small **Lake Marie Falls** *(see previous section).* Turning right the trail follows the canyon rim for 0.4 mi offering nice views up the canyon to the west. You can turn back here or descend 0.2 mi into the canyon and cross **South French Creek** on a footbridge. Stay left at the junction with the **French Creek Canyon Trail** to continue north through the forest. Upon reaching the **Miner's Cabin Trail**, turning left leads to the **Miner's Cabin** and turning right leads 1/4 mi climbing 100 ft to the **Red Mask Mine**. *Moderate; 2.2 mi one-way; 300 ft elev loss; 490 ft elev gain. To view the canyon only: Easy; 0.5 mi one-way; 150 ft elev loss.*
Cool Rating: *** *Crowds:* * *Time:* 2 hrs *Notes:* The parking area has 2 picnic tables.
Directions: Parking area on E side of hwy. Also accessed from the south end of the Lake Marie West parking area.

MM: 44.1 **GPS:** 41.31412/-106.35052 **Elev:** 10635 **Grid:** 67/92 **Land:** NF
Meadow Falls Trailhead **Type:** Trailhead
The start of the **Meadow Falls-Silver Lake Loop Trail**, which traverses meadows and forest clockwise around **Silver Lake** and past **Meadow Falls**, a small cascade. Good fishing in **Silver Lake**. *Moderately easy; 2.7 mi loop; 300 ft elev loss.*
Cool Rating: *** **Crowds:** * **Time:** 1.5 hrs **Directions:** SE side of hwy

MM: 46.0 **Dist:** 3.2 **GPS:** 41.32799/-106.36366 **Elev:** 10270 **Grid:** 67/92 **Land:** NF
FR-200 & FR-103 **Type:** Highway Junction
Forest roads on the west side of the **Snowy Range** north to **Dipper Lake** and **Quealy Lake**. This is a good OHV area. *560 ft elev gain. Dispersed camping.* A fourth hiking route 2.6 mi east to **Medicine Bow Peak** starts at **Dipper Lake**.
Road Desc: The gravel road turns to 4WD after 1.9 mi.
Directions: N on FR-200 0.9 mi; NE/R at fork on FR-103 1.0 mi to start of 4WD section; Continue 1.3 mi to Dipper Lake; Continue 1.5 mi to Quealy Lake.

MM: 53.1 **GPS:** 41.32714/-106.49321 **Elev:** 8430 **Grid:** 65/92 **Land:** NF
Ryan Park Campground **Type:** Campground
Composed of 3 loops with the first loop only for groups with reservations. The campground is the former location of a **Civilian Conservation Corps** (CCC) camp in the 1930s and a **POW Camp** from 1942 through 1945 for Italian and German prisoners. Interpretive signs at the campground entrance provide information about the camp. *Sparse conifer forest. Sites range from widely spaced with long aprons to being very close together. Most pull-thrus in upper section.*
Crowds: * **[FEE AREA]** **Notes:** Many of the trees have been beetle killed and removed. **Directions:** S side of hwy
Campsites: 48 **Shade:** * **Privacy:** ** **RV Size:** 40'+ **Other:** 1-877-444-6777:www.recreation.gov,Water

MM: 53.8 **GPS:** 41.32403/-106.50440 **Elev:** 8322 **Grid:** 65/92
Ryan Park **Type:** Town

MM: 55.5 **Dist:** 0.1 **GPS:** 41.34301/-106.52497 **Elev:** 8105 **Grid:** 65/91 **Land:** NF
Brush Creek Visitor Center **Type:** Visitor Center
A small visitor center with maps, brochures, passes, permits, books, and schedules for ranger-led interpretive programs. The building was built by the **Civilian Conservation Corps** (CCC) between 1937 and 1941 and was formerly the **Brush Creek Ranger Station**. The building is currently on the **National Register of Historic Places**.
Hours: 9am - 5pm (Late May - Sept) **Phone:** 307-326-5258 **Directions:** E 0.1 mi

MM: 55.8 **Dist:** 1.4 **GPS:** 41.34476/-106.50466 **Elev:** 8300 **Grid:** 65/91 **Land:** NF
South Brush Creek Campground **Type:** Campground
Along **Brush Creek** in 2 loops with separate entrances. *Conifer forest. 1 pull-thru in the first loop and 5 in the second loop. Level.*
Crowds: *** **[FEE AREA]** **Road Desc:** Gravel **Directions:** NE on Brush Creek Rd/FR-100 0.3 mi; SE/R on FR-200 1.1 mi.
Campsites: 20 **Shade:** *** **Privacy:** *** **RV Size:** 40' **Other:** Water

MM: 55.8 **Dist:** 2.6 **GPS:** 41.37434/-106.51452 **Elev:** 8093 **Grid:** 65/91 **Land:** NF
Lincoln Park Campground **Type:** Campground
North Brush Creek flows between 2 loops with a few sites near the creek. A good campground for RVs and is a good base camp for an OHV trip to **Kennaday Peak Lookout** *(see next section). Sparse conifer forest. Spacious sites. Little understory. Level.*
Crowds: *** **[FEE AREA]** **Road Desc:** Gravel **Directions:** NE on Brush Creek Rd/FR-100 2.6 mi
Campsites: 12 **Shade:** ** **Privacy:** * **RV Size:** 40' **Other:** Water

MM: 55.8 **Dist:** 12.6 **GPS:** 41.45239/-106.51809 **Elev:** 10825 **Grid:** 65/89 **Land:** NF
Kennaday Peak Lookout **Type:** Fire Lookout
A closed fire lookout that was one of six in the area built by the **Civilian Conservation Corps** (CCC) in the 1930s. Although the lookout is closed, the views of the surrounding mountains and the **North Platte River Valley** are excellent. This is not a great automobile road and the majority of the access is by OHV.
Cool Rating: **** **Crowds:** * **Road Desc:** Gravel, rough, narrow, steep & winding, high clearance
Notes: There are a few dispersed campsites in the first 3 miles of FR-215. There is a site at the intersection of FR-100 and FR-215 that is the most mosquito infested place that I have ever camped.
Directions: N on Brush Creek Rd/FR-100 5.9 mi; N/L on FR-215 6.7 mi.

MM: 56.2 **GPS:** 41.35166/-106.53353 **Elev:** 7992 **Grid:** 65/91 **Land:** NF
Snowy Range Scenic Byway (west end) **Type:** Scenic Byway
See description on MM 28.6.

MM: 68.1 **GPS:** 41.35743/-106.74203 **Elev:** 7002 **Grid:** 62/91
Wy-130/Wy-230 (Walcott to Riverside) *(see chapter)* **Type:** Hwy Junction w/Chapter
Wy-130 continues north to **Saratoga**; however, the mile markers count down from MM 28.2. **Wy-230** heads south to **Riverside**, also from MM 28.2. Highlights include: **Hobo Hot Pool**, **Saratoga National Fish Hatchery**.
Directions: N to Saratoga or S to Riverside from MM 28.3

MM: 68.1 **GPS:** 41.35743/-106.74203 **Elev:** 7002 **Grid:** 62/91
End of Highway **Type:** Highway End
68.1 mi highway from **Wy-130/Wy-230 (Walcott to Riverside)** (8 mi south of **Saratoga**) east over **Snowy Range Pass** to **Laramie**. Highlights include the many attractions along the 27 mi **Snowy Range Scenic Byway**.
Nearest Town: Saratoga 8 N **Directions:** E to Laramie from MM 68.1

Wy-130/Wy-230 (Walcott to Riverside)   N/S

MM: 0.0   *GPS:* 41.74135/-106.83036   *Elev:* 6791   *Grid:* 60/81
Wy-130/Wy-230 (Walcott to Riverside)   *Type:* Highway Description
38.2 mi highway from **Walcott** south to **Riverside**. The highway transitions from **Wy-130** to **Wy-230** at MM 28.3 (the junction with Wy-130 east) and the mile markers continue sequentially south on **Wy-230**. A 68.1 mi section of **Wy-130** heads east to **Laramie** but uses different mile markers and is handled by the book as a separate chapter *(see chapter Wy-130 (Laramie to Wy-130))*.
Highlights include: **Saratoga National Fish Hatchery**, **Hobo Hot Pool**.
Directions: I-80 exit 235; S to Saratoga from MM 0
Notes: From north to south the mile markers measure 0.2 mi short (e.g. MM 14 measures 13.8 mi) until MM 20 at Saratoga (there are 1.2 mi between MM 19 and MM 20).

MM: 0.0   *GPS:* 41.74135/-106.83036   *Elev:* 6791   *Grid:* 60/81
I-80 *(see chapter)*   *Type:* Hwy Junction w/Chapter
403 mi interstate highway through southern **Wyoming** from **Utah** east to **Nebraska**. Highlights include: **Bear River State Park**, **Fort Bridger State Historic Site**, **Wyoming Frontier Prison**, **Fort Fred Steele**, **Wyoming Territorial Prison State Historic Site**, **Pole Mountain Trails**, **Curt Gowdy State Park**, **Vedauwoo Recreation Area**, and much more.
Directions: E to Laramie or W to Rawlins from MM 235.3

MM: 0.0   *GPS:* 41.74135/-106.83036   *Elev:* 6791   *Grid:* 60/81
Walcott   *Type:* Town

MM: 9.1   *GPS:* 41.61433/-106.81532   *Elev:* 6940   *Grid:* 61/85
Overland Trail Historical Marker   *Type:* Historical Marker
A stone marker stating that a historic **North Platte River** crossing point along the **Overland Trail** is 9 mi west.
Cool Rating: *   *Crowds:* *   *Time:* 5 min   *Directions:* W side of hwy

MM: 13.9   *Dist:* 3.9   *GPS:* 41.53831/-106.88108   *Elev:* 6690   *Grid:* 60/86   *Land:* Wyoming G & F
Pick Bridge Public Access Area   *Type:* Recreation Area
Primitive camping on either side of the **North Platte River** just south of the river bridge. The first area on the east side of the river has 1 primary site under cottonwoods with a fire ring. Other camping is possible in the open with no fire rings. *Vault toilet.* On the west side of the river is 1 site in an open grassy area under cottonwoods with no facilities.
Crowds: *****   *Road Desc:* Gravel
Directions: W on CR-508/Pick Bridge Rd 3.9 mi. **Camping area on west side**: W 0.1 past the bridge; S/L 0.2 mi; E/L 0.1 mi.
Campsites: 2   *Shade:* ***   *Privacy:* *   *RV Size:* 40'   *Other:* None

MM: 13.9   *Dist:* 6.8   *GPS:* 41.55510/-106.91924   *Elev:* 6670   *Grid:* 59/86   *Land:* Wyoming G & F
Sanger Public Access Area   *Type:* Public Access Area
Primitive camping in grassy areas along the **North Platte River**. The mileages are measured from **Pick Bridge Rd** 5.3 mi west of **Wy-130**:

Area 1 - MI 1.5 (41.5551/-106.91924): Turn right and travel a short distance to a fork in the road. To the right it is 0.1 mi to a parking area with camping around the perimeter. *Vault toilet.* To the left it is 1/4 mi to a beautiful campsite next to the river and under cottonwoods. *Stone fire ring.* Past this site the road continues another 0.1 mi to an established grassy site near the river. *Rock fire ring.* Several other dispersed sites are located along this road.

Area 2 - MI 2.0 (41.55365/-106.92778): Forks to the right 0.1 mi dropping slightly into a grassy area near the river. Room for 3 campsites with somewhat compromised privacy. *1 rock fire ring.*

Area 3 - MI 2.6 (41.55655/-106.94001): A pullout just off the road, under trees, and near the river. *Rock fire ring.*

Area 4 - MI 2.8 (41.55707/-106.94274): A loop at the end of the road with 1 primary site near the boat launch. *Rock fire ring.* Room for 2 other sites around the loop. *Cottonwoods. Vault toilet. Boat launch.*
Crowds: **   *Road Desc:* Gravel. First 5.3 mi is wide,   *Directions:* W on Pick Bridge Rd 5.3 mi; N/R 1.5 mi - 2.8 mi.
Campsites: Dispersed   *Shade:* ***   *Privacy:* **   *RV Size:* 30'   *Other:* None

MM: 16.3   *Dist:* 1.6   *GPS:* 41.51348/-106.80609   *GPS2:* 41.50473/-106.78722   *Elev:* 6800   *Grid:* 61/87   *Land:* Federal
Saratoga National Fish Hatchery (southbound)   *Type:* Fish Hatchery
See MM 18.0.
Cool Rating: **   *Crowds:* *   *Time:* 30 min
Directions: E then S on Fish Hatchery Rd/CR-207 1.6 mi. The road continues 1.6 mi S and W back to Wy-130 MM 18.0.

MM: 16.5   *Dist:* 1.7   *GPS:* 41.50915/-106.83811   *Elev:* 6738   *Grid:* 60/87   *Land:* Wyoming G & F
Foote Public Access Area   *Type:* Recreation Area
2 undeveloped camping areas on the **North Platte River**. At the fork turn left to a small parking area under cottonwoods or right to 3 well-spaced grassy areas under cottonwoods with a vault toilet and float launch.
Crowds: ***   *Notes:* More crowded on weekends.   *Road Desc:* Gravel, washboard   *Directions:* W 1.7 mi to fork
Campsites: Dispersed   *Shade:* *****   *Privacy:* ***   *RV Size:* 20'   *Other:* None

MM: 18.0   *Dist:* 1.6   *GPS:* 41.48981/-106.80265   *GPS2:* 41.50473/-106.78722   *Elev:* 6800   *Grid:* 61/88   *Land:* State
Saratoga National Fish Hatchery (northbound)   *Type:* Fish Hatchery
A brood stock hatchery that since 1911 has raised various species of trout to breed and harvest eggs for distribution to federal, state, and tribal hatcheries. In 1984 the hatchery became involved in supplying lake trout eggs to the **Great Lakes** lake trout recovery program. The endangered **Wyoming** toad is also bred at the hatchery for reintroduction into the wild. A self-guided tour describes the process used to harvest the eggs as well as the management policies behind restocking depleted fish populations. Fish spawning can be observed from the end of September through October. The **Silver Sage Ranch Wetland** overlook and interpretive area is located behind the hatchery. The grounds are nicely grassed with some picnic tables.
Hours: 8am - 4pm   *Phone:* 307-326-5662   *Cool Rating:* **   *Crowds:* *   *Time:* 30 min
Directions: E then N on Fish Hatchery Rd/CR-207 1.6 mi. The road continues 1.6 mi N and W back to Wy-130 MM 16.3.

MM: 19.2   *Dist:* 1.1   *GPS:* 41.46828/-106.78972   *Elev:* 6800   *Grid:* 61/88   *Land:* City
Saratoga Lake Campground   *Type:* Campground
Camping on 3 levels above the west shore of **Saratoga Lake**. The electric sites are lined up on the top level, and the other sites are spread out below. The area is patrolled daily. *Sandy beach area. No trees. 25 electric sites. Boat dock. Playground.*
Crowds: **   **[FEE AREA]**   *Directions:* SE 1/4 mi;   SE/L 0.8 mi.
Campsites: 45   *Shade:* *   *Privacy:* *   *RV Size:* 40'+   *Other:* Water,Electric

MM: 20.3   *GPS:* 41.45479/-106.80766   *Elev:* 6787   *Grid:* 61/89
Saratoga   *Type:* Town

MM: 20.6   *Dist:* 0.3   *GPS:* 41.45022/-106.80338   *Elev:* 6790   *Grid:* 61/89   *Land:* City
Hobo Hot Pool   *Type:* Hot Springs
A 30 x 30 ft hot spring pool with changing rooms, showers, and restrooms. The pool is fairly shallow with a dirt bottom and is very hot with a temperature range from 106° to 119° F. The overflow from the hot pool runs into the adjacent **North Platte River**, which provides a cooler soaking area.
Hours: Always open   *Cool Rating:* **   *Crowds:* ***
Directions: E on Walnut St 1/4 mi to public swimming pool parking at end of street. The hot pool is behind the swimming pool.

MM: 28.3   *GPS:* 41.35743/-106.74203   *Elev:* 7002   *Grid:* 62/91
Wy-130 (Laramie to Wy-230) *(see chapter)*   *Type:* Hwy Junction w/Chapter
68.1 mi highway east over **Snowy Range Pass** to **Laramie**. Highlights include the many attractions along the 27 mi **Snowy Range Scenic Byway**.
Nearest Town: Saratoga 8 N   *Directions:* E to Laramie from MM 68.1

MM: 30.0   *Dist:* 1.0   *GPS:* 41.33171/-106.72806   *Elev:* 6934   *Grid:* 62/92   *Land:* Wyoming G & F
Treasure Island Public Access Area   *Type:* Public Access Area
Primitive camping on the edge of a large, clean, gravel parking area, which provides fishing access on the west bank of the **North Platte River**. *Vault toilet. Stone fire rings. Approximately 4 sites.* Upstream 250 yds to the southeast are 2 suspended footbridges that provide access to the 2 mi long **Treasure Island**, which provides additional fishing access and tent camping possibilities.
Crowds: ***   *Directions:* E on Cow Creek Rd 0.5 mi;   Keep right at fork 0.5 mi to parking area.
Road Desc: Gravel, rough spots. Wide and smooth for the first 0.5 mi. Last 0.5 mi is narrow and rutted with a 5 ton weight limit bridge and is not recommended when wet.
Campsites: Dispersed   *Shade:* *   *Privacy:* *   *RV Size:* 30'   *Other:* None

MM: 38.2   *GPS:* 41.21738/-106.78231   *Elev:* 7165   *Grid:* 61/95
Riverside   *Type:* Town

MM: 38.2   *GPS:* 41.21700/-106.78302   *Elev:* 7171   *Grid:* 61/95   *Land:* City
Carbon County Visitor Center   *Type:* Visitor Center
A small staffed visitor center.
Hours: 6am - 7pm   *Phone:* 307-327-5600   *Directions:* SW corner of Wy-230 and Wy-70 junction.

MM: 38.2   *GPS:* 41.21738/-106.78231   *Elev:* 7165   *Grid:* 61/95
Wy-230 (Riverside to Colorado) *(see chapter)*   *Type:* Hwy Junction w/Chapter
27.1 mi highway from **Riverside** southeast to **Colorado**. The highway is a continuation of **Wy-130/Wy-230 (Walcott to Riverside)** from the north; however, the highway turns to the east and the mile markers do not continue sequentially. Highlights include: **Indian Bathtubs**, **Platte River Trail**.
Directions: E then SE to Colorado from MM 100

MM: 38.2   *GPS:* 41.21738/-106.78231   *Elev:* 7165   *Grid:* 61/95
Wy-70 *(see chapter)*   *Type:* Hwy Junction w/Chapter
57.7 mi highway in south-central **Wyoming**, just north of **Colorado**, from **Riverside** southwest to **Baggs**. Most of the highway runs through the **Sierra Madre Mountains** in the **Medicine Bow National Forest** and provides abundant OHV roads and dispersed camping opportunities. Highlights include: **Grand Encampment Museum**, **Green Mountain Falls**, **Dillon** and **Rudefeha Ghost Towns**, **Aspen Alley**.
Directions: SW to Encampment from MM 57.7

MM: 38.2   *GPS:* 41.21738/-106.78231   *Elev:* 7165   *Grid:* 61/95
Wy-230/Wy-130 (Riverside to Walcott)   *Type:* Highway End
38.2 mi highway from **Riverside** north to **Walcott**. The highway transitions from **Wy-230** to **Wy-130** at MM 28.3 (the junction with Wy-130 east) and the mile markers continue sequentially north on **Wy-130**. Highlights include: **Hobo Hot Pool**, **Saratoga National Fish Hatchery**.
Directions: N to Saratoga from MM 38.2

Wy-131/FR-300/Louis Lake Rd   N/S

MM: 0.0/36.5   *GPS:* 42.83397/-108.73519   *Elev:* 5358   *Grid:* 33/54
Wy-131/FR-300/Louis Lake Rd   *Type:* Highway Description
36.5 mi route from **US-287 (Lander to US-26)** in **Lander** south to **Wy-28**. The road traverses **Sinks Canyon** and climbs 4,240 ft above the city of **Lander** along the southeastern end of the **Wind River Mountains**. 7 public campgrounds are located along this route plus many dispersed camping opportunities. The road is paved for 17.7 mi up to the **Worthen Meadows Campground** turnoff *(see road description)*. The first 10.5 mi provide access to **Sinks Canyon State Park** and **Popo Agie Falls** (pronounced "po-po-zsha"). Just past **Bruce's Bridge Trailhead** the road transitions to **FR-300** and continues 26.0 mi to **Wy-28**. *NOTE: If you are strictly using this route as a shortcut to Wy-28, continuing on FR-300 from Bruce's Bridge Trailhead to Wy-28 only saves about 14 mi over turning around and driving the paved roads.* The road climbs 1,390 ft up switchbacks then gradually climbs another 1,055 ft to the high point (where a trail leads to the **Blue Ridge Fire Lookout**) before gradually descending 1,000 ft to **Louis Lake**. The road then climbs steeply out of the valley before gradually descending to **Wy-28**, where the last 2 mi are wide and fairly smooth gravel. Highlights include: **Sinks Canyon State Park**, **Popo Agie Falls**, trailheads into the **Wind River Mountains**, **Blue Ridge Fire Lookout**, **Louis Lake**.
Directions: S to Wy-28 from MM 0
Notes: The last 5 mi of this route, north of Wy-28, offers abundant dispersed camping. This route driven counterclockwise with connections to Wy-28 northeast and US-287/Wy-789 northwest creates a 70 mi scenic loop route from Lander. A nice, inexpensive self-guided tour booklet fully documents this loop and is available at the Sinks Canyon State Park visitor center. This route is not recommended solely as a shortcut between Lander and Wy-28 as it is an extremely slow drive.
Road Desc: Wy-131/FR-300 is paved for the first 17.7 mi to Worthen Meadows. From there FR-300 is gravel, narrow, winding, and washboarded in spots. Large RVs and trailers should enter from Wy-28 to avoid tight switchbacks between Bruce's Bridge Trailhead and Frye Lake. The road that descends to Louis Lake from the south is narrow, steep, and washboarded.

MM: 0.0/36.5   *GPS:* 42.83397/-108.73519   *Elev:* 5358   *Grid:* 33/54
US-287 (Lander to US-26) *(see chapter)*   *Type:* Hwy Junction w/Chapter
31.6 mi highway northwest from **Lander** to **US-26**. The highway transitions from **US-287/Wy-789**; however, the mile markers start at MM 0. Highlights include: **Sacajawea's Grave**.
Directions: NW to Fort Washaki or SE to Rawlins from MM 0.4

MM: 0.0/36.5   *GPS:* 42.83397/-108.73519   *Elev:* 5358   *Grid:* 33/54
Lander   *Type:* Town

MM: 2.3/34.2   *GPS:* 42.80986/-108.75387   *Elev:* 5498   *Grid:* 33/55
Mortimore Ln   *Type:* Highway Junction
If heading southeast toward **Rawlins** or southwest toward **Farson**, this 2.6 mi cutoff road connects to **US-287/Wy-789** without driving through **Lander**.
Directions: E on Mortimore Ln 2.6 mi; SE on US-287/Wy-789 from MM 79.3

MM: 6.5/30.0   *GPS:* 42.76040/-108.79467   *GPS2:* 42.76026/-108.79538   *Elev:* 6090   *Grid:* 32/56   *Land:* State
Petroglyphs and Pictographs   *Type:* Petroglyphs
Petroglyphs and **Pictographs** on the sandstone cliff face that parallels the road. The majority of this rock is fairly weathered and not well-defined.
Cool Rating: ***   *Crowds:* *   *Time:* 15 min
Directions: Small, single vehicle paved parking area on W side of hwy next to a large boulder; Walk straight and then left about 80 ft along the cliff face.

MM: 6.8/29.7   *GPS:* 42.75740/-108.79971   *Elev:* 6150   *Grid:* 32/56   *Land:* State
Sawmill Campground: Sinks Canyon State Park   *Type:* Campground/Day Use Area
Located between the highway and the **Popo Agie River** at the mouth of **Sinks Canyon**. The campground features a designated handicapped accessible campsite and fishing pier. Another site has enough room to park a pickup camper or van. 3 other sites have picnic tables, but there doesn't appear to be enough room to reasonably park a vehicle. These sites are best suited as picnic sites. The campground appears to serve as a day use area, as it has a group picnic shelter and a nice playground. *Highway noise.*
Crowds: ***   *[FEE AREA]*   *Directions:* SE side of hwy
Notes: Unless using the handicapped accessible facilities, I would suggest camping at one of the other campgrounds farther up the canyon.
Campsites: 2   *Shade:* *   *Privacy:* *   *RV Size:* 30'   *Other:* Water

MM: 7.3/29.2   *GPS:* 42.75214/-108.80588   *Elev:* 6280   *Grid:* 32/56   *Land:* State
Rise of the Sinks: Sinks Canyon State Park   *Type:* State Park
A pool where the **Middle Fork Popo Agie River** (pronounced "po-po-zsha") "rises" after being underground from **The Sinks** 1/4 mi north *(see next section)*. A pier overlooks **The Rise**, also known as the **Trout Pool**, where a large number of trout congregate. A fish food dispenser is provided so visitors can drop food to the fish below. Interpretive signs provide information about **The Rise**, the canyon geology, and the trout.
Cool Rating: ****   *Crowds:* ***   *Time:* 15-30 min   *Directions:* NW side of hwy
Notes: If entering from the south, it is best to go to the visitor center first to get oriented and see The Sinks. From there you can walk the 1/4 mi trail or drive back to The Rise.

MM: 7.6/28.9　*GPS:* 42.74842/-108.80965　*Elev:* 6387　*Grid:* 32/56　*Land:* State
Sinks Canyon State Park and Visitor Center　　　*Type:* State Park
Sinks Canyon gets its name from an odd geological phenomenon. The **Middle Fork Popo Agie River** (pronounced "po-po-zsha")
rushes through the canyon and turns abruptly into a large limestone cavern. The water "sinks" into cracks and crevices at the back
of the cave then flows underground and emerges 1/4 mi down the canyon in a large calm pool called **The Rise**. Where the water
goes while underground is unknown, as the small, clogged passages are not large enough to explore. However, a dye test has
proven that **The Sinks** and **The Rise** are connected. During this test the water mysteriously took 2 hours to re-emerge. It was also
discovered that more water emerges than goes into **The Sinks**. During heavy run-off periods the water flow into the cavern
increases by up to 5 times. The cavern cannot handle this flow, so the water spills over into a seasonal streambed called the
overflow channel, which continues down the canyon.

The Sinks are located behind the visitor center, which provides general information plus signs and displays about **The Sinks** and
The Rise and the geology, wildlife, plants, and history of the canyon. An easy 1/4 mi trail connects the visitor center and **The Rise**
with an optional short loop that passes the **overflow channel**. Other than **Sinks Canyon** itself, the 1/4 mi between **The Sinks** and
The Rise comprise the main activities in **Sinks Canyon State Park**.
Hours: 9am - 7pm (Memorial - Labor Day)　*Phone:* 307-332-3077　*Cool Rating:* ****　*Crowds:* ***　*Time:* 15-60 min
Directions: SE side of hwy

MM: 8.3/28.1　*GPS:* 42.74277/-108.82015　*Elev:* 6650　*Grid:* 32/56　*Land:* State
Popo Agie Campground: Sinks Canyon State Park　　　*Type:* Campground
Spread out between the road and the **Middle Fork Popo Agie River** in **Sinks Canyon**. A footbridge crosses the river to access a
1.0 mi interpretive loop nature trail and a 4.0 mi loop trail. *Mixed forest. Bushy middlestory. Many sites not level. Paved loops and
parking areas. Sites 1 and 4 accommodate 40 ft RVs. 1 tent-only site.*
Crowds: ***　*[FEE AREA]*　*Directions:* SE side of hwy
Campsites: 24　*Shade:* *　*Privacy:* ****　*RV Size:* 30'　*Other:* Water BEARS

MM: 9.0/27.4　*GPS:* 42.73881/-108.83212　*Elev:* 6835　*Grid:* 32/57　*Land:* NF
Shoshone National Forest　　　*Type:* National Forest Boundary

MM: 9.3/27.2　*GPS:* 42.73746/-108.83665　*Elev:* 6880　*Grid:* 32/57　*Land:* NF
Sinks Canyon Campground　　　*Type:* Campground
Just outside of **Sinks Canyon State Park** in **Sinks Canyon** near the **North Fork Popo Agie River**. A footbridge crosses the river
to a hiking trail and fishing access. *Scattered short junipers and sagebrush. Paved road and parking areas. Not level. 3 tent-only
sites. Good spacing between sites.*
Crowds: ***　*[FEE AREA]*　*Directions:* S side of hwy
Campsites: 9　*Shade:* *　*Privacy:* *　*RV Size:* 30'　*Other:* Water BEARS

MM: 10.1/26.4　*GPS:* 42.73250/-108.85039　*Elev:* 7045　*Grid:* 31/57　*Land:* NF
Dispersed Camping: Sinks Canyon　　　*Type:* Campground
Primitive camping and fishing access in **Sinks Canyon** along the **North Fork Popo Agie River**. 2 separate areas with the north
end being larger and the road smoother than the south end. *Sites in the open and near trees. Vault toilet and portable toilet. Stone
fire rings.*
Crowds: ***　*Directions:* SE side of hwy
Campsites: Dispersed　*Shade:* **　*Privacy:* *　*RV Size:* 40'+　*Other:* BEARS

MM: 10.3/26.2　*GPS:* 42.73110/-108.85486　*Elev:* 7120　*Grid:* 31/57　*Land:* NF
Bruce Picnic Area　　　*Type:* Picnic Area
Near the **North Fork Popo Agie River**, but the trees along the river don't provide much shade. One site is close to the river and
near trees. *5 picnic tables with grills.*
Directions: W side of road

MM: 10.5/26.0　*GPS:* 42.72916/-108.85731　*Elev:* 7145　*Grid:* 31/57　*Land:* NF
Bruce's Bridge Trailhead　　　*Type:* Trailhead
Parking area for the trail to **Popo Agie Falls** *(see next section)*.
Notes: This is bear country.　*Directions:* S side of hwy inside a sharp curve.

MM: 10.5/26.0　*GPS:* 42.72212/-108.88118　*GPS2:* 42.71971/-108.88266　*Elev:* 7790　*Grid:* 31/57　*Land:* NF
Popo Agie Falls　　　*Type:* Waterfall
A series of waterfalls and cascades on the **Middle Fork Popo Agie River**, which drop and cascade a total of about 190 ft into the
head of **Sinks Canyon**. The falls initially drop over the top of the rocky canyon before cascading and splitting into 2 separate
channels that flow through a ravine behind a large rock outcropping. The north channel tumbles over rocks into the canyon, while
about 110 yds south the other channel makes a short drop into the canyon. The trail starts at river level then climbs along the
canyon edge above the river with beautiful views. Most of the trail is in the open with little shade. The first overlook is at 1.5 mi, but
there are several vantage points all the way to the south channel at 1.7 mi. *Moderate; 1.7 mi one-way; 630 ft elev gain.*
Cool Rating: *****　*Crowds:* **　*Time:* 1.5-2 hrs
Directions: From Bruce's Bridge Trailhead cross the road to the north, cross the bridge and turn left.

MM: 15.8/20.7　*GPS:* 42.70933/-108.86428　*Elev:* 8540　*Grid:* 31/57　*Land:* NF
Wind River Vista　　　*Type:* Scenic Viewpoint
Shortly after reaching the summit of the 1,400 ft climb from **Bruce's Bridge Trailhead**, a pullout offers views of **Wind River Peak**
(13,400 ft) in the distance and **Frye Lake** in the valley below.
Directions: S side of hwy

MM: 16.8/19.7　*GPS:* 42.70392/-108.88122　*Elev:* 8525　*Grid:* 31/57　*Land:* NF
Frye Lake　　　*Type:* Campground
A popular fishing lake that is also an irrigation reservoir, resulting in fluctuating water levels. On the southwest end of the lake, at
the edge of the forest, is a meadow that provides a large dispersed camping area. Other dispersed camping around the lake is
accessed at MM 15.9, just below the **Wind River Vista** *(see previous section)*.
Crowds: ***　*Directions:* NW side of road
Campsites: Dispersed　*Shade:* **　*Privacy:* *　*RV Size:* 40'+　*Other:* BEARS

MM: 17.7/18.8 *GPS:* 42.72858/-108.85834 *Elev:* 7162 *Grid:* 31/57
Pavement Ends (heading southwest)   *Type:* Pavement Change
Heading southwest, **FR-300** turns to gravel with washboard sections and begins climbing steeply up switchbacks.

MM: 17.7/18.8 *Dist:* 2.4 *GPS:* 42.69756/-108.92935 *Elev:* 8843 *Grid:* 30/58 *Land:* NF
Worthen Meadows Campground   *Type:* Campground/Picnic Area
2 separate camping areas on the southwest side of **Worthen Meadows Reservoir**. To the left is a forested loop with 20 sites, with a few that overlook the lake. The area to the right is more open and closer to the lake with 8 sites on the entrance road and an end loop. A picnic area is located between the boat ramp and the campground. The **Worthen Meadows Trailhead** lies just beyond the campground entrance *(see next section)*. Conifer forest. 7 pull-thrus. Boat ramp.
Crowds: *** *[FEE AREA] Directions:* W on FR-302 2.4 mi
Campsites: 28 *Shade:* **** *Privacy:* ** *RV Size:* 40' *Other:* Water BEARS

MM: 17.7/18.8 *Dist:* 2.6 *GPS:* 42.70021/-108.93178 *Elev:* 8845 *Grid:* 30/57 *Land:* NF
Worthen Meadows Trailhead   *Type:* Trailhead
Long trails into the **Popo Agie Wilderness** and **Wind River Mountains** via the **Sheep Bridge Trail**, **Middle Fork Trail**, and **Stough Creek Basin Trail**.
Crowds: ** *Directions:* W on FR-302 2.6 mi to end of the road just past campground.

MM: 18.1/18.4 *GPS:* 42.69110/-108.89147 *Elev:* 8764 *Grid:* 31/58 *Land:* NF
Dispersed Camping: Louis Lake Rd (southbound)   *Type:* Campground
If heading south there is about 1/2 mi of primitive camping in tree-lined meadows on both sides of the road.
Crowds: **
Campsites: Dispersed *Shade:* ** *Privacy:* ** *RV Size:* 40'+ *Other:* BEARS

MM: 18.6/17.8 *GPS:* 42.68470/-108.88641 *Elev:* 8764 *Grid:* 31/58 *Land:* NF
Dispersed Camping: Louis Lake Rd (northbound)   *Type:* Campground
If heading north there is about 1/2 mi of primitive camping in tree-lined meadows on both sides of the road.
Crowds: **
Campsites: Dispersed *Shade:* ** *Privacy:* ** *RV Size:* 40'+ *Other:* BEARS

MM: 22.1/14.4 *GPS:* 42.64611/-108.86811 *GPS2:* 42.64701/-108.87415 *Elev:* 9593 *Grid:* 31/59 *Land:* NF
Blue Ridge Fire Lookout   *Type:* Fire Lookout
An open rock fire lookout constructed in 1938 by the **Civilian Conservation Corps** (CCC) and on the **National Register of Historic Places**. This is the highest point on the route and provides outstanding views of the surrounding mountains (**Fiddlers Lake** is visible to the south). The lookout is still used by the **U.S. Forest Service** to check for fire after lightning strikes. A hiking trail winds through the forest to the base of the lookout, where reaching the top requires climbing over 80 steep rock stairs with no handrails. *Moderately easy; 0.6 mi one-way; 330 ft elev gain.*
Cool Rating: *** *Crowds:* * *Time:* 1 hr *Directions:* NW side of road. Parking on other side of road.
Notes: Climb the lookout at your own risk.

MM: 23.3/13.2 *Dist:* 0.4 *GPS:* 42.63347/-108.88146 *Elev:* 9437 *Grid:* 31/59 *Land:* NF
Fiddlers Lake Campground   *Type:* Campground
Campsites spread along the north and west shore of **Fiddlers Lake**, a shallow natural lake. The first 4 sites are walk-in tent sites on the north side of the lake. Continuing along the entrance road are 7 well-spaced pull-thrus, some next to the lake. The end of the campground consists of back-in sites along the road as well as in an end loop where the sites are closer together. *Conifer forest. Level. Boat ramp. Handicapped accessible facilities.*
Crowds: **** *[FEE AREA] Notes:* Power boats limited to electric motors. *Directions:* SW 0.4 mi
Campsites: 20 *Shade:* *** *Privacy:* *** *RV Size:* 40' *Other:* Water BEARS

MM: 23.9/12.6 *GPS:* 42.62684/-108.87594 *Elev:* 9390 *Grid:* 31/59 *Land:* NF
Christina Lake Trailhead   *Type:* Trailhead
This is the highest trailhead into the **Wind River Mountains** and as such offers shorter hikes to high mountain lakes. The trail heads southwest 1.8 mi, where it forks left to **Christina Lake**, and right into the **Popo Agie Wilderness** toward **Silas Canyon**. **Christina Lake Trail** to **Christina Lake**: 2.3 mi; 550 ft elev gain. **Silas Canyon Trail** to **Lower Silas Lake**: *Moderate; 2.5 mi one-way; 300 ft elev gain;* **Upper Silas Lake**: *Moderate; 3.2 mi one-way; 700 ft elev gain;* **Island Lake**: *Moderate; 4.5 mi one-way; 1200 ft elev gain.*
Cool Rating: **** *Crowds:* *** *Directions:* SW side of road

MM: 26.1/10.3 *GPS:* 42.60840/-108.85485 *Elev:* 8768 *Grid:* 31/60 *Land:* NF
Popo Agie Campground   *Type:* Campground
Camping in a small open cul-de-sac near the **Little Popo Agie River**. *Conifer forest. Tables and fire-rings with grates. Vault toilet.*
Crowds: * *Directions:* 0.1 mi S of river bridge; SW side of road.
Campsites: 4 *Shade:* ** *Privacy:* * *RV Size:* 20' *Other:* None

MM: 27.2/9.3 *Dist:* 0.3 *GPS:* 42.59913/-108.84497 *Elev:* 8615 *Grid:* 32/60 *Land:* NF
Louis Beach Picnic Area and Beach (east)   *Type:* Picnic and Day Use Area
A nice picnic area and nearby sand beach on the northeast side of **Louis Lake**. The picnic area is above the lake and below the road.
Crowds: *** *Directions:* SE then curve NW 1/4 mi to parking area.

MM: 27.6/8.8 *GPS:* 42.59858/-108.84973 *Elev:* 8603 *Grid:* 31/60 *Land:* NF
Louis Beach Picnic Area (west)   *Type:* Picnic Area
A nice picnic area on the northwest side of **Louis Lake**.
Crowds: *** *Directions:* E side of road

MM: 28.7/7.8   *Dist:* 0.8   *GPS:* 42.59200/-108.84376   *Elev:* 8586   *Grid:* 32/60   *Land:* NF

Louis Lake Campground   *Type:* Campground

Located on the south shore of **Louis Lake**, which gets heavy day use. Moose are commonly seen around the lake. *Single loop. Light conifer forest. Boat ramp.*

Crowds: *****   *[FEE AREA]   Road Desc:* The road to the south of Louis Lake is steep, narrow, and rough.

Directions: NE 0.8 mi

Campsites: 9   *Shade:* ***   *Privacy:* *   *RV Size:* 30'   *Other:* BEARS

MM: 36.5/0.0   *GPS:* 42.51494/-108.77765   *Elev:* 8440   *Grid:* 33/62

Wy-28 (Farson to US-287) *(see chapter)*   *Type:* Hwy Junction w/Chapter

66.3 mi highway from **US-287/Wy-789**, 8.4 mi southeast of **Lander**, southwest to **Farson**. Highlights include: **Red Canyon**, **Miner's Delight**, **Atlantic City**, **Carissa Mine**, **South Pass City State Historic Site**, **South Pass** and related historic markers.

Directions: NE to Lander or SW to Farson from MM 45.8

MM: 36.5/0.0   *GPS:* 42.51494/-108.77765   *Elev:* 8440   *Grid:* 33/62

Louis Lake Rd/FR-300/Wy-131   *Type:* Highway End

36.5 mi route from **Wy-28** north to **US-287 (Lander to US-26)** in **Lander**. The road begins as **FR-300/Louis Lake Rd** and traverses the southeastern end of the **Wind River Mountains** to a high point 4,240 ft above the city of **Lander** before it descends and becomes **Wy-131** through **Sinks Canyon**. 7 public campgrounds are located along this route plus many dispersed camping opportunities. The gravel road is wide and fairly smooth for the first 2 mi but narrows and gets rough as it starts into the mountains. The road descends steeply to **Louis Lake**, where it is particularly narrow and rough, before climbing gradually 1,000 ft to the high point (where a trail leads to the **Blue Ridge Fire Lookout**). The road descends gradually 1,050 ft to **Frye Lake** and then 1,390 ft down switchbacks. *The road is paved starting at the **Worthen Meadows Campground** turnoff for the final 17.7 mi.* At the bottom of the switchbacks is **Bruce's Bridge Trailhead**, which is the start of the trail to **Popo Agie Falls** (pronounced "po-po-zsha"). **Wy-131** descends gradually for the final 10.5 mi through **Sinks Canyon** and past **Sinks Canyon State Park**. Highlights include: **Louis Lake**, **Blue Ridge Fire Lookout**, trailheads into the **Wind River Mountains**, **Popo Agie Falls**, **Sinks Canyon State Park**.

Nearest Town: Atlantic City 6.0 SE   *Directions:* N to Lander from MM 36.5

Wy-134 & Wy-133

MM: 0.0 *GPS:* 43.18553/-108.24585 *Elev:* 4895 *Grid:* 40/45
Wy-134 & Wy-133   *Type:* Highway Description
28.3 mi on 2 highways from **US-26/Wy-789** west and south to **US-26**, which heads northwest to **Dubois**. If traveling west between **Shoshoni** and **Dubois**, this route is 4.7 mi shorter than continuing through **Riverton** and offers 3 primitive campgrounds on the north side of **Ocean Lake**.
Nearest Town: Shoshoni 8.3 NE *Notes:* The mile markers are not particularly accurate along Wy-134.
Directions: W on Wy-134 24.2 mi; S on Wy-133 4.1 mi.

MM: 0.0 *GPS:* 43.18553/-108.24585 *Elev:* 4895 *Grid:* 40/45
Wy-789 & US-26/Wy-789 *(see chapter)*   *Type:* Hwy Junction w/Chapter
46.2 mi highway from **Lander** northeast to **Shoshoni**. The highway heads northeast from **Lander** as **Wy-789** continuing the mile markers from **US-287/Wy-789**. After 24.1 mi the highway combines with **US-26** and continues northeast 22.1 mi to **Shoshoni** as **US-26/Wy-789**. Highlights include: access to **Castle Gardens**, **Wyoming Heritage Trail**.
Directions: NE to Shoshoni or SW to Riverton from MM 119.0

MM: 15.6 *Dist:* 5.9 *GPS:* 43.18569/-108.57009 *Elev:* 5242 *Grid:* 35/45 *Land:* Bureau of Reclamation
Ocean Lake Wildlife Habitat Management Area - Mills Point   *Type:* Wildlife Habitat Mgmt Area
Lake access and primitive camping on the east shore of **Ocean Lake**. *Vault toilet. Primitive boat launch.*
Crowds: * *Nearest Town:* Pavillion 16.4 NW *Road Desc:* 8 Mile Rd is paved. N Irishman Rd and beyond is gravel.
Directions: S on 8 Mile Rd 2.4 mi; W/R on N Irishman Rd 0.75 mi; Keep right to continue straight on the narrow gravel road 2.7 mi.
Campsites: Dispersed *Shade:* * *Privacy:* * *RV Size:* 20' *Other:* None

MM: 17.9 *Dist:* 1.1 *GPS:* 43.20477/-108.57823 *Elev:* 5247 *Grid:* 35/45 *Land:* Bureau of Reclamation
Ocean Lake Wildlife Habitat Management Area - Dickinson Park   *Type:* Wildlife Habitat Mgmt Area
Lake access and primitive camping in a large gravel parking area on the northeast shore of **Ocean Lake**. *Vault toilet. Boat ramp and pier.*
Crowds: * *Nearest Town:* Pavillion 9.5 NW *Road Desc:* Gravel, narrow
Directions: S on Walleye Rd 0.7 mi; SW/R at fork 0.35 mi.
Campsites: Dispersed *Shade:* * *Privacy:* * *RV Size:* 20' *Other:* None

MM: 20.4 *Dist:* 0.3 *GPS:* 43.21082/-108.62014 *Elev:* 5242 *Grid:* 35/45 *Land:* Bureau of Reclamation
Ocean Lake Wildlife Habitat Management Area - Stultz   *Type:* Wildlife Habitat Mgmt Area
Lake access and primitive camping in a small gravel parking area on the northwest shore of **Ocean Lake**. *Vault toilet. Primitive boat launch.*
Crowds: * *Nearest Town:* Pavillion 6.6 NW *Road Desc:* Gravel, narrow *Directions:* S 0.3 mi
Campsites: Dispersed *Shade:* * *Privacy:* * *RV Size:* 20' *Other:* None

MM: 24.2 *GPS:* 43.21432/-108.69617 *Elev:* 5418 *Grid:* 34/45
Wy-133   *Type:* Highway Junction
Connecting highway south to **US-26**.
Directions: S 4.1 mi to US-26

MM: 28.3 *GPS:* 43.15571/-108.69511 *Elev:* 5428 *Grid:* 34/46
US-26/287 & US-26 *(see chapter)*   *Type:* Hwy Junction w/Chapter
133.7 mi highway from **Riverton** northwest to **Moran Jct**. **US-26** merges with **US-287 (Lander to US-26)** at MM 98.8 and continues northwest as **US-26/287**. This is a primary access route to **Grand Teton National Park** and **Yellowstone National Park**. Heading northwest between **Dubois** and **Moran Jct** is along the **Centennial Scenic Byway**. Highlights include: **Trail Lake Rd Petroglyphs**, colorful badlands, **Dubois Recreation Area Scenic Overlook**, **Brooks Lake**, **Brooks Lake Creek Falls**, **Pinnacle Buttes**, **Wind River Lake**, **Breccia Cliffs**.
Directions: NW to Dubois or SE to Riverton from MM 114.6

MM: 28.3 *GPS:* 43.15571/-108.69511 *Elev:* 5428 *Grid:* 34/46
Wy-133 & Wy-134   *Type:* Highway End
28.3 mi on 2 highways from **US-26** north and east to **US-26/Wy-789**, which heads northeast to **Shoshoni**. If traveling east between **Dubois** and **Shoshoni**, this route is 4.7 mi shorter than continuing through **Riverton** and offers 3 primitive campgrounds on the north side of **Ocean Lake**.
Nearest Town: Riverton 19.1 SE *Directions:* N on Wy-133 4.1 mi; E on Wy-134 24.2 mi.

MM: 0.0 *GPS:* 43.00611/-108.37826 *Elev:* 4923 *Grid:* 38/50
Wy-135/136   *Type:* Highway Description
35.6 mi highway from **Wy-789**, just south of **Riverton**, southeast to **US-287/Wy-789**, which heads southeast to **Rawlins**. The route starts as **Wy-136** for 1.0 mi before transitioning to **Wy-135**. The landscape is prairie and badlands with no towns or services along the way. This highway saves 24.5 mi over driving through **Lander**. Highlights include: **Badlands Scenic Overlook**.
Nearest Town: Riverton 2.5 N *Directions:* SE on Wy-136 1.0 mi; Continue S on Wy-135.

MM: 0.0 *GPS:* 43.00611/-108.37826 *Elev:* 4923 *Grid:* 38/50
Wy-789 & US-26/Wy-789 *(see chapter)*   *Type:* Hwy Junction w/Chapter
46.2 mi highway from **Lander** northeast to **Shoshoni**. The highway heads northeast from **Lander** as **Wy-789** continuing the mile markers from **US-287/Wy-789**. After 24.1 mi the highway combines with **US-26** and continues northeast 22.1 mi to **Shoshoni** as **US-26/Wy-789**. Highlights include: access to **Castle Gardens**, **Wyoming Heritage Trail**.
Directions: N to Riverton or SW to Lander from MM 103.8

MM: 1.0 *GPS:* 42.99388/-108.37078 *Elev:* 4928 *Grid:* 38/50
Wy-135   *Type:* Highway Transition
The road transitions from **Wy-136** to **Wy-135**. **Wy-136** junctions and heads east.

MM: 24.3 *Dist:* 0.5 *GPS:* 42.68250/-108.18606 *Elev:* 6866 *Grid:* 41/58 *Land:* BLM
Badlands Scenic Overlook   *Type:* Scenic Viewpoint
An expansive view to the west from the **Beaver Rim** into the 1,400 ft deep badlands valley with the **Wind River Mountains** in the distance. Interpretive plaques are located along the cliff edge.
Cool Rating: *** *Crowds:* * *Time:* 15 min *Road Desc:* Gravel *Directions:* SW 0.5 mi

MM: 27.7 *Dist:* 1.6 *GPS:* 42.65858/-108.20952 *Elev:* 6779 *Grid:* 41/59 *Land:* BLM
Dispersed Camping: Wy-135   *Type:* Dispersed Camping
Just down the road from the **Badlands Scenic Overlook**, this road runs 1.6 mi up to the cliff edge with opportunities for primitive camping with an expansive view. *No trees. No facilities.*
Crowds: * *Road Desc:* Dirt *Directions:* NW on BLM 2302 1.6 mi
Campsites: Dispersed *Shade:* * *Privacy:* *** *RV Size:* 40'+ *Other:* None

MM: 33.5 *Dist:* 3.1 *GPS:* 42.56930/-108.22869 *Elev:* 6630 *Grid:* 40/61 *Land:* BLM
Carmody Lake   *Type:* Campground
Primitive camping near a shallow lake on the sagebrush plains. *No facilities. No trees.*
Crowds: * *Road Desc:* Dirt, primitive & impassable when wet, narrow *Directions:* W on unmarked dirt road 3.1 mi
Campsites: Dispersed *Shade:* * *Privacy:* ***** *RV Size:* 30' *Other:* None

MM: 34.5 *GPS:* 42.54425/-108.18815 *Elev:* 6562 *Grid:* 41/61
Sweetwater Station Rest Area   *Type:* Rest Area
A nice grassed rest area with picnic shelters and **Oregon Trail** historical markers about the **Sweetwater Valley**.
Directions: E side of hwy

MM: 34.6 *GPS:* 42.54320/-108.18949 *Elev:* 6562 *Grid:* 41/61
US-287/Wy-789 *(see chapter)*   *Type:* Hwy Junction w/Chapter
125 mi highway from **Lander** southeast to **Rawlins** near **I-80**. Highlights include: **Green Mountain**, **Split Rock**.
Directions: NW to Lander or SE to Rawlins from MM 42.1

MM: 34.6 *GPS:* 42.54320/-108.18949 *Elev:* 6562 *Grid:* 41/61
End of Highway   *Type:* Highway End
35.6 mi highway from **US-287/Wy-789** northwest to **Wy-789**, just south of **Riverton**. **Wy-135** transitions to **Wy-136** for the last mile. The landscape is prairie and badlands with no towns or services along the way. This highway saves 24.5 mi over driving through **Lander**. Highlights include: **Badlands Scenic Overlook**.
Nearest Town: Jeffrey City 18.9 E; Lander 39 NW *Directions:* N to Riverton from MM 34.6

Wy-160/Grayrocks Rd/Power Plant Rd   E/W

MM: 0.0/30.0 *GPS:* 42.21292/-104.51935 *Elev:* 4240 *Grid:* 93/70
Wy-160/Grayrocks Rd/Power Plant Rd   *Type:* Highway Description
30.0 mi route from **US-26 (I-25 to Nebraska)** MM 27.9 at **Fort Laramie** southwest to **I-25** exit 80 at **Wheatland**. Highlights include: **Fort Laramie Bridge**, **Old Bedlam Ruts**, **Fort Laramie**, **Grayrocks Reservoir**.
Road Desc: CR-54 is gravel. Grayrocks Rd between I-25 and Guernsey Rd is paved, but the section after the power plant is narrow with no shoulders and is a popular road for pickups with large trailers.
Directions: W on Wy-160/CR-53 3.4 mi; Continue SW/R on CR-54 6.3 mi; S/L on S Guernsey Rd 0.7 mi; W/R on Grayrocks Rd 17.2 mi; S/L on Wy-320 1.8 mi; W/R on Rompoon Rd 0.5 mi; Continue on Swanson Rd 0.1 mi.

MM: 0.0/30.0 *GPS:* 42.21292/-104.51935 *Elev:* 4240 *Grid:* 93/70
US-26 (I-25 to Nebraska) *(see chapter)*   *Type:* Hwy Junction w/Chapter
56.2 mi highway southeast from **I-25** exit 92 to **Nebraska**. Highlights include: **Guernsey State Park**, **Oregon Trail Ruts**, **Register Cliff**, **Fort Laramie National Historic Site**.
Directions: SE to Torrington or NW to Guernsey from MM 27.9

MM: 0.0/30.0 *GPS:* 42.21292/-104.51935 *Elev:* 4240 *Grid:* 93/70
Fort Laramie   *Type:* Town

MM: 0.9/29.1 *GPS:* 42.20957/-104.53445 *Elev:* 4224 *Grid:* 93/70 *Land:* NPS
Fort Laramie Bridge   *Type:* Historic Site
A bridge constructed in 1875 over the **North Platte River**, which consists of three 140 ft bowed iron spans. It is believed to be the oldest existing military bridge west of the **Mississippi River**. The bridge was a vital link between **Cheyenne**, **Fort Laramie**, and the military outposts, Indian agencies, and gold fields of the **Black Hills**. The bridge also influenced the establishment of the famous **Cheyenne and Black Hills Stage and Express Line**. The bridge remained in use until 1958 and is now preserved as a footbridge on the **National Register of Historic Places**.

Walk 160 yds northeast across the bridge to a concrete marker with a plaque. From the southeast side of the parking area a 1.6 mi one-way trail follows the **North Platte River** to the confluence with the **Laramie River**.
Cool Rating: ** *Crowds:* * *Time:* 15 min *Directions:* SE 60 yds on RD 15 (just SW of the river bridge)

MM: 1.0/29.0 *GPS:* 42.20923/-104.53768 *Elev:* 4227 *Grid:* 93/70
Fort Platte Historical Marker   *Type:* Historical Marker
A concrete marker and plaque locating **Fort Platte** 50 yds to the north. **Fort Platte** was a trading post built in 1841.
Cool Rating: * *Crowds:* * *Time:* 5 min *Directions:* Pullout on N side of hwy

MM: 1.5/28.5 *GPS:* 42.20990/-104.54716 *Elev:* 4271 *Grid:* 93/70
CR-50/RD 92/Tank Farm Rd   *Type:* Highway Junction
9.9 mi cutoff road that connects to **S Guernsey Rd** 3.8 mi south of **Guernsey**. **Register Cliff** and the **Oregon Trail Ruts** are accessed along **S Guernsey Rd** at 1.2 mi and 3.0 mi respectively. This road saves 5.9 mi over continuing on **Wy-160/Grayrocks Rd**. It save another 3.2 mi if already heading to the **Old Bedlam Ruts** along this road.
Road Desc: Partially paved. The first 7.4 mi is gravel. *Directions:* NW on CR-50/RD 92 9.8 mi; NE/R to Guernsey.

MM: 1.5/28.5 *Dist:* 1.5 *GPS:* 42.22207/-104.56657 *Elev:* 4290 *Grid:* 93/69 *Land:* BLM
Mary Homsley Grave   *Type:* Historic Site
Mary Homsley was buried in this grave in 1852. Soon after giving birth to her fifth child, she and her baby boy both developed measles. Perhaps seeking medical care, her wagon train decided to cross the river to go to **Fort Laramie**. The wagon overturned and she and the child were both thrown into the river. Although they were rescued they became severely chilled. Mary died the next day and the baby died several weeks later. Her broken headstone was discovered in 1925 by some passing cowboys. The headstone was enclosed in a monument the following year. An interpretive sign at the site tells her story.
Cool Rating: ** *Crowds:* * *Time:* 15 min *Directions:* NW on CR-50/RD 92 1.2 mi; NE/R 0.2 mi; NW/L 0.1 mi.
Road Desc: Gravel. The 0.2 mi road is narrow with not much room to turn around. The last 0.1 mi is sandy and narrow.

MM: 1.5/28.5 *Dist:* 1.6 *GPS:* 42.22015/-104.57402 *GPS2:* 42.22194/-104.57449 *Elev:* 4445 *Grid:* 93/69 *Land:* BLM
Old Bedlam Ruts   *Type:* Historic Site
A 150 yd trail leads to a sign "The Journey West Continues." Just beyond is the **Oregon Trail** marker and the wagon ruts.
Cool Rating: ** *Crowds:* * *Time:* 15 min *Directions:* NW on CR-50/RD 92 1.6 mi; N/R into parking loop.

MM: 2.3/27.7 *GPS:* 42.20908/-104.56190 *Elev:* 4275 *Grid:* 93/70
The Greatest Ride in History   *Type:* Historical Marker
In memory of the horse ridden by **John "Portugee" Phillips** from **Fort Phil Kearny** to **Fort Laramie** after the **Fetterman Massacre**. This was the last of several horses Phillips had run into the ground, and it collapsed shortly after arriving at **Fort Laramie**. *See John "Portugee" Phillips Monument on Wy-193/US-87 MM 100.2.*
Cool Rating: * *Crowds:* * *Time:* 5 min *Directions:* NW side of sharp curve in road

MM: 2.5/27.5 **Dist:** 0.2 **GPS:** 42.20413/-104.55831 **Elev:** 4242 **Grid:** 93/70 **Land:** NPS
Fort Laramie National Historic Site   **Type:** Historic Site
The original establishment was founded as a trading post in 1834 during the fur trade. The post was located inside a bend on the **Laramie River** 1.5 mi west of the confluence with the **North Platte River**. It operated under different names but eventually came to be known as **Fort Laramie**. In the 1840s the fort became a well-known stopping point along the **Emigrant Trails**. As emigration along the trail increased so did Indian hostilities. This led to the purchase of the fort by the **U.S. Army** in 1849 for the purpose of operating a military outpost to protect travelers. While the original fort was being used, a new post was built as a collection of buildings around a large parade ground. Because of the high cost of building a fence around the fort, it remained open and dependent upon its location and its garrison of troops for security.

Because of the difficult task of protecting vast distances of trail, treaties with the Indians were signed but did not last. Indian conflicts escalated in the 1850s and were made worse in the 1860s by travelers heading to the gold fields in **Montana** through Indian hunting grounds along the **Bozeman Trail**. **Fort Laramie** also served as a **Pony Express** and transcontinental telegraph station in the early 1860s. Since the stream of emigrants had diminished by the 1860s, the fort was used primarily as a launching point for Indian campaigns that eventually led to their confinement on reservations in the 1880s. The **Union Pacific Railroad** had bypassed the fort to the south, further diminishing its importance. The fort remained in use for a time but was finally closed in March of 1890. The land and buildings were sold at auction to civilians.

The fort today looks much as it did in the 1800s with many original buildings restored to their historical appearance. The visitor center shows an interesting 20 minute video on the history of the fort. The tour of the expansive fort grounds is generally self-guided using interpretive signs on the grounds as well as inside the furnished buildings. Additionally, park personnel occasionally lead guided tours. Chauffeured electric cart tours are available for the handicapped and the elderly. A short distance southwest of the parking area is a large park and picnic area that is well-shaded by large cottonwoods. *Located at mile 650 of the* **Oregon Trail**.
Cool Rating: *** **Crowds:** ** **Time:** 1-3 hrs *[FEE AREA]* **Directions:** E 0.2 mi to entrance station.

MM: 11.7/18.3 **Dist:** 0.2 **GPS:** 42.16095/-104.69329 **GPS2:** 42.16297/-104.69118 **Elev:** 4432 **Grid:** 91/71 **Land:** State
Grayrocks Reservoir Dam Overlook   **Type:** Scenic Viewpoint
An overlook of the dam at the east end of **Grayrocks Reservoir**. A public access area is located on the northwest side of the highway for the next 3.7 mi. A boat ramp is located 1.4 mi west. *See next section.*
Cool Rating: ** **Crowds:** * **Directions:** N then immediately E 0.2 mi on a gravel road at the base of a long hill

MM: 15.4/14.6 **GPS:** 42.13265/-104.74760 **Elev:** 4430 **Grid:** 90/72 **Land:** State
Grayrocks Reservoir (west end)   **Type:** Public Access Area
A 3.5 mi long x 3/4 mi wide reservoir on the **Laramie River**, which provides opportunities for fishing, boating, swimming, and waterskiing. Public facilities on the south side of the reservoir include parking areas, vault toilets, and 3 boat ramps. The access point on the west end of the lake has 2 large gravel parking areas, each with a boat ramp. Dispersed camping is located along the south side of the reservoir with 11 access points along a 2.8 mi stretch. The north shore may also be used for overnight camping by boaters. The reservoir provides quality habitat for a variety of wildlife, including ducks, geese, pelicans, pheasants, wild turkeys, sharp-tailed grouse, squirrels, rabbits, deer, and pronghorn. The reservoir contains walleye, catfish, smallmouth bass, freshwater drum, and black crappie.
Cool Rating: ** **Crowds:** ** **Notes:** Camping is restricted to the major parking areas. The area is subject to high wind. This reservoir is about halfway between I-25 and US-26 and is a good camping area if visiting Fort Laramie National Historic Site.
Campsites: Dispersed **Shade:** * **Privacy:** * **RV Size:** 40'+ **Other:** None

MM: 29.4/0.6 **Dist:** 1.9 **GPS:** 42.04765/-104.95263 **Elev:** 4750 **Grid:** 87/74 **Land:** City
Wheatland City Park/Lewis Park   **Type:** Park
A large city park that allows camping along the south end. The campground includes 9 closely spaced back-in RV sites plus a separate tent area on the west end. The location is near basketball courts, tennis courts, and a skateboard park. The main park is about 150 yds north. *Cottonwoods. A few tables and grills. Donations appreciated, particularly for electricity use. RV dump 0.1 mi north (see next section).*
Notes: Railroad tracks run along the east end of the park; however, in the couple of hours that I was there, I never saw a train.
Directions: From the intersection of Wy-320 and Rompoon Rd; S on Wy-320 0.5 mi; S/L on Swanson Rd and 9th St 0.9 mi; E/L on Gilchrist St 1 block; S/R on 8th St 0.5 mi.
Campsites: 9 **Shade:** ***** **Privacy:** * **RV Size:** 40'+ **Other:** Electric,RVDump

MM: 29.4/0.6 **Dist:** 1.8 **GPS:** 42.04941/-104.95219 **Elev:** 4750 **Grid:** 87/74 **Land:** City
RV Dump: Wheatland City Park/Lewis Park   **Type:** RV Dump
RV dump with non-potable water on the east side of **Wheatland City Park/Lewis Park**. *See previous section for directions.*

MM: 30.0/0.0 **GPS:** 42.07434/-104.96485 **Elev:** 4700 **Grid:** 87/73
I-25 *(see chapter)*   **Type:** Hwy Junction w/Chapter
300.1 mi interstate highway through east/central **Wyoming** from **Colorado** north to **I-90** (just past **Buffalo**), which continues northwest to **Montana**. Highlights include: **Pioneer Museum**, **Ayres Park and Natural Bridge**, **National Historic Trails Interpretive Center**, **Hole-in-the-Wall**, **Outlaw Cave**, **Indian Rock Art Cave**.
Directions: N to Glendo or S to Cheyenne from MM 80.9

MM: 30.0/0.0 **GPS:** 42.07434/-104.96485 **Elev:** 4700 **Grid:** 87/73
Grayrocks Rd/Power Plant Rd/Wy-160   **Type:** Highway End
30.0 mi route from **I-25** exit 80 at **Wheatland** northeast to **US-26** (I-25 to Nebraska) MM 27.9 at **Fort Laramie**. Highlights include: **Grayrocks Reservoir**, **Fort Laramie**, **Old Bedlam Ruts**, **Fort Laramie Bridge**.
Nearest Town: Wheatland 1.9 S
Directions: I-25 exit 80; E on Swanson Rd 0.1 mi; Slight left onto Rompoon Rd 0.5 mi; N/L on Wy-320 1.8 mi; E/R on Grayrocks Rd 17.2 mi; N/L on S Guernsey Rd 0.7 mi; E/R on Fort Laramie Rd/CR-54 6.3 mi; Continue NE/L on CR-53/Wy-160 3.4 mi.

Wy-193/US-87   S/N

MM: 98.2 *GPS:* 44.51933/-106.80052 *Elev:* 4700 *Grid:* 61/12
Wy-193/US-87   *Type:* Highway Description
14.0 mi side trip from **I-90** MM 44.7 north back to **I-90** MM 33.6. After 7.9 mi **Wy-193** MM 106.2 transitions to **US-87** MM 38.9 and
continues 5.0 mi to MM 34.0 (the mile markers change direction), which returns 1.1 mi to **I-90** exit 33. Continuing north on **US-87**
leads 12.8 mi to **Sheridan** and back to **I-90** exit 20. Highlights include: **Fetterman Massacre Monument and Battlefield, Fort
Phil Kearny, Wagon Box Fight Historic Site, Story Fish Hatchery, Wyoming State Bird Farm.**
Nearest Town: Buffalo 13 S; Sheridan 21.2 N
Directions: I-90 exit 44 to Piney Creek Rd/Wy-193; NW 7.9 mi to a transition with US-87; Continue N on US-87 5.0 mi; E/R on
Meade Creek Rd/Wy-342 1.1 mi to I-90 MM 33.6

MM: 100.0 *Dist:* 2.5 *GPS:* 44.57130/-106.84108 *Elev:* 4867 *Grid:* 60/11 *Land:* State
Fetterman Massacre Monument and Battlefield   *Type:* Historic Site
The **Fetterman Massacre** was precipitated by the **U.S. Army** building **Fort Phil Kearny** in violation of a treaty with the **Sioux
Indians**. On December 21, 1866, a band of **Arapaho, Cheyenne,** and **Sioux Indians**, led by **Chief Red Cloud** and **Crazy Horse**,
retaliated by leading **Captain William J. Fetterman** and 79 men over **Lodge Trail Ridge** into an ambush by 2000 **Indians**. There
were no white survivors. This was the worst loss suffered by the **U.S. Army** until the battle of the **Little Bighorn** a decade later. A
large stone monument stands atop a hill marking the site. Interpretive signs are spread along a 2.0 mi round-trip trail through the
battlefield site.
Cool Rating: ** *Crowds:* * *Time:* 10-60 min *Directions:* N on US-87 2.5 mi

MM: 100.2 *Dist:* 0.4 *GPS:* 44.53528/-106.82352 *Elev:* 4670 *Grid:* 60/12
John "Portugee" Phillips Monument   *Type:* Historical Marker
Following the **Fetterman Massacre** on December 21, 1866, **John "Portugee" Phillips** rode 190 mi in 3 days from **Fort Phil
Kearny** to **Horseshoe Station** near present day **Glendo**. This ride to summon help was made in subzero weather while eluding
Indians. Phillips was accompanied by **Daniel Dixon** to **Fort Reno** (northeast of Sussex). While there he received an additional
message to be delivered to **Fort Laramie**, which he reached on December 25 for a total ride of 236 mi in 4 days. Legend has it
that he rode to **Fort Laramie** in a raging blizzard. A pyramid-shaped rock monument memorializes this event.
Cool Rating: * *Crowds:* * *Time:* 5 min *Road Desc:* Gravel
Directions: SE on Kearny Ln 0.4 mi; SE corner of intersection.

MM: 100.2 *Dist:* 0.7 *GPS:* 44.53377/-106.82843 *Elev:* 4724 *Grid:* 60/12 *Land:* State
Fort Phil Kearny   *Type:* Historic Site
This was one of 3 forts being built on the **Bozeman Trail** under the direction of **Colonel Henry B. Carrington** to protect travelers
from Indian attacks. Much to the anger of **Sioux Indian Chief Red Cloud**, construction started on July 13, 1866. Because of
perceived treaty violations, Carrington was continually harassed and by December 17 soldiers and 58 civilians had been killed.
These events led up to the **Fetterman Massacre** on December 21, which led to fears that Indians would subsequently attack **Fort
Phil Kearny**. 2 civilians, **John "Portugee" Phillips** and **Daniel Dixon**, were sent to get reinforcements from **Fort Laramie**. These
reinforcements arrived in mid-January 1867, but the Indians never attacked the fort directly. By 1868 the **Union Pacific Railroad**
had reached far enough west that the dangerous **Bozeman Trail** was rendered obsolete. The fort was abandoned in 1868 and
burned by **Cheyenne Indians**.

At the front of the fort is a reproduction of the stockade, guard station, officer's gate, and artillery bastion as originally built. Inside
the fort are markers and signs that identify and explain the fort layout and usage. The fort area is approximately 270 x 190 yds and
the tour is self-guided. Also at the site is an interpretive center with exhibits, videos, and a bookstore, as well as a picnic area and
restroom.

Nearby attractions related to the fort are the monuments and battlefields for the **Fetterman Massacre** and **Wagon Box Fight**, and
the **John "Portugee" Phillips Monument**.
Hours: Interpretive Center: 8am - 6pm (Summer); 12pm - 4pm (offseason) *Phone:* 307-684-7629
Cool Rating: ** *Crowds:* * *Time:* 1-2 hrs *[FEE AREA]* *Road Desc:* Gravel
Directions: SE on Kearny Ln 0.4 mi; SW on Wagon Box Rd 0.3 mi.

MM: 100.2 *Dist:* 5.0 *GPS:* 44.55818/-106.89825 *Elev:* 5330 *Grid:* 59/11 *Land:* State
Wagon Box Fight Historic Site (south access)   *Type:* Historic Site
On August 2, 1867, in the summer following the **Fetterman Massacre**, **Captain James Powell** and 31 men were attacked by
several hundred **Sioux Indians** 5 mi east of **Fort Phil Kearny**. Most of the men survived repeated attacks by taking refuge in a
corral formed by laying 14 wagon bodies end-to-end in an oval configuration. The battle lasted 5 hours with 3 men killed and 2
wounded. **Powell** reported killing 60 Indians and wounding 120. The soldiers survived the attacks primarily due to the recent
addition of breech-loading rifles (re-loaded from the rear of the barrel). A monument and several interpretive signs are located
around a paved loop. A picnic shelter is located at the site.
Cool Rating: ** *Crowds:* * *Time:* 30 min *Nearest Town:* Story 1.7 N *Road Desc:* Gravel
Directions: SE on Kearny Ln 0.4 mi; SW on Wagon Box Rd 4.4 mi (past Fort Phil Kearny); W/L 0.2 mi.

MM: 103.9 *GPS:* 44.57455/-106.87914 *Elev:* 5040 *Grid:* 60/11
Story   *Type:* Town

MM: 103.9 *Dist:* 2.3 *Land:* State
Wagon Box Fight Historic Site (north access)   *Type:* Historic Site
See MM 100.2 above.
Directions: W on Wy-194/Fish Hatchery Rd 1.0 mi; S/L on CR-145/Wagon Box Rd 1.1 mi; W/R 0.2 mi.

MM: 103.9 **Dist:** 2.9 **GPS:** 44.56562/-106.92700 **Elev:** 5410 **Grid:** 59/11 **Land:** Wyoming G & F
Story Fish Hatchery   **Type:** Fish Hatchery
Built in 1908, this is the oldest and most popular fish hatchery in the state, receiving over 20,000 visitors per year. This newly renovated state-of-the-art facility has a visitor center with interpretive exhibits. The hatchery raises approximately 350,000 trout per year and processes millions of fish eggs. A beautiful wooded picnic area is located just north of the entrance.
Hours: 8am - 5pm (mid Apr - mid Sept) **Phone:** 307-683-2234 **Cool Rating:** *** **Crowds:** *** **Time:** 1 hr
Directions: W on Wy-194/Fish Hatchery Rd 2.9 mi

MM: 106.2 **GPS:** 44.60094/-106.86620 **Elev:** 4571 **Grid:** 60/10
US-87 (northbound)   **Type:** Highway Transition
If heading north, **Wy-193** transitions to **US-87** and the mile markers count down from MM 38.9. This transition happens at the junction with a highway that heads southeast. This highway is a continuation of **US-87**, but is closed after 1.5 mi.

MM: 38.9 **GPS:** 44.60094/-106.86620 **Elev:** 4571 **Grid:** 60/10
Wy-193 (southbound)   **Type:** Highway Transition
If heading south, **US-87** transitions to **Wy-193** and the mile markers count down from MM 106.2. This transition happens at the junction with a highway that heads southeast. This highway is a continuation of **US-87**, but is closed after 1.5 mi.

MM: 35.6 **Dist:** 3.4 **GPS:** 44.66027/-106.94830 **Elev:** 4230 **Grid:** 59/9 **Land:** Wyoming G & F
Wyoming State Bird Farm   **Type:** Game Farm
The bird farm raises 19,000 ring-necked pheasants per year to be released for hunting. The pheasants can be seen in a couple of large cages; however, the majority of the birds are in the back and are not accessible. Near the entrance are peacocks, turkeys, and sometimes ornamental pheasants on display. An interesting place for children and visitors are welcome.
Phone: 307-674-7701 **Cool Rating:** ** **Crowds:** * **Time:** 30 min **Nearest Town:** Sheridan 11 N **Road Desc:** Gravel
Directions: W on CR-28/Bird Farm Rd 3.4 mi; SW/L side of road just before curve (326 Bird Farm Road, Bighorn) **To return to US-87 MM 32.6;** NE/L on Bird Farm Rd/CR-28 1.4 mi; E/R on Kruse Creek Rd/CR-30 1.9 mi; N to Sheridan or S 1.3 mi to Wy-342 (see next section).

MM: 33.9 **GPS:** 44.66664/-106.90273 **Elev:** 4297 **Grid:** 59/8
Wy-342   **Type:** Highway Junction
Short 1.1 mi connecting road between **US-87** and **I-90**.
Directions: If heading N on US-87: Turn E/R to return to I-90 MM 33.6. **If heading west from I-90:** Turn S/L on US-87 MM 33.9.

MM: 32.8 **GPS:** 44.66553/-106.87981 **Elev:** 4281 **Grid:** 60/8
US-87/Wy-193   **Type:** Highway End
14.0 mi side trip from **I-90** MM 33.6 south back to **I-90** MM 44.7. After 6.1 mi **US-87** MM 38.9 transitions to **Wy-193** MM 106.2 (the mile markers change direction) and continues 7.9 mi to **I-90** exit 44. Highlights include: **Wyoming State Bird Farm, Story Fish Hatchery, Wagon Box Fight Historic Site, Fort Phil Kearny, Fetterman Massacre Monument and Battlefield.**
Nearest Town: Sheridan 8.2 N
Directions: I-90 exit 33; W on Meade Creek Rd/Wy-343 1.1 mi; S on US-87 5.0 mi to a transition with Wy-193; Continue S 7.9 mi to I-90 MM 44.7.

Wy-210/Happy Jack Rd   E/W

MM: 0.0 *GPS:* 41.13696/-104.84057 *Elev:* 6078 *Grid:* 89/97
Wy-210/Happy Jack Rd   *Type:* Highway Description
37.3 mi highway from **I-25** exit 10 in **Cheyenne** west to **I-80** exit 323, 10 mi southeast of **Laramie**. The primary use of this highway is access to the north entrance of **Curt Gowdy State Park** and the **Vedauwoo Recreation Area**.
Notes: The mile markers lose 0.5 mi between MM 0 and MM 3. *Directions:* I-25 exit 10; W from MM 0

MM: 0.0 *GPS:* 41.13696/-104.84057 *Elev:* 6078 *Grid:* 89/97
I-25 *(see chapter)*   *Type:* Hwy Junction w/Chapter
Directions: S to Colorado or N to Wheatland from MM 10.6

MM: 0.0 *GPS:* 41.13696/-104.84057 *Elev:* 6078 *Grid:* 89/97
Cheyenne   *Type:* Town

MM: 3.0 *GPS:* 41.13150/-104.88633 *Elev:* 6236 *Grid:* 88/97
I-80 *(see chapter)*   *Type:* Hwy Junction w/Chapter
If heading east on **Wy-210/Happy Jack Rd**, this provides easier and shorter access (saves 1.1 mi) to **I-80** and southbound **I-25** than continuing straight to **I-25**.
Directions: S on Wy-222/Round Top Rd 1.0 mi to I-80 MM 358.

MM: 14.5 *Dist:* 6.2 *GPS:* 41.15111/-105.19681 *Elev:* 7018 *Grid:* 84/96 *Land:* State
Curt Gowdy State Park - South Entrance   *Type:* State Park
The south entrance enters near **Crystal Reservoir**. *See next section.*
Road Desc: Gravel, washboard *Directions:* W on Crystal Lake Rd/CR-210 6.1 mi; N 0.1 to entrance station.

MM: 24.0 *Dist:* 0.9 *GPS:* 41.18020/-105.23883 *Elev:* 7265 *Grid:* 83/95 *Land:* State
Curt Gowdy State Park - North Entrance   *Type:* State Park
A beautiful park with varied landscapes and 3 small reservoirs. **Granite Reservoir**, near the north entrance, is the largest of the reservoirs with room for water sports and excellent rainbow trout and kokanee salmon fishing. The west end of the reservoir rises to lightly forest hills and granite outcrops, which make for fun hiking and climbing as well as providing miles of novice to expert mountain bike trails. **Crystal Reservoir**, near the south entrance, is situated amid rolling grassy hills with fishing for brown trout, rainbow trout, and kokanee salmon. It is the smallest reservoir allowing only small boats with under 15 hp motors. **North Crow Reservoir** is 5 mi northwest of the north entrance *(see section below)*.

The campsites are spread out in 18+ separate areas around the lakes. The majority are around **Granite Reservoir** on the north and south side with a couple farther from the lake to the west. The sites on the north are more exposed but have better boat ramp access. The sites on the south have more shade. The dozen or so sites around **Crystal Reservoir** are on the west shore with some trees for shade in several sites.

The camping areas include 35 reservable sites, 15 sites for larger RVs, and 7 tent-only sites. Drinking water is available at **Tumbleweeds**, **Granite Point**, and at the north entrance. The **RV dump** is just past the north entrance.
Cool Rating: *** *Crowds:* **** *Nearest Town:* Laramie 24.6 W; Cheyenne 24.8 E *[FEE AREA]*
Directions: S on Granite Springs Rd. 0.9 mi
Campsites: 125 *Shade:* ** *Privacy:* * *RV Size:* 40'+ *Other:* 1-877-996-7275:wyoparks.state.wy.us/reservations,Water,RVDump

MM: 24.5 *Dist:* 0.1 *GPS:* 41.19231/-105.25166 *Elev:* 7544 *Grid:* 83/95 *Land:* State
Curt Gowdy State Park Headquarters   *Type:* Visitor Center
Visitor information and camping permits.
Directions: N 0.1 mi

MM: 25.7 *Dist:* 2.9 *GPS:* 41.23074/-105.27496 *Elev:* 7502 *Grid:* 83/94 *Land:* State
North Crow Reservoir: Curt Gowdy State Park   *Type:* Lake
The third reservoir in **Curt Gowdy State Park** amid rolling sagebrush hills and light forest in a remote section of the park. This is an unimproved fishing area in a natural setting with no camping, picnic tables, water, or restrooms.
Directions: N on N Crow Rd 2.9 mi; NW/L to south shore or straight to north shore.

MM: 26.5 *GPS:* 41.19201/-105.29168 *Elev:* 7782 *Grid:* 82/95 *Land:* NF
Medicine Bow National Forest   *Type:* National Forest Boundary

MM: 26.7 *GPS:* 41.19154/-105.29573 *Elev:* 7759 *Grid:* 82/95
FR-700/Vedauwoo Glen Rd *(see chapter)*   *Type:* Hwy Junction w/Chapter
A 7.3 mi forest road southwest to **I-80** passing **Reynolds Hill Trailhead** (3.7 mi) and **Vedauwoo Recreation Area** (6.2 mi). This area is very scenic and provides dispersed camping and other recreational opportunities amid sparse pine forest and granite outcroppings. Camping in this area is very popular, particularly on weekends. The closer to **Vedauwoo** the more crowded it gets. This is a very popular area for OHVs.
Directions: S then SW on FR-700
Notes: If looking for a place to camp and you don't care about a lake, restrooms, and drinking water, this may be preferable to Curt Gowdy State Park.

MM: 35.7 *Dist:* 0.4 *GPS:* 41.25468/-105.42187 *Elev:* 8332 *Grid:* 80/94 *Land:* NF
Happy Jack Recreation Area   *Type:* Recreation Area
Formerly a ski area, this is now a trailhead for the **Pole Mountain Trails**. This is primarily a bicycling trailhead and requires a 250 ft climb from the base of the mountain. *See Pole Mountain Trails on I-80 MM 323.1.*
Crowds: * *[FEE AREA]* *Directions:* S on FR-719 0.4 mi; SW/R into parking area.

MM: 35.7 *Dist:* 1.3 *GPS:* 41.25430/-105.41010 *Elev:* 8335 *Grid:* 81/94 *Land:* NF
Yellow Pine Campground   *Type:* Campground
Single loop. Mixed forest. 8 pull-thrus. Good spacing between sites. Little understory.
Crowds: **** *[FEE AREA]* *Road Desc:* Gravel *Directions:* S on FR-719 1.0 mi; Keep left 0.3 mi.
Campsites: 19 *Shade:* ***** *Privacy:* ** *RV Size:* 30' *Other:* Water

MM: 36.8   *GPS:* 41.25276/-105.43682   *Elev:* 8580   *Grid:* 80/94   *Land:* NF

Tie City Trailhead   *Type:* Trailhead

A trailhead for the **Pole Mountain Trails**, which is located at the beginning of the **Tie City Campground** entrance road. The riding is fairly level from this trailhead. *See Pole Mountain Trails on I-80 MM 323.1.*

Crowds: **   *[FEE AREA]*   *Directions:* SE 80 yds.

MM: 36.8   *Dist:* 0.2   *GPS:* 41.25072/-105.43540   *Elev:* 8620   *Grid:* 80/94   *Land:* NF

Tie City Campground   *Type:* Campground

Sites are located in both forest and open grassy meadows. The campground provides direct access to the **Pole Mountain Trails** from the southeast side of the campground *(see Pole Mountain Trails on I-80 MM 323.1).* This results in walking and biking activity past the campground. Configured as a teardrop loop making a second pass difficult in a large RV or trailer. *Mixed forest. Not level.*

Crowds: *****   *[FEE AREA]*   *Road Desc:* The interior road is narrow and rough in places.   *Directions:* SE 0.2 mi

Campsites: 19   *Shade:* ****   *Privacy:* ***   *RV Size:* 30'   *Other:* None

---

MM: 37.8   *GPS:* 41.24005/-105.43791   *Elev:* 8643   *Grid:* 80/94

I-80 *(see chapter)*   *Type:* Hwy Junction w/Chapter

Directions: SE to Cheyenne or NW to Laramie from MM 323.1

MM: 37.8   *GPS:* 41.24005/-105.43791   *Elev:* 8643   *Grid:* 80/94

End of Highway   *Type:* Highway End

37.3 mi highway from **I-80** exit 323, 10 mi southeast of **Laramie**, east to **I-25** exit 10 in **Cheyenne**. The primary use of this highway is access to the north entrance of **Curt Gowdy State Park**. 2 National Forest campgrounds are located a short distance north of **I-80**.

Nearest Town: Laramie 10 NW   *Directions:* I-80 exit 323; E 0.1 mi; N/L from MM 37.8

MM: 0.0 *GPS:* 43.47349/-110.78848 *Elev:* 6160 *Grid:* 4/38
Wy-22   *Type:* Highway Description
17.7 mi highway from **Jackson** west over **Teton Pass** and northwest to **Idaho**. The highway transitions to **Id-33** in **Idaho**, which is the route to **Cave Falls** and **Bechler Falls** in **Yellowstone National Park**, **Upper Mesa Falls** and **Lower Mesa Falls** in **Idaho**, and ending at the west entrance of **Yellowstone National Park**. Other highlights include: hiking and biking around **Teton Pass**.
Directions: NW to Wilson from MM 0

MM: 0.0 *GPS:* 43.47349/-110.78848 *Elev:* 6160 *Grid:* 4/38
US-26/89/191 *(see chapter)*   *Type:* Hwy Junction w/Chapter
43.3 mi highway from **Hoback Jct** north to **Moran Jct**. The highway then connects to **US-89/191/287**, using sequential mile markers, and continues 27 mi to **Yellowstone National Park**. The entire length is along the **Centennial Scenic Byway**. Highlights include: **Jackson, Jackson Hole and Greater Yellowstone Visitor Center, Grand Teton National Park**.
Notes: The highway section between Hoback Jct and Jackson might be referred to as US-26/89/189/191.
Directions: N to Grand Teton National Park or S to Hoback Jct from MM 153.1

MM: 4.1 *GPS:* 43.49970/-110.84596 *Elev:* 6164 *Grid:* 3/38
Wy-390/Moose-Wilson Rd *(see chapter)*   *Type:* Hwy Junction w/Chapter
14.7 mi road from **Wy-22** north to **Teton Park Rd** in **Grand Teton National Park** at **Moose**. The mile markers for **Wy-390** end at the **Granite Canyon Entrance** to **Grand Teton National Park**, so the mile markers in the book are also shown as starting at zero at that point to allow the trip odometer to be reset. Highlights include: **Teton Village, Granite Canyon Trailhead, Laurance S. Rockefeller Preserve, Death Canyon Trailhead**.
Nearest Town: Wilson 1.4 W *Notes:* RVs and trailers are prohibited. *Directions:* N to Moose from MM 0

MM: 5.5 *GPS:* 43.49807/-110.87630 *Elev:* 6142 *Grid:* 3/38
Wilson   *Type:* Town

MM: 5.6 *Dist:* 4.9 *GPS:* 43.44245/-110.86525 *Elev:* 6111 *Grid:* 3/39 *Land:* NF
Mosquito Creek Rd   *Type:* National Forest Access
The **Wilson** area offers few camping options; however, some dispersed camping is available in the **Targhee National Forest** along **Mosquito Creek Rd**. The road traverses a side hill in a canyon for 2.4 mi until descending to **Mosquito Creek**. This sloping terrain limits the number of campsites and they are not level.
Crowds: *** *Notes:* Fall Creek Rd accesses other National Forest roads south of Mosquito Creek Rd.
Road Desc: Dirt, rough & impassable when wet, narrow. Fall Creek Rd is paved.
Directions: At the west end of Wilson; S on Fall Creek Rd 4.3 mi; W/R on Mosquito Creek Rd to forest information sign 0.6 mi.
Campsites: Dispersed *Shade:* **** *Privacy:* ***** *RV Size:* 20' *Other:* None

MM: 6.6 *Dist:* 0.9 *GPS:* 43.49196/-110.90764 *Elev:* 6510 *Grid:* 2/38 *Land:* NF
Trail Creek Trailhead   *Type:* Trailhead
The primary destination for a day hike is **Crater Lake**, located at the base of the "Glory Slide," which is an avalanche chute on the east side of **Mount Glory**. The trailhead provides 3 trail options: <u>History Trail</u> (left) - Forested and parallels the creek for a short distance and is the only trail that excludes bikes *(1.8 mi)*. <u>Trail Creek Trail</u> (center) - The first half is in the open just below the **Old Pass Rd**, then through forest and meadows *(1.5 mi)*. <u>Old Pass Rd</u> (right) - The old paved road up **Teton Pass** *(1.3 mi)*. Any of these trails can be taken out and back or combined to make a loop. A good option is **Trail Creek Trail** up and **History Trail** back. *Moderate; 3.3 mi loop; 630 ft elev gain.*

A bicycling option is riding on the **Old Pass Rd** past **Crater Lake** to the top of **Teton Pass**. This 3.5 mi route on old weathered pavement gains 1,910 ft in elevation using several switchbacks. Return by the same route or ride an advanced mountain bike loop by connecting to the **Pass Ridge Trail** and **Black Canyon Trail**. *See Teton Pass Summit and Trailhead at MM 11.0.*

The trailhead can be reached on a bicycle directly from **Wilson** by taking the bike path 1.0 mi northwest along **Wy-22** to **Old Pass Rd** and riding 0.9 mi southwest.
Cool Rating: *** *Crowds:* *** *Directions:* SW on Old Pass Rd 0.9 mi to parking area.

MM: 9.5 *GPS:* 43.50523/-110.92735 *Elev:* 7745 *Grid:* 2/37 *Land:* NF
Phillips Ridge Trailhead   *Type:* Trailhead
The trailhead provides access to **Phillips Ridge, Phillips Canyon, Phillips Pass,** and **Ski Lake**, plus several miles of singletrack mountain bike trails on the **Arrow Trail** and **Phillips Ridge Trail**.

<u>Phillips Ridge</u> is the southeast wall of **Phillips Canyon**, which overlooks the **Snake River** valley with views of the surrounding mountains. A dirt service road (FR-30972) along the ridge climbs to a fire lookout. A new singletrack trail is being constructed to connect 2 segments of the road. *Moderate; 4.4 mi round-trip; 700 ft elev gain.*
<u>Phillips Pass</u> is a high and wide saddle in the southern **Teton Range**, which provides access to the **Jedediah Smith Wilderness**. The hike climbs through forest and wildflower-filled meadows. Turn left at the junction with the service road after 0.4 mi. *Moderately strenuous; 8.0 mi round-trip; 1180 ft elev gain.*
<u>Ski Lake</u> is a small deep blue lake in a mountain cirque. Turn left at the junction with the service road after 0.4 mi and left at another trail junction to **Phillips Canyon** after 0.8 mi. *Moderate; 4.0 mi round-trip; 900 ft elev gain.*
<u>Arrow Trail</u> is a 2.5 mi singletrack mountain bike trail that roughly parallels the **Phillips Pass Trail** to **Phillips Canyon**.
Cool Rating: *** *Crowds:* ***
Directions: Parking along FR-30972 on NW side of hwy. Additional parking in a large gravel pullout on SE side of the highway.

MM: 11.0 *GPS:* 43.49741/-110.95510 *Elev:* 8435 *Grid:* 1/38 *Land:* NF
Teton Pass Summit and Trailhead   *Type:* Trailhead
Teton Pass runs between the **Teton Range** to the north and the **Snake River Range** to the south. Several hiking/biking options start from the summit:

Pass Ridge Trail - Heads south along a ridge on the **Snake River Range** through forest and meadows climbing to the 9,279 ft summit with excellent views of **Jackson Hole**, the **Snake River**, and the **Gros Ventre Range**. *Moderate; 4.0 mi round-trip; 850 ft elev gain.*
Black Canyon Trail - A continuation of the **Pass Ridge Trail**, which continues south then loops east 4.0 mi descending 2,700 ft through the **Black Canyon** to the **Trail Creek Trailhead**. The trail is primarily an advanced mountain bike route with steep sections, loose sections, ruts, roots, and rocks.
Teton Pass Trail - Located just to the east of the pullout, the trail descends down **Old Pass Rd** 3.6 mi and 1,910 ft in elevation on deteriorating pavement to the **Trail Creek Trailhead** parking area. The road continues 0.9 mi northeast to **Wy-22** where a paved path leads east 1.0 mi to **Wilson**.
Full Loop - Combining all of the above trails makes a good 9.6 mi advanced mountain biking loop, which can start at either the **Teton Pass Summit** or the **Lake Creek Trailhead**. Starting in **Wilson** extends the distance to 13.4 mi.
Cool Rating: **** *Crowds:* ** *Directions:* Large pullout on SW side of hwy

MM: 13.9 *GPS:* 43.51062/-110.98594 *Elev:* 7244 *Grid:* 1/37 *Land:* NF
Coal Creek Trailhead   *Type:* Trailhead
A trail northeast into the **Jedediah Smith Wilderness** through a valley between **Taylor Mountain** and **Mount Glory** and ending at **Coal Creek Meadows**. The trail enters the canyon and parallels **Coal Creek** for 1.1 mi gaining 670 ft. Cross the creek and climb up the hill where the trail continues north along a side hill to **Coal Creek Meadows**. *Moderately strenuous; 4.4 mi round-trip; 1620 ft elev gain.*
Cool Rating: *** *Crowds:* * *Time:* 2.5 hrs *Directions:* Trailhead parking on NE side of hwy

MM: 17.4 *GPS:* 43.54136/-111.04113 *Elev:* 6710 *Grid:* 0/36 *Land:* NF
Trail Creek Campground   *Type:* Campground
Located in a canyon between the **Snake River Range** to the south and the **Teton Range** to the north. The campground stretches along **Trail Creek** just below the highway. *Mixed forest. Roomy sites. Grass understory. Fairly level. Several sites are in the open. Heavy highway noise that starts in early morning. 7 pull-thrus.*
Crowds: *** *[FEE AREA]* *Directions:* SW side of hwy
Campsites: 10 *Shade:* *** *Privacy:* **** *RV Size:* 30' *Other:* 1-877-444-6777:www.recreation.gov,Water BEARS

MM: 17.7 *Dist:* 59.9 *GPS:* 44.13211/-111.01550 *Elev:* 6200 *Grid:* 1/22 *Land:* NF
Cave Falls Campground   *Type:* Campground
Along the **Falls River** just outside the southwest corner of **Yellowstone National Park**. The campground is just inside **Wyoming** and only accessible through **Idaho**. **Cave Falls** and **Bechler Falls** are in **Yellowstone National Park** a short distance northeast of the campground *(see next section)*. *Conifer forest. Roomy sites. Not level. Sites in the back are nicer. All pull-thrus.*
Crowds: *** *Nearest Town:* Ashton, ID 23.7 SW *[FEE AREA]* *Road Desc:* Narrow dirt road into campground.
Notes: Dispersed camping is available along the National Forest road.
Directions: See directions for Cave Falls in next section.
Campsites: 23 *Shade:* **** *Privacy:* *** *RV Size:* 30' *Other:* Water GRIZZLIES

MM: 17.7 *Dist:* 61.3 *GPS:* 44.14474/-110.99781 *GPS2:* 44.14374/-110.99718 *Elev:* 6290 *Grid:* 1/21 *Land:* NPS
Cave Falls & Bechler Falls & Upper and Lower Mesa Falls   *Type:* Waterfall
The southwest corner of **Yellowstone National Park** is known as "**Cascade Corners**" because of the numerous waterfalls and cascades found in this region. Most of these waterfalls are reachable by long hiking trails; however, **Cave Falls** can be driven to and **Bechler Falls** can be reached by a 2.6 mi round-trip trail.

This region is only reachable by roads near **Ashton, Idaho**, on routes that begin near **Jackson** and from the **Yellowstone National Park** west entrance. **Upper and Lower Mesa Falls** are located in **Idaho** and are on the way if continuing to or from the west entrance of **Yellowstone National Park**. This is a scenic alternative when heading to **Yellowstone National Park** from **Jackson**, or vice-versa, keeping in mind that it bypasses **Grand Teton National Park**. The total drive is 157 mi. *4 picnic tables. Vault toilet.*

Cave Falls - A spectacular waterfall, only 20 ft high but 220 ft across the **Falls River**. The falls are named after a small cave, which can be accessed on the west side of the falls. The small lower parking area is below the falls with a short trail to the brink of the falls. This trail offers the best front view of the falls. The upper parking area is larger with a short path to the brink of the falls.

Bechler Falls - From the **Cave Falls** upper parking area, an easy 2.6 mi round-trip trail leads to the less spectacular, but still nice, **Bechler Falls**. Take the trail along the **Falls River** to the confluence with the **Bechler River**. The trail continues along the **Bechler River** to the falls.

Other Waterfalls In Yellowstone - At least 9 other waterfalls (that are beyond the scope of this book) are accessed by long hikes that originate from the **Bechler River Trail** and the **Bechler River Ranger Station**.

Upper and Lower Mesa Falls - Spectacular waterfalls on the **Snake River** in **Idaho**, which are accessed from **Id-47/Mesa Falls Scenic Byway**. **Upper Mesa Falls** are 110 ft high in a developed fee area with boardwalks, stairs, and viewing platforms. The stunning and very unique **Lower Mesa Falls** are 85 ft high, where the river flows through a rocky gorge with several different drops in many directions. The falls are viewed from the **Grandview Overlook** on the canyon edge from about 500 yds.
Cool Rating: ***** *Crowds:* * *Nearest Town:* Ashton, ID 24.9 SW *[FEE AREA]*
Notes: Large RVs and trailers are not recommended. Abundant dispersed camping in the National Forest on FR-582 and Id-47.
Road Desc: All roads are paved until just past the National Forest boundary. The road is then gravel for 10.2 mi, then paved for the last 2.9 mi to the Cave Falls upper parking area.
Directions: NW on Id-33 23.8 mi; N/R on Id-32 11.7 mi; N/R on N 4700 E and N 4725 E 5.2 mi; W/L on E 1100 N 2.2 mi; N/R on N 4500 E 1.0 mi; E/R on E 1200 N 0.4 mi; N/L on N 4525 E 2.4 mi; E/R on E 1400 N 1.0 mi to National Forest boundary; Continue on FR-582 12.3 mi to **Cave Falls Campground**; Continue 1.1 mi to **Cave Falls lower parking area**; Continue 0.2 mi to **Cave Falls upper parking area**.

From Cave Falls to Yellowstone West Entrance past Lower Mesa Falls and Upper Mesa Falls (78 mi): SW on FR-582/E 1400 N 19.3 mi; N on Id-47 8.6 mi to **Lower Mesa Falls**; N on Id-47 0.7 mi to **Upper Mesa Falls**; N on Id-47 12.9 mi to US-20; N on US-20 35.9 mi; S/R on Canyon St 0.2 mi; E on Yellowstone Ave 0.4 mi to **Yellowstone West Entrance**.

MM: 17.7 *GPS:* 43.54369/-111.04597 *Elev:* 6700 *Grid:* 0/36
End of Highway - Idaho State Line   *Type:* Highway End
17.7 mi highway from **Idaho** southeast over **Teton Pass** and east to **Jackson**. Highlights include: hiking and biking around **Teton Pass**.
Directions: SE from the Idaho state line from MM 17.7

MM: 44.3 *GPS:* 42.36282/-107.44393 *Elev:* 6272 *Grid:* 52/66
Wy-220   *Type:* Highway Description
72.6 mi highway from **US-287/Wy-789** northeast to **Casper**. The highway transitions from **US-287/Wy-789** at MM 44.3 and the mile markers continue sequentially. Highlights include: **Martin's Cove**, **Devil's Gate**, **Independence Rock**, **Pathfinder Reservoir**, **Alcova Reservoir**, **Bessemer Bend National Historic Site**, **Fort Caspar Museum and Historic Site**.
Nearest Town: Rawlins 44.3 S *Directions:* NE to Casper from MM 44.3

MM: 44.3 *GPS:* 42.36282/-107.44393 *Elev:* 6272 *Grid:* 52/66
US-287/Wy-789 *(see chapter)*   *Type:* Hwy Junction w/Chapter
Continue straight to transition to **US-287/Wy-789** and head south 44.3 mi to **Rawlins** with the mile markers continuing sequentially. Turn right to head 80.5 mi northwest to **Lander**. Highlights include: **Split Rock**, **Green Mountain**.
Directions: NW to Lander from MM 0 or S to Rawlins from MM 44.3

MM: 56.5 *Dist:* 0.8 *GPS:* 42.44182/-107.21884 *Elev:* 5977 *Grid:* 55/64 *Land:* Private
Mormon Handcart Historic Site: Martin's Cove & Devil's Gate   *Type:* Historic Site
In 1856 a group of 1,620 converts to the **Mormon** religion sailed to America intent on reaching **Salt Lake City** before winter. Unable to afford wagons, many of these destitute emigrants pulled small handcarts instead. The fifth group of 576 led by **Edward Martin** left Iowa City dangerously late on July 28. In October they waded across the freezing **North Platte River** and soon a blizzard dumped 18 inches of snow and it became bitterly cold. People died along 60 mi of trail before a rescue wagon finally arrived from **Salt Lake City** on November 1 and found the survivors huddled in **Martin's Cove**. They finally reached **Salt Lake City** on November 30 with a loss of over 145 members. The fourth group led by **James G. Willie** met a similar fate at **Rocky Ridge** *(see Willie Handcart Company Tragedy Memorial on Atlantic City Rd/CR-237 MM 2.9/5.3).*

This section of the historic **Sun Ranch** near **Martin's Cove** was purchased by the **Mormon Church** and opened to visitors in the late 1990s. The old ranch house has been converted to a visitor center, which contains historical displays and artifacts from the **Sun Ranch**. The visitor center is staffed by members of the **Mormon Church** who explain the history of the handcart companies. The ranch site also contains other historic buildings. A 4.9 mi round-trip hike leads to **Martin's Cove**, and handcarts are available to provide the true pioneer experience.

Devil's Gate is on **BLM** land and is accessible via a 0.9 mi (one-way) hiking trail. The trail starts at the visitor center and follows the **Martin's Cove** trail just past the bridge over the **Sweetwater River** before splitting off and heading east. An interpretive sign is located near the mouth of the gorge. *See next section for a description and GPS coordinates.*
Hours: 8am - 7pm (Summer); 9am - 4pm (offseason) *Phone:* 307-328-2953 *Cool Rating:* *** *Crowds:* ** *Time:* 1-4 hrs
Road Desc: Gravel *Directions:* NW then NE at the Mormon Handcart Historic Site sign 0.8 mi

MM: 57.2 *Dist:* 0.3 *GPS:* 42.43712/-107.21739 *GPS2:* 42.44669/-107.21225 *Elev:* 6080 *Grid:* 55/64 *Land:* BLM
Devil's Gate Historic Site   *Type:* Historic Site
Devil's Gate is a split in a ridge called the **Sweetwater Rocks**, which was created by volcanic activity and eroded by the **Sweetwater River** leaving a narrow gorge 300 ft deep and 1,500 ft in length. This was a major geographical landmark on the **Oregon Trail** and was visible from 15 mi east. The trail passed to the south; however, many emigrants camped near **Devil's Gate** and explored the gorge, some leaving inscriptions on the walls.

This historic site is 3/4 mi southwest of the gorge, providing views along a 1/3 mi paved interpretive loop trail. **Devil's Gate** is on **BLM** land and is accessible via a 0.9 mi hiking trail that starts at the **Mormon Handcart Visitor Center** 0.7 mi west on **Wy-220** *(see previous section)*. Vault toilet.
Cool Rating: *** *Crowds:* * *Time:* 30 min *Directions:* NW 0.3 mi to parking area

MM: 63.0 *GPS:* 42.49346/-107.13764 *Elev:* 5893 *Grid:* 56/63
Independence Rock Rest Area   *Type:* Rest Area
A nice grassed rest area with picnic shelters and an **RV dump** on the east side. **Independence Rock State Historic Site** is behind the rest area. *See next section.*
Directions: SE side of hwy

MM: 63.0 *GPS:* 42.49303/-107.13654 *GPS2:* 42.49400/-107.13300 *Elev:* 5892 *Grid:* 56/63 *Land:* State
Independence Rock State Historic Site   *Type:* Historic Site
This famous landmark is 1 of 3 major sites along the **Oregon Trail** where emigrants left inscriptions (the others being Register Cliff and Names Hill). This large granite dome is approximately 100 ft high, 200 yds wide, and 600 yds long. It was clearly visible from **Prospect Hill** to the east and was a favorite emigrant campsite. This is the best of the 3 sites, where the best-preserved inscriptions are found by climbing to the top of the rock. An estimated 50,000 names are etched on the rock with the oldest known from 1824. A common theory is the rock got its name from an **Independence Day** celebration held here in 1830 (although the plaque on the rock says 1825). It was also thought that the emigrants needed to reach this point by **Independence Day** in order to reach **Oregon** on schedule. On the way into the site from the rest area are several interpretive panels about **Independence Rock** and the westward migration. Several plaques and markers are located on the east side of the rock inside a fence. A 1.0 mi footpath circles the rock where a few inscriptions can be seen without climbing. *Located at mile 815 of the Oregon Trail.*
Cool Rating: **** *Crowds:* ** *Time:* 1-2 hrs *Directions:* SE side of hwy behind the rest area. *Notes:* A steep climb can be made to the top of the rock from the west side; however, it is easier from the east side. Beware of rattlesnakes on the footpath.

MM: 68.0 *GPS:* 42.54985/-107.08162 *Elev:* 5946 *Grid:* 57/61
Interpretive Pullout: Steamboat Lake   *Type:* Point of Interest
A pullout on the north side of **Steamboat Lake** with 6 interpretive signs about the area wildlife.
Cool Rating: * *Crowds:* * *Time:* 5 min *Directions:* SE side of hwy

MM: 72.8   *GPS:* 42.56673/-106.99060   *Elev:* 5926   *Grid:* 58/61
Oregon Trail Rd *(see chapter)*   *Type:* Hwy Junction w/Chapter
An interesting alternative route from **Wy-220** northeast to **Casper** following the actual **Oregon Trail** 40.4 mi to **US-20/26**. The road passes the historic sites **Prospect Hill** (a BLM interpretive site), **Willow Springs**, **Rock Avenue**, and **Emigrant Gap** in the opposite direction that the emigrants traveled. The route to **Casper** is roughly the same distance as taking **Wy-220** but is much slower and bypasses **Alcova Reservoir** and **Pathfinder Reservoir**.
Nearest Town: Alcova 13.7 E   *Directions:* NE on CR-319/Oregon Trail Rd from MM 40.4

MM: 80.7   *GPS:* 42.55471/-106.83480   *Elev:* 6296   *Grid:* 60/61
Alcova/Pathfinder Reservoir Loop *(see chapter)*   *Type:* Hwy Junction w/Chapter
20 mi loop from **Wy-220** past **Pathfinder Reservoir**, **Fremont Canyon**, and **Alcova Reservoir**. This route starts at **Wy-220** MM 80.7 and ends at **Wy-220** MM 86.5 at the town of **Alcova**, 5.8 mi east of the starting point. The campgrounds in the area are primarily for boaters and provide little shade. Highlights include: **Pathfinder Interpretive Center and Trail**, **Pathfinder Dam Overlook**, **Fremont Canyon Bridge and Overlook**, **Alcova Reservoir**.
Cool Rating: ***   *Crowds:* *   *Nearest Town:* Alcova 5.8 E   *Directions:* S on CR-409/Pathfinder Rd from MM 20

MM: 84.7   *GPS:* 42.56250/-106.76083   *Elev:* 5668   *Grid:* 61/61
CR-406/Lakeshore Drive *(see chapter)*   *Type:* Hwy Junction w/Chapter
5.2 mi road south along the west side of **Alcova Reservoir** to a paved parking area above the lake. This route provides access to a marina, 3 public campgrounds, 1 private RV park near the marina, and a scenic overlook of the reservoir. The camping along this road is more for boaters, and the campgrounds tend to be pretty full. However, **Okie Beach** has sites away from the lake that are slower to fill. Better overnight camping is located on the east side of the reservoir, south of MM 86.5 at **Alcova**.
Directions: S on CR-406/Lakeshore Dr from MM 0

MM: 86.5   *GPS:* 42.56102/-106.72524   *Elev:* 5377   *Grid:* 62/61
Alcova   *Type:* Town

MM: 86.5   *GPS:* 42.56102/-106.72524   *Elev:* 5377   *Grid:* 62/61
Alcova/Pathfinder Reservoir Loop *(see chapter)*   *Type:* Hwy Junction w/Chapter
20 mi loop from **Wy-220** past **Alcova Reservoir**, **Fremont Canyon**, and **Pathfinder Reservoir**. This route starts at **Wy-220** MM 86.5 at the town of **Alcova** and ends at **Wy-220** MM 80.7, 5.8 mi west of the starting point. The campgrounds in the area are primarily for boaters and provide little shade. Highlights include: **Alcova Reservoir**, **Fremont Canyon Bridge and Overlook**, **Pathfinder Dam Overlook**, **Pathfinder Interpretive Center and Trail**.
Cool Rating: ***   *Crowds:* *   *Directions:* SE on CR-407/Kortes Rd from MM 0

MM: 86.5   *GPS:* 42.56102/-106.72524   *Elev:* 5377   *Grid:* 62/61
Seminoe-Alcova Back Country Byway *(see chapter)*   *Type:* Hwy Junction w/Chapter
73.0 mi route from **Wy-220** MM 86.5 at **Alcova** south to **I-80** exit 219 at **Sinclair**. The route passes through prairie, rolling hills, and over the **Seminoe Mountains**. The distance is 18 mi shorter than taking the highways through **Rawlins**; however, it takes much longer to drive and there are no services along the way. Highlights include: **Alcova Reservoir**, the **Miracle Mile**, **Seminoe State Park** and **Seminoe Reservoir**, **White Sand Dunes**.
Directions: S on CR-407 following various county roads 73.0 mi to Sinclair. W/R on Lincoln Ave 0.2 mi to I-80 exit 219.
Notes: The road is suitable for passenger cars but not recommended for large RVs or trailers.

MM: 87.1   *Dist:* 0.8   *GPS:* 42.56754/-106.70319   *Elev:* 5323   *Grid:* 62/61   *Land:* Bureau of Reclamation
Gray Reef Reservoir Campground   *Type:* Campground
Gray Reef Reservoir is the fifth of 7 reservoirs on the **North Platte River**. This small reservoir supports fishing (but is not stocked) and is good for small boats and canoes. The campground is just below the dam. *No trees.*
Crowds: *   *[FEE AREA]*   *Directions:* SE on CR-412/Gray Reef Rd 0.7 mi; SE 0.1 mi.
Campsites: 10   *Shade:* *   *Privacy:* *   *RV Size:* 40'   *Other:* None

MM: 87.1   *Dist:* 1.5   *GPS:* 42.57460/-106.69613   *Elev:* 5318   *Grid:* 62/61   *Land:* Bureau of Reclamation
Trapper's Route Number One Campground   *Type:* Campground
Primitive camping and day use fishing area on the **North Platte River** below **Gray Reef Reservoir**. The river is also popular with floaters. Walk-in tent camping near the river. *2 tables. Vault toilet.*
Crowds: *   *Directions:* SE on CR-412/Gray Reef Rd 1.4 mi; SE 0.1 mi.
Campsites: Dispersed   *Shade:* *   *Privacy:* *   *RV Size:* 40'+   *Other:* None

MM: 97.3   *Dist:* 16.7   *GPS:* 42.67530/-106.58866   *Elev:* 5364   *Grid:* 64/58
Casper Mountain Rd/Wy-251 *(see chapter)*   *Type:* Hwy Junction w/Chapter
If heading northeast, this is a shorter route to **Muddy Mountain** and **Casper Mountain**. **CR-505/Circle Dr** traverses a scenic red-hilled area crossing BLM and state public lands with some side roads for possible dispersed camping. *See Casper Mountain Rd/Wy-251 MM 13.9.*
Road Desc: Wy-487 is paved. CR-505 is gravel and washboard and rutted in spots. Not recommended when wet.
Directions: SE on Wy-487 8.4 mi to MM 64.3; NE on CR-505/Circle Drive Rd 8.3 mi.

MM: 103.6   *Dist:* 2.1   *GPS:* 42.74725/-106.52121   *GPS2:* 42.77322/-106.53147   *Elev:* 5241   *Grid:* 65/56   *Land:* BLM
Bessemer Bend National Historic Site (heading northeast)   *Type:* Historic Site
If heading northeast, this is a shorter route to **Bessemer Bend**. *See next section.*
Road Desc: Gravel   *Directions:* NW then N on Bessemer Bend South Rd/CR-309 1.5 mi; Continue 0.6 mi (just past river bridge)

MM: 105.3 **Dist:** 2.1 **GPS:** 42.76352/-106.49763 **GPS2:** 42.77322/-106.53147 **Elev:** 5183 **Grid:** 65/56 **Land:** BLM
Bessemer Bend National Historic Site (heading southwest)   **Type:** Historic Site
The famous landmark **Red Buttes** stand above this bend in the **North Platte River**, which the emigrants followed for nearly 500 mi on their journey west. At this low-water crossing the river turns south and became impassable without a ferry or bridge, which weren't established until 1847. Even after safer means of crossing were established, some emigrants who didn't want to pay the tolls or wait in line still chose to cross here. This included the **Martin Handcart Company** and **Willie Handcart Company** who had many members perish when a blizzard blew in after they had crossed at this point. Interpretive signs along a short loop trail explain the history of the area. *Picnic tables. Restroom.*
Cool Rating: ** **Crowds:** * **Time:** 30 min **Nearest Town:** Casper 10.2 NE
Directions: W on Bessemer Bend Rd/CR-308 2.1 mi just past the river bridge. **Road Desc:** Paved

MM: 105.3 **Dist:** 7.4 **GPS:** 42.76352/-106.49763 **GPS2:** 42.80622/-106.59365 **Elev:** 5335 **Grid:** 65/56 **Land:** BLM
Oregon Trail Rd (heading southwest)   **Type:** Historic Site
An interesting 35.8 mi side trip past the **Bessemer Bend National Historic Site** and then following the historic **Oregon Trail Rd** southwest back to **Wy-220** MM 72.8. This is only 3.5 mi farther than following the highway but is on dirt roads and bypasses **Alcova Reservoir** and **Pathfinder Reservoir**. If already visiting **Bessemer Bend National Historic Site** this route is actually shorter. *After reaching the end of CR-308/Bessemer Bend Rd, see Oregon Trail Rd MM 11.9.*
Cool Rating: ** **Crowds:** *
Road Desc: Bessemer Bend Rd/CR-308 is paved east of Bessemer Bend and gravel to the west. The Oregon Trail Rd is impassable when wet.
Directions: W on Bessemer Bend Rd/CR-308 2.1 mi *(just past the river bridge)* to Bessemer Bend National Historic Site *(see previous section);* Continue N and W 2.3 mi; N and W 3.0 mi; SW on Oregon Trail Rd from MM 11.9

MM: 113.4 **GPS:** 42.82098/-106.36957 **Elev:** 5175 **Grid:** 67/54
Casper   **Type:** Town

MM: 113.4 **Dist:** 1.3 **GPS:** 42.83555/-106.37092 **Elev:** 5123 **Grid:** 67/54 **Land:** State
Fort Caspar Museum and Historic Site   **Type:** Historic Site
A reconstructed military post that was active from 1862-1867 and located at a major river crossing on the emigrant, **Pony Express**, and transcontinental telegraph trails. The **Mormons** established a ferry operation at this point in 1847, and **Louis Guinard** established a toll bridge and trading post in 1859-1860. The fort was taken over by the **U.S. Army** primarily to protect emigrants and the telegraph office. It was named in honor of **Lt. Caspar Collins** who was killed while protecting a supply train from an Indian attack. Hostility with the Indians increased over time so the fort was expanded and about 100 soldiers were eventually garrisoned here.

The first stop is the museum, which features exhibits on prehistoric peoples, **Plains Indians**, western **Emigrant Trails**, the frontier army, ranching, the energy industry, and the city of **Casper**. Outside of the museum is a reconstruction of the fort along with a memorial cemetery and a carriage shed with a collection of wagons and other vehicles from the late 19th and early 20th centuries. North of the fort near the **North Platte River** is a replica of the **Mormon Ferry** and a partial reconstruction of the 810 ft **Guinard Bridge**, both with interpretive signs. Directly west of the museum is **Centennial Park**, which was added in 1990 to commemorate the **Wyoming** state centennial. A concrete path leads through the park to picnic shelters, grills, and a playground. Along this path is a series of 16 interpretive signs, called the **"History Walk,"** that explain the history of central **Wyoming**. **Fort Caspar Park** is just east of the fort along **Wyoming Blvd SW**.
Cool Rating: *** **Crowds:** ** **Time:** 1-2 hrs *[FEE AREA]*
Notes: A campground is located just west of Centennial Park. This campground is marked with brown signs in several places along the highways, which usually means a public campground. However, this is a crowded private RV park and campground.
Directions: N on SW Wyoming Blvd/Wy-258 1.1 mi; W/L on Fort Caspar Rd 0.2 mi

MM: 113.4 **Dist:** 2.7 **GPS:** 42.82098/-106.36957 **Elev:** 5175 **Grid:** 67/54
Casper Mountain Rd/Wy-251 *(see chapter)*   **Type:** Hwy Junction w/Chapter
18.4 mi series of roads from **Casper** south over **Casper Mountain** (nearly 3,000 ft above Casper) down through the **Red Valley** and up to **Muddy Mountain**. Activities on **Casper Mountain** include camping, hiking, and mountain biking, as well as downhill and cross-country skiing in the winter. Much of **Casper Mountain** is private property; however, **Casper Mountain Park** is a large public access area with 5 campgrounds. Highlights include: **Garden Creek Falls**, **Bridle Trail**, scenic overlook of **Casper**, **Casper Mountain Park**, **Crimson Dawn Park and Museum**, **Muddy Mountain Environmental Education Area**.
Directions: S and E on SE Wyoming Blvd/Wy-258 2.6 mi; S on Casper Mountain Rd/Wy-251 from MM 3.0.
Notes: The roads up and down the mountains are steep and winding and few of the campsites accommodate large RVs and trailers.

MM: 116.9 **GPS:** 42.85693/-106.33429 **Elev:** 5122 **Grid:** 67/54
I-25 *(see chapter)*   **Type:** Hwy Junction w/Chapter
300.1 mi interstate highway through east/central **Wyoming** from **Colorado** north to **I-90** (just past **Buffalo**), which continues northwest to **Montana**. Highlights include: **Pioneer Museum**, **Ayres Park and Natural Bridge**, **National Historic Trails Interpretive Center**, **Hole-in-the-Wall**, **Outlaw Cave**, **Indian Rock Art Cave**.
Directions: N to Buffalo or E to Glenrock from MM 188.6

MM: 116.9 **GPS:** 42.85693/-106.33429 **Elev:** 5122 **Grid:** 67/54
End of Highway   **Type:** Highway End
72.6 mi highway from **Casper** southwest to **US-287/Wy-789** and **Rawlins**. The highway transitions to **US-287/Wy-789** at MM 44.3 and the mile markers continue sequentially to **Rawlins**. Highlights include: **Fort Caspar Museum and Historic Site**, **Bessemer Bend National Historic Site**, **Alcova Reservoir**, **Pathfinder Reservoir**, **Independence Rock**, **Devil's Gate**, **Martin's Cove**.
Directions: I-25 exit 188B; SW on N Poplar St/Wy-220 to Alcova from MM 116.9

Wy-230 (Laramie to Colorado)   NE/SW

MM: 0.0   *GPS:* 41.31480/-105.59319   *Elev:* 7160   *Grid:* 78/92
Wy-230 (Laramie to Colorado)   *Type:* Highway Description
42.0 mi highway from the junction with **US-30/287** in **Laramie** southwest to **Colorado**. 4 fishing and camping lakes, including one large reservoir, are located along this route.
Directions: W from the intersection of N 3rd St/US-30/287 and Clarke St from MM 0
Notes: Intersects a north/south section of I-80 at MM 1.3.

MM: 0.0   *GPS:* 41.31480/-105.59319   *Elev:* 7160   *Grid:* 78/92
US-30/287 & US-287 (Laramie to Colorado)   *Type:* Highway Junction
Northwest on **US-30/287** to **Medicine Bow** and **Hanna** or south on **US-287** to **Colorado**.

MM: 0.0   *GPS:* 41.31480/-105.59319   *Elev:* 7160   *Grid:* 78/92
Laramie   *Type:* Town

MM: 1.0   *GPS:* 41.31076/-105.60988   *Elev:* 7144   *Grid:* 78/92   *Land:* State
Wyoming Territorial Prison State Historic Site   *Type:* Historic Site
A restored prison that was in use from 1872-1902 and held some of the most notorious outlaws in the region, including **Butch Cassidy**. *See I-80 MM 311.8 for a complete description.*
Cool Rating: ***   *Crowds:* **   *Directions:* NW side of hwy

MM: 1.3   *GPS:* 41.30900/-105.61419   *Elev:* 7150   *Grid:* 78/92
I-80 *(see chapter)*   *Type:* Hwy Junction w/Chapter
403 mi interstate highway through southern **Wyoming** from **Utah** east to **Nebraska**. Highlights include: **Bear River State Park**, **Fort Bridger State Historic Site**, **Wyoming Frontier Prison**, **Fort Fred Steele**, **Wyoming Territorial Prison State Historic Site**, **Pole Mountain Trails**, **Curt Gowdy State Park**, **Vedauwoo Recreation Area**, and much more.
Directions: E to Cheyenne or W to Rawlins from MM 311.8

MM: 2.1   *GPS:* 41.30892/-105.62925   *Elev:* 7172   *Grid:* 77/92
Wy-130 (Laramie to Wy-230) *(see chapter)*   *Type:* Hwy Junction w/Chapter
68.1 mi highway from **Laramie** west over **Snowy Range Pass** to **Wy-130/Wy-230 (Walcott to Riverside)** (8 mi south of **Saratoga**). Highlights include the many attractions along the 27 mi **Snowy Range Scenic Byway**.
Directions: N then W on Wy-130 from MM 0.

MM: 10.0   *GPS:* 41.23334/-105.74110   *Elev:* 7213   *Grid:* 76/94
CR-422/Phalow Ln & CR-44/Harmony Ln (heading southwest) *(see chapter)*   *Type:* Hwy Junction w/Chapter
If heading southwest on Wy-230: A 10.2 mi paved route west with access to 2 small lakes and 2 larger reservoirs. The road reconnects with **Wy-230 (Laramie to Colorado)** at MM 17.8.
Directions: W on CR-422/Phalow Ln 6.9 mi; Continue S on CR-44/Harmony Ln 3.3 mi to Wy-230 MM 17.8.

MM: 17.8   *GPS:* 41.17148/-105.86295   *Elev:* 7315   *Grid:* 74/96
CR-422/Phalow Ln & CR-44/Harmony Ln (heading northeast) *(see chapter)*   *Type:* Hwy Junction w/Chapter
If heading northeast on Wy-230: A 10.2 mi paved route east with access to 2 small lakes and 2 larger reservoirs. The road reconnects with **Wy-230 (Laramie to Colorado)** at MM 10.0.
Directions: N on CR-44/Harmony Ln 3.3 mi; Continue E on CR-422/Phalow Ln 6.9 mi to Wy-230 MM 10.0.

MM: 27.4   *GPS:* 41.11132/-106.01281   *Elev:* 7481   *Grid:* 72/97
Woods Landing   *Type:* Town

MM: 28.5   *GPS:* 41.11318/-106.03283   *Elev:* 7744   *Grid:* 72/97   *Land:* NF
Medicine Bow National Forest   *Type:* National Forest Boundary

MM: 33.8   *GPS:* 41.07423/-106.10453   *Elev:* 8956   *Grid:* 71/98   *Land:* NF
Chimney Park Trailhead   *Type:* Trailhead
4 hiking and biking loops along forest roads, which are used as cross-country ski trails in the winter: **Woods Creek Loop** - 2.9 mi north loop closest to the highway. **Porter Loop** - 4.4 mi northeast loop. **Lodgepole Loop** - 3.5 mi southeast loop. **Jelm View Loop** - 3.2 mi southwest loop. The roads are interconnected and it is 8.5 mi around the outside of the 4 loops. *Moderately easy; 160 ft elev loss.*
Cool Rating: **   *Crowds:* *   *[FEE AREA]*   *Directions:* Large pullout on SE side of hwy

MM: 36.2   *Dist:* 1.1   *GPS:* 41.07018/-106.15552   *Elev:* 9060   *Grid:* 70/98   *Land:* NF
Miller Lake Campground   *Type:* Campground
A small campground near **Miller Lake**. *Single loop. Roomy sites. 2 sites with long parking areas.*
Crowds: ***   *[FEE AREA]*   *Road Desc:* Gravel   *Directions:* N on FR-512 0.8 mi; SW/L 0.3 mi.
Notes: This campground was closed in 2009 because of beetle killed trees. If it re-opens it will have few trees for shade.
Campsites: 7   *Shade:* *   *Privacy:* *   *RV Size:* 20'   *Other:* Water

MM: 40.2   *GPS:* 41.00790/-106.17191   *Elev:* 8770   *Grid:* 70/100
Mountain Home   *Type:* Town

MM: 42.0   *GPS:* 40.99735/-106.20378   *Elev:* 8819   *Grid:* 69/100
End of Highway - Colorado State Line   *Type:* Highway End
42.0 mi highway from **Colorado** northeast to the junction with **US-30/287** in **Laramie**. 4 fishing and camping lakes, including one large reservoir, are located along this route.
Nearest Town: Mountain Home 1.8 NE   *Directions:* NE from the Colorado state line from MM 42

MM: 100.0 **GPS:** 41.21738/-106.78231 **Elev:** 7165 **Grid:** 61/95

Wy-230 (Riverside to Colorado)   **Type:** Highway Description

27.1 mi highway from **Riverside** southeast to **Colorado**. The highway is a continuation of **Wy-130/Wy-230 (Walcott to Riverside)** from the north; however, the highway turns to the east and the mile markers do not continue sequentially. Highlights include: **Indian Bathtubs**, **Platte River Trail**.

Directions: E then SE to Colorado from MM 100

MM: 100.0 **GPS:** 41.21738/-106.78231 **Elev:** 7165 **Grid:** 61/95

Wy-130/Wy-230 (Walcott to Riverside) *(see chapter)*   **Type:** Hwy Junction w/Chapter

38.2 mi highway from **Riverside** north to **Walcott**. The highway transitions from **Wy-230** to **Wy-130** at MM 28.3 (the junction with Wy-130 east) and the mile markers continue sequentially north on **Wy-130**. Highlights include: **Hobo Hot Pool**, **Saratoga National Fish Hatchery**.

Directions: N to Saratoga from MM 38.2

MM: 100.0 **GPS:** 41.21738/-106.78231 **Elev:** 7165 **Grid:** 61/95

Wy-70 *(see chapter)*   **Type:** Hwy Junction w/Chapter

57.7 mi highway in south-central **Wyoming**, just north of **Colorado**, from **Riverside** southwest to **Baggs**. Most of the highway runs through the **Sierra Madre Mountains** in the **Medicine Bow National Forest** and provides abundant OHV roads and dispersed camping opportunities. Highlights include: **Grand Encampment Museum**, **Green Mountain Falls**, **Dillon** and **Rudefeha Ghost Towns**, **Aspen Alley**.

Directions: SW to Encampment from MM 57.7

MM: 100.0 **GPS:** 41.21738/-106.78231 **Elev:** 7165 **Grid:** 61/95

Riverside   **Type:** Town

MM: 100.0 **GPS:** 41.21700/-106.78302 **Elev:** 7171 **Grid:** 61/95 **Land:** City

Carbon County Visitor Center   **Type:** Visitor Center

A small staffed visitor center.

Hours: 6am - 7pm **Phone:** 307-327-5600 **Directions:** SW corner of Wy-230 and Wy-70 junction.

MM: 100.9 **Dist:** 0.9 **GPS:** 41.20443/-106.76478 **GPS2:** 41.20356/-106.77217 **Elev:** 7343 **Grid:** 61/95

Indian Bathtubs   **Type:** Point of Interest

The **Encampment River Valley** was a gathering place for Indian tribes in the 1800s as they hunted during the summer months. To the east of the **Encampment River** is a granite outcrop with deep holes that fill with water and act as natural bathtubs. A 1/2 mi trail leads west to the site across sagebrush flats for 1/4 mi before dropping in and out of a tree-lined ravine crossing **Cottonwood Creek**.

Cool Rating: *** **Crowds:** * **Time:** 1 hr **Notes:** The section of trail into the ravine is steep and rocky.

Road Desc: Gravel **Directions:** S on Blackhall Mountain Rd/CR-211 0.9 mi; Parking area on W side of road.

MM: 123.0 **Dist:** 2.0 **GPS:** 41.04418/-106.40103 **Elev:** 7797 **Grid:** 66/99 **Land:** NF

Six Mile Gap Campground   **Type:** Campground

A loop road with 2 separate sections. On the north side are 3 pull-thru RV sites in the open with no trees. On the south side are 6 walk-in tent sites up a rise in an aspen grove. Just past the campground is the parking area for the **Platte River Trail** into the **Platte River Wilderness**. *See next section.*

Crowds: *** [FEE AREA] **Road Desc:** Gravel, narrow **Directions:** E on FR-492 2.0 mi

Campsites: 9 **Shade:** *** **Privacy:** ** **RV Size:** 40' **Other:** Water

---

MM: 123.0 **Dist:** 2.2 **GPS:** 41.04452/-106.39662 **Elev:** 7725 **Grid:** 67/99 **Land:** NF

Platte River Trail   **Type:** Hiking Trail

A 7 mi trail through **North Gate Canyon**, which follows the **North Platte River** into the **Platte River Wilderness**. This stretch of the river is popular for white-water rafting as well as being a blue ribbon fishery. *Moderate; 7.0 mi one-way; 300 ft elev loss.*

Cool Rating: *** **Crowds:** *

Notes: Some accounts have it that the ticks are bad along this trail. **Road Desc:** Gravel, narrow

Directions: E on FR-492 2.2 mi. Just past the Six Mile Gap Campground

---

MM: 127.1 **GPS:** 41.00147/-106.40319 **Elev:** 7950 **Grid:** 66/100

End of Highway - Colorado State Line   **Type:** Highway End

27.1 mi highway from **Colorado** northwest to **Riverside**. **Wy-130/Wy-230 (Walcott to Riverside)** continues north; however, the mile markers do not continue sequentially. Highlights include: **Platte River Trail**, **Indian Bathtubs**.

Directions: NW from the Colorado state line from MM 127.1

MM: 0.0 *GPS:* 44.50255/-104.69047 *Elev:* 4184 *Grid:* 91/12
Wy-24   *Type:* Highway Description
46.3 mi highway from **US-14 (east)**, 6 mi south of **Devils Tower**, north and east to **South Dakota**. The primary purpose of this highway is access to **Devils Tower National Monument**. Other highlights include: access to **Cook Lake Recreation Area, Aladdin Tipple Historical Park**.
Nearest Town: Hulett 15.5 N *Directions:* N to Devils Tower from MM 0

MM: 4.3 *GPS:* 44.56003/-104.68644 *Elev:* 4308 *Grid:* 91/11
Devils Tower Overlook and Historical Marker   *Type:* Scenic Viewpoint
Long pullouts on both sides of the highway provide a nice mid-range view of **Devils Tower** and the surrounding hills. A historical marker provides some history and other information. The highway is not in the photo from the southwest pullout.
Cool Rating: **** *Crowds:* ** *Time:* 10 min

MM: 6.0 *GPS:* 44.58218/-104.69560 *Elev:* 3941 *Grid:* 91/10
Wy-110/Devils Tower Rd (Devils Tower National Monument) *(see chapter)*   *Type:* Hwy Junction w/Chapter
3.4 mi road west into **Devils Tower National Monument** ending at **Devils Tower** and the visitor center parking area.
Directions: W from MM 0

MM: 15.5 *GPS:* 44.68249/-104.59944 *Elev:* 3754 *Grid:* 92/8
Hulett   *Type:* Town

MM: 25.4 *GPS:* 44.69447/-104.44068 *Elev:* 3980 *Grid:* 94/8
Alva   *Type:* Town

MM: 30.3 *GPS:* 44.65652/-104.36465 *Elev:* 4284 *Grid:* 96/9
Cook Lake Recreation Area and Scenic Drive *(see chapter)*   *Type:* Hwy Junction w/Chapter
Access to the **Cook Lake Recreation Area** along a 26.3 mi scenic drive through the **Bear Lodge Mountains** and **Black Hills National Forest** from **Wy-24** MM 30.3 south to **US-14 (east)** MM 199.5 (1.0 mi west of **I-90**). The **Warren Peak Lookout** is at the highest elevation of the drive. Dispersed camping along **FR-830**, **FR-843**, and **FR-838**.
Nearest Town: Alva 4.9 NW *Directions:* SW on FR-838 from MM 26.3

MM: 32.2 *Dist:* 0.1 *GPS:* 44.65450/-104.32742 *Elev:* 4685 *Grid:* 96/9 *Land:* NF
Bearlodge Campground   *Type:* Campground
A quiet, little-used campground in the **Bear Lodge Mountains**. *Single loop. Conifer forest.*
Crowds: * *[FEE AREA]* *Directions:* S 0.1 mi
Campsites: 8 *Shade:* **** *Privacy:* *** *RV Size:* 30' *Other:* None

MM: 36.6 *GPS:* 44.65022/-104.24680 *Elev:* 3952 *Grid:* 97/9
Custer Expedition Historic Marker   *Type:* Historical Marker
In 1874 **Lt. Colonel George A. Custer** led an expedition into the **Black Hills** to verify rumors of gold. His party consisted of 1,000 men, 110 wagons, and 200 animals. The expedition violated the Indian treaty of 1868.
Cool Rating: * *Crowds:* * *Time:* 5 min *Directions:* S side of hwy
Notes: There are supposed to be visible wagon ruts at the site; however, I could not see them.

MM: 39.4 *GPS:* 44.64050/-104.19267 *Elev:* 3721 *Grid:* 98/9
Wy-111   *Type:* Highway Junction
8.6 mi highway that connects **Wy-24** south to **I-90**.

MM: 39.9 *GPS:* 44.63975/-104.18238 *Elev:* 3688 *Grid:* 98/9
Aladdin   *Type:* Town

MM: 40.8 *GPS:* 44.63851/-104.16361 *Elev:* 3633 *Grid:* 98/9 *Land:* State
Aladdin Tipple Historical Park   *Type:* Historic Site
This primitive wooden tipple was used to sort and grade coal and load it into rail cars from 1898 to 1942. An 18 mi short line railroad was built to connect the coal mine to the main rail line in **Belle Fourche**, **South Dakota**. By 1911 the industrial coal production was dwindling so the mine produced only domestic coal. This is one of the last wooden coal tipples left in the west and is an example of mine engineering technology used in the late 1800s and early 1900s. The tipple, hoist house, and mine opening were saved from near collapse and the site was restored and developed as a historical interpretive park. It is 75 yds along a paved path to the tipple and an additional 0.1 mi up a somewhat steep hill to the hoist house and adit (a horizontal entrance). Several signs explain the structure, history, operation, and restoration of the tipple. The only other coal tipple in the state is the **Reliance Tipple** north of Rock Springs *(see US-191 MM 4.5)*.
Cool Rating: *** *Crowds:* * *Time:* 40 min *Directions:* 0.9 mi E of Aladdin on N side of hwy
Notes: This operation is particularly interesting in contrast to the Eagle Butte Coal Mine in Gillette, which provides free tours.

MM: 46.8 *GPS:* 44.64149/-104.05641 *Elev:* 3391 *Grid:* 100/9
End of Highway - South Dakota State Line   *Type:* Highway End
46.3 mi highway from **South Dakota** west and south to **US-14 (east)**, 6 mi south of **Devils Tower**. The primary purpose of this highway is access to **Devils Tower National Monument**. Other highlights include: **Aladdin Tipple Historical Park**, access to **Cook Lake Recreation Area**.
Nearest Town: Aladdin 6.9 W *Directions:* W to Aladdin from MM 46.8

Wy-28 (Farson to US-287)   SW/NE

MM: 0.0   **GPS:** 42.10859/-109.44899   **Elev:** 6595   **Grid:** 23/72
Wy-28 (Farson to US-287)   **Type:** Highway Description
66.3 mi highway from **Farson** northeast to **US-287/Wy-789**, 8.4 mi southeast of **Lander**. Highlights include: **South Pass** and related historic markers, **Carissa Mine**, **South Pass City State Historic Site**, **Miner's Delight**, **Atlantic City**, **Red Canyon**.
Directions: NE to Lander from MM 0
Notes: **Wy-28** runs 94.6 mi northeast from **Wy-372** to **US-287/Wy-789**; however, because of the mile marker change at **US-191**, this book has divided the highway into 2 chapters, **Wy-28 (Wy-372 to Farson)** and **Wy-28 (Farson to US-287)**. The mile markers gain 1.8 mi between MM 49 and MM 52.

MM: 0.0   **GPS:** 42.10859/-109.44899   **Elev:** 6595   **Grid:** 23/72
US-191 *(see chapter)*   **Type:** Hwy Junction w/Chapter
109.2 mi highway from **I-80** exit 104 in **Rock Springs** northwest past **Pinedale** to a transition with **US-189/191**, which continues 53.2 mi to **Hoback Jct** (south of **Jackson**) using sequential mile markers. Highlights include: **Reliance Tipple**, **White Mountain Petroglyphs**, **Boar's Tusk**, **Killpecker Sand Dunes**, **Pilot Butte Wild Horse Tour**, **Fremont Lake**, **Green River Lakes**.
Directions: NW to Pinedale or S to Rock Springs from MM 40.5

MM: 0.0   **GPS:** 42.10859/-109.44899   **Elev:** 6595   **Grid:** 23/72
Farson   **Type:** Town

MM: 23.5   **GPS:** 42.28495/-109.05913   **Elev:** 7025   **Grid:** 29/68
Parting of the Ways   **Type:** Historical Marker
A decision point for travelers along the **Oregon Trail**. The traditional route traveled southwest to **Fort Bridger**, then northwest. An alternative route, which saved 85 mi and 5-6 days of travel, headed due west through 50 mi of hot desert before crossing mountains. This route was particularly popular with the **"Forty-Niners"** who were in a hurry to reach the **California** gold fields. The biggest obstacle was a 40 mi waterless stretch between the **Big Sandy River** and the **Green River**. This shortcut was originally known as the **Greenwood Cutoff** but later became known as the **Sublette Cutoff**. A monument and interpretive signs mark the site; however, one sign explains that the **Parting of the Ways** is actually 10 mi west.
Cool Rating: *   **Crowds:** *   **Time:** 10 min   **Directions:** Pullout on NW side of hwy. Short path NW to marker.

MM: 28.9   **GPS:** 42.33045/-108.97371   **Elev:** 7230   **Grid:** 30/67   **Land:** BLM
South Pass Overlook   **Type:** Scenic Viewpoint
South Pass offered a broad, gradual ascent over the **Continental Divide**, which was the key to the entire **Oregon-Mormon-California Trail** system. Every emigrant heading westward traveled over this pass, which also provided a dependable supply of grass and water. A loop pullout provides a walking loop with 8 interpretive signs, trail ruts, and a panoramic view of **South Pass**, **Pacific Springs**, and the **Oregon Buttes**. *Located at mile 914 of the **Oregon Trail**.*
Cool Rating: ***   **Crowds:** *   **Time:** 20 min   **Directions:** Parking loop on SE side of hwy

MM: 34.2   **GPS:** 42.38200/-108.89731   **Elev:** 7465   **Grid:** 31/65
South Pass Rest Area   **Type:** Rest Area
A nice grassed rest area with covered picnic shelters.
Directions: NW side of hwy

MM: 37.4   **GPS:** 42.42289/-108.87221   **Elev:** 7797   **Grid:** 31/64   **Land:** BLM
Lander Cutoff   **Type:** Historical Marker
Built in 1857-1858 as a shortcut wagon road between **South Pass** and the **Snake River** country for those traveling to the **Pacific Northwest** on the **Oregon Trail**. This route traversed a sparsely-forested high altitude region at the southern edge of the **Wind River Mountains**, which provided better water, wood, and forage than the southern desert route. Surveyed by **Frederick W. Lander** for the Department of the Interior, this was the only stretch of the **Oregon Trail** system ever to be subsidized and constructed by the **U.S. Government**. The new route cut nearly 7 days off the travel time; however, the mountainous terrain and unpredictable weather still proved challenging. More than 13,000 emigrants utilized the new **Lander Trail** in its first year, and it remained in use until 1912 when automobiles made it obsolete. *A historical monument is located at the other end of the Lander Cutoff on US-89 MM 72.2, 103 mi west.*
Cool Rating: *   **Crowds:** *   **Time:** 5 min   **Directions:** Long pullout on SE side of hwy

MM: 43.5   **GPS:** 42.49302/-108.80958   **Elev:** 8264   **Grid:** 32/63
South Pass and South Pass City Historical Marker   **Type:** Historical Marker
A sign about the importance of **South Pass** and the gold rush that created **South Pass City**.
Cool Rating: *   **Crowds:** *   **Time:** 5 min   **Directions:** SE side of hwy at the junction with South Pass City Rd

MM: 43.5   **GPS:** 42.49295/-108.80993   **Elev:** 8264   **Grid:** 32/63
Atlantic City Rd/CR-237 & South Pass City Rd (heading northeast) *(see chapter)*   **Type:** Hwy Junction w/Chapter
8.2 mi route that loops from **Wy-28** MM 43.5 south past **South Pass City**, northeast through **Atlantic City**, and north to **Wy-28** MM 49.0. Highlights include: **Carissa Mine**, **South Pass City**, **Willie Handcart Company Tragedy Memorial**, **Atlantic City**, **Miner's Delight Ghost Town**.
Directions: SE on South Pass City Rd/CR-479 from MM 8.2

MM: 45.8   **GPS:** 42.51494/-108.77765   **Elev:** 8440   **Grid:** 33/62
Wy-131/FR-300/Louis Lake Rd *(see chapter)*   **Type:** Hwy Junction w/Chapter
36.5 mi route from **Wy-28** north to **US-287 (Lander to US-26)** in **Lander**. The road traverses the southeastern end of the **Wind River Mountains** to a high point 4,240 ft above the city of **Lander** before descending and traveling through **Sinks Canyon**. 7 public campgrounds are located along this route plus many dispersed camping opportunities. Highlights include: **Louis Lake**, **Blue Ridge Fire Lookout**, trailheads into the **Wind River Mountains**, **Popo Agie Falls**, **Sinks Canyon State Park**.
Nearest Town: Atlantic City 6.0 SE   **Notes:** The first 5 miles of FR-300 provides abundant dispersed camping.
Directions: N to Lander from MM 36.5

MM: 46.9   *Dist:* 2.2   *GPS:* 42.52736/-108.72232   *Elev:* 8277   *Grid:* 33/62
Atlantic City Rd/CR-237 & South Pass City Rd (heading northeast) *(see chapter)*   *Type:* Hwy Junction w/Chapter
This route should only be used if heading northeast and only visiting **Atlantic City**, the **Willie Handcart Company Tragedy Memorial**, or camping in the campgrounds along the way. If the intent is to drive the entire **Atlantic City** loop, start at MM 43.5 *See next section.*
Directions: SE 2.2 mi;   S on Atlantic City Rd/CR-237 from MM 0
Notes: Atlantic City Rd does not connect directly to Wy-28. The old highway loops southeast to the junction and then north back to Wy-28 at MM 49.

MM: 49.0   *Dist:* 1.5   *GPS:* 42.52736/-108.72232   *Elev:* 8277   *Grid:* 33/62
Atlantic City Rd/CR-237 & South Pass City Rd (heading southwest) *(see chapter)*   *Type:* Hwy Junction w/Chapter
8.2 mi route that loops from **Wy-28** MM 49.0 southwest through **Atlantic City**, past **South Pass City**, and north back to **Wy-28** MM 43.5. Highlights include: **Miner's Delight Ghost Town, Atlantic City, Willie Handcart Company Tragedy Memorial, Carissa Mine, South Pass City**.
Directions: S 1.5 mi;   S on Atlantic City Rd/CR-237 from MM 0
Notes: Atlantic City Rd does not connect directly to Wy-28. A side road loops south to the junction and then northwest back to Wy-28 at MM 46.9.

MM: 49.0
Mile Marker Discrepancy   *Type:* MM Discrepancy
Wy-28 used to loop southeast to **Atlantic City Rd/CR-237**; however, this loop was replaced by a straight section of highway between MM 46.9 and MM 49.0. This made **Wy-28** 1.8 miles shorter, which is realized at MM 49.0, which jumps to MM 50.8 at the turnoff to **Atlantic City** *(see previous section).*

MM: 57.2   *GPS:* 42.59474/-108.63344   *Elev:* 7070   *Grid:* 35/60   *Land:* State
Red Canyon Rd/CR-235 (heading northeast)   *Type:* Backcountry Byway
A 10.1 mi scenic backcountry route through the **Red Canyon**. *See next section.* This route is the same distance as staying on the highway but much slower.
Cool Rating: **   *Crowds:* *   *Directions:* N on Red Canyon Rd/CR-235 10.1 mi
Road Desc: Gravel, rough spots & impassable when wet, narrow. The road descends steeply into the canyon.

MM: 58.5   *GPS:* 42.60328/-108.61419   *Elev:* 6993   *Grid:* 35/60   *Land:* BLM
Red Canyon Overlook   *Type:* Scenic Viewpoint
A colorful view of the brick red cliffs of the **Red Canyon**, which are part of the **Chugwater Formation**. The bottom of the canyon is 1,400 ft below the overlook. A portion of this area is the **Red Canyon Wildlife Habitat Management Area**, which provides a crucial wintering range for elk.
Cool Rating: ***   *Crowds:* *   *Time:* 10 min   *Nearest Town:* Lander 18.4 N   *Directions:* NW side of hwy

MM: 67.3   *GPS:* 42.71575/-108.64416   *Elev:* 5485   *Grid:* 34/57   *Land:* State
Red Canyon Rd/CR-235 (southbound)   *Type:* Backcountry Byway
A 10.1 mi scenic backcountry route through the **Red Canyon**. *See previous section.* This route is the same distance as staying on the highway but much slower.
Cool Rating: **   *Crowds:* *   *Road Desc:* Gravel, rough spots & impassable when wet, narrow
Directions: SW on Red Canyon Rd/CR-235 10.1 mi

MM: 68.2   *GPS:* 42.72881/-108.64653   *Elev:* 5546   *Grid:* 34/57
US-287/Wy-789 *(see chapter)*   *Type:* Hwy Junction w/Chapter
125 mi highway from **Lander** southeast to **Rawlins** near **I-80**. Highlights include: **Green Mountain, Split Rock**.
Directions: Continue straight N 8.4 mi to Lander or SE/R to Rawlins from MM 72.9

MM: 68.2   *GPS:* 42.72881/-108.64653   *Elev:* 5546   *Grid:* 34/57
End of Highway   *Type:* Highway End
66.3 mi highway from **US-287/Wy-789**, 8.4 mi southeast of **Lander**, southwest to **Farson**. Highlights include: **Red Canyon, Miner's Delight, Atlantic City, Carissa Mine, South Pass City State Historic Site, South Pass** and related historic markers.
Nearest Town: Lander 8.4 NW   *Directions:* SW to Farson from MM 68.2

MM: 100.0 *GPS:* 41.86803/-109.85848 *Elev:* 6309 *Grid:* 17/78
Wy-28 (Wy-372 to Farson) *Type:* Highway Description
28.3 mi highway from **Wy-372** northeast to **Farson**. At the junction with **US-191**, **Wy-28** continues northeast toward **Lander**; however, the mile markers start over at 0.0. *See chapter: Wy-28 (Farson to US-287).* Highlights include: **Lombard/Mormon Ferry**, **Pilot Butte Emigrant Trails Interpretive Site**, **Simpson's Hollow**.
Nearest Town: Farson 28.3 NE *Directions:* NE to Farson from MM 100
Notes: **Wy-28** runs 94.6 mi northeast from **Wy-372** to **US-287/Wy-789**; however, because of the mile marker change at **US-191**, this book has divided the highway into 2 chapters, **Wy-28 (Wy-372 to Farson)** and **Wy-28 (Farson to US-287)**.

MM: 100.0 *GPS:* 41.86803/-109.85848 *Elev:* 6309 *Grid:* 17/78
Wy-372 *(see chapter)* *Type:* Hwy Junction w/Chapter
48.6 mi highway from **I-80** exit 83 northwest to **US-189** MM 61.3. This is primarily a connecting road to **Wy-28** and **US-189** northbound. 3 BLM campgrounds are located near **Fontenelle Reservoir** 40.4 mi northwest. Highlights include: **Lombard/Mormon Ferry**, **Seedskadee National Wildlife Refuge**.
Directions: NW to US-189 or SE to I-80 from MM 26.8

MM: 102.7 *Dist:* 0.1 *GPS:* 41.87952/-109.80797 *Elev:* 6275 *Grid:* 18/78 *Land:* BLM
Lombard/Mormon Ferry *Type:* Historic Site
A popular crossing point of the **Green River** where a ferry was first established by mountain men and then operated by the **Mormons** during the peak emigration years of the1850s. When the water level was low in late summer and early fall, many people would ford the river to avoid the ferry tolls. Unfortunately, some would attempt to ford when the current was too strong, often with disastrous results. The site includes 6 interpretive signs about this crossing point and a short paved trail to a replica of the ferry.
Cool Rating: ** *Crowds:* * *Time:* 20 min *Road Desc:* Gravel
Directions: Just southwest of the river bridge; SE 0.1 mi.

MM: 116.0 *GPS:* 41.99837/-109.62282 *Elev:* 6590 *Grid:* 20/75 *Land:* BLM
Pilot Butte Emigrant Trails Interpretive Site *Type:* Historical Marker
An interpretive walking loop with 8 signs about the history of the **Oregon-Mormon-California-Pony Express Trails** plus actual trail ruts. 3 of the signs are about death and burial on the trail complete with 2 simulated graves for effect. The landmark **Pilot Butte** is visible 25 mi south.
Cool Rating: ** *Crowds:* * *Time:* 20 min *Directions:* Parking loop on SE side of hwy

MM: 118.1 *GPS:* 42.01801/-109.59087 *Elev:* 6554 *Grid:* 21/75 *Land:* BLM
Simpson's Hollow *Type:* Historical Marker
One of only 3 significant engagements in a war between the **U.S. Government** and the people in the **Utah Territory**. This conflict took place in 1857-1858 and was known as the **Utah War**. At this point **U.S. Army** supply wagons were burned by **Utah Militia** men. 3 interpretive signs and a granite monument tell this interesting story. A 200 yd footpath leads to a trail marker.
Cool Rating: ** *Crowds:* * *Time:* 10 min *Directions:* NW side of hwy

MM: 128.1 *GPS:* 42.10797/-109.45322 *Elev:* 6586 *Grid:* 23/72
Little Sandy Crossing *Type:* Historical Marker
A fording and camping location on the **Big Sandy River** for emigrants taking the southern route of the **Oregon Trail** toward **Fort Bridger**. A monument recounts a conversation from 1847 between **Jim Bridger** and **Brigham Young** about the route and the ability to sustain a large population in the **Great Salt Lake Valley**.
Cool Rating: * *Crowds:* * *Time:* 5 min *Directions:* N side of hwy 0.2 mi W of US-191

MM: 128.3 *GPS:* 42.10859/-109.44899 *Elev:* 6595 *Grid:* 23/72
Farson *Type:* Town

MM: 128.3 *GPS:* 42.10859/-109.44899 *Elev:* 6595 *Grid:* 23/72
US-191 *(see chapter)* *Type:* Hwy Junction w/Chapter
109.2 mi highway from **I-80** exit 104 in **Rock Springs** northwest past **Pinedale** to a transition with **US-189/191**, which continues 53.2 mi to **Hoback Jct** (south of **Jackson**) using sequential mile markers. Highlights include: **Reliance Tipple**, **White Mountain Petroglyphs**, **Boar's Tusk**, **Killpecker Sand Dunes**, **Pilot Butte Wild Horse Tour**, **Fremont Lake**, **Green River Lakes**.
Directions: NW to Pinedale or S to Rock Springs from MM 40.5

MM: 128.3 *GPS:* 42.10859/-109.44899 *Elev:* 6595 *Grid:* 23/72
End of Highway *Type:* Highway End
28.3 mi highway from **Farson** southwest to **Wy-372**. This is a continuation of **Wy-28** from the northeast; however, the mile markers change from 0.0 to 128.3 at the intersection with **US-191**. Highlights include: **Simpson's Hollow**, **Pilot Butte Emigrant Trails Interpretive Site**, **Lombard/Mormon Ferry**.
Directions: SW to Wy-372 from MM 128.3

Wy-296 (Chief Joseph Scenic Highway)   NW/SE

MM: 0.0   *GPS:* 44.93001/-109.72608   *Elev:* 7115   *Grid:* 19/2
Wy-296 (Chief Joseph Scenic Highway)   *Type:* Highway Description
46.2 mi highway from **US-212** southeast to **Wy-120**. The highway follows the route of the historic pursuit of **Chief Joseph** and the **Nez Perce Indians** by the **United States 7th Cavalry** in 1877. This is one of the most scenic highways in **Wyoming**. Highlights include: **Sunlight Gorge**, overlooks from **Dead Indian Pass**.
Nearest Town: Cooke City, MT 13.8 NW   *Notes:* No towns or services.   *Directions:* SE to Wy-120 from MM 0

MM: 0.0   *GPS:* 44.93001/-109.72608   *Elev:* 7115   *Grid:* 19/2
US-212 (Beartooth Scenic Byway) *(see chapter)*   *Type:* Hwy Junction w/Chapter
43.6 mi highway east from the northeast entrance of **Yellowstone National Park**, briefly into **Montana**, across far northern **Wyoming**, and back into **Montana** on Beartooth Pass. This is a remote section of highway with only a single small town, **Cooke City, Montana**, and only a single highway junction to **Wy-296**, another remote highway with no towns. Highlights include: **Crazy Creek Falls, Lake Creek Falls, Clay Butte Fire Lookout, Beartooth Falls, Beartooth Pass**.
Directions: W to Yellowstone National Park or E to Beartooth Pass and Red Lodge, Montana from MM 17.8.

MM: 1.2   *GPS:* 44.92096/-109.70723   *Elev:* 6930   *Grid:* 19/2   *Land:* NF
Lake Creek Campground   *Type:* Campground
Located on a hillside near **Lake Creek**, which flows near the west side of the campground and is closest to the site at the end. *Dense conifer forest. Roomy sites. Not level. 2 sites close to highway.*
Crowds: ** *[FEE AREA]* *Notes:* A cattle grate on the highway clangs loudly as vehicles pass by.
Directions: NE side of hwy
Campsites: 6   *Shade:* *****   *Privacy:* ****   *RV Size:* 20'   *Other:* GRIZZLIES

MM: 2.4   *GPS:* 44.90811/-109.68964   *Elev:* 6728   *Grid:* 20/2   *Land:* NF
Chief Joseph Scenic Highway Sign   *Type:* Visitor Information
A long half-loop pullout that provides a sign with a map of **Wy-296** identifying the campgrounds and attractions along this scenic highway. Historical information is also provided about how **Chief Joseph** and the **Nez Perce Indians** eluded the 7th Cavalry along this route. More detailed information on the **Nez Perce Indians** is available on top of **Dead Indian Pass**. *See MM 32.7.*
Cool Rating: * *Crowds:* * *Time:* 5 min *Directions:* SW side of hwy

MM: 4.7   *GPS:* 44.88617/-109.65535   *Elev:* 6533   *Grid:* 20/3   *Land:* NF
Hunter Peak Campground   *Type:* Campground
Located between the highway and the **Clarks Fork Yellowstone River**, which has excellent fishing. The campsites are located on the entrance road and around an end loop. The campground is named after the 9,025 ft **Hunter Peak**, located 1.6 mi southwest. *Mixed forest. Roomy sites. Wide, back-in parking areas that accommodate a trailer and the towing vehicle parked side by side. Meat hanging racks for hunters.*
Crowds: *** *[FEE AREA]* *Directions:* SW side of hwy
Campsites: 8   *Shade:* ***   *Privacy:* **   *RV Size:* 30'   *Other:* 1-877-444-6777;www.recreation.gov,Water   GRIZZLIES

MM: 7.9   *Dist:* 0.2   *GPS:* 44.84705/-109.63493   *Elev:* 6502   *Grid:* 20/4   *Land:* NF
Crandall Ranger Station   *Type:* Visitor Center
Maps, driving directions, and local area information.
Directions: SW 0.2 mi

MM: 9.4   *GPS:* 44.84580/-109.60151   *Elev:* 6615   *Grid:* 21/4   *Land:* NF
Cathedral Cliffs Viewpoint   *Type:* Scenic Viewpoint
A pullout with a view of the eroded limestone **Cathedral Cliffs** to the south.
Cool Rating: * *Crowds:* * *Time:* 5 min *Directions:* S side of hwy

MM: 11.6   *GPS:* 44.84462/-109.56174   *Elev:* 6666   *Grid:* 21/4   *Land:* NF
Reef Creek Picnic Area   *Type:* Picnic Area
A small picnic area in a half-loop pullout. *No toilet.*
Directions: SE side of hwy

MM: 23.0   *GPS:* 44.76940/-109.42517   *Elev:* 6136   *Grid:* 23/6   *Land:* NF
Sunlight Gorge   *Type:* Canyon
The highest bridge in **Wyoming** at 300 ft above **Sunlight Creek** across a vertical rock walled gorge. Pedestrian walkways are located on both sides of the bridge allowing views directly into the gorge. *Vault toilet.*
Cool Rating: **** *Crowds:* ** *Time:* 30 min *Directions:* Parking area on E side of hwy just past S end of bridge.

MM: 23.4   *Dist:* 6.0   *GPS:* 44.73939/-109.52951   *GPS2:* 44.73813/-109.55577   *Elev:* 6745   *Grid:* 22/7   *Land:* State
Sunlight Wildlife Habitat Management Area   *Type:* Wildlife Habitat Mgmt Area
A beautiful setting in **Sunlight Basin** below a mountain that rises 1,000 ft above 2 established primitive camping areas. **Sunlight** is a large unshaded parking area just off the left side of the road *(see GPS)*. **Grizzly** is nice and shady in a stand of cottonwoods along **Little Sunlight Creek** *(see GPS2)*. *Vault toilets. Stone fire rings.*
Crowds: *** *Nearest Town:* Cody 45 SE *Road Desc:* Gravel. FR-127 is a narrow 2-track dirt road
Directions: SW on FR-101/Sunlight Rd 5.9 mi; N/R 0.1 mi to Sunlight on left; Continue N and W on FR-127 1.8 mi to Grizzly (crossing a single lane bridge over Little Sunlight Creek at 0.3 mi).
Campsites: Dispersed   *Shade:* ***   *Privacy:* **   *RV Size:* 30'   *Other:* GRIZZLIES

MM: 23.4   *Dist:* 10.5   *GPS:* 44.71852/-109.59026   *Elev:* 6913   *Grid:* 21/7   *Land:* NF
Little Sunlight Campground   *Type:* Campground
A small campground at the **Little Sunlight Trailhead** with a trail into the **Absaroka Wilderness**. *Roomy sites. Tables. Fire rings with grates. Vault toilet. Horse corrals.*
Crowds: *** *Road Desc:* Gravel *Directions:* SW on FR-101/Sunlight Rd 10.5 mi
Campsites: 4   *Shade:* ***   *Privacy:* ***   *RV Size:* 30'   *Other:* GRIZZLIES

MM: 25.0 **Dist:** 0.2 **GPS:** 44.75024/-109.42170 **Elev:** 6083 **Grid:** 23/6 **Land:** NF
Dead Indian Creek Trailhead **Type:** Trailhead
Long trails into the **Absaroka Mountains** and **Absaroka Wilderness**. Corrals, feeding stalls, and hitching rails are provided, and camping is allowed for people with horses.
Crowds: *** **Directions:** SW 0.2 mi
Campsites: Dispersed **Shade:** ** **Privacy:** ** **Other:** GRIZZLIES

MM: 25.1 **GPS:** 44.75262/-109.41955 **Elev:** 6012 **Grid:** 23/6 **Land:** NF
Dead Indian Campground (north section) **Type:** Campground
Located on the inside of a sharp curve in the highway at the western base of **Dead Indian Pass**. The campground is divided into 2 sections, separated by **Dead Indian Creek**, with separate entrances *(see next section)*. *Mixed forest. Grass understory. Most sites are in the open. Fairly level. 1 tent-only site. Highway noise.*
Crowds: *** **[FEE AREA]** **Directions:** Inside of curve on NE side of hwy
Campsites: 10 **Shade:** ** **Privacy:** ** **RV Size:** 40' **Other:** GRIZZLIES

MM: 25.2 **GPS:** 44.75294/-109.41693 **Elev:** 6012 **Grid:** 23/6 **Land:** NF
Dead Indian Campground (south section) **Type:** Campground
The entrance to the south section of **Dead Indian Campground** across **Dead Indian Creek**. *See previous section.*
Directions: NW side of hwy

MM: 25.7 **Dist:** 0.3 **GPS:** 44.76028/-109.40511 **Elev:** 6140 **Grid:** 24/6 **Land:** NF
Dead Indian Trail **Type:** Hiking Trail
A hiking trail to an overlook of the **Clarks Fork Canyon**. *Moderately easy; 200 ft elev loss; 2.0 mi one-way.* The trail continues along the canyon rim.
Cool Rating: *** **Crowds:** * **Time:** 2 hrs **Road Desc:** Dirt, rough & impassable when wet, narrow
Directions: NW then NE 0.3 mi to parking area.

MM: 31.8 **GPS:** 44.75620/-109.38330 **Elev:** 7788 **Grid:** 24/6 **Land:** NF
Dead Indian Pass Overlook **Type:** Scenic Viewpoint
A nice view of the **Clarks Fork Canyon** to the northwest.
Cool Rating: *** **Crowds:** * **Time:** 10 min **Directions:** N side of hwy on outside of a hairpin curve.

MM: 32.7 **GPS:** 44.74346/-109.38324 **Elev:** 8078 **Grid:** 24/6 **Land:** NF
Dead Indian Pass Summit **Type:** Scenic Viewpoint
A large parking area that provides spectacular views of the **Absaroka Mountains** to the west and into the **Clarks Fork Canyon** to the northwest. The overlook includes signs explaining the 1877 escape over this pass by **Chief Joseph** and the **Nez Perce Indians** while being pursued by **General Oliver O. Howard** and the 7th Cavalry. On the north end of the parking area are 2 metal sculptures of an Indian man and woman on horses. *Vault toilets are on the south side of the pullout.*
Cool Rating: ***** **Crowds:** ** **Time:** 30 min **Directions:** W side of hwy

MM: 39.1 **GPS:** 44.72953/-109.31025 **Elev:** 6440 **Grid:** 25/7 **Land:** NF
Scenic Overlook **Typo:** Scenic Viewpoint
A view of red cliffs and into the valley.
Cool Rating: ** **Crowds:** * **Time:** 5 min **Directions:** N side of hwy on outside of a hairpin curve.

MM: 46.2 **GPS:** 44.72716/-109.21737 **Elev:** 4983 **Grid:** 26/7
Wy-120 *(see chapter)* **Type:** Hwy Junction w/Chapter
118.7 mi highway from **Montana** southeast through **Cody** to **Thermopolis**. Highlights include: Attractions in **Cody** *(see US-14/16/20 MM 52.4)*, **Gooseberry Badlands Scenic Area**, **Legend Rock Petroglyphs**.
Directions: N to Montana or S to Cody from MM 116.5

MM: 46.2 **GPS:** 44.72716/-109.21737 **Elev:** 4983 **Grid:** 26/7
End of Highway **Type:** Highway End
46.2 mi highway from **Wy-120** northwest to **US-212**. The highway follows the route of the historic pursuit of **Chief Joseph** and the **Nez Perce Indians** by the **United States 7th Cavalry** in 1877. This is one of the most scenic highways in **Wyoming**. Highlights include: overlooks from **Dead Indian Pass**, **Sunlight Gorge**.
Nearest Town: Cody 16.5 SE **Directions:** NW to US-212 from MM 46.2

Wy-352/FR-10091   S/N

MM: 0.0 *GPS:* 42.88084/-109.97460 *Elev:* 7262 *Grid:* 15/53
Wy-352/FR-10091   *Type:* Highway Description
43.9 mi route north from **US-191** ending at the **Green River Lakes** area. **Wy-352** is paved and heads north 25.3 mi before becoming gravel at the **Bridger-Teton National Forest** boundary. At this point the road transitions to **FR-10091** and loops east then south to the **Green River Lakes Trailhead** at the end of the road. The mile markers for **Wy-352** end at MM 25.3, so they are also shown as starting at zero from **FR-10091** to allow the trip odometer to be reset. Along the way are 4 public campgrounds as well as numerous dispersed camping options after entering the National Forest. This route also connects to the 44.6 mi road over **Union Pass** that connects to **US-26/287** 8 mi northwest of **Dubois**. Highlights include: **New Fork Lake**, **Kendall Warm Springs**, **Green River Lakes area**, **Clear Creek Falls**, **Clear Creek Natural Bridge**, **Porcupine Falls**, **Slide Lake**.
Nearest Town: Pinedale 5.9 E *Directions:* N from MM 0
Notes: If the wind isn't blowing the evening mosquitoes are awful in the National Forest area along this route.
Road Desc: The first 25.3 mi are paved but then changes to a wide gravel road that is extremely washboarded for long stretches.

MM: 14.2 *Dist:* 3.4 *GPS:* 43.08104/-109.96794 *Elev:* 7847 *Grid:* 16/48 *Land:* NF
New Fork Lake Campground   *Type:* Campground
New Fork Lake is a long terminal moraine dammed lake at the end of **New Fork Canyon**, a glacial valley formed by ice flowing out of the **Wind River Mountains**. The lake measures 3.2 mi long, 0.8 mi wide, and up to 210 ft deep. It is divided into 2 sections where water passes through a narrow neck known as **The Narrows**. The campground is located on the southwest shore of the lake, where several sites have a good view of the lake and the canyon but none are on the lake. A boat ramp is located 1.4 mi farther up **New Fork Lake Rd**. *Single loop. Young aspen forest. Dense middlestory. Good spacing between sites. Primitive boat launch.*
Crowds: *** *[FEE AREA]* *Road Desc:* Gravel *Directions:* NE on New Fork Lake Rd/CR-162 3.3 mi; E/R 0.1 mi.
Notes: There are dispersed camping options between this campground and the Narrows campground.
Campsites: 15 *Shade:* *** *Privacy:* **** *RV Size:* 20' *Other:* 1-877-444-6777:www.recreation.gov

MM: 14.2 *Dist:* 6.0 *GPS:* 43.10525/-109.94223 *Elev:* 7914 *Grid:* 16/47 *Land:* NF
New Fork Lake Trailhead   *Type:* Trailhead
A trail into the **Wind River Mountains** and **Bridger Wilderness** that is less crowded than the trail from the **Green River Lakes Trailhead**. The **New Fork Trail** travels along the **New Fork River** into the open **New Fork Canyon**, where scattered forests are situated below granite walls that rise over 2,500 ft. The trail junctions with the **Palmer Canyon Trail** at 8.2 mi, the **Porcupine Trail** at 9.3 mi, and the **Highline Trail** in **Trail Creek Park** at 16.5 mi. The parking area provides corrals and horse trailer parking.
Cool Rating: **** *Crowds:* *** *Time:* Days *Road Desc:* Gravel *Directions:* NE on New Fork Lake Rd/CR-162 6.0 mi

MM: 14.2 *Dist:* 6.0 *GPS:* 43.10479/-109.94258 *Elev:* 7888 *Grid:* 16/47 *Land:* NF
Narrows Campground   *Type:* Campground
Located on a rise above the north side of **New Fork Lake** near **The Narrows** *(see New Fork Campground for a description of New Fork Lake)*. The campground is composed of 2 loops that are near different shorelines on either side of **The Narrows**. Many sites have a view of the lake. The **New Fork Lake Trailhead** is located at the campground entrance *(see previous section)*. A boat ramp is located off the road 1.2 mi west of the campground. *Aspen forest. Grass understory. Sites are close together.*
Crowds: *** *[FEE AREA]* *Road Desc:* Gravel *Directions:* NE on New Fork Lake Rd 6.0 mi
Campsites: 19 *Shade:* *** *Privacy:* * *RV Size:* 30' *Other:* 1-877-444-6777:www.recreation.gov,Water BEARS

MM: 25.3 (0.0/18.6) *GPS:* 43.22155/-110.00825 *Elev:* 7658 *Grid:* 15/44
FR-10091   *Type:* Highway Transition
At the Bridger-Teton National Forest boundary the pavement ends and the road becomes gravel.
Road Desc: Gravel, washboard sections

MM: 25.7 (0.5/18.2) *GPS:* 43.22702/-110.01301 *Elev:* 7687 *Grid:* 15/44
First Tie Drive on the Green River   *Type:* Historical Marker
A sign commemorating the "first tie drive on the **Green River**." Between 1867 and 1869 several hundred thousand railroad ties were sent 130 mi down the **Green River** to the city of **Green River**, where they were caught and loaded into railcars to supply neighboring states where timber was scarce.
Cool Rating: * *Crowds:* * *Time:* 5 min *Directions:* SW side of hwy just NW of where the pavement ends.

MM: 27.6 (2.4/16.3) *Dist:* 0.5 *GPS:* 43.25570/-110.02579 *Elev:* 7700 *Grid:* 15/44 *Land:* NF
Whiskey Grove Campground   *Type:* Campground
Located on a bend of the **Green River** in a shallow river valley hidden from the road. A few sites are along the river bank, some have no shade, and some are not very nice. *Small stand of pine trees. Medium understory. OK spacing between sites.*
Crowds: *** *[FEE AREA]* *Road Desc:* Gravel *Directions:* W 0.5 mi
Campsites: 9 *Shade:* *** *Privacy:* *** *RV Size:* 30' *Other:* Water

MM: 28.1 (2.8/15.9) *GPS:* 43.26002/-110.01643 *Elev:* 7750 *Grid:* 15/43
Union Pass Rd *(see chapter)*   *Type:* Hwy Junction w/Chapter
44.6 mi route on National Forest and county roads that connect **Wy-352/FR-10091**, in the **Upper Green River Valley**, north to **US-26/287** by climbing over the 9,643 ft **Union Pass**. This drive offers nice scenery and a chance to see wildlife and wildflowers. The area is popular for ATVs and provides many dispersed camping opportunities. The north side of the pass offers great views across the valley to the northeast. Using this route and **Wy-352/FR-10091** between **US-191** and **US-26/287** saves 74 mi over driving the paved roads.
Nearest Town: Pinedale 34 SE *Directions:* NW on Union Pass Rd from MM 0
Notes: This is a seasonal road and is typically open from July through September. I would only recommend this route for recreational purposes or travel between Wy-352 & US-26/287, as the road is fairly slow and the scenery is not that spectacular.

MM: 29.6 (4.3/14.3) *GPS:* 43.28114/-110.02216 *Elev:* 7805 *Grid:* 15/43 *Land:* NF
Kendall Warm Springs   *Type:* Hot Springs
The only place in the world where the tiny **Kendall Dace** fish are found. These endangered fish only grow up to 2 in long and are particularly striking during the summer breeding season when the males turn purple in contrast with the green females. The area where the warmer water flows is colorful and somewhat interesting.
Cool Rating: ** *Crowds:* * *Time:* 15 min *Directions:* E side of road. Parking on W side of road.
Notes: To protect the fish, no wading is allowed. I couldn't actually see any of these fish.

MM: 34.0 (8.7/10.0) *GPS:* 43.33986/-110.00317 *Elev:* 7825 *Grid:* 15/42 *Land:* NF
Dispersed Camping: Dollar Lake   *Type:* Campground
A large and well-used primitive camping area across and just southeast of **Dollar Lake**. *Stone fire rings.*
Crowds: * *Directions:* E side of road
Campsites: Dispersed *RV Size:* 40' *Other:* None

MM: 43.7 (18.4/0.2) *GPS:* 43.31559/-109.86306 *Elev:* 8012 *Grid:* 17/42 *Land:* NF
Green River Lake Campground   *Type:* Campground
Located on a hillside that rises 100 ft above **Lower Green River Lake**. The sites have no view of the lake, but some have a view of **Squaretop Mountain**. *2 loops. Thin mixed forest. 5 pull-thrus. Fairly level. Bear-proof containers. 3 group sites holding 35, 35, and 50 people.*
Crowds: ***** *[FEE AREA]* *Directions:* SW side of road
Notes: Numerous free dispersed camping options are located along the National Forest access road.
Campsites: 39 *Shade:* ** *Privacy:* ** *RV Size:* 40' *Other:* 1-877-444-6777:www.recreation.gov,Water GRIZZLIES

MM: 43.9 (18.6/0.0) *GPS:* 43.31445/-109.85802 *Elev:* 8047 *Grid:* 17/42 *Land:* NF
Green River Lakes Trailhead   *Type:* Trailhead

The **Green River Lakes** area is one of the most popular areas in the **Wind River Mountains**. The glacially created lower lake along with the much smaller upper lake sit below the headwaters of the **Green River**, a major tributary to the **Colorado River**. Just north of the lower lake is the **Green River Lakes Trailhead**, with popular trails into the **Wind River Mountains** and the **Bridger Wilderness**, passing impressive peaks, granite crags, and sheer canyon walls. The **Lower Green River Lake** is highly photographed with its landmark backdrop of **Squaretop Mountain**. 2 trails start from the trailhead and connect to other trails:

Highline Trail - The main trail that runs most of the length of the **Wind River Mountains**. The trail parallels the east shore of **Lower Green River Lake** and continues south through **Green River Canyon**. *From the Green River Lakes Trailhead,* turn left and descend to the **Green River**. Cross the bridge and continue southeast above the lakeshore, which is in the open with nice views of **Squaretop Mountain**. *Trail junctions and destinations:* **Clear Creek Trail** junction (MI 1.9), **Cutoff Trail** junction (MI 2.7), **Upper Green River Lake** (MI 3.0), **Three Forks Park** (MI 11.0), **Summit Lake** (16.3 mi).

Lakeside Trail - Parallels the west shore of **Lower Green River Lake** to the junction with the **Porcupine Trail** and the **Cutoff Trail** (MI 2.7). *From the Green River Lakes Trailhead,* turn right and head southwest 0.3 mi to the southwest corner of the campground and continue south into the forest above the lake. The trail stays mostly in the forest, limiting views.

Connecting trails:

Porcupine Trail - Heads southwest from the **Lakeside Trail** into **Porcupine Creek Canyon** past **Porcupine Creek Falls** (MI 0.5), over **Porcupine Pass** (MI 7.1), to **New Fork Lake** (MI 9.3).

Clear Creek Trail - Heads east from the **Highline Trail** into **Clear Creek Canyon** past **Clear Creek Falls** (MI 0.2), past the **Slide Lake Trail** junction (MI 1.0), to **Clear Creek Natural Bridge** (MI 2.2).

Slide Lake Trail - Heads southeast from the **Clear Creek Trail** into **Slide Canyon**, past **Slide Creek Falls** (~MI 0.9), to **Slide Lake** (MI 2.6).

Cutoff Trail - Runs 0.3 mi east/west, north of **Lower Green River Lake**, connecting the **Highline Trail** to the **Lakeside Trail**. The trail crosses the **Green River** and is the north end of the loop trail around **Lower Green River Lake**.

Following are 5 day hikes:

Lower Green River Lake loop:
Loop trail around **Lower Green River Lake**. To maximize views of the canyon, mountains, and **Squaretop Mountain**, travel clockwise on the **Highline Trail** 2.7 mi to the **Cutoff Trail** junction. *Continue straight for a 0.6 mi round-trip option to* **Upper Green River Lake**. Turn right 0.3 mi to connect to the **Lakeside Trail**. *Turn left for a 1.8 mi round-trip option to* **Porcupine Creek Falls** *(see next hike).* Turn right 2.7 mi to complete the loop. **Basic Loop**: *Easy; 5.7 mi loop; Mostly level.* **With options**: *Moderate; 8.1 mi round-trip; 320 ft elev gain.*

Porcupine Creek Falls:
Overlook of **Porcupine Creek Falls**, a rushing cascade through a rocky canyon. Follow the **Lakeside Trail** 2.7 mi to the junction with the **Porcupine Trail**. Turn right 0.4 mi across a tree-lined meadow to a crossing of **Porcupine Creek** on logs or rocks. The trail climbs steeply 0.5 mi to a faint side path on the right, which leads to the edge of **Porcupine Creek Canyon** and a view of the falls. *Moderate; 7.2 mi round-trip; 320 ft elev gain.*

Clear Creek Falls:
Follow the **Highline Trail** 1.9 mi southeast above **Lower Green River Lake** to the junction with the **Clear Creek Trail**. Turn left 0.2 mi to the cascading **Clear Creek Falls**. *Easy; 4.2 mi round-trip; 130 ft elev gain.*

Clear Creek Natural Bridge:
A gradual climb through **Clear Creek Canyon** ending at the **Clear Creek Natural Bridge**. The natural bridge was formed by water undercutting and penetrating a resistant wall of limestone sedimentary rock. From **Clear Creek Falls**, continue east 2.0 mi to the south side of the natural bridge, which is not very large (20 ft wide x 4 ft high) and not very impressive. Continue 0.1 mi around the rocks to the other side of the opening, which is much larger (40 ft wide x 15 ft high) and much more impressive. *Moderate; 8.4 mi round-trip; 350 ft elev gain.*

Slide Lake:
A beautiful subalpine lake situated in a deep cirque below **Flat Top Mountain** to the north and **Lost Eagle Peak** to the southeast, which tower over 2,000 ft above the lake. From **Clear Creek Falls**, continue east 0.8 mi to the **Slide Lake Trail**. Turn right and cross the bridge over **Clear Creek** before turning southeast 0.3 mi across a tree-lined meadow to **Slide Creek**. Cross the creek and climb up switchbacks through the forested canyon past **Slide Creek Falls**, a long cascade about halfway up. The trail levels out with just over a mile to the lake. After crossing a meadow, the trail heads back into the forest and passes **Fish Bowl Spring**, a small spring-fed pool that contains small trout. The trail then climbs steeply to **Slide Lake**. *Moderately strenuous; 11.0 mi round-trip; 1530 ft elev gain.*
Cool Rating: **** **Crowds:** *** **Time:** Hours to days
Notes: Consult other books for detailed information on extended hikes or contact the **U.S. Forest Service**.
Directions: *At the end of the road;* E/L into trailhead parking keeping right at fork.

MM: 43.9 (18.6/0.0) *GPS:* 43.31392/-109.86012 *Elev:* 8042 *Grid:* 17/42 *Land:* NF
End of Highway   *Type:* Highway End

Wy-37 (Bighorn Canyon National Recreation Area)   S/N

MM: 0.0 *GPS:* 44.84063/-108.33153 *Elev:* 3795 *Grid:* 39/4
Wy-37 (Bighorn Canyon National Recreation Area)   *Type:* Highway Description
16.2 mi highway north to the **Bighorn Canyon National Recreation Area**, which is partially in **Montana**. This is not a through highway, so the return is by the same route. The mile markers for **Wy-37** end at MM 9.0, so they are also shown as starting at zero from the fee station to allow the trip odometer to be reset. Highlights include: **Sykes Mountain Trail**, **Mouth of the Canyon Trail**, **Devil Canyon Overlook**.
Nearest Town: Lovell 2.8 W *Directions:* N to Bighorn Canyon National Recreation Area from MM 0
Notes: Only a few miles have been covered on the Montana side, even though the road continues several more miles. There is not much of interest beyond Sullivan's Knob, so check the map and brochure for more details.

MM: 0.0 *GPS:* 44.84063/-108.33153 *Elev:* 3795 *Grid:* 39/4
US-14A *(see chapter)*   *Type:* Hwy Junction w/Chapter
Directions: E to Burgess Jct or W to Lovell from MM 49.2

MM: 9.6 (0.6/6.6) *GPS:* 44.95755/-108.29091 *Elev:* 3760 *Grid:* 39/1 *Land:* NPS
Bighorn Canyon National Recreation Area   *Type:* Recreation Area
Established in 1966 following the construction of the **Yellowtail Dam** by the **Bureau of Reclamation**. This dam on the **Bighorn River** created **Bighorn Lake**, which extends approximately 71 mi through **Wyoming** and **Montana**, 55 mi of which are contained within the spectacular **Bighorn Canyon**. The **Pryor Mountain Wild Horse Range** is located on the west side of the National Recreation Area.
Cool Rating: *** *Crowds:* * *[FEE AREA] Notes:* The National Parks annual pass can be used for entry.
Directions: Self-pay fee station on SE side of hwy

MM: 9.6 (0.6/6.5) *GPS:* 44.95859/-108.29073 *Elev:* 3748 *Grid:* 39/1 *Land:* NPS
Bighorn Canyon Ranger Station   *Type:* Visitor Center
Information and trail maps for **Bighorn Canyon National Recreation Area**.
Directions: NW side of hwy

MM: 9.7 (0.7/6.5) *GPS:* 44.95859/-108.28953 *Elev:* 3752 *Grid:* 39/1 *Land:* NPS
Sykes Mountain Trail   *Type:* Hiking Trail
A rugged hike up a desert mountain for views into **Bighorn Canyon** and **Horseshoe Bend**. Follow the trail around the hill to the first drainage, then follow a game trail and rock cairns to the overlook at about 1.3 mi. Turn around at the overlook or continue on a clockwise loop around **Crooked Creek Summit**, with the option of a short spur trail to the top for fine views of the **Bighorn Basin**. *Moderately strenuous; 2.6 to 4.0 mi round-trip; 700-800 ft elev gain.*
Cool Rating: **** *Crowds:* * *Time:* 1.5-2.5 hrs
Notes: Watch out for rattlesnakes. Best hiked in non-summer months or early or late in the day when it is not so hot. The morning is less windy with less chance of lightning. Take plenty of water.
Directions: Park at the Ranger Station on the NW side of the road. Cross the road and walk 90 yds NE to the trailhead.

MM: 9.8 (0.8/0.4) *Dist.* 1.3 *GPS.* 44.90188/-108.20007 *Elev.* 3681 *Grid:* 40/1 *Land:* NPS
RV Dump   *Type:* RV Dump
Directions: SE 1.3 mi; NE side of road just before the campground entrance.

MM: 9.8 (0.8/6.4) *Dist:* 1.5 *GPS:* 44.96252/-108.26441 *Elev:* 3720 *Grid:* 40/1 *Land:* NPS
Horseshoe Bend Campground   *Type:* Campground
A large campground with 3 loops in an open grass and sagebrush setting. Strong winds are common at this campground. Camping is **free** except for the sites with water and electricity that are marked "fee site." *No trees. Some sheltered picnic tables. Paved roads and gravel parking areas. 4 long pull-thrus. Flush toilets.*
Hours: Open year-round *Crowds:* * *[FEE AREA] Directions:* SE 1.4 mi; NE/L 0.1 mi.
Campsites: 59 *Shade:* * *Privacy:* * *RV Size:* 40'+ *Other:* Water,Electric,RVDump

MM: 9.8 (0.8/6.4) *Dist:* 1.6 *GPS:* 44.96350/-108.26131 *Elev:* 3758 *Grid:* 40/1 *Land:* NPS
Mouth of the Canyon Trail   *Type:* Hiking Trail
A hike along a 2-track road that climbs gradually to a colorful and scenic view 275 ft above a point where a side canyon, fed by **Crooked Creek**, joins with **Bighorn Lake**. This viewpoint is just north of the main body of **Bighorn Lake** as it enters the mouth of the steep walled canyon. From the overlook the trail continues west into a shallow ravine, then turns south creating a partial loop that reconnects with the main trail after 0.4 mi. This part of the trail is faint and only marked by a few signposts. It doesn't really offer anything of particular interest, so it is easier to simply return by the same route. *Moderately easy; 1.9 mi round-trip; 190 ft elev gain.*
Cool Rating: **** *Crowds:* * *Time:* 1 hr
Directions: SE 1.4 mi to campground turnoff; NE/L 0.15 mi to Loop B; Enter Loop B and take the first left 0.1 mi to the parking area; The trail starts 80 yds southeast.

MM: 9.8 (0.8/6.4) *Dist:* 1.6 *GPS:* 44.95871/-108.26250 *Elev:* 3670 *Grid:* 40/1 *Land:* NPS
Horseshoe Bend   *Type:* Recreation Area
The **Bighorn Lake** access area on the **Wyoming** side of **Bighorn Canyon National Recreation Area**, which includes a picnic area, playground, beach, volleyball, horseshoes, marina, boat ramp, boat docks, boat rentals, store, restaurant, gas, and propane.
Crowds: ** *Directions:* SE 1.6 mi to marina area

MM: 11.0 (2.0/5.2) *GPS:* 44.96950/-108.26795 *Elev:* 3670 *Grid:* 40/1 *Land:* NPS
Pryor Mountain Wild Horse Range   *Type:* Wildlife Area
The southern boundary of the **Pryor Mountain Wild Horse Range**. **Wild Horses** may sometimes be seen near the road. A signed pullout has detailed information about the wild horse range *(see next section)*.

MM: 12.3 (3.3/3.8) *GPS:* 44.98689/-108.26160 *Elev:* 3983 *Grid:* 40/0 *Land:* NPS
Pryor Mountain Wild Horse Range Sign   *Type:* Wildlife Area
3 signs with information on the **Pryor Mountain Wild Horse Range**.
Cool Rating: ** *Crowds:* * *Directions:* Pullout on W side of hwy

MM: 13.3 (4.3/2.8) *GPS:* 45.00009/-108.26459 *Elev:* 4305 *Grid:* 40/0
Montana State Line   *Type:* State Line

MM: 13.4 (4.4/2.8) *GPS:* 45.00094/-108.26557 *Elev:* 4315 *Grid:* 40/0 *Land:* NPS
State Line Trail   *Type:* Hiking Trail
A short hike to a view 800 ft above a sharp bend in **Bighorn Canyon**. A 0.3 mi trail north along the canyon rim connects to the **Ranger Delight Trail**. *Easy; 3/4 mi round-trip; 140 ft elev gain.*
Cool Rating: **** *Crowds:* * *Time:* 30-60 min *Notes:* The view is similar to that of the Ranger Delight Trail.
Directions: Small pullout on NE side of hwy

MM: 14.0 (5.0/2.2) *GPS:* 45.00903/-108.26861 *Elev:* 4446 *Grid:* 40/0 *Land:* NPS
Ranger Delight Trail   *Type:* Hiking Trail
A short hike to a view 800 ft above a sharp bend in **Bighorn Canyon**. At 1/4 mi a 0.3 mi trail south along the canyon rim connects to the **State Line Trail**. *Easy; 0.7 mi round-trip; 125 ft elev gain.*
Cool Rating: **** *Crowds:* * *Time:* 30-60 min *Notes:* The view is similar to that of the State Line Trail.
Directions: Large pullout on W side of hwy. The trail starts across the hwy from the south end of the pullout.

MM: 15.3 (6.3/0.8) *Dist:* 0.8 *GPS:* 45.02169/-108.25108 *Elev:* 4557 *Grid:* 40/-1 *Land:* NPS
Devil Canyon Overlook   *Type:* Scenic Area
An overlook situated on a point above a bend in **Bighorn Lake** where **Devil Canyon** joins **Bighorn Canyon**. The overlook offers views up and down **Bighorn Canyon** as well as into **Devil Canyon** where colorful canyon walls rise 900 ft above the lake. This is the only overlook that doesn't require hiking to the canyon rim. Several interpretive signs about the canyon geology and wildlife are located on both sides of the overlook.
Cool Rating: ***** *Crowds:* ** *Time:* 30 min *Directions:* E/R 0.8 mi to large parking area.

MM: 16.2 (7.2/0.0) *GPS:* 45.03610/-108.25653 *Elev:* 4382 *Grid:* 40/-1 *Land:* NPS
Sullivan's Knob Trail   *Type:* Hiking Trail
A loop road and parking area around **Sullivan's Knob**, a rock formation that looks like a giant anthill. A short hike leads to views into the **Bighorn Canyon**. *Easy; 3/4 mi round-trip; 140 ft elev loss.*
Cool Rating: **** *Crowds:* * *Time:* 30-60 min *Directions:* E side of hwy

MM: 0.0 **GPS:** 41.55540/-109.59076 **Elev:** 6443 **Grid:** 21/86

Wy-372   **Type:** Highway Description

48.6 mi highway from **I-80** exit 83 northwest to **US-189** MM 61.3. This is primarily a connecting road to **Wy-28** and **US-189** northbound. 3 BLM campgrounds are located near **Fontenelle Reservoir** 40.4 mi northwest. Highlights include: **Lombard/Mormon Ferry, Seedskadee National Wildlife Refuge.**
Nearest Town: Green River 6.5 E **Directions:** I-80 exit 83; NW to US-189 from MM 0

MM: 0.0 **GPS:** 41.55540/-109.59076 **Elev:** 6443 **Grid:** 21/86

I-80 *(see chapter)*   **Type:** Hwy Junction w/Chapter

403 mi interstate highway through southern **Wyoming** from **Utah** east to **Nebraska**. Highlights include: **Bear River State Park, Fort Bridger State Historic Site, Wyoming Frontier Prison, Fort Fred Steele, Wyoming Territorial Prison State Historic Site, Pole Mountain Trails, Curt Gowdy State Park, Vedauwoo Recreation Area,** and much more.
Directions: E to Rock Springs or W to Evanston from MM 83.0

MM: 26.8 **GPS:** 41.86803/-109.85848 **Elev:** 6309 **Grid:** 17/78

Wy-28 (Wy-372 to Farson) *(see chapter)*   **Type:** Hwy Junction w/Chapter

28.3 mi highway from **Wy-372** northeast to **Farson**. At the junction with **US-191**, **Wy-28** continues northeast toward **Lander**; however, the mile markers start over at 0.0. *See chapter: Wy-28 (Farson to US-287).* Highlights include: **Lombard/Mormon Ferry, Pilot Butte Emigrant Trails Interpretive Site, Simpson's Hollow.**
Nearest Town: Farson 28.3 NE **Directions:** NE to Farson from MM 100

MM: 26.8 **Dist:** 2.7 **GPS:** 41.87952/-109.80797 **Elev:** 6275 **Grid:** 18/78 **Land:** BLM

Lombard/Mormon Ferry   **Type:** Historic Site

A popular crossing point of the **Green River** where a ferry was first established by mountain men and then operated by the **Mormons** during the peak emigration years of the1850s. When the water level was low in late summer and early fall, many people would ford the river to avoid the ferry tolls. Unfortunately, some would attempt to ford when the current was too strong, often with disastrous results. The site includes 6 interpretive signs about this crossing point and a short paved trail to a replica of the ferry.
Cool Rating: ** **Crowds:** * **Time:** 20 min **Road Desc:** Gravel
Directions: NE on Wy-28 2.7 mi; SE 0.1 mi before the river bridge.

MM: 27.3 **Dist:** 2.4 **GPS:** 41.90548/-109.85112 **Elev:** 6315 **Grid:** 17/77 **Land:** Public Lands

Seedskadee National Wildlife Refuge   **Type:** Wildlife Area

A 26,400 acre wildlife refuge that protects riparian, wetland, and upland shrub habitats along 36 mi of the **Green River**. The refuge was established in 1965 as mitigation for the loss of habitat when **Fontenelle Dam** and **Flaming Gorge Dam** were constructed on the **Green River** above and below this area. The riparian corridor is an important migration route and nesting area for a wide variety of migratory waterfowl and passerine (perching) bird species.
Cool Rating: ** **Crowds:** * **Road Desc:** Gravel **Directions:** NE on Seedskadee Rd 2.4 mi to NWR headquarters.

MM: 40.4 **Dist:** 0.8 **GPS:** 41.98115/-110.04703 **Elev:** 6380 **Grid:** 14/75 **Land:** BLM

Slate Creek Campground   **Type:** Campground

A large dispersed camping area on the inside of a bend on the west side of the **Green River**. A handful of designated sites provide tables, fire rings, and grills; however, the area is huge with plenty of dispersed camping outside of the established sites. The campground is popular for ATVs. *Scattered cottonwoods. Native grass understory. Stone fire rings. Primitive float ramp. The campground is big enough to provide some distance between sites. Approximately 30 sites.*
Crowds: *** **Notes:** ATVs may be running around the campground at all hours of the day and evening. **Road Desc:** Gravel
Directions: At the sharp curve SW; NE on Fontenelle Townsite Rd/CR-311 0.8 mi
Campsites: Dispersed **Shade:** ** **Privacy:** ** **RV Size:** 40'+ **Other:** None

---

MM: 40.4 **Dist:** 5.3 **GPS:** 42.02476/-110.06113 **Elev:** 6404 **Grid:** 14/74 **Land:** BLM

Tailrace Campground   **Type:** Campground

A small campground along the **Green River** just below the spillway from **Fontenelle Dam**. A couple of sites have tables, fire rings, and grills. *Cottonwoods. Stone fire rings. Primitive float ramp. Approximately 10 sites.*
Crowds: * **Road Desc:** Gravel
Directions: At the sharp curve SW; NE on Fontenelle Townsite Rd/CR-311 0.9 mi (past Slate Creek Campground); Just across the river bridge NE/L on County Line Rd/CR-52; Follow signs 4.4 mi to campground.
Campsites: Dispersed **Shade:** *** **Privacy:** ** **RV Size:** 40' **Other:** None

---

MM: 40.4 **Dist:** 4.3 **GPS:** 42.02070/-110.04963 **Elev:** 6400 **Grid:** 14/74 **Land:** BLM

Weeping Rock Campground   **Type:** Campground

Below **Fontenelle Dam** southwest of a bend in the **Green River**. A handful of designated sites provide tables, fire rings, and grills. *Scattered cottonwoods. Native grass understory. Stone fire rings. Primitive float ramp. Approximately 20 sites.*
Crowds: ** **Road Desc:** Gravel
Directions: At the sharp curve SW; Continue N on Fontenelle North Rd/CR-316 2.9 mi; E/R 1.4 mi. **To continue N on US-189:** Return to CR-316; NW around curve, then W on Fontenelle Dam Rd/CR-313 4.0 mi.
Campsites: Dispersed **Shade:** ** **Privacy:** ** **RV Size:** 40'+ **Other:** None

---

MM: 48.6 **GPS:** 41.96807/-110.21309 **Elev:** 6895 **Grid:** 12/76

US-189 *(see chapter)*   **Type:** Hwy Junction w/Chapter

131.5 mi highway from **I-80** exit 18 north to the junctions with **US-189/191**, which heads northwest toward **Jackson**, and **US-191**, which heads east to **Pinedale**. Highlights include: **Names Hill, Father DeSmet Monument.**
Directions: N to La Barge or S to Kemmerer from MM 61.3

MM: 48.6 **GPS:** 41.96807/-110.21309 **Elev:** 6895 **Grid:** 12/76

End of Highway   **Type:** Highway End

48.6 mi highway from **US-189** MM 61.3 southeast to **I-80** exit 83. This is primarily a connecting road to **Wy-28** and **I-80** eastbound. 3 BLM campgrounds are located near **Fontenelle Reservoir** 8.2 mi east. Highlights include: **Seedskadee National Wildlife Refuge, Lombard/Mormon Ferry.**
Nearest Town: Kemmerer 24 SW **Directions:** SE to I-80 from MM 48.6

Wy-390/Moose-Wilson Rd   S/N

MM: 0.0 *GPS:* 43.49970/-110.84596 *Elev:* 6164 *Grid:* 3/38
Wy-390/Moose-Wilson Rd   *Type:* Highway Description
14.7 mi road from **Wy-22** north to **Teton Park Rd** in **Grand Teton National Park** at **Moose**. The mile markers for **Wy-390** end at the **Granite Canyon Entrance** to **Grand Teton National Park**, so the mile markers in the book are also shown as starting at zero at that point to allow the trip odometer to be reset. Highlights include: **Teton Village**, **Granite Canyon Trailhead**, **Laurance S. Rockefeller Preserve**, **Death Canyon Trailhead**.
Nearest Town: Wilson 1.4 W *Notes:* RVs and trailers are prohibited. *Directions:* N to Moose from MM 0
Road Desc: The road from the Grand Teton NP entrance station is mostly paved but narrow with no shoulders. A 1.4 mi section is dirt with potholes.

MM: 0.0 *GPS:* 43.49970/-110.84596 *Elev:* 6164 *Grid:* 3/38
Wy-22 *(see chapter)*   *Type:* Hwy Junction w/Chapter
17.7 mi highway from **Jackson** west over **Teton Pass** and northwest to **Idaho**. The highway transitions to **Id-33** in **Idaho**, which is the route to **Cave Falls** and **Bechler Falls** in **Yellowstone National Park**, **Upper Mesa Falls** and **Lower Mesa Falls** in **Idaho**, and ending at the west entrance of **Yellowstone National Park**. Other highlights include: hiking and biking around **Teton Pass**.
Directions: W to Wilson or E to Jackson from MM 4.1

MM: 6.7 *Dist:* 0.3 *GPS:* 43.58655/-110.82608 *Elev:* 6300 *Grid:* 3/35
Teton Village   *Type:* Town
A European-style village with restaurants, lodging, fuel, and shops at the base of **Rendezvous Mountain** in the **Teton Range**. This is the home of **Jackson Hole Mountain Resort**, the largest and most popular ski resort in **Wyoming**.

The most popular summer activity is riding the aerial tram, which can carry 100 passengers 4,139 vertical ft in 9 minutes to the top of **Rendezvous Mountain** at 10,450 ft elevation. The top of the mountain provides stunning views of the **Teton Range**, **Jackson**, and **Jackson Hole**, as well as hiking trails and tandem paragliding. One of the trails is a 12.4 mi loop down the mountain through **Granite Canyon** and returning to **Teton Village** on the **Valley Trail**.

Other summer activities at the village and on the lower mountain include hiking, mountain biking, fishing, horseback riding, a climbing wall, and a kid's camp. The **Teewinot Chairlift** to the lower mountain provides easy access to 7 mi of single track trails augmented with a dual track system that offers 15 different mountain bike trails.

It is free to park, walk around the village, and hike and bike from the bottom of the mountain; however, every other activity charges a fee.
Crowds: **** *[FEE AREA]* *Directions:* W 0.3 mi to parking area

MM: 7.8 (0.0/6.9) *GPS:* 43.59694/-110.80350 *Elev:* 6344 *Grid:* 4/35 *Land:* NPS
Grand Teton National Park - Granite Canyon Entrance   *Type:* National Park
Pay the National Park entrance fee that covers both **Grand Teton National Park** and **Yellowstone National Park**. *See chapter: Grand Teton National Park.*
[FEE AREA] *Notes:* No RVs or trailers through this entrance.
Road Desc: Partially paved. Heading north the road is narrow and paved except for a 1.4 mi hard-packed dirt section with some ruts and potholes.

MM: 8.6 (0.8/6.1) *GPS:* 43.60436/-110.79315 *Elev:* 6355 *Grid:* 4/35 *Land:* NPS
Pavement Ends (northbound)   *Type:* Pavement Change
1.4 mi section of hard-packed dirt with some ruts and potholes.

MM: 8.8 (1.0/5.9) *GPS:* 43.60737/-110.79293 *Elev:* 6386 *Grid:* 4/35 *Land:* NPS
Granite Canyon Trailhead   *Type:* Trailhead
A hike through **Granite Canyon**, a U-shaped canyon between **Rendezvous Mountain** on the south and **Mount Hunt** on the north. The first destination is the **Upper Granite Canyon Patrol Cabin**, which was built around 1935 by the **Civilian Conservation Corps** (CCC). At this point it is an additional 2.6 mi to **Marion Lake** at the end of the canyon or 5.2 mi to the aerial tramway at the top of **Rendezvous Mountain** (2,370 ft elev gain). A shorter option is hiking to the mouth of the canyon or partially up the canyon.
To the canyon: Moderately easy; 1.7 mi one-way; 200 ft elev gain. *To the patrol cabin:* Strenuous; 6.4 mi one-way; 1700 ft elev gain. *To Marion Lake:* Strenuous; 8.8 mi one-way; 2850 ft elev gain.
Cool Rating: *** *Crowds:* * *Directions:* W side of road
Road Desc: Partially paved, narrow. This is on a 1.4 mi section of hard-packed dirt with some ruts and potholes.

MM: 10.0 (2.2/4.8) *GPS:* 43.62316/-110.78680 *Elev:* 6467 *Grid:* 4/34 *Land:* NPS
Pavement Ends (southbound)   *Type:* Pavement Change
1.4 mi section of hard-packed dirt with some ruts and potholes.

MM: 11.0 (3.2/3.7) *Dist:* 0.3 *GPS:* 43.62725/-110.77311 *Elev:* 6405 *Grid:* 4/34 *Land:* NPS

Laurance S. Rockefeller Preserve   *Type:* Wildlife Area

Starting in 1927 **John D. Rockefeller, Jr.** purchased much of the land in **Jackson Hole** to be donated to the expansion of **Grand Teton National Park**. A small portion of this land was retained as a family retreat and named the **JY Ranch**. The ranch was passed down to **Laurance S. Rockefeller** who donated about 2/3 of the ranch to the National Park. The final 1,106 acres (1.7 sq mi) were donated in 2001 to become the **Laurance S. Rockefeller Preserve**. This donation came with the condition that the property should serve as a model of public use and enjoyment in balance with land conservation and environmental stewardship. Between 2004 and 2007 buildings, roads, and utilities were removed, native habitats were reclaimed, and equestrian trails were restored as pedestrian trails.

The Preserve includes the shoreline of the southern 2/3 of **Phelps Lake** and features 8 mi of trails through sagebrush meadows, forest, and wetlands. These trails provide access to **Phelps Lake** and views of the **Teton Range**. An easy 2.9 mi loop trail accesses the south end of **Phelps Lake**. A moderate 5.8 mi loop trail climbs up the ridges on the east and west side of the lake. A moderately easy 7.0 mi trail loops around the lake. A 1/3 mi trail provides an opportunity for visitors with limited mobility to experience the **Lake Creek** riparian community.

The **visitor center** contains a series of visual and audio experiences, including a large relief map of the area, a 4 screen high-definition video display of scenery and wildlife, a mural of **Phelps Lake** and the **Teton Range** made up of a mosaic of thousands of small nature pictures, a sound room with nature recordings from the preserve, and a walkway with recordings of **Laurance S. Rockefeller** speaking about the importance of conservation. On the west side of the center is a resource room where visitors can relax and learn about the preserve through books, albums, and maps.

The Preserve was designed with a limited amount of parking, thereby reducing congestion and providing an opportunity for solitude and reflection. The downside is that once the lot is full, visitors have to wait in line or come back at a later time. Early morning or late afternoon are the best times to visit.

The Preserve provides easy access to **Phelps Lake** as an alternative to driving on the high-clearance road to the **Death Canyon Trailhead** and taking a moderately strenuous 4.0 mi round-trip hike *(see next section)*.
Cool Rating: *** *Crowds:* ***** *Road Desc:* Gravel *Directions:* S 0.3 mi
Notes: I didn't personally find the visitor center itself worth sitting in line very long to see.

MM: 11.7 (3.9/3.0) *Dist:* 2.2 *GPS:* 43.64877/-110.76861 *GPS2:* 43.65600/-110.78135 *Elev:* 6793 *Grid:* 4/34 *Land:* NPS

Death Canyon Trailhead   *Type:* Trailhead

A hike through partial forest to a beautiful overlook of **Phelps Lake**, the fourth largest lake in the park. *Moderate; 0.9 mi one-way; 410 ft elev gain.* From the overlook the trail descends down switchbacks to **Phelps Lake**. *Moderate; 1.1 mi one-way (from the overlook); 570 ft elev loss.* At 0.7 mi along the descent to **Phelps Lake** is a junction with the **Death Canyon Trail**, which traverses the scenic **Death Canyon**, where the canyon walls rise over 2,500 ft. This hike ends at the **Death Canyon Patrol Cabin**, a small log structure built in the 1930s. *Strenuous; 2.1 mi one-way (from the trail jct); 1030 ft elev gain (1200 ft elev gain from Phelps Lake).* The entire hike to **Phelps Lake** and **Death Canyon** is 8.2 mi round-trip.
Cool Rating: **** *Crowds:* ***** *Time:* 1-5 hrs
Notes: No RVs or trailers. Although the road is rough and 4WD is recommended by the park, plenty of sedans were seen in all parking areas. Phelps Lake can also be reached from the Laurance S. Rockefeller Preserve *(see previous section)*.
Road Desc: Dirt, rough & potholed, narrow, high clearance. First 0.6 mi is paved.
Directions: N on Whitegrass Ranch Rd 0.6 mi; NW/l 1.6 mi; There are several parking areas for this trailhead. The first is the Whitegrass Ranch Trailhead at 1.1 mi and might be the best for low clearance vehicles. A medium size parking area is located at 1.5 mi (with a picnic table) and the larger trailhead parking at 1.6 mi (with a vault toilet). 4 small parking areas are interspersed between the larger areas.

MM: 14.7 (6.9/0.0) *GPS:* 43.65635/-110.71891 *Elev:* 6455 *Grid:* 5/34

Moose *Type:* Town

MM: 14.7 (6.9/0.0) *GPS:* 43.65635/-110.71891 *Elev:* 6455 *Grid:* 5/34

Teton Park Rd: Grand Teton National Park *(see chapter)*   *Type:* Hwy Junction w/Chapter

20.8 mi road north through the main section of **Grand Teton National Park**, which traverses the central-eastern base of the **Teton Range** and offers the closest access and views. Highlights include: the **Craig Thomas Discovery and Visitor Center**, **Chapel of the Transfiguration and Menor's Ferry Historic District**, **Jenny Lake**, **Hidden Falls**, **Inspiration Point**, **Signal Mountain**, **Jackson Lake**.
Directions: NW to Jenny Lake or SE to Moose from MM 0.7

MM: 14.7 (6.9/0.0) *GPS:* 43.65635/-110.71891 *Elev:* 6455 *Grid:* 5/34 *Land:* NPS

Moose-Wilson Rd/Wy-390   *Type:* Highway End

14.7 mi road from **Teton Park Rd** in **Grand Teton National Park**, at **Moose**, south to **Wy-22**, 1.4 mi east of **Wilson**. The mile markers don't start for **Wy-390** until leaving **Grand Teton National Park** at the **Granite Canyon Entrance**, so set the trip odometer to zero at **Teton Park Rd** and use the mile markers in parenthesis. Highlights include: **Death Canyon Trailhead**, **Laurance S. Rockefeller Preserve**, **Granite Canyon Trailhead**, **Teton Village**.
Directions: S to Wy-22, 1.4 mi E of Wilson, from MM 14.7

Wy-70   SW/NE

MM: 0.0 *GPS:* 41.03418/-107.65780 *Elev:* 6246 *Grid:* 49/99
Wy-70   *Type:* Highway Description
57.7 mi highway in south-central **Wyoming**, just north of **Colorado**, from **Wy-789** at **Baggs** northeast to **Riverside**. Most of the highway runs through the **Sierra Madre Mountains** in the **Medicine Bow National Forest** and provides abundant OHV roads and dispersed camping opportunities. Highlights include: **Aspen Alley**, **Dillon** and **Rudefeha Ghost Towns**, **Green Mountain Falls**, **Grand Encampment Museum**.
Directions: E to Encampment from MM 0

MM: 0.0 *GPS:* 41.03418/-107.65780 *Elev:* 6246 *Grid:* 49/99
Baggs   *Type:* Town

MM: 32.4 *Dist:* 2.2 *GPS:* 41.09382/-107.16004 *Elev:* 7300 *Grid:* 56/98 *Land:* NF
Battle Creek Campground   *Type:* Campground
Along **West Fork Battle Creek** at the end of a valley on the western base of the **Sierra Madre Mountains**. *Cottonwoods. Tables. Fire rings. Vault toilet.*
Crowds: *** *Road Desc:* The narrow, steep and winding gravel road descends 1,000 ft.
Notes: There is a nice camping area 0.1 mi along FR-807. With all of the dispersed camping possibilities along Wy-70, it may not be worth the drive down this steep road for an overnight campground.
Directions: E then S on FR-807 2.2 mi
Campsites: 3 *Shade:* *** *Privacy:* *** *RV Size:* 30' *Other:* None

MM: 32.8 *GPS:* 41.11867/-107.15783 *Elev:* 8330 *Grid:* 56/97
Wy-71   *Type:* Highway Junction
54.8 mi route from **Wy-70** north to **Rawlins** at **I-80** crossing **National Forest** and **BLM** lands and losing 1,560 ft in elevation. The lone highlight is **Aspen Alley**, which is just north *(see next section)*, so the primary purpose of this route is saving 30 mi over driving the paved highways through **Saratoga**. 2 free campgrounds are located along this route: **Little Sandstone Campground** at 2.4 mi and **Teton Reservoir Recreation Site** at 40.2 mi.
Directions: NE on FR-801/CR-401/Wy-71 54.8 mi
Road Desc: The first 30.2 mi is gravel with washboard sections. The last 24.6 mi is paved with some of the pavement being rough and bumpy.

MM: 32.8 *Dist:* 0.8 *GPS:* 41.12549/-107.16818 *Elev:* 8104 *Grid:* 56/97 *Land:* NF
Aspen Alley   *Type:* Scenic Area
50+ ft tall aspen trees line both sides of the narrow road for about 1/3 mi forming an "alley" and even a canopy in places. This highly photographed location is particularly beautiful in the fall when the leaves turn.
Cool Rating: *** *Crowds:* * *Time:* 15 min *Road Desc:* Gravel *Directions:* NE on FR-801 0.8 mi

MM: 32.8 *Dist:* 2.4 *GPS:* 41.14011/-107.18841 *Elev:* 7925 *Grid:* 55/96 *Land:* NF
Little Sandstone Campground   *Type:* Campground
Primitive camping in a native grassed area with room for about 6-10 camps. *Almost all of the scattered pine trees are beetle-killed. Some stone fire rings. Level. No toilet.*
Crowds: * *Road Desc:* Gravel *Directions:* NE on FR-801 2.4 mi
Campsites: Dispersed *Shade:* ** *Privacy:* ** *RV Size:* 40' *Other:* None

MM: 35.5 *Dist:* 3.1 *GPS:* 41.14323/-107.12236 *GPS2:* 41.17714/-107.09233 *Elev:* 8376 *Grid:* 56/96 *Land:* NF
Dillon Ghost Town & Rudefeha Ghost Town   *Type:* Historic Site
2 worn-out signs provide information about the **Rudefeha Mine** (later renamed **Ferris-Haggarty Mine**) and the **Ferris-Haggarty Tramway**. The mine operated from 1898 to 1908 and was the major development in the region. **FR-862** parallels **Haggarty Creek** northeast and climbs through a valley 3.1 mi to the **Dillon Ghost Town** (700 ft elev gain) and about another 1.4 mi to the **Rudefeha Ghost Town** (1,400 ft elev gain). Many building foundations still remain. The mine itself is on private property, so don't trespass.
Cool Rating: *** *Crowds:* * *Time:* 5 min - 2 hrs *Road Desc:* Dirt, rough & impassable when wet, narrow, 4WD
Notes: FR-862 is better for OHVs. The beginning of the road crosses private property and had a closed gate in 2011.
Directions: Signs on N side of hwy. Ghost towns N on FR-862 3.1 mi to Dillon and 4.5 mi to Rudefeha.

MM: 37.9 *GPS:* 41.14091/-107.07943 *Elev:* 8710 *Grid:* 57/96 *Land:* NF
Lost Creek Campground   *Type:* Campground
Lost Creek flows nearby with **Baby Lake Trail** to the **Huston Park Wilderness** across from the campground. The sites are spread along a road and a teardrop loop. Many sites are in the open with tables in the tall grass. *Mixed forest. Good spacing between sites. Grass understory. Some sites are in the open. 1 pull-thru.*
Crowds: ** *[FEE AREA]* *Directions:* N side of hwy
Campsites: 13 *Shade:* ** *Privacy:* *** *RV Size:* 30' *Other:* Water

MM: 42.4 *GPS:* 41.15870/-107.01000 *Elev:* 9485 *Grid:* 58/96 *Land:* NF
Battle Lake Overlook & Thomas Edison Monument   *Type:* Scenic Viewpoint
A scenic overlook of **Battle Lake** located in the beautiful valley below. Also at the pullout is a plaque stating that **Thomas Edison** was camping near this spot in 1878 when his attention was directed to the fiber from his bamboo fishing pole, which he tested as a suitable filament for his incandescent electric lamp.
Cool Rating: *** *Crowds:* * *Time:* 10 min *Directions:* Pullout on S side of hwy

MM: 44.7 *GPS:* 41.15626/-106.98171 *Elev:* 9939 *Grid:* 58/96 *Land:* NF
Continental Divide Overlook   *Type:* Scenic Viewpoint
A loop pullout with views of the **Sierra Madre Mountains**. There is a hill above the parking area that offers a view to the west that is actually better than the official viewpoint. *Vault toilet.*
Directions: E side of hwy

MM: 50.7 **Dist:** 0.3 **GPS:** 41.17493/-106.89850 **Elev:** 8684 **Grid:** 59/96 **Land:** NF
Bottle Creek Campground   Type: Campground
Bottle Creek flows through a canyon south of the campground. The shade has been diminished by beetle-killed trees, which have been removed. A short path leads to an unspectacular view of the beetle-killed forest from the **Memorial Overlook**. *Good spacing between sites. Reservable group picnic site.*
Crowds: *** **[FEE AREA] Road Desc:** Gravel **Directions:** S on Hog Park Rd/FR-550 0.1 mi; W/R 0.2 mi.
Campsites: 12 **Shade:** *** **Privacy:** ** **RV Size:** 40' **Other:** Water

MM: 50.7 **Dist:** 2.0 **GPS:** 41.16003/-106.89119 **GPS2:** 41.13893/-106.93520 **Elev:** 8210 **Grid:** 59/96 **Land:** NF
Green Mountain Falls   Type: Waterfall
A hike southwest along the **North Fork Encampment River** through a conifer and aspen forest to a beautiful series of tumbling cascades that flow along a channel cut through a long stretch of slickrock. The falls flow out of a side canyon into the **North Fork Encampment River**. The best view of the falls is from the top, and a complete front view of the falls is difficult. The location is out of the way and receives only a modest amount of traffic. It is 2.0 mi from the parking area to the trailhead (41.14951/-106.92141) along a narrow and bumpy forest road with a 300 ft elevation gain. The falls are 1.2 mi from the trailhead on what starts out as a fairly level hiking path. The trail then climbs gradually 200 ft to a river bridge before a short, steep climb to the top of the falls. The main trail continues past this point into the **Huston Park Wilderness** area, where bicycles are not permitted. *From parking area: Moderate; 3.2 mi one-way; 580 ft elev gain. From trailhead: Moderately easy; 1.2 mi one-way; 280 ft elev gain.*
Cool Rating: **** **Crowds:** ** **Time:** 2-4 hrs **Road Desc:** Gravel
Notes: Small 4WD vehicles, OHVs, and bicycles can drive/ride the forest road to the trailhead. Bicycles can continue to the falls; however, continuing all the way to the falls may require walking the bike in places, so it might be best to walk the last half mile or so. Riding the road back to the parking area on a bicycle is fun.
Directions: S on Hog Park Rd/FR-550 2.0 mi; W/R into parking area.

MM: 56.1 **Dist:** 1.6 **GPS:** 41.18421/-106.79708 **Elev:** 7225 **Grid:** 61/95 **Land:** BLM
Encampment River Campground   Type: Campground
Located along the **Encampment River** in the foothills of the **Sierra Madre Mountains**. The first 3 sites are located in a small loop at the entrance and are not as shady as the other 5, which are shaded by large trees. The **Encampment River Trail** starts at the bridge at the end of the campground and travels 16 mi into the mountains and the **Encampment River Wilderness**. *Level.*
Crowds: *** **[FEE AREA] Notes:** Steepness of the gravel road may make it difficult to get out when wet.
Road Desc: Gravel. 300 ft elevation drop. **Directions:** S on CR-353 0.7 mi; Keep left onto BLM-3407 0.9 mi.
Campsites: 8 **Shade:** **** **Privacy:** *** **RV Size:** 40'+ **Other:** Water

MM: 56.8 **GPS:** 41.20664/-106.79174 **Elev:** 7318 **Grid:** 61/95
Encampment   Type: Town

MM: 56.8 **Dist:** 0.2 **GPS:** 41.20505/-106.78845 **Elev:** 7304 **Grid:** 61/95 **Land:** City
Grandview Park   Type: Park
A sheltered picnic area and playground next to the **Grand Encampment Museum**.
Directions: In the center of town; SE on 6th St 3 blocks to Barnett Ave.

MM: 56.8 **Dist:** 0.3 **GPS:** 41.20396/-106.78929 **Elev:** 7322 **Grid:** 61/95 **Land:** City
Grand Encampment Museum   Type: Museum
In the late 1890s, **Grand Encampment** was a rich copper mining town. However, in 1908 the mine was shut down over questionable bookkeeping and fraudulent stock sales. The towns of **Encampment** ("Grand" was dropped) and **Riverside** survived, but the smaller surrounding towns became ghost towns. This museum captures some of this history with displays in the main **"Doc" Culleton Building** plus a collection of over a dozen historic buildings filled with artifacts representing the timber, mining, and agricultural history of the **Encampment River Valley**. Outside are several items of interest, including a lookout tower and a segment of the aerial tramway that supplied the smelter. Some of the more unusual exhibits include a two-story outhouse, folding oak bathtub, and a square grand piano.
Hours: 10am - 5pm, Mon-Sat; 1pm - 5pm, Sun (Memorial Day - Sept and weekends in Oct) **Phone:** 307-327-5308
Cool Rating: *** **Crowds:** ** **Time:** 1-2 hrs **Road Desc:** Gravel
Directions: In the center of town; SE on 6th St 3 blocks; SW/R 1 block on Barnett Ave.

MM: 57.1 **Dist:** 0.2 **GPS:** 41.21122/-106.79213 **Elev:** 7287 **Grid:** 61/95 **Land:** City
Encampment RV Campground   Type: Campground
A street-corner lot with a natural landscape of dirt, grass, and weeds. Sites are lined up in parallel with a medium-sized tree between each site. A donation box is located at the site. *Some picnic tables.*
Crowds: *** **Road Desc:** Gravel
Directions: NE corner of town; NW on 4th St 0.2 mi (3 blocks) to Winchell Ave; Right side of road.
Campsites: 7 **Shade:** * **Privacy:** * **RV Size:** 40' **Other:** Water,Electric

MM: 57.7 **GPS:** 41.21738/-106.78231 **Elev:** 7165 **Grid:** 61/95
Riverside   Type: Town

MM: 57.7 **GPS:** 41.21700/-106.78302 **Elev:** 7171 **Grid:** 61/95 **Land:** City
Carbon County Visitor Center   Type: Visitor Center
A small staffed visitor center.
Hours: 6am - 7pm **Phone:** 307-327-5600 **Directions:** SW corner of Wy-70 and Wy-230 junction.

MM: 57.7 **Dist:** 1.8 **GPS:** 41.20443/-106.76478 **GPS2:** 41.20356/-106.77217 **Elev:** 7343 **Grid:** 61/95
Indian Bathtubs   Type: Point of Interest
The **Encampment River Valley** was a gathering place for Indian tribes in the 1800s as they hunted during the summer months. To the east of the **Encampment River** is a granite outcrop with deep holes that fill with water and act as natural bathtubs. A 1/2 mi trail leads west to the site across sagebrush flats for 1/4 mi before dropping in and out of a tree-lined ravine crossing **Cottonwood Creek**.
Cool Rating: *** **Crowds:** * **Time:** 1 hr **Notes:** The section of trail into the ravine is steep and rocky.
Road Desc: Gravel
Directions: E on Wy-230 0.9 mi; S on Blackhall Mountain Rd 0.9 mi; Parking area on W side of road.

MM: 57.7   *GPS:* 41.21738/-106.78231   *Elev:* 7165   *Grid:* 61/95
Wy-130/Wy-230 (Walcott to Riverside) *(see chapter)*   *Type:* Hwy Junction w/Chapter
38.2 mi highway from **Riverside** north to **Walcott**. The highway transitions from **Wy-230** to **Wy-130** at MM 28.3 (the junction with Wy-130 east) and the mile markers continue sequentially north on **Wy-130**. Highlights include: **Hobo Hot Pool**, **Saratoga National Fish Hatchery**.
Directions: N to Saratoga from MM 38.2

MM: 57.7   *GPS:* 41.21738/-106.78231   *Elev:* 7165   *Grid:* 61/95
Wy-230 (Riverside to Colorado) *(see chapter)*   *Type:* Hwy Junction w/Chapter
27.1 mi highway from **Riverside** southeast to **Colorado**. The highway is a continuation of **Wy-130/Wy-230 (Walcott to Riverside)** from the north; however, the highway turns to the east and the mile markers do not continue sequentially. Highlights include: **Indian Bathtubs**, **Platte River Trail**.
Directions: E then SE to Colorado from MM 100

MM: 57.7   *GPS:* 41.21738/-106.78231   *Elev:* 7165   *Grid:* 61/95
End of Highway   *Type:* Highway End
57.7 mi highway in south-central **Wyoming**, just north of **Colorado**, from **Riverside** southwest to **Baggs**. Most of the highway runs through the **Sierra Madre Mountains** in the **Medicine Bow National Forest** and provides abundant OHV roads and dispersed camping opportunities. Highlights include: **Grand Encampment Museum**, **Green Mountain Falls**, **Dillon** and **Rudefeha Ghost Towns**, **Aspen Alley**.
Directions: SW to Encampment from MM 57.7

MM: 81.1 *GPS:* 42.83107/-108.72393 *Elev:* 5384 *Grid:* 33/54
Wy-789 & US-26/Wy-789   *Type:* Highway Description
46.2 mi highway from **Lander** northeast to **Shoshoni**. The highway heads northeast from **Lander** as **Wy-789** continuing the mile markers from **US-287/Wy-789**. After 24.1 mi the highway combines with **US-26** and continues northeast 22.1 mi to **Shoshoni** as **US-26/Wy-789**. Highlights include: access to **Castle Gardens**, **Wyoming Heritage Trail**.
Directions: NE to Riverton from MM 81.1

MM: 81.1 *GPS:* 42.83107/-108.72393 *Elev:* 5384 *Grid:* 33/54
US-287/Wy-789 *(see chapter)*   *Type:* Hwy Junction w/Chapter
125 mi highway from **Lander** southeast to **Rawlins** near **I-80**. Highlights include: **Green Mountain**, **Split Rock**.
Directions: SE to Rawlins from MM 81.1

MM: 81.1 *GPS:* 42.83107/-108.72393 *Elev:* 5384 *Grid:* 33/54
US-287 (Lander to US-26) *(see chapter)*   *Type:* Hwy Junction w/Chapter
31.6 mi highway northwest from **Lander** to **US-26**. The highway transitions from **US-287/Wy-789**; however, the mile markers start at MM 0. Highlights include: **Sacajawea's Grave**.
Directions: NW to Fort Washaki from MM 0

MM: 81.1 *GPS:* 42.83107/-108.72393 *Elev:* 5384 *Grid:* 33/54
Lander   *Type:* Town

MM: 103.8 *GPS:* 43.00611/-108.37826 *Elev:* 4923 *Grid:* 38/50
Wy-135/136 *(see chapter)*   *Type:* Hwy Junction w/Chapter
35.6 mi highway from **Wy-789**, just south of **Riverton**, southeast to **US-287/Wy-789**, which heads southeast to **Rawlins**. The route starts as **Wy-136** for 1.0 mi before transitioning to **Wy-135**. The landscape is prairie and badlands with no towns or services along the way. This highway saves 24.5 mi over driving through **Lander**. Highlights include: **Badlands Scenic Overlook**.
Nearest Town: Riverton 2.5 N *Directions:* SE on Wy-136 1.0 mi; Continue S on Wy-135.

MM: 103.8 *Dist:* 49.5 *GPS:* 42.93109/-107.61748 *Elev:* 6131 *Grid:* 49/52 *Land:* BLM
Castle Gardens   *Type:* Scenic Area
Cliffs and outcroppings of colorful eroded sandstone that resemble the towers of a castle. The cliffs and hills form a small valley of rock outcrops and boulders in colorful soil dotted with juniper and pine trees. Along the northern cliffs is a fenced in area with **Petroglyphs** that are done in the regional **Castle Gardens Shield Style**, the oldest recognizable example of shields and shield-bearing warrior figures. After viewing the **Petroglyphs** spend some time walking around this beautiful area, which is particularly nice in the evening. Although no official campsites are provided, you can camp along the road or in the parking area. This is the second **Castle Gardens** in **Wyoming**, the other being off **US-16** about 70 mi north.
Cool Rating: ***** *Crowds:* * *Time:* 1-2 hrs
Road Desc: Gravel, impassable when wet. The BLM road is dirt and not as well-maintained.
Directions: SE on Wy-136 1.0 mi; E/L to continue on Wy-136 36.3 mi; N on CR-459/Castle Gardens Rd 6.3 mi; E/R at BLM sign on BLM-2107 5.9 mi. *If continuing north to US-20/26 see US-20/26 MM 78.5 and reverse directions.*

MM: 105.2 *GPS:* 43.02463/-108.38063 *Elev:* 4952 *Grid:* 38/49
Riverton   *Type:* Town

MM: 105.2 *GPS:* 43.02463/-108.38063 *Elev:* 4952 *Grid:* 38/49
US-26/287 & US-26 *(see chapter)*   *Type:* Hwy Junction w/Chapter
133.7 mi highway from **Riverton** northwest to **Moran Jct**. **US-26** merges with **US-287 (Lander to US-26)** at MM 98.8 and continues northwest as **US-26/287**. This is a primary access route to **Grand Teton National Park** and **Yellowstone National Park**. Heading northwest between **Dubois** and **Moran Jct** is along the **Centennial Scenic Byway**. Highlights include: **Trail Lake Rd Petroglyphs**, colorful badlands, **Dubois Recreation Area Scenic Overlook**, **Brooks Lake**, **Brooks Lake Creek Falls**, **Pinnacle Buttes**, **Wind River Lake**, **Breccia Cliffs**.
Directions: NW to Dubois from MM 133.7

MM: 105.7 *GPS:* 43.03292/-108.38183 *GPS2:* 43.23275/-108.11818 *Elev:* 4964 *Grid:* 38/49
Wyoming Heritage Trail (southwest access)   *Type:* Trailhead
This **"Rails to Trails"** trail runs 22.8 mi from the **Wind River** in southwest **Riverton** (43.01306/-108.40197) northeast to **Shoshoni**, where the trail ends at **Shoshoni City Park** *(see GPS2 and MM 127)*. The path through **Riverton** is a paved walking and biking trail for 3.7 mi. The pavement ends and turns to gravel northeast of town where the trail follows a former railroad bed for the final 19.1 mi. This section of the trail can be used by OHVs. A good parking area in **Riverton** is at the north center of town at (MI 1.6). From this parking area the trail is paved for 2.1 mi before turning to gravel. The trail crosses a large historic truss bridge over the **Wind River** (MI 7.1) that makes a good destination for a nice 11 mi round-trip bike ride from the parking area. Continuing 3.2 mi past the bridge you will again reach the river and a break in the trail that requires a short steep climb up and over a hill (MI 10.3). From here the landscape turns primarily to rolling sagebrush prairie. At (MI 14.4) the trail crosses a large sand wash that is fun to ride in on an ATV. Heading northwest in this wash 1/4 mi leads to the edge of the **Wind River**.
Cool Rating: *** *Crowds:* * *Time:* 2-10 hrs
Notes: The **Riverton** end of the trail is more accommodating for walking and bicycling, whereas the **Shoshoni** end is probably better for OHV usage.
Directions: The turnoff is about halfway between E Pershing Ave to the south and E Sunset Dr to the north, opposite the intersection with Forest Dr. This is the parking lot for the Riverton city building, where a sign on the street reads "City of Riverton". W through the parking lot and keep right into a dirt parking area next to the Police station.

MM: 119.0 *GPS:* 43.18553/-108.24585 *Elev:* 4895 *Grid:* 40/45
Wy-134 & Wy-133 *(see chapter)*   *Type:* Hwy Junction w/Chapter
28.3 mi on 2 highways from **US-26/Wy-789** west and south to **US-26**, which heads northwest to **Dubois**. If traveling west between **Shoshoni** and **Dubois**, this route is 4.7 mi shorter than continuing through **Riverton** and offers 3 primitive campgrounds on the north side of **Ocean Lake**.
Nearest Town: Shoshoni 8.3 NE *Directions:* W on Wy-134 24.2 mi; S on Wy-133 4.1 mi.

MM: 121.8 *Dist:* 0.5 *GPS:* 43.22276/-108.21966 *Elev:* 4774 *Grid:* 40/44 *Land:* State
West Shoreline Drive: Boysen State Park   *Type:* Campground
Located on the west side of **Boysen Reservoir** with 2 loops that contain several small camping areas with close access to the lake. **Fremont Bay** and **Cottonwood Bay** have drinking water, a boat ramp, and a reservable group picnic shelter. The rest of the sites are primitive with few shade trees.
<u>Loop 1</u> - 9.3 mi loop that reconnects to **Bass Lake Rd** with 3 camping areas: **Fremont Bay** (MI 3.4), **Sandy Hills** (MI 4.7), and **South Muddy** (MI 5.2). *Approximately 20 sites.*
<u>Loop 2</u> - 13.4 mi loop that starts from **Bass Lake Rd** (MI 8.7), just north of the end of **Loop 1** (MI 8.4), and reconnects with **Bass Lake Rd** (MI 11.6). The loop begins with 2 free camping areas at **Lake Cameahwait**. The first is located on the south shore and just north of the road (MI 2.5). The second is located on the east shore 0.5 mi north of the turnoff (MI 3.1). Continuing into the state park are 4 camping areas: **North Muddy** (MI 4.2), **Sand Mesa** (MI 7.1), **Trout Bay** (MI 7.7), and **Cottonwood Bay** (MI 10.1). *Approximately 30 sites.*
Crowds: * *[FEE AREA]* *Road Desc:* Partially paved
Directions: NW on Bass Lake Rd 0.5 mi; N on West Shore Dr for Loop 1; Continue on Bass Lake Rd 8.7 mi to Loop 2.
Campsites: 50 *Shade:* * *Privacy:* * *RV Size:* 30' *Other:* Water

MM: 123.6 *GPS:* 43.21884/-108.17923 *Elev:* 4747 *Grid:* 41/45 *Land:* State
Lakeside Day Use Area: Boysen State Park   *Type:* Day Use Area
Day use area at the southern end of **Boysen State Park** with a picnic area, group shelter, and boat ramp.
Crowds: ** *[FEE AREA]* *Directions:* Just E of the bridge over Boysen Reservoir. N side of hwy.

MM: 125.8 *Dist:* 1.9 *GPS:* 43.24698/-108.16213 *Elev:* 4740 *Grid:* 41/44 *Land:* State
Poison Creek Campground: Boysen State Park   *Type:* Campground/Day Use Area
Primitive camping just south of the inlet of **Poison Creek** to the southeast end of **Boysen Reservoir**. *A few trees. Vault toilet. Stone fire rings.*
Crowds: * *[FEE AREA]* *Road Desc:* Gravel *Directions:* NW 1.3 mi; N/R 0.6 mi.
Campsites: Dispersed *Shade:* * *Privacy:* * *RV Size:* 40' *Other:* None

MM: 127.0 *Dist:* 0.1 *GPS:* 43.23361/-108.11710 *Elev:* 4826 *Grid:* 42/44 *Land:* City
Shoshoni City Park   *Type:* Park
A city park with a few shade trees, sheltered picnic tables, a restroom, and a playground. The north end of the **Wyoming Heritage Trail** starts just south of the park. Camping is permitted at the southwest end of the park.
Crowds: * *Directions:* On the west end of Shoshoni; S on Maple St 2 blocks.
Campsites: Dispersed *Shade:* * *Privacy:* * *RV Size:* 40' *Other:* Water

MM: 127.0 *Dist:* 0.2 *GPS:* 43.23275/-108.11818 *Elev:* 4824 *Grid:* 42/44
Wyoming Heritage Trail (northeast access)   *Type:* Trailhead
This **"Rails to Trails"** trail runs 22.8 mi from **Shoshoni** southwest to **Riverton** *(see MM 105.7)*, where the trail ends at the **Wind River** (43.01306/-108.40197). The gravel trail follows a former railroad bed for 19.1 mi before changing to a paved walking and biking trail for the final 3.7 mi through **Riverton**. The gravel section of the trail can be used by OHVs. The first 12.3 mi from **Shoshoni** is primarily rolling sagebrush prairie, but becomes more vegetated upon reaching the river. At (MI 8.4) the trail crosses a large sand wash that is fun to ride in on an ATV. Heading northwest in this wash 1/4 mi leads to the edge of the **Wind River**. Upon reaching the Wind River at (MI 12.3), you will reach a break in the trail that requires a short steep climb up and over a hill. The trail crosses several old bridges including a large historic truss bridge over the **Wind River** at (MI 15.7). You can continue another 3.4 mi on an OHV or continue into **Riverton** on a bicycle.
Cool Rating: *** *Crowds:* * *Time:* 2-10 hrs
Notes: The **Shoshoni** end of the trail is more accommodating to OHVs, whereas the **Riverton** end is best for walking and bicycling,
Directions: On the west end of Shoshoni; S on Maple St 3 blocks to the south end of City Park. The trail starts just south of the park.

MM: 127.3 *GPS:* 43.23552/-108.11071 *Elev:* 4841 *Grid:* 42/44
Shoshoni   *Type:* Town

MM: 127.3 *GPS:* 43.23552/-108.11071 *Elev:* 4841 *Grid:* 42/44
US-20/Wy-789 & US-16/20/Wy-789 & US-14/16/20/Wy-789 *(see chapter)*   *Type:* Hwy Junction w/Chapter
157 mi highway from **Shoshoni** north to **Montana**. Highlights include: **Boysen State Park**, **Wind River Canyon**, **Hot Springs State Park**, **Medicine Lodge State Archaeological Site**, **Devil's Kitchen Geological Site**, **Museum of Flight and Aerial Firefighting**.
Directions: N to Thermopolis from MM 100

MM: 127.3 *GPS:* 43.23552/-108.11071 *Elev:* 4841 *Grid:* 42/44
US-20/26 *(see chapter)*   *Type:* Hwy Transition w/Chapter
96.9 mi highway from **Shoshoni** southeast to **Casper**. Highlights include: **Castle Gardens**, **Hole-in-the-Wall**, **Hell's Half Acre**.
Directions: Continue straight to head SE to Casper from MM 100

MM: 127.3 *GPS:* 43.23552/-108.11071 *Elev:* 4841 *Grid:* 42/44
US-26/Wy-789 & Wy-789   *Type:* Highway End
46.2 mi highway from **Shoshoni** southwest to **Lander**. The highway heads southwest from **Shoshoni** as **US-26/Wy-789**. After 22.1 mi **US-26** heads northwest and the highway continues 24.1 mi to **Lander** as **Wy-789**. Highlights include: **Wyoming Heritage Trail**, access to **Castle Gardens**.
Directions: SW to Riverton from MM 127.3

Yellowstone National Park

History
Indigenous people have lived in the Yellowstone area for thousands of years. However, the area was unknown to the new Americans until **Lewis and Clark Expedition** member **John Colter** split away from the party on the return trip from the northwest and visited the area in 1806. Colter returned with stories of "fire and brimstone," which few people believed, so the area became cynically known as "**Colter's Hell**." However, a few people did believe him and the area was subsequently visited by mountain men during the early to mid 1800s. The **Civil War** distracted from further exploration until the first organized and privately funded exploration by the **Cook-Folsom-Peterson Expedition** of 1869. This was followed by the **Washburn-Langford-Doane Expedition** in 1870. In 1871 the government finally sent its own team of explorers led by **Ferdinand V. Hayden** and including photographer **William H. Jackson** and artist **Thomas Moran**. Upon their return they verified all of the previous accounts of this spectacular area and Hayden joined with Washburn, Doane, and Langford in lobbying Congress to preserve Yellowstone from future development. Congress eventually passed the **Yellowstone Park Bill**, which **President Ulysses S. Grant** signed on March 1, 1872, making **Yellowstone** the nation's first National Park. Although the park had been created, it was not protected from poaching, vandalism, souvenir collecting, and forest fires. In 1886 the **U.S. Army** was sent to Yellowstone to protect the park. **Fort Yellowstone** was built in 1891 and occupied until 1913 when Yellowstone was turned over to the **National Park Service**.

Geography and Geology
Yellowstone is the second largest National Park in the continental U.S. behind **Death Valley National Park**. The park is roughly 63 mi north to south and 54 mi east to west, with an area of 3,472 sq mi, making it larger than the states of **Rhode Island** and **Delaware** combined. The majority of the park is located in **Wyoming**, although it extends slightly into **Montana** and **Idaho**. The elevations range from 5,314 ft near the north entrance's sagebrush flats to 11,358 ft at the summit of **Eagle Peak**, part of the **Absaroka Range** on the southeast edge of the park. The average elevation is 8,000 ft.

Yellowstone is best known for **Old Faithful Geyser** and its other geothermal features. The park contains over half of the world's geothermal features, including over 10,000 geysers and hot springs, colorful hot pools, hot lakes, mudpots, steam vents, fumaroles, and travertine terraces and mounds. **Steamboat Geyser**, in the **Norris Geyser Basin**, is the tallest active geyser in the world, although major eruptions are rare. None of the surface water in the hot springs and mud pots is actually boiling (212°). Volcanic gas bubbles give this appearance.

A large section at about the center of the park, including most of **Yellowstone Lake**, is within the **Yellowstone Caldera**, a large 45 mi x 34 mi and 2/3 mi deep crater left by a massive volcanic eruption 640,000 years ago. This eruption was 1000 times larger than the eruption of **Mount St. Helens** in 1980. This and other volcanic activity are responsible for **Yellowstone**'s geothermal features as well as the **Grand Canyon of the Yellowstone**.

In addition to the geothermal features, the park offers 290 waterfalls of at least 15 ft (the highest being the **Lower Falls** at 308 ft), several deep canyons, 13 major rivers and creeks, and 4 major lakes. **Yellowstone Lake** is North America's largest high elevation lake occupying an area of 136 sq mi with 141 mi of shoreline and a maximum depth of 430 ft.

Wildlife
Yellowstone is part of the **Greater Yellowstone Ecosystem**. This is the largest remaining nearly intact ecosystem in the Earth's northern temperate zone and provides habitat for abundant wildlife. Over 60 species of mammals live in Yellowstone, including bison, deer, elk, pronghorn, moose, coyote, fox, grizzly bear, black bear, bighorn sheep, mountain goat, and beaver. Less seen mammals are the wolf, mountain lion, and lynx.

One of the most commonly seen mammals in the park is the bison, despite the fact that they were almost hunted to extinction in the early 1900s. Once the park began protecting these animals their population increased from less than 50 in 1902 to over 4000 in the 2000s. The bison at Yellowstone are believed to be one of only 4 free roaming and genetically pure herds on public lands in North America.

In the 1990s the gray wolf was controversially re-introduced to Yellowstone. Ironically, they were eliminated by the government in the early 1900s out of fear that elk and moose populations would be wiped out by these predators.

Over 300 species of birds have been reported in the park, including bald eagles, ospreys, cranes, herons, pelicans, and swans.

Forest Fires
Forest fires are a natural part of maintaining healthy forests, particularly the lodgepole pine forests in Yellowstone. Fire is needed to open the lodgepole pine cones and release the seeds as well as to clear out dead and downed wood.

Natural fires are allowed to extinguish themselves naturally unless they threaten people, structures, or will burn out of control. However, until the 1970s forest fires were seen as destructive and were always suppressed. This led to an increase in dead and dying forests, which would later provide the fuel for fires that would be much harder, and in some cases, impossible to control.

This unfortunately became reality in the summer of 1988, when the worst fires in Yellowstone history were caused by a wet spring followed by the driest summer on record, which turned green grass to dry tinder. The **National Park Service** began firefighting efforts in July to keep the fires under control, but they spread quickly throughout the entire region, including areas outside the park. By the end of the month the fires were out of control. Large fires burned together and on August 20, 1988, the single worst day of the fires, more than 150,000 acres (230 sq mi) were consumed. In all 793,000 acres (1,239 sq mi) were burned over a 2 month period. The snowfall in September helped finally extinguish the fire, which smoldered until November. By 1992 Yellowstone had adopted a new fire management plan observing stricter guidelines for the management of natural fires.

General

Yellowstone receives more than 3 million visitors per year. The park has 12 campgrounds with over 1,750 campsites. 5 of these campgrounds take reservations. The campground at **Fishing Bridge** is for hard-sided RVs only and requires reservations 1 to 2 years in advance.

The primary tourist areas are around the **Grand Loop Road**, a 152 mi, figure-8 shaped road in the center of the park. Following are the main attractions clockwise from the south entrance: **Upper Geyser Basin** and **Lower Geyser Basin** to the southwest; **Norris Geyser Basin** to the west; **Mammoth Hot Springs** area to the northwest; **Tower Fall** to the northeast; **Grand Canyon of the Yellowstone** with **Upper Falls** and **Lower Falls** to the east; **Mud Volcano Area** to the east; **Yellowstone Lake** to the southeast. The majority of the tourist activity is at **Upper Geyser Basin** and the **Grand Canyon of the Yellowstone**.

Tips For Visiting

• **Upon entering the park, read the Yellowstone Today Newspaper to understand the park rules and regulations, safety tips, and help plan your time**. The paper contains considerable information on the park.

• When making camping or lodging reservations, space them around the **Grand Loop Road** depending on the next day's destinations. **The Grand Loop Road** is long and slow, so it is not advisable to have to drive out and back every day. Remember that the geyser basins and the **Grand Canyon of the Yellowstone** take the most time to visit.

• The geyser basins on the southwest side of the park require several days to explore. The **Upper Geyser Basin** itself requires at least a long day to walk the trails and boardwalks and see some eruptions. If time is limited, spend time at the **Upper Geyser Basin**, see the large hot springs at **Midway Geyser Basin**, and the **Fountain Paint Pot** at the **Lower Geyser Basin**.

• Geyser eruption predictions can be obtained at the **Old Faithful Visitor Center** or **Madison Information Station** or by calling 307-344-2751.

• Check on road construction for both Yellowstone and Grand Teton National Parks.

• Check for any fires burning in Yellowstone.

• The road signs for the picnic areas are shaped with an arrow pointing to the side of the road where the picnic area is located.

• Do not stop in the roadway to observe wildlife.

• Gas and groceries in **Gardiner, Montana** are considerably cheaper than in the park, and it is only 5 mi north of **Mammoth Hot Springs**. The only other town near Yellowstone is **West Yellowstone, Montana** near the west entrance. Prices for gas, groceries, and other supplies are expensive in the park.

• Drinking water is available in many areas of the park.

• It is best to not bring pets to Yellowstone. They are not allowed on any of the trails and boardwalks.

• If hiking in the backcountry, bring bear pepper spray and know how to use it. Learn what to do in case of a bear encounter.

How to Use This Book in Yellowstone

• Since the **Grand Loop Road** is not a regular highway with mile markers, the book splits the loop road into 7 sections that are separated by the entrance roads plus the connecting road between **Norris** and **Canyon Village**. These 7 sections, the connecting road, 5 entrance roads, plus 3 side roads comprise 16 chapters. The mile markers on the loop sections advance clockwise. The mile markers on the entrance roads start at the entrance stations. All mile markers are shown in either direction being traveled. *See the Yellowstone National Park map on page 13.*

• Trail guidebooks are available at all of the major attractions, and therefore great detail on each thermal feature is beyond the scope of this book.

• The cool ratings for the geysers are based on seeing them erupt.

• Geyser eruption information includes the **type** of geyser *(see next bullet)*, the **interval** between eruptions, the **height** of the eruption, and the **duration** of the eruption. For example: Type: *Cone;* Interval: *3 hrs;* Height: *45 ft;* Duration: *30 min*

• Geyser Types: **Cone** - Shoots a steady jet of water from a cone or mound. **Fountain** - Shoots water in various directions, usually from a pool of water and often in a series of bursts. They may be mistaken for hot springs when they aren't erupting. **Vent** - My own term for a geyser that is neither Cone nor Fountain. Erupts from a crater with no cone.

MM: 0.0/15.4 **GPS:** 44.73591/-110.49325 **Elev:** 7915 **Grid:** 8/7 **Land:** NPS
Yellowstone - Canyon Village to Fishing Bridge　　**Type:** Highway Description
15.4 mi east-central section of the **Grand Loop Road** from **Canyon Village** south to **Fishing Bridge**. Highlights include: **Grand Canyon of the Yellowstone**, **Upper Falls**, **Lower Falls**, **Sulphur Caldron**, **Mud Volcano Area**, **LeHardy Rapids**.
Nearest Town: Canyon Village 0.1 E **Directions:** S to Fishing Bridge from MM 0

MM: 0.0/15.4 **GPS:** 44.73591/-110.49325 **Elev:** 7915 **Grid:** 8/7
Yellowstone - Tower-Roosevelt to Canyon Village (see chapter)　　**Type:** Hwy Transition w/Chapter
18.3 mi northeast section of the **Grand Loop Road** from **Canyon Village** north to **Tower-Roosevelt**. Highlights include: **Mount Washburn**, **Tower Fall**, **Devil's Den**, **Calcite Springs**.
Directions: N to Tower-Roosevelt from MM 18.3

MM: 0.0/15.4 **GPS:** 44.73591/-110.49325 **Elev:** 7915 **Grid:** 8/7
Yellowstone - Norris to Canyon Village (see chapter)　　**Type:** Hwy Junction w/Chapter
11.6 mi cutoff road at the center of the **Grand Loop Road** connecting **Canyon Village** west to **Norris**. If just visiting the attractions along this highway, they are much closer from the **Norris** end. Highlights include: **Little Gibbon Falls** and **Virginia Cascade**.
Directions: W to Norris from MM 11.6

MM: 0.0/15.4 **Dist:** 0.1 **GPS:** 44.73547/-110.48945 **Elev:** 7940 **Grid:** 8/7 **Land:** NPS
Canyon Village　　**Type:** Town & Campground
Visitor services located on the east central section of the **Grand Loop Road** and on the north end of **Grand Canyon of the Yellowstone**, including an ATM, general store, gift shop, sporting goods store, fuel, auto repair, restaurant, cafeteria, fast food, laundry, showers, hotel, cabins, post office, horseback riding, backcountry and fishing permits, and a **Ranger Station**. On the west side of the complex is the large **Canyon Visitor Education Center**, which contains a staffed information desk, bookstore, a large theatre, and several elaborate exhibits about **Yellowstone's** supervolcano and other aspects of the park geology.

The campground is one of 4 large modern campgrounds that take reservations. *10 loops. Conifer forest. Paved roads and parking areas. Restrooms with flush toilets, running water, and electricity. Generators permitted. Amphitheater for ranger programs. 3 wheelchair accessible sites.*
Hours: Visitor center: 8am - 8pm (307-344-2550) **Crowds:** ***** *[FEE AREA]*
Directions: E 0.1 mi and right to Visitor Center and stores; Continue E 0.1 mi and left to campground or right to hotel.
Campsites: 272 **Shade:** ***** **Privacy:** * **RV Size:** 30' **Other:** 1-866-439-7375,Water,RVDump BEARS

MM: 1.2/14.2 **GPS:** 44.72057/-110.49959 **Elev:** 7836 **Grid:** 8/7 **Land:** NPS
Yellowstone - North Rim Drive *(see chapter)*　　**Type:** Side Loop Road w/Chapter
2.0 mi one-way half-loop along the **North Rim of the Grand Canyon of the Yellowstone** ending at **Canyon Village**. The road provides access to 4 canyon overlooks, 3 of which require only a short walk. The parking areas at the overlooks tend to be pretty full. Highlights include: canyon viewpoints, **North Rim Trail**, **Lower Falls**, **Brink of the Lower Falls**.
Nearest Town: Canyon Village 1.3 N **Directions:** S then E from MM 0

MM: 1.6/13.8 **Dist:** 0.3 **GPS:** 44.71573/-110.50161 **GPS2:** 44.71659/-110.50149 **Elev:** 7630 **Grid:** 8/7 **Land:** NPS
Crystal Falls　　**Type:** Waterfall
A beautiful 129 ft 3-tiered waterfall on **Cascade Creek**. The first drop is 5 ft, followed by a 15 ft drop into **Grotto Pool**, a deep pool in a cavern from where the river emerges for the final 110 ft drop. The short trail forks right a short distance to a viewpoint of the falls. The left fork leads to the top of the falls and a bridge over the creek.
Cool Rating: ***** **Crowds:** ** **Time:** 30 min
Directions: SE 1/4 mi to Upper Falls parking area; Walk back up the road about 70 yds; Turn right on the North Rim Trail 100 yds to a fork in the trail.

MM: 1.6/13.8 **Dist:** 0.3 **GPS:** 44.71431/-110.50102 **GPS2:** 44.71304/-110.49969 **Elev:** 7690 **Grid:** 8/7 **Land:** NPS
Brink of the Upper Falls　　**Type:** Waterfall
Paved trail to a platform overlooking the 109 ft **Upper Falls**. *Easy; 0.1 ml; 70 ft elev loss.*
Cool Rating: ***** **Crowds:** ***** **Time:** 30 min **Directions:** SE 0.3 mi to parking area.

MM: 2.3/13.1 **GPS:** 44.70813/-110.50371 **Elev:** 7720 **Grid:** 8/7
Yellowstone - South Rim Drive *(see chapter)*　　**Type:** Hwy Junction w/Chapter
1.6 mi side road that provides access to the **South Rim of the Grand Canyon of the Yellowstone** ending at the **Artist Point** parking area. The **South Rim Trail** to **Artist Point**, including the descent down **Uncle Tom's Trail** to a close-up view of the **Lower Falls**, provides as good or better views of the canyon and waterfalls than that from the **North Rim Drive** or the **North Rim Trail**. The missing attractions to be seen from the **North Rim** are the **Brink of the Upper Falls**, **Brink of the Lower Falls**, and **Crystal Falls**, all of which are short hikes from the road. Highlights include: **North Rim Trail**, **South Rim Trail**, **Upper Falls**, **Lower Falls**, **Uncle Tom's Trail** to the **Lower Falls**, **Artist Point**.
Nearest Town: Canyon Village 2.4 N **Directions:** E then NE from MM 0

MM: 3.0/12.4 **GPS:** 44.69846/-110.50310 **Elev:** 7696 **Grid:** 8/8 **Land:** NPS
Otter Creek Picnic Area　　**Type:** Picnic Area
A nice forested picnic area near the **Yellowstone River**. *8 tables. No toilet.*
Directions: Parking area along NE side of hwy

MM: 4.6/10.8 **GPS:** 44.67898/-110.48780 **Elev:** 7683 **Grid:** 8/8 **Land:** NPS
Wildlife Exhibit　　**Type:** Point of Interest
A broad, slow moving, shallow bend in the **Yellowstone River** where trout and aquatic vegetation can thrive. This attracts bald eagles, ospreys, and pelicans, as well as ducks and geese that feed on underwater plants. View the area from a pullout with an interpretive sign.
Cool Rating: ** **Crowds:** * **Time:** 10 min **Directions:** NE side of hwy

MM: 5.8/9.6 *GPS:* 44.66821/-110.47005 *Elev:* 7778 *Grid:* 8/8 *Land:* NPS
Grizzly Overlook   *Type:* Wildlife Area
An overlook directly above the **Yellowstone River**, which is a good place to view wildlife.
Cool Rating: ** *Crowds:* * *Time:* 10 min *Directions:* NE side of hwy

MM: 7.7/7.7 *GPS:* 44.64341/-110.45730 *Elev:* 7710 *Grid:* 9/9 *Land:* NPS
Trout Creek Overlook   *Type:* Point of Interest
Trout Creek winds through the meadows below this overlook.
Cool Rating: * *Crowds:* * *Time:* 5 min *Directions:* SW side of hwy

MM: 8.5/6.9 *GPS:* 44.63470/-110.44811 *Elev:* 7772 *Grid:* 9/9 *Land:* NPS
Wildlife Overlook   *Type:* Wildlife Area
Below this overlook the **Yellowstone River** flows through the **Hayden Valley** and provides habitat for bison, elk, moose, deer, grizzly bears, large birds, and ducks.
Cool Rating: ** *Crowds:* * *Time:* 10 min *Directions:* NE side of hwy

MM: 9.1/6.3 *GPS:* 44.63029/-110.43913 *Elev:* 7760 *Grid:* 9/9 *Land:* NPS
Interpretive Pullout: Hayden Valley   *Type:* Point of Interest
A sign about the **Hayden Valley**, a former lakebed from ancient **Lake Yellowstone**. The valley is an excellent place to view wildlife, particularly bison and large birds. Additional pullouts provide viewing areas for the next few miles heading north.
Cool Rating: ** *Crowds:* * *Time:* 5 min *Directions:* NE side of hwy

MM: 9.5/5.9 *GPS:* 44.62797/-110.43335 *Elev:* 7760 *Grid:* 9/9 *Land:* NPS
Sulphur Caldron   *Type:* Thermal Area
An overlook from above a large churning pool, which is one of the most acidic springs in **Yellowstone National Park** with about the same acidity as battery acid. Sulphur and microorganisms produce the yellowish color and pungent odor.
Cool Rating: **** *Crowds:* *** *Time:* 15 min
Directions: Main parking on E side of hwy just north and across from the Mud Volcano area. Another small pullout is located 0.1 mi NW just past the Sulphur Caldron.

MM: 9.6/5.8 *GPS:* 44.62481/-110.43342 *Elev:* 7760 *Grid:* 9/9 *Land:* NPS
Mud Volcano Area   *Type:* Thermal Area
Unlike the underground water-driven geyser areas to the west, the water in the **Mud Volcano Area** comes from rain and snowmelt and is reused by the underground steam-driven vents. This water is very acidic with iron sulfide producing a dark color, hydrogen sulfide producing a rotten egg smell, and volcanic gases causing a "boiling" action.

Just off the south end of the parking area is **Mud Caldron**, a bubbling lake of gray mud. On the north end is a short handicapped accessible loop trail with 2 main features: **Dragon's Mouth** is a turbulent hot spring where steam and gas sloshes water rhythmically in and out of a cavern. **Mud Volcano** was once a violent mud spring but is now a churning caldron.

The 0.6 mi upper loop climbs 100 ft to **Black Dragon's Caldron**, a churning mass of black mud that exploded in 1948, blowing trees out by their roots and covering the surrounding forest with mud. It has since shifted 200 ft along a natural crack from where it first formed. Other features include **Mud Geyser**, **Churning Caldron**, and **Sour Lake**. The climb is more gradual by walking the loop counterclockwise. A trail brochure provides more details on individual features.
Cool Rating: ***** *Crowds:* *** *Time:* 1 hr *Directions:* W side of hwy

MM: 10.4/5.0 *GPS:* 44.61839/-110.42091 *Elev:* 7723 *Grid:* 9/10 *Land:* NPS
Nez Perce Ford Picnic Area   *Type:* Picnic Area
A nice large picnic area along a 1/4 mi road with several loops, some individual sites, and 5 tables in the open near the **Yellowstone River**. *17 tables. Vault toilet. Handicapped accessible.*
Directions: NE up to 1/4 mi

MM: 10.6/4.8 *GPS:* 44.61675/-110.41656 *Elev:* 7720 *Grid:* 9/10 *Land:* NPS
Cascade Picnic Area   *Type:* Picnic Area
A short loop road in a shady conifer forest. *6 tables. Vault toilet. Handicapped accessible.*
Directions: SW side of hwy

MM: 11.3/4.1 *GPS:* 44.61064/-110.40746 *Elev:* 7715 *Grid:* 9/10 *Land:* NPS
LeHardy Picnic Area   *Type:* Picnic Area
A long half-loop pullout in a sparse conifer forest. *6 tables. No toilet.*
Directions: SW side of hwy

MM: 12.3/3.1 *GPS:* 44.60768/-110.38675 *GPS2:* 44.60728/-110.38415 *Elev:* 7726 *Grid:* 10/10 *Land:* NPS
LeHardy Rapids (northwest access)   *Type:* Point of Interest
An unofficial pullout to the northwest of **LeHardy Rapids** with a non-wheelchair accessible dirt trail. *See next section.*
Directions: NE side of hwy

MM: 12.5/2.9 *GPS:* 44.60587/-110.38366 *GPS2:* 44.60728/-110.38415 *Elev:* 7726 *Grid:* 10/10 *Land:* NPS
LeHardy Rapids (south access)   *Type:* Point of Interest
A paved wheelchair accessible trail leads to rapids on the **Yellowstone River**, where in June and early July cutthroat trout can be observed jumping up the rapids for spawning in **Yellowstone Lake**.
Cool Rating: *** *Crowds:* * *Time:* 20+ min *Notes:* The time depends on whether the fish are jumping.
Directions: E side of hwy

MM: 15.4/0.0 *GPS:* 44.56808/-110.38831 *Elev:* 7824 *Grid:* 10/11

Yellowstone - Fishing Bridge to West Thumb *(see chapter)*   *Type:* Hwy Transition w/Chapter

20.6 mi southeast section of the **Grand Loop Road** from **Fishing Bridge** southwest to **West Thumb**. The entire length of this section follows the shore of **Yellowstone Lake**, which is North America's largest high elevation lake occupying an area of 136 sq mi with 141 mi of shoreline and a maximum depth of 430 ft. The southern end of this route travels along a protrusion in the lake known as the **West Thumb**. Highlights include: **Elephant Back Mountain**, **Natural Bridge**, **West Thumb Geyser Basin**, **Duck Lake**.

Nearest Town: Fishing Bridge 0.7 E; Lake Village 2.1 SW *Directions:* SW to West Thumb from MM 0

MM: 15.4/0.0 *GPS:* 44.56808/-110.38831 *Elev:* 7824 *Grid:* 10/11

Yellowstone - East Entrance to Fishing Bridge *(see chapter)*   *Type:* Hwy Junction w/Chapter

25.8 mi highway from **Fishing Bridge** east out of **Yellowstone National Park** to **US-14/16/20**. There is hiking and **Yellowstone Lake** access but very little thermal activity. Highlights include: **Fishing Bridge**, **Steamboat Point**, **Lake Butte Overlook**.

Nearest Town: Fishing Bridge 0.7 E *Directions:* E to Cody from MM 25.8

MM: 15.4/0.0 *GPS:* 44.56808/-110.38831 *Elev:* 7824 *Grid:* 10/11 *Land:* NPS

Yellowstone - Fishing Bridge to Canyon Village   *Type:* Highway End

15.4 mi east-central section of the **Grand Loop Road** from **Fishing Bridge** north to **Canyon Village**. Highlights include: **LeHardy Rapids**, **Mud Volcano Area**, **Sulphur Caldron**, **Grand Canyon of the Yellowstone**, **Upper Falls**, **Lower Falls**.

Nearest Town: Fishing Bridge 0.7 E *Directions:* N to Canyon Village from MM 15.4

Yellowstone - East Entrance to Fishing Bridge

MM: 0.0/25.8 *GPS:* 44.48859/-110.00382 *Elev:* 6946 *Grid:* 15/13 *Land:* NPS
Yellowstone - East Entrance to Fishing Bridge   *Type:* Highway Description
25.8 mi highway from the east entrance of **Yellowstone National Park**, via **US-14/16/20**, west to **Fishing Bridge**. There is hiking and **Yellowstone Lake** access but very little thermal activity. Highlights include: **Lake Butte Overlook, Steamboat Point, Fishing Bridge**.
Nearest Town: Pahaska 2 E; Fishing Bridge 25.1 W *Directions:* W to Fishing Bridge from MM 0

MM: 0.0/25.8 *GPS:* 44.48973/-110.00129 *Elev:* 6946 *Grid:* 15/13
US-14/16/20 (*see chapter*)   *Type:* Hwy Transition w/Chapter
100.1 mi highway east from the east entrance of **Yellowstone National Park** to either a transition east to **Greybull** or a junction north to **Lovell**. The **Buffalo Bill Cody Scenic Byway** runs 27.4 mi from the east entrance of **Yellowstone National Park** to the east boundary of the **Shoshone National Forest**. Highlights include: interesting volcanic rock formations, **Firefighters Memorial and Trail, Holy City, Buffalo Bill Dam and Visitor Center, Old West Miniature Village and Museum, Buffalo Bill Historical Center**.
Nearest Town: Pahaska 2 E *Directions:* E to Cody from MM 0

MM: 0.0/25.8 *GPS:* 44.48859/-110.00382 *Elev:* 6946 *Grid:* 15/13 *Land:* NPS
Yellowstone National Park - East Entrance   *Type:* National Park
Pay the National Park entrance fee, which covers both **Yellowstone National Park** and **Grand Teton National Park**. *See chapter: Yellowstone National Park.*
Nearest Town: Pahaska 2 E; Fishing Bridge 25.1 W *[FEE AREA]*

MM: 7.7/18.1 *GPS:* 44.47056/-110.14270 *Elev:* 8475 *Grid:* 13/13 *Land:* NPS
Eleanor Lake Picnic Area   *Type:* Picnic Area
A small picnic area in a stand of trees just west of **Eleanor Lake**. This is also the parking area for the **Avalanche Peak Trailhead** *(see next section). 2 tables. No toilet.*
Directions: S side of hwy

MM: 7.7/18.1 *GPS:* 44.47072/-110.14259 *Elev:* 8480 *Grid:* 13/13 *Land:* NPS
Avalanche Peak Trailhead   *Type:* Trailhead
A rugged and steep hike through thick forest, wildflower filled meadows, and a whitebark pine forest, before climbing a talus slope and crossing a rocky ridge to the 10,566 ft **Avalanche Peak**, which is part of the **Absaroka Range**. The view from the top offers spectacular panoramas of rugged mountains, tall mountain peaks, and **Yellowstone Lake**. The trail is best hiked after mid-July and before September as snow can linger well into the summer, and the grizzlies move in to feast on the whitebark pine cones in the fall. Loose rocks on the talus slope can make the footing unstable. *Strenuous with few switchbacks; 2.0 mi one-way; 2100 ft elev gain.*
Cool Rating: ***** *Crowds:* * *Time:* 3-4 hrs
Directions: Park at **Eleanor Picnic Area** on S side of hwy; Trail starts across the hwy.

MM: 8.7/17.1 *GPS:* 44.47825/-110.15812 *Elev:* 8425 *Grid:* 13/13 *Land:* NPS
Sylvan Lake Picnic Area   *Type:* Picnic Area
The main picnic area is located on the northeast side of the highway with tables in a forested area. *8 tables. Vault toilet. Handicapped accessible.* On the southwest side is a pullout next to **Sylvan Lake** with 2 tables sitting on a point overlooking the lake.
Directions: NE side of hwy

MM: 16.3/9.5 *Dist:* 0.8 *GPS:* 44.51002/-110.27463 *Elev:* 8335 *Grid:* 11/12 *Land:* NPS
Lake Butte Overlook   *Type:* Scenic Viewpoint
A short side road that climbs up **Lake Butte** to an overlook 300 ft above the northeast end of **Yellowstone Lake**. The surrounding area was burned in 2003. A sign at the overlook identifies locations on the horizon and explains the remoteness of this area.
Cool Rating: *** *Crowds:* ** *Time:* 15 min *Directions:* N then NW 0.8 mi

MM: 18.0/7.8 *GPS:* 44.51972/-110.27856 *Elev:* 7735 *Grid:* 11/12 *Land:* NPS
Sedge Bay Picnic Area   *Type:* Picnic Area
A long pullout with a mile of gravel shoreline on the northeast shore of **Yellowstone Lake**. The picnic area is located in a small sparse stand of trees near a canoe and kayak launching area. *3 tables. Vault toilet. Handicapped accessible.*
Directions: SW side of hwy

MM: 19.3/6.5 *GPS:* 44.52985/-110.29731 *Elev:* 7803 *Grid:* 11/12 *Land:* NPS
Steamboat Point   *Type:* Thermal Area
A point on the northeast end of **Yellowstone Lake** where steam rises near the water's edge. This point is located at the south end of **Mary Bay**, a hydrothermal explosion crater where heat flow measurements are among the highest recorded in the park. A fracture line runs from the hills to the northwest straight through the lake bed and across **Steamboat Point**, producing heat from deep magma chambers. The point is observed from a pullout above the lake with an interpretive sign.
Cool Rating: *** *Crowds:* * *Time:* 10 min *Directions:* W side of hwy

MM: 19.5/6.3 *GPS:* 44.53240/-110.29655 *Elev:* 7773 *Grid:* 11/12 *Land:* NPS
Steamboat Point Picnic Area   *Type:* Picnic Area
A nice picnic area overlooking **Yellowstone Lake**. *2 tables. Vault toilet. Handicapped accessible.*
Directions: W side of hwy

MM: 22.6/3.2   *GPS:* 44.55967/-110.32632   *Elev:* 7788   *Grid:* 10/11   *Land:* NPS

Indian Pond & Storm Point Nature Trail   *Type:* Hiking Trail

The **Indian Pond** was formed by a hydrothermal explosion leaving a crater filled with water. An informational sign explains this event. The pond gets its name from being a historic Indian campsite.

The **Storm Point Nature Trail** follows the west shore of **Indian Pond**, then proceeds through meadows and forest to **Storm Point**, an elevated rocky point overlooking the northeast shore of **Yellowstone Lake**. The trail continues 0.2 mi along the bluff above the lakeshore before heading back into the woods to complete the loop. *Easy; 2.3 mi loop; 40 ft elev loss.*

Cool Rating: ***   *Crowds:* **   *Time:* 1 hr   *Directions:* S side of hwy. Additional trail parking is located 0.1 mi W.

MM: 24.3/1.5   *GPS:* 44.56018/-110.36067   *Elev:* 7750   *Grid:* 10/11   *Land:* NPS

Pelican Creek Nature Trail   *Type:* Hiking Trail

A nature trail across a marsh and through forest to a sandy beach on **Yellowstone Lake** near the mouth of **Pelican Creek**. This is a good area for birdwatching where white pelicans can be seen fishing at the mouth of **Pelican Creek**. *Easy; 1.0 mi loop; Level.*

Cool Rating: ***   *Crowds:* ***   *Time:* 30 min   *Directions:* SW side of hwy

---

MM: 24.8/1.0   *GPS:* 44.56287/-110.36999   *Elev:* 7780   *Grid:* 10/11   *Land:* NPS

Fishing Bridge RV Park   *Type:* Campground

Yellowstone National Park's only RV park with full hookups. Located on the north end of **Yellowstone Lake**. Generally requires reservations 1 to 2 years in advance. *No tables or fire rings. Spaces are tight. Flush toilets and electricity. Showers. Generators permitted. Hard-sided RVs only.*

Crowds: *****   *[FEE AREA]*   *Directions:* NE side of hwy

Campsites: 346   *Shade:* *   *Privacy:* *   *RV Size:* 40'+   *Other:* 1-866-439-7375,Water,Electric,RVDump   BEARS

MM: 25.1/0.7   *Dist:* 0.1   *GPS:* 44.56664/-110.37342   *Elev:* 7748   *Grid:* 10/11   *Land:* NPS

Howard Eaton Trail to LeHardy Rapids Overlook   *Type:* Hiking Trail

A hike along a portion of the **Howard Eaton Trail** with frequent views of the **Yellowstone River**. The trail traverses meadows, forest, and sage flats to an overlook of the **LeHardy Rapids**. Past the rapids the trail continues all the way to the **Grand Canyon of the Yellowstone**, approximately 10 mi northwest. The first half of the trail is level and roughly follows the river. The trail gradually climbs a hill into the forest before dropping to the overlook of **LeHardy Rapids**. *Moderate; 3.4 mi one-way; 150 ft elev gain, 100 ft elev loss.*

Cool Rating: ***   *Crowds:* *   *Notes:* This is grizzly habitat, so check for trail closures and don't hike alone.

Directions: Just SE of the Yellowstone General Store; NE 1 block to parking area (if full, park anywhere around here); The trail starts 0.1 mi NE of the parking area. Alternatively, park in the parking area just E of Fishing Bridge (see MM 25.4).

MM: 25.1/0.7   *GPS:* 44.56455/-110.37577   *Elev:* 7747   *Grid:* 10/11   *Land:* NPS

Fishing Bridge Village   *Type:* Town

Visitor services located on the north end of **Yellowstone Lake**, including an ATM, general store, fuel, auto repair, propane, laundry, showers, fishing permits, and a **Ranger Station**.

Directions: NE side of hwy

MM: 25.2/0.6   *GPS:* 44.56360/-110.37734   *Elev:* 7745   *Grid:* 10/11   *Land:* NPS

Fishing Bridge Visitor Center   *Type:* Visitor Center

This **National Historic Landmark** on the north shore of **Yellowstone Lake** was built in 1931 using a distinctive stone and log architecture known as "parkitecture," which became a prototype for park buildings all around the country. Inside the center is a staffed information desk, a large bookstore in the east wing, and a museum containing a large exhibit of taxidermied birds of the **Yellowstone** region and taxidermied wildlife displays, including a grizzly sow and 2 cubs (in the bookstore), and a family of river otters. In front of the building is an amphitheatre for ranger programs; however, the center has no theater for audio-visual programs. Behind the building is a short walkway to the lakeshore complete with benches for enjoying the view.

Hours: 8am - 7pm   *Phone:* 307-242-2450   *Directions:* SW side of hwy at end of parking area.

MM: 25.2/0.6   *GPS:* 44.56403/-110.37749   *Elev:* 7745   *Grid:* 10/11   *Land:* NPS

Fishing Bridge Picnic Area   *Type:* Picnic Area

A shady picnic area at the **Fishing Bridge Visitor Center**. *11 tables.*

Directions: SW side of hwy; On the SW side of the visitor center parking area.

MM: 25.4/0.4   *GPS:* 44.56593/-110.38013   *Elev:* 7745   *Grid:* 10/11   *Land:* NPS

Howard Eaton Trail   *Type:* Hiking Trail

The trail follows the **Yellowstone River** for a short distance before paralleling a service road to the trailhead. *See earlier section on Howard Eaton Trail to LeHardy Rapids Overlook at MM 25.1.*

Directions: NE side of road just SE of Fishing Bridge.

MM: 25.4/0.4   *GPS:* 44.56638/-110.38157   *Elev:* 7740   *Grid:* 10/11   *Land:* NPS

Fishing Bridge   *Type:* Point of Interest

A famous bridge over the **Yellowstone River** from which visitors could fish prior to 1973. This fishing was decimating the trout population as well as causing other problems. Interpretive signs explain why fishing from the bridge is no longer allowed.

Cool Rating: ***   *Crowds:* ***   *Time:* 20 min

Directions: Parking areas on both ends of the bridge; however, the northwest end is closer.

MM: 25.6/0.2   *GPS:* 44.56697/-110.38295   *Elev:* 7745   *Grid:* 10/11   *Land:* NPS

Lakeshore Trail   *Type:* Hiking Trail

An easy hiking trail that starts from the northwest end of **Fishing Bridge** and heads southwest along the mouth of the **Yellowstone River** and **Yellowstone Lake** to **Lake Village**. *Easy; 2.0 mi round-trip; Level.*

Cool Rating: ***   *Crowds:* *   *Time:* 45 min

Directions: Park in the Fishing Bridge northwest parking area; Walk to the near end of Fishing Bridge and cross the road to a set of wood and dirt steps up a hill.

MM: 25.8/0.0 *GPS:* 44.56808/-110.38831 *Elev:* 7824 *Grid:* 10/11

Yellowstone - Fishing Bridge to West Thumb *(see chapter)*   *Type:* Hwy Junction w/Chapter

20.6 mi southeast section of the **Grand Loop Road** from **Fishing Bridge** southwest to **West Thumb**. The entire length of this section follows the shore of **Yellowstone Lake**, which is North America's largest high elevation lake occupying an area of 136 sq mi with 141 mi of shoreline and a maximum depth of 430 ft. The southern end of this route travels along a protrusion in the lake known as the **West Thumb**. Highlights include: **Elephant Back Mountain, Natural Bridge, West Thumb Geyser Basin, Duck Lake**.

Nearest Town: Fishing Bridge 0.7 E; Lake Village 2.1 SW *Directions:* SW to West Thumb from MM 0

MM: 25.8/0.0 *GPS:* 44.56808/-110.38831 *Elev:* 7824 *Grid:* 10/11

Yellowstone - Canyon Village to Fishing Bridge *(see chapter)*   *Type:* Hwy Junction w/Chapter

15.4 mi east-central section of the **Grand Loop Road** from **Fishing Bridge** north to **Canyon Village**. Highlights include: **LeHardy Rapids, Mud Volcano Area, Sulphur Caldron, Grand Canyon of the Yellowstone, Upper Falls, Lower Falls**.

Nearest Town: Fishing Bridge 0.7 E *Directions:* N to Canyon Village from MM 15.4

MM: 25.8/0.0 *GPS:* 44.56808/-110.38831 *Elev:* 7824 *Grid:* 10/11 *Land:* NPS

Yellowstone - Fishing Bridge to East Entrance   *Type:* Highway End

25.8 mi highway from **Fishing Bridge** east out of **Yellowstone National Park** to **US-14/16/20**. There is hiking and **Yellowstone Lake** access but very little thermal activity. Highlights include: **Fishing Bridge, Steamboat Point, Lake Butte Overlook**.

Nearest Town: Fishing Bridge 0.7 E *Directions:* E to Cody from MM 25.8

Yellowstone - Fishing Bridge to West Thumb   NE/SW

MM: 0.0/20.6   *GPS:* 44.56808/-110.38831   *Elev:* 7824   *Grid:* 10/11   *Land:* NPS
Yellowstone - Fishing Bridge to West Thumb   *Type:* Highway Description
20.6 mi southeast section of the **Grand Loop Road** from **Fishing Bridge** southwest to **West Thumb**. The entire length of this section follows the shore of **Yellowstone Lake**, which is North America's largest high elevation lake occupying an area of 136 sq mi with 141 mi of shoreline and a maximum depth of 430 ft. The southern end of this route travels along a protrusion in the lake known as the **West Thumb**. Highlights include: **Elephant Back Mountain**, **Natural Bridge**, **West Thumb Geyser Basin**, **Duck Lake**.
Nearest Town: Fishing Bridge 0.7 E; Lake Village 2.1 SW   *Directions:* SW to West Thumb from MM 0

MM: 0.0/20.6   *GPS:* 44.56808/-110.38831   *Elev:* 7824   *Grid:* 10/11
Yellowstone - Canyon Village to Fishing Bridge *(see chapter)*   *Type:* Hwy Transition w/Chapter
15.4 mi east-central section of the **Grand Loop Road** from **Fishing Bridge** north to **Canyon Village**. Highlights include: **LeHardy Rapids**, **Mud Volcano Area**, **Sulphur Caldron**, **Grand Canyon of the Yellowstone**, **Upper Falls**, **Lower Falls**.
Nearest Town: Fishing Bridge 0.7 E   *Directions:* N to Canyon Village from MM 15.4

MM: 0.0/20.6   *GPS:* 44.56808/-110.38831   *Elev:* 7824   *Grid:* 10/11
Yellowstone - East Entrance to Fishing Bridge *(see chapter)*   *Type:* Hwy Junction w/Chapter
25.8 mi highway from **Fishing Bridge** east out of **Yellowstone National Park** to **US-14/16/20**. There is hiking and **Yellowstone Lake** access but very little thermal activity. Highlights include: **Fishing Bridge**, **Steamboat Point**, **Lake Butte Overlook**.
Nearest Town: Fishing Bridge 0.7 E   *Directions:* E to Cody from MM 25.8

MM: 1.1/19.5   *GPS:* 44.55672/-110.40160   *Elev:* 7821   *Grid:* 9/11   *Land:* NPS
Elephant Back Mountain Trailhead   *Type:* Trailhead
A hike on a popular and well-maintained trail to the top of **Elephant Back Mountain** for panoramic views of the **Yellowstone Lake** area. The trail parallels the highway southwest 130 yds before turning north into an old growth lodgepole pine forest. Continue to climb 300 ft in 0.9 mi to a trail junction that begins a loop trail over the summit. Turn left to travel clockwise and climb 500 ft up switchbacks in 0.9 mi to the overlook. Looking east on the left side of the lake is the **Yellowstone River** outlet, **Pelican Valley**, and **Storm Point**. The island to the right is **Stevenson Island** and the **Absaroka Range** rises up beyond the lake. Continue across the top of the mountain and descend back to the trail junction. Turn left to return to the parking area. *Moderate; 4.0 mi loop; 800 ft elev gain.*
Cool Rating: ****   *Crowds:* ****   *Time:* 1.5 hrs   *Notes:* Grizzly bears frequent this area in the early season.
Directions: Parking pullout on NW side of hwy

MM: 1.6/19.0   *Dist:* 0.5   *GPS:* 44.55183/-110.40274   *Elev:* 7786   *Grid:* 9/11   *Land:* NPS
Lake Village & Lakeshore Trail   *Type:* Town
Visitor services located on the northwest end of **Yellowstone Lake**, including an ATM, general store, gift shop, restaurant, cafeteria, fast food, laundry, the elegant **Lake Yellowstone Hotel**, cabins, post office, medical clinic, fishing permits, and a **Ranger Station**.

The easy 2.0 mi round-trip **Lakeshore Trail** starts at **Lake Lodge** and travels northeast to **Fishing Bridge**. *See Lakeshore Trail in chapter. Yellowstone - East Entrance to Fishing Bridge MM 25.6.*
Directions: E 0.5 - 0.9 mi

MM: 3.3/17.3   *GPS:* 44.53628/-110.43251   *Elev:* 7750   *Grid:* 9/12   *Land:* NPS
Yellowstone Lake Access   *Type:* Lake
Unmarked road for fishing and lake access.
Directions: SE side of hwy

MM: 3.4/17.2   *Dist:* 0.1   *GPS:* 44.53317/-110.43602   *Elev:* 7755   *Grid:* 9/12   *Land:* NPS
Bridge Bay Picnic Area   *Type:* Picnic Area
Located in a forested area on the east end of the **Bridge Bay Marina** parking area. *23 tables. 3 grills. Vault toilet. Handicapped accessible.*
Directions: W 0.1 mi; S/L 90 yds.

MM: 3.4/17.2   *Dist:* 0.2   *GPS:* 44.53379/-110.43757   *Elev:* 7770   *Grid:* 9/12   *Land:* NPS
Bridge Bay Campground   *Type:* Campground
One of 4 large modern campgrounds that take reservations. This is **Yellowstone National Park**'s largest campground. It is located on the northwest end of **Yellowstone Lake** just north of the **Bridge Bay Marina** on the southeast section of the **Grand Loop Road**. The first 4 loops are in the open with no view of the lake. The other loops are forested and higher up, where several sites have views of the lake. *10 loops. 3 tent-only loops (79 sites). 1 loop for groups and hiker/biker walk-ins. Conifer forest. Paved roads and parking areas. Restrooms with flush toilets, running water, and electricity. Generators permitted. Amphitheater for ranger programs.*
Crowds: *****   *[FEE AREA]*   *Directions:* W 0.2 mi; N into campground.
Campsites: 431   *Shade:* ***   *Privacy:* *   *RV Size:* 30'   *Other:* 1-866-439-7375,Water,RVDump   BEARS

MM: 3.4/17.2   *Dist:* 0.2   *GPS:* 44.53342/-110.43897   *Elev:* 7750   *Grid:* 9/12   *Land:* NPS
Bridge Bay Ranger Station   *Type:* Visitor Center
Information and permits.
Directions: W 0.2 mi; S/L into parking area.

MM: 3.4/17.2   *Dist:* 0.2   *GPS:* 44.53342/-110.43897   *Elev:* 7750   *Grid:* 9/12   *Land:* NPS
Bridge Bay Marina   *Type:* Marina
A commercial marina and visitor services located on the northwest end of **Yellowstone Lake**, including a general store, sporting goods store, marina, boat rentals, dock rentals, boat cruises, backcountry and fishing permits, and a **Ranger Station**.
Directions: W 0.2 mi

MM: 3.4/17.2 *Dist:* 0.2 *GPS:* 44.53376/-110.43884 *GPS2:* 44.52615/-110.45520 *Elev:* 7840 *Grid:* 9/12 *Land:* NPS
Natural Bridge   *Type:* Natural Feature
The only natural bridge in **Yellowstone National Park**. The 40 ft high by 30 ft wide arch was cut by **Bridge Creek** through a 51 ft cliff of rhyolite lava. A short trail leads to an interpretive sign and continues to the arch opening. Another short but steep trail leads to the top of the natural bridge; however, visitors are not allowed to walk across the top. The natural bridge can be accessed by either hiking or biking from the **Bridge Bay Marina** parking area. The actual hiking trailhead starts at the west end of the **Bridge Bay Campground**. *Easy; 3.0 mi round-trip bike route from parking area; 2.0 mi round-trip hike from parking area; 2.4 mi round-trip hike from campground; Level.*
Cool Rating: **** *Crowds:* ** *Time:* 1-2 hrs
Notes: The trail is closed from late spring to early summer due to grizzlies feeding on spawning trout in Bridge Creek.
Directions: W 0.2 mi to Bridge Bay Marina parking area. **Biking:** From the parking area head east back to the Grand Loop Road 0.2 mi; S/R along the shoulder of the road and over the bridge 0.3 mi; W/R on old road 0.9 mi; Right at fork 0.1 mi. **Hiking:** From the west end of the parking area head west into the woods about 70 yds to find the trail. From the campground the trailhead starts on the west side. The trail heads SW 0.5 mi (0.7 from campground); W/R on old road 0.4 mi; Right at fork 0.1 mi.

MM: 3.7/16.8 *Dist:* 1.3 *GPS:* 44.53044/-110.43600 *GPS2:* 44.52519/-110.41795 *Elev:* 7780 *Grid:* 9/12 *Land:* NPS
Gull Point Picnic Area (southbound)   *Type:* Picnic Area
A large, shady picnic area at **Gull Point**, which is a peninsula on the south end of **Bridge Bay** at the northwest end of **Yellowstone Lake**. **Gull Point** is just outside the forested picnic area with a sandy/rocky shoreline around a small marshy pond. A 2.0 mi side road through forest and along the lakeshore provides access and loops back to the main highway. *21 tables. Vault toilet. Handicapped accessible.*
Directions: NE then S 1.3 mi to picnic area. 0.7 mi to finish loop back to hwy.

MM: 5.3/15.3 *Dist:* 0.7 *GPS:* 44.51532/-110.41895 *Elev:* 7780 *Grid:* 9/12 *Land:* NPS
Gull Point Picnic Area (northbound)   *Type:* Picnic Area
See previous section.
Directions: NE 0.7 mi to picnic area. 1.3 mi to finish loop back to hwy.

MM: 6.6/14.0 *GPS:* 44.49816/-110.42030 *Elev:* 7794 *Grid:* 9/13 *Land:* NPS
Sand Point Picnic Area   *Type:* Picnic Area
A large shady picnic area. *18 tables. Vault toilet.*
Directions: E side of hwy

MM: 9.8/10.8 *GPS:* 44.46759/-110.46668 *Elev:* 7770 *Grid:* 8/13 *Land:* NPS
Interpretive Pullout: Contrasting Forests and Picnic Area   *Type:* Point of Interest
A sign that contrasts the forests of spruce and fir to the lodgepole pine forests, explaining how Mother Nature keeps the lodgepole pine the predominate tree. The long pullout is along the rocky lakeshore with 4 picnic tables.
Cool Rating: * *Crowds:* * *Time:* 5 min *Directions:* S side of hwy

MM: 11.9/8.6 *GPS:* 44.45265/-110.50350 *Elev:* 7766 *Grid:* 8/14 *Land:* NPS
Pumice Point   *Type:* Scenic Area
A large half-loop pullout on a point into the north end of the **West Thumb of Yellowstone Lake**.
Cool Rating: ** *Crowds:* * *Time:* 10 min *Directions:* S side of hwy

MM: 12.7/7.9 *Dist:* 0.3 *GPS:* 44.45983/-110.51642 *Elev:* 7770 *Grid:* 8/14 *Land:* NPS
Picnic Area   *Type:* Picnic Area
Picnic tables along a 100 yd path that leads to a 30 ft cliff overlooking **Yellowstone Lake**. *3 tables. Vault toilet.*
Directions: S on unmarked road 0.3 mi

MM: 13.1/7.5 *GPS:* 44.46664/-110.51683 *Elev:* 7745 *Grid:* 8/13 *Land:* NPS
Yellowstone Lake Sandbar   *Type:* Scenic Area
A 1.0 mi long natural sandbar across the north end of the **West Thumb of Yellowstone Lake**. The walk across the sandbar is pleasant with good views across the lake.
Cool Rating: ** *Crowds:* * *Time:* 20 min *Directions:* Pullout on W side of hwy above sandbar

MM: 13.8/6.8 *GPS:* 44.47325/-110.52611 *Elev:* 7748 *Grid:* 8/13 *Land:* NPS
Pullout with Vault Toilet   *Type:* Restroom
A half-loop pullout with a vault toilet.
Directions: SW side of hwy

MM: 18.0/2.5 *GPS:* 44.44075/-110.57220 *Elev:* 7750 *Grid:* 7/14 *Land:* NPS
Interpretive Pullout: An Exploded Bay   *Type:* Point of Interest
A sign explaining that **West Thumb** was created by a massive explosion.
Cool Rating: * *Crowds:* * *Time:* 5 min *Directions:* SE side of hwy

MM: 18.9/1.7 *GPS:* 44.43301/-110.58480 *Elev:* 7812 *Grid:* 7/14 *Land:* NPS
Potts Hot Spring Basin   *Type:* Geyser Basin
The northernmost group of geysers and hot springs from the **West Thumb** area. This very old thermal area is not accessible. There are no signs, so it is just a point of interest.
Cool Rating: * *Crowds:* * *Time:* Drive by *Directions:* Pullout on E side of hwy

MM: 20.4/0.1 *Dist:* 0.2 *GPS:* 44.41557/-110.57657 *Elev:* 7790 *Grid:* 7/15 *Land:* NPS
West Thumb Geyser Basin   *Type:* Geyser Basin
Located on the west shore of the **West Thumb of Yellowstone Lake**, this is one of the most scenic geyser basins in **Yellowstone National Park**, although one of the smallest. A 3/4 mi boardwalk leads to hot springs, pools, mud pots, fumaroles, and lakeshore geysers (with little actual geyser activity). Highlights include **Fishing Cone**, which is popular because of its unusual location along the lakeshore and its symmetrical cone, and the **Abyss Pool**, noted for its depth and colors. A small information station with a bookstore is located near the start of the trail. 2 hikes start from the parking area *(see next 2 sections)*.
Hours: Information Station: 9am - 5pm *Cool Rating:* ***** *Crowds:* ***** *Time:* 1 hr *Directions:* SE into parking area.

MM: 20.4/0.1 *Dist:* 0.2 *GPS:* 44.41557/-110.57515 *Elev:* 7792 *Grid:* 7/15 *Land:* NPS

Yellowstone Lake Overlook Trail   *Type:* Hiking Trail

A short hike through meadows, a burn area, and a regenerating forest to an overlook of **West Thumb Geyser Basin** and **Yellowstone Lake**. The trail heads southwest out of the parking area and crosses the highway before joining the loop trail at 1/4 mi. Turning left to hike clockwise, the trail climbs gradually 3/4 mi through sparse forest before leaving the trees and climbing steeply 150 ft in the next 1/4 mi to the overlook. Turn left at the bench to climb 50 yds to the top. To complete the loop return to the bench and continue left. *Moderately easy; 1.8 mi loop; 240 ft elev gain.*

Cool Rating: *** *Crowds:* * *Time:* 1 hr

Directions: SE into West Thumb Geyser Basin parking area. Trail is on the SW side.

MM: 20.4/0.1 *Dist:* 0.2 *GPS:* 44.41631/-110.57501 *Elev:* 7795 *Grid:* 7/15 *Land:* NPS

Duck Lake Trail   *Type:* Hiking Trail

A short hike through a regenerating forest to a tranquil lake with a large sandy beach, which is actually an explosion crater filled with water. Head north and climb straight up a hill gaining 100 ft in 1/4 mi, then descend 100 ft to the lakeshore in another 0.2 mi. *Moderately easy; 0.9 mi round-trip; 100 ft elev gain.*

Cool Rating: *** *Crowds:* * *Time:* 45 min

Directions: SE into West Thumb Geyser Basin parking area. Trail is on the NW side.

MM: 20.4/0.1 *Dist:* 0.2 *GPS:* 44.41545/-110.57321 *Elev:* 7788 *Grid:* 7/15 *Land:* NPS

West Thumb Picnic Area   *Type:* Picnic Area

A nice shady picnic area. *5 tables. Vault toilet. Handicapped accessible.*

Directions: SE into West Thumb Geyser parking area; End of parking area on NE side.

MM: 20.6/0.0 *GPS:* 44.41403/-110.57848 *Elev:* 7808 *Grid:* 7/15

Yellowstone - West Thumb to Madison *(see chapter)*   *Type:* Hwy Junction w/Chapter

33.5 mi southwest section of the **Grand Loop Road** from **West Thumb** northwest to **Madison**. The majority of the geyser activity is along this section. Highlights include: **Lone Star Geyser**, **Kepler Cascades**, **Upper Geyser Basin**, **Old Faithful**, **Black Sand Basin**, **Mystic Falls**, **Biscuit Basin**, **Fairy Falls**, **Midway Geyser Basin**, **Firehole Lake Drive Geysers**, **Lower Geyser Basin**, **Firehole Falls**.

Nearest Town: Grant Village 2.8 S *Directions:* NW to Madison from MM 0

MM: 20.6/0.0 *GPS:* 44.41403/-110.57848 *Elev:* 7808 *Grid:* 7/15

Yellowstone - South Entrance to West Thumb *(see chapter)*   *Type:* Hwy Junction w/Chapter

21.2 mi highway from **West Thumb** south out of **Yellowstone National Park** to **US-89/191/287**. Highlights include: **Lewis Falls**, **Moose Falls**.

Nearest Town: Grant Village 2.8 S *Directions:* S to Grand Teton National Park from MM 21.2

MM: 20.6/0.0 *GPS:* 44.41403/-110.57848 *Elev:* 7808 *Grid:* 7/15 *Land:* NPS

Yellowstone - West Thumb to Fishing Bridge   *Type:* Highway End

20.6 mi southeast section of the **Grand Loop Road** from **West Thumb** northeast to **Fishing Bridge**. The entire length of this section follows the shore of **Yellowstone Lake**, which is North America's largest high elevation lake occupying an area of 136 sq mi with 141 mi of shoreline and a maximum depth of 430 ft. The southern end of this route travels along a protrusion in the lake known as the **West Thumb**. Highlights include: **West Thumb Geyser Basin**, **Duck Lake**, **Natural Bridge**, **Elephant Back Mountain**.

Nearest Town: Grant Village 2.8 S *Directions:* NE to Fishing Bridge from MM 20.6

MM: 0.0/13.4 **GPS:** 44.64540/-110.85846 **Elev:** 6836 **Grid:** 3/9 **Land:** NPS
Yellowstone - Madison to Norris   **Type:** Highway Description
13.4 mi west-central section of the **Grand Loop Road** from **Madison** northeast to **Norris**. Highlights include: **Gibbon Falls, Beryl Spring, Monument Geyser Basin, Artist Paint Pots, Chocolate Pots, Norris Geyser Basin**.
Nearest Town: West Yellowstone, MT 14.0 W **Directions:** NE to Norris from MM 0

MM: 0.0/13.4 **GPS:** 44.64540/-110.85846 **Elev:** 6836 **Grid:** 3/9
Yellowstone - West Thumb to Madison *(see chapter)*   **Type:** Hwy Transition w/Chapter
33.5 mi southwest section of the **Grand Loop Road** from **Madison** southeast to **West Thumb**. The majority of the geyser activity is along this section. Highlights include: **Firehole Falls, Lower Geyser Basin, Firehole Lake Drive Geysers, Midway Geyser Basin, Fairy Falls, Biscuit Basin, Mystic Falls, Black Sand Basin, Upper Geyser Basin, Old Faithful, Kepler Cascades, Lone Star Geyser**.
Nearest Town: West Yellowstone, MT 14.0 W **Directions:** SE to West Thumb from MM 33.5

MM: 0.0/13.4 **GPS:** 44.64540/-110.85846 **Elev:** 6836 **Grid:** 3/9
Yellowstone - West Entrance to Madison *(see chapter)*   **Type:** Hwy Junction w/Chapter
13.6 mi highway from **Madison** west out of **Yellowstone National Park** to **US-20** and **West Yellowstone, Montana**. The road follows the **Madison River** with minor points of interest and scenic views along the way.
Nearest Town: West Yellowstone, MT 14.0 W **Directions:** W to West Yellowstone, MT from MM 13.6

MM: 0.2/13.2 **GPS:** 44.64650/-110.85501 **Elev:** 6850 **Grid:** 3/9 **Land:** NPS
Purple Mountain Trailhead   **Type:** Trailhead
A hike up **Purple Mountain** through a partially burned lodgepole pine forest for nice views of the lower **Gibbon River Valley, Firehole Valley**, and the **Madison** area. *Moderately strenuous; 6.0 mi round-trip; 1500 ft elev gain.*
Cool Rating: *** **Crowds:** * **Time:** 3 hrs
Directions: Parking for 4 or 5 vehicles at a small pullout on S side of hwy. Trail starts across the road about 30 yds E of the pullout at the "Purple Mountain" sign. It can also be accessed by walking about 0.3 mi NE to the trailhead from the Madison Campground or the Madison Information Station.

MM: 0.8/12.6 **GPS:** 44.64994/-110.84513 **Elev:** 6900 **Grid:** 3/9 **Land:** NPS
Terrace Spring Thermal Area   **Type:** Thermal Area
A 0.2 mi wheelchair accessible boardwalk to **Bath Spring** and **Terrace Spring**, a large hot lake.
Cool Rating: ** **Crowds:** * **Time:** 20 min **Directions:** NE into parking area

MM: 1.6/11.8 **GPS:** 44.65049/-110.82911 **Elev:** 6860 **Grid:** 3/9 **Land:** NPS
Tuff Cliff Picnic Area   **Type:** Picnic Area
A nice picnic area below **Tuff Cliff** with an interpretive sign about its formation. The handicapped accessible table is in the open and the other 2 tables are located in a stand of lodgepole pines. *3 tables. Vault toilet. Handicapped accessible.*
Directions: N side of hwy

MM: 4.4/9.0 **GPS:** 44.64925/-110.77427 **Elev:** 7025 **Grid:** 4/9 **Land:** NPS
Gibbon Falls Picnic Area   **Type:** Picnic Area
Near the **Gibbon River** just downriver from **Gibbon Falls**. *7 tables. Vault toilet. Handicapped accessible.*
Directions: S side of hwy

MM: 4.8/8.6 **GPS:** 44.65387/-110.77181 **Elev:** 7090 **Grid:** 4/9 **Land:** NPS
Gibbon Falls   **Type:** Waterfall
An 84 ft waterfall on the **Gibbon River**, which cascades through a canyon over smooth volcanic rock. Walking south 100 yds leads to a more straight-on view where parking is not allowed.
Cool Rating: **** **Crowds:** ***** **Time:** 15 min **Directions:** SE side of hwy

MM: 5.3/8.1 **GPS:** 44.65964/-110.76624 **Elev:** 7185 **Grid:** 4/9 **Land:** NPS
Iron Spring Picnic Area   **Type:** Picnic Area
A picnic and parking area that provides views of **Gibbon Canyon** and the **Gibbon River**. *5 tables. Vault toilet. Handicapped accessible.*
Directions: NW side of hwy

MM: 6.2/7.2 **GPS:** 44.65962/-110.75071 **Elev:** 7350 **Grid:** 4/9 **Land:** NPS
Caldera Rim Picnic Area   **Type:** Picnic Area
A picnic and parking area that provides views of **Gibbon Canyon** and the **Gibbon River**. *3 tables. Vault toilet. Handicapped accessible.*
Directions: NE side of hwy

MM: 8.2/5.2 **GPS:** 44.67866/-110.74651 **Elev:** 7315 **Grid:** 4/8 **Land:** NPS
Beryl Spring   **Type:** Thermal Area
Named after the similarity in color to the blue-green color of the gemstone beryl. This is one of the hottest springs in **Yellowstone National Park** at 196° F. This is below the boiling point of water and the violent agitation of the water is from volcanic gases. Dense clouds of steam make this difficult to photograph.
Cool Rating: *** **Crowds:** ** **Time:** 15 min **Directions:** W side of hwy on S end of bridge

MM: 8.6/4.8 **GPS:** 44.68368/-110.74466 **GPS2:** 44.68438/-110.75366 **Elev:** 7333 **Grid:** 4/8 **Land:** NPS
Monument Geyser Basin Trailhead   **Type:** Geyser Basin
A nearly dormant geyser basin that contains oddly shaped geyser cones. The most distinct is the tall thin cone of **Monument Geyser**, also known as **Thermos Bottle Geyser**, which is still slightly active. This colorful area also contains steaming fumaroles, bubbling pools, and mud pots. The trail follows the **Gibbon River** for 0.5 mi before climbing steeply with a few switchbacks to scenic views and this very interesting and unusual thermal area. The forest along the way was burned in the 1988 fires and the regenerating forest offers little shade. *Moderately strenuous; 1.3 mi one-way; 650 ft elev gain.*
Cool Rating: ***** **Crowds:** * **Time:** 1.5-2 hrs
Directions: Main pullout on NW side of hwy just SW of bridge. Another pullout on SE side of hwy NE of bridge.

MM: 9.6/3.8 ***Dist:*** 0.2 ***GPS:*** 44.69654/-110.74185 ***GPS2:*** 44.69283/-110.73762 ***Elev:*** 7343 ***Grid:*** 4/8 ***Land:*** NPS
Artist Paint Pots   ***Type:*** Thermal Area
An easy 1.0 mi round-trip path leads to small geysers, hot pools, steam vents, and pastel multicolored mud pots at the top of
Paintpots Hill, which provides an overlook of the area below.
Cool Rating: **** ***Crowds:*** ***** ***Time:*** 1 hr ***Directions:*** E 0.2 mi to parking area.

MM: 10.2/3.2 ***GPS:*** 44.70621/-110.74557 ***Elev:*** 7342 ***Grid:*** 4/7 ***Land:*** NPS
Gibbon Meadows Picnic Area   ***Type:*** Picnic Area
A nice forested picnic area next to the **Gibbon River**. *9 tables. Vault toilet. Handicapped accessible.*
Directions: Half-loop on NW side of hwy

MM: 10.5/2.9 ***GPS:*** 44.70965/-110.74210 ***Elev:*** 7352 ***Grid:*** 4/7 ***Land:*** NPS
Chocolate Pots   ***Type:*** Thermal Area
2 dark brown cones on either side of the **Gibbon River**. The cones are several feet tall and are formed on the hillsides at the edge
of the river. Hot springs feed a constant flow of water to the cones, which are streaked green, yellow, and orange by warm water
bacteria and algae. Mineral oxides are responsible for the dark-brown color of the cones. The best cone is across the river from the
middle of the pullout (44.70992/-110.74248). The other cone is located on the near side of the river about 40 yds past the
northeast end of the parking area (44.71008/-110.74141).
Cool Rating: *** ***Crowds:*** * ***Time:*** 15 min ***Directions:*** NW side of hwy

MM: 13.4/0.0 ***GPS:*** 44.72559/-110.69999 ***Elev:*** 7580 ***Grid:*** 5/7 ***Land:*** NPS
Norris Geyser Basin and Museum   ***Type:*** Geyser Basin
The oldest, hottest, and most extreme and changeable thermal area in **Yellowstone National Park**. 2.2 mi of trails in 2 loops lead
past geysers, hot springs, hot lakes, and fumaroles. Most springs and all geysers are hot enough to release boiling water. The
water at **Norris Geyser Basin** is *acidic* in nature, as opposed to most other thermal areas in **Yellowstone National Park** and
around the world, which are *alkaline*.

Upon entering the geyser basin, the walking path passes a small bookstore and through a stone archway designed as a gateway
to the overlooks and trails of the geyser basin. This archway is part of the **Norris Geyser Basin Museum**, one of the park's
original trailside museums opened to the public in 1930. The rustic architecture is an excellent example of the stone and log
architecture of the period. The museum is now a **National Historic Landmark**. It contains a staffed information desk and several
exhibits related to the **Norris** area's geothermal wonders. Ranger-led programs are offered several times each day. A trail
brochure provides a map and detailed descriptions of the main features.

The **Norris Geyser Basin** is divided into 2 separate basins:

Porcelain Basin to the north is named for the milky color of the mineral deposits and is the fastest changing area. The 3/4 mi trail
from the **Norris Geyser Basin Museum** drops into a vast, nearly treeless, open terrain with hundreds of densely packed
geothermal features and colorful runoff areas. Highlighted features: **Congress Pool**, **Whirligig Geyser**, **Whale's Mouth**,
Crackling Lake, and **Blue Geyser**.

Back Basin to the south is in stark contrast with thermal features scattered around a 1.5 mi trail in a forested terrain. Highlighted
features: **Steamboat Geyser** - The world's tallest active geyser, but major eruptions are rare. Minor eruptions can reach 40 ft.
Cistern Spring - Linked to Steamboat Geyser, this pool constantly overflows depositing up to 1/2 in of gray sinter around the lip
per year. **Echinus Geyser** - The largest frequently active acid geyser in the world. Eruptions used to be predictable before 1997,
but it now erupts a few times a day, 40-60 ft for 4 min. **Porkchop Geyser** - The geyser exploded on September 5 1989, throwing
rocks surrounding the vent more than 216 ft and turning it into a hot spring. **Minute Geyser** - Used to erupt every minute before its
larger vent was clogged with rocks tossed in by early visitors.
Hours: Museum: 9am - 6pm ***Phone:*** 307-344-2812 ***Cool Rating:*** ***** ***Crowds:*** ***** ***Time:*** 1-3 hrs ***Directions:*** W 0.3 mi

MM: 13.4/0.0 ***GPS:*** 44.72735/-110.69656 ***Elev:*** 7526 ***Grid:*** 5/7
Yellowstone - Norris to Mammoth Hot Springs *(see chapter)*   ***Type:*** Hwy Transition w/Chapter
20.9 mi northwest section of the **Grand Loop Road** from **Norris** north to **Mammoth Hot Springs**. Highlights include: **Norris
Geyser Basin**, **Osprey Falls**, **Bunsen Peak**, **The Hoodoos**, **Rustic Falls**, **Mammoth Hot Springs Terraces**.
Nearest Town: Canyon Village 11.7 E ***Directions:*** N to Mammoth Hot Springs from MM 0

MM: 13.4/0.0 ***GPS:*** 44.72735/-110.69656 ***Elev:*** 7526 ***Grid:*** 5/7
Yellowstone - Norris to Canyon Village *(see chapter)*   ***Type:*** Hwy Junction w/Chapter
11.6 mi cutoff road at the center of the **Grand Loop Road** connecting **Norris** east to **Canyon Village**. If just visiting the attractions
along this highway, they are much closer from this end. Highlights include: **Virginia Cascade** and **Little Gibbon Falls**.
Nearest Town: Canyon Village 11.7 E ***Directions:*** E to Canyon Village from MM 0

MM: 13.4/0.0 ***GPS:*** 44.72735/-110.69656 ***Elev:*** 7526 ***Grid:*** 5/7 ***Land:*** NPS
Yellowstone - Norris to Madison   ***Type:*** Highway End
13.4 mi west-central section of the **Grand Loop Road** from **Norris** southwest to **Madison**. Highlights include: **Norris Geyser
Basin**, **Chocolate Pots**, **Artist Paint Pots**, **Monument Geyser Basin**, **Beryl Spring**, **Gibbon Falls**.
Nearest Town: Canyon Village 11.7 E ***Directions:*** SW to Madison from MM 13.4

Yellowstone - Mammoth Hot Springs to Tower-Roosevelt   W/E

MM: 0.0/18.1 *GPS:* 44.97631/-110.70088 *Elev:* 6243 *Grid:* 5/1 *Land:* NPS
Yellowstone - Mammoth Hot Springs to Tower-Roosevelt   *Type:* Highway Description
18.1 mi north section of the **Grand Loop Road** from **Mammoth Hot Springs** east to **Tower-Roosevelt**. Highlights include:
Undine Falls, Wraith Falls, Hellroaring Creek Trail, Petrified Tree.
Nearest Town: Gardiner, MT 5.5 N *Directions:* E to Tower-Roosevelt from MM 0

MM: 0.0/18.1 *GPS:* 44.97631/-110.70088 *Elev:* 6243 *Grid:* 5/1
Yellowstone - Norris to Mammoth Hot Springs *(see chapter)*   *Type:* Hwy Junction w/Chapter
20.9 mi northwest section of the **Grand Loop Road** from **Mammoth Hot Springs** south to **Norris**. Highlights include: **Mammoth Hot Springs Terraces, Rustic Falls, Osprey Falls, Bunsen Peak, The Hoodoos, Norris Geyser Basin.**
Nearest Town: Gardiner, MT 5.5 N *Directions:* S to Norris from MM 20.9

MM: 0.0/18.1 *GPS:* 44.97631/-110.70088 *Elev:* 6243 *Grid:* 5/1
Yellowstone - North Entrance to Mammoth Hot Springs *(see chapter)*   *Type:* Hwy Junction w/Chapter
5.3 mi highway from **Mammoth Hot Springs** north out of **Yellowstone National Park** to **US-89** in **Montana**. **Gardiner, Montana** is located just outside the north park entrance. A few minor points of interest along the way.
Nearest Town: Gardiner, MT 5.5 N *Directions:* N to Gardiner, MT from MM 5.3

MM: 0.0/18.1 *GPS:* 44.97631/-110.70088 *Elev:* 6243 *Grid:* 5/1 *Land:* NPS
Mammoth Hot Springs   *Type:* Town
Visitor services located on the northwest end of the **Grand Loop Road**, including an ATM, general store, gift shop, hotel, cabins, fuel, restaurant and fast food, showers, horseback riding, medical clinic, backcountry and fishing permits, **Ranger Station**. This is also the location of the **Yellowstone National Park** headquarters. A resident herd of elk frequent the grassy areas around the development. Across from the visitor center are 5 unshaded picnic tables in the grass. 2 more picnic tables are located under trees 0.1 mi north next to the medical clinic.

The **U.S. Army** arrived in **Yellowstone** in 1886 to protect the park from poaching, vandalism, souvenir collecting, and forest fires. **Fort Yellowstone** was built here by the **U.S. Army** in 1891 and occupied until 1913, when **Yellowstone** was turned over to the **National Park Service**. On the east end of town is a large group of red-roofed buildings that were part of the fort. These buildings include the **Albright Visitor Center**, where a brochure can be obtained for a self-guided walking tour of the **Fort Yellowstone Historic District**. The visitor center also contains a staffed information desk, bookstore, theatre, historical displays about the early exploration of **Yellowstone**, dioramas of **Yellowstone**'s wildlife and history, historic paintings by **Thomas Moran**, and original **United States Geological Survey** photos by **William H. Jackson**, who was the photographer to the **Hayden Expedition** of 1871.
Hours: Albright Visitor Center: 8am - 7pm (May 23 - Sept 30); 9am - 6pm (offseason) *Phone:* 307-344-2263
Directions: The Visitor Center is 1 block NE of the turnoff to Norris and the North Entrance.

MM: 4.0/14.1 *GPS:* 44.94356/-110.64047 *GPS2:* 44.94406/-110.63852 *Elev:* 6581 *Grid:* 6/1 *Land:* NPS
Undine Falls   *Type:* Waterfall
A 60 ft waterfall on **Lava Creek** that drops in 3 steps into **Lava Creek Canyon**. The overlook is just below the parking pullout and is ~150 yds from the falls. A 1/2 mi trail leads to the north side of the falls *(see next section)*.
Cool Rating: **** *Crowds:* *** *Time:* 15 min *Directions:* NE side of hwy

MM: 4.4/13.7 *GPS:* 44.94090/-110.63214 *Elev:* 6562 *Grid:* 6/2 *Land:* NPS
Lava Creek Trail to Undine Falls   *Type:* Trailhead
A short hike along the **Lava Creek Trail** to the north side and brink of **Undine Falls** *(see previous section)*. Beyond the falls the trail continues west 3.4 mi to the **Boiling River Trailhead** and the **Mammoth Hot Springs** area. The trail descends 700 ft and parallels the base of **Mount Everts** and **Lava Creek** through **Lava Creek Canyon**. From the trailhead, head north 0.1 mi then turn left and follow the trail 1/3 mi northwest to the falls. *Easy; 0.9 mi round-trip; 50 ft elev loss.*
Cool Rating: **** *Crowds:* * *Time:* 45 min
Directions: Park at the picnic area on S side of hwy. The trail is across the hwy, just E of the bridge.

MM: 4.4/13.7 *GPS:* 44.94073/-110.63268 *Elev:* 6562 *Grid:* 6/2 *Land:* NPS
Lava Creek Picnic Area   *Type:* Picnic Area
A nice small picnic area next to **Lava Creek**. *5 tables. Vault toilet. Handicapped accessible.*
Directions: S side of hwy

MM: 4.9/13.2 *GPS:* 44.94231/-110.62354 *GPS2:* 44.93695/-110.62202 *Elev:* 6690 *Grid:* 6/1 *Land:* NPS
Wraith Falls   *Type:* Waterfall
A 90 ft waterfall on **Lupine Creek**, which is really more of a cascade that fans out over a gently sloping section of smooth rock. Follow a trail south through **Lupine Meadows** with a short climb to a view of the falls from ~100 yds. *Easy; 0.4 mi one-way; 80 ft elev gain.*
Cool Rating: *** *Crowds:* * *Time:* 30 min *Directions:* Parking pullout on S side of hwy

MM: 8.2/9.9 *GPS:* 44.95940/-110.56649 *Elev:* 6923 *Grid:* 7/1 *Land:* NPS
Forces of the Northern Range Trail   *Type:* Hiking Trail
A 1/2 mi boardwalk loop trail that passes interpretive displays about the geology and nature in the northern range of **Yellowstone National Park**, which is unique from the rest of the park. *Wheelchair accessible.*
Cool Rating: ** *Crowds:* * *Time:* 30 min *Directions:* NW side of hwy

MM: 9.5/8.6 *GPS:* 44.95807/-110.54170 *Elev:* 6909 *Grid:* 7/1 *Land:* NPS
Blacktail Deer Plateau Drive   *Type:* Scenic Drive
A 6.8 mi side trip along a one-way dirt road over a high plateau of sagebrush and forest. This was part of the first road through the area and the route of early explorations. The road climbs through mostly grassland and scattered trees 670 ft in 4.0 mi. The road then descends 980 ft in 2.8 mi through a small canyon and a semi-forested valley, passing a display about the effects of the 1988 fire on the area, before connecting back to the main highway. This route is actually slightly shorter than the main road but much slower.
Cool Rating: ** *Crowds:* * *Time:* 1 hr *Road Desc:* Gravel, impassable when wet, winding & steep in spots
Notes: Closed after rain or snowstorms. No RVs or trailers. Not really a lot to see on this route.
Directions: S side of hwy

MM: 14.5/3.7 *Dist:* 0.3 *GPS:* 44.94902/-110.45068 *Elev:* 6463 *Grid:* 9/1 *Land:* NPS
Hellroaring Creek Trailhead   *Type:* Trailhead
A hiking and horse trail to the **Yellowstone River** and **Hellroaring Creek**:

To the suspension bridge over the Yellowstone River - Descend along a steep, smooth trail through sparse forest to a suspension bridge over the **Yellowstone River**, which flows through the **Black Canyon of the Yellowstone**, a narrow steep walled canyon. *Moderate; 1.0 mi one-way; 570 ft elev loss.*

Continuing to Hellroaring Creek - After the bridge, the trail climbs 90 ft in 1/4 mi to a small forested valley before descending 0.65 mi down sagebrush hills to a trail junction. Turn left 100 yds then right 0.1 mi past a small pond to **Hellroaring Creek**. *Moderately easy; 1.0 mi one-way; 90 ft elev gain, 140 ft elev loss.*
Cool Rating: *** *Crowds:* * *Time:* 1-2 hrs *Road Desc:* Gravel *Directions:* N 1/4 mi
Notes: Horses use this trail and the suspension bridge actually has a dirt surface.

MM: 16.6/1.6 *GPS:* 44.92202/-110.44409 *Elev:* 6597 *Grid:* 9/2 *Land:* NPS
Blacktail Deer Plateau Drive (end)   *Type:* Scenic Drive
End of the one-way side road that starts at MM 9.5/8.6.

MM: 16.7/1.4 *Dist:* 0.5 *GPS:* 44.91628/-110.43938 *Elev:* 6743 *Grid:* 9/2 *Land:* NPS
Petrified Tree   *Type:* Point of Interest
A relatively tall petrified redwood tree stump behind a protective fence. There were previously 2 others, but they were removed a piece at a time by park visitors. The trees were petrified when their organic structure was replaced by minerals while they were slowly buried by volcanic ash.
Cool Rating: *** *Crowds:* ** *Time:* 15 min *Notes:* No room to turn around large RVs and trailers. *Directions:* S 0.5 mi

MM: 16.9/1.3 *GPS:* 44.92166/-110.43847 *Elev:* 6581 *Grid:* 9/2 *Land:* NPS
Interpretive Pullout: North Fork Fire   *Type:* Point of Interest
A sign explains how the 1988 **North Fork Fire** was so hot that it scorched and sterilized the soil.
Cool Rating: ** *Crowds:* * *Time:* 5 min *Directions:* N side of hwy

MM: 17.9/0.2 *GPS:* 44.91643/-110.41991 *Elev:* 6267 *Grid:* 9/2 *Land:* NPS
Tower Ranger Station   *Type:* Visitor Center
Information, maps, and backcountry and fishing permits. This 1923 building is a reconstruction of a 1907 soldier station.
Directions: SE 90 yds.

MM: 18.1/0.0 *Dist:* 0.2 *GPS:* 44.91300/-110.41640 *Elev:* 6318 *Grid:* 9/2 *Land:* NPS
Roosevelt   *Type:* Town
Visitor services located on the northeast end of the **Grand Loop Road**, including a general store, gift shop, fuel, restaurant, showers, cabins (historic **Roosevelt Lodge**), horseback riding, backcountry and fishing permits, and a **Ranger Station**.

MM: 18.1/0.0 *GPS:* 44.91601/-110.41577 *Elev:* 6262 *Grid:* 9/2
Yellowstone - Tower-Roosevelt to Canyon Village *(see chapter)*   *Type:* Hwy Transition w/Chapter
18.3 mi northeast section of the **Grand Loop Road** from **Tower-Roosevelt** south to **Canyon Village**. Highlights include: **Calcite Springs**, **Devil's Den**, **Tower Fall**, **Mount Washburn**.
Directions: SE to Canyon Village from MM 0

MM: 18.1/0.0 *GPS:* 44.91601/-110.41577 *Elev:* 6262 *Grid:* 9/2
Yellowstone - Northeast Entrance to Tower-Roosevelt *(see chapter)*   *Type:* Hwy Junction w/Chapter
28.2 mi highway from **Tower-Roosevelt** northeast out of **Yellowstone National Park** to **US-212** in **Montana**. A few minor points of interest along the way.
Directions: NE to Cooke City, MT from MM 28.2

MM: 18.1/0.0 *GPS:* 44.91601/-110.41577 *Elev:* 6262 *Grid:* 9/2 *Land:* NPS
Yellowstone - Tower-Roosevelt to Mammoth Hot Springs   *Type:* Highway End
18.1 mi north section of the **Grand Loop Road** from **Tower-Roosevelt** west to **Mammoth Hot Springs**. Highlights include: **Petrified Tree**, **Hellroaring Creek Trail**, **Wraith Falls**, **Undine Falls**.
Directions: W to Mammoth Hot Springs from MM 18.1

Yellowstone - Norris to Canyon Village   E/W

MM: 0.0/11.6 **GPS:** 44.72735/-110.69656 **Elev:** 7526 **Grid:** 5/7 **Land:** NPS
Yellowstone - Norris to Canyon Village   **Type:** Highway Description
11.6 mi cutoff road at the center of the **Grand Loop Road** connecting **Norris** east to **Canyon Village**. If just visiting the attractions along this highway, they are much closer from this end. Highlights include: **Virginia Cascade** and **Little Gibbon Falls**.
Nearest Town: Canyon Village 11.7 E **Directions:** E to Canyon Village from MM 0

MM: 0.0/11.6 **GPS:** 44.72735/-110.69656 **Elev:** 7526 **Grid:** 5/7
Yellowstone - Norris to Mammoth Hot Springs (see chapter)   **Type:** Hwy Junction w/Chapter
20.9 mi northwest section of the **Grand Loop Road** from **Norris** north to **Mammoth Hot Springs**. Highlights include: **Norris Geyser Basin, Osprey Falls, Bunsen Peak, The Hoodoos, Rustic Falls, Mammoth Hot Springs Terraces.**
Nearest Town: Canyon Village 11.7 E **Directions:** N to Mammoth Hot Springs from MM 0

MM: 0.0/11.6 **GPS:** 44.72735/-110.69656 **Elev:** 7526 **Grid:** 5/7
Yellowstone - Madison to Norris (see chapter)   **Type:** Hwy Junction w/Chapter
13.4 mi west-central section of the **Grand Loop Road** from **Norris** southwest to **Madison**. Highlights include: **Norris Geyser Basin, Chocolate Pots, Artist Paint Pots, Monument Geyser Basin, Beryl Spring, Gibbon Falls.**
Nearest Town: Canyon Village 11.7 E **Directions:** SW to Madison from MM 13.4

MM: 0.5/11.0 **Dist:** 0.3 **GPS:** 44.73020/-110.68905 **Elev:** 7486 **Grid:** 5/7 **Land:** NPS
Norris Meadows Picnic Area   **Type:** Picnic Area
A nice shady and flat picnic area. *16 tables. 4 grills. Vault toilet. Handicapped accessible.*
Directions: N 1/4 mi

MM: 1.6/9.9 **Dist:** 0.9 **GPS:** 44.71402/-110.65033 **GPS2:** 44.71310/-110.64764 **Elev:** 7750 **Grid:** 6/7 **Land:** NPS
Virginia Cascade   **Type:** Waterfall
A pretty waterfall on the **Gibbon River**, which cascades 60 ft down a gradual slope into a forested canyon. A 2.0 mi one-way road leaves the main highway, loops past the falls, and returns to the highway 1.9 mi east. Drive down the road 0.9 mi to the viewpoint of the falls from ~200 yds away. Unfortunately at this point the road is narrow with steep drop-offs and little room to park. Continue 0.2 mi to the top of the falls just off the southwest side of the road. A picnic area is located near the end of the road. *6 tables. Vault toilet. Handicapped accessible.*
Cool Rating: *** **Crowds:** ** **Time:** 20 min **Road Desc:** Paved, narrow & winding
Notes: No RVs or trailers. The road past the falls is about the same distance as the main highway.
Directions: SE on the 2.0 mi one-way half-loop road

MM: 3.1/8.5 **GPS:** 44.71727/-110.63960 **Elev:** 7923 **Grid:** 6/7 **Land:** NPS
Fire and Blowdown Exhibit   **Type:** Point of Interest
In 1984, a violent wind shear uprooted and toppled thousands of lodgepole pine trees in this area. This was followed a few years later by the big fire in 1988. Lodgepole pines actually depend on fire to melt resin, releasing the seeds and starting a new generation of trees. 20+ years of growth can now be seen on these new trees. Observe the area on a 50 yd boardwalk with an interpretive sign.
Cool Rating: ** **Crowds:** * **Time:** 15 min
Directions: SW side of hwy. Narrow pullouts on both sides of hwy. No road signs identify the site, but there is a crosswalk.

MM: 3.4/8.2 **GPS:** 44.71674/-110.63382 **Elev:** 7877 **Grid:** 6/7 **Land:** NPS
Ice Lake   **Type:** Lake
A short hike north along the west end of the long and narrow **Ice Lake**. The southwest tip of the lake is at 0.2 mi and the northwest end is at 0.5 mi. This is also the junction with the **Howard Eaton Trail**, which heads east 0.7 mi along the north end of the lake and continues to 3 more lakes: **Wolf Lake** (3.1 mi), **Grebe Lake** (4.2 mi), and **Cascade Lake** (6.9 mi). This area was almost completely burned by the 1988 fires leaving remarkable piles of downed trees. In some places it looks as if there is a wood fence along the trail. The wood piles are the attraction here, as Ice Lake is a fairly typical lake. *Easy; 0.5 mi one-way; 20 ft elev gain;*
Cool Rating: ** **Crowds:** * **Time:** 30 min **Directions:** Parking area on N side of hwy
Notes: The downed trees are similar to the "Fire and Blowdown Exhibit" in the previous section.

MM: 3.5/8.1 **GPS:** 44.71501/-110.63148 **Elev:** 7855 **Grid:** 6/7 **Land:** NPS
East End of Virginia Cascade Drive   **Type:** Highway Junction
End of the one-way loop (see Virginia Cascade at MM 1.6/9.9).

MM: 3.8/7.8 **GPS:** 44.71269/-110.62692 **GPS2:** 44.71665/-110.61570 **Elev:** 7796 **Grid:** 6/7 **Land:** NPS
Little Gibbon Falls   **Type:** Waterfall
A hike along the **Wolf Lake Trail**, roughly paralleling the meandering **Little Gibbon River** to **Little Gibbon Falls**, which drops 25 ft into a small canyon. The trail starts through forest and follows the base of a hill for about 0.4 mi before crossing an open meadow. At the end of the meadow the trail climbs to an overlook of the falls from the edge of the canyon. A short distance farther the trail descends to an overlook above the falls where a side trail leads to the brink of the falls. *Easy; 3/4 mi one-way; 95 ft elev gain.*
Cool Rating: *** **Crowds:** * **Time:** 1 hr
Directions: Parking area on SW side of hwy; Cross the hwy and walk SE 40 yds to the **Wolf Creek Trailhead**.

MM: 11.6/0.0 *Dist:* 0.1 *GPS:* 44.73547/-110.48945 *Elev:* 7940 *Grid:* 8/7 *Land:* NPS
Canyon Village   *Type:* Town & Campground
Visitor services located on the east central section of the **Grand Loop Road** and on the north end of **Grand Canyon of the Yellowstone**, including an ATM, general store, gift shop, sporting goods store, fuel, auto repair, restaurant, cafeteria, fast food, laundry, showers, hotel, cabins, post office, horseback riding, backcountry and fishing permits, and a **Ranger Station**. On the west side of the complex is the large **Canyon Visitor Education Center**, which contains a staffed information desk, bookstore, a large theatre, and several elaborate exhibits about **Yellowstone**'s supervolcano and other aspects of the park geology.

The campground is one of 4 large modern campgrounds that take reservations. 10 loops. Conifer forest. Paved roads and parking areas. Restrooms with flush toilets, running water, and electricity. Generators permitted. Amphitheater for ranger programs. 3 wheelchair accessible sites.
Hours: Visitor center: 8am - 8pm (307-344-2550)
Directions: E 0.1 mi and right to Visitor Center and stores; E 0.1 mi and left to campground or right to hotel.

MM: 11.6/0.0 *GPS:* 44.73591/-110.49325 *Elev:* 7915 *Grid:* 8/7
Yellowstone - Canyon Village to Fishing Bridge *(see chapter)*   *Type:* Hwy Junction w/Chapter
15.4 mi east-central section of the **Grand Loop Road** from **Canyon Village** south to **Fishing Bridge**. Highlights include: **Grand Canyon of the Yellowstone**, **Upper Falls**, **Lower Falls**, **Sulphur Caldron**, **Mud Volcano Area**, **LeHardy Rapids**.
Nearest Town: Canyon Village 0.1 E *Directions:* S to Fishing Bridge from MM 0

MM: 11.6/0.0 *GPS:* 44.73591/-110.49325 *Elev:* 7915 *Grid:* 8/7
Yellowstone - Tower-Roosevelt to Canyon Village *(see chapter)*   *Type:* Hwy Junction w/Chapter
18.3 mi northeast section of the **Grand Loop Road** from **Canyon Village** north to **Tower-Roosevelt**. Highlights include: **Mount Washburn**, **Tower Fall**, **Devil's Den**, **Calcite Springs**.
Directions: N to Tower-Roosevelt from MM 18.3

MM: 11.6/0.0 *GPS:* 44.73591/-110.49325 *Elev:* 7915 *Grid:* 8/7 *Land:* NPS
Yellowstone - Canyon Village to Norris   *Type:* Highway End
11.6 mi cutoff road at the center of the **Grand Loop Road** connecting **Canyon Village** west to **Norris**. If just visiting the attractions along this highway, they are much closer from the **Norris** end. Highlights include: **Little Gibbon Falls** and **Virginia Cascade**.
Directions: W to Norris from MM 11.6

Yellowstone - Norris to Mammoth Hot Springs · S/N

MM: 0.0/20.9 *GPS:* 44.72735/-110.69656 *Elev:* 7526 *Grid:* 5/7 *Land:* NPS
Yellowstone - Norris to Mammoth Hot Springs   *Type:* Highway Description
20.9 mi northwest section of the **Grand Loop Road** from **Norris** north to **Mammoth Hot Springs**. Highlights include: **Norris Geyser Basin, Osprey Falls, Bunsen Peak, The Hoodoos, Rustic Falls, Mammoth Hot Springs Terraces**.
Nearest Town: Canyon Village 11.7 E *Directions:* N to Mammoth Hot Springs from MM 0

MM: 0.0/20.9 *GPS:* 44.72735/-110.69656 *Elev:* 7526 *Grid:* 5/7
Yellowstone - Norris to Canyon Village *(see chapter)*   *Type:* Hwy Junction w/Chapter
11.6 mi cutoff road at the center of the **Grand Loop Road** connecting **Norris** east to **Canyon Village**. If just visiting the attractions along this highway, they are much closer from this end. Highlights include: **Virginia Cascade** and **Little Gibbon Falls**.
Nearest Town: Canyon Village 11.7 E *Directions:* E to Canyon Village from MM 0

MM: 0.0/20.9 *GPS:* 44.72735/-110.69656 *Elev:* 7526 *Grid:* 5/7
Yellowstone - Madison to Norris *(see chapter)*   *Type:* Hwy Transition w/Chapter
13.4 mi west-central section of the **Grand Loop Road** from **Norris** southwest to **Madison**. Highlights include: **Norris Geyser Basin, Chocolate Pots, Artist Paint Pots, Monument Geyser Basin, Beryl Spring, Gibbon Falls**.
Nearest Town: Canyon Village 11.7 E *Directions:* SW to Madison from MM 13.4

MM: 0.0/20.9 *Dist:* 0.3 *GPS:* 44.72559/-110.69999 *Elev:* 7580 *Grid:* 5/7 *Land:* NPS
Norris Geyser Basin and Museum   *Type:* Geyser Basin
The oldest, hottest, and most extreme and changeable thermal area in **Yellowstone National Park**. 2.2 mi of trails in 2 loops lead past geysers, hot springs, hot lakes, and fumaroles. Most springs and all geysers are hot enough to release boiling water. The water at **Norris Geyser Basin** is *acidic* in nature, as opposed to most other thermal areas in **Yellowstone National Park** and around the world, which are *alkaline*.

Upon entering the geyser basin, the walking path passes a small bookstore and through a stone archway designed as a gateway to the overlooks and trails of the geyser basin. This archway is part of the **Norris Geyser Basin Museum**, one of the park's original trailside museums opened to the public in 1930. The rustic architecture is an excellent example of the stone and log architecture of the period. The museum is now a **National Historic Landmark**. It contains a staffed information desk and several exhibits related to the **Norris** area's geothermal wonders. Ranger-led programs are offered several times each day. A trail brochure provides a map and detailed descriptions of the main features.

The **Norris Geyser Basin** is divided into 2 separate basins:

Porcelain Basin to the north is named for the milky color of the mineral deposits and is the fastest changing area. The 3/4 mi trail from the **Norris Geyser Basin Museum** drops into a vast, nearly treeless, open terrain with hundreds of densely packed geothermal features and colorful runoff areas. Highlighted features: **Congress Pool, Whirligig Geyser, Whale's Mouth, Crackling Lake**, and **Blue Geyser**.

Back Basin to the south is in stark contrast with thermal features scattered around a 1.5 mi trail in a forested terrain. Highlighted features: **Steamboat Geyser** - The world's tallest active geyser, but major eruptions are rare. Minor eruptions can reach 40 ft. **Cistern Spring** - Linked to Steamboat Geyser, this pool constantly overflows depositing up to 1/2 in of gray sinter around the lip per year. **Echinus Geyser** - The largest frequently active acid geyser in the world. Eruptions used to be predictable before 1997, but it now erupts a few times a day, 40-60 ft for 4 min. **Porkchop Geyser** - The geyser exploded on September 5 1989, throwing rocks surrounding the vent more than 216 ft and turning it into a hot spring. **Minute Geyser** - Used to erupt every minute before its larger vent was clogged with rocks tossed in by early visitors.
Hours: Museum: 9am - 6pm *Phone:* 307-344-2812 *Cool Rating:* ***** *Crowds:* ***** *Time:* 1-3 hrs *Directions:* W 0.3 mi

MM: 0.8/20.1 *Dist:* 0.2 *GPS:* 44.73771/-110.69637 *Elev:* 7476 *Grid:* 5/7 *Land:* NPS
Museum of the National Park Ranger   *Type:* Museum
The **U.S. Army** arrived in **Yellowstone** in 1886 to protect the park from poaching, vandalism, souvenir collecting, and forest fires. They stayed until 1916, when the job was turned over to the **National Park Service**. This museum is dedicated to the men and women who have served as stewards of America's national parks, beginning from these military roots to their present-day roles. Inside are historical exhibits, including photographs, uniforms, equipment, and a 25 minute laser-disc historical documentary "American Legacy." The building stands on the site of the original 1886 soldier station, which was replaced after a fire in 1897 and modified in 1908. After the **National Park Service** took over, the building was used as a ranger station until being destroyed by an earthquake in 1959. It was restored in 1991 to reflect the station's original layout. The museum is staffed by retired National Park Service staff.
Hours: 9am - 5pm *Cool Rating:* ** *Crowds:* * *Time:* 30 min *Directions:* E 0.2 mi on the road to Norris Campground.

MM: 0.8/20.1 *Dist:* 0.3 *GPS:* 44.73781/-110.69373 *Elev:* 7513 *Grid:* 5/7 *Land:* NPS
Norris Campground   *Type:* Campground
A beautiful campground with evening presentations at Campfire Circle. *3 loops with a few walk-in sites and sites for longer rigs. Conifer forest. Roomy sites. Flush toilets. Generators permitted. Firewood and ice for sale. Cheaper than the large campgrounds that take reservations. Fills early in the morning.*
Crowds: ***** *[FEE AREA]* *Directions:* E 0.3 mi
Campsites: 116 *Shade:* **** *Privacy:* * *RV Size:* 30' *Other:* Water BEARS

MM: 2.7/18.2 *GPS:* 44.75368/-110.72492 *Elev:* 7532 *Grid:* 5/6 *Land:* NPS
Nymph Lake   *Type:* Scenic Viewpoint
A pretty view of a small, fishless lake located in a small valley in the midst of a colorful thermal landscape.
Cool Rating: ** *Crowds:* * *Time:* 5 min *Directions:* SW side of hwy

MM: 4.9/16.0 **GPS:** 44.78122/-110.74082 **GPS2:** 44.77940/-110.73400 **Elev:** 7575 **Grid:** 4/6 **Land:** NPS

Roaring Mountain   *Type:* Thermal Area

Originally named for the loud hissing of numerous steam vents on the 400 ft mountainside. The mountain is relatively quiet now; however, some steam can still be seen, particularly when the weather is cool. The leaching of sulfuric acid has produced the stark, barren environment. In front of the mountain is **Lemonade Lake**, which is usually dry.

Cool Rating: ** **Crowds:** * **Time:** 5 min **Directions:** E side of hwy

MM: 6.3/14.6 **GPS:** 44.79893/-110.74523 **Elev:** 7442 **Grid:** 4/5 **Land:** NPS

Grizzly Lake Trailhead and Twice Burned Interpretive Sign   *Type:* Trailhead

At the north end of this parking area is a trail to the long and narrow **Grizzly Lake**. The trail leads through a burn area and meadows to good fishing in the lake or in **Straight Creek**. The trail climbs 410 ft, including a steep 1/4 mi section that climbs 200 ft up switchbacks, before descending along switchbacks 340 ft to the lake in the last 1/2 mi. *Moderate; 3.6 mi round-trip; 410 ft elev gain, 340 ft elev loss.*

Also at the pullout is an interpretive sign explaining how the hillside was burned twice by fires in 1976 and 1988, and how the regrowth of the lodgepole pines was affected. The first trees that burned left fire-dependent cones to regenerate the forest; however, the young trees were subsequently burned before they were mature enough to produce cones.

Cool Rating: *** **Crowds:** * **Time:** 5 min - 2 hrs **Directions:** W side of hwy

MM: 7.5/13.5 **GPS:** 44.81133/-110.73210 **Elev:** 7400 **Grid:** 5/5 **Land:** NPS

Beaver Lake Picnic Area   *Type:* Picnic Area

A shady picnic area along a loop road. *9 tables. Vault toilet. Handicapped accessible.*

Directions: NW 80 yds

MM: 8.4/12.5 **GPS:** 44.82404/-110.72924 **Elev:** 7382 **Grid:** 5/4 **Land:** NPS

Obsidian Cliff   *Type:* Geological Feature

A pullout with signs about **Obsidian Cliff**, a vertical cliff that extends 1/2 mi and rises 150-200 ft above **Obsidian Creek**. Obsidian is volcanic glass that forms from rapidly cooling lava. Obsidian has formed at several locations within **Yellowstone National Park**; however, this is the largest concentration and easiest to access. Obsidian was a highly valued trade commodity among the native peoples of North America for many centuries, as it is easily shaped and forms sharp edges for cutting tools, projectile points, and decorative items.

Cool Rating: ** **Crowds:** * **Time:** 10 min **Notes:** It is against the law to remove obsidian from the park.

Directions: Pullout on W side of hwy. Obsidian Cliff on E side extending south.

MM: 9.7/11.2 **GPS:** 44.84247/-110.73352 **Elev:** 7343 **Grid:** 5/4 **Land:** NPS

Apollinaris Spring   *Type:* Point of Interest

Travertine steps laid in 1925 climb to a cold-water spring and interpretive signs. The spring was named after German spring water with a similar mineral content. The water is not safe to drink.

Cool Rating: ** **Crowds:** * **Time:** 10 min

Directions: NE side of hwy just SW of the spring in a small gravel pullout. Parking is also available at the end of the picnic area across the road. The spring is not marked with a road sign.

MM: 9.9/11.1 **Dist:** 0.1 **GPS:** 44.84405/-110.73436 **Elev:** 7338 **Grid:** 5/4 **Land:** NPS

Apollinaris Spring Picnic Area   *Type:* Picnic Area

6 tables. Flush toilet.

Directions: SW 0.1 mi

MM: 10.3/10.6 **GPS:** 44.85086/-110.73629 **Elev:** 7320 **Grid:** 5/4 **Land:** NPS

Interpretive Pullout: Moose Boggs   *Type:* Point of Interest

A stream running through a meadow with a nearby pine forest, which provide moose with willow shrubs to eat and forest for shelter. A sign explains more about moose habitat.

Cool Rating: * **Crowds:** * **Time:** 5 min **Directions:** W side of hwy

MM: 12.5/8.5 **Dist:** 0.5 **GPS:** 44.88080/-110.73400 **Elev:** 7284 **Grid:** 5/3 **Land:** NPS

Indian Creek Campground   *Type:* Campground

The campground is composed of an upper and lower loop. The lower loop is about twice as big as the upper loop, has some pull-thrus, and is better for RVs. Many of the sites in the upper loop are unlevel and better for tents. *Sparse conifer forest. Vault toilets. 5 pull-thrus. Generators not permitted. Firewood for sale. Cheaper than the large campgrounds that take reservations. Last campground on the Grand Loop Road to fill.*

Crowds: ***** **[FEE AREA]** **Directions:** NW 0.5 mi

Campsites: 75 **Shade:** *** **Privacy:** ** **RV Size:** 40' **Other:** Water BEARS

MM: 13.0/7.9 **Dist:** 0.3 **GPS:** 44.89125/-110.72986 **Elev:** 7267 **Grid:** 5/3 **Land:** NPS

Sheepeater Cliff Picnic Area   *Type:* Picnic Area

The **Sheepeater Cliffs** are basalt lava cliffs that formed columnar joints when they cooled nearly 500,000 years ago. The picnic area is situated in a sparse forest below these cliffs, near the **Gardner River** at the mouth of **Sheepeater Canyon**. *5 tables. Vault toilet. Handicapped accessible.*

Directions: NE 1/4 mi

MM: 15.3/5.7 **GPS:** 44.92043/-110.73180 **Elev:** 7277 **Grid:** 5/2 **Land:** NPS

Swan Lake   *Type:* Scenic Area

A shallow lake in a basin with an interpretive sign identifying the peaks of the **Gallatin Range** to the west. **Trumpeter Swans** are sometimes seen on the lake.

Cool Rating: * **Crowds:** * **Time:** 5 min **Directions:** W side of hwy

MM: 16.2/4.8   *GPS:* 44.93222/-110.72804   *GPS2:* 44.93309/-110.70744   *Elev:* 7276   *Grid:* 5/2   *Land:* NPS

Bunsen Peak   *Type:* Hiking Trail

A scenic hike to the 8,570 ft **Bunsen Peak**, which is an ancient volcano cone. The 1988 fires have left a regenerating burn mosaic that offers little shade along the way. Along the trail are views to the north of **Rustic Falls**, **Cathedral Rocks**, **Terrace Mountain**, **The Hoodoos**, **Golden Gate Canyon**, **Mammoth Hot Springs**, and the **Gardner River Valley** to **Gardiner, Montana**. Switchbacks cross talus slopes below the summit where bighorn sheep are often seen. From the top are great views in all directions of the surrounding mountains, peaks, and valleys, including the **Gallatin Range** to the west, **Electric Peak** (8 mi northwest), **Mount Holmes** (10 mi southwest), the **Washburn Range** to the east, and the **Absaroka Range** to the east and northeast. Return by the same route or continue another 2.1 mi east to connect to the road near the **Osprey Falls Trail** (*see next section*). Continue straight to the 2.8 mi round-trip trail to **Osprey Falls** or turn right to take the road back to the parking area and complete the loop. *Out and back: Moderate; 4.2 mi round-trip; 1290 ft elev gain. Loop: Moderate; 7.4 mi loop; 1290 ft elev gain.*
Loop with side trip to Osprey Falls: Moderately strenuous; 10.2 mi round-trip; 1290 ft elev gain, 875 ft elev loss to Osprey Falls.
Cool Rating: *****   *Crowds:* ****   *Time:* 2-6 hrs
Notes: Time depends on whether you hike the loop and/or hike to Osprey Falls.
Directions: Glen Creek Trailhead parking on SE side of hwy; Hike SE and turn left just past the service road barrier.

MM: 16.2/4.8   *GPS:* 44.93222/-110.72804   *GPS2:* 44.92871/-110.68096   *Elev:* 7276   *Grid:* 5/2   *Land:* NPS

Osprey Falls   *Type:* Waterfall

A spectacular 150 ft waterfall on the **Gardner River**, which flows through the deep **Sheepeater Canyon**. The first 3.2 mi of the trail is along open terrain on an old 2-track service road that skirts the southern base of **Bunsen Peak**. This road can be hiked or biked and is reasonably level except the last 0.1 mi, which descends 95 ft to the **Osprey Falls Trail** (MI 3.2). If a bike was ridden to this point leave it here. Follow the level footpath, which after a short distance parallels the canyon rim for 1/2 mi (MI 3.7). The trail then descends steeply 720 ft along 12 switchbacks into the canyon for 0.7 mi (MI 4.4). This part of the trail is narrow but fairly smooth. The final 0.2 mi to the falls overlook is along the base of the hillside above the river (MI 4.6). *Moderately strenuous; 4.6 mi one-way; 875 ft elev loss.*
Cool Rating: *****   *Crowds:* *   *Time:* 3-5 hrs
Notes: From the Osprey Falls Trail the road continues north descending 700 ft in another 2.6 mi to a residential area near Mammoth Hot Springs. The time depends on whether you hike or bike to the Osprey Falls Trail.
Directions: Glen Creek Trailhead parking on SE side of hwy; Head SE on the dirt service road.

MM: 16.2/4.8   *GPS:* 44.93222/-110.72804   *GPS2:* 44.94578/-110.72325   *Elev:* 7276   *Grid:* 5/2   *Land:* NPS

The Hoodoos   *Type:* Hiking Trail

A hike above the **Golden Gate Canyon** to **The Hoodoos**, a jumbled pile of rocks that have slid off **Terrace Mountain**. The rocks are primarily travertine, like those in **Mammoth Hot Springs**, which were formed by a hot spring system that existed several hundred thousand years ago. The trail climbs through forest 180 ft in 0.8 mi to the high point of the trail, which overlooks the **Golden Gate Canyon** and **Rustic Falls** with **Bunsen Peak** across the canyon. The trail then descends 215 ft into **The Hoodoos** area along a steep hillside under a rocky cliff face on the east side of **Terrace Mountain**. At 1.5 mi the trail crosses the main slide area. *Moderate; 1.5 mi one-way; 180 ft elev gain, 215 ft elev loss.*
Cool Rating: ****   *Crowds:* *   *Time:* 1.5 hrs
Notes: Fallen rocks can also be seen from a short drive-through located below the slide area at MM 17.3/3.7.
Directions: Glen Creek Trailhead parking on SE side of hwy; Cross the hwy and follow the Glen Creek Trail NW 0.2 mi to a junction with the Howard Eaton Trail. Turn right and follow this trail 1.3 mi.

MM: 16.3/4.6   *GPS:* 44.93377/-110.72622   *Elev:* 7252   *Grid:* 5/2   *Land:* NPS

Rustic Falls   *Type:* Waterfall

A 47 ft waterfall on **Glen Creek**. The parking area is at the top of the falls. The next pullout to the northeast for **Golden Gate** provides a slightly distant front view of the falls.
Cool Rating: ***   *Crowds:* *   *Time:* 15 min   *Directions:* SE side of hwy

MM: 16.4/4.5   *GPS:* 44.93470/-110.72440   *Elev:* 7210   *Grid:* 5/2   *Land:* NPS

Golden Gate at Kingman Pass & Rustic Falls   *Type:* Pass

A canyon cut by **Glen Creek** through volcanic tuff, which is stained reddish-yellow by iron oxide. A sign explains the history of travel through this canyon beginning with a wooden trestle built in 1885. A slightly distant front view of **Rustic Falls** is seen from the southwest end of the pullout.
Cool Rating: ***   *Crowds:* *   *Time:* 10 min   *Directions:* SE side of hwy

MM: 17.3/3.7   *GPS:* 44.94433/-110.71652   *Elev:* 7078   *Grid:* 5/1   *Land:* NPS

Silver Gate/The Hoodoos   *Type:* Geological Feature

A tight 125 yd one-way half-loop road through the remains of a large landslide off **Terrace Mountain**. The rocks are primarily travertine, like those in **Mammoth Hot Springs**, which were formed by a hot spring system that existed several hundred thousand years ago. *See The Hoodoos at MM 16.2/4.8 for a hike above this area.*
Cool Rating: **   *Crowds:* *   *Time:* Drive through   *Notes:* No RVs or trailers. No place to park.   *Directions:* NW side of hwy

MM: 17.9/3.1   *GPS:* 44.95165/-110.71321   *Elev:* 6895   *Grid:* 5/1   *Land:* NPS

Interpretive Pullout: The Burn Mosaic   *Type:* Point of Interest

A sign explains the uneven burn of the forest on **Bunsen Peak**. Below and to the south of the pullout is **Africa Lake**, named for its shape.
Cool Rating: *   *Crowds:* *   *Time:* 5 min   *Directions:* SE side of hwy

MM: 18.9/2.0   *GPS:* 44.96528/-110.70769   *Elev:* 6625   *Grid:* 5/1

Yellowstone - Upper Terrace Drive (*see chapter*)   *Type:* Side Loop Road w/Chapter

1.6 mi one-way loop road that provides automobile access to the **Mammoth Hot Springs Upper Terrace** as well as alternate access to the **Main Terrace** and **Canary Spring** without climbing stairs from below. The **Upper Terrace** contains individual thermal features spaced out along the road.
Cool Rating: *****   *Crowds:* ****   *Time:* 1/2 to 2 hrs   *Nearest Town:* Mammoth Hot Springs 2 N
Notes: No vehicles over 25 ft.   *Directions:* NW on loop road from MM 0

MM: 19.1/1.8 *GPS:* 44.96625/-110.70515 *Elev:* 6555 *Grid:* 5/1 *Land:* NPS
Canary Spring Overlook   *Type:* Scenic Viewpoint
A good view of the water pouring over the top of the terrace at **Canary Spring**. Trees limit the view; however, the view of the top of the terrace is better than what can be seen from the boardwalk.
Cool Rating: ** *Crowds:* * *Time:* 5 min *Directions:* NE side of hwy

MM: 20.4/0.6 *GPS:* 44.96947/-110.70213 *Elev:* 6353 *Grid:* 5/1 *Land:* NPS
Mammoth Hot Springs Terraces Parking   *Type:* Thermal Area
The southernmost parking area for the **Mammoth Hot Springs Terraces** close to **Jupiter Terrace**. *See section below for a description.*
Directions: W side of hwy

MM: 20.5/0.4 *GPS:* 44.97135/-110.70318 *Elev:* 6320 *Grid:* 5/1 *Land:* NPS
Mammoth Hot Springs Terraces Parking   *Type:* Thermal Area
Middle parking area for the **Mammoth Hot Springs Terraces** close to **Minerva Terrace**. *See next section for a description.*
Directions: W side of hwy

MM: 20.6/0.3 *GPS:* 44.97283/-110.70383 *Elev:* 6283 *Grid:* 5/1 *Land:* NPS
Mammoth Hot Springs Terraces   *Type:* Thermal Area
The **Mammoth Hot Springs Terraces** are a large area of white, gray, and colorful travertine terraces that rise 450 ft up the northeast side of **Terrace Mountain**. The terraces are divided into 3 sections, the **Lower Terrace**, **Main Terrace**, and **Upper Terrace**, which is part of the **Upper Terrace Drive** *(see MM 18.9/2.0 and chapter: Yellowstone - Upper Terrace Drive)*. The most popular formations along the boardwalks are **Palette Spring**, **Minerva Terrace**, **Jupiter Terrace**, and **Canary Spring**. This area has no geysers.

This is the northernmost and main parking area for the **Mammoth Hot Springs Terraces** close to **Liberty Cap**. 3 interconnected loops on boardwalks lead 1.0 mi around the **Lower Terrace** with a 190 ft elevation gain. It is an additional 0.4 mi and 105 ft elevation gain to reach the **Main Terrace** and **Angel Terrace**. This climb can be avoided by using the parking area on the **Upper Terrace Drive** and walking down. A trail brochure provides more details on individual features.

The terraces were created by rain and snow seeping deep underground through a series of small cracks, where geothermal activity heats the water and forces it back above the surface. During this cycle the water joins forces with carbon dioxide gases to form an acidic solution that dissolves and picks up underground limestone deposits. Upon reaching the oxygenated surface, the carbon dioxide gasses escape leaving the liquefied limestone to harden into white travertine terraces. Microorganisms and living bacteria grow in the hot water creating beautiful shades of oranges, pinks, yellows, greens, and browns. As these formations grow, water is forced to flow in different directions resulting in a constantly changing environment that grows 8-24 inches per year. This change includes areas where the water ceases to flow, causing the area to dry up and the organisms to die, which result in a gray color.
Cool Rating: ***** *Crowds:* ***** *Time:* 1-2 hrs *Directions:* W side of hwy
Notes: As of 2009 the active and colorful areas were at opposite ends at Palette Spring and Canary Spring, which is currently the highlight of the area.

MM: 20.6/0.3 *GPS:* 44.97283/-110.70383 *Elev:* 6283 *Grid:* 5/1 *Land:* NPS
Liberty Cap & Opal Terrace   *Type:* Thermal Area
Just west of the parking area stands **Liberty Cap**, a 37 ft cone created by mineral deposits from a hot spring that remained in one location for a long period of time, but is now dormant. The cone got its name in 1871 because of the resemblance to caps worn during the French Revolution.

Opal Terrace is located on the east side of the road. After years of dormancy, **Opal Spring** became active in 1926 and began depositing up to one foot of travertine per year, which required a tennis court to be removed in 1947. Sandbags and an earthen wall were put in place to protect a historic home built in 1908. The terrace is currently inactive and filled with native grass. A herd of elk often sit on the terrace, which makes for a good picture.
Cool Rating: *** *Crowds:* *** *Time:* 15 min

MM: 20.7/0.3 *GPS:* 44.97377/-110.70356 *Elev:* 6273 *Grid:* 5/1 *Land:* NPS
Mammoth Picnic Area   *Type:* Picnic Area
Across from the **Mammoth Hot Springs Terraces**. *4 tables. Some shade.*
Directions: E side of road, just north of Mammoth Terraces parking at Liberty Cap

MM: 20.8/0.2 *GPS:* 44.97472/-110.70402 *Elev:* 6276 *Grid:* 5/1 *Land:* NPS
Mammoth Public Restrooms   *Type:* Restroom
Nice restrooms with flush toilets and running water. Only handicapped parking is located at the restrooms. Other parking is located to the south just past the **Mammoth Hot Springs Terraces**.
Directions: W side of road.

MM: 20.9/0.0 *GPS:* 44.97631/-110.70088 *Elev:* 6243 *Grid:* 5/1 *Land:* NPS
Mammoth Hot Springs   *Type:* Town
Visitor services located on the northwest end of the **Grand Loop Road**, including an ATM, general store, gift shop, hotel, cabins, fuel, restaurant and fast food, showers, horseback riding, medical clinic, backcountry and fishing permits, **Ranger Station**. This is also the location of the **Yellowstone National Park** headquarters. A resident herd of elk frequent the grassy areas around the development. Across from the visitor center are 5 unshaded picnic tables in the grass. 2 more picnic tables are located under trees 0.1 mi north next to the medical clinic.

The **U.S. Army** arrived in **Yellowstone** in 1886 to protect the park from poaching, vandalism, souvenir collecting, and forest fires. **Fort Yellowstone** was built here by the **U.S. Army** in 1891 and occupied until 1913, when **Yellowstone** was turned over to the **National Park Service**. On the east end of town is a large group of red-roofed buildings that were part of the fort. These buildings include the **Albright Visitor Center**, where a brochure can be obtained for a self-guided walking tour of the **Fort Yellowstone Historic District**. The visitor center also contains a staffed information desk, bookstore, theatre, historical displays about the early exploration of **Yellowstone**, dioramas of **Yellowstone**'s wildlife and history, historic paintings by **Thomas Moran**, and original **United States Geological Survey** photos by **William H. Jackson**, who was the photographer to the **Hayden Expedition** of 1871.
Hours: Albright Visitor Center: 8am - 7pm (May 23 - Sept 30); 9am - 6pm (offseason) *Phone:* 307-344-2263
Directions: The Visitor Center is 1 block NE of the turnoff to Tower-Roosevelt.

MM: 20.9/0.0 *GPS:* 44.97631/-110.70088 *Elev:* 6243 *Grid:* 5/1
Yellowstone - Mammoth Hot Springs to Tower-Roosevelt *(see chapter)*   *Type:* Hwy Junction w/Chapter
18.1 mi north section of the **Grand Loop Road** from **Mammoth Hot Springs** east to **Tower-Roosevelt**. Highlights include: **Undine Falls**, **Wraith Falls**, **Hellroaring Creek Trail**, **Petrified Tree**.
Nearest Town: Gardiner, MT 5.5 N *Directions:* E to Tower-Roosevelt from MM 0

MM: 20.9/0.0 *GPS:* 44.97631/-110.70088 *Elev:* 6243 *Grid:* 5/1
Yellowstone - North Entrance to Mammoth Hot Springs *(see chapter)*   *Type:* Hwy Transition w/Chapter
5.3 mi highway from **Mammoth Hot Springs** north out of **Yellowstone National Park** to **US-89** in **Montana**. **Gardiner, Montana** is located just outside the north park entrance. A few minor points of interest along the way.
Nearest Town: Gardiner, MT 5.5 N *Directions:* N to Gardiner, MT from MM 5.3

MM: 20.9/0.0 *GPS:* 44.97631/-110.70088 *Elev:* 6243 *Grid:* 5/1 *Land:* NPS
Yellowstone - Mammoth Hot Springs to Norris   *Type:* Highway End
20.9 mi northwest section of the **Grand Loop Road** from **Mammoth Hot Springs** south to **Norris**. Highlights include: **Mammoth Hot Springs Terraces**, **Rustic Falls**, **Osprey Falls**, **Bunsen Peak**, **The Hoodoos**, **Norris Geyser Basin**.
Nearest Town: Gardiner, MT 5.5 N *Directions:* S to Norris from MM 20.9

MM: 0.0/5.3 *GPS:* 45.02950/-110.70866 *Elev:* 5323 *Grid:* 5/-1 *Land:* NPS
Yellowstone - North Entrance to Mammoth Hot Springs *Type:* Highway Description
5.3 mi highway from the **Roosevelt Arch**, at the north boundary of **Yellowstone National Park**, via **US-89** in **Montana**, south to **Mammoth Hot Springs**. A few minor points of interest along the way.
Nearest Town: Gardiner, MT 0.2 N *Directions:* S to Mammoth Hot Springs from MM 0

MM: 0.0/5.3 *GPS:* 45.02950/-110.70866 *Elev:* 5323 *Grid:* 5/-1 *Land:* NPS
Roosevelt Arch *Type:* National Park
This is the only highway into **Yellowstone National Park** that doesn't start at the entrance station. At the park boundary, 1/2 mile north of the entrance station on the Montana state line, stands the **Roosevelt Arch**, which was built in 1903 and named for **President Theodore Roosevelt**. Inscribed in the top of the arch is "For the Benefit and Enjoyment of the People."

Just to the north of the arch is the **Gardiner Community Park** with 3 open picnic tables and 4 more under a shelter.
Cool Rating: *** *Crowds:* * *Nearest Town:* Gardiner, MT 0.2 N

MM: 0.5/4.8 *GPS:* 45.02534/-110.70077 *Elev:* 5352 *Grid:* 5/-1 *Land:* NPS
Yellowstone National Park - North Entrance *Type:* National Park
Pay the National Park entrance fee, which covers both **Yellowstone National Park** and **Grand Teton National Park**. *See chapter: Yellowstone National Park.*
[FEE AREA]

MM: 0.9/4.4 *GPS:* 45.02073/-110.69679 *Elev:* 5340 *Grid:* 5/0 *Land:* NPS
Interpretive Pullout: Northern Range *Type:* Point of Interest
3 signs about the landscape and wildlife of the **Yellowstone Northern Range**.
Cool Rating: * *Crowds:* * *Time:* 10 min *Directions:* NE side of hwy

---

MM: 1.1/4.1 *GPS:* 45.01768/-110.69369 *Elev:* 5365 *Grid:* 5/0 *Land:* NPS
Interpretive Pullout: Wildlife Migrations *Type:* Point of Interest
A sign about the winter migration of large mammals into the **Gardner River Valley**, which lies at the lowest elevation in the park. This is also the **Rescue Creek Trailhead** with a trail that travels 7.7 mi southeast to the **Grand Loop Road**, northeast of **Wraith Falls**.
Cool Rating: * *Crowds:* * *Time:* 5 min *Directions:* E side of hwy

---

MM: 1.6/3.6 *GPS:* 45.01073/-110.69388 *GPS2:* 45.00999/-110.69382 *Elev:* 5430 *Grid:* 5/0 *Land:* NPS
Eagle Nest Rock and Split Rock *Type:* Point of Interest
2 points of interest near the north end of **Gardner Canyon**. On a side hill on the east side of the highway is **Eagle Nest Rock**, a rock needle where ospreys nest. Just to the south and on the west side of the highway is **Split Rock**, a large boulder that rolled down the mountain and split in half in the **Gardner River** *(see GPS2)*.
Cool Rating: ** *Crowds:* * *Time:* 15 min
Directions: The parking area is just south of the river bridge on the east side of the hwy. **Eagle Nest Rock** is directly above. Cross the road and walk 90 yds south to **Split Rock**.

MM: 2.0/3.3 *GPS:* 45.00616/-110.69350 *Elev:* 5490 *Grid:* 5/0 *Land:* NPS
Sliding Hill *Type:* Point of Interest
Directly to the southwest is a foothill of **Sepulcher Mountain** from which large amounts of dirt and rock occasionally slide into the **Gardner River**.
Cool Rating: ** *Crowds:* * *Time:* Drive by *Directions:* W side of hwy

---

MM: 2.2/3.1 *GPS:* 45.00332/-110.69231 *Elev:* 5570 *Grid:* 5/0 *Land:* NPS
45th Parallel *Type:* Point of Interest
The halfway point between the equator and the **North Pole**. This is the **45th parallel** of latitude. A pullout with a wooden sign marks the spot.
Time: 5 min *Directions:* W side of hwy

MM: 2.9/2.3 *GPS:* 44.99289/-110.69280 *Elev:* 5623 *Grid:* 5/0 *Land:* NPS
45th Parallel Picnic Area *Type:* Picnic Area
A large gravel parking area amid sagebrush hills near the **Gardner River**. On the edge of the parking area are 2 picnic tables, each located under a medium-sized tree. *See previous section about the 45th Parallel. Vault toilet across the road at the Boiling River Trailhead.*
Directions: W side of hwy

MM: 3.0/2.3 *GPS:* 44.99249/-110.69140 *GPS2:* 44.98621/-110.68993 *Elev:* 5670 *Grid:* 5/0 *Land:* NPS
Boiling River Trail and Swimming Hole *Type:* Hot Springs
A 1/2 mi walk (one-way) along the **Gardner River** to an area where a hot spring heats the river and soaking is allowed. The trail continues 1.1 mi to a connection with the **Lava Creek Trail**. *Vault toilet.*
Cool Rating: *** *Crowds:* ***** *Notes:* Keep your head above water because of dangerous bacteria. *Directions:* E 100 yds

---

MM: 4.0/1.3 *GPS:* 44.97859/-110.69212 *Elev:* 5967 *Grid:* 5/1 *Land:* NPS
Interpretive Pullout: Mount Everts Rock Slides *Type:* Point of Interest
A sign with an explanation about mud and rock slides off **Mount Everts** to the east. A 1/4 mi trail leads east to the **Boiling River Trail** with access to the **Gardner River**.
Cool Rating: * *Crowds:* * *Time:* 5 min *Directions:* E side of hwy

MM: 4.4/0.8   *GPS:* 44.97281/-110.69306   *Elev:* 6040   *Grid:* 5/1   *Land:* NPS

Mammoth Campground   *Type:* Campground

Located in a sagebrush valley at the base of a hill below **Mammoth Hot Springs**. Scattered conifer and deciduous trees provide shade for some sites with the north end having more trees than the south end. The campground is just off the highway situated inside a hairpin curve. *2 long loops with parking loops or pullouts. Flush toilets. Level. Generators permitted. Open year-round. Cheaper than the large campgrounds that take reservations.*

Crowds: *****   *[FEE AREA]*   *Directions:* NW from the E side of the hairpin curve

Campsites: 85   *Shade:* *   *Privacy:* *   *RV Size:* 40'+   *Other:* Water BEARS

MM: 5.3/0.0   *GPS:* 44.97631/-110.70088   *Elev:* 6243   *Grid:* 5/1   *Land:* NPS

Mammoth Hot Springs   *Type:* Town

Visitor services located on the northwest end of the **Grand Loop Road**, including an ATM, general store, gift shop, hotel, cabins, fuel, restaurant and fast food, showers, horseback riding, medical clinic, backcountry and fishing permits, **Ranger Station**. This is also the location of the **Yellowstone National Park** headquarters. A resident herd of elk frequent the grassy areas around the development. Across from the visitor center are 5 unshaded picnic tables in the grass. 2 more picnic tables are located under trees 0.1 mi north next to the medical clinic.

The **U.S. Army** arrived in **Yellowstone** in 1886 to protect the park from poaching, vandalism, souvenir collecting, and forest fires. **Fort Yellowstone** was built here by the **U.S. Army** in 1891 and occupied until 1913, when **Yellowstone** was turned over to the **National Park Service**. On the east end of town is a large group of red-roofed buildings that were part of the fort. These buildings include the **Albright Visitor Center**, where a brochure can be obtained for a self-guided walking tour of the **Fort Yellowstone Historic District**. The visitor center also contains a staffed information desk, bookstore, theatre, historical displays about the early exploration of **Yellowstone**, dioramas of **Yellowstone**'s wildlife and history, historic paintings by **Thomas Moran**, and original **United States Geological Survey** photos by **William H. Jackson**, who was the photographer to the **Hayden Expedition** of 1871.

Hours: Albright Visitor Center: 8am - 7pm (May 23 - Sept 30); 9am - 6pm (offseason)   *Phone:* 307-344-2263

MM: 5.3/0.0   *GPS:* 44.97631/-110.70088   *Elev:* 6243   *Grid:* 5/1

Yellowstone - Norris to Mammoth Hot Springs *(see chapter)*   *Type:* Hwy Transition w/Chapter

20.9 mi northwest section of the **Grand Loop Road** from **Mammoth Hot Springs** south to **Norris**. Highlights include: **Mammoth Hot Springs Terraces, Rustic Falls, Osprey Falls, Bunsen Peak, The Hoodoos, Norris Geyser Basin.**

Nearest Town: Gardiner, MT 5.5 N   *Directions:* S to Norris from MM 20.9

MM: 5.3/0.0   *GPS:* 44.97631/-110.70088   *Elev:* 6243   *Grid:* 5/1

Yellowstone - Mammoth Hot Springs to Tower-Roosevelt *(see chapter)*   *Type:* Hwy Junction w/Chapter

18.1 mi north section of the **Grand Loop Road** from **Mammoth Hot Springs** east to **Tower-Roosevelt**. Highlights include: **Undine Falls, Wraith Falls, Hellroaring Creek Trail, Petrified Tree.**

Nearest Town: Gardiner, MT 5.5 N   *Directions:* E to Tower-Roosevelt from MM 0

MM: 5.3/0.0   *GPS:* 44.97631/-110.70088   *Elev:* 6243   *Grid:* 5/1   *Land:* NPS

Yellowstone - Mammoth Hot Springs to North Entrance   *Type:* Highway End

5.3 mi highway from **Mammoth Hot Springs** north out of **Yellowstone National Park** to **US-89** in **Montana**. **Gardiner, Montana** is located just outside the north park entrance. A few minor points of interest along the way.

Nearest Town: Gardiner, MT 5.5 N   *Directions:* N to Gardiner, MT from MM 5.3

Yellowstone - North Rim Drive

MM: 0.0 **GPS:** 44.72057/-110.49959 **Elev:** 7836 **Grid:** 8/7 **Land:** NPS
Yellowstone - North Rim Drive **Type:** Highway Description
2.0 mi one-way half-loop along the **North Rim of the Grand Canyon of the Yellowstone** ending at **Canyon Village**. The road provides access to 4 canyon overlooks, 3 of which require only a short walk. The parking areas at the overlooks tend to be pretty full. Highlights include: canyon viewpoints, **North Rim Trail**, **Lower Falls**, **Brink of the Lower Falls**.
Nearest Town: Canyon Village 1.3 N **Directions:** S then E from MM 0

MM: 0.1 **GPS:** 44.71954/-110.49745 **GPS2:** 44.71811/-110.49634 **Elev:** 7810 **Grid:** 8/7 **Land:** NPS
Brink of the Lower Falls **Type:** Waterfall
A paved trail that descends steeply along switchbacks to the top of the 308 ft **Lower Falls**. At 0.3 mi is a view of the **Grand Canyon of the Yellowstone** to the east. At the end of the trail a viewing platform is located directly above the brink of the falls. An additional viewing platform is located higher up for a different perspective. Below the overlook across the canyon is the viewing platform from **Uncle Tom's Trail**. *Moderate; 0.4 mi one-way; 360 ft elev loss.*

At the far end of the parking area are 3 overlooks. The third overlook has the best view of the **Lower Falls**, although the falls are partially obstructed. *Vault toilet.*
Cool Rating: ***** **Crowds:** ***** **Time:** 30-45 min
Notes: The sign at the top of the trail says that it is a 600 ft descent, but that is wrong.

MM: 0.7 **GPS:** 44.72141/-110.48751 **Elev:** 7770 **Grid:** 8/7 **Land:** NPS
Lookout Point & Red Rock Point **Type:** Scenic Viewpoint
Lookout Point provides the best canyon-top view of the 308 ft **Lower Falls** from the **North Rim**. An interpretive sign explains how ospreys build nests on the cliffs below this overlook.

For an even better view of the falls, a short but **very steep** paved trail descends to **Red Rock Point** for an eye-level view about 550 yds from the falls. *Moderate; 1/4 mi one-way; 270 ft elev loss.*
Cool Rating: ***** **Crowds:** ***** **Time:** 15 min - 1 hr
Notes: Several views from the South Rim Trail are similar to Lookout Point, and Uncle Tom's Trail gets you to within about 150 yds of the falls. *See Yellowstone - South Rim Drive MM 0.6.*

MM: 0.9 **GPS:** 44.72335/-110.48454 **Elev:** 7852 **Grid:** 8/7 **Land:** NPS
Grand View **Type:** Scenic Viewpoint
A viewpoint into the **Grand Canyon of the Yellowstone** without views of the waterfalls. Just past the north end of the main parking area is a smaller parking area that provides access to the last 1.1 mi of the **North Rim Trail** to **Inspiration Point**. This pleasant trail turns to dirt and follows the canyon rim 1/3 mi before heading into the forest until reaching **Inspiration Point**. *Easy; 1.1 mi one-way; Level.*
Cool Rating: **** **Crowds:** **** **Time:** 10 min
Notes: If taking the trail to Inspiration point, move your vehicle to the north parking area so others can park at the Grand View. This is a nice alternative to driving.

MM: 1.3 **Dist:** 0.4 **GPS:** 44.72957/-110.47272 **GPS2:** 44.73170/-110.45600 **Elev:** 7895 **Grid:** 8/7 **Land:** NPS
Glacial Boulder Trailhead & Glacial Boulder **Type:** Trailhead
A hiking trail east to a view of the **Silver Cord Cascade** across the **Grand Canyon of the Yellowstone**, where **Surface Creek** drops and cascades 1,200 ft into the **Yellowstone River**. After a short distance the trail drops steeply to a small creek before climbing back up to a view into the **Grand Canyon of the Yellowstone** (MI 0.25). Following along and near the edge of the canyon another 0.4 mi leads to a short trail ending with a very nice view into the canyon (MI 0.65). The trail continues 1/3 mi leaving the canyon edge and heading into the forest before emerging again at the **Silver Cord Cascade** viewpoint across the canyon (MI 1.0). The overlook is not marked, but the sound of water can be heard from the approach. The best view is obtained by climbing down a hill a short distance, but be careful as the hill is located on the edge of the canyon. *Easy; 1.0 mi one-way; 160 ft elevation change.*

Just south of the **Glacial Boulder Trailhead** is an out of place, house-sized granite boulder, which was carried some 15 mi southwest by a glacier around 80,000 years ago.
Cool Rating: **** **Crowds:** ** **Time:** 1 hr
Directions: At the Inspiration Point turnoff; E/R to parking area on NE side of road 0.4 mi.

MM: 1.3 **Dist:** 0.8 **GPS:** 44.72511/-110.46976 **Elev:** 7790 **Grid:** 8/7 **Land:** NPS
Inspiration Point **Type:** Scenic Viewpoint
A view up the **Grand Canyon of the Yellowstone** with the **Lower Falls** in the distance. The canyon can be viewed from the parking area, or for a much better view descend down 50+ concrete steps to a natural observation point, where the canyon wall juts out 120 ft allowing views over 2 sides both up and down the canyon. The observation point extended another 100 ft before it was destroyed by a 1975 earthquake.
Cool Rating: ***** **Crowds:** ***** **Time:** 30 min **Directions:** E/R 0.8 mi

MM: 1.3 *Dist:* 0.8 *GPS:* 44.72509/-110.47019 *Elev:* 7780 *Grid:* 8/7 *Land:* NPS

North Rim Trail   *Type:* Hiking Trail

A partially paved hiking trail that follows the **North Rim of the Grand Canyon of the Yellowstone** from **Inspiration Point** to **Chittenden Bridge**. All of the attractions along the trail are reachable by car; however, the parking areas tend to be very crowded. A shuttle vehicle can be parked at various points to prevent re-tracing the same route. Shorter versions of this hike can be made by starting at the **Grand View** parking area and/or skipping the last section to **Chittenden Bridge**. *See Canyon Village to Fishing Bridge Junction MM 1.6 for descriptions of Brink of the Upper Falls and Crystal Falls. See previous sections for descriptions of the other viewpoints.*

Head northwest on the dirt trail into the forest, which curves back to the southwest 0.8 mi before emerging at the canyon rim. Continue 1/3 mi to **Grand View** (MI 1.2) and then southwest to **Lookout Point** (MI 1.4). Continue west to **Brink of the Lower Falls** parking area, where the trail turns left 0.1 mi to a junction with the steep 0.6 mi round-trip trail to the **Brink of the Lower Falls** (MI 2.0). The trail continues 1/4 mi to the top of **Crystal Falls** and **Grotto Pool**, then another 0.1 mi to a fork where a short distance left is the viewpoint for **Crystal Falls**. Continue 100 yds to the road to the **Brink of the Upper Falls** parking area (MI 2.4). Turn left and continue through the parking area to the trail to the **Brink of the Upper Falls**. Follow the trail 0.1 mi, where a viewing platform from the brink is a short distance to the left (MI 2.7). Continue south 0.5 mi on an old road along the west bank of the **Yellowstone River** to the main road (MI 3.1). Turn left, cross **Chittenden Bridge** and continue to the **Wapiti Lake Trailhead** parking area (MI 3.2). *Moderately easy; 3.2 mi one-way; Mostly level.* **With 2 steep side trails to Lower Falls overlooks***: Moderate; 4.3 mi one-way; 630 ft elev loss.*

Cool Rating: ***** *Crowds:* *** *Time:* 1.5-4 hrs

Directions: E/L 0.8 mi to the SW side of the Inspiration Point parking area. Optionally park at the Glacial Boulder trailhead and walk down the road 0.4 mi.

MM: 2.0 *GPS:* 44.73547/-110.48945 *Elev:* 7940 *Grid:* 8/7 *Land:* NPS

Canyon Village   *Type:* Town & Campground

Visitor services located on the east central section of the **Grand Loop Road** and on the north end of **Grand Canyon of the Yellowstone**, including an ATM, general store, gift shop, sporting goods store, fuel, auto repair, restaurant, cafeteria, fast food, laundry, showers, hotel, cabins, post office, horseback riding, backcountry and fishing permits, and a **Ranger Station**. On the west side of the complex is the large **Canyon Visitor Education Center**, which contains a staffed information desk, bookstore, a large theatre, and several elaborate exhibits about **Yellowstone**'s supervolcano and other aspects of the park geology.

The campground is one of 4 large modern campgrounds that take reservations. *10 loops. Conifer forest. Paved roads and parking areas. Restrooms with flush toilets, running water, and electricity. Generators permitted. Amphitheater for ranger programs. 3 wheelchair accessible sites.*

Hours: Visitor center: 8am - 8pm (307-344-2550) *Crowds:* ***** *[FEE AREA]*

Directions: Right to campground or left to hotel, stores, and visitor center

Campsites: 272 *Shade:* ***** *Privacy:* * *RV Size:* 30' *Other:* 1-866-439-7375,Water,RVDump BEARS

Yellowstone - Northeast Entrance to Tower-Roosevelt — NE/SW

MM: 0.0/28.2 **GPS:** 45.00451/-110.01040 **Elev:** 7355 **Grid:** 15/0 **Land:** NPS
Yellowstone - Northeast Entrance to Tower-Roosevelt **Type:** Highway Description
28.2 mi highway from the northeast entrance of **Yellowstone National Park**, via **US-212** in **Montana**, southwest to **Tower-Roosevelt**. A few minor points of interest along the way.
Nearest Town: Cooke City, MT 4.1 NE **Directions:** SW to Tower-Roosevelt from MM 0

MM: 0.0/28.2 **GPS:** 45.00451/-110.01040 **Elev:** 7355 **Grid:** 15/0
US-212 (Beartooth Scenic Byway) *(see chapter)* **Type:** Hwy Transition w/Chapter
43.6 mi highway east from the northeast entrance of **Yellowstone National Park**, briefly into **Montana**, across far northern **Wyoming**, and back into **Montana** on **Beartooth Pass**. This is a remote section of highway with only a single small town, **Cooke City, Montana**, and only a single highway junction to **Wy-296**, another remote highway with no towns. Highlights include: **Crazy Creek Falls, Lake Creek Falls, Clay Butte Fire Lookout, Beartooth Falls, Beartooth Pass**.
Nearest Town: Cooke City, MT 4.1 NE **Directions:** NE then SE from the northeast entrance of Yellowstone from MM 0

MM: 0.0/28.2 **GPS:** 45.00451/-110.01040 **Elev:** 7355 **Grid:** 15/0 **Land:** NPS
Yellowstone National Park - Northeast Entrance **Type:** National Park
Pay the National Park entrance fee, which covers both **Yellowstone National Park** and **Grand Teton National Park**. *See chapter: Yellowstone National Park.*
Nearest Town: Cooke City, MT 4.1 NE *[FEE AREA]*

MM: 1.1/27.1 **GPS:** 45.00360/-110.02915 **Elev:** 7280 **Grid:** 15/0 **Land:** NPS
Warm Creek Picnic Area **Type:** Picnic Area
Sites are spread out along a 0.2 mi road on the edge of the forest with an end loop near **Soda Butte Creek**. One table sits in the open at the end of the loop by the creek. *7 tables. Vault toilet. Handicapped accessible.*
Directions: SE up to 0.2 mi

MM: 7.1/21.1 **GPS:** 44.93482/-110.08373 **Elev:** 6960 **Grid:** 14/2 **Land:** NPS
Soda Butte Creek Picnic Area **Type:** Picnic Area
Located in a meadow with a few pine trees next to **Soda Butte Creek**. One table is next to the creek at the end of a wooden boardwalk. One table is in the open and the other 3 are near trees, which may offer some shade during part of the day. *4 tables. Vault toilet. Handicapped accessible.*
Directions: W side of hwy

MM: 9.2/18.9 **Dist:** 0.2 **GPS:** 44.91673/-110.11392 **Elev:** 6840 **Grid:** 13/2 **Land:** NPS
Pebble Creek Campground **Type:** Campground
The campground is located in a combination of grassy meadows and pine forest. The western edge of the campground, including the tent-only sites, are along **Pebble Creek**. *Sparse conifer forest. 8 tent-only sites. Vault toilets. Generators not permitted. Cheaper than the large campgrounds that take reservations.* The 12 mi **Pebble Creek Trail** starts at the campground and ends at **Warm Creek Picnic Area**.
Crowds: ***** *[FEE AREA]* **Notes:** A better overnight or sportsman campground than a base camp for touring Yellowstone.
Directions: NW 0.2 mi
Campsites: 32 **Shade:** *** **Privacy:** * **RV Size:** 30' **Other:** Water BEARS

MM: 12.5/15.6 **GPS:** 44.87792/-110.15273 **Elev:** 6650 **Grid:** 13/3 **Land:** NPS
Soda Butte **Type:** Thermal Area
A travertine mound that was formed more than a century ago by a hot spring, which now has very little hydrothermal activity. This is the only thermal feature in this area.
Cool Rating: ** **Crowds:** * **Time:** 10 min **Directions:** SE side of hwy

MM: 15.7/12.4 **GPS:** 44.87463/-110.20955 **Elev:** 6574 **Grid:** 12/3 **Land:** NPS
Interpretive Pullout: Fences in the Wilderness **Type:** Point of Interest
A sign about a fenced-in area that researchers constructed east of this point to study the effect on the land of large herbivores such as elk and bison.
Cool Rating: * **Crowds:** * **Time:** 5 min **Directions:** SW side of hwy

MM: 15.9/12.2 **GPS:** 44.87637/-110.21186 **Elev:** 6570 **Grid:** 12/3 **Land:** NPS
Interpretive Pullout: An American Eden **Type:** Point of Interest
A sign about how the **Lamar Valley** effectively supports elk and bison herds.
Cool Rating: * **Crowds:** * **Time:** 5 min **Directions:** SW side of hwy

MM: 17.6/10.5 **GPS:** 44.89438/-110.23524 **Elev:** 6559 **Grid:** 12/3 **Land:** NPS
Interpretive Pullout: Buffalo Ranch **Type:** Historic Site
A sign about the **Lamar Buffalo Ranch**, which was started in 1907 to help restore the **Yellowstone** buffalo herd that was nearly wiped out by poachers in the 1880s. The ranch is across the highway.
Cool Rating: * **Crowds:** * **Time:** 5 min **Directions:** SW side of hwy

MM: 22.3/5.9 **Dist:** 2.3 **GPS:** 44.94861/-110.30675 **Elev:** 6266 **Grid:** 11/1 **Land:** NPS
Slough Creek Campground **Type:** Campground
The campground is located in a grassy meadow with pine trees along **Slough Creek**. The sites are spread along a road that runs parallel to the creek. Except for tent sites along the river, most of the sites are in the open. *Vault toilets. Generators not permitted. Cheaper than the large campgrounds that take reservations.*
Crowds: ***** *[FEE AREA]* **Road Desc:** Gravel, rough **Directions:** N 2.3 mi
Notes: A better overnight or sportsman campground than a base camp for touring Yellowstone.
Campsites: 29 **Shade:** ** **Privacy:** * **RV Size:** 30' **Other:** Water GRIZZLIES

MM: 26.9/1.2 **GPS:** 44.91722/-110.39986 **Elev:** 6237 **Grid:** 9/2 **Land:** NPS
Yellowstone River Picnic Area **Type:** Picnic Area
A combination picnic area and trailhead in an area of grass, sagebrush, and light forest. Sites are spread out with individual parking areas. *9 tables. 4 grills. Vault toilet. Handicapped accessible.*
Directions: W side of hwy

MM: 26.9/1.2 *GPS:* 44.91670/-110.40021 *Elev:* 6240 *Grid:* 9/2 *Land:* NPS
Yellowstone River Trail   *Type:* Hiking Trail
A hiking trail that follows the east rim of the **Grand Canyon of the Yellowstone** through open terrain to the **Specimen Ridge Trail**. The trail heads south 0.4 mi, climbing 200 ft out of the picnic area before leveling off (MI 0.4). Continue 0.4 mi to reach a view across the canyon of **Calcite Springs** at the base of the flat-topped **Bumpus Butte** (MI 0.8). This is an area where geothermal discharge reaches the earth surface, which has turned the cliff white, yellow, and orange (MI 0.8). Continuing 0.4 mi is the narrowest point of the **Grand Canyon of the Yellowstone**, called **The Narrows**, with the **Calcite Springs Overlook** on the other side of the canyon (MI 1.2). In another 0.4 mi the canyon and the trail turns east (MI 1.6) to the junction with the **Specimen Ridge Trail** (MI 1.9). Along this stretch are views across the canyon of **Devil's Den** and the **Tower Fall** area, but no view of the falls. Return by the same route. *Easy; 1.6-1.9 mi one-way; 200 ft elev gain.*
Cool Rating: **** *Crowds:* * *Time:* 2 hrs *Directions:* W side of hwy

MM: 28.2/0.0 *Dist:* 0.2 *GPS:* 44.91300/-110.41640 *Elev:* 6318 *Grid:* 9/2 *Land:* NPS
Roosevelt   *Type:* Town
Visitor services located on the northeast end of the **Grand Loop Road**, including a general store, gift shop, fuel, restaurant, showers, cabins (historic **Roosevelt Lodge**), horseback riding, backcountry and fishing permits, and a **Ranger Station**.
Directions: SW 0.2 mi

MM: 28.2/0.0 *GPS:* 44.91601/-110.41577 *Elev:* 6262 *Grid:* 9/2
Yellowstone - Tower-Roosevelt to Canyon Village *(see chapter)*   *Type:* Hwy Junction w/Chapter
18.3 mi northeast section of the **Grand Loop Road** from **Tower-Roosevelt** south to **Canyon Village**. Highlights include: **Calcite Springs**, **Devil's Den**, **Tower Fall**, **Mount Washburn**.
Directions: SE to Canyon Village from MM 0

MM: 28.2/0.0 *GPS:* 44.91601/-110.41577 *Elev:* 6262 *Grid:* 9/2
Yellowstone - Mammoth Hot Springs to Tower-Roosevelt *(see chapter)*   *Type:* Hwy Junction w/Chapter
18.1 mi north section of the **Grand Loop Road** from **Tower-Roosevelt** west to **Mammoth Hot Springs**. Highlights include: **Petrified Tree**, **Hellroaring Creek Trail**, **Wraith Falls**, **Undine Falls**.
Directions: W to Mammoth Hot Springs from MM 18.1

MM: 28.2/0.0 *GPS:* 44.91601/-110.41577 *Elev:* 6262 *Grid:* 9/2 *Land:* NPS
Yellowstone - Tower-Roosevelt to Northeast Entrance   *Type:* Highway End
28.2 mi highway from **Tower-Roosevelt** northeast out of **Yellowstone National Park** to **US-212** in **Montana**. A few minor points of interest along the way.
Directions: NE to Cooke City, MT from MM 28.2

Yellowstone - South Entrance to West Thumb   S/N

MM: 0.0/21.2 **GPS:** 44.13331/-110.66521 **Elev:** 6885 **Grid:** 6/22 **Land:** NPS
Yellowstone - South Entrance to West Thumb   **Type:** Highway Description
21.2 mi highway from the south entrance of **Yellowstone National Park**, via **US-89/191/287**, north to **West Thumb**. Highlights include: **Moose Falls**, **Lewis Falls**.
Nearest Town: Grant Village 20.4 N **Directions:** N to West Thumb from MM 0

MM: 0.0/21.2 **GPS:** 44.13331/-110.66521 **Elev:** 6885 **Grid:** 6/22
US-89/191/287 (see chapter)   **Type:** Hwy Transition w/Chapter
27 mi highway from the south entrance of **Yellowstone National Park** south through **Grand Teton National Park** to **Moran Jct**. Highlights include: views of **Jackson Lake** and the **Teton Range**, **Oxbow Bend**.
Nearest Town: Grant Village 20.4 N **Directions:** S to Grand Teton NP from MM 211.6 (27)
Notes: There are no mile markers along this highway, so some rivers and creeks have been included as points of reference. The official mile markers are provided as well as the mileages starting at zero in both directions.

MM: 0.0/21.2 **GPS:** 44.13331/-110.66521 **Elev:** 6885 **Grid:** 6/22 **Land:** NPS
Yellowstone National Park - South Entrance   **Type:** National Park
Pay the National Park entrance fee, which covers both **Yellowstone National Park** and **Grand Teton National Park**. See chapter: Yellowstone National Park.
Nearest Town: Grant Village 20.4 N **[FEE AREA]**

MM: 0.1/21.1 **Dist:** 0.1 **GPS:** 44.13706/-110.66775 **Elev:** 6887 **Grid:** 6/22 **Land:** NPS
Snake River Picnic Area   **Type:** Picnic Area
A sparsely forested picnic area near the **Snake River**. 15 tables. 8 grills. Vault toilet. Handicapped accessible.
Directions: NE 0.1 mi

MM: 1.2/20.0 **GPS:** 44.15218/-110.67373 **GPS2:** 44.15185/-110.67264 **Elev:** 6970 **Grid:** 5/21 **Land:** NPS
Moose Falls   **Type:** Waterfall
A 30 ft waterfall over hardened lava on **Crawfish Creek**. The falls are accessed by a short 100 yd trail.
Cool Rating: *** **Crowds:** ** **Time:** 20 min **Directions:** Parking pullout on NE side of hwy

MM: 6.4/14.8 **GPS:** 44.22183/-110.65532 **Elev:** 7713 **Grid:** 6/19 **Land:** NPS
Interpretive Pullout: Forest Fire   **Type:** Point of Interest
A sign about the 80 mph winds that caused the 1988 forest fire to jump the **Lewis Canyon** and continue burning.
Cool Rating: ** **Crowds:** * **Time:** 5 min **Directions:** SE side of hwy

MM: 9.9/11.3 **GPS:** 44.26752/-110.63487 **GPS2:** 44.26736/-110.63684 **Elev:** 7720 **Grid:** 6/18 **Land:** NPS
Lewis Falls   **Type:** Waterfall
A 30 ft waterfall on the **Lewis River** less than a mile downstream from where the river flows out of the south end of **Lewis Lake**. The falls are 250 yds upstream, west of the highway, and can be viewed from either end of the bridge. The southwest end has a large parking area with a viewpoint; however, the view of the falls is partially blocked. A full view of the falls can be seen from the northeast end of the bridge. This can be reached by walking across the bridge from the southwest parking area or from a long parking area located on the northeast end of the bridge. The falls were named after **Merlwether Lewis** even though he never actually passed through the area.
Cool Rating: *** **Crowds:** *** **Time:** 20 min **Directions:** Parking on both ends of the bridge

MM: 11.1/10.1 **GPS:** 44.28325/-110.62657 **Elev:** 7809 **Grid:** 6/18 **Land:** NPS
Lewis Lake Campground and Picnic Area   **Type:** Campground/Picnic Area
Located on a forested hilltop above the southeast shore of **Lewis Lake**. 3 paved loops plus a section with 17 walk-in tent-sites. Conifer forest. Vault toilets. Boat ramp. Generators not permitted. Self-registration. Cheaper than the large campgrounds that take reservations. Slowest campground to fill.

A **Ranger Station** and shady picnic area are located at the campground entrance. 9 tables. Vault toilet. Handicapped accessible.
Crowds: ^^^^^ **[FEE AREA]** **Notes:** A better overnight or sportsman campground than a base camp for touring Yellowstone.
Directions: SW side of hwy
Campsites: 85 **Shade:** ***** **Privacy:** *** **RV Size:** 25' **Other:** Water BEARS

MM: 19.4/1.8 **Dist:** 1.0 **GPS:** 44.39019/-110.55631 **Elev:** 7805 **Grid:** 7/15 **Land:** NPS
Grant Village   **Type:** Town & Campground
Visitor services located on the southwest shore of the **West Thumb of Yellowstone Lake**, including an ATM, general store, gift shop, fuel, auto repair, propane, restaurant, laundry, showers, hotel, post office, backcountry and fishing permits, and a **Ranger Station**. Named after **President Ulysses S. Grant**, the 18th U.S. president, who signed the bill creating **Yellowstone National Park** in 1872. The visitor center has a staffed information desk, bookstore, and exhibits and video on the role of fire in **Yellowstone National Park**. A picnic area is located at the beginning of the campground. 17 tables. 12 grills. Vault toilet.

The campground is one of 4 large modern campgrounds that take reservations. 13 loops. 1 tent-only loop. 1 reserved group and hiker/biker loop. 2 loops are wheelchair accessible. Conifer forest. Paved roads and parking areas. Restrooms with flush toilets, running water, and electricity. Most sites have short pull-thrus. Good spacing between sites. Generators permitted. Amphitheater for ranger programs. RV dumps at campground and gas station.
Hours: Visitor center: 8am - 7pm **Phone:** 307-242-2650 **Crowds:** ***** **[FEE AREA]**
Directions: SE 1.0 mi; The campground is 0.4 mi NW.
Campsites: 425 **Shade:** **** **Privacy:** * **RV Size:** 30' **Other:** 1-866-439-7375,Water,RVDump BEARS

MM: 21.2/0.0 *GPS:* 44.41403/-110.57848 *Elev:* 7808 *Grid:* 7/15
Yellowstone - West Thumb to Madison *(see chapter)*   *Type:* Hwy Transition w/Chapter
33.5 mi southwest section of the **Grand Loop Road** from **West Thumb** northwest to **Madison**. The majority of the geyser activity is along this section. Highlights include: **Lone Star Geyser, Kepler Cascades, Upper Geyser Basin, Old Faithful, Black Sand Basin, Mystic Falls, Biscuit Basin, Fairy Falls, Midway Geyser Basin, Firehole Lake Drive Geysers, Lower Geyser Basin, Firehole Falls**.
Nearest Town: Grant Village 2.8 S *Directions:* NW to Madison from MM 0

MM: 21.2/0.0 *GPS:* 44.41403/-110.57848 *Elev:* 7808 *Grid:* 7/15
Yellowstone - Fishing Bridge to West Thumb *(see chapter)*   *Type:* Hwy Junction w/Chapter
20.6 mi southeast section of the **Grand Loop Road** from **West Thumb** northeast to **Fishing Bridge**. The entire length of this section follows the shore of **Yellowstone Lake**, which is North America's largest high elevation lake occupying an area of 136 sq mi with 141 mi of shoreline and a maximum depth of 430 ft. The southern end of this route travels along a protrusion in the lake known as the **West Thumb**. Highlights include: **West Thumb Geyser Basin, Duck Lake, Natural Bridge, Elephant Back Mountain**.
Nearest Town: Grant Village 2.8 S *Directions:* NE to Fishing Bridge from MM 20.6

MM: 21.2/0.0 *GPS:* 44.41403/-110.57848 *Elev:* 7808 *Grid:* 7/15 *Land:* NPS
Yellowstone - West Thumb to South Entrance   *Type:* Highway End
21.2 mi highway from **West Thumb** south out of **Yellowstone National Park** to **US-89/191/287**. Highlights include: **Lewis Falls, Moose Falls**.
Nearest Town: Grant Village 2.8 S *Directions:* S to Grand Teton National Park from MM 21.2

Yellowstone - South Rim Drive · SW/NE

MM: 0.0 **GPS:** 44.70813/-110.50371 **Elev:** 7720 **Grid:** 8/7 **Land:** NPS
Yellowstone - South Rim Drive **Type:** Highway Description
1.6 mi side road that provides access to the **South Rim of the Grand Canyon of the Yellowstone** ending at the **Artist Point** parking area. The **South Rim Trail** to **Artist Point**, including the descent down **Uncle Tom's Trail** to a close-up view of the **Lower Falls**, provides as good or better views of the canyon and waterfalls than that from the **North Rim Drive** or the **North Rim Trail**. The missing attractions to be seen from the **North Rim** are the **Brink of the Upper Falls**, **Brink of the Lower Falls**, and **Crystal Falls**, all of which are short hikes from the road. Highlights include: **North Rim Trail**, **South Rim Trail**, **Upper Falls**, **Lower Falls**, **Uncle Tom's Trail** to the **Lower Falls**, **Artist Point**.
Nearest Town: Canyon Village 2.4 N **Directions:** E then NE from MM 0

MM: 0.0 **GPS:** 44.70806/-110.50259 **Elev:** 7710 **Grid:** 8/7 **Land:** NPS
Chittenden Memorial Bridge **Type:** Historic Site
Named in 1962 for **Hiram Martin Chittenden** who wrote the first history of the park. He was an engineer with the **U.S. Army Corps of Engineers** and was responsible for building many of the roads in **Yellowstone National Park**, including the original bridge where the memorial bridge now stands.
Cool Rating: * **Crowds:** * **Time:** Drive by

MM: 0.1 **GPS:** 44.70859/-110.50119 **Elev:** 7734 **Grid:** 8/7 **Land:** NPS
Chittenden Bridge Picnic Area & Wapiti Lake Trailhead **Type:** Picnic Area and Trailhead
A shady picnic area that also serves as the parking area for the **South Rim Trail** and **North Rim Trail**, as well as long backcountry hikes to **Howard Eaton Lake** and **Wapiti Lake**. *4 tables. Vault toilet.*
Directions: SE side of road.

MM: 0.1 **GPS:** 44.70824/-110.50307 **Elev:** 7705 **Grid:** 8/7 **Land:** NPS
North Rim Trail **Type:** Hiking Trail
A partially paved hiking trail that follows the **North Rim of the Grand Canyon of the Yellowstone** from **Chittenden Bridge** to **Inspiration Point**. All of the attractions along the trail are reachable by car; however, the parking areas tend to be very crowded. A shuttle vehicle can be parked at various points to prevent re-tracing the same route. Shorter versions of this hike can be made by starting at the **Brink of the Upper Falls** parking area and/or skipping the last section to **Inspiration Point**. *See Canyon Village to Fishing Bridge Junction MM 1.6 for descriptions of Brink of the Upper Falls and Crystal Falls. See chapter: North Rim Drive for descriptions of the other viewpoints.*

Head west from the **Wapiti Lake Trailhead** across the **Chittenden Bridge** to the start of the **North Rim Trail** (MI 0.1). The trail heads north 0.5 mi on an old road along the west bank of the **Yellowstone River**, where the river rushes to the **Brink of the Upper Falls**, which has a viewing platform a short distance to the right (MI 0.5). Finish the climb to the parking area and continue around the right side then up the road about 60 yds to reconnect to the **North Rim Trail** (MI 0.8). Follow the trail north 100 yds to a fork, where a short distance to the right is the viewpoint for **Crystal Falls**. Keep left 0.1 mi to the top of the falls and **Grotto Pool**. Continue 0.3 mi to a junction with the steep 0.6 mi round-trip trail to the **Brink of the Lower Falls** (MI 1.2). Climb 0.1 mi to the parking area and turn right to follow the road and trail to **Lookout Point** (MI 1.8) and **Grand View** (MI 2.0). Shortly past the parking area the trail turns to dirt and after 1/3 mi heads into the forest before emerging at **Inspiration Point** (MI 3.2). *Without side trails: Moderately easy; 3.2 mi one-way; Mostly level.* **With 2 steep side trails to Lower Falls overlooks**: Moderate; 4.3 mi one-way; 630 ft elev loss.
Cool Rating: ***** **Crowds:** *** **Time:** 1.5-4 hrs
Directions: Park at Wapiti Trailhead/Chittenden Picnic Area parking area. Trail starts at W end of Chittenden Bridge.

MM: 0.6 **GPS:** 44.71482/-110.49634 **GPS2:** 44.71460/-110.49721 **Elev:** 7737 **Grid:** 8/7 **Land:** NPS
Uncle Tom's Overlook of the Upper Falls **Type:** Waterfall
A short wheelchair accessible trail to an overlook of the **Upper Falls**. **Crystal Falls** can be seen across the canyon by looking through the trees between the parking area and the overlook.
Cool Rating: ***** **Crowds:** ***** **Time:** 20 min **Directions:** NW to parking area.

MM: 0.6 **GPS:** 44.71529/-110.49630 **Elev:** 7777 **Grid:** 8/7 **Land:** NPS
South Rim Trail **Type:** Hiking Trail
This hiking trail follows the south rim of the spectacular **Grand Canyon of the Yellowstone** northeast to **Artist Point** and beyond. The loop trail starts on the west side of **Uncle Tom's Parking Area**, but can also be started from the **Wapiti Lake Trailhead/Chittenden Bridge Picnic Area** 0.6 mi southwest. From **Uncle Tom's Parking Area** follow the trail 0.1 mi to the junction with **Uncle Tom's Trail** *(see next section)* (MI 0.1). Continue 0.8 mi northeast to the **Artist Point** parking area, passing 3 overlooks of the **Lower Falls** (MI 0.9). Continue across the parking area to **Artist Point** for spectacular views *(see Artist Point at MM 1.6)* (MI 1.1). Continue east 0.6 mi to a trail junction to **Point Sublime** or **Lily Pad Lake** (MI 1.7):

Out-and-back spur trail to Point Sublime: Continue straight 0.4 mi to a cool view of river rapids deep in the canyon or 0.8 mi to **Point Sublime**. I would recommend turning around at the rapids, as **Point Sublime** is probably the worst vantage point on the entire trail. It has only a mediocre view to the northeast, and the rest is blocked by trees.

Continuing the loop to Lily Pad Lake: Turn right and hike 0.3 mi past **Lily Pad Lake** to a second trail junction. Turn right to pass by a **thermal area** containing mud pots, hot pools, and steam vents. Continue past the emerald green **Clear Lake** to a third trail junction (MI 2.8). Keep right to return to the parking area (MI 3.5). *Moderately easy with a few short steep sections;* **Basic Loop:** 3.5 mi; **Loop with river rapids option:** 4.3 mi; **Loop with Point Sublime option:** 5.1 mi; 60 ft elevation gain.

From **Lily Pad Lake**, there is also a 1.3 mi trail north to **Ribbon Lake** and the top of **Silver Cord Cascade**. However, this adds 2.6 mi to the hike and may not be worth the extra effort.
Cool Rating: ***** **Crowds:** *** **Time:** 1.5-3 hrs **Directions:** NW into parking area.
Notes: A good portion of the trail is close to steep drop-offs, so keep kids under control. The section past Clear Lake has early season bear activity.

MM: 0.6 *GPS:* 44.71529/-110.49630 *GPS2:* 44.71753/-110.49452 *Elev:* 7777 *Grid:* 8/7 *Land:* NPS
Uncle Tom's Trail to the Lower Falls   *Type:* Waterfall
Originally constructed in 1898 by **"Uncle" Tom Richardson** with steps, ropes, and ladders, this trail now consists of 328 stairs and paved inclines that drop steeply into the **Grand Canyon of the Yellowstone** for a close-up view of the **Lower Falls**. From the west side of the parking area, head north to descend on the paved **South Rim Trail** 0.1 mi to the junction with **Uncle Tom's Trail**. The paved path and stairs then descend another 320 ft in 0.3 mi to the viewing platform. *Moderately strenuous; 0.4 mi; 390 ft elev loss.*
Cool Rating: ***** **Crowds:** ***** **Time:** 1 hr **Directions:** NW into parking area.
Notes: Not recommended for those with health concerns. Wear flat-soled shoes, as much of the walkway is made from meshed steel.

MM: 1.6 *GPS:* 44.71979/-110.48015 *GPS2:* 44.72123/-110.47945 *Elev:* 7643 *Grid:* 8/7 *Land:* NPS
Artist Point   *Type:* Scenic Viewpoint
A legendary overlook of the **Lower Falls** in the vividly colored **Grand Canyon of the Yellowstone**. This is one of the most majestic views in the United States and is one of the most crowded attractions in the park. This is along the **South Rim Trail**, which heads east and southwest from here. *See earlier section.*
Cool Rating: ****** **Crowds:** ***** **Time:** 30 min
Directions: End of road at parking area; Walk NE 0.1 mi to the overlook.

MM: 0.0/18.3 **GPS:** 44.91601/-110.41577 **Elev:** 6262 **Grid:** 9/2 **Land:** NPS
Yellowstone - Tower-Roosevelt to Canyon Village   **Type:** Highway Description
18.3 mi northeast section of the **Grand Loop Road** from **Tower-Roosevelt** south to **Canyon Village**. Highlights include: **Calcite Springs**, **Devil's Den**, **Tower Fall**, **Mount Washburn**.
Directions: SE to Canyon Village from MM 0

MM: 0.0/18.3 **GPS:** 44.91601/-110.41577 **Elev:** 6262 **Grid:** 9/2
Yellowstone - Mammoth Hot Springs to Tower-Roosevelt *(see chapter)*   **Type:** Hwy Transition w/Chapter
18.1 mi north section of the **Grand Loop Road** from **Tower-Roosevelt** west to **Mammoth Hot Springs**. Highlights include: **Petrified Tree**, **Hellroaring Creek Trail**, **Wraith Falls**, **Undine Falls**.
Directions: W to Mammoth Hot Springs from MM 18.1

MM: 0.0/18.3 **GPS:** 44.91601/-110.41577 **Elev:** 6262 **Grid:** 9/2
Yellowstone - Northeast Entrance to Tower-Roosevelt *(see chapter)*   **Type:** Hwy Junction w/Chapter
28.2 mi highway from **Tower-Roosevelt** northeast out of **Yellowstone National Park** to **US-212** in **Montana**. A few minor points of interest along the way.
Directions: NE to Cooke City, MT from MM 28.2

MM: 0.0/18.3 **Dist:** 0.1 **GPS:** 44.91643/-110.41991 **Elev:** 6267 **Grid:** 9/2 **Land:** NPS
Tower Ranger Station   **Type:** Visitor Center
Information, maps, and backcountry and fishing permits. This 1923 building is a reconstruction of a 1907 soldier station.
Directions: W toward Mammoth Hot Springs 0.1 mi; S 90 yds.

MM: 0.0/18.3 **Dist:** 0.2 **GPS:** 44.91300/-110.41640 **Elev:** 6318 **Grid:** 9/2 **Land:** NPS
Roosevelt   **Type:** Town
Visitor services located on the northeast end of the **Grand Loop Road**, including a general store, gift shop, fuel, restaurant, showers, cabins (historic **Roosevelt Lodge**), horseback riding, backcountry and fishing permits, and a **Ranger Station**.
Directions: SW 0.2 mi

MM: 0.0/18.3 **Dist:** 0.2 **GPS:** 44.91244/-110.41666 **GPS2:** 44.90982/-110.41897 **Elev:** 6325 **Grid:** 9/2 **Land:** NPS
Lost Creek Falls & Lost Lake   **Type:** Waterfall
Lost Creek Falls is a 40 ft high waterfall on **Lost Creek**, which falls into a steep canyon. **Lost Lake** is a narrow 1/4 mi long lake partially covered with lily pads and located in a shallow valley. The following directions provide for a short hike to a viewpoint of the falls or a longer trip to a second overlook of the falls and to the lake. From the south side of the lodge, walk southwest 85 yds to the trailhead. Turn left and climb steeply 0.2 mi, gaining 140 ft to an overlook of the falls. Return to the trailhead and continue west 0.6 mi, crossing **Lost Creek** and climbing 340 ft to a trail junction. Turn left for a 1.2 mi round-trip to a second overlook of the falls or turn right to continue 0.2 mi through a shallow valley to **Lost Lake**. Continuing 1.0 mi past the lake leads to the **Petrified Tree**.
Lost Creek Falls only: Easy; 0.4 mi round-trip; 140 ft elev gain. *First falls overlook and Lost Lake:* Moderately easy; 2.1 mi round-trip; 460 ft elev gain. *Both falls overlooks and Lost Lake:* Moderately easy; 3.3 mi round-trip; 480 ft elev gain.
Cool Rating: *** **Crowds:** * **Time:** 30 min - 2 hrs
Directions: SW 0.2 mi to the Roosevelt Lodge parking area The trail starts on the south side of the lodge.

MM: 1.6/16.7 **GPS:** 44.90187/-110.39313 **GPS2:** 44.90649/-110.39492 **Elev:** 6505 **Grid:** 9/2 **Land:** NPS
Calcite Springs Overlook   **Type:** Scenic Viewpoint
A 230 yd boardwalk loop trail with interpretive signs and views of **Calcite Springs**, which is 1/4 mi north up the **Grand Canyon of the Yellowstone** at the base of the flat-topped **Bumpus Butte**. This area is next to the **Yellowstone River** where geothermal discharge reaches the surface, which has turned the cliff white, yellow, and orange. On the west end of the loop is an interpretive sign about the volcanic formation of hexagonal columns of basalt that line the upper edge of the canyon. This formation can be seen directly across the canyon.

A better view of **Calcite Springs** can be seen along the **Yellowstone River Trail** on the northeast entrance road, 1.2 mi east of **Tower Junction**. *See Yellowstone - Northeast Entrance to Tower-Roosevelt MM 26.9/1.2.*
Cool Rating: *** **Crowds:** ** **Time:** 20 min **Directions:** NE side of hwy

MM: 2.2/16.1 **GPS:** 44.89452/-110.38807 **Elev:** 6450 **Grid:** 10/3 **Land:** NPS
Devil's Den   **Type:** Point of Interest
Just to the south of the pullout, **Tower Creek** winds through a canyon of volcanic rock pinnacles to the brink of **Tower Fall**. This canyon continues east to the **Yellowstone River** and is called **Devil's Den**.
Cool Rating: *** **Crowds:** * **Time:** 10 min **Directions:** Pullout on E side of hwy

MM: 2.4/15.9 **Dist:** 0.3 **GPS:** 44.89190/-110.38731 **GPS2:** 44.88962/-110.39074 **Elev:** 6585 **Grid:** 10/3 **Land:** NPS
Tower Fall Campground   **Type:** Campground
Located on a 0.6 mi half-loop road southwest of **Tower Fall** near **Tower Creek**. The campground is situated on a hillside and most of the sites are unlevel and cramped with no privacy. *Single loop with a tight curve. Conifer forest. Amphitheater for ranger programs. Cheaper than the large campgrounds that take reservations. Fills early.*

Just east of the campground is a trail that heads 3.5 mi southwest along **Tower Creek** or 2.1 mi north to a junction with the **Lost Lake Trail**. From this trail junction the trail turns right 0.7 mi to **Roosevelt Lodge** or left 1.4 mi to **Lost Lake**.
Crowds: ***** **[FEE AREA]** **Directions:** Across from the Tower Fall parking area; W on a one-way loop 0.3 mi.
Notes: In my opinion, this is the worst campground in Yellowstone.
Campsites: 32 **Shade:** **** **Privacy:** * **RV Size:** 30' **Other:** Water BEARS

MM: 2.4/15.9 **GPS:** 44.89158/-110.38685 **GPS2:** 44.89373/-110.38695 **Elev:** 6430 **Grid:** 10/3 **Land:** NPS
Tower Fall   **Type:** Waterfall
A magnificent 132 ft waterfall on **Tower Creek**. At the brink of the falls are pinnacles sculpted from rhyolitic basalt from which the falls gets its name. A 0.1 mi trail leads to a viewing platform of the falls across the canyon. The trail continues 0.4 mi dropping steeply 240 ft to the base of the waterfall where it is shady and cool. From the base of the falls, **Tower Creek** flows 0.2 mi through a canyon called **Devil's Den** into the **Yellowstone River**. Where the trail passes closest to the river, a short trail continues along the river bank. *Moderately easy; 0.5 mi one-way; 240 ft elev loss.*
Cool Rating: ***** **Crowds:** ***** **Time:** 1.5 hr **Notes:** A general store and restrooms are located at the parking area.
Directions: E side of hwy

MM: 7.0/11.2 **GPS:** 44.85132/-110.42258 **Elev:** 7767 **Grid:** 9/4 **Land:** NPS
Interpretive Pullout: Grizzly Bears   **Type:** Point of Interest
A sign about grizzly bear habitat. Grizzly bears, moose, and elk may be seen in the valley below.
Cool Rating: * **Crowds:** * **Time:** 10 min **Directions:** SE side of hwy

MM: 8.5/9.8 **Dist:** 1.3 **GPS:** 44.82455/-110.44468 **GPS2:** 44.79756/-110.43386 **Elev:** 8750 **Grid:** 9/4 **Land:** NPS
Mount Washburn Trail from Chittenden Rd   **Type:** Hiking Trail
A hiking or bike trail on an unshaded service road up the northeast side of **Mount Washburn**. At the 10,243 ft summit is the finest 360° panoramic view in the park, which includes views of the surrounding mountains, high peaks, **Grand Canyon of the Yellowstone**, and **Yellowstone Lake**. This trail also offers wildlife viewing, including a resident herd of bighorn sheep, and beautiful wildflowers in July and early August. **Mount Washburn** is the northernmost point of the **Yellowstone Caldera**. At the summit is a 3-story structure, including a manned fire lookout, which is not accessible to visitors. On the ground floor are restrooms and an indoor interpretive center and viewing room, which includes interpretive panels identifying the surrounding landscape and a telescope for viewing. On the second floor is an observation deck with additional interpretive signs. *See later section at MM 13.5 for the southern route to the summit. Strenuous; 2.8 mi one-way; 1490 ft elev gain.*
Cool Rating: ***** **Crowds:** *** **Time:** 3-5 hrs **Directions:** S 1.3 mi on Chittenden Rd to parking area.
Notes: Be aware of changing weather, including wind, rain, and lightning storms. Stay on the trail and off the fragile alpine tundra. Stay alert for grizzly bears.
Road Desc: Gravel, rough, washboard, & potholed, narrow & steep. Climbs 660 ft to parking area.

MM: 8.7/9.5 **GPS:** 44.83855/-110.44226 **Elev:** 8215 **Grid:** 9/4 **Land:** NPS
Restroom   **Type:** Restroom
A half-loop pullout with a vault toilet.
Directions: NW side of hwy

MM: 10.4/7.8 **GPS:** 44.81692/-110.45030 **Elev:** 8625 **Grid:** 9/5 **Land:** NPS
Mount Washburn View Pullout (north)   **Type:** Scenic Viewpoint
A view of the northwest side of **Mount Washburn** and into a valley to the west. Grizzly bears can sometimes be seen on **Mount Washburn**.
Cool Rating: ** **Crowds:** *** **Time:** 10 min **Directions:** W side of hwy

MM: 13.5/4.8 **GPS:** 44.78501/-110.45346 **GPS2:** 44.79756/-110.43386 **Elev:** 8867 **Grid:** 9/5 **Land:** NPS
Mount Washburn Trail from Dunraven Pass   **Type:** Hiking Trail
A hiking only route that climbs up switchbacks on an unused service road to the top of the 10,243 ft **Mount Washburn**. This route travels up the southwest side, offering a more forested and interesting terrain plus better views than those on the north side. This trail is less steep but slightly longer and provides some shade. *See earlier section at MM 8.5 for the northern route and a description at the summit. Strenuous; 3.5 mi one-way; 1375 ft elev gain.*
Cool Rating: ***** **Crowds:** **** **Time:** 3-5 hrs **Directions:** Parking area on E side of hwy
Notes: Be aware of changing weather, including wind, rain, and lightning storms. Stay alert for grizzly bears.

MM: 13.9/4.4 **GPS:** 44.77963/-110.45667 **Elev:** 8780 **Grid:** 9/6 **Land:** NPS
Mount Washburn View Pullout (south)   **Type:** Scenic Viewpoint
A pullout below **Dunraven Peak** with a view of the south side of **Mount Washburn** and the valley below. Bring the binoculars to look for wildlife. *Vault toilet.*
Cool Rating: ** **Crowds:** *** **Time:** 5 min **Directions:** SE side of hwy

MM: 14.9/3.4 **GPS:** 44.76780/-110.45531 **Elev:** 8532 **Grid:** 9/6 **Land:** NPS
Interpretive Pullout: Yellowstone Caldera   **Type:** Point of Interest
A sign about the **Yellowstone Caldera**, which formed the ridge line on the horizon. A caldera is a large basin-like depression (crater) resulting from the explosion or collapse of the center of a volcano.
Cool Rating: ** **Crowds:** * **Time:** 5 min **Directions:** SE side of hwy

MM: 15.8/2.4 **GPS:** 44.76184/-110.47120 **Elev:** 8327 **Grid:** 8/6 **Land:** NPS
Dunraven Road Picnic Area   **Type:** Picnic Area
A large picnic area with individual sites. *12 tables. Vault toilet.*
Directions: NW side of hwy

MM: 16.9/1.3 **GPS:** 44.75154/-110.48600 **Elev:** 8025 **Grid:** 8/6 **Land:** NPS
Cascade Lake Picnic Area and Trail   **Type:** Picnic Area and Trailhead
A large picnic area with individual sites. *16 tables. 5 grills. Vault toilet.*

This is also the trailhead for a hike through meadows and forest west to **Cascade Lake**, which is situated in a large meadow. The lake is a better fishing lake than a hiking destination. *Easy; 5.0 mi round-trip; 70 ft elevation loss.*
Cool Rating: ** **Crowds:** *** **Directions:** NW side of hwy

MM: 17.2/1.0 **GPS:** 44.75015/-110.49172 **Elev:** 8015 **Grid:** 8/6 **Land:** NPS
Cascade Lake Trailhead   **Type:** Trailhead
If not picnicking, this provides alternate parking for the trail to **Cascade Lake**. *See previous section.*
Directions: NW side of hwy

MM: 18.3/0.0 *Dist:* 0.1 *GPS:* 44.73547/-110.48945 *Elev:* 7940 *Grid:* 8/7 *Land:* NPS

Canyon Village   *Type:* Town & Campground

Visitor services located on the east central section of the **Grand Loop Road** and on the north end of **Grand Canyon of the Yellowstone**, including an ATM, general store, gift shop, sporting goods store, fuel, auto repair, restaurant, cafeteria, fast food, laundry, showers, hotel, cabins, post office, horseback riding, backcountry and fishing permits, and a **Ranger Station**. On the west side of the complex is the large **Canyon Visitor Education Center**, which contains a staffed information desk, bookstore, a large theatre, and several elaborate exhibits about **Yellowstone's** supervolcano and other aspects of the park geology.

The campground is one of 4 large modern campgrounds that take reservations. *10 loops. Conifer forest. Paved roads and parking areas. Restrooms with flush toilets, running water, and electricity. Generators permitted. Amphitheater for ranger programs. 3 wheelchair accessible sites.*

Hours: Visitor center: 8am - 8pm (307-344-2550)

Directions: E 0.1 mi and right to Visitor Center and stores; E 0.1 mi and left to campground or right to hotel.

MM: 18.3/0.0 *GPS:* 44.73591/-110.49325 *Elev:* 7915 *Grid:* 8/7

Yellowstone - Canyon Village to Fishing Bridge *(see chapter)*   *Type:* Hwy Transition w/Chapter

15.4 mi east-central section of the **Grand Loop Road** from **Canyon Village** south to **Fishing Bridge**. Highlights include: **Grand Canyon of the Yellowstone, Upper Falls, Lower Falls, Sulphur Caldron, Mud Volcano Area, LeHardy Rapids**.

Nearest Town: Canyon Village 0.1 E *Directions:* S to Fishing Bridge from MM 0

MM: 18.3/0.0 *GPS:* 44.73591/-110.49325 *Elev:* 7915 *Grid:* 8/7

Yellowstone - Norris to Canyon Village *(see chapter)*   *Type:* Hwy Junction w/Chapter

11.6 mi cutoff road at the center of the **Grand Loop Road** connecting **Canyon Village** west to **Norris**. If just visiting the attractions along this highway, they are much closer from the **Norris** end. Highlights include: **Little Gibbon Falls** and **Virginia Cascade**.

Directions: W to Norris from MM 11.6

MM: 18.3/0.0 *GPS:* 44.73591/-110.49325 *Elev:* 7915 *Grid:* 8/7 *Land:* NPS

Yellowstone - Canyon Village to Tower-Roosevelt   *Type:* Highway End

18.3 mi northeast section of the **Grand Loop Road** from **Canyon Village** north to **Tower-Roosevelt**. Highlights include: **Mount Washburn, Tower Fall, Devil's Den, Calcite Springs**.

Directions: N to Tower-Roosevelt from MM 18.3

Yellowstone - Upper Terrace Drive
Loop

MM: 0.0 **GPS:** 44.96528/-110.70769 **Elev:** 6625 **Grid:** 5/1 **Land:** NPS
Yellowstone - Upper Terrace Drive **Type:** Highway Description
1.6 mi one-way loop road that provides automobile access to the **Mammoth Hot Springs Upper Terrace** as well as alternate access to the **Main Terrace** and **Canary Spring** without climbing stairs from below. The **Upper Terrace** contains individual thermal features spaced out along the road.
Nearest Town: Mammoth Hot Springs 2 N **Notes:** No vehicles over 25 ft. **Directions:** NW on loop road from MM 0

MM: 0.1 **GPS:** 44.96615/-110.70803 **Elev:** 6600 **Grid:** 5/1 **Land:** NPS
Wheelchair Access to Main Terrace and Canary Spring **Type:** Thermal Area
A 0.1 mi gradually descending boardwalk for wheelchair access to the **Main Terrace** and **Canary Spring**.

MM: 0.2 **GPS:** 44.96842/-110.70766 **Elev:** 6575 **Grid:** 5/1 **Land:** NPS
Upper Parking for Main Terrace and Canary Spring **Type:** Thermal Area
Parking just above the **Main Terrace** and **Canary Spring** for an easier alternative to climbing from the lower parking areas. *See Mammoth Hot Springs Terraces in chapter: Yellowstone - Norris to Mammoth Hot Springs MM 20.6/0.3.*
Cool Rating: ***** **Crowds:** ***** **Time:** 30 min

MM: 0.3 **GPS:** 44.96923/-110.70823 **Elev:** 6570 **Grid:** 5/1 **Land:** NPS
Mammoth Hot Springs Overlook **Type:** Scenic Viewpoint
A view from 330 ft above **Mammoth Hot Springs**, the former sight of **Fort Yellowstone**. An interpretive sign explains some history of the fort. *See Mammoth Hot Springs in chapter: Yellowstone - Mammoth Hot Springs to Tower MM 20.9 for more on Fort Yellowstone.*
Cool Rating: ** **Crowds:** * **Time:** 5 min **Directions:** Right side of road

MM: 0.4 **GPS:** 44.96820/-110.70926 **Elev:** 6600 **Grid:** 5/1 **Land:** NPS
Prospect Terrace **Type:** Thermal Area
Prospect Spring is a foot tall gray cone. The parking area can be used to access the **Narrow Gauge Terrace** trail. *See next section.*
Cool Rating: * **Crowds:** * **Time:** 5 min **Directions:** Right side of road

MM: 0.4 **Dist:** 0.1 **GPS:** 44.96816/-110.71019 **GPS2:** 44.96931/-110.71026 **Elev:** 6630 **Grid:** 5/1 **Land:** NPS
Narrow Gauge Terrace **Type:** Thermal Area
A short trail to a long, narrow, and colorful travertine terrace, which has engulfed a section of the forest. A small parking area is located at the trailhead or the trail can also be accessed 75 yds up the road from the **Prospect Terrace** parking area.
Cool Rating: **** **Crowds:** * **Time:** 15 min
Directions: Trail to the right 65 yds to the Howard Eaton Trail; Right 50 yds.

MM: 0.6 **GPS:** 44.96735/-110.71358 **Elev:** 6720 **Grid:** 5/1 **Land:** NPS
New Highland Terrace **Type:** Thermal Area
Once a wooded hillside, in the early 1950s **New Highland Spring** became active and rapidly formed a massive deposit of travertine. This activity engulfed and killed the trees, which still stand today.
Cool Rating: *** **Crowds:** ** **Time:** 10 min **Directions:** Left side of road

MM: 0.8 **GPS:** 44.96618/-110.71504 **Elev:** 6755 **Grid:** 5/1 **Land:** NPS
Orange Spring Mound **Type:** Thermal Area
A large white and orange travertine mound (50 ft x 20 ft) created by very slow water flow and mineral deposition. The streaks of orange were created by bacteria and algae. The road and a boardwalk allow views from 3 sides.
Cool Rating: **** **Crowds:** ** **Time:** 15 min **Directions:** Left side of road

MM: 1.2 **GPS:** 44.96295/-110.71387 **Elev:** 6795 **Grid:** 5/1 **Land:** NPS
White Elephant Back Terrace **Type:** Thermal Area
Water flowing from a fissure in the earth's crust has built a long ridge that resembles the back of an elephant. This feature is at the high-point of **Upper Terrace Drive**.
Cool Rating: *** **Crowds:** ** **Time:** 5 min **Directions:** Left side of road

MM: 1.5 **GPS:** 44.96515/-110.70853 **Elev:** 6630 **Grid:** 5/1 **Land:** NPS
Angel Terrace **Type:** Thermal Area
Once snowy white and colorful, this unpredictable formation was dry and crumbling for decades. More recently hot springs have been intermittently active in parts of the formation.
Cool Rating: **** **Crowds:** ** **Time:** 5 min **Directions:** Left side of road

Yellowstone - West Entrance to Madison   W/E

MM: 0.0/13.6   **GPS:** 44.65727/-111.09200   **Elev:** 6677   **Grid:** -1/9   **Land:** NPS
Yellowstone - West Entrance to Madison   **Type:** Highway Description
13.6 mi highway from the west entrance of **Yellowstone National Park**, via **US-20** in **Montana**, east to **Madison**. The road follows the **Madison River** with minor points of interest and scenic views along the way.
Nearest Town: West Yellowstone, MT 0.4 W   **Directions:** E to Madison from MM 0

MM: 0.0/13.6   **GPS:** 44.65727/-111.09200   **Elev:** 6677   **Grid:** -1/9   **Land:** NPS
Yellowstone National Park - West Entrance   **Type:** National Park
Pay the National Park entrance fee, which covers both **Yellowstone National Park** and **Grand Teton National Park**. *See chapter: Yellowstone National Park.*
Nearest Town: West Yellowstone, MT 0.4 W   *[FEE AREA]*

MM: 0.0/13.6   **Dist:** 78.0   **GPS:** 44.14474/-110.99781   **Elev:** 6290   **Grid:** 1/21   **Land:** NPS
Cave Falls & Bechler Falls & Upper and Lower Mesa Falls   **Type:** Waterfall
The southwest corner of **Yellowstone National Park** is known as "**Cascade Corners**," because of the numerous waterfalls and cascades found in this region. Most of these waterfalls are reachable by long hiking trails; however, **Cave Falls** can be driven to and **Bechler Falls** can be reached by a 2.6 mi round-trip trail.

This region is only reachable by roads near **Ashton, Idaho**, on routes that start from the **Yellowstone National Park** west entrance and near **Jackson**. If leaving **Yellowstone National Park** from the west, the directions below lead past 2 spectacular **Idaho** waterfalls, **Upper Mesa Falls** and **Lower Mesa Falls**. **Cave Falls Campground** as well as dispersed camping is located just outside of the park.

See sections on **Cave Falls & Bechler Falls & Upper and Lower Mesa Falls** *and* **Cave Falls Campground** *in chapter: Wy-22 MM 17.7.*
Directions: From **Yellowstone West Entrance**; W 0.4 mi; N/R on Canyon St 0.2 mi; W/L on Firehole Ave/US-20 35.9 mi; SE/L on Id-47 12.9 mi to **Upper Mesa Falls**; S on Id-47 0.7 mi to **Lower Mesa Falls**; S on Id-47 8.6 mi; E/L on E 1400 N/Cave Falls Hwy 5.7 mi to National Forest boundary; Continue on FR-582 12.3 mi to **Cave Falls Campground**; Continue 1.1 mi to **Cave Falls lower parking area**; Continue 0.2 mi to **Cave Falls upper parking area**.

From Cave Falls upper parking area to Jackson (79 mi):
W on FR-582/E 1400 N 14.6 mi; S/L on N 4525 E 2.4 mi; W/R on E 1200 N 0.4 mi; S/L on N 4500 E 1.0 mi; E/L on E 1100 N 2.2 mi; S/R on N 4725 E and N 4700 E 5.2 mi; E/L on Id-32 11.7 mi; E/L on Id-33/Wy-22 41.5 mi to **Jackson**.

MM: 2.8/10.9   **GPS:** 44.65222/-111.03762   **Elev:** 6700   **Grid:** 0/9   **Land:** NPS
Two Ribbons Nature Trail (west end)   **Type:** Point of Interest
A 3/4 mi handicapped accessible boardwalk loop trail through a 1988 burn area. An interpretive sign at the trailhead explains why the area was not completely scorched. The north end of the trail is near the **Madison River**.
Cool Rating: ** **Crowds:** * **Time:** 30 min **Directions:** NE side of hwy

---

MM: 3.1/10.5   **GPS:** 44.65150/-111.03082   **Elev:** 6700   **Grid:** 0/9   **Land:** NPS
Two Ribbons Nature Trail (east end)   **Type:** Point of Interest
See previous section.
Directions: N side of hwy

MM: 4.6/9.0   **GPS:** 44.65086/-111.00186   **Elev:** 6750   **Grid:** 1/9   **Land:** NPS
Riverside Drive (west end)   **Type:** Fishing Area
A 1.1 mi half-loop road along the **Madison River** that provides fishing access.
Cool Rating: * **Crowds:** * **Directions:** NW side of hwy

MM: 5.7/7.9   **GPS:** 44.66201/-110.99150   **Elev:** 6743   **Grid:** 1/8   **Land:** NPS
Riverside Drive (east end)   **Type:** Fishing Area
See previous section.
Cool Rating: * **Crowds:** * **Directions:** W side of hwy

MM: 7.2/6.4   **GPS:** 44.66486/-110.96680   **Elev:** 6750   **Grid:** 1/8   **Land:** NPS
Madison River Picnic Area   **Type:** Picnic Area
A half-loop road next to the **Madison River**. Scattered trees provide some shade. *7 tables. Vault toilet. Handicapped accessible.*
Directions: NE side of hwy

MM: 7.5/6.1   **GPS:** 44.66188/-110.96252   **Elev:** 6760   **Grid:** 1/8   **Land:** NPS
Interpretive Pullout: Trumpeter Swans   **Type:** Point of Interest
2 signs on the opposite ends of the pullout about trumpeter swans and the historical use of the west entrance road.
Cool Rating: * **Crowds:** * **Time:** 5 min **Directions:** SW side of hwy

---

MM: 9.7/3.9   **GPS:** 44.64666/-110.93089   **Elev:** 6765   **Grid:** 2/9   **Land:** NPS
Interpretive Pullout: Talus   **Type:** Point of Interest
A sign about **Talus**, which can be seen on the hill across the river. **Talus** is a slope formed by an accumulation of rock debris at the base of a cliff. This pullout also provides fishing access.
Cool Rating: * **Crowds:** * **Time:** 5 min **Directions:** SW side of hwy

---

MM: 10.1/3.5   **GPS:** 44.64449/-110.92332   **Elev:** 6769   **Grid:** 2/9   **Land:** NPS
Mount Hayes Overlook and Fishing Access   **Type:** Fishing Area
A view to the south of the 8,231 ft **Mount Hayes**. A 120 yd wheelchair accessible boardwalk provides access to a 70 ft long fishing platform.
Cool Rating: * **Crowds:** * **Time:** 5 min **Directions:** S side of hwy

MM: 11.9/1.7 *GPS:* 44.63991/-110.88867 *Elev:* 6804 *Grid:* 2/9 *Land:* NPS
Harlequin Lake Trail   *Type:* Hiking Trail
A hike through burned and regenerating forest to **Harlequin Lake**, which is covered with lily pads and has no fish. *Easy; 1.0 mi round-trip; 120 ft elev gain.*
Cool Rating: ** *Crowds:* * *Time:* 30 min
Directions: Park on S side of hwy; Trailhead is across the road from the east end of the pullout.

MM: 12.2/1.4 *GPS:* 44.63985/ 110.88239 *Elev:* 6806 *Grid:* 2/9 *Land:* NPS
Interpretive Pullout: Beetle-killed Forest   *Type:* Point of Interest
A sign about how the 1988 fire aided the regeneration of this former beetle-killed forest.
Cool Rating: * *Crowds:* * *Time:* 5 min *Directions:* S side of hwy

MM: 12.5/1.1 *GPS:* 44.64156/-110.87668 *Elev:* 6795 *Grid:* 3/9 *Land:* NPS
Interpretive Pullout: Madison Elk Herd   *Type:* Point of Interest
A sign about the summer and winter range of the **Madison Elk Herd**.
Cool Rating: * *Crowds:* * *Time:* 5 min *Directions:* SE side of hwy

MM: 13.5/0.2 *GPS:* 44.64620/-110.86106 *Elev:* 6830 *Grid:* 3/9 *Land:* NPS
Madison Campground   *Type:* Campground
One of 4 large modern campgrounds that take reservations. Located just north of the **Madison River** on the west central section of the **Grand Loop Road**. *10 loops, 2 for tents only near the river. Conifer forest. Paved roads and parking areas. Restrooms with flush toilets, running water, and electricity. Generators permitted. Amphitheater for ranger programs. Firewood and ice for sale.*
Crowds: ***** *[FEE AREA] Directions:* S side of hwy
Campsites: 277 *Shade:* ***** *Privacy:* * *RV Size:* 30' *Other:* 1-866-439-7375,Water,RVDump BEARS

MM: 13.6/0.0 *GPS:* 44.64540/-110.85846 *Elev:* 6836 *Grid:* 3/9
Yellowstone - Madison to Norris *(see chapter)*   *Type:* Hwy Junction w/Chapter
13.4 mi west-central section of the **Grand Loop Road** from **Madison** northeast to **Norris**. Highlights include: **Gibbon Falls, Beryl Spring, Monument Geyser Basin, Artist Paint Pots, Chocolate Pots, Norris Geyser Basin**.
Nearest Town: West Yellowstone, MT 14.0 W *Directions:* NE to Norris from MM 0

MM: 13.6/0.0 *GPS:* 44.64540/-110.85846 *Elev:* 6836 *Grid:* 3/9
Yellowstone - West Thumb to Madison *(see chapter)*   *Type:* Hwy Junction w/Chapter
33.5 mi southwest section of the **Grand Loop Road** from **Madison** southeast to **West Thumb**. The majority of the geyser activity is along this section. Highlights include: **Firehole Falls, Lower Geyser Basin, Firehole Lake Drive Geysers, Midway Geyser Basin, Fairy Falls, Biscuit Basin, Mystic Falls, Black Sand Basin, Upper Geyser Basin, Old Faithful, Kepler Cascades, Lone Star Geyser**.
Nearest Town: West Yellowstone, MT 14.0 W *Directions:* SE to West Thumb from MM 33.5

MM: 13.6/0.0 *GPS:* 44.64540/-110.85846 *Elev:* 6836 *Grid:* 3/9 *Land:* NPS
Yellowstone - Madison to West Entrance   *Type:* Highway End
13.6 mi highway from **Madison** west out of **Yellowstone National Park** to **US-20** and **West Yellowstone, Montana**. The road follows the **Madison River** with minor points of interest and scenic views along the way.
Nearest Town: West Yellowstone, MT 14.0 W *Directions:* W to West Yellowstone, MT from MM 13.6

MM: 0.0/33.5 *GPS:* 44.41403/-110.57848 *Elev:* 7808 *Grid:* 7/15 *Land:* NPS

Yellowstone - West Thumb to Madison   *Type:* Highway Description

33.5 mi southwest section of the **Grand Loop Road** from **West Thumb** northwest to **Madison**. The majority of the geyser activity is along this section. Highlights include: **Lone Star Geyser**, **Kepler Cascades**, **Upper Geyser Basin**, **Old Faithful**, **Black Sand Basin**, **Mystic Falls**, **Biscuit Basin**, **Fairy Falls**, **Midway Geyser Basin**, **Firehole Lake Drive Geysers**, **Lower Geyser Basin**, **Firehole Falls**.

Nearest Town: Grant Village 2.8 S *Directions:* NW to Madison from MM 0

MM: 0.0/33.5 *GPS:* 44.41403/-110.57848 *Elev:* 7808 *Grid:* 7/15

Yellowstone - South Entrance to West Thumb *(see chapter)*   *Type:* Hwy Transition w/Chapter

21.2 mi highway from **West Thumb** south out of **Yellowstone National Park** to **US-89/191/287**. Highlights include: **Lewis Falls**, **Moose Falls**.

Nearest Town: Grant Village 2.8 S *Directions:* S to Grand Teton National Park from MM 21.2

MM: 0.0/33.5 *GPS:* 44.41403/-110.57848 *Elev:* 7808 *Grid:* 7/15

Yellowstone - Fishing Bridge to West Thumb *(see chapter)*   *Type:* Hwy Junction w/Chapter

20.6 mi southeast section of the **Grand Loop Road** from **West Thumb** northeast to **Fishing Bridge**. The entire length of this section follows the shore of **Yellowstone Lake**, which is North America's largest high elevation lake occupying an area of 136 sq mi with 141 mi of shoreline and a maximum depth of 430 ft. The southern end of this route travels along a protrusion in the lake known as the **West Thumb**. Highlights include: **West Thumb Geyser Basin**, **Duck Lake**, **Natural Bridge**, **Elephant Back Mountain**.

Nearest Town: Grant Village 2.8 S *Directions:* NE to Fishing Bridge from MM 20.6

MM: 3.7/29.7 *GPS:* 44.43249/-110.63294 *Elev:* 8350 *Grid:* 6/14 *Land:* NPS

Divide Picnic Area   *Type:* Picnic Area

A shady loop road with individual sites. *14 tables. Vault toilet. Handicapped accessible.*

Directions: NE side of hwy

MM: 8.2/25.2 *GPS:* 44.44831/-110.69193 *Elev:* 8072 *Grid:* 5/14 *Land:* NPS

Shoshone Point   *Type:* Scenic Viewpoint

A distant view to the south of **Shoshone Lake**, the second largest lake in **Yellowstone National Park**.

Cool Rating: * *Crowds:* * *Time:* 5 min *Directions:* S side of hwy

MM: 8.6/24.9 *GPS:* 44.44799/-110.69808 *Elev:* 7990 *Grid:* 5/14 *Land:* NPS

DeLacy Creek Picnic Area   *Type:* Picnic Area

A shady half-loop road with individual sites. *9 tables. Vault toilet.*

Directions: NW side of hwy

MM: 8.7/24.7 *GPS:* 44.44668/-110.70097 *Elev:* 7952 *Grid:* 5/14 *Land:* NPS

DeLacy Creek Trailhead   *Type:* Trailhead

A hike south through forest and meadows on the edge of the forest to the north end of **Shoshone Lake**, the second largest lake in **Yellowstone National Park**. The remote **Shoshone Geyser Basin** is located on the southwest end of the lake 7.6 mi farther. *Moderately easy; 3.0 mi one-way; 150 ft elev loss.*

Cool Rating: ** *Crowds:* * *Time:* 3 hrs

Directions: N side of hwy; The trailhead is on the S side of hwy at the W end of the parking area.

MM: 9.9/23.6 *GPS:* 44.44201/-110.71837 *Elev:* 8275 *Grid:* 5/14 *Land:* NPS

Isa Lake   *Type:* Point of Interest

At the summit of **Craig Pass**, this lily pad-covered lake straddles the **Continental Divide** and drains to different watersheds on either end of the 0.2 mi long lake. The east end drains to the **Pacific Ocean**, while the west end drains to the **Gulf of Mexico**. The road crosses diagonally over the lake with parking areas at either end. The east parking area is much larger with an interpretive sign.

Cool Rating: ** *Crowds:* * *Time:* 10 min *Directions:* Main pullout on NW side of hwy at NE end of lake.

MM: 12.0/21.5 *GPS:* 44.43080/-110.75310 *Elev:* 7955 *Grid:* 4/14 *Land:* NPS

Spring Creek Picnic Area   *Type:* Picnic Area

A nice shady loop road with individual sites. *10 tables. 2 grills. Vault toilet. Handicapped accessible.*

Directions: SW side of hwy

MM: 15.0/18.4 *GPS:* 44.44526/-110.80462 *GPS2:* 44.41824/-110.80679 *Elev:* 7590 *Grid:* 4/14 *Land:* NPS

Lone Star Geyser   *Type:* Geyser

Type: *Cone;* Interval: *3 hrs;* Height: *45 ft;* Duration: *30 min.* Frequent splashing of the geyser during its minor eruption phase has built up a steep 12 ft tall cone, which is one of the largest in **Yellowstone National Park**. A log book is provided for visitors to record the very predictable eruption times, which allows subsequent visitors to predict the next eruption. *Eruption cycle: Splashing starts 60 to 90 min after a major eruption and leads to one or more minor eruptions that last about 5 min and reach 45 ft; After a rest of 25 to 35 min, renewed splashing builds into the major eruption that lasts 30 min and reaches 45 ft; Followed by a powerful and loud steam phase.*

The geyser is reached by hiking or biking on an abandoned paved road along the **Firehole River**. *Easy; 2.5 mi one-way; 50 ft elev gain.*

Cool Rating: ***** *Crowds:* *** *Time:* 2-4 hrs

Directions: Parking area on SW side of hwy just S of Kepler Cascades; S on old paved road.

MM: 15.1/18.4 *GPS:* 44.44610/-110.80598 *GPS2:* 44.44564/-110.80617 *Elev:* 7570 *Grid:* 4/14 *Land:* NPS

Kepler Cascades   *Type:* Waterfall

A beautiful series of cascades and falls on the **Firehole River** that drop over 100 ft with the longest drop being 50 ft.

Cool Rating: **** *Crowds:* ***** *Time:* 15 min *Directions:* Large parking area on SW side of hwy

MM: 16.7/16.8   *GPS:* 44.45408/-110.82973   *GPS2:* 44.44684/-110.84368   *Elev:* 7378   *Grid:* 3/14   *Land:* NPS
Fern Cascades   *Type:* Waterfall
A 3 step cascade on **Iron Spring Creek** that drops 10, 20, and 70 ft. The name comes from the ferns that grow in this moist area. Getting a good view of the 70 ft section requires scrambling down a somewhat loose and rocky hill. The loop can be hiked in either direction; however, the climb is much more gradual traveling clockwise. Parking is at either the **Howard Eaton Trailhead** or at the **Old Faithful Village** at the ranger station.

Traveling clockwise from the **Howard Eaton Trailhead**, head southwest up a 2-track service road, which after a short distance turns into a footpath through a regenerating burned forest with little shade. This half of the loop gains 150 ft in 1.3 mi to the **Fern Cascades** sign. Turn left about 40 yds to a fork in the trail. The left fork heads down to **Iron Spring Creek** but not to the cascades. Instead, turn right and follow the trail about 70 yds down a loose rocky hill for the best view of **Fern Cascades**. The viewpoint has plenty of room, but don't get too close to the edge. Return to the sign on the loop and turn left to complete the 1.2 mi second half of the loop. The trail is fairly level for 0.3 mi and then drops 175 ft in another 0.3 mi to the employee housing area. Turn right and follow the paved road northeast toward the exit onto the main highway. About 100 ft before a stop sign, crosswalk, and paved walking path, turn right onto a gravel trail that connects to the **Howard Eaton Trail** and heads east 1/3 mi back to the trailhead.
Moderate; 2.5 mi loop; 170 ft elev gain.
Cool Rating: *** *Crowds:* * *Time:* 1.5 hrs *Notes:* Descend to the Fern Cascades overlook at your own risk.
Directions: SW side of hwy into the small Howard Eaton Trailhead parking area. *To alternate parking at Old Faithful Village;* Exit to Old Faithful Village and continue SE 1.1 mi to a fork in the road (at 0.8 mi is the crosswalk); Fork left 1/4 mi to a stop sign; W/L 0.15 mi; S/L 0.1 mi; Right into parking area; The paved trail to the employee housing is on the west end of the parking area next to the ranger station; Walk SW 300 yds across the highway to the concrete path; After a short distance, cut south through the trees 40 yds to the Howard Eaton Trail and turn left; Continue 1/4 mi to the Howard Eaton Trailhead parking area.

MM: 17.6/15.9   *Dist:* 1.1   *GPS:* 44.45691/-110.82687   *Elev:* 7370   *Grid:* 3/14   *Land:* NPS
Old Faithful Village   *Type:* Town
Adjacent to **Old Faithful Geyser**, this is the most developed area of the park and includes an ATM, general store, gift shop, fuel, auto repair, restaurant, cafeteria, fast food, showers, hotels (including the historic **Old Faithful Inn**), cabins, post office, medical clinic, backcountry and fishing permits, and a **Ranger Station**. A large, shady picnic area is located at the far end of the large RV parking lot southeast of **Old Faithful**. *15 tables. Vault toilet.*

A state-of-the-art visitor education center features exhibits and programs to help visitors understand and appreciate the geysers, hot springs, and other hydrothermal features in **Yellowstone National Park**. The center also contains a staffed information desk with geyser eruption predictions, auditorium, bookstore, research library, multi-purpose classroom, and ranger-led programs.
Hours: Visitor Center: 8am - 7pm *Phone:* 307-344-2750 *Crowds:* ***** *Directions:* NE then SE 1.1 mi

MM: 17.6/15.9   *Dist:* 1.1   *GPS:* 44.45960/-110.82880   *Elev:* 7360   *Grid:* 3/14   *Land:* NPS
Upper Geyser Basin and Old Faithful   *Type:* Geyser Basin
Along with the **Grand Canyon of the Yellowstone**, the **Upper Geyser Basin** is the highlight of **Yellowstone National Park**. This area contains the largest concentration of geysers in the world and takes a fair amount of time to explore. Start by visiting the **Old Faithful Visitor Center** (or call 307-344-2751) to get eruption times for 6 predicted geysers: **Old Faithful Geyser**, **Castle Geyser**, **Grand Geyser**, **Daisy Geyser**, and **Riverside Geyser**. The sixth, **Great Fountain Geyser**, is located at the **Lower Geyser Basin**. The pattern of activity for infrequent and unpredictable geysers can also be checked. Plan your tour around the geyser predictions, taking into account that **Old Faithful** erupts frequently and can always be seen later.

The **Upper Geyser Basin** is accessible by over 6 mi of trails and boardwalks. Following are descriptions and distances (where applicable) of the 6 primary trails. Under each trail are the primary features. Geyser information includes the type of geyser, interval between eruptions, and the height and duration of the eruption (* denotes predictable geysers). The **Old Faithful Area Trail Guide** provides a map and further information.

<u>OLD FAITHFUL LOOP</u> - A 0.7 mi loop boardwalk around **Old Faithful**.
***Old Faithful Geyser** - Type: *Cone;* Interval: *35-120 min;* Height: *90-184 ft;* Duration: *1.5-5 min*. The most famous geyser in Yellowstone with the most frequent eruptions of the big geysers.

<u>OBSERVATION POINT LOOP</u> - A 0.6 mi trail that starts northeast of the visitor center and climbs 220 ft to the **Observation Point** overlooking **Old Faithful** and the **Upper Geyser Basin**. The loop continues 0.6 mi past **Solitary Geyser** and connects with the **Geyser Hill** loop. (Take the boardwalk 0.3 mi NE from visitor center; Just across the Firehole River, turn right on the dirt trail: *1.2 mi out and back; 2.1 mi loop)*
Solitary Geyser - Type: *Fountain;* Interval: *4-8 min;* Height: *<6 ft;* Duration: *1 min*.

<u>GEYSER HILL LOOP</u> - A 0.5 mi loop around a variety of geysers. (Take the boardwalk 0.4 mi NE from visitor center to the loop: *1.3 mi round-trip)*. Walk the loop clockwise.
Anemone Geyser - Type: *Vent;* Interval: *6-10 min;* Height: *6-8 ft;* Duration: *25-45 sec*. Short interval provides an excellent opportunity to observe a typical geyser eruption cycle.
Beehive Geyser - Type: *Cone;* Interval: *8-24 hrs;* Height: *130-190+ ft;* Duration: *5 min*. 4 ft tall cone that resembles a beehive with a small opening that acts like a nozzle shooting a high narrow stream. Near the cone is a small 10-15 ft geyser that usually starts 10-25 min prior to an eruption.
Depression Geyser - Type: *Fountain;* Interval: *8-12 hrs;* Height: *4-10 ft;* Duration: *5 min*. Erupts from a small, deep pool.
Plume Geyser - Type: *Vent;* Interval: *9-15 hrs;* Height: *25 ft;* Duration: *3-5 quick bursts*. Created by a steam explosion in 1922.
Little Cub Geyser - Type: *Cone;* Interval: *60-90 min;* Height: *10 ft;* Duration: *10 min*. Part of the **Lion Group** of interconnected geysers, including **Lion Geyser**.
Lion Geyser - Type: *Cone;* Interval: *6-24 hrs;* Height: *50-90 ft;* Duration: *1-7 min*. Erupts in a series of up to 7 eruptions, about an hour apart. Eruptions often preceded by sudden gushes of steam and a deep roaring sound.

CONTINUED ON NEXT PAGE ...

MM: 17.6/15.9   **Dist:** 1.1   **GPS:** 44.45960/-110.82880   **Elev:** 7360   **Grid:** 3/14   **Land:** NPS

Upper Geyser Basin and Old Faithful (continued)   **Type:** Geyser Basin

Aurum Geyser - Type: *Cone;* Interval: *3-7 hrs;* Height: *15-25 ft;* Duration: *90 sec.*

Plate Geyser - Type: *Fountain;* Interval: *1-8 hrs;* Height: *15 ft;* Duration: *5 min.* The pool is behind **Sponge Geyser** and difficult to see.

Doublet Pool - Elaborate border ledges and deep blue waters. Periodically produces vibrations and audible thumps.

Giantess Geyser - Type: *Fountain;* Interval: *2-6 time per year;* Height: *200+ ft;* Duration: *Phases lasting 3 hrs to 2 days.* One of the largest geysers in Yellowstone. Best part starts 30 min - 6 hrs into the eruption. Eruption cycle includes a very loud steam phase.

BOARDWALK FROM GEYSER HILL TO PAVED TRAIL - A 0.9 mi boardwalk northwest past many more geysers and pools, ending near **Riverside Geyser** and **Daisy Geyser**.

Sawmill Geyser - Type: *Fountain;* Interval: *1-3 hrs;* Height: *35+ ft;* Duration: *30-50+ min.* Named after the water that spins in its crater as it erupts, which looks somewhat like a rotating saw blade.

*Grand Geyser - Type: *Fountain;* Interval: *8-12 hrs;* Height: *150-180 ft;* Duration: *10-12 min.* World's tallest predictable geyser. Erupts from a large pool with powerful bursts rather than a steady column.

Beauty Pool - Noted for its rich, blue water framed by rainbow-colored bacteria. The pool is connected to the neighboring **Chromatic Spring**.

Oblong Geyser - Type: *Fountain;* Interval: *3-12+ hrs;* Height: *25+ ft;* Duration: *5 min.* Eruption is more of a raised boiling than bursts.

Giant Geyser - Type: *Cone;* Interval: *days to years;* Height: *250 ft;* Duration: *1+ hr.* Second largest geyser in the world behind **Steamboat Geyser**. Erupts over a million gallons of water.

VISITOR CENTER TO BISCUIT BASIN - A paved path, which allows bicycles, from the visitor center to **Morning Glory Pool** (1.5 mi one-way). A gravel trail continues 0.8 mi to **Biscuit Basin**. A gravel bike path that leads 1.4 mi to **Biscuit Basin** is located about 120 yds west on the north end of the **Daisy Geyser** loop.

(0.5 mi) ***Castle Geyser** - Type: *Cone;* Interval: *9-11 hrs;* Height: *60-90 ft;* Duration: *20 min.* Eruption followed by a noisy 30-40 min steam phase. The 12 ft cone is the largest and may be the oldest of all geysers in the basin.

(0.5 mi) **Tilt Geyser** - Type: *Vent;* Interval: *50 min;* Height: *<6 ft;* Duration: *2 min.* Makes sucking and gurgling noises at end of the eruption. Just past **Castle Geyser**.

(0.5 mi) **Crested Pool** - 42 ft deep clear blue superheated pool that when boiling violently may rise to heights of 8-10 ft.

(1.1 mi) *Trail to Black Sand Basin - See next section*

(1.2 mi) **Grotto Geyser** - Type: *Fountain;* Interval: *7-24+ hrs;* Height: *10 ft;* Duration: *1.5-2+ hrs.* Part of the **Grotto Group** of connected geysers, which also connect to **Giant Geyser**. Erupts simultaneously with neighboring **Rocket Geyser**. The pool is hidden inside a strange shaped formation of sinter covered tree trunks that once grew here.

(1.3 mi) ***Riverside Geyser** - Type: *Cone;* Interval: *5.5-7 hrs;* Height: *75 ft;* Duration: *20 min.* One of the most beautiful and predictable geysers in Yellowstone. Water runs over the edge of the cone for an hour or two before each eruption. During the eruption a fountain of water arches over the **Firehole River**. Eruption is followed by a 10 min steam phase.

(1.4 mi) **Fan and Mortar Geyser** - Type: *Vent;* Interval: *3 days to months;* Height: *80-125 ft;* Duration: *1 hr.* These 2 geysers are close together and almost always erupt together. Many vents cause a spray resembling a fan. The main vent of **Fan Geyser** often shoots an angled jet of water across the trail.

(1.5 mi) **Morning Glory Pool** - This beautiful and popular pool was originally named for its remarkable likeness to its namesake flower. However, the water circulation and appearance has been effected by people throwing objects into the pool. As the temperature dropped, orange and yellow bacteria that were once only on the perimeter have spread toward the center of the pool. The clarity of the pool has also been affected.

(1.8 mi) **Artemisia Geyser** - Type: *Fountain;* Interval: *9-28+ hrs;* Height: *30 ft;* Duration: *15-25 min.* One of the most beautiful pools in the Upper Geyser Basin and one of the most interesting eruption cycles. Named for the sagebrush color of the sinter around the pool. *Eruption cycle: Pool drops about 2 ft after an eruption, then slowly rises and reaches overflow in about 5 hrs; Gently overflows many hours until it abruptly starts to erupt; Water rises and starts a ~5 min massive overflow before the pool starts to boil; A few minutes of strong underground thumping can be felt and heard before the eruption.*

(1.8 mi) **Atomizer Geyser** - Type: *Cone;* Interval: *12-17 hrs;* Height: *40-50 ft;* Duration: *8-10 min.* Named after one of the 3 ft cones that emits a fine spray. *Eruption cycle: Pool overflows every few minutes for 2-4 hrs; 6-8 minor eruptions at 1 hr intervals at 30 ft and last 1 min; Major eruption start 15-75 min later; 4 hrs for pool to refill.*

(1.9 mi) **Gem Pool** - Small colorful hot pool.

(2.1 mi) **Mirror Pool** - Large steaming sapphire blue hot pool.

(2.3 mi) **Grand Loop Road** at **Biscuit Basin**

TRAIL TO BLACK SAND BASIN - A 0.5 mi trail from the **Upper Geyser Basin** to **Black Sand Basin**. The trail is accessed from the paved trail, 1.1 mi north of the visitor center *(see previous section)*.

(0.1 mi) ***Daisy Geyser** - Type: *Cone;* Interval: *100-130 min;* Height: *60-75 ft;* Duration: *3-4 min.*

(0.1 mi) **Splendid Geyser** - Type: *Vent;* Interval: *rare;* Height: *200 ft;* Duration: *1-9+ min.* Tied closely to the activity of **Daisy Geyser**, but is mostly dormant.

(0.3 mi) **Punch Bowl Spring** - Hot spring contained by a 12 ft diameter, 3 ft high circular lip.

(0.5 mi) **Black Sand Pool** - Beautiful sapphire blue pool with a colorful runoff area

(0.9 mi) **Black Sand Basin** - *See next section*

Cool Rating: ******   **Crowds:** *****   **Time:** 1 hr to 2 days

Directions: Exit ramp to Old Faithful Village; NE then SE 1.1 mi.

MM: 18.0/15.5 **Dist:** 0.1 **GPS:** 44.46216/-110.85328 **Elev:** 7286 **Grid:** 3/13 **Land:** NPS

Black Sand Basin   **Type:** Geyser Basin

A small collection of geysers and hot springs. The geyser basin gets its name from the patches of fine black obsidian sand. A short trail north leads to **Opalescent Pool**, a calm rainbow-colored pool that killed a stand of lodgepole pines and left the dead, white remains. The main trail heads 0.1 mi southwest to **Cliff Geyser** on the bank of **Iron Spring Creek**, which erupts 30 to 40 ft high at irregular intervals. An indication of a pending eruption is when the crater nearly fills with water. A 0.1 mi trail to the left leads to **Emerald Pool** and a 0.1 mi trail to the right leads to **Rainbow Pool** and **Sunset Lake**, the biggest pool in the basin.

Cool Rating: ****   **Crowds:** *****   **Time:** 1 hr   **Directions:** SW 0.1 mi to parking area

MM: 18.0/15.5 *Dist:* 0.1 *GPS:* 44.46355/-110.85222 *GPS2:* 44.46995/-110.84397 *Elev:* 7294 *Grid:* 3/13 *Land:* NPS
Daisy Geyser & North Upper Geyser Basin   *Type:* Geyser Basin
An alternative route to **Daisy Geyser** and the northern section of the **Upper Geyser Basin**. From the **Black Sand Basin** parking area, head northeast 0.1 mi and cross the highway. Continue northeast to **Black Sand Pool**, a beautiful blue pool with a colorful runoff area (MI 0.4). The next stop is **Punch Bowl Spring**, a hot spring contained by a 12 ft diameter, 3 ft high circular lip (MI 0.6). In another 0.1 mi the trail forks right to **Daisy Geyser** (MI 0.8). Continue 0.1 mi where the trail ends at the **Upper Geyser Basin** paved path from the visitor center (MI 0.9), which heads north to **Grotto Geyser** (MI 0.95), **Riverside Geyser** (MI 1.1), and **Morning Glory Pool** (MI 1.3). *For attractions on this route see VISITOR CENTER TO BISCUIT BASIN and TRAIL TO BLACK SAND BASIN in the earlier section on the Upper Geyser Basin. Easy; 0.8-1.3 mi one-way; 40 ft elev gain.*
Cool Rating: ***** *Crowds:* **** *Time:* 1+ hrs *Directions:* SW 0.1 mi into Black Sand Basin parking area.
Notes: Stop at the Old Faithful or Madison visitor center or call 307-344-2751 to get the Daisy Geyser eruption prediction.

MM: 19.3/14.2 *GPS:* 44.48042/-110.85400 *Elev:* 7280 *Grid:* 3/13 *Land:* NPS
Bicycle Trailhead to Upper Geyser Basin   *Type:* Trailhead
A 1.4 mi gravel bicycle trail southeast to the **Daisy Geyser** loop in the **Upper Geyser Basin**. Upon reaching the **Daisy Geyser** trail, turn left to connect to the 1.5 mi paved path north 0.3 mi to **Morning Glory Pool** or south 1.2 mi to **Old Faithful**. *For attractions on this route see VISITOR CENTER TO BISCUIT BASIN in the earlier section on the Upper Geyser Basin.*
Directions: Parking pullout on SE side of hwy

MM: 19.6/13.9 *Dist:* 0.1 *GPS:* 44.48501/-110.85253 *Elev:* 7263 *Grid:* 3/13 *Land:* NPS
Biscuit Basin   *Type:* Geyser Basin
Named for biscuit-shaped deposits that once surrounded **Sapphire Pool** but were destroyed by an earthquake in 1959. This pool is bright blue and considered one of the most beautiful in **Yellowstone National Park**. The majority of the 0.6 mi loop contains small pools and geysers. **Jewel Geyser** erupts every 10 minutes in a series of busts to a height of 10 to 25 ft.
Cool Rating: **** *Crowds:* ***** *Time:* 1 hr *Directions:* NW 0.1 mi into parking area.

MM: 19.6/13.9 *Dist:* 0.1 *GPS:* 44.48501/-110.85253 *GPS2:* 44.48399/-110.87358 *Elev:* 7264 *Grid:* 3/13 *Land:* NPS
Mystic Falls   *Type:* Waterfall
A hike to 2 main viewpoints of the spectacular **Mystic Falls**, where the powerful water of the **Little Firehole River** cascades and drops 70 ft over several benches through a narrow canyon. Notice the thermal activity resulting in steam around the edges of the falls. The official overlook of the falls (at a small sign) is a short distance and minor climb after the initial viewpoint. Return by the same route or continue on the loop trail to the top of a ridge. Once on the top, at the east end is a spectacular overlook of **Biscuit Basin** and **Upper Geyser Basin**, including **Old Faithful** about 2.5 mi southeast.

From the parking area, cross the river and walk west across **Biscuit Basin** on the boardwalk 0.3 mi to a trail junction. Continue straight west 0.3 mi to another trail junction. This is the end of the loop, which climbs steeply 0.6 mi to the overlook. Keep left 0.6 mi to the falls. *Mystic Falls overlook: Easy; 1.2 mi one-way; 160 ft elev gain. Full Loop: Moderate; 3.3 mi; 530 ft elev gain.*
Cool Rating: ***** *Crowds:* *** *Time:* 1-2 hrs *Directions:* NW 0.1 mi into Biscuit Basin parking area.

MM: 19.6/13.9 *Dist:* 0.1 *GPS:* 44.48414/-110.85141 *Elev:* 7272 *Grid:* 3/13 *Land:* NPS
Trail from Biscuit Basin to Upper Geyser Basin   *Type:* Trailhead
A gravel trail to the north end of the **Upper Geyser Basin**. The trail passes pools and geysers, including: **Mirror Pool** (MI 0.2), **Gem Pool** (MI 0.45), **Atomizer Geyser** and **Artemisia Geyser** (MI 0.5), and **Morning Glory Pool** (MI 0.8). The trail continues 1.5 mi to the **Old Faithful Visitor Center**. *For attractions on this route see VISITOR CENTER TO BISCUIT BASIN in the earlier section on the Upper Geyser Basin. Easy; 0.5-0.8 mi one-way; Level.*
Cool Rating: **** *Crowds:* ** *Time:* 1 hr
Directions: NW 0.1 mi into Biscuit Basin parking area. Cross the hwy to the trail, which heads southeast and then south.

MM: 21.9/11.5 *Dist:* 0.1 *GPS:* 44.51543/-110.83259 *GPS2:* 44.52451/-110.87024 *Elev:* 7245 *Grid:* 3/12 *Land:* NPS
Trail to Fairy Falls and Imperial Geyser   *Type:* Hiking Trail
A hike to **Fairy Falls**, a narrow 197 ft waterfall that splashes off the rock face into a small pool. **Spray Geyser** and **Imperial Geyser** (44.53174/-110.87639) are 0.4 and 0.6 mi farther along the trail and are worth the walk. From the trailhead, walk north on the paved path 1.0 mi to the signed junction for the **Fairy Falls Trail**. The trail passes within 130 yds above **Grand Prismatic Spring** to the northeast. Turn west/left and continue on the dirt path 1.5 mi. *Easy; 2.5 mi one-way; 100 ft elev gain.*
Cool Rating: **** *Crowds:* * *Time:* 2-3 hrs *Directions:* NW 0.1 mi to parking area.

MM: 23.4/10.1 *GPS:* 44.52839/-110.83631 *Elev:* 7212 *Grid:* 3/12 *Land:* NPS
Midway Geyser Basin   *Type:* Geyser Basin
A 0.5 mi loop trail leads to 2 of the largest hot springs in the world. **Excelsior Geyser** was once the largest geyser in the world with a massive 300 ft eruption. It went dormant after 1890, but briefly came back to life for 2 days in 1985 with smaller eruptions less than 100 ft. It is now considered a hot spring situated in a massive 240 x 340 ft crater that discharges more than 4000 gallons of water per minute. This water overflows and runs through a colorful yellow, orange, and brown channel into the **Firehole River**. **Grand Prismatic Spring** is the largest hot spring in the U.S. and third largest in the world, measuring 250 x 300 ft. Prismatic means brilliantly colored, and with blue, blue-green, yellow, and orange colors, it certainly is that.
Cool Rating: ***** *Crowds:* ***** *Time:* 45 min *Directions:* NW into parking area.

MM: 23.8/9.7 *GPS:* 44.53285/-110.82754 *Elev:* 7267 *Grid:* 3/12 *Land:* NPS
Whiskey Flats Picnic Area   *Type:* Picnic Area
A shady forest with individual sites along a 0.1 mi road and end loop. *13 tables. 1 grill. Vault toilet. Handicapped accessible.*
Notes: No RVs or trailers. *Road Desc:* Gravel *Directions:* SE side of hwy

MM: 24.3/9.1 *GPS:* 44.53534/-110.81776 *Elev:* 7263 *Grid:* 3/12 *Land:* NPS
Firehole Lake Drive   *Type:* Geyser Basin
Part of **Lower Geyser Basin**, this 3.3 mi one-way loop road runs from south to north and includes **Great Fountain Geyser**, **White Dome Geyser**, and **Pink Cone Geyser**.
Cool Rating: ***** *Crowds:* ***** *Directions:* E on one-way Firehole Lake Drive.

MM: 24.3/9.1 **Dist:** 0.8 **GPS:** 44.53511/-110.80201 **Elev:** 7331 **Grid:** 4/12 **Land:** NPS
Firehole Spring   **Type:** Hot Springs
A perpetual spouter in a pretty blue pool with a large colorful runoff area.
Cool Rating: *** **Crowds:** ** **Directions:** E on Firehole Lake Dr 0.8 mi

MM: 24.3/9.1 **Dist:** 1.0 **GPS:** 44.53656/-110.80010 **Elev:** 7322 **Grid:** 4/12 **Land:** NPS
Great Fountain Geyser   **Type:** Geyser
Type: *Fountain;* Interval: *9-15 hrs;* Height: *75-200+ ft;* Duration: *1+ hr.* One of the largest geysers in the park and the only predictable geyser in the **Lower Geyser Basin**. The short term predictions are usually accurate within 1-2 hrs and are posted at the **Old Faithful Visitor Center**, **Madison Information Station**, at the geyser itself, or call 307-344-2751. The 16 ft diameter crater is situated amid elaborately edged reflecting pools on sinter terraces, which makes the geyser worth visiting even when not active. The reflecting pools make a beautiful sunset picture.

About 70-100 min prior to an eruption, the crater begins overflowing into the pools. The eruption is a series of distinctly spaced bursts of about 10 min with a 5 min quiet period. The bursts shoot water in all directions at heights often under 100 ft with the first 2 or 3 periods being the largest.
Cool Rating: ***** **Crowds:** ***** **Directions:** E on Firehole Lake Dr 1.0 mi

MM: 24.3/9.1 **Dist:** 1.2 **GPS:** 44.53895/-110.80197 **Elev:** 7303 **Grid:** 4/12 **Land:** NPS
White Dome Geyser   **Type:** Geyser
Type: *Cone;* Interval: *Unpredictable 10 min - 35 min up to 3 hrs;* Height: *30 ft;* Duration: *2 min.* A massive 12 ft high white/gray/pink cone that erupts a narrow flow of water through a small opening. The eruption can be seen from **Great Fountain Geyser**.
Cool Rating: **** **Crowds:** *** **Directions:** E on Firehole Lake Dr 1.2 mi; Right side of road.

MM: 24.3/9.1 **Dist:** 1.6 **GPS:** 44.54287/-110.79630 **Elev:** 7325 **Grid:** 4/11 **Land:** NPS
Pink Cone Geyser   **Type:** Geyser
Type: *Cone;* Interval: *9-22 hrs;* Height: *30 ft;* Duration: *1.5-2 hrs.* Named after the color of its small cone.
Cool Rating: **** **Crowds:** *** **Directions:** E on Firehole Lake Dr 1.6 mi; Left side of road.

MM: 24.3/9.1 **Dist:** 2.2 **GPS:** 44.54423/-110.78544 **Elev:** 7377 **Grid:** 4/11 **Land:** NPS
Firehole Lake Area   **Type:** Thermal Area
Boardwalks to thermal areas on both sides of the road. Highlights on the west side include **Steady Geyser**, a perpetual spouter that reaches a height of 15 ft. It is located on the edge of **Black Warrior Lake**, which in turn flows over the **Hot Cascades** into **Hot Lake**, a large collecting pool for runoff. On the east side around **Firehole Lake** are several spouting springs and small geysers, including **Artesia Geyser**, a perpetual spouter that reaches a height of 5 ft.
Cool Rating: **** **Crowds:** **** **Time:** 30 min **Directions:** E on Firehole Lake Dr 2.2 mi

MM: 25.3/8.1 **GPS:** 44.54775/-110.80793 **Elev:** 7286 **Grid:** 4/11 **Land:** NPS
Lower Geyser Basin   **Type:** Geyser Basin
The largest geyser basin in **Yellowstone National Park**, covering approximately 11 sq mi. In comparison, the **Upper Geyser Basin** covers about 1 sq mi. Because of its large size the thermal features tend to be clumped in widely spaced groups. The easiest and most interesting grouping to get to is the **Fountain Paint Pot** area, where very good examples of most types of thermal features can be seen along a 0.5 mi loop path. These features include hot pools, steaming fumaroles, erupting geysers, and mudpots. The area is highly active and at least one geyser is usually erupting at all times.

Highlighted features: **Fountain Paint Pot** - The largest easily accessible paint pot in Yellowstone, 0.1 mi from the parking area. **Jet Geyser** - Erupts every 7 to 30 minutes at 20 ft from at least 5 vents in an elongated cone. **Clepsydra Geyser** - Erupts almost constantly at 45 ft. **Morning Geyser** - One of the largest geysers in the world, but is seldom active and last erupted in 1994. When active it can erupt as often as every 4 hrs at 200 ft high and 100 ft wide and last up to 1/2 hr.
Cool Rating: ***** **Crowds:** ***** **Time:** 1 hr **Directions:** NW into large parking area

MM: 27.4/6.0 **GPS:** 44.57407/-110.82284 **Elev:** 7182 **Grid:** 3/11 **Land:** NPS
Nez Perce Indian Signs   **Type:** Historical Marker
A 2-sided historical sign about the **Nez Perce Indian** battles.
Cool Rating: * **Crowds:** * **Time:** 10 min **Directions:** SW side of hwy

MM: 27.8/5.6 **Dist:** 0.2 **GPS:** 44.57840/-110.83102 **Elev:** 7165 **Grid:** 3/11 **Land:** NPS
Nez Perce Picnic Area   **Type:** Picnic Area
A nice shady picnic area between **Nez Perce Creek** and the **Firehole River**. *12 tables. 3 grills. Vault toilet. Handicapped accessible.*
Directions: SW on Fountain Flat Dr 0.1 mi; NW/R 0.1 mi.

MM: 27.8/5.6 **Dist:** 0.8 **GPS:** 44.56711/-110.83522 **Elev:** 7193 **Grid:** 3/11 **Land:** NPS
Fountain Freight Rd Trailhead   **Type:** Trailhead
A 4.0 mi hiking and bicycling trail south to the **Fairy Falls** parking area, which passes within 130 yds above **Grand Prismatic Spring** at 3.3 mi. Thermal areas are located within 1/2 mi of the parking area. On the west side of the main trail, just before it crosses the **Firehole River** (at 0.3 mi), is **Ojo Caliente Spring**, a beautiful blue hot spring. On the east side are unmaintained trails that lead a few tenths of a mile to some interesting thermal activity along both sides of the **Firehole River** (enter at your own risk).

Just past the bridge, on the west side, is a trail past **Sentinel Meadows** to **Queens Laundry**. The trail through **Sentinel Meadows** is dotted with tall hot spring mounds and hot pools. **Queens Laundry** is a large hot spring pool with a drainage channel cool enough for bathing. It was discovered in 1880 by Superintendent Norris, who later proposed a 2 room log bathhouse at the site. The bathhouse was started in 1881, but never finished. The ruins are still standing today. The trail can be wet and swampy in spots. *Easy; 3.8 mi round-trip; 50 ft elev gain.*
Cool Rating: *** **Crowds:** * **Directions:** SW on Fountain Flat Dr 0.8 mi.

MM: 29.0/4.5 **GPS:** 44.59333/-110.83122 **Elev:** 7152 **Grid:** 3/10 **Land:** NPS
Firehole River Picnic Area   **Type:** Picnic Area
A shady picnic area on a half-loop road. *12 tables. Vault toilet.*
Directions: W side of hwy

MM: 31.1/2.4 **GPS:** 44.61652/-110.85464 **GPS2:** 44.61636/-110.85526 **Elev:** 7116 **Grid:** 3/10 **Land:** NPS
Firehole Cascade   **Type:** Waterfall
A 40 ft cascade on the **Firehole River**. The cascade is located about 40 yds west of the highway. It can also be seen at the end of the **Firehole Canyon Drive**.
Cool Rating: *** **Crowds:** ** **Time:** 10 min **Directions:** Pullout on W side of hwy

MM: 32.9/0.6 **GPS:** 44.63888/-110.85862 **Elev:** 6853 **Grid:** 3/9 **Land:** NPS
Firehole Canyon Drive   **Type:** Side Loop Road
A 2.2 mi one-way half-loop road south through **Firehole Canyon**, which was formed by lava flows. Highlights include: **Firehole Falls** (MI 1.0), a warm water swimming area (MI 1.9), and **Firehole Cascade** (MI 2.2).
Cool Rating: **** **Crowds:** **** **Notes:** Not recommended for large RVs and trailers. **Road Desc:** Paved, narrow & winding
Directions: SW on one-way Firehole Canyon Rd.

MM: 32.9/0.6 **Dist:** 1.0 **GPS:** 44.62949/-110.86275 **GPS2:** 44.62876/-110.86344 **Elev:** 6965 **Grid:** 3/9 **Land:** NPS
Firehole Falls   **Type:** Waterfall
A pretty 40 ft waterfall on the **Firehole River**. The parking pullout also has an interpretive display about the rhyolite lava flows that formed the canyon.
Cool Rating: **** **Crowds:** *** **Time:** 10 min **Directions:** SW on Firehole Canyon Rd 1.0 mi

MM: 32.9/0.6 **Dist:** 1.9 **GPS:** 44.61838/-110.86035 **Elev:** 7080 **Grid:** 3/10 **Land:** NPS
Firehole River Swimming Area   **Type:** Swimming Area
A warm water area of the **Firehole River** (75° F) where swimming is allowed. A stairway leads down to the river and a vault toilet in the parking area provides a place to change. Keep your head above water to avoid harmful microorganisms.
Cool Rating: *** **Crowds:** ***** **Directions:** SW on Firehole Canyon Rd 1.9 mi
Notes: No climbing on, jumping, or diving off cliffs or trees. No glass containers or inflatable objects. $100 fine for violations.

MM: 32.9/0.6 **Dist:** 2.2 **GPS:** 44.61718/-110.85550 **GPS2:** 44.61636/-110.85526 **Elev:** 7107 **Grid:** 3/10 **Land:** NPS
Firehole Cascade   **Type:** Waterfall
A 40 ft cascade on the **Firehole River**. A short paved trail to the cascade is located just before the end of **Firehole Drive**.
Cool Rating: *** **Crowds:** ** **Time:** 10 min
Directions: SW on Firehole Canyon Rd 2.2 mi; Pullout on right side just before the end of the road; A paved path leads about 70 yds south.

MM: 33.3/0.2 **GPS:** 44.64278/-110.86075 **Elev:** 6815 **Grid:** 3/9 **Land:** NPS
Madison Information Station and Picnic Area   **Type:** Visitor Center
A staffed information station and picnic area located a short distance north of the **Madison River**. The information station provides books, maps, and information, including current eruption predictions for the **Upper Geyser Basin** and **Great Fountain Geyser**. An amphitheater is used for ranger programs and can be walked to from the southeast end of the **Madison Campground**. The picnic area has scattered tables in a sparse forest. *14 tables. Flush toilet.*
Hours: 9am - 6pm **Phone:** 307-344-2821
Directions: W into parking area. Information station is at SW end of parking area. Restrooms are on the right when entering.

MM: 33.5/0.0 **Dist:** 0.1 **GPS:** 44.64620/-110.86106 **Elev:** 6830 **Grid:** 3/9 **Land:** NPS
Madison Campground   **Type:** Campground
One of 4 large modern campgrounds that take reservations. Located just north of the **Madison River** on the west central section of the **Grand Loop Road**. *10 loops, 2 for tents only near the river. Conifer forest. Paved roads and parking areas. Restrooms with flush toilets, running water, and electricity. Generators permitted. Amphitheater for ranger programs. Firewood and ice for sale.*
Crowds: ***** **[FEE AREA]** **Directions:** W 0.1 mi at Madison Junction; S/L into campground.
Campsites: 277 **Shade:** ***** **Privacy:** * **RV Size:** 30' **Other:** 1-866-439-7375,Water,RVDump BEARS

MM: 33.5/0.0 **GPS:** 44.64540/-110.85846 **Elev:** 6836 **Grid:** 3/9
Yellowstone - Madison to Norris *(see chapter)*   **Type:** Hwy Transition w/Chapter
13.4 mi west-central section of the **Grand Loop Road** from **Madison** northeast to **Norris**. Highlights include: **Gibbon Falls, Beryl Spring, Monument Geyser Basin, Artist Paint Pots, Chocolate Pots, Norris Geyser Basin**.
Nearest Town: West Yellowstone, MT 14.0 W **Directions:** NE to Norris from MM 0

MM: 33.5/0.0 **GPS:** 44.64540/-110.85846 **Elev:** 6836 **Grid:** 3/9
Yellowstone - West Entrance to Madison *(see chapter)*   **Type:** Hwy Junction w/Chapter
13.6 mi highway from **Madison** west out of **Yellowstone National Park** to **US-20** and **West Yellowstone**, **Montana**. The road follows the **Madison River** with minor points of interest and scenic views along the way.
Nearest Town: West Yellowstone, MT 14.0 W **Directions:** W to West Yellowstone, MT from MM 13.6

MM: 33.5/0.0 **GPS:** 44.64540/-110.85846 **Elev:** 6836 **Grid:** 3/9 **Land:** NPS
Yellowstone - Madison to West Thumb   **Type:** Highway End
33.5 mi southwest section of the **Grand Loop Road** from **Madison** southeast to **West Thumb**. The majority of the geyser activity is along this section. Highlights include: **Firehole Falls, Lower Geyser Basin, Firehole Lake Drive Geysers, Midway Geyser Basin, Fairy Falls, Biscuit Basin, Mystic Falls, Black Sand Basin, Upper Geyser Basin, Old Faithful, Kepler Cascades, Lone Star Geyser**.
Nearest Town: West Yellowstone, MT 14.0 W **Directions:** SE to West Thumb from MM 33.5

GLOSSARY

alkali - Any of various soluble mineral salts found in natural water and arid soils.

arroyo - A deep gully cut by an intermittent stream.

Astorians - A group of explorers hired by America's richest man, John Jacob Astor, to establish a route to the Pacific Northwest to set up a fur trading enterprise at the mouth of the Columbia River.

ATV – This is an "All Terrain Vehicle" which is generally a 4-wheel off road only vehicle.

basalt - A hard, dense, dark volcanic rock.

bastion - A projecting part of a fortification.

BLM - Bureau of Land Management. Public land for general use, including free camping. Some land is developed with parking areas, camping areas, and vault toilets. The land is generally prairie, badlands, or desert.

broodstock - A group of sexually mature individuals of a cultured species that is kept separate for breeding purposes.

calcite - Calcium carbonate. A major constituent of limestone, marble, and chalk.

caldera - A large basin-like depression (crater) resulting from the explosion or collapse of the center of a volcano.

caldron - A large vessel, such as a kettle or vat, used for boiling.

chasm - A deep, steep-sided opening in the earth's surface.

Chugwater Formation - Bedrock consisting primarily of red sandstone. Named for Chugwater, Wyoming.

columnar - Having the shape of a column.

confluence - A flowing together of two or more rivers or streams.

conifer - Evergreen cone-bearing trees or shrubs, including pine, fir, spruce, and juniper.

deciduous - Trees and shrubs that shed their leaves annually.

emigrant - The American people who traveled west along the Oregon/Mormon/California Trails in the mid-19th century on their way to Oregon, Utah, and California.

escarpment - A steep slope or long cliff that results from erosion or faulting and separates two relatively level areas of differing elevations.

forage - Food for horses or cattle.

fumarole - A hole in the Earth's surface from which steam and volcanic gases escape.

garrison - The troops stationed at a military post.

herbivore - A plant eating animal.

hew - To make, shape, smooth, etc., with cutting blows.

moor - To secure a boat by a cable, anchor, or line.

moraine - Deposits of boulders, gravel, sand, and clay left by a glacier.

OHV - An "Off Highway Vehicle" including ATVs and motorcycles.

paleontology - The study of the prehistoric fossils.

philanthropist - A person who desires to increase the well-being of humankind, as by charitable aid or donations.

pronghorn - A fleet, antelope-like ruminant (even-toed, hoofed mammal) of the plains of western North America. Named for their black forked horns. The fastest mammal in North America that can reach a top speed of 60 mph. Often mistakenly referred to as antelope.

rhyolite - Volcanic rock similar to granite in composition.

scree - *See talus*

sinter - A chemical sediment or crust, as of porous silica, deposited by a mineral spring.

talus - The loose rock that lies on a steep mountainside or at the base of a cliff.

terminal moraine - A moraine at the end of the advance of a glacier.

travertine - Limestone deposits from a hot spring.

tuff - Rock composed of compacted volcanic ash in varying in sizes.

vault toilet - a cement underground pit with a toilet and building on top. The vault is seeded with chemicals to prevent odor and disease and regularly the entire thing is pumped out and retreated.

WHMA - Wildlife Habitat Management Area. Mostly undeveloped public land with parking and free camping areas. Some areas provide vault toilets.

ATTRACTIONS AT A GLANCE

ATTRACTIONS OF NOTE

Alcova/Pathfinder Reservoir Loop
9.9	Fremont Canyon Bridge and Overlook
13.6	Pathfinder Dam Overlook
13.8	Pathfinder Interpretive Trail

Atlantic City Rd/CR-237 & South Pass City Rd/CR-479
0.6	Miner's Delight Ghost Town
2.6	Atlantic City
6.6	Carissa Mine
6.6	South Pass City State Historic Site

Brooklyn Lake Rd/FR-317
1.7	Sheep Lake Trail
1.9	Lost Lake Trail

Brooks Lake Rd/FR-515
4.9	Brooks Lake
4.9	Brooks Lake Trailhead

Buffalo Valley Rd/FR-30050
8.7	Box Creek Trailhead: Turpin Meadow Recreation Area

Casper Mountain Rd/Wy-251
4.9	Garden Creek Falls & Bridle Trail
10.2	Crimson Dawn Park and Museum
18.4	Muddy Mountain Environmental Education Area

Chilton Rd
13.6	White Mountain Petroglyphs
15.9	Boar's Tusk
20.3	Killpecker Sand Dunes

Cook Lake Recreation Area and Scenic Drive
7.0	Warren Peak Lookout
18.0	Cook Lake Recreation Area

Fossil Butte National Monument
0.9	Historic Quarry Trail
3.5	Fossil Butte National Monument Visitor Center
5.9	Fossil Lake Trail

FR-27/Ten Sleep Rd
7.1	Tensleep Falls
7.1	West Tensleep Trailhead

FR-700/Vedauwoo Glen Rd
1.1	Vedauwoo Recreation Area
3.6	Reynolds Hill Trail

Fremont Lake Rd/Skyline Drive
11.1	Fremont Lake Scenic Overlook
13.7	Wind River Mountains Scenic Overlook
14.4	Elkhart Park Trailheads

Gros Ventre Rd/FR-30400
5.0	Blacktail Butte Trailhead: Grand Teton National Park
12.7	Gros Ventre Slide Geological Area
18.2	Red Hills Trail

Guernsey State Park - Lakeshore Drive/Wy-317
0.9	Guernsey State Park
1.7	Guernsey Dam

Guernsey State Park - Skyline Drive
2.1	Brimmer Point
2.1	The Castle

I-25
140.1	Pioneer Museum
151.2	Ayres Park and Natural Bridge
188.6	Fort Caspar Museum and Historic Site
189.5	National Historic Trails Interpretive Center
249.7	Hole-in-the-Wall
254.3	Outlaw Cave

I-80
6.3	Bear River State Park
23.9	Piedmont Charcoal Kilns
34.7	Fort Bridger State Historic Site
53.3	Church Butte
103.8	Western Wyoming Natural History Museum
104.8	Reliance Tipple
211.8/215.6	Wyoming Frontier Prison
228.3	Fort Fred Steele
311.8	Wyoming Territorial Prison State Historic Site
323.1	Curt Gowdy State Park
323.1	Abraham Lincoln Monument
323.1	Pole Mountain Trails
329.3	Ames Monument

I-90
66.0	Dry Creek Petrified Tree Environmental Education Area
126.4	Eagle Butte Coal Mine Tour
199.3/205.9	Vore Buffalo Jump

Jenny Lake Loop Rd: Grand Teton National Park
0.8	Cathedral Group Turnout
1.5	Leigh Lake Trail
1.5	String Lake Trail
3.0	Jenny Lake Overlook

Pilot Butte Wild Horse Tour
13.0	Pilot Butte

Sugarloaf Recreation Area/FR-346
1.0	Lewis Lake
1.0	Medicine Bow Peak Trail from Lewis Lake
1.0	Gap Lakes Trail

Teton Park Rd: Grand Teton National Park
1.2	Chapel of the Transfiguration & Menor's Ferry Historic District
3.4	Taggart Lake Trailhead
7.9	Jenny Lake and Trails
16.7	Signal Mountain Rd

Trail Lake Rd/CR-411
2.2	Whiskey Basin WHMA
2.3	Bighorn Sheep Observation Parking Area
6.4	Trail Lake Rd Petroglyphs
9.1	Torrey Creek Trailhead

US-14
0.7/7.4	Devil's Kitchen Geological Site (eastbound)
10.5	Red Gulch Dinosaur Tracksite
10.5	Medicine Lodge State Archaeological Site
26.5	Shell Falls
83.6	Tongue River Recreation Area

US-14/16/20
15.3	Firefighters Memorial Trail
25.1	Holy City & Goose Rock
44.7	Buffalo Bill Dam and Visitor Center
49.6	Tecumseh's Trading Post
51.5	Buffalo Bill Historical Center

US-14A
13.1	Heart Mountain Relocation Center
68.6	Five Springs Falls
78.1	Medicine Wheel National Historic Landmark
80.5	Porcupine Falls
80.5	Bucking Mule Falls

US-16
17.0	The Honeycombs
24.4	Castle Gardens (north)
48.6	High Park Lookout
64.5	Crazy Woman Canyon

US-189
79.2	Names Hill

US-189/191
152.1	Granite Falls
152.1	Granite Hot Springs

US-191
4.5	Reliance Tipple
10.3	*See Chilton Rd*

US-20/26
45.2	Hell's Half Acre
50.7	Hole-in-the-Wall
78.5	Castle Gardens

US-20/Wy-789 & US-16/20/Wy-789 & US-14/16/20/Wy-789
116.1	Wind River Canyon (south end)
127.6	Wind River Canyon (north end)
133.0	Hot Springs State Park
133.6	Hot Springs State Park Scenic Overlook
156.6	Gooseberry Badlands Scenic Area
185.0	Medicine Lodge State Archaeological Site
204.1	Devil's Kitchen Geological Site
206.6	Museum of Flight and Aerial Firefighting

US-212 (Beartooth Scenic Byway)
15.2	Crazy Creek Falls
19.0	Lake Creek Falls and Historic Bridge
25.4	Clay Butte Fire Lookout
26.4	Beartooth Falls
30.0	Island Lake Trailhead
37.3	Beartooth Pass Summit

US-26 (I-25 to Nebraska)
14.4	Guernsey State Park - South Entrance
15.3	Oregon Trail Ruts
15.3	Register Cliff

US-26/287 & US-26
21.8	Breccia Cliffs & Lost Lake
25.9	Wind River Lake and Picnic Area
32.3	Brooks Lake Creek Falls
54.4	Dubois Recreation Area Scenic Overlook

US-26/89/191
154.9 Jackson Hole and Greater Yellowstone Visitor Center
167.7 Blacktail Butte Trailhead: Grand Teton National Park
168.0 Shadow Mountain
168.1 Blacktail Ponds Overlook
170.2 Glacier View Turnout
170.8 Schwabacher Landing
172.2 Teton View Turnout
175.1 Snake River Overlook
US-287 (Lander to US-26)
14.8/15.7 Sacajawea's Grave (northbound)
US-287/Wy-789
8.2 Split Rock Historic Site
11.5 Split Rock Historical Marker
US-89
85.5 Intermittent Spring
US-89/191/287
187.4 Oxbow Bend
189.1 Willow Flats Overlook
190.5 Grand View Point Trail
Wy-110/Devils Tower Rd (Devils Tower National Monument)
2.8 Joyner Ridge Trail
3.4 Devils Tower
3.4 Red Beds Trail
Wy-120
20.2 Legend Rock Petroglyphs
32.3 Gooseberry Badlands Scenic Area
Wy-130 (Laramie to Wy-230)
29.9 Corner Mountain Trails
30.9 Little Laramie Trails
33.7 Libby Creek Falls
34.0 Greenrock Trailhead
38.7 Sugarloaf Recreation Area
39.2 Libby Observation Point
39.6 Medicine Bow Peak Overlook & Miner's Cabin Trail
40.9 Mirror Lake and Lake Marie Parking and Picnic Area
40.9 Lakes Trail w/option to Medicine Bow Peak
41.5 Lake Marie West Trailhead to Medicine Bow Peak
41.5 Lake Marie Falls
41.7 Tipple Trail
44.1 Meadow Falls Trailhead
55.8 Kennaday Peak Lookout
Wy-131/FR-300/Louis Lake Rd
7.3 Rise of the Sinks: Sinks Canyon State Park
7.6 Sinks Canyon State Park and Visitor Center
10.5 Popo Agie Falls
22.1 Blue Ridge Fire Lookout
23.9 Christina Lake Trailhead
Wy-135/136
24.3 Badlands Scenic Overlook
Wy-160/Grayrocks Rd/Power Plant Rd
2.5 Fort Laramie National Historic Site
Wy-193/US-87
103.9 Story Fish Hatchery
Wy-210/Happy Jack Rd
24.0 Curt Gowdy State Park
Wy-22
6.6 Trail Creek Trailhead
9.5 Phillips Ridge Trailhead
11.0 Teton Pass Summit and Trailhead
13.9 Coal Creek Trailhead
17.7 Cave Falls & Bechler Falls & Upper and Lower Mesa Falls
Wy-220
56.5 Mormon Handcart Historic Site: Martin's Cove & Devil's Gate
57.2 Devil's Gate Historic Site
63.0 Independence Rock State Historic Site
113.4 Fort Caspar Museum and Historic Site
Wy-230 (Riverside to Colorado)
100.9 Indian Bathtubs
Wy-24
4.3 Devils Tower Overlook and Historical Marker
6.0 Devils Tower National Monument
40.8 Aladdin Tipple Historical Park
Wy-28 (Farson to US-287)
28.9 South Pass Overlook
58.5 Red Canyon Overlook
Wy-296 (Chief Joseph Scenic Highway)
23.0 Sunlight Gorge
32.7 Dead Indian Pass Summit
Wy-352/FR-10091
43.9 Green River Lakes Trailhead

Wy-37 (Bighorn Canyon National Recreation Area)
9.7 Sykes Mountain Trail
9.8 Mouth of the Canyon Trail
13.4 State Line Trail
14.0 Ranger Delight Trail
15.3 Devil Canyon Overlook
16.2 Sullivan's Knob Trail
Wy-390/Moose-Wilson Rd
11.0 Laurance S. Rockefeller Preserve
11.7 Death Canyon Trailhead
Wy-70
32.8 Aspen Alley
50.7 Green Mountain Falls
56.8 Grand Encampment Museum
57.7 Indian Bathtubs
Wy-789 & US-26/Wy-789
103.8 Castle Gardens
105.7/127.0 Wyoming Heritage Trail
Yellowstone - Canyon Village to Fishing Bridge
1.6 Crystal Falls
1.6 Brink of the Upper Falls
9.5 Sulphur Caldron
9.6 Mud Volcano Area
12.5 LeHardy Rapids
Yellowstone - East Entrance to Fishing Bridge
7.7 Avalanche Peak Trailhead
16.3 Lake Butte Overlook
25.4 Fishing Bridge
Yellowstone - Fishing Bridge to West Thumb
1.1 Elephant Back Mountain Trailhead
3.4 Natural Bridge
20.4 West Thumb Geyser Basin
Yellowstone - Madison to Norris
4.8 Gibbon Falls
8.2 Beryl Spring
8.6 Monument Geyser Basin Trailhead
9.6 Artist Paint Pots
10.5 Chocolate Pots
13.4 Norris Geyser Basin and Museum
Yellowstone - Mammoth Hot Springs to Tower-Roosevelt
4.0 Undine Falls
4.4 Lava Creek Trail to Undine Falls
4.9 Wraith Falls
14.5 Hellroaring Creek Trailhead
16.7 Petrified Tree
Yellowstone - Norris to Canyon Village
1.6 Virginia Cascade
3.8 Little Gibbon Falls
Yellowstone - Norris to Mammoth Hot Springs
0.0 Norris Geyser Basin and Museum
16.2 Bunsen Peak
16.2 Osprey Falls
16.2 The Hoodoos
16.3 Rustic Falls
18.9 Yellowstone - Upper Terrace Drive
20.6 Mammoth Hot Springs Terraces
Yellowstone - North Entrance to Mammoth Hot Springs
0.0 Roosevelt Arch
3.0 Boiling River Trail and Swimming Hole
Yellowstone - North Rim Drive
0.1 Brink of the Lower Falls
0.7 Lookout Point & Red Rock Point
0.9 Grand View
1.3 Glacial Boulder Trailhead & Glacial Boulder
1.3 Inspiration Point
1.3 North Rim Trail
Yellowstone - Northeast Entrance to Tower-Roosevelt
26.9 Yellowstone River Trail
Yellowstone - South Entrance to West Thumb
1.2 Moose Falls
9.9 Lewis Falls
Yellowstone - South Rim Drive
0.1 North Rim Trail
0.6 Uncle Tom's Overlook of the Upper Falls
0.6 South Rim Trail
0.6 Uncle Tom's Trail to the Lower Falls
1.6 Artist Point

Attractions at a Glance

Yellowstone - Tower-Roosevelt to Canyon Village
0.0   Lost Creek Falls & Lost Lake
1.6   Calcite Springs Overlook
2.2   Devil's Den
2.4   Tower Fall
8.5   Mount Washburn Trail from Chittenden Rd
13.5 Mount Washburn Trail from Dunraven Pass

Yellowstone - Upper Terrace Drive
0.2   Main Terrace and Canary Spring
0.4   Narrow Gauge Terrace
0.8   New Highland Terrace
0.8   Orange Spring Mound
1.2   White Elephant Back Terrace
1.5   Angel Terrace

Yellowstone - West Thumb to Madison
15.0 Lone Star Geyser
15.1 Kepler Cascades
17.6 Upper Geyser Basin and Old Faithful
18.0 Black Sand Basin
18.0 Daisy Geyser & North Upper Geyser Basin
19.6 Biscuit Basin
19.6 Mystic Falls
19.6 Trail from Biscuit Basin to Upper Geyser Basin
21.9 Trail to Fairy Falls and Imperial Geyser
23.4 Midway Geyser Basin
24.3 Firehole Lake Drive
24.3 Great Fountain Geyser
24.3 White Dome Geyser
24.3 Firehole Lake Area
25.3 Lower Geyser Basin
32.9 Firehole Canyon Drive
32.9 Firehole Falls

CAMPGROUNDS

Alcova/Pathfinder Reservoir Loop
3.0   Black Beach Campground: Alcova Reservoir
5.0   Cottonwood Creek Campground: Alcova Reservoir
9.9   Fremont Canyon Bridge and Overlook
12.7 Dispersed Camping: Pathfinder Reservoir
13.8 Weiss Campground: Pathfinder Reservoir
13.8 Sage Campground: Pathfinder Reservoir
13.8 Diabase Campground: Pathfinder Reservoir
16.4 Bishops Point Campground: Pathfinder Reservoir

Atlantic City Rd/CR-237 & South Pass City Rd/CR-479
0.6   Big Atlantic Gulch Campground
0.9   Atlantic City Campground

Brooklyn Lake Rd/FR-317
0.1   Nash Fork Campground
1.9   Brooklyn Lake Campground

Brooks Lake Rd/FR-515
4.3   Pinnacles Campground
4.9   Brooks Lake Campground

Buffalo Valley Rd/FR-30050
8.7   Box Creek Campground: Turpin Meadow Recreation Area
9.7   Turpin Meadow Campground: Turpin Meadow Recreation Area

Casper Mountain Rd/Wy-251
9.9   Skunk Hollow Park Campground: Casper Mountain
9.9   Elkhorn Springs Park Campground: Casper Mountain
10.2 Tower Hill Park Campground: Casper Mountain
10.3 Beartrap Meadow Park: Casper Mountain
10.3 Deerhaven Park Campground: Casper Mountain
18.4 Lodgepole Campground: Muddy Mountain
18.4 Rim Campground: Muddy Mountain

Chilton Rd
20.3 Killpecker Sand Dunes Recreation Site

Cook Lake Recreation Area and Scenic Drive
2.5   Reuter Campground
18.0 Cook Lake Recreation Area

CR-406/Lakeshore Drive
2.3   Okie Beach Campground: Alcova Reservoir
4.4   Westside Campground: Alcova Reservoir
4.9   Fremont Campground: Alcova Reservoir

CR-422/Phalow Ln & CR-44/Harmony Ln
4.5   Meeboer Lake Public Access Area
5.1   Gelatt Lake Public Access Area
5.5   Twin Buttes Reservoir Public Access Area
6.9   Lake Hattie Public Access Area

FR-27/Ten Sleep Rd
0.2   Boulder Park Campground
3.0   Island Park Campground
6.1   Deer Park Campground
7.3   West Tensleep Lake Campground

FR-700/Vedauwoo Glen Rd
1.1   Vedauwoo Recreation Area

Fremont Lake Rd/Skyline Drive
3.2   Dispersed Camping: Fremont Lake
3.2   Fremont Lake Campground
6.9   Half Moon Lake Campground
14.5 Trails End Campground

Glendo Park Rd (Glendo State Park)
1.4   Waters Point Campground
1.4   Colter Bay Campground
1.4   Custer Cove Campground
1.4   Soldier Rock Campground
1.4   Reno Cove Campground
1.4   Red Hills Campground
2.0   Whiskey Gulch Campground
2.6   Sagebrush Campground
3.6   Shelter Point Campground
4.4   Two Moon Campground
13.4 Sandy Beach Campground

Greys River Rd/FR-10138
2.5   Bridge Campground
12.4 Lynx Creek Campground
14.2 Murphy Creek Campground
22.5 Moose Flat Campground
34.6 Forest Park Campground

Gros Ventre Rd/FR-30400
4.6   Gros Ventre Campground: Grand Teton National Park
14.1 Atherton Creek Campground
19.6 Red Hills Campground
19.9 Crystal Creek Campground

Guernsey State Park - Lakeshore Drive/Wy-317
2.7   Spotted Tail Campground (Upper)
2.8   Spotted Tail Campground (Lower)
3.1   Red Cloud Campground
3.5   Black Canyon Cove Campground
3.7   Black Canyon Point Campground
4.3   Fish Canyon Campground
4.3   Fish Canyon Cove Campground
5.2   Deadman's Cove Campground
6.9   Long Canyon Campground

Guernsey State Park - Skyline Drive
0.4   Skyline Drive Campground
2.0   Newell Bay Campground
2.1   Davis Bay Campground
2.8   Sandy Beach Campground
3.3   Cottonwood Cove Campground
3.4   Sandy Point Campground
3.6   Sandy Cove Campground

I-25
73.0 Rock Lake
73.0 Wheatland Reservoir #1 (heading north)
78.9 Wheatland Reservoir #1 (southbound)
78.9 Wheatland City Park/Lewis Park
80.9 Festo Lake
111.7 Elkhorn Campground: Glendo State Park
111.7 Glendo State Park Airport Entrance
140.1 Riverside Park
140.1 Fort Fetterman State Historic Site
160.9 Bixby Public Access Area (southbound)
165.9 Glenrock South Recreation Complex
254.3 Kaycee Town Park

I-80
267.2 Wick WHMA
279.9 Diamond Lake Public Access Area
323.1 *See Wy-210/Happy Jack Rd*

I-90
9.9   Connor Battlefield State Park and Historic Site
51.4 Lake DeSmet Recreation Area
185.7 Reuter Campground
189.0 Sundance Campground
205.9 Sand Creek Campground

Keyhole State Park via CR-205/CR-180
3.6   Coulter Bay Campground
3.6   Wind Creek Campground
5.6   Arch Rock Campground
5.6   Tatanka Campground
5.6   Pat's Point Campground
5.6   Pronghorn Campground
5.6   Beach Area Campground
6.2   Homestead Campground
7.0   Cottonwood Campground
7.0   Rocky Point Campground

Seminoe-Alcova Back Country Byway
8.0   Dugway Recreation Site
31.4 Sunshine Beach Campground: Seminoe State Park
32.4 South Red Hills Campground: Seminoe State Park
32.6 North Red Hills Campground: Seminoe State Park
42.5 Miracle Mile
43.1 Miracle Mile
67.9 Cottonwood Creek Campground: Alcova Reservoir
69.9 Black Beach Campground: Alcova Reservoir
Teton Park Rd: Grand Teton National Park
7.9   Jenny Lake Campground
17.8 Signal Mountain Campground
Trail Lake Rd/CR-411
6.1   Ring Lake Campground
6.4   Torrey Creek Campground
6.9   Trail Lake Campground
8.5   Trail Meadow Campground
9.1   Glacier Trail Campground
Union Pass Rd
39.2 Warm Springs Creek Campground
US-14
31.3 Cabin Creek Meadows Campground
31.3 Cabin Creek Campground
31.3 Shell Creek Campground
31.3 Ranger Creek Campground
42.6 Tie Flume Campground
42.6 Dead Swede Campground
42.8 Owen Creek Campground
47.7 North Tongue Campground (heading north)
57.1 North Tongue Campground (southbound)
60.9 Prune Creek Campground
62.4 Sibley Lake Campground
83.6 Tongue River Recreation Area & Amsden Wildlife Habitat
89.0 Connor Battlefield State Park and Historic Site
US-14/16/20
3.0   Three Mile Campground
6.8   Eagle Creek Campground
14.4 Newton Creek Campground
16.6 Rex Hale Campground
19.9 Clearwater Campground
22.2 Elk Fork Campground
22.3 Wapiti Campground
23.1 Big Game Campground
37.3 North Fork Campground: Buffalo Bill State Park
42.0 North Shore Bay Campground: Buffalo Bill State Park
US-14A
24.9 Homesteader Park and Rest Area
46.4 Lovell Camper Park
55.5 Yellowtail WHMA: Kane Ponds
59.2 Yellowtail WHMA: Mason-Lovell Ranch
60.1 Yellowtail WHMA - Crystal Creek Rd
68.6 Five Springs Falls Campground
68.7 Dispersed Camping
78.5 Porcupine Campground
78.8 Bald Mountain Campground
98.6 North Tongue Campground
US-16
24.4 Castle Gardens (north)
31.6 Wigwam Rearing Station Access Area
34.0 Leigh Creek Campground
34.0 Tensleep Creek Campground
46.4 Sitting Bull Campground
46.7 Lakeview Campground
62.4 Lost Cabin Campground
63.4 Doyle Campground
64.9 Crazy Woman Campground
75.6 South Fork Campground
76.0 Tie Hack Campground
76.4 Circle Park Campground
78.4 Middle Fork Campground
US-189
38.1 Kemmerer Tent Park
61.3 Slate Creek Campground
61.3 Tailrace Campground
66.5 Weeping Rock Campground
70.0 Fontenelle Creek Campground
US-189/191
114.1 Daniel Public Access Area
120.1 Warren Bridge Campground
120.3 Warren Bridge Public Fishing Area
150.7 Kozy Campground
152.1 Granite Creek Campground
155.5 Hoback Campground and Picnic Area

US-191
49.6 Big Sandy Recreation Area
87.8 Stokes Crossing Campground
87.8 Boulder Lake (dispersed)
87.8 Boulder Lake Campground
88.8 Boulder Lake North Campground
100.0 Soda Lake WHMA
100.0 Willow Lake Campground
US-20/26
25.4 Goldeneye Wildlife and Recreation Area
100.0 Shoshoni City Park
US-20/Wy-789 & US-16/20/Wy-789 & US-14/16/20/Wy-789
106.2 Tough Creek Campground: Boysen State Park
113.3 Brannon Campground: Boysen State Park
113.3 Tamarask Campground: Boysen State Park
115.4 Upper Wind River Campground: Boysen State Park
116.0 Lower Wind River Campground: Boysen State Park
236.4 Lovell Camper Park
US-212 (Beartooth Scenic Byway)
5.0   Soda Butte Campground: Montana
6.1   Colter Campground: Montana
7.5   Chief Joseph Campground: Montana
11.4 Fox Creek Campground
15.2 Crazy Creek Campground
17.8 Lake Creek Campground
26.9 Beartooth Lake Campground
30.0 Island Lake Campground
US-26 (I-25 to Nebraska)
15.3 Larson Park
27.9 Fort Laramie City Park
48.3 Pioneer Park
US-26/287 & US-26
8.2   Hatchet Campground
32.3 Falls Campground
38.2 Sheridan Creek Campground
115.5 Ocean Lake WHMA - Lindholm
115.5 Ocean Lake WHMA - South Cove
115.5 Ocean Lake WHMA - Long Point
US-26/89
118.3 Alpine Campground
124.8 Wolf Creek Campground
128.6 Station Creek Campground
130.1 East Table Creek Campground
US-26/89/191
154.5 Curtis Canyon Campground
168.0 Shadow Mountain
US-287 (Lander to US-26)
0.4   Lander City Park
US-287/Wy-789
16.9 Green Mountain Park Campground: Green Mountain
16.9 Cottonwood Campground: Green Mountain
42.1 Carmody Lake (westbound)
46.9 Carmody Lake (eastbound)
US-30
10.6 Cokeville City Park
54.6 Kemmerer Tent Park
US-30/287
271.9 East Allen Lake - East Shore
271.9 East Allen Lake - South Shore
US-85
67.4 Hawk Springs State Recreation Area
77.5 Springer WHMA (northbound)
92.9 Pioneer Park
247.3 Beaver Creek Campground
US-89
65.2 Allred Flat Campground
71.1 Smiths Fork Rd/FR-10072
77.2 Cottonwood Lake Campground
85.5 Swift Creek Campground
97.3 Upper Salt River Public Access Area
104.4 Tin Cup Campground
112.0 Lower Salt River Public Access Area
118.3 Alpine Campground
US-89/191/287
185.8 Pacific Creek Campground
188.6 Signal Mountain Campground
194.1 Colter Bay Village and Campground: Grand Teton National Park
202.0 Lizard Creek Campground: Grand Teton National Park
209.6 Grassy Lake Rd
Wy-110/Devils Tower Rd (Devils Tower National Monument)
1.5   Belle Fourche Campground

Wy-120

32.3	Gooseberry Badlands Scenic Area
118.1	Hogan Reservoir

Wy-130 (Laramie to Wy-230)

29.3	Aspen Campground
29.3	Pine Campground
29.3	Willow Campground
29.5	Spruce Campground
31.2	North Fork Campground
38.7	Sugarloaf Campground
53.1	Ryan Park Campground
55.8	South Brush Creek Campground
55.8	Lincoln Park Campground

Wy-130/Wy-230 (Walcott to Riverside)

13.9	Pick Bridge Public Access Area
13.9	Sanger Public Access Area
16.5	Foote Public Access Area
19.2	Saratoga Lake Campground
30.0	Treasure Island Public Access Area

Wy-131/FR-300/Louis Lake Rd

6.8	Sawmill Campground: Sinks Canyon State Park
8.3	Popo Agie Campground: Sinks Canyon State Park
9.3	Sinks Canyon Campground
10.1	Dispersed Camping: Sinks Canyon
16.8	Frye Lake
17.7	Worthen Meadows Campground
18.1	Dispersed Camping: Louis Lake Rd (southbound)
18.6	Dispersed Camping: Louis Lake Rd (northbound)
23.3	Fiddlers Lake Campground
26.1	Popo Agie Campground
28.7	Louis Lake Campground

Wy-134 & Wy-133

15.6	Ocean Lake WHMA - Mills Point
17.9	Ocean Lake WHMA - Dickinson Park
20.4	Ocean Lake WHMA - Stultz

Wy-135/136

27.7	Dispersed Camping
33.5	Carmody Lake

Wy-160/Grayrocks Rd/Power Plant Rd

15.4	Grayrocks Reservoir (west end)
29.4	Wheatland City Park/Lewis Park

Wy-210/Happy Jack Rd

24.0	Curt Gowdy State Park - North Entrance
35.7	Yellow Pine Campground
36.8	Tie City Campground

Wy-22

5.6	Mosquito Creek Rd
17.4	Trail Creek Campground

Wy-220

87.1	Gray Reef Reservoir Campground
87.1	Trapper's Route Number One Campground

Wy-230 (Laramie to Colorado)

10.0	See CR-422/Phalow Ln & CR-44/Harmony Ln
17.8	See CR-422/Phalow Ln & CR-44/Harmony Ln
36.2	Miller Lake Campground

Wy-230 (Riverside to Colorado)

123.0	Six Mile Gap Campground

Wy-24

32.2	Bearlodge Campground

Wy-296 (Chief Joseph Scenic Highway)

1.2	Lake Creek Campground
4.7	Hunter Peak Campground
23.4	Sunlight WHMA
25.0	Dead Indian Creek Trailhead
25.1	Dead Indian Campground

Wy-352/FR-10091

14.2	New Fork Lake Campground
14.2	Narrows Campground
27.6	Whiskey Grove Campground
34.0	Dispersed Camping: Dollar Lake
43.7	Green River Lake Campground

Wy-37 (Bighorn Canyon National Recreation Area)

9.8	Horseshoe Bend Campground

Wy-372

40.4	Slate Creek Campground
40.4	Tailrace Campground
40.4	Weeping Rock Campground

Wy-70

32.4	Battle Creek Campground
32.8	Little Sandstone Campground
37.9	Lost Creek Campground
50.7	Bottle Creek Campground
56.1	Encampment River Campground
57.1	Encampment RV Campground

Wy-789 & US-26/Wy-789

121.8	West Shoreline Drive: Boysen State Park
125.8	Poison Creek Campground: Boysen State Park
127.0	Shoshoni City Park

Yellowstone - Canyon Village to Fishing Bridge

0.0	Canyon Village

Yellowstone - East Entrance to Fishing Bridge

24.8	Fishing Bridge RV Park

Yellowstone - Fishing Bridge to West Thumb

3.4	Bridge Bay Campground

Yellowstone - Norris to Canyon Village

11.6	Canyon Village

Yellowstone - Norris to Mammoth Hot Springs

0.8	Norris Campground
12.5	Indian Creek Campground

Yellowstone - North Entrance to Mammoth Hot Springs

3.9	Mammoth Campground

Yellowstone - Northeast Entrance to Tower-Roosevelt

9.2	Pebble Creek Campground
22.3	Slough Creek Campground

Yellowstone - South Entrance to West Thumb

11.1	Lewis Lake Campground and Picnic Area
19.4	Grant Village

Yellowstone - Tower-Roosevelt to Canyon Village

2.4	Tower Fall Campground
18.3	Canyon Village

Yellowstone - West Entrance to Madison

13.5	Madison Campground

Yellowstone - West Thumb to Madison

33.5	Madison Campground

PICNIC AREAS AND REST AREAS

Alcova/Pathfinder Reservoir Loop

9.9	Fremont Canyon Bridge and Overlook
10.0	Pathfinder Interpretive Center

Casper Mountain Rd/Wy-251

4.9	Garden Creek Falls

Cook Lake Recreation Area and Scenic Drive

18.0	Cook Lake Recreation Area

CR-406/Lakeshore Drive

4.1	Natrona County Park

Fossil Butte National Monument

5.8	Chicken Creek Picnic Area

FR-700/Vedauwoo Glen Rd

1.1	Vedauwoo Recreation Area

Guernsey State Park - Lakeshore Drive/Wy-317

1.6	Picnic Shelter and Vault Toilet
1.7	Guernsey Dam
3.1	Sitting Bull Day Use Area

Guernsey State Park - Skyline Drive

2.1	The Castle Day Use Area

I-25

7.9	Cheyenne Rest Area
54.5	Chugwater Rest Area
92.4	Dwyer Junction Rest Area
126.5	Orin Junction Rest Area
140.1	Douglas Railroad Interpretive Center
140.1	Jackalope Square
151.2	Ayres Park and Natural Bridge
182.5	Edness Wilkins State Park
188.6	Fort Caspar Museum and Historic Site
254.3	Kaycee Rest Area
254.3	Kaycee Town Park

I-80
6.3 Bear River State Park
6.3 Bear River Welcome Center
42.0 Lyman Rest Area
89.5 Green River Visitor Information Center
91.5 Expedition Island
91.5 Scott's Bottom Nature Area
143.7 Bitter Creek Rest Area (westbound)
144.5 Bitter Creek Rest Area (eastbound)
228.3 Fort Steele Rest Area
267.2 Wagonhound Rest Area
311.8 Optimist Park
323.1 Summit Rest Area
401.5 Pine Bluffs Rest Area

I-90
23.2 Sheridan Visitor Center and Rest Area
88.7 Powder River Rest Area
153.4 Moorcroft Rest Area
189.0 Sundance Rest Area

Jenny Lake Loop Rd: Grand Teton National Park
1.5 String Lake Picnic Area

Oregon Trail Rd
11.9 Bessemer Bend National Historic Site

Seminoe-Alcova Back Country Byway
25.9 Sand Mountain Day Use Area: Seminoe State Park

Sugarloaf Recreation Area/FR-346
0.7 Libby Lake Picnic Ground
1.0 Lewis Lake

Teton Park Rd: Grand Teton National Park
3.8 Cottonwood Creek Picnic Area
16.7 Signal Mountain Rd
18.4 Picnic Area and Jackson Lake Access
19.8 Picnic Area and Snake River Access below Jackson Lake Dam

Trail Lake Rd/CR-411
9.1 Torrey Creek Trailhead

US-14
0.6 East Bridge Rest Area and Boat Ramp
10.5 Red Gulch Dinosaur Tracksite
42.6 Dead Swede Campground
47.7 Burgess Picnic Area (northbound)
57.1 Burgess Picnic Area (southbound)
62.4 Sibley Lake Picnic Areas

US-14/16/20
3.9 Sleeping Giant Picnic Area
14.7 Newton Springs Picnic Area
15.2 Firefighters Memorial
24.2 Forest Creek Picnic Area
51.8 Cody City Park

US-14A
24.9 Homesteader Park and Rest Area
46.8 Bighorn Canyon National Recreation Area Visitor Center
68.6 Five Springs Falls Campground
98.6 Burgess Picnic Area

US-16
1.3 Worland City Park
26.8 Ten Sleep City Park
45.1 Willow Park Group Picnic Area
45.4 Lake Point Picnic Area
46.7 Lakeview Campground and Picnic Area
76.0 Tie Hack Reservoir
76.9 Hettinger Picnic Area
85.9 Mosier Gulch Recreation Area

US-189
70.0 Fontenelle Creek Campground

US-189/191
155.5 Hoback Campground and Picnic Area

US-191
33.8 Roadside Table
36.6 Bicentennial Park

US-20/26
25.4 Goldeneye Wildlife and Recreation Area
53.2 Waltman Rest Area
99.7 Shoshoni Picnic Area
100.0 Shoshoni City Park

US-20/Wy-789 & US-16/20/Wy-789 & US-14/16/20/Wy-789
119.8 Picnic Area: Wind River Canyon
127.5 Picnic Area: Wind River Canyon
133.0 Hot Springs State Park
206.6 Greybull Rest Area

US-212 (Beartooth Scenic Byway)
26.9 Beartooth Lake Campground and Picnic Area

US-26 (I-25 to Nebraska)
0.5 Dwyer Junction Rest Area
17.7 Guernsey Rest Area
27.9 Fort Laramie City Park
38.3 Whipple Park
48.3 Pioneer Park

US-26/287 & US-26
13.0 Four Mile Meadows Picnic Area
25.9 Wind River Lake and Picnic Area
32.3 Brooks Lake Creek Falls Trailhead
96.4 Diversion Dam Rest Area
115.5 Ocean Lake WHMA - South Cove

US-26/89
129.3 West Table Boat Ramp and Picnic Area

US-26/89/191
154.9 Jackson Hole and Greater Yellowstone Visitor Center

US-287/Wy-789
8.2 Split Rock Historic Site
42.0 Sweetwater Station Rest Area

US-30
10.6 Cokeville City Park
44.5 Fossil Butte National Monument: Chicken Creek Picnic Area

US-30/287
252.7 Hanna Memorial Park
289.8 Rock River City Park

US-85
53.8 Meriden Rest Area
72.6 Roadside Table
92.9 Pioneer Park
103.1 Whipple Park
149.3 Lusk Rest Area
159.4 Roadside Table
196.2 Mule Creek Jct Rest Area

US-89
85.5 Intermittent Spring parking area
97.6 Star Valley Rest Area

US-89/191/287
196.0 Sargent's Bay Picnic Area
198.3 Arizona Island Picnic Area
199.4 Lake View Picnic Area
201.4 Northern Teton Range Overlook
209.6 Flagg Ranch Information Station

Wy-120
37.1 Gooseberry Creek Rest Area
81.2 *See US-14/16/20: Cody City Park*

Wy-130 (Laramie to Wy-230)
29.3 Fir Picnic Ground
29.3 Barber Lake Picnic Ground
34.0 Greenrock Trailhead and Picnic Ground
38.7 *See Sugarloaf Recreation Area/FR-346*
40.9 Mirror Lake and Lake Marie Parking and Picnic Area

Wy-130/Wy-230 (Walcott to Riverside)
18.0 Saratoga National Fish Hatchery (northbound)

Wy-131/FR-300/Louis Lake Rd
6.8 Sawmill Campground: Sinks Canyon State Park
10.3 Bruce Picnic Area
17.7 Worthen Meadows Campground
27.2 Louis Beach Picnic Area and Beach (east)
27.6 Louis Beach Picnic Area (west)

Wy-135/136
34.5 Sweetwater Station Rest Area

Wy-160/Grayrocks Rd/Power Plant Rd
2.5 Fort Laramie National Historic Site

Wy-193/US-87
100.2 Fort Phil Kearny
100.2 Wagon Box Fight Historic Site (south access)
103.9 Story Fish Hatchery

Wy-220
63.0 Independence Rock Rest Area
105.3 Bessemer Bend National Historic Site (heading southwest)
103.6 Bessemer Bend National Historic Site (heading northeast)
113.4 Fort Caspar Museum and Historic Site

Wy-28 (Farson to US-287)
34.2 South Pass Rest Area

Wy-296 (Chief Joseph Scenic Highway)
11.6 Reef Creek Picnic Area

Wy-37 (Bighorn Canyon National Recreation Area)
9.8 Horseshoe Bend

Wy-70
56.8 Grandview Park

Attractions at a Glance

Wy-789 & US-26/Wy-789
123.6 Lakeside Day Use Area: Boysen State Park
127.0 Shoshoni City Park
Yellowstone - Canyon Village to Fishing Bridge
2.3 *See Yellowstone - South Rim Drive: Chittenden Bridge Picnic Area*
3.0 Otter Creek Picnic Area
10.4 Nez Perce Ford Picnic Area
10.6 Cascade Picnic Area
11.3 LeHardy Picnic Area
Yellowstone - East Entrance to Fishing Bridge
7.7 Eleanor Lake Picnic Area
8.7 Sylvan Lake Picnic Area
18.0 Sedge Bay Picnic Area
19.5 Steamboat Point Picnic Area
25.2 Fishing Bridge Picnic Area
Yellowstone - Fishing Bridge to West Thumb
3.4 Bridge Bay Picnic Area
3.7 Gull Point Picnic Area (southbound)
5.3 Gull Point Picnic Area (northbound)
6.6 Sand Point Picnic Area
9.8 Interpretive Pullout: Contrasting Forests and Picnic Area
12.7 Picnic Area
20.4 West Thumb Picnic Area
Yellowstone - Madison to Norris
1.6 Tuff Cliff Picnic Area
4.4 Gibbon Falls Picnic Area
5.3 Iron Spring Picnic Area
6.2 Caldera Rim Picnic Area
10.2 Gibbon Meadows Picnic Area
Yellowstone - Mammoth Hot Springs to Tower-Roosevelt
0.0 Mammoth Hot Springs
4.4 Lava Creek Picnic Area
Yellowstone - Norris to Canyon Village
0.5 Norris Meadows Picnic Area
1.6 Virginia Cascade
Yellowstone - Norris to Mammoth Hot Springs
7.5 Beaver Lake Picnic Area
9.9 Apollinaris Spring Picnic Area
13.0 Sheepeater Cliff Picnic Area
20.7 Mammoth Picnic Area
20.9 Mammoth Hot Springs
Yellowstone - North Entrance to Mammoth Hot Springs
0.0 Gardiner Community Park
2.5 45th Parallel Picnic Area
Yellowstone - Northeast Entrance to Tower-Roosevelt
1.1 Warm Creek Picnic Area
7.1 Soda Butte Creek Picnic Area
26.9 Yellowstone River Picnic Area
Yellowstone - South Entrance to West Thumb
0.1 Snake River Picnic Area
11.1 Lewis Lake Campground and Picnic Area
19.4 Grant Village
Yellowstone - South Rim Drive
0.1 Chittenden Bridge Picnic Area
Yellowstone - Tower-Roosevelt to Canyon Village
15.8 Dunraven Road Picnic Area
16.9 Cascade Lake Picnic Area and Trail
Yellowstone - West Entrance to Madison
7.2 Madison River Picnic Area
Yellowstone - West Thumb to Madison
3.7 Divide Picnic Area
8.6 DeLacy Creek Picnic Area
12.0 Spring Creek Picnic Area
17.6 Old Faithful Village
23.8 Whiskey Flats Picnic Area
27.8 Nez Perce Picnic Area
29.0 Firehole River Picnic Area
33.3 Madison Information Station and Picnic Area

VISITOR CENTERS

Casper Mountain Rd/Wy-251
9.7 Casper Mountain Trail Center
Fremont Lake Rd/Skyline Drive
14.3 U.S. Forest Service Visitor Center
I-25
7.9 Cheyenne Rest Area
254.3 Kaycee Visitor Center

I-80
6.3 Bear River Welcome Center
89.5 Green River Visitor Information Center
323.1 Summit Rest Area & Abraham Lincoln Monument
401.5 Pine Bluffs Rest Area
I-90
23.2 Sheridan Visitor Center and Rest Area
126.4 Gillette Visitor Center
189.0 Sundance Rest Area
Pilot Butte Wild Horse Tour
0.0 Green River Visitor Information Center
Teton Park Rd: Grand Teton National Park
0.5 Craig Thomas Discovery and Visitor Center
7.9 Jenny Lake Visitor Center
US-14
58.4 Burgess Jct Visitor Center
US-14/16/20
22.7 Wapiti Wayside Visitor Center and Ranger Station
44.7 Buffalo Bill Dam and Visitor Center
US-14A
46.8 Bighorn Canyon National Recreation Area Visitor Center
US-20/Wy-789 & US-16/20/Wy-789 & US-14/16/20/Wy-789 & US-310/Wy-789
113.1 Boysen State Park Headquarters
US-26 (I-25 to Nebraska)
15.3 Guernsey Visitor Center and Museum
US-26/287 & US-26
8.3 Black Rock Ranger Station
54.8 National Bighorn Sheep Interpretive Center
US-26/89/191
154.9 Jackson Hole and Greater Yellowstone Visitor Center
US-89
85.5 City of Afton Information Center
US-89/191/287
194.1 Colter Bay Visitor Center & Indian Arts Museum
209.6 Flagg Ranch Information Station
Wy-130 (Laramie to Wy-230)
28.8 Centennial Visitor Center
55.5 Brush Creek Visitor Center
Wy-130/Wy-230 (Walcott to Riverside)
38.2 Carbon County Visitor Center
Wy-210/Happy Jack Rd
24.5 Curt Gowdy State Park Headquarters
Wy-230 (Riverside to Colorado)
100.0 Carbon County Visitor Center
Wy-296 (Chief Joseph Scenic Highway)
7.9 Crandall Ranger Station
Wy-37 (Bighorn Canyon National Recreation Area)
9.6 Bighorn Canyon Ranger Station
Wy-70
57.7 Carbon County Visitor Center
Yellowstone - Canyon Village to Fishing Bridge
0.0 Canyon Visitor Education Center
Yellowstone - East Entrance to Fishing Bridge
25.2 Fishing Bridge Visitor Center
Yellowstone - Fishing Bridge to West Thumb
3.4 Bridge Bay Ranger Station
Yellowstone - Mammoth Hot Springs to Tower-Roosevelt
0.0 Albright Visitor Center
17.9 Tower Ranger Station
Yellowstone – Norris to Canyon Village
11.6 Canyon Visitor Education Center
Yellowstone - Norris to Mammoth Hot Springs
20.9 Albright Visitor Center
Yellowstone - South Entrance to West Thumb
19.4 Grant Village
Yellowstone - Tower-Roosevelt to Canyon Village
0.0 Tower Ranger Station
18.3 Canyon Visitor Education Center
Yellowstone - West Thumb to Madison
17.6 Old Faithful Visitor Center
33.3 Madison Information Station and Picnic Area

INDEX

-- 4 --

40 Rod Rd to Wy-352; 104
45th Parallel; 219
45th Parallel Picnic Area: Yellowstone National Park; 219

-- A --

Abraham Lincoln Monument; 57
Absaroka Mountains; 39, 88, 119, 125, 126, 183, 197, 202, 205, 216
Absaroka Volcanic Field; 88
Absaroka Wilderness; 182, 183
Abyss Pool; 206
Adams, Ansel; 131
Africa Lake; 216
Afton; 143
Afton Information Center; 143
Aladdin; 178
Aladdin Tipple; 53, 106
Aladdin Tipple Historical Park; 178
Albright View Turnout; 130
Albright Visitor Center; 210, 218, 220
Albright, Horace; 130
Alcova; 14, 16, 27, 70, 72, 174
Alcova Dam; 14
Alcova Reservoir; 14, 16, 27, 66, 67, 70-72, 175
Alcova/Pathfinder Reservoir Loop; 14, 70
Alder Trail; 57
Allred Flat Campground; 143
Alpine; 37, 144
Alpine Campground; 128, 144
Alpine Jct; 128, 143, 144
Alva; 178
Ames Brothers; 57
Ames Monument; 57
Amsden Wildlife Habitat Management Area; 85
Anemone Geyser; 236
Angel Terrace; 217, 232
Antelope Flats Rd; 38, 130
Antelope Springs Reservoir; 136
Anvil Draw; 53
Apollinaris Spring; 215
Apollinaris Spring Picnic Area: Yellowstone National Park; 215
Arch Rock Campground: Keyhole State Park; 64
Arizona Island Picnic Area; 146
Arrow Trail; 170
Artemisia Geyser; 237, 238
Artesia Geyser; 239
Artist Paint Pots; 209
Artist Point; 227, 228
Ashton, Idaho; 172, 233
Aspen Alley; 26, 54, 192
Aspen Campground; 151
Aspen Meadow Loop Trail; 24
Aspen Trail; 57
Astorians; 104, 126
Atherton Creek Campground; 38
Atlantic City; 17, 18, 136, 180
Atlantic City Campground; 17
Atlantic City Rd/CR-237; 17, 18, 180
Atomizer Geyser; 237, 238
Aurum Geyser; 237
Avalanche Canyon; 75
Avalanche Peak Trailhead; 202
Avenue of Rocks (Devil's Backbone); 66
Ayres Park and Natural Bridge; 47

-- B --

Baby Lake Trail; 192
Back Basin; 209, 214
Badlands Scenic Overlook; 163
Baggs; 54, 192, 194
Bald Mountain Campground; 94
Bald Mountain Pass; 51
Bald Ridge; 30, 150
Bald Ridge Trailhead; 150
Bar Flying U Ranch; 131
Barber Lake; 152, 153
Barber Lake Picnic Ground; 152
Barber Lake Rd; 152
Barber Lake Trail; 153
Basin; 116

Bass Lake Rd; 196
Bath Spring; 208
Battle Creek Campground; 192
Battle Lake Overlook; 192
Beach Area Campground: Keyhole State Park; 64
Bear Lake; 153
Bear Lodge Mountains; 26, 27, 62, 178
Bear River State Park; 51
Bear River Welcome Center; 51
Bear's Claw; 64
Bearlodge Campground; 178
Bearpaw Lake; 63
Beartooth Butte; 120
Beartooth Creek; 119
Beartooth Falls; 119
Beartooth Lake; 119
Beartooth Lake Campground and Picnic Area; 120
Beartooth Mountains; 120
Beartooth Pass; 118, 120, 149, 150
Beartooth Plateau; 119
Beartrap Meadow Park: Casper Mountain; 23
Beauty Lake; 120
Beauty Pool; 237
Beaver Creek Campground; 142
Beaver Creek Fire; 75
Beaver Lake Picnic Area: Yellowstone National Park; 215
Beaver Ponds Day Use Area; 31
Beaver Rim; 136, 163
Bechler Falls; 170-172, 233
Bechler River; 172
Bechler River Trail; 172
Becker Lake; 120
Beehive Geyser; 236
Belle Fourche; 178
Belle Fourche Campground: Devils Tower National Monument; 148
Belle Fourche River; 148
Beryl Spring; 208
Bessemer Bend National Historic Site; 66, 174, 175
Bicentennial Park; 106
Big Atlantic Gulch Campground; 17
Big Game Campground; 88
Big Horn Mountains; 101
Big Sandy Pony Express Station; 107
Big Sandy Recreation Area; 107
Big Sandy Reservoir; 107
Big Sandy River; 107, 179, 181
Big Sandy Station; 107
Big Spring; 115
Bighorn Basin; 81, 82, 85, 91-97, 116, 117, 149, 187
Bighorn Canyon; 114, 187, 188
Bighorn Canyon National Recreation Area; 92, 187, 188
Bighorn Lake; 187, 188
Bighorn Mountains; 30, 81, 82, 84, 85, 94, 96, 98-101, 110, 111
Bighorn National Forest; 82-85, 93, 95, 98, 101
Bighorn Peak; 30
Bighorn River; 81, 93, 114, 115, 149, 187
Bighorn Scenic Byway; 81, 82, 85
Bighorn Sheep; 78, 114, 126
Bighorn Sheep Observation Parking Area; 78
Bill Menor's Cabin; 74
Bingham Post Office and Stage Station; 85
Biscuit Basin; 237, 238
Bishops Point Campground: Pathfinder Reservoir; 16
Bitter Creek Rest Area; 54
Bixby Public Access Area; 46, 47
Black Beach Campground: Alcova Reservoir; 14, 72
Black Canyon; 171
Black Canyon Cove Campground: Guernsey State Park; 41
Black Canyon of the Yellowstone; 211
Black Canyon Point Campground: Guernsey State Park; 41
Black Canyon Trail; 170, 171
Black Dragon's Caldron; 200
Black Hills; 64, 140, 142, 164, 178
Black Hills National Forest; 26, 27
Black Sand Basin; 237, 238
Black Sand Pool; 237, 238
Black Warrior Lake; 239
Blacktail Butte; 131, 146
Blacktail Butte Trailhead: Grand Teton National Park; 38, 130
Blacktail Deer Plateau Drive; 211
Blacktail Ponds Overlook; 131
Blackwater Fire; 88
BLM; 32, 54, 66, 68, 69, 81, 104, 173, 192

BLM Ridge Wintering Site; 78
Blue Geyser; 209, 214
Blue Ridge Fire Lookout; 158, 160, 161
Blue Rim Rd; 69
Boar's Tusk; 25, 68
Boiling River Trail; 219
Boiling River Trail and Swimming Hole; 219
Boiling River Trailhead; 210
Bomber Falls; 79
Bomber Lake Trail; 79
Bottle Creek Campground; 193
Boulder; 107
Boulder Canyon; 108
Boulder Canyon Trail; 108
Boulder Lake; 107, 108
Boulder Lake Campground; 108
Boulder Lake North Campground; 108
Boulder Lake Rd; 108
Boulder Lake Trailhead; 108
Boulder Park Campground; 30
Box Canyon; 31
Box Canyon Trail; 31
Box Creek Campground: Turpin Meadow Recreation Area; 21
Box Creek Trailhead: Turpin Meadow Recreation Area; 21
Boysen Dam; 113
Boysen Reservoir; 113, 196
Boysen State Park; 113, 114, 196
Boysen State Park Headquarters; 113
Bozeman Trail; 46, 59, 85, 165, 166
Bradley Lake; 36, 75
Bradley Lake Trail; 75
Braille Trail; 23
Brannon Campground: Boysen State Park; 113
Breccia Cliffs; 125
Bridge Bay; 206
Bridge Bay Campground: Yellowstone National Park; 205
Bridge Bay Marina; 205, 206
Bridge Bay Picnic Area: Yellowstone National Park; 205
Bridge Campground; 37
Bridger Tender House; 55
Bridger Wilderness; 32, 108, 184, 186
Bridger, Jim; 48, 52, 102, 107, 181
Bridger-Teton National Forest; 21, 38, 124, 130, 145, 184
Bridle Trail; 22
Brimmer Point: Guernsey State Park; 42
Brimmer, George; 42
Brooklyn Lake; 19, 73, 152
Brooklyn Lake Campground; 19
Brooklyn Lake Rd/FR 317; 10, 163
Brooklyn Lake Trailhead; 19
Brooks Lake; 20
Brooks Lake Campground; 20
Brooks Lake Cliffs; 20
Brooks Lake Creek; 20
Brooks Lake Creek Falls; 125
Brooks Lake Rd/FR-515; 20
Brooks Lake Trailhead; 20
Browns Landing Trail; 57
Browns Peak; 19, 73
Bruce Picnic Area; 159
Bruce's Bridge Trailhead; 158, 159, 161
Brush Creek Visitor Center; 155
Buckboard Crossing Campground; 53
Buckboard South; 53
Bucking Mule Falls; 94
Buffalo; 44, 49, 60, 96, 101
Buffalo Bill; 87, 89, 90
Buffalo Bill Cody Scenic Byway; 87, 89, 90
Buffalo Bill Dam and Visitor Center; 89
Buffalo Bill Historical Center; 90
Buffalo Bill Museum; 90
Buffalo Bill Reservoir; 89
Buffalo Bill State Park; 89
Buffalo Creek Campground; 99, 110
Buffalo Creek Rd; 99
Buffalo Fork River; 21
Buffalo Fork Valley; 21
Buffalo Valley Rd/FR-30050; 21
Bump Sullivan Reservoir; 140
Bumpus Butte; 224, 229
Bunsen Peak; 216
Bureau of Reclamation; 187
Burgess Jct; 83, 84, 91, 93, 95

Burgess Jct Visitor Center; 84
Burgess Picnic Area; 83, 84, 95
Burlington Northern; 91
Butch Cassidy; 49, 56, 176
Butch Cassidy and the Sundance Kid; 49, 111
Byrne Family Cemetery; 51
Byrne, Moses; 51
Byron; 92
Byron Sessions Statue; 92

-- C --
Cabin Creek Campground; 82
Cabin Creek Meadows Campground; 82
Calcite Springs; 224, 229
Caldera Rim Picnic Area: Yellowstone National Park; 208
California; 48, 107, 179
California Trail; 48, 51, 52, 102, 134, 179, 181
Canary Spring; 217, 232
Canyon Village; 198, 199, 201, 212, 213, 221, 222, 229, 231
Canyon Visitor Education Center; 199, 212, 222, 231
Carbon County Visitor Center; 157, 177, 193
Cariso Lode; 18
Carissa Mine; 18
Carmody Lake; 136, 163
Carrington, Colonel Henry B.; 166
Cascade Canyon; 75
Cascade Canyon Turnout; 76
Cascade Corners; 172, 233
Cascade Lake; 212, 230
Cascade Lake Picnic Area and Trail; 230
Cascade Lake Trailhead; 230
Cascade Picnic Area: Yellowstone National Park; 200
Casper; 22, 47, 48, 66, 67, 110, 112, 134, 173, 175
Casper Mountain; 22-24, 138, 139
Casper Mountain Park; 22, 23
Casper Mountain Rd/Wy-251; 22
Casper Mountain Scenic Overlook; 22
Casper Mountain Trail Center; 22
Casper Nordic Center; 22
Castle Gardens; 97, 111, 195
Castle Gardens (north); 97
Castle Geyser; 236, 237
Cathedral Cliffs; 182
Cathedral Group; 36, 63, 75, 131
Cathedral Group Turnout; 63
Cathedral Rocks; 216
Cave Falls; 170-172, 233
Cave Falls Campground; 171, 233
Centennial; 151
Centennial Park; 48, 175
Centennial Scenic Byway; 104, 105, 124, 127, 129, 131
Centennial Valley; 151
Centennial Visitor Center; 151
Chapel of the Sacred Heart; 76
Chapel of the Transfiguration; 74
Cheyenne and Black Hills Stage and Express Line; 164
Cheyenne and Black Hills Stage Road; 141
Cheyenne Rest Area; 44
Cheyenne to Deadwood Stage Route; 142
Cheyenne-Black Hills Trail Monument; 122
Chicago and Northwestern Railroad; 46, 125
Chicken Creek Picnic Area: Fossil Butte National Monument; 29
Chicken Creek Rd; 29
Chief Black Bear; 59, 85
Chief Joseph; 182, 183
Chief Joseph Campground: Montana; 118
Chief Joseph Scenic Highway; 182
Chief Red Cloud; 166
Chief Washakie; 125, 126, 132
Chilton Rd; 25
Chimney Park Trailhead; 176
Chimney Rock; 82, 87
Chinese Wall; 89
Chittenden Memorial Bridge; 222, 227
Chittenden Memorial Bridge Picnic Area; 227
Chittenden, Hiram Martin; 227
Chocolate Pots; 209
Christina Lake Trailhead; 160
Chromatic Spring; 237
Chugwater; 44
Chugwater Formation; 180
Chugwater Rest Area; 44
Church Butte; 52

Churning Caldron; 200
Circle Dr; 22, 23
Circle Park Campground; 100
Circle Park Trailhead; 100
Cistern Spring; 209, 214
Civil War; 54, 197
Civilian Conservation Corps; 40-42, 99, 105, 119, 121, 155, 160, 190
Clarks Fork Canyon; 183
Clarks Fork Overlook; 119
Clarks Fork River Valley; 119
Clarks Fork Yellowstone River; 118, 119, 182
Clay Butte Fire Lookout; 119
Clayton, William; 66
Clear Creek Canyon; 186
Clear Creek Falls; 186
Clear Creek Natural Bridge; 186
Clear Creek Trail; 21, 186
Clear Lake; 227
Clearwater Campground; 88
Clepsydra Geyser; 239
Cliff Geyser; 237
Cliff Swallow Trail; 26
Cloud Peak; 98, 101
Cloud Peak Skyway; 96, 98, 101
Cloud Peak Wilderness; 30, 99, 100
Clover Mist Fire; 119
Cloverly Formation; 81, 116
Coal Creek Meadows; 171
Coal Creek Trailhead; 171
Cody; 89-91, 95, 120, 149, 150
Cody City Park; 90
Cody Firearms Museum; 90
Cody Gunfighters; 90
Cody Peak; 87
Cody, Colonel William F.; 89, 90
Cokeville; 137
Cokeville City Park; 137
Colby Mammoth Kill Site; 96
Collins, Lt. Caspar; 48, 175
Colorado; 44, 50, 54, 133, 138, 153, 176, 177, 192, 194
Colorado River; 52, 186
Colter Bay Campground: Glendo State Park; 34
Colter Bay Village; 36
Colter Bay Village and Campground: Grand Teton National Park; 146
Colter Bay Visitor Center; 36, 146
Colter Campground: Montana; 118
Colter's Hell; 89, 197
Colter, John; 89, 197
Columbia River; 126
Como Bluffs; 138
Como Ridge; 138
Congress Pool; 209, 214
Connor Battlefield State Park and Historic Site; 59, 85
Connor, General Patrick E.; 59, 85
Continental Divide; 25, 125, 179, 235
Cook Lake Recreation Area; 26, 27, 62, 86, 178
Cook Lake Recreation Area and Scenic Drive; 26
Cook Lake Trail; 26
Cook-Folsom-Peterson Expedition; 197
Cooke City, Montana; 118, 120
Coolidge, President Calvin; 36
Corner Mountain Trails; 12, 152
Cottonwood Bay; 64, 65
Cottonwood Campground: Green Mountain; 135
Cottonwood Campground: Keyhole State Park; 65
Cottonwood Cove Campground: Guernsey State Park; 43
Cottonwood Creek Campground: Alcova Reservoir; 14, 71
Cottonwood Creek Dinosaur Trail; 14, 72
Cottonwood Creek Picnic Area: Grand Teton National Park; 75
Cottonwood Lake Campground; 143
Coulter Bay Campground: Keyhole State Park; 64
Cowley; 117
CR-105/Buffalo Creek Rd; 99
CR-110; 99
CR-14/Blue Rim Rd; 69
CR-149/40 Rod Rd to Wy-352; 104
CR-180; 64
CR-188; 103
CR-205; 86
CR-235; 180
CR-237; 17, 18, 180
CR-319/Oregon Trail Rd; 66
CR-406/Lakeshore Drive; 27

CR-407/Kortes Rd; 14
CR-408/Fremont Canyon Rd; 14, 15
CR-409/Pathfinder Rd; 15
CR-411; 78
CR-422/Phalow Ln; 28
CR-44/Harmony Ln; 28
CR-479; 17, 18
CR-50/RD 92/Tank Farm Rd; 164
CR-505/Circle Dr; 22, 23
CR-53/White Mountain Rd; 69
CR-83; 97
CR-84; 99
Crackling Lake; 209, 214
Craig Pass; 235
Craig Thomas Discovery and Visitor Center; 36, 74, 75
Crater Lake; 170
Crazy Creek Campground; 119
Crazy Creek Falls; 118, 119
Crazy Horse; 166
Crazy Lakes Trail; 118
Crazy Woman Campground; 100
Crazy Woman Canyon; 99
Crested Pool; 237
Crimson Dawn Park and Museum; 22, 23
Crooked Creek Summit; 187
Crowheart Butte; 126
Crystal Creek Campground; 38, 39
Crystal Creek Rest Area; 93
Crystal Falls; 199, 222, 227
Crystal Reservoir; 57, 58, 168
Cundick Ridge; 29
Cunningham Cabin; 36, 131
Cunningham, J. Pierce; 131
Curt Gowdy State Park; 31, 57, 58, 168, 169
Curt Gowdy State Park Headquarters; 168
Curtis Canyon Campground; 129
Curtis Canyon Overlook; 129
Custer Cove Campground: Glendo State Park; 34
Custer, Lt. Colonel George A.; 178
Cutthroat Lake; 19, 73

-- D --
Daisy Geyser; 236-238
Daniel Fish Hatchery; 104
Daniel Public Access Area; 104
Darton Peak; 30
Davis Bay Campground: Guernsey State Park; 42
Dayton; 82, 84, 85
Dayton Bell Tower; 85
Dead Indian Campground; 183
Dead Indian Creek Trailhead; 183
Dead Indian Pass; 149, 182, 183
Dead Indian Trail; 183
Dead Swede Campground; 83
Deadman's Bar; 131
Deadman's Cove Campground: Guernsey State Park; 41
Death Canyon Patrol Cabin; 191
Death Canyon Trailhead; 191
Deep Lake Trail; 19, 73
Deer Park Campground; 30
Deer Path Interpretive Hiking Trail; 116
Deerhaven Park Campground: Casper Mountain; 23
DeLacy Creek Picnic Area: Yellowstone National Park; 235
DeLacy Creek Trailhead; 235
Depression Geyser; 236
DeSmet, Father Pierre Jeane; 60, 103
Devil Canyon; 94, 188
Devil Canyon Overlook: Bighorn Canyon National Recreation Area; 188
Devil's Backbone; 66
Devil's Den; 224, 229, 230
Devil's Gate; 67, 134, 173
Devil's Gate Historic Site; 173
Devil's Kitchen Geological Site; 81, 116
Devils Tower; 86, 148, 178
Devils Tower National Monument; 86, 148, 178
Devils Tower Rd (Devils Tower National Monument); 148
Diabase Campground: Pathfinder Reservoir; 16
Diamond Lake Public Access Area; 56
Dillon Ghost Town; 192
Dinosaur Tracks; 81
Dinwoody Glacier; 79
Dinwoody Petroglyphs; 149

Diplodocus; 138
Dipper Lake; 155
Dipper Lake Trail; 154
Disaster Wall; 154
Dispersed Camping: Dollar Lake; 185
Dispersed Camping: Fremont Lake; 32
Dispersed Camping: Louis Lake Rd; 160
Dispersed Camping: Pathfinder Reservoir; 15
Dispersed Camping: Sinks Canyon; 159
Dispersed Camping: US-14A; 93
Dispersed Camping: Wy-135; 163
Diversion Dam Rest Area; 127
Divide Picnic Area: Yellowstone National Park; 235
Dixon, Daniel; 166
Doc Culleton Building; 193
Dollar Lake; 185
Doublet Pool; 237
Douglas; 46, 47
Douglas Railroad Interpretive Center; 46
Downar Bird Farm; 140
Doyle Campground; 99
Dragon's Mouth; 200
Draper Museum of Natural History; 90
Dream Lake; 108
Dry Creek Petrified Tree Environmental Education Area; 60
Dry Medicine Lodge Canyon; 116
Dry Medicine Lodge Creek; 116
Dubois; 78, 124, 126, 127, 162, 184
Dubois Recreation Area Scenic Overlook; 126
Dubois State Fish Hatchery; 126
Duck Lake Trail; 207
Dugway Recreation Site; 70
Dull Knife Battle; 49
Dullknife Reservoir; 99
Dunraven Peak; 230
Dunraven Road Picnic Area: Yellowstone National Park; 230
Dwyer Junction Rest Area; 45, 121

-- E --
Eagle Butte Coal Mine; 61
Eagle Butte Coal Mine Tour; 61
Eagle Creek Campground; 87
Eagle Lake Rainbow Trout; 97
Eagle Nest Rock and Split Rock; 219
Eagle Peak; 107
East Allen Lake; 138
East Bridge Rest Area and Boat Ramp; 81
East Glacier Lake; 19
East Table Creek Campground; 128
Easter Island Statue; 53
Echinus Geyser; 209, 214
Eden; 106
Edison, Thomas; 192
Edness Wilkins State Park; 47, 110
Egbert Hill; 31
Eleanor Lake Picnic Area: Yellowstone National Park; 202
Electric Peak; 216
Elephant Back Mountain Trailhead; 205
Elk Fork Campground; 88
Elk Fork Trailhead; 88
Elk Ranch Flats Turnout; 131
Elkhart Park; 32
Elkhart Park Trailhead; 32, 33
Elkhorn Campground: Glendo State Park; 45
Elkhorn Canyon; 23
Elkhorn Springs Park Campground: Casper Mountain; 23
Elva Ingram Grave and Trail Ruts; 41
Emblem; 90
Emerald Pool; 237
Emigrant Gap; 66, 67
Emigrant Hill; 41
Emigrant Ridge; 66
Emigrant Trails; 48, 165, 175
Emma Matilda Lake; 146
Encampment; 193
Encampment River; 177, 193
Encampment River Campground; 193
Encampment River Trail; 193
Encampment River Valley; 177, 193
Encampment River Wilderness; 193
Encampment RV Campground; 193
Enos Lake; 21
Episcopal Church; 19, 74

Eskridge Draw Monument; 69
Evanston; 51
Excelsior Geyser; 238
Expedition Island; 52, 53

-- F --
Fairy Falls; 238, 239
Fallen City; 84
Falls Campground; 125
Falls River; 171, 172
Fan and Mortar Geyser; 237
Farson; 106, 158, 179-181
Father DeSmet Monument; 60
Father DeSmet's Prairie Mass Monument; 103
Featherlegs Monument and Grave; 141
Fern Cascades; 236
Ferris-Haggarty Mine; 192
Festo Lake; 45
Fetterman City; 46
Fetterman Massacre; 164, 166
Fetterman Massacre Monument and Battlefield; 166
Fetterman, Captain William J.; 166
Fick, Jerry; 89
Fiddlers Lake; 160
Fiddlers Lake Campground; 160
Fir Picnic Ground; 151
Fire and Blowdown Exhibit; 212
Firefighters Memorial; 88, 99
Firefighters Memorial Trail; 88
Firefighters Monument; 88
Firehole Canyon; 240
Firehole Canyon Campground; 53
Firehole Canyon Drive; 240
Firehole Cascade; 240
Firehole Drive; 240
Firehole Falls; 240
Firehole Lake; 239
Firehole Lake Drive; 238
Firehole River; 235, 237-240
Firehole River Picnic Area: Yellowstone National Park; 240
Firehole River Swimming Area; 240
Firehole Spring; 239
Firehole Valley; 208
Fish Bowl Spring; 186
Fish Canyon Campground: Guernsey State Park; 41
Fish Canyon Cove Campground: Guernsey State Park; 41
Fish Creek; 80
Fishing Bridge; 198, 199, 201-205, 207
Fishing Bridge Picnic Area: Yellowstone National Park; 203
Fishing Bridge RV Park: Yellowstone National Park; 203
Fishing Bridge Village; 203
Fishing Bridge Visitor Center; 203
Fishing Cone; 206
Fitzpatrick Wilderness; 79
Five Springs Falls; 93
Five Springs Falls Campground; 93
Flagg Ranch Information Station; 147
Flaming Gorge Dam; 189
Flaming Gorge National Recreation Area - Buckboard Crossing; 53
Flaming Gorge National Recreation Area - Firehole Canyon; 53
Flaming Gorge Reservoir; 53
Flat Top Mountain; 186
Flemish Revival Architecture; 59
FMC Park; 52, 53
Fontenelle Creek Campground; 102
Fontenelle Dam; 102, 189
Fontenelle Reservoir; 102, 189
Foote Creek Rim Wind Energy Project; 56, 139
Foote Public Access Area; 156
Forces of the Northern Range Trail; 210
Forest Creek Picnic Area; 88
Forest Park Campground; 37
Forsling, Neal; 23
Fort Bridger; 52, 107, 179, 181
Fort Bridger State Historic Site; 52
Fort Caspar Museum and Historic Site; 48, 175
Fort Caspar Park; 48, 175
Fort Fetterman State Historic Site; 46, 47
Fort Fred Steele; 55
Fort Hat Creek Stage Station; 142
Fort Laramie; 60, 122, 164-166
Fort Laramie Bridge; 164
Fort Laramie City Park; 122

Fort Laramie National Historic Site; 165
Fort Laramie Treaty; 122
Fort Phil Kearny; 164, 166
Fort Platte; 164
Fort Reno; 166
Fort Sanders; 133
Fort Steele Rest Area; 55
Fort Washakie; 132
Fort Washakie Cemetery; 132
Fort Yellowstone; 197, 210, 218, 220, 232
Fort Yellowstone Historic District; 210, 218, 220
Forty-Niners; 48, 179
Fossil Butte National Monument; 29
Fossil Cabin Museum; 138
Fossil Lake Trail: Fossil Butte National Monument; 29
Fountain Freight Rd Trailhead; 239
Fountain Paint Pot; 198, 239
Four Mile Meadows Picnic Area; 124
Fox Creek Campground; 118
FR-10/Hunt Mountain Rd; 82, 94
FR-10072; 37, 143
FR-10091; 80, 104, 184
FR-101/Sand Lake Rd; 19, 152
FR-10138; 37
FR-103; 155
FR-200; 155
FR-27/Ten Sleep Rd; 30
FR-300/Louis Lake Rd; 158, 160, 161
FR-30050; 21
FR-30400; 38
FR-317; 19, 153
FR-330; 152
FR-332/Towner Lake Rd; 19, 153
FR-346; 73
FR-515; 20
FR-516; 20
FR-532; 80
FR-700/Vedauwoo Glen Rd; 31
FR-705; 57
FR-707; 57
FR-830; 26, 27
FR-838; 26, 27
FR-843; 26, 27
FR-862; 192
FR-863; 62, 142
Frannie; 117
Fremont Campground: Alcova Reservoir; 27
Fremont Canyon; 14-16, 70
Fremont Canyon Bridge and Overlook; 14
Fremont Canyon Rd; 14, 15
Fremont County Pioneer Museum; 132
Fremont Lake; 32, 108
Fremont Lake Campground; 32
Fremont Lake Rd/Skyline Drive; 32
Fremont Trail; 108
Fremont, John C.; 48
French Creek Canyon; 154
French Creek Canyon Trail; 154
Frye Lake; 159, 161

-- G --
Gallatin Range; 215, 216
Gap Lakes Trail; 19, 73
Garden Creek Falls; 22
Gardiner, Montana; 198, 216, 220
Gardner Canyon; 219
Gardner River; 215, 216, 219
Garnet Canyon; 75
Gelatt Lake Public Access Area; 28
Gem Pool; 237, 238
George Lathrop Monument; 141
Geyser Hill; 236
Giant Geyser; 237
Giantess Geyser; 237
Gibbon Canyon; 208
Gibbon Falls; 208
Gibbon Falls Picnic Area: Yellowstone National Park; 208
Gibbon Meadows Picnic Area: Yellowstone National Park; 209
Gibbon River; 208, 209, 212
Gillette; 61
Gillette Visitor Center; 61
Glacial Boulder; 221
Glacial Boulder Trailhead; 221

Glacier Trail; 79
Glacier Trail Campground; 79
Glacier View Turnout; 131
Glendo; 34, 45, 166
Glendo Dam; 35
Glendo Park Rd (Glendo State Park); 34
Glendo Reservoir; 34, 45
Glendo State Park; 34, 35, 45
Glendo State Park - Airport Entrance; 45
Glenrock; 46, 47, 110
Glenrock South Recreation Complex; 47
Glimpse Lake; 32
Glory Slide; 170
Golden Gate at Kingman Pass; 216
Golden Gate Canyon; 216
Goldeneye Reservoir; 110
Goldeneye Wildlife and Recreation Area; 110
Goose Rock; 88
Gooseberry Badlands Scenic Area; 115, 149
Gooseberry Creek Rest Area; 149
Goshen Hole Reservoir; 140
Grand Canyon; 62, 142
Grand Canyon of the Yellowstone; 197-199, 203, 212, 221, 222, 224, 227-231, 236
Grand Encampment; 193
Grand Encampment Museum; 193
Grand Geyser; 236, 237
Grand Loop Road; 198, 199, 201, 205, 207-214, 218-220, 222, 224, 229, 231, 234, 235, 237, 240
Grand Prismatic Spring; 238, 239
Grand Teton; 36, 63, 74, 75, 131
Grand Teton National Park; 36, 38, 63, 74-77, 124, 127, 130, 145-147, 172, 190, 191, 202, 219, 223, 225, 233
Grand Teton National Park - Buffalo Entrance; 145
Grand Teton National Park - Granite Canyon Entrance; 190
Grand Teton National Park - Moose Entrance; 74
Grand View; 221, 222, 227
Grand View Point Trail; 146
Grandview Overlook; 172
Grandview Park; 193
Granite Canyon; 190
Granite Canyon Trailhead; 190
Granite Creek Campground; 105
Granite Falls; 105
Granite Hot Springs; 105
Granite Pass; 82, 85, 94
Granite Reservoir; 57, 168
Grant Village; 225
Grant, President Ulysses S.; 197, 225
Grassy Lake Rd; 147
Grave Springs Campground; 99, 111
Gravel Mountain; 21
Gravel Ridge; 21
Gray Reef Reservoir; 174
Gray Reef Reservoir Campground; 174
Grayrocks Rd/Power Plant Rd/Wy-160; 165
Grayrocks Reservoir; 165
Grayrocks Reservoir Dam Overlook; 165
Great Divide Basin; 25
Great Fountain Geyser; 236, 238-240
Great Lakes; 156
Great Salt Lake Valley; 48, 107, 181
Great Skyroad; 151
Greater Sand Dunes; 25
Greater Yellowstone Ecosystem; 36, 90, 129, 131, 197
Grebe Lake; 212
Green Mountain; 135
Green Mountain Falls; 193
Green Mountain Park Campground: Green Mountain; 135
Green River; 52, 53, 68, 69, 102-104, 179, 181, 184, 186, 189
Green River Basin; 25, 68
Green River Canyon; 186
Green River Formation; 29
Green River Lake Campground; 185
Green River Lakes; 80, 104, 184, 186
Green River Lakes Trailhead; 184, 186
Green River Rendezvous; 103
Green River Visitor Information Center; 52, 68
Greenrock Trailhead and Picnic Ground; 153
Greenwood Cutoff; 179
Greybull; 81, 85, 87, 90, 113, 116, 117
Greybull Rest Area; 116
Greys River; 37

Greys River Rd/FR-10138; 37, 143
Greys River Valley; 37
Grizzly Lake; 215
Gros Ventre Campground: Grand Teton National Park; 38
Gros Ventre Mountains; 36, 38, 39, 75, 130, 146, 171
Gros Ventre Rd/FR-30400; 36, 38, 39, 130
Gros Ventre River; 38, 39
Gros Ventre Slide; 38, 74
Grotto Geyser; 237, 238
Grotto Pool; 199, 222, 227
Guernsey; 34, 41, 42, 121, 164
Guernsey Dam; 40
Guernsey Museum; 40, 121
Guernsey Reservoir; 40, 42, 121
Guernsey Rest Area; 122
Guernsey State Park; 40-43, 121, 122
Guernsey State Park - Lakeshore Drive/Wy-317; 40
Guernsey State Park - Skyline Drive; 42
Guernsey Visitor Center and Museum; 121
Guild Reservoir; 51
Guinard Bridge; 48, 175
Guinard, Louis; 48, 175
Gull Point; 206
Gull Point Picnic Area: Yellowstone National Park; 206

-- H --
Half Moon Lake Campground; 32
Hamilton City; 17
Hanna; 138
Hanna Cemetery; 138
Hanna Memorial Park; 138
Hanna VFW War Memorial; 138
Happy Jack Rd; 31, 57, 168
Happy Jack Recreation Area; 168
Happy Jack Trailhead; 57
Harlequin Lake Trail; 234
Harmony Ln; 28
Hat Creek Station; 142
Hatchet Campground; 124
Hawk Springs; 140
Hawk Springs Reservoir; 140
Hawk Springs State Recreation Area; 140
Hayden Expedition; 210, 218, 220
Hayden Valley; 200
Hayden, Ferdinand V.; 197
Hazelton Rd; 99
Headquarters Trail; 57
Heart Mountain Relocation Center; 91
Hell's Half Acre; 110
Hellroaring Creek Trailhead; 211
Her Lake; 100
Hettinger Picnic Area; 100
Hidden Falls; 75
High Park Lookout; 99
Highline Trail; 32, 108, 184, 186
Highway Beautification Act; 141
Historic Downtown Douglas Walking Tour; 46
Historic Fossil Quarry; 29
Historic Quarry Trail: Fossil Butte National Monument; 29
History Trail; 170
History Walk; 48, 175
Hoback Campground and Picnic Area; 105
Hoback Canyon; 104, 105
Hoback Jct; 104-106, 128, 129, 131
Hoback River; 104, 105
Hobo Hot Pool; 157
Hogadon Rd; 22
Hogan Reservoir; 150
Hole-in-the-Wall; 49, 99, 110, 111
Hole-in-the-Wall Fight; 111
Holy City; 88
Homestead Campground: Keyhole State Park; 65
Homesteader Museum; 91
Homesteader Park and Rest Area; 91
Homesteaders Museum; 123, 140
Horse Creek Campground; 126
Horseshoe Bend; 187
Horseshoe Bend Campground: Bighorn Canyon National Recreation Area; 187
Horseshoe Station; 166
Hot Cascades; 239
Hot Lake; 239
Hot Springs State Park; 115

Howard Eaton Lake; 227
Howard Eaton Trail; 203, 212, 236
Howard Eaton Trail to LeHardy Rapids Overlook; 203
Howard Eaton Trailhead; 236
Howard, General Oliver O.; 183
Hulett; 178
Hunt Mountain Rd; 82, 94
Hunter Peak Campground; 182
Huston Park Wilderness; 192, 193
Hyattville; 81, 97, 115

-- I --
I-25; 22, 44, 49, 59, 99, 110, 121, 123, 142, 164, 165, 168, 169
I-80; 31, 51, 53, 54, 56-58, 68-70, 72, 102, 103, 106, 109, 133, 134, 136-139, 168, 169, 189, 192
I-90; 26, 27, 44, 50, 59, 62, 64, 86, 142, 166, 167, 178
Ice Lake; 212
Ice Slough; 135
Id-33; 170
Id-47/Mesa Falls Scenic Byway; 172
Idaho; 77, 92, 128, 137, 143, 144, 170-172, 197, 233
Imperial Geyser; 238
Independence Rock; 66, 67, 102, 134, 173
Independence Rock Rest Area; 173
Independence Rock State Historic Site; 173
Index Peak; 119
Indian Arts Museum; 146
Indian Bathtubs; 177, 193
Indian Creek Campground: Yellowstone National Park; 215
Indian Pond; 203
Indian Rock Art Cave; 49
Indians; See Native Americans
Ingram, Elva; 41
Inscription Wall; 48
Inspiration Point; 75, 221, 222, 227
Intermittent Spring; 143, 144
Iron Spring Picnic Area: Yellowstone National Park; 208
Isa Lake; 235
Island Lake; 120, 160
Island Lake Campground; 120
Island Lake Trailhead; 120
Island Park Campground; 30

-- J --
Jackalope Square; 46
Jackson; 36, 102, 129, 170, 172, 190, 233
Jackson Hole; 36, 38, 76, 129-131, 146, 171, 190, 191
Jackson Hole and Greater Yellowstone Visitor Center; 129
Jackson Hole Mountain Resort; 190
Jackson Hole National Monument; 36
Jackson Hole Valley; 36
Jackson Lake; 36, 76, 77, 145, 146
Jackson Lake Dam; 77
Jackson Point Overlook; 76, 145
Jackson, William H.; 76, 197, 210, 218, 220
Jade Lakes, 20
Jade Lakes Trail; 20
Japanese; 91
Jedediah Smith Wilderness; 170, 171
Jenny Lake; 36, 63, 75
Jenny Lake and Trails; 75
Jenny Lake Campground: Grand Teton National Park; 75
Jenny Lake Loop Rd: Grand Teton National Park; 63
Jenny Lake Loop Trail; 63, 75
Jenny Lake Overlook; 63
Jenny Lake Visitor Center; 36, 74, 75
Jet Geyser; 239
Jewel Geyser; 238
John "Portugee" Phillips Monument; 166
John D. Rockefeller, Jr. Memorial Parkway; 146, 147
Joy, Henry B.; 57
Joyner Ridge Trail: Devils Tower National Monument; 148
Jupiter Terrace; 217
JY Ranch; 191

-- K --

Kamas; 51
Kamloops Rainbow Trout; 150
Kane Ponds; 92
Kaycee; 49, 110
Kaycee Rest Area; 49
Kaycee Town Park; 49
Kaycee Visitor Center; 49
Kelly; 38
Kelly Warm Spring; 38
Kemmerer; 102, 137
Kemmerer Tent Park; 102, 137
Kendall Dace; 185
Kendall Warm Springs; 185
Kendrick, John B.; 59
Kennaday Peak Lookout; 155
Kepler Cascades; 235
Keyhole Reservoir; 64
Keyhole State Park; 64, 65, 86
Keyhole State Park via CR-205/CR-180; 64
Killpecker Sand Dunes; 25, 68
Kortes Dam; 71
Kortes Rd; 14
Kozy Campground; 104

-- L --

Lake Absarraca; 44
Lake Butte; 202
Lake Cameahwait; 196
Lake Creek Bridge; 119
Lake Creek Campground; 119, 182
Lake Creek Falls and Historic Bridge; 119
Lake Creek Trailhead; 171
Lake DeSmet; 60
Lake DeSmet Rd; 60
Lake DeSmet Recreation Area; 60
Lake Gosiute; 68
Lake Hattie Public Access Area; 28
Lake Helen; 30
Lake Lodge; 205
Lake Louise; 79
Lake Marie; 154
Lake Marie Falls; 154
Lake Marie West Trailhead to Medicine Bow Peak; 154
Lake Marion; 30
Lake of the Woods; 80
Lake Point Picnic Area; 98
Lake Solitude; 75
Lake Vera; 108
Lake View Picnic Area; 146
Lake Village; 203, 205
Lake Yellowstone; 200
Lake Yellowstone Hotel; 205
Lakes Trail; 73, 154
Lakeshore Drive; 27, 45
Lakeshore Drive Campgrounds: Glendo State Park; 34
Lakeshore Trail; 203, 205
Lakeside Day Use Area: Boysen State Park; 196
Lakeside Trail; 186
Lakeview Campground and Picnic Area; 98
Lamar Buffalo Ranch; 223
Lamar Valley; 223
Lander; 132-134, 136, 158, 161, 163, 179-181, 195, 196
Lander City Park; 132
Lander Cutoff; 143, 179
Lander Trail; 179
Lander, Frederick W.; 179
Laramie; 56, 133, 138, 139, 151, 155, 156, 168, 169, 176
Laramie Peak; 40, 42
Laramie Range; 40, 42
Laramie River; 56, 164, 165
Laramie River Greenbelt Trail; 56
Larson Park; 121
Lathrop, George; 141
Laurance S. Rockefeller Preserve; 191
Lava Creek Canyon; 210
Lava Creek Picnic Area: Yellowstone National Park; 210
Lava Creek Trail; 210, 219
Legend Rock Petroglyphs; 149
LeHardy Picnic Area: Yellowstone National Park; 200
LeHardy Rapids; 200, 203
Leigh Canyon; 98
Leigh Creek Campground; 97

Leigh Creek Monument; 98
Leigh Lake; 36, 63
Leigh Lake Trail; 63
Leigh, Gilbert E.; 98
Lemonade Lake; 215
Lewis and Clark Expedition; 89, 132, 197
Lewis Canyon; 225
Lewis Falls; 225
Lewis Lake; 73, 154, 225
Lewis Lake Campground and Picnic Area: Yellowstone National Park; 225
Lewis Lake Trailhead; 19
Lewis Park; 45, 165
Lewis River; 225
Lewis, Meriwether; 225
Libby Creek; 152, 153
Libby Creek Canyon; 153
Libby Creek Falls; 153
Libby Creek Trail; 153
Libby Flats; 153
Libby Lake; 73
Libby Lake Picnic Ground; 73
Libby Observation Point; 153
Liberty Cap; 217
Lightning Lakes; 108
Lily Pad Lake; 227
Lincoln Highway; 57, 68
Lincoln Highway Association; 57
Lincoln Park Campground; 155
Lincoln, Abraham; 57
Lingle; 122, 140-142
Lion Geyser; 236
Lion Group; 236
Little Bighorn; 166
Little Cub Geyser; 236
Little Divide Lake; 108
Little Firehole River; 238
Little Gibbon Falls; 212
Little Gibbon River; 212
Little Laramie Trails; 12, 152
Little Popo Agie River; 160
Little Sandstone Campground; 54, 192
Little Sandy Crossing; 107, 181
Little Sunlight Campground; 182
Little Sunlight Trailhead; 182
Lizard Creek Campground: Grand Teton National Park; 146
Loaf Mountain Overlook; 100
Lodge Trail Ridge; 166
Lodgepole Campground: Muddy Mountain; 24
Lodgepole Loop; 152
Lodgepole Pine Trail; 24
Lombard/Mormon Ferry; 181, 189
Lone Star Geyser; 235
Long Canyon Campground: Guernsey State Park; 41
Long Lake; 32, 120
Long Point Campground; 127
Long Point Rd; 127
Lookout Lake; 154
Lookout Point; 221, 222, 227
Lost Cabin Campground; 99
Lost Creek Campground; 192
Lost Creek Falls; 229
Lost Eagle Peak; 186
Lost Lake; 19, 73, 125, 229
Lost Lake Trail; 19, 73, 229
Lost Twin Lakes; 30
Louis Beach Picnic Area; 160
Louis Lake; 158, 160, 161
Louis Lake Campground; 161
Louis Lake Rd/FR-300/Wy-131; 158, 160, 161
Lovell; 87, 90-92, 95, 113, 117
Lovell Camper Park; 92, 117
Lower Geyser Basin; 198, 236, 238, 239
Lower Green River Lake; 185, 186
Lower Jade Lake; 20
Lower Mesa Falls; 170, 172, 233
Lower Salt River Public Access Area; 144
Lower Shell Schoolhouse; 81
Lower Silas Lake; 160
Lower Slide Lake; 38
Lower Terrace; 217
Lower Wind River Campground: Boysen State Park; 114
Lower Yellowstone Falls; 197, 198, 221, 222, 227, 228

Luce Reservoir; 150
Lucite Hills; 68
Lupine Meadows; 210
Lusk; 122, 141
Lusk Rest Area; 141
Lyman Rest Area; 52
Lynx Creek Campground; 37

-- M --
Madison; 208, 209, 233-235, 240
Madison Campground: Yellowstone National Park; 234, 240
Madison Information Station; 198, 239, 240
Madison River; 233, 234, 240
Madison River Picnic Area: Yellowstone National Park; 233
Main Terrace; 217, 232
Mammoth Campground: Yellowstone National Park; 220
Mammoth Hot Springs; 198, 210, 211, 214, 216, 218-220, 232
Mammoth Hot Springs Terraces; 217
Mammoth Hot Springs Upper Terrace; 232
Mammoth Picnic Area: Yellowstone National Park; 217
Manderson; 115
Manila; 53
Manville; 34
Marion Lake; 190
Martin Handcart Company; 17, 48, 66, 175
Martin's Cove; 173
Martin, Edward; 173
Mary Bay; 202
Mary Homsley Grave; 164
Mason-Lovell Ranch; 93
Maude Noble's Cabin; 74
Meadow Falls; 155
Meadow Falls Trailhead; 155
Meadow Falls-Silver Lake Loop Trail; 155
Meadow Loop; 152
Meadowlark Lake; 98, 99
Medicine Bow; 138, 139
Medicine Bow National Forest; 31, 151, 168, 176, 192, 194
Medicine Bow Peak; 73, 151, 154, 155
Medicine Bow Peak Overlook; 154
Medicine Bow Peak Trail from Lewis Lake; 73
Medicine Lodge Nature Trail; 116
Medicine Lodge State Archaeological Site; 81, 82, 97, 115, 116
Medicine Lodge Wildlife Habitat Management Area; 116
Medicine Mountain; 94
Medicine Wheel National Historic Landmark; 93-95
Medicine Wheel Passage; 91, 93-95
Meeboer Lake Public Access Area; 28
Meeteetse; 149
Menor's Ferry Historic District; 74
Meriden Rest Area; 140
Mesa Falls Scenic Byway; 172
Mid-Summer's Eve Celebration; 23
Middle Aspen Trail; 57
Middle Fork Campground; 100
Middle Fork Popo Agie River; 158, 159
Middle Fork Powder River Campground; 99
Middle Fork Trail; 160
Middle Jurassic; 81
Midway Geyser Basin; 198, 238
Miller Lake; 32, 176
Miller Lake Campground; 176
Million Dollar Biffy; 42
Miner's Cabin Trail; 154
Miner's Delight; 17, 18
Miner's Memorial; 138
Minerva Terrace; 217
Minute Geyser; 209, 214
Miracle Mile; 70, 71
Mirror Lake; 30, 154
Mirror Lake Picnic Area; 154
Mirror Lake Scenic Byway; 51
Mirror Pool; 237, 238
Mistymoon Lake; 30
Moneta; 111
Montana; 44, 59, 62, 85, 89, 90, 113, 114, 117, 118, 120, 149, 150, 165, 187, 188, 197, 198, 219, 220, 223, 224, 233, 234
Monument Geyser Basin; 208
Moorcroft; 61, 86
Moorcroft Rest Area; 61
Moose; 36, 74, 190, 191
Moose Falls; 225
Moose Flat Campground; 37

Moose-Wilson Rd/Wy-390; 190, 191
Moran Jct; 36, 124, 127, 129, 131, 145, 147
Moran, Thomas; 197, 210, 218, 220
Mormon Church; 92, 135, 173
Mormon Colonists Monument; 92, 117
Mormon Ferry; 48, 66, 175
Mormon Handcart Historic Site: Martin's Cove; 173
Mormon Handcart Historic Site: Willie Center Sixth Crossing; 135
Mormon Row; 130
Mormon Trail; 48, 51, 52, 102, 134, 179, 181
Mormons; 17, 48, 52, 92, 117, 173, 175, 181, 189
Morning Geyser; 239
Morning Glory Pool; 237, 238
Morrison Formation; 14, 72
Mortimore Ln; 136, 158
Mosier Gulch Recreation Area; 101
Mosquito Creek Rd; 170
Mosquito Lake; 80
Mother Featherlegs Shepherd; 141
Mount Everts; 210, 219
Mount Glory; 170, 171
Mount Hayes Overlook and Fishing Access; 233
Mount Holmes; 216
Mount Hunt; 190
Mount Moran; 76, 145
Mount Moran Turnout; 76
Mount Owen; 36, 63, 75
Mount Sublette; 20
Mount Washburn; 230
Mount Washburn Trail; 230
Mountain Home; 176
Mountain View Turnout; 76
Mouth of the Canyon Trail: Bighorn Canyon National Recreation Area; 187
Mud Caldron; 200
Mud Geyser; 200
Mud Volcano Area; 198, 200
Muddy Creek Camp and Crossing; 51
Muddy Mountain; 22, 24, 138, 139
Muddy Mountain Environmental Education Area; 23, 24
Muddy Mountain Rd; 23, 24
Mule Creek Jct Rest Area; 142
Murphy Creek Campground; 37
Museum of Flight and Aerial Firefighting; 117
Museum of the National Park Ranger; 214
Mystic Falls; 238

-- N --
Names Hill; 102
Narrow Gauge Terrace; 232
Narrows Campground; 184
Nash Fork Campground; 19
National Bighorn Sheep Interpretive Center; 78, 126
National Elk Refuge; 129
National Historic Landmark; 40, 121, 203, 209, 214
National Historic Trails Interpretive Center; 48
National Park Service; 197, 210, 214, 218, 220
National Register of Historic Places; 87, 88, 109, 131, 138, 155, 160, 164
Native Americans; 31, 42, 44, 46, 48, 58, 59, 62, 85, 94, 96, 125, 140, 142, 164, 166, 168, 169, 175, 182, 183, 239
Natrona; 110
Natrona County; 23, 27
Natural Bridge; 206
Nebraska; 51, 58, 121, 123, 140, 142
Needles Eye Arch; 85
New Fork Canyon; 184
New Fork Lake; 184, 186
New Fork Lake Campground; 184
New Fork Lake Rd; 184
New Fork Lake Trailhead; 184
New Fork River; 103, 107, 184
New Fork River Campground; 103, 107
New Fork Trail; 184
New Highland Spring; 232
New Highland Terrace; 232
New York Museum of Natural History; 138
Newcastle; 142
Newell Bay Campground: Guernsey State Park; 42
Newton Creek Campground; 87
Newton Springs Picnic Area; 87
Nez Perce Ford Picnic Area: Yellowstone National Park; 200
Nez Perce Picnic Area: Yellowstone National Park; 239

Nici Self Historical Museum; 151
Night Lake; 120
Noble, Maude; 74
Norris; 198, 208, 209, 212-214, 218
Norris Campground: Yellowstone National Park; 214
Norris Geyser Basin; 197, 198, 209, 214
Norris Geyser Basin Museum; 209, 214
Norris Meadows Picnic Area: Yellowstone National Park; 212
North Butte; 96
North Cove Boat Ramp; 98
North Crow Reservoir: Curt Gowdy State Park; 57, 168
North Fork Campground; 152
North Fork Campground: Buffalo Bill State Park; 89
North Fork Cottonwood Trail; 143
North Fork Encampment River; 193
North Fork Fire; 211
North Fork Little Laramie River; 152
North Fork Popo Agie River; 159
North Fork Shoshone River; 87-89
North Fork Trail; 152
North Fork Yellowstone River; 119
North Gap Lake; 19, 73
North Gate Canyon; 177
North Platte River; 14, 15, 34, 35, 40, 46-48, 55, 66, 70, 71, 121, 123, 140, 156, 157, 164, 165, 173-175, 177
North Platte River Valley; 66, 121, 155
North Platte Valley Overlook; 122
North Red Hills Campground: Seminoe State Park; 70
North Rim Drive; 227
North Rim of the Grand Canyon of the Yellowstone; 221, 222, 227
North Rim Trail; 221, 222, 227
North Shore Bay Campground: Buffalo Bill State Park; 89
North Tongue Campground; 83, 84, 94
North Tongue River; 83, 94, 95
North Twin Lakes; 19
Nymph Lake; 214

-- O --
Oblong Geyser; 237
Obsidian Cliff; 215
Ocean Lake; 127, 162
Ocean Lake Wildlife Habitat Management Area - Dickinson Park; 162
Ocean Lake Wildlife Habitat Management Area - Lindholm; 127
Ocean Lake Wildlife Habitat Management Area - Long Point; 127
Ocean Lake Wildlife Habitat Management Area - Mills Point; 162
Ocean Lake Wildlife Habitat Management Area - South Cove; 127
Ocean Lake Wildlife Habitat Management Area - Stultz; 162
Ojo Caliente Spring; 239
Okie Beach Campground: Alcova Reservoir; 27
Old Bedlam Ruts; 164
Old Crow Lake; 100
Old Faithful Geyser; 197, 236, 238
Old Faithful Inn; 236
Old Faithful Village; 236
Old Faithful Visitor Center; 198, 236, 238, 239
Old Pass Rd; 170, 171
Old West Miniature Village and Museum; 89
Old Wyoming State Penitentiary; 54
Opal Spring; 217
Opal Terrace; 217
Opalescent Pool; 237
Optimist Park; 56
Orange Spring Mound; 232
Oregon; 107
Oregon Buttes; 179
Oregon Trail; 46, 48, 52, 54, 66, 67, 102, 103, 107, 122, 134, 135, 143, 163-165, 173, 179, 181
Oregon Trail Rd; 66, 175
Oregon Trail Ruts; 121, 164
Orin Junction Rest Area; 46
Osprey Falls; 216
Otter Creek Picnic Area: Yellowstone National Park; 199
Otter Lake; 100
Our Lady of Peace Shrine; 58
Outlaw Cave; 49
Overland Stage Route; 54
Overland Trail; 51, 54, 133, 151, 156
Owen Creek Campground; 83
Owl Creek Mountains; 114
Oxbow Bend; 145

-- P --
Pacific Creek Campground; 145
Pacific Creek Trailhead; 145
Pacific Northwest; 143, 179
Pacific Springs; 179
Pahaska Teepee; 87
Paintpots Hill; 209
Palette Spring; 217
Palisades Reservoir; 128, 144
Palmer Canyon Trail; 184
Parting of the Ways; 179
Pass Ridge Trail; 170, 171
Pat's Point Campground: Keyhole State Park; 64
Pathfinder Dam; 14, 15
Pathfinder Dam Overlook; 15
Pathfinder Interpretive Center; 15
Pathfinder Interpretive Trail; 14, 15
Pathfinder Rd; 15
Pathfinder Reservoir; 14-16, 66, 67, 70, 175
Pathfinder Wildlife Refuge; 71
Pearl Harbor; 85, 91
Pebble Creek Campground: Yellowstone National Park; 223
Pebble Creek Trail; 223
Pelican Creek Nature Trail; 203
Pelican Valley; 205
Periodic Spring; 143, 144
Petrified Tree; 211, 229
Petroglyphs; 25, 78, 82, 97, 111, 116, 149, 158, 195
Phalow Ln; 28
Phelps Lake; 36, 191
Phillips Canyon; 170
Phillips Pass Trail; 170
Phillips Ridge Trailhead; 170
Phillips, John "Portugee"; 164, 166
Photographer's Point; 32
Pick Bridge Public Access Area; 156
Pick Bridge Rd; 156
Pictographs; 49, 82, 97, 116, 158
Piedmont Charcoal Kilns; 51
Pilot Butte; 68, 69, 181
Pilot Butte Wild Horse Tour; 54, 68, 69
Pilot Index Overlook; 119
Pilot Peak; 119
Pine Bluffs; 58
Pine Bluffs Rest Area; 58
Pine Campground; 152
Pine Creek Canyon; 32
Pine Creek Trail; 32, 33
Pine Haven; 64, 86
Pine Haven Rd; 86
Pine Ridge Rd/CR-205; 86
Pinedale; 32, 33, 102, 106, 108
Pink Cone Geyser; 238, 239
Pinnacle Buttes; 20, 125
Pinnacles Campground; 20
Pioneer Museum; 46
Pioneer Park; 123, 140
Pioneer Square; 96
Plains Indian Museum; 90
Plate Geyser; 237
Platte River Trail; 177
Platte River Wilderness; 177
Plume Geyser; 236
Point of Rocks Stagecoach Station; 54
Point Sublime; 227
Poison Creek Campground: Boysen State Park; 196
Pole Creek Trail; 32, 57
Pole Mountain Trails; 11, 57, 168, 169
Pony Express; 48, 107, 122, 165, 175
Pony Express Trail; 48, 51, 52, 122, 181
Popo Agie Campground; 160
Popo Agie Campground: Sinks Canyon State Park; 159
Popo Agie Falls; 158, 159, 161
Popo Agie River; 158
Popo Agie Wilderness; 160
Porcelain Basin; 209, 214
Porcupine Campground; 94
Porcupine Creek Canyon; 186
Porcupine Creek Falls; 186
Porcupine Falls; 94
Porcupine Pass; 186
Porcupine Trail; 184, 186
Porkchop Geyser; 209, 214

Potholes Turnout; 76
Potts Hot Spring Basin; 206
POW Camp; 155
Powder River Basin; 60, 61, 82, 85
Powder River Expedition; 59, 85
Powder River Pass; 98, 99, 101
Powder River Rest Area; 60
Powell; 52, 91
Powell, Captain James; 166
Powell, John Wesley; 52
Power Plant Rd; 164, 165
Prairie Dog Town: Devils Tower National Monument; 148
Pronghorn Campground: Keyhole State Park; 64
Prospect Hill; 66, 67, 173
Prospect Spring; 232
Prospect Terrace; 232
Prune Creek Campground; 84
Pryor Mountain Wild Horse Range; 187
Pumice Point; 206
Punch Bowl Spring; 237, 238
Purple Mountain Trailhead; 208

-- Q --
Quealy Lake; 73, 155
Quealy Lake Trail; 73
Queens Laundry; 239

-- R --
Rails to Trails; 195, 196
Rainbow Pool; 237
Rainbow Terrace; 115
Rainy Lake; 100
Ralston; 91
Ralston Bridges; 91
Ranchester; 59, 81, 85
Ranger Creek Campground; 82
Ranger Delight Trail: Bighorn Canyon National Recreation Area; 188
Ranger Station; 88, 199, 203, 205, 210-212, 218, 220, 222, 224, 225, 229, 231, 236
Ranger Station: Bechler River; 172
Ranger Station: Bighorn Canyon; 187
Ranger Station: Black Rock; 124
Ranger Station: Bridge Bay; 206
Ranger Station: Brush Creek; 155
Ranger Station: Crandall; 182
Ranger Station: Tower; 211, 229
Ranger Station: Wapiti; 88
Rattlesnake Range; 134
Rawhide Buttes; 141
Rawlins; 55, 56, 70, 72, 134, 136, 158, 163, 175, 192
RD 92; 164
Red Beds Trail: Devils Tower National Monument; 148
Red Butte; 142
Red Buttes; 66, 175
Red Canyon; 180
Red Canyon Overlook; 180
Red Canyon Rd/CR-235; 180
Red Canyon Wildlife Habitat Management Area; 180
Red Cliff Trail; 40
Red Cloud Campground: Guernsey State Park; 41
Red Desert; 25, 68
Red Gulch Dinosaur Tracksite; 81
Red Gulch/Alkali National Back Country Byway; 81
Red Hills; 39
Red Hills Campground: Glendo State Park; 34
Red Hills Campground: Gros Ventre Rd; 39
Red Hills Trail; 39
Red Lodge; 120
Red Mask Mine; 154
Red Rock Point; 221
Red Valley; 22
Red Wall; 49, 111
Redwood Water Tank; 141
Reef Creek Picnic Area; 182
Register Cliff; 102, 122, 164
Reliance Tipple; 53, 106, 178
Rendezvous Mountain; 190
Renner Reservoir; 97
Renner Wildlife Management Area; 97
Rescue Creek Trailhead; 219
Reservoir Lake; 73
Reuter Campground; 26, 61

Rex Hale Campground; 88
Reynolds Hill Trail; 31
Ribbon Lake; 227
Richardson, "Uncle" Tom; 228
Rim Campground: Muddy Mountain; 24
Rim Trail; 24
Ring Lake; 78
Ring Lake Campground; 78
Ripley's Believe It or Not; 91
Rise of the Sinks: Sinks Canyon State Park; 158
River Trail; 152
Riverside; 156, 157, 177, 192-194
Riverside Drive; 233
Riverside Geyser; 236-238
Riverside Park; 46
Riverton; 124, 125, 127, 162, 163, 195, 196
Roaring Mountain; 215
Roberts, Reverend John; 132
Rock Avenue; 66, 67
Rock Creek Hollow; 17
Rock in the Glen; 47
Rock Lake; 44
Rock River; 139
Rock River City Park; 139
Rock Springs; 53, 68, 69, 106, 109
Rockchuck Peak; 63
Rockefeller, John D. Jr.; 36, 130, 146, 147, 191
Rockefeller, Laurance S.; 191
Rocket Geyser; 237
Rocky Mountains; 36, 66, 67, 136
Rocky Point Campground: Keyhole State Park; 65
Rocky Ridge; 17, 135, 136, 173
Roosevelt; 211, 224, 229
Roosevelt Arch; 219
Roosevelt Lodge; 211, 224, 229
Roosevelt, President Franklin D.; 36, 91
Roosevelt, President Theodore; 219
Ross Lake; 79
Rotary Park; 22
Rotary Snowplow Locomotive; 138
Rudefeha Ghost Town; 192
Rudefeha Mine; 192
Rustic Falls; 216
RV Dump: Afton; 143
RV Dump: Alcova Reservoir; 27
RV Dump: Bear River Welcome Center; 51
RV Dump: Bighorn Canyon National Recreation Area; 187
RV Dump: Bighorn National Forest; 84, 99
RV Dump: Boysen State Park; 113
RV Dump: Buffalo Bill State Park; 89
RV Dump: Cheyenne Rest Area; 44
RV Dump: Chugwater Rest Area; 44
RV Dump: Cody; 90
RV Dump: Curt Gowdy State Park; 57, 168
RV Dump: Dwyer Junction Rest Area; 45, 121
RV Dump: Glendo State Park; 35
RV Dump: Grant Village; 225
RV Dump: Green River; 53
RV Dump: Guernsey State Park; 40
RV Dump: Independence Rock Rest Area; 173
RV Dump: Keyhole State Park; 64
RV Dump: Lake Absarraca - Cheyenne; 44
RV Dump: Lander; 132
RV Dump: Lusk Rest Area; 141
RV Dump: Orin Junction Rest Area; 46
RV Dump: Overland Express Mart - Basin; 116
RV Dump: Pathfinder Reservoir; 15
RV Dump: Sheridan Rest Area; 59
RV Dump: Sundance Rest Area; 62
RV Dump: Warren Bridge Campground; 104
RV Dump: Wheatland City Park/Lewis Park; 45, 165
RV Dump: Wyoming Territorial Prison; 56
Ryan Hill; 67
Ryan Park; 155
Ryan Park Campground; 155

Index

-- S --

Sacajawea's Grave; 132, 133
Sage Campground: Pathfinder Reservoir; 15
Sage Creek Campground; 136
Sagebrush Campground: Glendo State Park; 35
Salt Lake City; 17, 51, 173
Salt River; 144
Salt River Pass; 143
Salt River Range; 37, 143
Sand Creek Campground; 62, 142
Sand Creek Canyon Scenic Drive; 62, 142
Sand Creek Rd/FR-863; 62
Sand Dunes Recreation Site; 25
Sand Lake; 19, 73
Sand Lake Rd; 19, 152
Sand Mountain Day Use Area: Seminoe State Park; 70
Sand Point Picnic Area: Yellowstone National Park; 206
Sanders, Brigadier General William P.; 133
Sandy Beach Campground: Glendo State Park; 35
Sandy Beach Campground: Guernsey State Park; 42
Sandy Cove Campground: Guernsey State Park; 43
Sandy Point Campground: Guernsey State Park; 43
Sanger Public Access Area; 156
Sapphire Pool; 238
Saratoga; 54, 157, 192
Saratoga Lake Campground; 157
Saratoga National Fish Hatchery; 156
Sargent's Bay Picnic Area; 146
Sawmill Campground: Sinks Canyon State Park; 158
Sawmill Geyser; 237
Sawyer Expedition Bozeman Trail; 85
Sawyer, Colonel James; 85
Scab Creek Campground; 108
Scab Creek Trailhead; 108
Schwabacher Landing; 131
Scott Bicentennial Park; 85
Scott's Bottom Nature Area; 52, 53
SE Wyoming Blvd/Wy-258; 22
Sedge Bay Picnic Area: Yellowstone National Park; 202
Seedskadee National Wildlife Refuge; 189
Seminoe Dam; 71
Seminoe Mountains; 70-72
Seminoe Rd; 71
Seminoe Reservoir; 70, 71
Seminoe State Park; 70, 71
Seminoe-Alcova Back Country Byway; 70
Sentinel Meadows; 239
Sepulcher Mountain; 219
Sessions, Byron; 92
Shadow Mountain; 38, 130
Sheep Bridge Trail; 160
Sheep Lake; 19, 73
Sheep Lake Trail; 19, 73
Sheep Mountain; 38, 74
Sheep Springs Canyon; 116
Sheepeater Canyon; 215, 216
Sheepeater Cliff Picnic Area: Yellowstone National Park; 215
Sheepeater Cliffs; 215
Shelf Lakes Trail; 73
Shell; 81, 82, 85
Shell Canyon; 82
Shell Creek Campground; 82
Shell Falls; 82
Shelter Point Campground: Glendo State Park; 35
Sherd Lake; 100
Sheridan; 59, 166
Sheridan Creek Campground; 126
Sheridan Visitor Center and Rest Area; 59
Shoshone Episcopal Mission Boarding School; 132, 133
Shoshone Forest Fire; 99
Shoshone Geyser Basin; 235
Shoshone Lake; 235
Shoshone National Forest; 87, 89, 90, 126, 159
Shoshone Point; 235
Shoshone Reclamation Project; 91
Shoshone River; 89
Shoshone Valley; 92
Shoshoni; 90, 110-113, 117, 162, 195, 196
Shoshoni City Park; 112, 195, 196
Shoshoni Picnic Area; 111
Sibley Dam; 84
Sibley Lake Campground; 84
Sibley Lake Picnic Areas; 84

Sidon Canal; 92
Sierra Madre Mountains; 192-194
Signal Mountain; 76, 145
Signal Mountain Campground: Grand Teton National Park; 36, 76, 145
Signal Mountain Lodge; 76, 145
Signal Mountain Rd; 76
Signal Mountain Trail; 76, 145
Silas Canyon Trail; 160
Silver Cord Cascade; 221, 227
Silver Creek Reservoir; 136
Silver Gate/The Hoodoos; 216
Silver Lake; 155
Silver Run Lake; 153
Silver Sage Ranch Wetland; 156
Silver Springs Rd; 141
Simpson's Hollow; 181
Sinclair; 55, 70, 72
Sinks Canyon; 158, 159, 161
Sinks Canyon Campground; 159
Sinks Canyon State Park; 136, 158, 159, 161
Sitting Bull Campground; 98
Sitting Bull Day Use Area: Guernsey State Park; 41
Six Mile Gap Campground; 177
Ski Lake; 170
Skunk Hollow Park Campground: Casper Mountain; 22
Skyline Drive; 32, 40, 121
Skyline Drive Campground: Guernsey State Park; 42
Slate Creek Campground; 102, 189
Sleeping Giant Picnic Area; 87
Slide Canyon; 186
Slide Creek Falls; 186
Slide Lake; 186
Slide Lake Trail; 186
Sliding Hill; 219
Slough Creek Campground: Yellowstone National Park; 223
Smiths Fork Rd/FR-10072; 37, 143
Smokey Row Cemetery; 115
Snake River; 36, 74, 76, 77, 128, 131, 143, 145-147, 170-172, 179, 225
Snake River Canyon; 128, 144
Snake River Cutthroat Trout; 97
Snake River Picnic Area: Yellowstone National Park; 225
Snake River Range; 128, 171
Snow King Mountain; 129
Snowy Range; 73, 151, 153-155
Snowy Range Pass; 73, 151, 153-155
Snowy Range Scenic Byway; 151, 155
Soda Butte; 223
Soda Butte Campground: Montana; 118
Soda Butte Creek Picnic Area: Yellowstone National Park; 223
Soda Lake Wildlife Habitat Management Area; 109
Soldier Rock Campground: Glendo State Park; 34
Solitary Geyser; 236
Sour Lake; 200
South Brush Creek Campground; 155
South Dakota; 26, 59, 62, 140, 142, 178
South Fork Campground; 100
South Gap Lake; 19, 73
South Pass; 17, 18, 134, 143, 179
South Pass City; 17, 18, 179
South Pass City Rd/CR-479; 17, 18
South Pass City State Historic Site; 18
South Pass Rest Area; 179
South Red Hills Campground: Seminoe State Park; 70
South Rim of the Grand Canyon of the Yellowstone; 227
South Rim Trail; 227, 228
South Tongue River; 83
Spanish Diggings; 34
Specimen Ridge Trail; 224
Splendid Geyser; 237
Split Rock; 67, 134, 219
Split Rock Historic Site; 134
Sponge Geyser; 237
Spotted Tail Campground: Guernsey State Park; 40, 41
Spray Geyser; 238
Spring Creek Picnic Area: Yellowstone National Park; 235
Springer Wildlife Habitat Management Area; 140
Spruce Campground; 152
Squaretop Mountain; 185, 186
Squaw Hollow; 53
St. Alban's Chapel; 19
St. Christopher's in the Bighorns Episcopal Chapel; 99

Star Valley Rest Area; 144
State Bath House; 115
State Line Trail: Bighorn Canyon National Recreation Area; 188
Station Creek Campground; 128
Steady Geyser; 239
Steamboat Geyser; 197, 209, 214, 237
Steamboat Lake; 173
Steamboat Point; 202
Steamboat Point Picnic Area: Yellowstone National Park; 202
Stephens, W.H.; 66
Stevenson Island; 205
Stinking Springs; 105
Stokes Crossing Campground; 107
Storm Point; 203, 205
Storm Point Nature Trail; 203
Story; 166
Story Fish Hatchery; 167
Stough Creek Basin Trail; 160
String Lake; 36, 63
String Lake Picnic Area; 63
String Lake Trail; 63
Sublette Cutoff; 102, 179
Sugarloaf Campground; 73
Sugarloaf Mountain; 73, 154
Sugarloaf Recreation Area; 19
Sugarloaf Recreation Area/FR-346; 73
Sullivan's Knob Trail: Bighorn Canyon National Recreation Area; 188
Sulphur Caldron; 200
Summer Solstice; 23
Summit Lake; 186
Summit Rest Area; 57
Summit Trailhead; 57
Sun Ranch; 173
Sundance; 62, 86
Sundance Campground; 62
Sundance Rest Area; 62
Sundance Trail System; 62
Sunlight Basin; 182
Sunlight Gorge; 182
Sunlight Wildlife Habitat Management Area; 182
Sunset Lake; 237
Sunshine Beach Campground: Seminoe State Park; 70
Swan Lake; 215
Sweetwater River; 66, 134, 135, 173
Sweetwater Rocks; 173
Sweetwater Station Rest Area; 135, 163
Sweetwater Valley; 67, 134, 135, 163
Swift Creek Campground; 143
Swift Creek Canyon; 143
Swinging Bridge; 14, 115
Sykes Mountain Trail: Bighorn Canyon National Recreation Area; 187
Sylvan Lake Picnic Area: Yellowstone National Park; 202

-- T --
Taggart Lake; 36, 75
Taggart Lake Trailhead; 75
Tailrace Campground; 102, 189
Tamarask Campground: Boysen State Park; 113
Tank Farm Rd; 164
Tatanka Campground: Keyhole State Park; 64
Taylor Mountain; 171
Tecumseh's Trading Post; 89
Teepee Fountain; 115
Teewinot Chairlift; 190
Teewinot Mountain; 36, 63, 75
Telephone Lakes; 19
Ten Sleep; 97
Ten Sleep City Park; 97
Ten Sleep Fish Hatchery; 98
Ten Sleep Rd; 30
Tensleep Canyon; 97, 98
Tensleep Creek Campground; 98
Tensleep Falls; 30
Terrace Mountain; 216, 217
Terrace Spring Thermal Area; 208
Teton Glacier; 75, 131
Teton Glacier Turnout; 75
Teton Park Rd: Grand Teton National Park; 36, 63, 74, 190, 191
Teton Pass; 170-172
Teton Pass Trail; 171
Teton Range; 21, 36, 38, 39, 63, 74-77, 124, 129-131, 145, 146, 170, 171, 190, 191
Teton Reservoir Recreation Site; 54, 192

Teton View Turnout; 131
Teton Village; 190
Teton Wilderness; 21, 88, 145
Teton-Yellowstone Tornado; 21
Thayne; 144
The Castle; 40, 42, 121
The Castle Day Use Area: Guernsey State Park; 42
The Greeting and the Gift; 44
The Honeycombs; 96, 97
The Hoodoos; 216
The Narrows; 184, 224
The Open Door; 105
The Prairie of the Mass; 103
The Rise; 158, 159
The Sinks; 158, 159
Thermopolis; 113, 114, 117, 149, 150
Thermos Bottle Geyser; 208
Thirty Three Mile Rd; 99
Thomas Edison Monument; 192
Three Forks Park; 186
Three Mile Campground; 87
Three Waters Mountain; 80
Tie City Campground; 169
Tie City Trailhead; 57, 169
Tie Flume Campground; 83
Tie Hack Campground; 100
Tie Hack Monument; 125
Tie Hack Reservoir; 100
Tie Hacks; 125
Tilt Geyser; 237
Tin Cup Campground; 144
Tipple Trail; 154
Togwotee Overlook; 124
Togwotee Pass; 125
Tongue River; 59, 85
Tongue River Canyon; 85
Tongue River Recreation Area; 85
Tongue River Trail; 85
Torrey Creek Campground; 78
Torrey Creek Trailhead; 78, 79
Torrington; 122, 140-142
Toth, Peter; 96
Tough Creek Campground: Boysen State Park; 113
Tower Creek; 229, 230
Tower Fall; 198, 224, 229, 230
Tower Fall Campground: Yellowstone National Park; 229
Tower Hill Park Campground: Casper Mountain; 23
Tower Junction; 229
Tower Trail; 148
Tower-Roosevelt; 210, 211, 223, 224, 229, 231
Towner Lake Rd; 19, 153
Trail Creek Campground; 171
Trail Creek Trailhead; 170, 171
Trail End State Historic Site; 59
Trail Fork Trail; 143
Trail Lake; 78, 79
Trail Lake Campground; 78, 79
Trail Lake Rd Petroglyphs; 78
Trail Lake Rd/CR-411; 78
Trail Meadow Campground; 79
Trail of the Whispering Giants; 96
Trails End Campground; 32, 33
Transcontinental Railroad; 151
Trapper's Route Number One Campground; 174
Trappers Point; 109
Treasure Island Public Access Area; 157
Trigger Lake; 100
Trona Patch; 68
Trout Cabin; 123, 140
Trout Creek Overlook; 200
Trout Pool; 158
Truman, President Harry S.; 36
Trumpeter Swans; 80, 215
Tuff Cliff Picnic Area: Yellowstone National Park; 208
Turpin Meadow Campground: Turpin Meadow Recreation Area; 21
Turpin Meadow Ranch; 21
Turpin Meadow Recreation Area; 21
Turpin Meadow Trailhead; 21
Turtle Rock Trail; 31
Twin Buttes Reservoir Public Access Area; 28
Two Moon Campground: Glendo State Park; 35
Two Ocean Lake; 146
Two Ribbons Nature Trail; 233

-- U --

U.S. Army; 46, 48, 52, 142, 165, 166, 175, 181, 197, 210, 214, 218, 220
U.S. Army Corps of Engineers; 227
U.S. Forest Service; 88, 160
U.S. Government; 52, 55, 123, 125, 140, 179, 181
Uinta Mountains; 51
Uncle Tom's Overlook of the Upper Falls; 227
Uncle Tom's Parking Area; 227
Uncle Tom's Trail; 221, 227, 228
Undine Falls; 210
Union Pacific Depot; 123, 140
Union Pacific Gallery; 123, 140
Union Pacific Railroad; 46, 57, 133, 151, 165, 166
Union Pass; 80, 126, 184
Union Pass National Historic Site; 80
Union Pass Rd; 80
United States 7th Cavalry; 182, 183
United States Geological Survey; 210, 218, 220
University of Wyoming; 58
Upper Brooks Lake; 20
Upper Geyser Basin; 198, 236-240
Upper Granite Canyon Patrol Cabin; 190
Upper Green River Lake; 186
Upper Green River Valley; 80, 103, 109
Upper Jade Lake; 20
Upper Mesa Falls; 170, 172, 233
Upper Salt River Public Access Area; 144
Upper Silas Lake; 160
Upper Terrace; 217, 232
Upper Terrace Drive; 217, 232
Upper Wind River Campground: Boysen State Park; 113
Upper Yellowstone Falls; 198, 199, 222, 227
US-14; 81, 82, 85, 86, 94, 113, 117
US-14 (east); 26, 27, 64, 86, 178
US-14/16/20; 87, 113, 117, 149, 202, 204
US-14/16/20/Wy-789; 90, 113, 117
US-14A; 82, 83, 91-95, 150
US-16; 30, 96, 99, 111, 113, 117, 195
US-16/20/Wy-789; 113, 117
US-18; 140
US-18/20; 122, 141
US-189; 102, 104, 105, 189
US-189/191; 102-104, 106, 109
US-191; 25, 32, 53, 68, 69, 80, 102-106, 181, 184
US-20; 113, 233, 234
US-20/26; 49, 66, 67, 99, 110
US-20/26/87; 110
US-20/Wy-789; 113, 117
US-212 (Beartooth Scenic Byway); 118, 120, 149, 150, 182, 183, 223, 224
US-26; 124, 127, 132, 133, 162, 195, 196
US-26 (I-25 to Nebraska); 40-42, 121, 122, 140, 142, 164, 165
US-26/287; 20, 21, 80, 124, 127, 184
US-26/89; 128, 131, 143, 144
US-26/89/191; 36, 38, 128, 129, 143, 145
US-26/Wy-789; 162, 195, 196
US-287 (Lander to US-26); 124, 127, 132, 158, 161
US-287 (Laramie to Colorado); 133, 138, 139, 176
US-287/Wy-789; 132, 134, 136, 158, 163, 173, 175, 179, 180, 195
US-30; 137
US-30/287; 56, 138, 139, 176
US-310/Wy-789; 90, 92, 113, 117
US-85; 34, 62, 122, 140-142
US-87/Wy-193; 166, 167
US-89; 37, 128, 137, 143, 219, 220
US-89/191/287; 36, 129, 143, 145, 225, 226
US-89/N Washington St; 143
USAF Portable Medium 1 Nuclear Power Plant; 26
Ut-44; 53
Utah; 51, 53, 58, 92
Utah Militia; 181
Utah Territory; 181
Utah War; 181

-- V --

Valley Trail; 190
Vasquez, Louis; 52
Vedauwoo Climbing Area; 31
Vedauwoo Glen Rd; 31
Vedauwoo Recreation Area; 31, 168
Virgin Mary; 58
Virginia Cascade; 212
Vore Buffalo Jump; 62

-- W --

Wagon Box Fight Historic Site; 166
Wagonhound Rest Area; 55
Walcott; 55, 138, 139, 151, 156, 157
Waltman; 49, 110
Wapiti; 89
Wapiti Campground; 88
Wapiti Lake Trailhead; 222, 227
Wapiti Wayside Visitor Center and Ranger Station; 88
Warm Creek Picnic Area: Yellowstone National Park; 223
Warm Springs Creek Campground; 80
Warm Springs Creek Rd/FR-532; 80
Warren Bridge Campground; 104
Warren Bridge Public Fishing Area; 104
Warren Peak Lookout; 26, 27, 86
Washakie Museum; 96
Washakie Wilderness; 88
Washburn Range; 216
Washburn-Langford-Doane Expedition; 197
Waterfalls Canyon; 146
Waters Point Campground: Glendo State Park; 34
Wedding of the Waters; 114
Weeping Rock Campground; 102, 189
Weiss Campground: Pathfinder Reservoir; 15
Welcome Center; 44, 51, 58, 59, 62
Werner Memorial Shelter; 46
West Glacier Lake; 19
West Sandy Beach Day Use Area: Guernsey State Park; 43
West Shoreline Drive: Boysen State Park; 196
West Table Boat Ramp and Picnic Area; 128
West Tensleep Falls; 30
West Tensleep Lake; 30
West Tensleep Lake Campground; 30
West Tensleep Trailhead; 30
West Thumb; 205-207, 225, 226, 235, 240
West Thumb Geyser Basin; 206, 207
West Thumb of Yellowstone Lake; 206, 225
West Thumb Picnic Area: Yellowstone National Park; 207
West Yellowstone; 198, 234
Western Wyoming Community College; 53
Western Wyoming Natural History Museum; 53
Westside Campground: Alcova Reservoir; 27
Whale's Mouth; 209, 214
Wheatland; 45, 164, 165
Wheatland City Park/Lewis Park; 45, 165
Wheatland Reservoir #1; 44, 45
Whipple Park; 122, 141
Whirligig Geyser; 209, 214
Whiskey Basin Wildlife Habitat Management Area; 78, 126
Whiskey Flats Picnic Area: Yellowstone National Park; 238
Whiskey Grove Campground; 184
Whiskey Gulch Campground: Glendo State Park; 34
Whiskey Mountain; 78
Whiskey Mountain Trail; 79
White Dome Geyser; 238, 239
White Elephant Back Terrace; 232
White Mountain; 25, 68, 69
White Mountain Petroglyphs; 25
White Mountain Rd; 69
White Mountain Wild Horse Herd; 68
White Sand Dunes; 70
White Sulphur Spring; 115
Whitman, Narcissa; 48
Whitney Gallery of Western Art; 90
Wick Wildlife Habitat Management Area; 55
Wigwam Rearing Station; 97
Wigwam Rearing Station Access Area; 97
Wild and Scenic River; 119
Wild Bunch Gang; 49, 111
Wild Horse and Burrow Act; 106
Wild Horse Canyon Rd; 52, 68
Wild Horse Corrals; 106
Wild Horse Point; 135
Wild Horse Program; 68, 69

Wild Horses; 68, 69, 106, 135, 187
Wilkins Peak; 68
William Clayton's Slough (Poison Springs); 66
Willie Center Sixth Crossing; 135
Willie Handcart Company; 17, 66, 135, 175
Willie Handcart Company Tragedy Memorial; 17, 136
Willie, James G.; 17, 173
Willow Campground; 152
Willow Flats; 146
Willow Lake Campground; 109
Willow Park Group Picnic Area; 98
Willow Springs; 66, 67
Willow Springs Pony Express Station; 66
Wilson; 170, 171, 191
Wind Creek Campground: Keyhole State Park; 64
Wind River; 113, 114, 125, 195, 196
Wind River Canyon; 113, 114
Wind River Lake and Picnic Area; 125
Wind River Mountains; 32, 78, 79, 108, 109, 126, 136, 158, 160, 161, 163, 179, 184, 186
Wind River Vista; 159
Window Rock Arch; 87
Windows of the Past; 58
Windy Point Turnout; 74
Wolf Creek Campground; 128
Wolf Lake; 212
Wolf Lake Trail; 212
Woods Landing; 176
Woolf Point; 15
Worland; 96, 101, 113, 115, 117
Worland City Park; 96
World War II; 91, 117, 123, 140
World's Largest Elk Antler Arch; 143
Worthen Meadows Campground; 160, 161
Worthen Meadows Reservoir; 160
Worthen Meadows Trailhead; 160
Wraith Falls; 210, 219
Wy-110/Devils Tower Rd (Devils Tower National Monument); 148
Wy-111; 178
Wy-113; 86
Wy-120; 120, 149, 150, 182, 183
Wy-13; 56, 139
Wy-130; 19, 151-154, 156, 157
Wy-130 (Laramie to Wy-230); 151
Wy-130/Wy-230 (Walcott to Riverside); 151, 155, 156, 177
Wy-131/FR-300/Louis Lake Rd; 136, 158, 161
Wy-133; 162
Wy-134; 162
Wy-135; 136, 163
Wy-135/136; 163
Wy-136; 163
Wy-160/Grayrocks Rd/Power Plant Rd; 164, 165
Wy-193/US-87; 166, 167
Wy-196; 99
Wy-210/Happy Jack Rd; 31, 57, 168
Wy-22; 170, 171, 190, 191
Wy-220; 14, 16, 22, 27, 66, 67, 70, 72, 134, 136, 138, 139, 173, 175
Wy-230; 151, 156, 157
Wy-230 (Laramie to Colorado); 28, 176
Wy-230 (Riverside to Colorado); 177
Wy-230/Wy-130 (Riverside to Walcott); 157
Wy-24; 26, 27, 86, 178
Wy-251; 22
Wy-258; 22
Wy-270; 41, 122
Wy-28; 17, 18, 158, 161, 180, 181, 189
Wy-28 (Farson to US-287); 179
Wy-28 (Wy-372 to Farson); 181
Wy-296 (Chief Joseph Scenic Highway); 118, 120, 149, 182
Wy-31; 81, 115
Wy-317; 40
Wy-319; 45
Wy-342; 167
Wy-351; 103, 107
Wy-352/FR-10091; 80, 104, 184
Wy-37 (Bighorn Canyon National Recreation Area); 187
Wy-372; 181, 189
Wy-390/Moose-Wilson Rd; 190, 191
Wy-487; 23, 138
Wy-530; 53
Wy-70; 54, 192
Wy-71; 54, 192

Wy-789; 54, 90, 92, 113, 117, 132, 134, 136, 158, 162, 163, 173, 175, 179, 180, 192, 195, 196
Wy-89; 137
Wyoming Backway shortcut from I-25 to US-20/26; 49
Wyoming Backway shortcut from US-20/26 to I-25; 110
Wyoming Frontier Prison; 54
Wyoming Game and Fish; 104, 140
Wyoming Heritage Trail; 112, 195, 196
Wyoming Range; 37
Wyoming State Bird Farm; 167
Wyoming Territorial Prison State Historic Site; 56, 176
Wyoming Tie and Timber Company; 125

-- Y --
Yellow Pine Campground; 168
Yellowstone - Canyon Village to Fishing Bridge; 199
Yellowstone - Canyon Village to Norris; 213
Yellowstone - Canyon Village to Tower-Roosevelt; 231
Yellowstone - East Entrance to Fishing Bridge; 202
Yellowstone - Fishing Bridge to Canyon Village; 201
Yellowstone - Fishing Bridge to East Entrance; 204
Yellowstone - Fishing Bridge to West Thumb; 205
Yellowstone - Madison to Norris; 208
Yellowstone - Madison to West Entrance; 234
Yellowstone - Madison to West Thumb; 240
Yellowstone - Mammoth Hot Springs to Norris; 218
Yellowstone - Mammoth Hot Springs to North Entrance; 220
Yellowstone - Mammoth Hot Springs to Tower-Roosevelt; 210
Yellowstone - Norris to Canyon Village; 212
Yellowstone - Norris to Madison; 209
Yellowstone - Norris to Mammoth Hot Springs; 214
Yellowstone - North Entrance to Mammoth Hot Springs; 219
Yellowstone - North Rim Drive; 221
Yellowstone - Northeast Entrance to Tower-Roosevelt; 223
Yellowstone - South Entrance to West Thumb; 225
Yellowstone - South Rim Drive; 227
Yellowstone - Tower-Roosevelt to Canyon Village; 229
Yellowstone - Tower-Roosevelt to Mammoth Hot Springs; 211
Yellowstone - Tower-Roosevelt to Northeast Entrance; 224
Yellowstone - Upper Terrace Drive; 232
Yellowstone - West Entrance to Madison; 233
Yellowstone - West Thumb to Fishing Bridge; 207
Yellowstone - West Thumb to Madison; 235
Yellowstone - West Thumb to South Entrance; 226
Yellowstone Caldera, 197, 230
Yellowstone Cutthroat Trout; 98
Yellowstone Lake; 197, 198, 200, 202-207, 230
Yellowstone Lake Overlook Trail; 207
Yellowstone Lake Sandbar; 206
Yellowstone National Park; 21, 36, 74, 87, 89, 90, 118-120, 127, 129, 143, 145-147, 149, 150, 170-172, 190, 197, 199, 200, 202-210, 212, 214, 215, 217-220, 222-227, 229-231, 233-236, 238-240
Yellowstone National Park - East Entrance; 202
Yellowstone National Park - North Entrance; 219
Yellowstone National Park - Northeast Entrance; 223
Yellowstone National Park - South Entrance; 225
Yellowstone National Park - West Entrance; 233
Yellowstone Northern Range; 219
Yellowstone Park Bill; 197
Yellowstone River; 114, 199, 200, 203, 205, 211, 221, 222, 227, 229, 230
Yellowstone River Picnic Area: Yellowstone National Park; 223
Yellowstone River Trail; 224, 229
Yellowstone Today Newspaper; 198
Yellowtail Dam; 187
Yellowtail Wildlife Habitat Management Area - Crystal Creek Rd; 93
Yellowtail Wildlife Habitat Management Area: Kane Ponds; 92
Yellowtail Wildlife Habitat Management Area: Mason-Lovell Ranch; 93
Young, Brigham; 107, 181

Made in the USA
Lexington, KY
24 February 2015